LAURA V. LOUMEAU

The Psychoanalytic Study
of the Child

VOLUME XXV

The Psychoanalytic Study

of the Child

VOLUME XXV

INTERNATIONAL UNIVERSITIES PRESS, INC.

New York   New York

ISBN   0   8236   4962   8

Manufactured in the United States of America

CONTENTS

Aspects of Normal and Pathological Development

Applications of Psychoanalysis

Education

Pediatrics

Heinz Hartmann died on May 17, 1970 at the age of 75. He founded *The Psychoanalytic Study of the Child,* together with Anna Freud and Ernst Kris in 1945. His vision and his active participation as editor and scientific contributor gave this publication its direction and its standard.

With this volume, the twenty-fifth of the series, we thought to celebrate his twenty-five years of editorship. His death is an irreparable loss to us.

RUTH S. EISSLER
ANNA FREUD
MARIANNE KRIS
SEYMOUR L. LUSTMAN
LOTTIE M. NEWMAN

IN MEMORIAM: HEINZ HARTMANN

Most readers of this Annual will by now have learned of Heinz Hartmann's death and read the obituaries that described his life and the significance of his work. Yet, for all of us who worked with him on this Annual the event of his death has retained its shocking newness, since we re-experience our loss whenever we turn to those tasks which we were so used to share with him.

It was always a particular satisfaction to me that every year the first copy of the new volume of *The Psychoanalytic Study of the Child* was ready for Heinz Hartmann's birthday on November 4th. The fact that he will never see this or any future volume compounds the awareness of present emptiness and irreparable loss.

I shall always regard it as a rare privilege to have been allowed to work with Heinz Hartmann so closely for so many years and to share so many areas of his work and interests.

I met Heinz Hartmann for the first time in 1933, immediately after I had left Nazi Germany to begin my psychoanalytic training in Vienna. He was then in charge of one of the departments of the University Psychiatric Clinics and I was very fortunate to be able to participate in the daily morning rounds which he conducted. The term "rounds," though, does not reflect what actually took place on these occasions. I can compare them only to a psychiatric seminar of a quality that was far beyond my expectations and hopes after the interruption of my own psychiatric career in Germany. Heinz Hartmann had one of those rare minds which integrated classical psychiatry, its fascinating phenomenological, philosophical, and diagnostic problems and their historical aspects with the broad range of psychoanalytic knowledge.

At the bedside of patients with the most severe psychiatric disorders he synthesized the best that the past had to offer with the best that the new psychiatry had introduced; for in his everyday contacts with patients one could observe Heinz Hartmann as the great clinician and diagnostician he was. His quiet humanity, his tender consideration of individual expressions, his empathy with the patients' conflicts, and his immediate understanding even of very bizarre thought processes transformed the hospital routine of rounds into a unique experience.

After these rounds the members of his staff as well as colleagues and students from other departments gathered around Heinz Hartmann in his office to listen to his discourses on a great variety of subjects—including not only psychiatry, psychoanalysis, and hospital affairs, but also politics, art, literature, music, and daily events in the city. The brilliance, knowledge, and wit with which he discussed these subjects aroused admiration and envy in many of his listeners.

When Heinz Hartmann left the University Clinics because he would not compromise his personal and scientific convictions for the sake of a university professorship which a reactionary government otherwise refused to bestow on him, the scientific level and clinical work in the department changed markedly; some members of his staff preferred to work in other hospitals rather than accept this change.

As a student at the Vienna Psychoanalytic Institute I did not lose contact with him but had the opportunity to attend his seminars, hear him present his own papers, and listen to his discussions of other papers read at the meetings of the Psychoanalytic Society.

My own psychoanalytic thinking was greatly influenced by his brilliant book, *Die Grundlagen der Psychoanalyse*. When many years later, I, together with a group at the University of Chicago, suggested a translation of this book, Heinz Hartmann refused because he felt he would no longer present the material in precisely the same way he had done in 1927. He did not wish to be treated as a "historical person" whose works should be republished unaltered, regardless of new insights which had been formulated and added to the basic concepts of psychoanalysis.

The Nazi occupation of Austria seemed to separate us forever: I finding refuge in the United States, and Heinz Hartmann and his family staying in Europe, first in Paris and later settling in Switzerland. However, when during the Second World War he came to New York, our previous contacts were resumed. After I moved to New

York, I was immensely proud to be invited to join the managing editors of *The Psychoanalytic Study of the Child*, which had been founded by him, Anna Freud, and Ernst Kris a few years earlier. This invitation, which I gratefully accepted, offered a new opportunity for close cooperation with him.

Heinz Hartmann was one of those very rare beings who carried a self-imposed assignment out to perfection. While earlier I had had the opportunity to observe his exquisite talents as clinician, teacher, and theoretician, I now had occasion to admire his talents in a different area (as some time later I again was privileged to do when we worked together on the Central Executive Committee of the International Psycho-Analytical Association). His ability to read and digest any number of manuscripts regardless of length, the conciseness and precision of judgment, the tact when forced to refuse a contribution, the encouragement of productivity in others—all this made him an ideal editor whose guidance was a great help to me and an unforgettable experience.

The high standards, which I believe this Annual has achieved, are due largely to Heinz Hartmann. This is true not only because of his own contributions; he read almost all papers submitted, and whenever counsel was asked of him, he was available for discussion and advice. Yet he never imposed his opinion and did not interfere once he had delegated authority. There were occasions when we differed in the evaluation of certain contributions, but the ensuing discussions actually heightened the appreciation of and confidence in the collaboration with him, since they were proof of his interest and concern for the work. Now, when so many decisions have to be made without him, I frequently think of his wisdom and tolerance.

The death of a great man is always tragic and leaves the survivors inconsolable. But, as Freud maintained after the death of a close collaborator, the development and growth of psychoanalysis may not depend on individual minds and must continue unrelentingly. Heinz Hartmann's activity as an editor has created a tradition of the highest order, and even though he will be irreplaceable, all of us were enriched by his presence and the splendid example he gave us, and some of this will go on living in generations to come.

Ruth S. Eissler

HEINZ HARTMANN

On June 9 of this year, only a few weeks after Heinz Hartmann's death, I read a tribute to him at a meeting of the New York Psychoanalytic Society. So close to his death, it would have been very difficult for me to speak of him in a relatively detached way. I could honor him at that time mainly as a friend, and less as a psychoanalyst or scientist. I was not alone in this. Those who spoke of him at the funeral service stressed predominantly his charm, his many talents, his character and personality: all that endeared him to so many. But even then it was impossible not to mention some of the characteristics which revealed themselves in Hartmann's mode of thinking and working.

In his earlier years his interest already was decidedly in psychoanalytic theory. His book *Die Grundlagen der Psychoanalyse* (1927) was and has remained a unique systematic statement of psychoanalytic theory and methodology valid at that time.

My closer personal contact with Hartmann in the scientific field started in August, 1939. It so happened that we and our families spent the summer holidays, the last before the outbreak of the War, in the same place in Brittany. As Editor of the *Internationale Zeitschrift für Psychoanalyse,* he wanted to publish the German translation of a paper of mine dealing with the theory of the aggressive drive. In my first draft I had used the term "instinct of self-preservation." He cogently criticized this term, so that I was able to add the necessary remarks which clarified what I had intended to convey, namely, the various instinctual forces entering into the behavior which leads to self-preservation. He was satisfied with the text, and the paper was published in the *Zeitschrift* as well as in the *International Journal for Psycho-Analysis.* At a later date, however, he pointed out that in this paper I had stressed the opposite of his own view; i.e., that he considered the ego to be the essential "organ of self-preservation." This attitude was an example of Hartmann's remarkable objectivity and absence of dogmatism.

Anna Freud, Heinz Hartmann, and Ernst Kris were the founders and the original managing editors of *The Psychoanalytic Study of the Child,* and very many of Hartmann's papers over the last twenty-five years appeared in this Annual. His was not a particular interest in child analysis, but he realized the eminent importance of psychoanalytic studies of children for the understanding of human behavior. And he always had an open mind for approaching the study of man from various angles, and not exclusively from that of the analytic situation with adult patients. He knew that in the analysis of adults, genetic interpretations and reconstructions centering around drive development were more convincing than reconstructions of ego functioning at various periods of childhood. Therefore he found it very important to apply analytic observations and thinking at, so to say, the other end of the development: studying the child not only as seen retroactively, but as the main object, for the understanding of subsequent development.

I often wondered how it came about that Hartmann and Kris asked me to collaborate with them in their joint work. Their invitation made me very happy, and I was flattered by it, since I had the greatest respect and admiration for them both. This was in the winter of 1943-1944. It was preceded by some incidents which I feel might have contributed to their decision.

At a meeting of the New York Psychoanalytic Society a paper was presented, consisting essentially in the discussion of a clinical vignette in which a symbolic interpretation of a dream was the main point. The paper in itself appeared interesting and the conclusions plausible, but at the end of the evening I found myself saying to Hartmann that if scientific contributions of such kind were all that analysts could produce, it would be the end of analysis in twenty years; that we needed, in psychoanalysis, what in medicine is achieved by physiology. He looked at me pensively, but did not say anything.

Shortly afterward, at the makeshift French university in New York, where French refugees were teaching various subjects, I invited Dr. Katherine Wolf, who had for many years been in training with Heinz Hartmann and subsequently collaborated with René A. Spitz, to give a joint seminar on psychoanalysis and genetic psychology. To my surprise and pleasure, Hartmann and Kris audited this seminar. At the end of the last session, they invited me to join them in their common work. It was quite clear, although not stated, that the main theme would be ego psychology and that its base of departure would be Hartmann's *Ego Psychology and the Problem of Adaptation* as well as Kris's contributions to ego psychology.

An interesting incident occurred at the beginning of our weekly evening meetings, which threw a light on a side of Hartmann that is hardly known and seems to contradict the image most people have of him. On the first evening Kris spoke most of the time, offering brilliant new suggestions and hypotheses. The next week I arrived at Hartmann's home early, so that I felt free to tell him that I had strong inferiority feelings since the previous meeting. He generously replied: "You are not the only one." As time went on, it was mostly Hartmann who would, after we discussed various clinical and theoretical problems, summarize some point in a succinct theoretical formulation.

Some believe that Hartmann was *a theoretician only*. But he was equally an excellent and farsighted clinician, and there were always data of observation underlying his generalizations. On the other hand, he was well aware that even ordinary clinical observation tacitly includes theoretical assumptions and hypotheses. What was characteristic of Hartmann's thought was that he would formulate his ideas in general or abstract terms, without mentioning the observations related to them. But in all our joint writings there was not a single statement that had not been confronted with or based upon data of observation on which all three of us had agreed during our discussions. Moreover, Hartmann would always consider any new hypothesis in the light of existing analytic theories, so as not to lose previous theoretical acquisitions for the sake of a new one. He would try to formulate a new theoretical view so as to add something without sacrificing what was known before. He was well aware of the complexities of the human mind; and he eschewed reductionism in theory, oversimplification for the mere sake of clarity.

These are, I believe, among the main reasons why Hartmann, a revolutionary in analytic theory, did not originate a splinter group, but on the contrary, immensely enriched and broadened the mainstream of psychoanalytic theory, clinical practice, and therapy.

Rudolph M. Loewenstein

THE SYMPTOMATOLOGY OF CHILDHOOD

THE SYMPTOMATOLOGY OF CHILDHOOD

A Preliminary Attempt at Classification

ANNA FREUD, LL.D., D.Sc. (London)

INTRODUCTION
THE MISLEADING QUALITY OF MANIFEST SYMPTOMATOLOGY

Analysts have always been proud of the distinction that theirs is a causal therapy, aiming directly at the conflicts and stresses which are hidden in the patients' personalities and underlie their symptomatology. Inevitably, with this approach they find themselves at cross-purposes with many of the adult neurotics under analysis who are intent only on being relieved of the suffering caused by painful anxieties and crippling obsessions, and who regard these as the only logical starting point for investigation; or with the parents of child patients who are concerned only with removing the disturbing manifestations in the child and completely disregard the pathological turn in the child's development which is revealed by the disturbances that trouble them.

Naturally, neither the adult neurotics themselves nor the parents of these endangered children possess the analyst's knowledge of the deceiving nature of overt symptomatology. They lack the experience of how quickly anxieties can be shifted from one apparently all-important object to another; or how easily one particular compulsion can be substituted for by a different one. Therefore, they cannot appreciate that symptoms are no more than symbols, to be taken merely as indications that some mental turmoil is taking place in

The material for this paper was gathered at the Hampstead Child-Therapy Clinic, an organization which at present is maintained by the Field Foundation, the Anna Freud Foundation, the Freud Centenary Fund, the Grant Foundation, the Flora Haas Estate, the National Institute for Mental Health, the Newland Foundation, the Andrew Mellon Foundation, the Psychoanalytic Research and Development Fund, and a number of private supporters.

the lower strata of the mind. Many symptoms, important and un-assailable as they seem if untreated, give way fairly easily to many types of therapy. But if they are removed by measures which do not reach to their roots, their place may be taken almost instantaneously by other pathological formations which, although overtly different, express the same latent content and may be no less aggravating for the individual's life.

On the other hand, symptoms are negligible in the analyst's view only for the purposes of the technique of therapy; in their eyes, too, symptoms have retained full significance so far as diagnostic classifi-cation is concerned. Whether a patient is assessed as a hysteric or phobic subject, as suffering from an obsessional neurosis or a para-noid state, is decided wholly on the basis of his manifest symptoma-tology, i.e., on the overt evidence of bodily conversions, anxiety attacks, avoidance mechanisms, compulsive acts, ruminations, projec-tions, etc.

There is an incongruity here between the analyst's therapeutic thinking, which is metapsychological, i.e., directed toward the dy-namic, economic, genetic, and structural aspects of psychic function-ing, and his thinking as a diagnostician, which proceeds on the basis of concepts and categories which are descriptive.[1] The differ-ence between these viewpoints is so fundamental that it has caused many analysts to withdraw their interest altogether from diagnostic assessment as from an area which is neither essential nor very signifi-cant for their field of work, and has caused some others to regard all their patients' abnormalities as mere variations of the many vagaries and complexities of human behavior.[2]

But before subscribing to a diagnostic nihilism of this extreme kind, the attempt seems worthwhile to bridge the gap between the two contrasting approaches and to use the vast array of overt symp-toms themselves for the purpose of forging links between them. There is no reason, after all, why the very classification of symptoma-tology should not go beyond enumeration and description and why probing into dynamic clashes and genetic antecedents should be ex-

[1] Or, at best, on the basis of unconscious content converted into conscious symbols.

[2] An outstanding example of the latter is Karl Menninger who is known to con-demn all psychiatric labels and classifications as unjustified offenses against the pa-tient's human dignity, i.e., as "name-calling."

cluded from it, to be reserved for scrutiny within the analytic procedure. It is inevitable, of course, that such a different mode of classification will sacrifice the neatness and order of any system based on phenomenology. It is only to be expected that in many instances there will be no one-to-one correlation between underlying unconscious constellation and manifest symptom. The former, as shown in Part I of this paper, can give rise to a variety of manifestations; the latter, as demonstrated in Part II, are the result of a variety of causes. Far from this being confusing for the analyst, it can only help to sharpen his diagnostic acumen.

When one is dealing with the psychopathology of childhood, a descriptive survey of symptomatology is even less rewarding. As is well known, in the immature personality, isolated symptoms are no reliable guide to any specific type of underlying pathology, nor are they a measure of its severity. Symptoms may be no more than the child's answer to some developmental stress and as such transitory, i.e., liable to pass away together with the maturational phase which has given rise to them. Or symptoms may represent a permanent countercathexis against some threatening drive derivative and as such be crippling to further development. Or symptoms, though pathological in origin, may nevertheless be ego-syntonic, and merged with the structure of the child's personality to a degree which makes it difficult to distinguish between such manifestations as outward evidence of ongoing pathological involvement or as more or less normal, stable features of the individual's character. There is no doubt that in any classification system based on phenomenology, these widely different classes of symptom appear as if on a par.

Moreover, if we scrutinize what children's clinics list under the heading of "referral symptoms," we feel doubtful whether in all instances these manifestations deserve to be classified as symptomatology, or whether the meaning of the term "symptom" is not extended here beyond its proper use. What is grouped together in such surveys are on the one hand the true signs or residues of present or past pathological processes; on the other hand such complaints by parents and disruptions of the child's life as, for example, multiplicity of fears; disturbances of intake, digestion, and elimination; sleep, respiratory or skin disturbances; aches and pains, motor disturbances; unusual sexual behavior; self-injurious acts and habits; disturbances of mood, affect, and object relatedness; failure of learning processes and/or poor quality of other ego functions; behavior disorders including antisocial reactions; moral indifference; failures of adaptation; failure to comply with parental demands or to fulfill parental expectation in general; etc.

Although an enumeration of this kind promises a first orientation in the field, and seems to satisfy the clinicians' immediate need at the stage of intake of cases, what it does, in fact, is to defeat its own purpose. By remaining strictly on the descriptive level, regardless of genetic roots, dynamic, structural, and economic complications, such an initial approach discourages analytic thinking and blocks the road to diagnostic assessment proper instead of facilitating it. Last but not least, it provides no clue for the diagnostician with regard to the choice of adequate therapeutic method.[3]

There is no warning implied in such a phenomenological survey that many of the items listed in it may belong genetically to any one of two, three, or more analytic categories. A *behavior disorder*, such as lying, for example, may be rooted in the child's stage of ego development, i.e., express the immature individual's inability to distinguish between reality and fantasy, or may signify a delay in acquiring and perfecting this important ego function. But, equally, lying may betray the level and quality of the child's object relations and express his fear of punishment and loss of love. As fantasy lying it may be evidence of persistent denial of unpalatable realities, with the function of reality testing fundamentally intact. As a feature of the child's character, it may denote weakness or failure of superego function.[4]

Disturbance of elimination such as extreme withholding of feces may have its roots in a very early vulnerability of the digestive system (i.e., psychosomatic); or it may be symbolic of the child's imitation of and identification with a pregnant mother (hysterical); or it may signify his revolt against inappropriate forms of toilet training (behavioral); or it may express phallic sexual needs and fantasies on a regressed anal level (obsessional).

Similarly, *enuresis* may be the sign either of simple failure of

---

[3] This may be the explanation why many clinics for children provide only one type of treatment, i.e., once weekly psychotherapy.

[4] See also Hedy Schwarz, "On Lying" (unpublished manuscript).

control in a generally impulsive personality structure,[5] or a highly complex reaction on the level of penis envy and castration anxiety. *Learning failures* may point to developmental arrest or, conversely, to blocking and inhibitions interfering with basically intact intellectual functions. *Antisocial reactions,* such as aggressve outbursts, may be the mark of defusion or insufficient fusion between libido and aggression; or of insufficient control of drives in an impulsive character; or of a violent defensive reaction against underlying passive-feminine leanings in boys striving overtly for masculinity.

In short, manifest symptoms may be identical so far as their appearance is concerned, but may differ widely in respect to latent meaning and pathological significance. According to the latter, they may require very different types of therapeutic handling.

Ideally, the solution for the analytic clinician in the children's field is a classification of symptoms which, on the one hand, embodies consideration of the various metapsychological aspects, while, on the other hand, maintains links with and pointers to the descriptive diagnostic categories as they are in common use. It is obvious nevertheless that no complex system of this kind will lend itself to the quick, almost automatic application to which diagnosticians are used so long as they remain within the framework of phenomenology. What is needed to make such a new classification of symptomatology profitable is, already at the diagnostic stage, a thorough investigation of the child's personality which makes it possible to pinpoint each symptom's relevance with regard to developmental level, structure, dynamic significance, etc.

I. SYMPTOMATOLOGY PROPER

As indicated above, for a first attempt of ordering the clinical material, it seems useful to separate symptoms, in the narrow sense of the term, from other signs of disturbance and other reasons for a child's referral for diagnosis and treatment. In this restricted field it becomes more possible to survey the relevant range of pathological processes and to correlate them with the various forms of mental illness which correspond to them.

[5] See J. J. Michaels (1955).

1. SYMPTOMS RESULTING FROM INITIAL NONDIFFERENTIATION
   BETWEEN SOMATIC AND PSYCHOLOGICAL PROCESSES:
   PSYCHOSOMATICS

At the beginning of life, before somatic and psychological processes are separated off from each other, bodily excitations such as
hunger, cold, pain, etc., are discharged as easily via mental pathways
in the form of unpleasure, anxiety, anger, rage, as mental upsets of
any kind are discharged via disturbances of the body surface, of intake, digestion, elimination, breathing, etc. Such "psychosomatic"
reactions are developmentally determined at this time of life. It is
important for later events which particular bodily outlets are given
preference by the individual since this choice gives rise to increased
sensitivity and vulnerability in the organ system concerned, i.e., the
skin, the respiratory system, the intestinal system, the sleep rhythm,
etc.

Normally, this easy access from mind to body (and vice versa)
diminishes with advancing ego development and the opening up of
new, purely mental pathways of discharge by means of action,
thought, speech. Where it remains more than usually open, on the
other hand, it accounts directly for the range of *psychosomatic symptomatology*, i.e., for *asthma, eczema, ulcerative colitis, headaches,
migraine*, etc.

It is also responsible for the creation of the so-called "somatic
compliance" which, in later and more complex hysterical symptom
formation, facilitates the conversion of mental processes into physical manifestations with symbolic meaning.

2. SYMPTOMS RESULTING FROM COMPROMISE FORMATIONS BETWEEN
   ID AND EGO: NEUROTIC SYMPTOMATOLOGY

Since basic psychoanalytic training takes place in the area of
theory and therapy of the neuroses, analysts feel most knowledgeable
about the specific structure of neurotic symptomatology. In fact, so
far as the neuroses are concerned, the term "symptom" has become
synonymous with the conception of the ego acting as intermediary
and finding solutions for the clashes between drive derivatives on the
one hand and other, rational or moral, claims of the individual on
the other hand. The complex route of symptom formation along a

line of danger-anxiety-regression-defense-compromise has become familiar.

The resulting symptomatic structures may prove ego-dystonic and continue to produce mental pain and discomfort; or they may be accepted as ego-syntonic and become part of the individual's character. The latter outcome depends largely on economic factors, i.e., on the varying degrees to which elements from id, ego, and superego sides are embodied in the final symptomatic result. It depends also on the ego's willingness to become distorted itself by accommodating the pathological manifestation within its structure. This last-mentioned solution, not to treat the symptoms as a foreign body, is one often adopted by children.

Since compromise formations of this kind depend for their existence on established boundaries between id and ego, unconscious and conscious, we do not expect to find neurotic symptoms in the unstructured personality, i.e., in early infancy. Neurotic symptom formation waits until the ego has divided itself off from the id, but does not need to wait until ego and superego also have become two independent agencies. The first id-ego conflicts, and with them the first neurotic symptoms as conflict solutions, are produced with the ego under pressure from the environment, i.e., threatened not by guilt feelings arising internally from the superego but by dangers arising from the object world such as loss of love, rejection, punishment.

The neurotic manifestations of this phase are *hysterical* in nature so far as the body areas involved have oral or oral-aggressive value and the symptom implies a primitive defense against these drive representatives (*affection of single limbs, motor disturbances, aches and pains, food fads and avoidances, vomiting*). They are *obsessional* in nature so far as they defend against anal-sadistic strivings (first appearance of *compulsive cleanliness, orderliness, repetitiveness, avoidance of touch*).

With the emergence and dissolution of the phallic-oedipal strivings and the superego as an independent source of guilt these isolated symptoms become organized into the syndromes which form the familiar infantile neuroses, i.e., the full-blown *phobias* (of animals, of separation, of doctor, dentist, of the lavatory, of school, etc.) as well as the true *obsessional neuroses*, complete with *doubting, repeating, rituals*, bedtime *ceremonials, ruminations, compulsive ac-*

tions. Crippling *inhibitions, ego restrictions,* and *self-injurious tendencies* appear as character defenses against aggression at this time.

3. SYMPTOMS RESULTING FROM THE IRRUPTION OF ID DERIVATIVES
   INTO THE EGO

Neurotic symptomatology comes about only where the border between id and ego is intact. This may be lacking for a variety of reasons: the ego may be constitutionally weak; or the id strivings may be constitutionally increased in intensity; damage may have been done to the ego through traumatic events which have put it out of action; or through phase-determined alterations of the inner equilibrium. In any case, the result will be failure to control id content and the entrance of id elements into the ego organization, with disruptive consequences for the latter.

Where the irrupting elements are part of primary process functioning and take the place of the rational secondary process thinking which is characteristic for the ego otherwise, the corresponding manifest symptoms such as *disturbances of thought and language, misidentifications, delusions,* etc., are significant for the differential diagnosis between neurosis and psychosis; if only partially in evidence, they are a hallmark of the borderline states between the two diagnostic categories.

Where the irrupting elements are from the area of the drives, the resulting symptoms consist of the *undefended* (or unsuccessfully defended) *acting out of drive derivatives* with disregard for reality considerations which is characteristic for certain types of delinquency and criminality.

The combination of both leakages from the id produces those ominous types of abnormal behavior which on the one hand carry the individual beyond the confines of what is legally permissible and, on the other hand, characterize him as mentally ill and for this reason absolved from responsibility for his actions.

4. SYMPTOMS RESULTING FROM CHANGES IN THE LIBIDO ECONOMY
   OR DIRECTION OF CATHEXIS

Although all symptom formation implies pathological upsets to the dynamics and structural aspects of the personality, these may be secondary to alterations in the economy of the libido and the direction of its employment.

Where, for example, the narcissistic cathexis of the self is increased unduly, the corresponding symptomatic results are *egotism*, *self-centeredness, overvaluation* of the self, in extreme cases *megalomania*. Where such cathexis is decreased unduly, the symptoms are *bodily neglect, self-derogation, inferiority feelings, depressive states, depersonalization* (in childhood).

Direction of cathexis may be altered in three respects with corresponding symptomatology. Narcissistic libido may move from the individual's mind to his body, where the increased cathexis of specific body parts creates *hypochrondriacal* symptoms. Object libido may be withdrawn from the external world, changed into narcissistic libido, and employed wholly in cathexis of the self. Or, conversely, all narcissistic libido may be added to the existing object libido and become concentrated on an external love object with consequences for its overvaluation; in extreme cases for complete *emotional surrender* to it.

5. SYMPTOMS RESULTING FROM CHANGES IN THE
    QUALITY OR DIRECTION OF AGGRESSION

What is significant for symptomatology in this respect are the changes in intensity as well as the frequent changes in aim direction, from mind to body, from self to object, and vice versa.

The former, the quantitative changes, are brought about mainly by the vagaries within the defense organization, in childhood by the varying quality of the defense mechanisms which are employed, from crudely primitive to highly sophisticated. These decide about the availability or nonavailability of the necessary aggressive contributions to ego functioning and to sublimations. Some of the resulting symptomatic manifestations are *inhibitions* and *failure* in play, learning, and work.

The type of defense used against aggression is also responsible for the swings between *self-injurios behavior*, which corresponds to aggression turned against the self, and violent *aggressive-destructive outbursts* against animate and inanimate objects in the environment.

6. SYMPTOMS RESULTING FROM UNDEFENDED REGRESSIONS

In our work with children we have become alerted to a type of pathological manifestation which equals a prestage of neurotic symptom formation, but remains abortive so far as the infantile neuroses are concerned. Its point of origin is the phallic phase, its precipitating cause is danger and anxiety arising from the oedipus and castration complexes, followed by regression to oral and anal fixation points.

While in neurotic symptom formation such regressions are rejected by the ego and defended against, in these cases they are accepted and treated as ego-syntonic, i.e., they do not give rise to further conflict. The result is a lowering of all aspects of the personality (drive activity as well as ego functioning). The clinical pictures which correspond to this are *infantilism* and a form of *pseudodebility,* accompanied by behavioral symptoms such as *whining, clinging,* prolonged *dependency, passive-feminine traits* in boys, *inefficiency,* etc.

7. SYMPTOMS RESULTING FROM ORGANIC CAUSES

The foregoing enumeration leaves to the last those disturbances of psychic function which have an organic origin such as brain damage due to prenatal influences or to birth injury or to later inflammatory processes or to traumatic accidents. A whole range of symptoms is attributable to these causes such as a *delay in developmental milestones, difficulties in locomotion,* difficulties with *speech, poor* quality of *intellectual functions, interference with concentration, flatness or lability of affect, distractability,* etc. Many of these symptoms bear a close resemblance to the result of inhibitions, compromise formations, or any other of the categories described above, and the correct diagnosis is difficult in those cases where the neurological tests prove inconclusive. Doubtless, mistakes in differential diagnosis occur here in both directions, either mental or organic damage being discounted unjustifiably, or a combination between both factors being overlooked.

What should also be added here are those symptomatic manifestations or deviations from the norm which are the direct or indirect consequence of physical handicaps, whether inborn or acquired ones. It is well known by now that where vision is missing, ego development is thrown into confusion, the balance between autoerotism and object relatedness disturbed, aggression inhibited, passivity enhanced, etc. Where hearing is absent or grossly defective, not only speech development but secondary process thinking and, with it, higher development of the personality are interfered with. Missing limbs, spasticity bring with them their own psychopathology which needs to be explored further.

II. OTHER SIGNS OF DISTURBANCE AND OTHER REASONS FOR A CHILD'S CLINICAL REFERRAL

As discussed before, not all the manifestations which lead to a child's clinical examination are evidence of true pathology, nor do they all form part of recognized clinical pictures. There are other disturbances, upsets, and malfunctions, and, consequently, other reasons for referral. What they all have in common is that they represent interferences with normal processes, with adequate growth and development, with reasonable behavior, with contentment and enjoyment of life, with adaptation to environmental conditions and requirements. Since the causes for them are diffuse, and the same overt manifestation may be due to a variety of underlying constellations, the attempt seems justified to approach their classification from a different angle. The method adopted before consisted of following certain psychic processes ongoing in the depth to their various expressions on the surface of the mind. The procedure applied to what follows is the opposite one, namely, to start out from the surface signs of disturbance and, from there, to trace back the links to whichever upheaval, involvement or failure may be responsible for them.

1. THE FEARS AND ANXIETIES

The mere number of children who are referred to clinics with fears and anxieties of all kinds and intensities justifies the attempt to classify these manifestations as such, i.e., apart from the active role which they play in the formation of a variety of clinical syndromes.

It is well known to analysts, of course, that anxiety, experienced by the ego, is a regular accompaniment to development in childhood, occasioned on the one hand by the helplessness of the immature being, on the other hand by structuralization, higher development, and the resultant rising tension between the inner agencies. Its absence rather than its presence in the picture is considered as an ominous sign. Nevertheless, even though anxiety is normal and the disturbance in many instances no more than a quantitative exacerbation of expectable reactions, anxiety states remain one of the most common and potent causes of suffering in childhood.

To arrive at their understanding, these manifestations have to be viewed from a number of angles. For example, their classification can be, and has been, attempted from the *developmental* point of view, by creating a chronological sequence according to which the common fears and anxieties are allocated to the various instinctual phases in which they arise and, connected with these, the external or internal dangers toward which they are directed. Classification has also been carried out from the aspect of *dynamic* vicissitude, i.e., from the side of the defenses employed to keep fear and anxiety in check, and the *economic* factors which determine the success or failure of these coping mechanisms. What has been done most frequently by analytic authors, without doubt, is to explore the role played by the various kinds of anxiety in *structural* conflict and the responsibility which has to be ascribed to them for the swings between mental health and illness since it is at their instigation that the ego's defensive mechanisms and, following on them, the ego's compromises with the id are put into action.

Obviously, it is the diagnostician's task to explore each of these avenues in greater detail.

(i) *The Chronology of Fears and Anxieties*

Where the clinician arrives at ordering the child's manifest fears and anxieties according to the developmental stages in which they arise and according to the dangers represented by these stages, many of the quantitative increases in them can be understood as due to unsatisfied developmental needs or to unjustifiable developmental interferences (see Nagera, 1966).

The initial stages of ego development, in this view, become correlated with the so-called *archaic fears* of the infant. These are inevitable while the ego has no resources of its own to cope either with the massive stimuli which arrive from the environment or with the equally disturbing tensions in the inner world. These fears increase in intensity and range when a child's ego is unusually sensitive or when a child's mother is unusually unable to provide the comfort and reassurance to which the infant is entitled at this stage. Where ego development is slow, the archaic fears last beyond infancy. Their undue persistence and prominence can be taken as diagnostic indicators for retardation or arrest in the area of ego functioning.

The symbiotic stage, i.e., the phase of biological unity between infant and mother, is relevant for the arousal of *separation anxiety*, i.e., fear of object loss, whenever this unity is threatened. Separation anxiety becomes overwhelming if the infant experiences actual separations from the mother, or if in other ways the mother proves unreliable as a stable object. Separation anxiety can be prolonged unduly, which points diagnostically to fixation in the symbiotic phase or arrests in it.[6]

When the parental objects become representatives of the demand for drive control, the child's difficulty of complying with this arouses *fear of rejection* by the object and fear of the loss of the object's love. As such, these fears are signs of beginning moral adjustment and positive prestages of superego development; their nonemergence points to developmental failure in these respects. They become excessive for environmental reasons if the parents commit errors in either the timing or the harshness of their demands. But even where no blame can be attached to the environment in this respect, oversensitivity of the ego or excessive dependency on being loved can bring about the same result for internal reasons.

The arrival of a boy in the phallic phase, which as such is a welcome event, commonly reveals itself at the same time in a heightened fear for the intactness of his sex organ, i.e., in *castration anxiety*. The frequent exacerbations of this correspond directly to the strivings of the oedipus complex and depend on the defenses and compromise formations which the ego employs to deal with them. Castration

[6] There are fears of object loss in later childhood which manifest themselves as difficulties in separating from the parental objects, especially the mother. Although phenomenologically identical, they are different in dynamic and structural respects, i.e., due to internal rejection of aggression and death wishes directed against the parents.

anxiety represents a specific threat for development owing to the drive regressions initiated by it and their further role for neurosis and character formation.

The child's first moves from family to community and his new dependency on the opinions of his peers give rise to an additional *fear,* that of *social disgrace,* which is especially experienced in school.

According to the individual child's structural development, i.e., with the establishment of the superego's independence and authority (whenever this happens), the advance from anxiety to *guilt* is made as the crowning step in this chronology of infantile fears.

Obviously, such a chronology of fears and anxieties is helpful as a diagnostic tool since observation of the presenting disturbance leads directly to the corresponding phase of development in which the child's mental upset is rooted. Nevertheless, it fails to serve the diagnostician in other respects, since it does not include an important anxiety which neither originates in any particular phase nor bears the characteristics of any one, but persists through the whole period of development and reappears at all times of later life, not for reasons of fixation or regression but whenever the inner structural balance is upset. This anxiety denotes the ego's concern for the intactness of its own organization, at whatever level; it is due to economic reasons, i.e., to the uneven distribution of energy between id and ego; and it gains in intensity whenever the strength of the drive derivatives increases or ego strength diminishes for some reason.

In contrast to other anxieties, this *fear of the id* is not favorably influenced by the lightening of external pressure. Much to the parents' disappointment, it is increased rather than decreased by excessive educational leniency or by educational nihilism.

When fear of the id is more than usually in evidence, it arouses the diagnostic suspicion of a borderline or prepsychotic state.

(ii) *The Manifest and Latent Content of Fears and Anxieties*

While in these childhood cases described, the affect of anxiety is manifest and brought directly to the clinician's notice, the latent meaning of the fear is obscured by the fact that almost any type of anxiety can find symbolic expression in almost any mental representation, or can remain free-floating and unattached. Nevertheless, in most instances it is possible to correlate fear and symbol as follows:

Archaic fears:	of darkness, noise, strangers, solitude, etc.
separation anxiety:	of annihiliation, starvation, loneliness, helplessness, etc.
fear of loss of love:	of punishment, rejection, desertion, earth quakes, thunderstorms, death, etc.
castration anxiety:	of operation, mutilation, doctor, dentist, illness, poverty, robbers, witches, ghosts, etc.

On the whole, these symbols are also interchangeable and, by themselves, an insufficient guide to diagnosis.

(iii) *Defense against Anxiety, Absence of Defense,*
      Its Role within the Structure

So far as a classification of the various fates of anxieties is concerned, the study of childhood cases is more productive than that of adult ones since the defensive moves against anxiety are more often incomplete, i.e., partly unsuccessful. This allows both sides to be visible on the conscious surface, on the one hand the manifest expression of the anxiety affect, on the other hand the ego's attempts to deal with the danger situations and their affective consequences by means of denial or avoidance, displacement or projection, repression, reaction formation, or any other available defense mechanism or defensive move, or a combination of several of them.

There is also the possibility for defense against anxiety to be lacking altogether, or to be wholly unsuccessful, in which case the affect reigns supreme in the form of *panic states* and full-blown *anxiety attacks.*[7] The occurrence of these is indicative that the child's ego has failed to acquire the important ability to reduce harmful panic anxiety to structurally useful signal anxiety, i.e., to the much smaller amount which is necessary to set defense in motion. Panics and anxiety attacks are not only extremely painful for the total personality of the child, they are, in fact, actually harmful for the

---

[7] For the clinician it is important to differentiate between such states and the common temper tantrums of childhood, which are manifestly similar but different as regards origin.

ego which is swamped by them. Similar to true traumatic events, they temporarily put ego functioning out of action and thereby constitute a threat to the stability of the ego organization.

Classification of anxiety according to defense activity also provides clues for predicting the direction in which the child's further course is set: toward more or less normal adjustment; toward social or dissocial character formation; toward hysterical, or phobic, or obsessional or paranoid symptom formation or character development, etc.

2. THE DELAYS OR FAILURES IN DEVELOPMENT

It is well known by now that the developmental age of a child does not need to coincide with his chronological age and that fairly wide discrepancies in this respect are within the normal range. Children may be either fast or slow developers throughout. One also frequently sees that they change their rate of growing between one developmental phase and the succeeding one.

Nevertheless, a large number of children arrive in the clinic with the "referral symptoms" of unsatisfactory development, which, on clinical examination, may be found to range from the merest delay to the complete cessation of all forward movement on the lines of progress. A child's failure to reach the expected level of growth may show up anywhere within the structure of his personality. It may concern the so-called milestones in the first year of life, i.e., the advances in motor development, the beginning of speech, etc. On the side of the drives it may concern a lagging behind on the prephallic libidinal and aggressive stages, in extreme instances a failure to reach the phallic-oedipal level at all. So far as the ego is concerned, the arrest may reveal itself in the quality of object relatedness, for example, in the persistence of anaclitic relationships at a time of life when object constancy is to be expected; or in the retardation of functions such as control of motility, reality testing, memory, learning capacity which remain below par; or in the defense organization which may remain at a primitive level of functioning via somatization, denial, projection, avoidance, etc., instead of advancing to repression, reaction formations, and sublimations. The superego may be retarded either with respect to its autonomy, or its effectiveness, or with regard to the quality of its content, i.e., the crudeness of the internalized commands and prohibitions.

Developmental irregularities and failures of this kind confront the clinician with many problems, foremost among them the need to differentiate between the causes for them. Retardation of milestones in the first year of life raises the suspicion of *organic* damage (see Part I, 7). Delay in drive development may either be due to *constitutional* factors or may be determined *environmentally* by inadequate response from the parental objects. Ego retardation is frequently due to poor *endowment* but, as the study of many underprivileged children has revealed, equally often the consequence of lack of proper *environmental* stimulation. Arrested superego development may be part of general ego retardation (and share its causations); or it may be due to the lack of adequate objects in the child's *environment;* or to separations from them; or to *internal* failure to form relations to objects; or to the *qualities* of the parental personalities with whom the child identifies. Traumatic experiences may at any time endanger progress in any direction or, at worst, bring forward development to a complete standstill.

It remains as a task then to distinguish between these developmental delays and failures and another type of damage to development which, though superficially similar, is different in kind. While the former refer to expected developmental steps not being taken, the latter represents the undoing of developmental achievements after they have been acquired and is due to regressions and inhibitions, i.e., based on conflict (see Part I,2, neurotic symptomatology). Although the differential diagnosis here is important, and becomes all-important when the choice of therapy comes into question, confusion—especially between the effects of arrest and regression—is frequent. There are few criteria to guide the clinician when, for example, he has to decide whether a boy has retreated from the phallic to the anal level (due to castration anxiety), or whether he has never reached the phallic stage; whether a child's superego has never proceeded beyond a primitive, crude level or whether it has become so at a later, more sophisticated stage of development, due to aggression turned inward and/or sexualization of its demands, etc. The most reliable hallmarks of neurosis are anxiety, guilt, and conflict, while in contrast to this the various types of developmental arrest may remain internally undisputed, especially in those cases where the arrest affects more than one sector of the personality. But this diagnostic indicator too cannot be trusted in all instances. Retarded children frequently react with anxiety and a semblance of guilt to the disapproval of their disappointed parents, while neurotic children are well able to deny conflict and guilt and thereby make them disappear from the manifest picture.

3. THE SCHOOL FAILURES

While all developmental failures are apt to arouse the parents' concern, usually they seek clinical advice most urgently when the child lags behind in age-adequate intellectual achievement and becomes a school failure. While the parents' concern exists regardless of the origin of the defect, in clinical examination it proves most important to distinguish between the different types of causation which can be subsumed under almost any of the different diagnostic categories discussed above.

Thus, learning difficulties, although they may be identical in their manifest appearance, may have to be allocated to any of the following categories:

to *arrested development,* affecting either the person of the child as a whole, or the ego in general, or the ego's intellectual function in particular;

to *undefended ego regression,* either global or particular to the intellect;

to *sexualization or aggressive symbolization,* either of the learning process as such, or of the particular subject to which the learning difficulty is attached;

to *defense* against the symbolic dangers implied, especially by means of *inhibition* and ego restriction;

to *symptom formation* of the neurotic types and its crippling effect on ego activity in general and sublimation in particular.

4. FAILURES IN SOCIAL ADAPTATION

In this respect, as in the previous one, there is a marked discrepancy between the parents' concern which is easily alerted when a child fails to respond to moral standards, and their ignorance with regard to the causes which, either singly or combined, lead to the asocial, or dissocial, or delinquent or even criminal behavior which is produced.

On the basis of the reasoning which has gone before, failures in social adaptation can be seen in the following lights:

as the logical outcome of adverse environmental circumstances such as neglect, lack of stability in object relations, separations and other traumatic events, undue parental pressure, failure of parental guidance, etc.;

as the result of defects in the ego functions and the defense organization due to developmental arrests or neurotic regressions;

as the result of economic alterations in the balance between id and ego;

as the result of defects in the superego, caused by failures in object relatedness, identifications, internalizations, or by aggression used in its entirety against the external world instead of being in part at the disposal of the superego;

as the result of faulty ego ideals, due to deviant parental models for identification.

In fact, causation of social failure is extremely varied in its nature, ranging, as it does, from the purely environmental to the near-psychotic. This has led to doubts among clinicians and some law teachers whether it is permissible at all to use the terms "dissociality" or "delinquency" as diagnostic labels, instead of speaking merely of dissocial or delinquent actions committed by individuals who may belong to any number of diagnostic categories.[8]

5. ACHES AND PAINS

What remains are the multiple aches and pains of childhood for which no organic cause can be found in physical examination. They alarm the parents, and distress the child. Incidentally, they also lead to innumerable absences from school and, if massive, may constitute a serious threat to formal education. They are also the most frequent reason for a child's medical referral to a child guidance clinic or, in general, for a pediatrician's interest in the intricacies of child psychology.

[8] See, for example, Joseph Goldstein of the Yale Law School who opposes violently the use of "delinquency" as a meaningful diagnostic term.

According to the metapsychological classification of symptoms in Part I of this paper, the various aches and pains of nonorganic origin can be traced back to three or four of the categories enumerated there:

to category 1, so far as they are the direct somatic expression of mental processes;

to category 2, so far as the affected body parts are symbolic of mental content and as such involved in mental conflict;

to categories 3 or 4, so far as the affection of the body part is due to changes of cathexis, either qualitative or quantitative.

The diffuse aches and pains of childhood can be characterized accordingly as either psychosomatic, or hysterical, or hypochondriacal. It hardly needs stressing that these different origins have a significant bearing on the evaluation of the presenting symptom, on the therapeutic approach to it, as well as on the prognosis with regard to its transience or permanency.

CONCLUSIONS

The Diagnostic Profile, as it is in use in the Hampstead Child-Therapy Clinic at present, is intended to draw the diagnostician's concentration away from the child's pathology and to return it instead to an assessment of his developmental status and the picture of his total personality. The present attempt at classifying the symptomatology of childhood may serve to amend and amplify this procedure by returning to the symptoms themselves a measure of diagnostic significance. If symptoms are viewed merely as manifest phenomena, dealing with them remains arid so far as analytic interest is concerned. If the clinician is alerted to see opening up behind these the whole range of possible derivations, causations, and developmental affiliations, the field becomes fascinating, and scrutinizing a child's symptomatology becomes a truly analytic task.

Besides, so far as work with children is concerned, diagnostic assessment is more than a mere intellectual exercise for the clinician. It is, in fact, the only true guide to the choice of therapeutic method.

As matters stand now, the form of treatment available for a disturbed child depends usually not on the specific category of his disorder but on the resources of the department or clinical facility to which he has been referred: institutional or foster parent provision if he is taken in care; residential treatment if, legally, found out of control; weekly psychotherapy if referred to a child guidance clinic; family psychiatry, where this is the clinic's orientation; full-scale child analysis in a psychoanalytic clinic. It is only too frequent that the specific type of treatment applied is insufficiently matched with the specific type of disorder which should have been ascertained. Where this happens, children find themselves in institutions while they are in urgent need of individual, one-to-one relationships to develop their libidinal potentialities. Or they find themselves adopted, or in foster care, in spite of being far removed from the possibility of producing the child-to-parent attitudes which are an indispensable requirement of these situations. Or they receive analysis when education and guidance are needed; or guidance, when only analysis can solve their internal conflicts.

It is also futile to expect that any single method, whether superficial or deep, educational or therapeutic, will prove effective with disorders which are as different from each other as, for example, the neurotic compromise formations and the developmental arrests; or, so far as the learning failures are concerned, those caused by arrest, by undefended regression, and by inhibitions. Arrested children have to be treated educationally on their own mental level, an approach which fails disastrously where the therapeutic need is for the undoing of regressions or of lifting conflicts to consciousness, i.e., of freeing in the child an existing intellectual potentiality. Where the diagnostician remains on the phenomenological level and remains oblivious of the underlying fundamental differences, such therapeutic misapplications become inevitable.

The same plea for therapeutic differentiation (following diagnostic differentiation) is justified where the child's fears and anxieties are concerned. It is as futile therapeutically to reassure a child in the throes of castration anxiety and guilt as it would be futile to approach separation anxiety at the symbiotic stage with analytic efforts. Fear of loss of love can be diminished by removal of external pressure, but only in those instances where its origin is due largely to environmental causes; not in others. Where fear of the id is present, as said before, parental leniency acts as an aggravating factor, not as a relieving one.

Where children commit delinquent acts, it is perhaps more obvious than with other disturbances that treatment has to be selected according to the cause being either environmental, or developmental, or neurotic, or psychotic. No single type of therapy, however elaborate, or costly, or easily available, can possibly fit these widely different circumstances.

It is reasonable to expect that any step forward in the refinement of diagnostic assessment will, in the long run, lead to improvements in matching disorder and therapy in the children's field. The present paper is meant to represent a move in this direction.

APPENDIX

THE SYMPTOMATOLOGY OF CHILDHOOD

I. Symptomatology Proper

1. Symptoms resulting from the initial nondifferentiation between somatic and psychological processes=psychosomatic manifestations.

2. Symptoms resulting from compromise formations between id and ego=neurotic manifestations.

3. Symptoms resulting from the irruption of id derivatives into the ego=infantile psychosis, borderline states, delinquent states.

4. Symptoms resulting from changes in the libido economy or direction of cathexis=upsets in self and object valuation, depressive states, autism, emotional surrender.

5. Symptoms resulting from changes in the quality or direction of aggression=inhibition of functioning, accident proneness, self-injury, aggressive outbursts.

6. Symptoms resulting from undefended regressions=infantilisms, pseudodebility.

7. Symptoms resulting from organic causes:

   (a) from brain damage = delay of milestones, reduced quality of ego functioning, affective changes, etc.;
   (b) from sensory or anatomical handicaps = deviations in drive and ego development, multiple upsets of inner equilibrium.

II. *Other Signs of Disturbance*

1. The fears and anxieties (origin, content, defense, bearing on pathology).

2. The delays and failures in development (organic, constitutional, environmental, traumatic; differentiation from regressions).

3. The school failures (developmental arrest, undefended ego regression, sexualization or aggressive symbolization and defense against it, neurotic inhibition, ego restriction, neurotic symptom formation).

4. Failures in social adaptation (environmental, developmental, economic, structural, neurotic, psychotic).

5. Aches and pains (psychosomatic, hysterical, hypochondriacal).

BIBLIOGRAPHY

Freud, A. (1965), *Normality and Pathology in Childhood.* New York: International Universities Press.
Michaels, J. J. (1955), *Disorders of Character.* Springfield, Ill.: Charles C Thomas.
Nagera, H. (1966), *Early Childhood Disturbances, the Infantile Neurosis, and the Adulthood Disturbances.* New York: International Universities Press.

CONTRIBUTIONS TO PSYCHOANALYTIC THEORY

PSYCHOANALYTIC THEORY AND THE PSYCHOANALYTIC PROCESS

HANS W. LOEWALD, M.D. (New Haven)

I

An investigation of the relationship of psychoanalytic theory to the psychoanalytic process and method is fraught with difficulties and pitfalls, as the many recent efforts to elucidate and, where necessary, to redefine and revise, theoretical concepts and formulations have demonstrated. In this attempt it is important that psychoanalytic theory (or metapsychology), though being on a high level of abstraction and generalization, keep faith with our work as analysts. This work, whether we consider it as scientific or as therapeutic or as both, has given us the insights into psychic reality, into the processes and structures of the human mind, on which the theory is founded. Yet, in the attempt to arrive at a general body of theory, following the lead and premises of other sciences, we have come to divorce, to a significant degree, theory from method and process of investigation; we have neglected the implications which the unique conditions in our field—that aspect of reality which psychoanalysis deals with— have for our method and for theory formation. To evolve theory as though our methods and processes of study were essentially the same, or could be the same, as those of other sciences, or could be disregarded when it comes to theory, implies a view of reality that is no longer tenable, least of all in that ambiguous area which we call psychic reality. Nevertheless, all of us are still more or less captives of an erroneous understanding of objectivity and objective reality, and this is one reason for the difficulties.

Based on a lecture presented at the Plenary Session of the Regional Conference arranged by the Chicago Psychoanalytic Society, Chicago, February 21-22, 1970.

I gratefully acknowledge a grant by the Robert P. Knight Fund which helped support part of the work on which this paper is based.

I mentioned that the unique conditions prevailing in our field of study have specific implications for its method and theory. The scientific fiction—I use that word here in its nonpejorative sense—of a field of study to which we are in the relation of extraneous observers cannot be maintained in psychoanalysis. We become part and participant of and in the field as soon as we are present in our role as analysts. The unit of a psychoanalytic investigation is the individual human mind or personality. We single it out—for reasons deeply rooted in that human mind of which we ourselves are specimens—as a subject worthy of study, as a universe in its own right. "Universe" has been defined as "any distinct field or province of thought or reality conceived as forming a closed system or self-inclusive and independent organization." The individual's status in this regard, however, is questionable and cannot be taken for granted. If nothing else, the phenomena of transference and resistance, encountered in both analysand and analyst during the investigation of our object of study, demonstrate the precariousness of that status and show that the individual cannot be studied psychoanalytically as though he were simply a closed system investigated by another closed system. In fact, a psychoanalytic investigation must take into account and include in its investigation the phenomena of transference and resistance as essential parts of what we want to study and of our investigative method.

For the purpose of study, we have to become an integral, though in certain ways detached, part of the "field of study." The object of investigation, the analysand, as well as the investigator, the analyst, although each has a considerable degree of internal psychic organization and relative autonomy in respect to the other, can enter a psychoanalytic investigation only by virtue of their being relatively open systems, and open to each other. And each in his own ways must renounce a degree of autonomy for the sake of the investigation. Neither the object of investigation nor the investigator can be dealt with theoretically as though a simple subject-object confrontation obtained. We even have to qualify our speaking of investigator and object, insofar as the object, by the very nature of the psychoanalytic process, becomes an investigator of himself, and the investigator-analyst becomes an object of study to himself. At the same time the analysand, although not in a scientifically and professionally informed and skilled way, "studies" the analyst in the analytic process, and the analyst must hold himself open as an object of the analysand's search (by this, of course, I do not mean that he must answer questions and tell the analysand about himself). The analysand's search proceeds under the surface, often unconsciously, and the analyst is not always aware of being the object of such a search. That the analytic relationship is an asymmetrical one, and that it has to be that if analysis is to proceed, is unquestioned.

All this is confusing—our customary categories and distributions of role and our traditional views on the constellation of an investigation do not fit. Implied in the foregoing considerations, but to be made more explicit, is that the two systems, the two would-be universes, the one which is studied and the one which investigates, are the same kinds of organizations: individual psychic organizations. The mental processes and structures we study in our patients are essentially the same as our own and of the same order of reality (psychic reality), as well as of the same order as the processes and structures by means of which we study them. Our traditional standard of objectivity implies that making something an object of investigation means to subject it to procedures, ultimately mental ones, which are in principle extraneous and superordinated to the processes inherent in the object. There are differences between analysand and analyst in the degree to which their mental processes are developed and organized, and these differences make for the possibility of relative objectivity. But the differences must not be too great; if they are, the psychic processes in the object of investigation are no longer within the ken of psychoanalytic investigation. The case of the infant or of the deeply regressed psychotic (as extreme examples) introduces factors which interfere with psychoanalytic investigation, because the latter is based on the premise that analysand and analyst are both participants and that the analysand, too, is capable of a measure of objectivity toward himself as well as toward the analyst. The analysand must, at least to some extent, have developed an "observing ego" in order to get the analytic investigation off the ground.

In contrast to physics or biology, for instance, psychoanalytic knowledge and explanation depend not so much on the differences between the processes obtaining in the scientist and those obtaining in his object, but on their similarity and interrelatedness. It is a com-

monplace that introspection and empathy are essential tools of psychoanalysis, and that we can analyze others only as far as we have
been analyzed ourselves and understand ourselves. To this there is
the corollary: we understand ourselves phychoanalytically by seeing
ourselves as others (objectivating introspection), and our self-understanding is greatly enhanced by analyzing others, as every analyst
knows. This is so not only because in the external other we can
often see ourselves more clearly, but also because in this concentrated and minutely scrutinized relationship, in this specially focused
and heightened field of psychic forces, the analyst's intrapsychic field
gains in vitality and vivid outline. The analysand in this respect can
be compared to the child who—if he can allow himself that freedom
—scrutinizes with his unconscious antennae the parents' motivations
and moods and in this way may contribute—if the parent or analyst
allows himself that freedom—to the latter's self-awareness. Internal
communication, on which self-understanding is based, and communication with another organization of the same rank of reality—the
psychic reality of another individual—are inextricably interwoven.

There are still other important elements inherent in the analytic
process and method of psychoanalytic research and these should be
encompassed in a psychoanalytic theory worthy of that name. One
such fundamental characteristic of the human psyche is the capacity
to change. "Where id was, there ego shall become" (Freud, 1933)[1]
is not simply a statement of therapeutic goals. This dictum says that
by being understood psychoanalytically and by understanding ourselves we tend to change. Our psychic organization tends to increase
its range and level of functioning or, on the other hand, to become
disorganized by virtue of the investigation itself. Disorganization
and higher organization often go hand in hand; the balance or confluence of the two may be precarious or disrupted, but they are part
of the investigative process itself. By opening up the channels of
intrapsychic and interpsychic communication our psychic life is altered, even if this opening up has only increased anxiety and guilt
and heightened defenses. Here we have the problem of our conventional distinction between scientific investigation and therapy, be-

[1] Strachey's translation, "Where id was, there ego shall *be*" (p. 80) does not do
justice to the original, "Wo Es war, soll Ich *werden*" (*Gesammelte Werke*, Vol. 15,
p. 86).

tween psychoanalysis as a "research tool" and as treatment. Again, the facts of psychic life and of what the psychoanalytic study of another person involves do not fit these traditional distinctions. The dichotomy of pure and applied science may be applicable, to quite a degree at least, in other scientific disciplines; it is not applicable in ours.

Psychoanalyzing someone means to intervene in his psychic life. For this reason we enter into such an investigation only upon the request and with the active consent of the analysand (and we attempt to make sure that the consent is as informed as it can be at the outset of the venture). We must decide as best we can, beforehand or during the initial stage, whether such an intervention "makes sense" for the other person or is contraindicated because of the dangers involved in the process. If psychoanalysis is not indicated in a given case, this is not only a matter of the patient's being too vulnerable or not sufficiently able to be part of the analytic process; the investigation per se would not get very far without the patient's active participation and capacity for psychic work.

From each individual investigation, of course, we learn a great deal about human nature, about psychic reality in general. In this process we use not only the data accumulated by others and the theories that have been constructed on the basis of these data. In addition to using these as guidelines, we may also try to contribute further empirical data and/or to refine or revise or enlarge the theory. But in our field the theory has to encompass and organize not only what we consider the "objective data" observed or inferred by us from what the analysand presents, but more fundamentally also what we learn about the nature of psychic reality from the investigative process itself. This requirement increases in measure as the level of abstraction becomes higher.

The investigative process furnishes insights into the formation, disorganization, maintenance, enrichment, and impoverishment of psychic processes and structure, into the determinants of conflict and conflict resolution, etc.—all being of the greatest relevance precisely for psychoanalytic theory; more so, I believe, than, for instance, the sorting out, definition, and clarification of the various "functions" (from the point of view of adaptation) of the psyche and its substructures. I agree with Hartmann and Loewenstein (1962) who stress the difference between genesis and present level and range of functions of a substructure such as the superego and emphasize that these two points of view should not be confused. But it is the genesis and history of the superego which can explain the dynamic and economic processes that go into forming its functions and constitute the superego as a structure. This is not a preference of the genetic point of view over other "metapsychological points of view." When Rapaport and Gill (1959) added the genetic and adaptive points of view to the three others, they considered that these two might be on a different level of discourse. I believe this to be true, but cannot explore the question further in this context.

I only wish to emphasize here that genetic-historical understanding is of the essence of psychoanalysis as a science and as a form of treatment. From the scientific point of view, the genetic approach makes possible the mental reconstruction of psychic structures and processes and of their functions, a unique undertaking and contribution of psychoanalysis, comparable only to the reconstructive analysis of physical structure and physical processes of modern physics, in its implications both for understanding and for altering, i.e., destroying and composing or recomposing, structure. Psychoanalysis is in this sense as dangerous and as promising an undertaking as atomic physics, depending on how we use this emerging power of understanding the formation, composition, decomposition, and reorganization of the human psyche.

The psychoanalytic data we obtain from the analysand are forever "contaminated" by transference and resistance, but they can be obtained only through transference and resistance. The three structures (id, ego, superego) postulated by Freud are, from all we know, mutually interdependent. They have been formed and they are maintained and, within limits, can change by intercourse with other persons: they are not only mutually interdependent but also interdependent with the psyches of others. The genesis of the individual psyche and of its substructures is thus not merely something that happened in the past but an ongoing process, granted that it slows down after childhood and adolescence and that this genesis may and often does come to a relative standstill as time goes on. But insofar as psychic life is active and does not proceed by rote alone and automatically, the genesis of psychic structure continues, although more imperceptibly. When Freud said: where id was, there ego shall become, he had in mind this growth potential, especially in regard to the analytic process, where the genesis and the vicissitudes of the genesis of psychic organization become perceptible again in the transference illness and its resolution.

As does early psychic development, the resumption of psychic development in the concentrated form of analysis takes place within a psychic matrix: the psychoanalytic situation. Recently the similarities between that situation and the early mother-child relationship have been stressed by Stone (1961), Gitelson (1962), Greenacre (1966), myself (1960), and others. As happens frequently, in emphasizing certain aspects of a problem, other aspects tend to be neglected or not sufficiently stressed to keep a balanced view. There are radical differences between the two situations which deserve careful consideration and further elucidation; moreover, the preoedipal, diadic matrix has been stressed at the expense of the oedipal situation and its much more familiar similarities to the analytic situation as evinced in the classical transference neurosis. Changes in our perspective on psychic development, probably changes in our case material, and other factors such as increased interest in the earliest phases, have contributed to this slant, which needs correction. Nevertheless, through analytic work with so many patients who clearly show differences and deviations from the classical neuroses—even though perhaps sometimes not as many as we tend to think—we have gained deeper insight into the genesis of the psychic substructures and into the defects and deformations of ego and superego particularly.

This insight has come to us primarily, although not exclusively, from the often painful and laborious work of understanding what goes into and what interferes with the analytic process when we attempt to analyze such patients. Transference and resistance are again our guiding lights, but on deeper, more primitive levels, and therefore on levels of less differentiation, intrapsychically, i.e., between id, ego, and superego, but also interpsychically. The differentiation between patient and analyst, between object of investigation and investigator, is less, sometimes minimally, advanced, and primitive levels of psychic functioning are called into operation. It is important to realize that the analysand's operating on such levels en-

tails the analyst's operating on such levels—if he can and will do it—
although the analyst, of course, does so within the secure framework
of and steered by his mature overall organization. This implies, by
the nature of such psychic primitivity, a loosening or even suspension of the subject-object split. Communication with the other person then tends to approximate the kind of deep mutual empathy
which we see in the mother-child relationship. By the same token,
lack of communication tends to approximate an event of annihilation, insofar as the insufficiently differentiated matrix is disrupted.

Empathy, whether in this intense form or others, involves, in
contrast to sympathy, a suspension of the subject-object split. A
psychic organization operating on such a level experiences lack of
communication, of empathic understanding, as a disruption of organization, and not simply as being separate from another person.
While the analyst is easily capable of calling forth or ascending to
higher levels of psychic functioning, the patient cannot do so to the
same degree. For the theoretical grasp of that aspect of analytic work
which involves empathy, the notion of the loosening or suspension
of the subject-object split is essential, as it is for the understanding
of true identification. The subject-object split can be suspended because it did not always exist in psychic development, because psychic
development takes its beginning in a psychic matrix which comprises, stated from the viewpoint of an outside observer—a nonpsychoanalytic observer—mother and infant. Stated from a reconstructive, psychoanalytic viewpoint, this matrix is a psychic field
from which the infantile psyche gradually becomes differentiated as
a relatively autonomous focus of psychic activity, by processes of internalization and externalization taking place within the total original field.

What we call object relations represents a highly developed form
of psychic interactions in which relatively autonomous and in themselves highly organized centers of psychic activity interact with each
other. But each such center originates in a primitive interactional
field and depends for its further development and maintenance on
remaining within the compass of increasingly wider and more complex interactional fields, even though it is now itself a comparatively
autonomous, highly organized psychic field within such fields.

The psychoanalytic situation, in this regard, represents a novel interpsychic field in which more fully developed features of psychic fields, object relations, merge with or are strongly influenced by co-existing primitive features. Not that more primitive features do not form part of ordinary adult relationships; they do, as analysts well know. But the analytic method and process, by focusing on intra-psychic and interpsychic events and forces per se and on their genetic reconstruction, intervene in the very organization of the individual psyche because such special focusing and care themselves alter the field we study. As analysts we become, whether we want to or not, a weighty element and force in it. The tension, during significant periods of analysis, is in the direction of transformations from intrapsychic organization toward re-externalization of internal relationships and conflicts, and from there toward reconstitution of the psychic characteristics of the primitive matrix.

Psychoanalysis is an activity of the human mind which we as analysts exercise upon and in conjunction and cooperation with another person and his mental activity—whether we think in terms of "pure" psychoanalytic investigation or in terms of therapeutic analysis. The method we employ comprises prominently the use of verbal symbols as the means of communication, free association, free-floating attention, self-reflection and introspection, confrontation, clarification, interpretation, etc. And psychoanalysis is the body of knowledge and theory resulting from this activity and method. When I say: "the method we employ," it means not only: we as analysts, but: we, analyst and analysand. If the analytic process "takes" at all, the method becomes common good, although with significant differences between analyst and analysand. There can be no analysis as a going process in which the analysand, after a period of time which we may call the time of induction, does not engage to a varying extent in the procedures listed above. In respect to some of them, such as free-floating attention, interpretation, self-reflection, this may happen only in identifying conjunction with the analyst, whereby an interpretation, for instance, is "accepted" by the analysand. Such acceptance, if genuine, involves the free reproduction of the interpretive act on the part of the analysand. An advanced analysand may and often does perform such acts on his own. The analyst, on the other hand, does not merely engage in free-floating attention, interpretations, etc., but he uses introspection, self-reflection as well as free association (although usually not verbalized) in the service of understanding the patient.

While verbalization is the prominent means of communication (and this itself, of course, involves far more than the uttering and hearing of words and sentences), the range of communicative interaction is vast. It actually excludes only visual means, especially the visual eye-to-eye contact and grasp of facial expression, and body contact and locomotion. The psychic range may vary from the most intimate mutual understanding and empathic merging to highly abstract dialogue and argumentation. I recently had the—for me at least—unique experience of an analytic hour by telephone. The particular situation was such that I consented to the patient's request, made over the phone when he called me at the time of the beginning of his regular hour—he had to be in another city on that day—to have us proceed with his analytic hour then and there. I was struck by the fact that the funneling of communication exclusively through voice and ear seemed so extraordinary, although we are apt to think that this is what more or less happens in every analytic hour. What was lacking was personal presence, the simple being together in the same room, whether visible or not. The hour was not unproductive, but it seemed clear to me that it could be only an exception within the context of the usual analytic situation. I mention this incident because it vividly brought home to me the global nature of personal presence and the likelihood that such presence involves more than the usually listed perceptual and communicative modalities. There was—this is the best way I can describe it—a contraction of the operational psychic field which entailed a far greater effort of concentration on my part, with a deficit of free-floating attention.

II

The investigations which led to the creation of psychoanalysis were carried out as psychotherapeutic endeavors to cure emotionally disturbed patients, and psychoanalysis, once its outlines as a method *sui generis* were established, continued along this path. Transference and resistance came into view by this route. But by whatever route they might have been discovered, there can be no question that they are basic phenomena, interactional phenomena, of psychic life, and that no psychoanalytic investigation is possible without their making their appearance and being taken into account. Looked at from the viewpoint of scientific research, the object of investigation, the analysand, develops a particular kind of relationship with the analyst-investigator. This fact is part of the investigative process and of the situation in which it is carried out. In fact, a significant part of the investigation increasingly devolves on just that relationship, albeit as a vehicle for a more general understanding of the analysand's psychic processes and as a means for decontaminating, as it were, our field of vision. But it must be noted immediately that transference and resistance "contaminations" are themselves, of course, psychic phenomena and therefore part of what we want to study; that they are actually not contaminants but determinants of psychic behavior; and that such "decontamination" affects, and is intended to affect, the object no less than the investigator. The particular relationship, clinically described as transference neurosis or transference illness, develops by the nature of psychic processes, whether or not the analysand is suffering from an illness in a psychiatrically definable sense. A viable psychoanalytic process and investigation cannot develop without the development of transference. Transference and its correlate, resistance, however, not only are elements of what we intend to study, they also are the processes by which we study them ("countertransference" and "counterresistance" would be the terms applicable here, but these are open to many misunderstandings).

If transference and resistance are basic ingredients and determinants of a psychoanalytic investigation, the extent to which such an investigation is "objective" is limited by them. The investigative process itself, being carried out by the analyst who inevitably takes on all kinds of crucially important features for the analysand—and this happens not only if the latter is "sick"—continually affects the analysand's psychic processes. The analyst's interpretations, whether transference interpretations or not, are essential elements of the investigation. From the research point of view, they test and verify surmised connections and relationships between different aspects of the psychic material we perceive, and open up new avenues of approach and new psychic layers. In order to proceed with the investigative work, they have to be communicated to the analysand. If an interpretation is correct and resistance does not interfere—and this we judge from the patient's response—this communication not only verifies a connection or clarifies a piece of material for the analyst, it does the same for the analysand; better, it establishes or re-establishes connections within him, i.e., it changes something in the nexus of his psychic processes. As investigators we have, then, an object which is and must be affected by the investigative process itself if the investigation is to proceed.

Transference and resistance are basic determinants of a psychoanalytic investigation in regard to the analyst as well. Since a psychoanalytic investigation can be carried out only by a human mind, we cannot conceive of one in which the analyst's transference and resistance are not the warp and woof of his activity. Through his own analytic experience and training he has a significant measure of insight into this dynamic source of his motivations, is capable of allowing for this dynamism and of a considerable degree of self-regulation. But far from eliminating his transference and resistance, these capacities enable him to use them in the service of his work.

The phenomena of transference and resistance alone make something particularly clear in our field—though it is becoming increasingly clear in other sciences too—namely, the inextricable interrelationship between what we call subject and object. In psychoanalysis the object of study is an object in the psychoanalytic sense, another individual. In forming a theory about that object, we cannot abstract from the method we use to make it available to us, nor from what we learn from the method, more than from any other instrumentality, about the interrelationship and complementarity of subject and object. At the same time, the theory has to encompass the genesis of the subject-object split and cannot start from a basis which presupposes the latter, especially since the psychoanalytic process is based on as well as documents the merely relative existence of that split in terms of psychic reality.

Other psychoanalytic insights, gained in the pursuit of the analytic process itself and from analytically informed observation of early developmental stages and of psychotic material, point even more in the same direction. The formulation and elaboration of the concepts of narcissism, identification, introjection, and internalization represent milestones on the path toward a more adequate foundation of psychoanalytic theory. As a consequence the model of the psyche no longer is an apparatus which processes stimuli in certain ways or which, in its encounter with objects, uses them to discharge energy potentials (satisfaction=abolition of excitation in a closed system). The psyche now is conceived as an emerging organization which evolves through an active and ever more complex interchange[2] with developed organizations of the same kind—i.e., people, from whom it becomes differentiated as a separate psychic entity by slow and gradual processes of individuation. Implicit and essential in this new conception are that interaction processes between what initially are focal elements in a unitary psychic field become internalized within one focal element, which by this process increasingly assumes the properties of a psychic field in its own right. This newly established intrapsychic field then entertains modified and more complex interactions with what has become external to it. The first outline of such an idea of the formation of intrapsychic structure was given by Freud (1921) in his discussions on the formation of the superego. Speaking of the ego ideal as "a differentiating grade in the ego," he writes:

> The assumption of this kind of differentiating grade in the ego as a first step in an analysis of the ego must gradually establish its justification in the most various regions of psychology. In my paper on narcissism I have put together all the pathological material that could at the moment be used in support of this differentiation. But it may be expected that when we penetrate deeper into the psychology of the psychoses its significance will be discovered to be far greater. *Let us reflect that the ego now enters into the relation of an object to the ego ideal which has been developed out of it, and that all the interplay between an external object and the ego as a whole, with which our study of the neuroses has made us acquainted, may possibly be repeated upon this new scene of action within the ego* [p. 130; my italics].

The interplay between an external object and the ego as a whole is repeated upon a new, internal scene of action: this is internalization. Freud's formulation applies specifically to the superego. Only

[2] In this conception, the processes of introjection, identification, and internalization as well as projection and externalization are prominent examples of this interchange.

on the level of superego formation can one speak of an established
ego and of external objects. But this formulation can be generalized
to the effect that ego formation, too, is governed by comparable
processes of internalization, with the proviso that by these primitive
internalizations (and externalizations) internality and externality
become constituted, whereas the more complex ones augment and
enrich internality and externality.

The concept of internalization envisaged here—I can comment
on this only in passing—is different from, although related to, Hartmann's (1939) and Hartmann and Loewenstein's (1962) definition
of internalization. The main though not the only difference is that
in their definition they include thought processes and what Rapaport (1957) has termed the internal map of external events and
phenomena (representations), while I hold that thought processes
and ideas are not of the same order as the processes which lead to
ego and superego formation and, therefore, should not be subsumed
under the same term.

The concept of internalization, as the essential process in intrapsychic structure formation or, to put it differently, in individuation,
presupposes neither the subject-object split nor the assumption of a
separate psychic apparatus or organization, however primitive, from
the beginning; it posits an original psychic field or matrix, the
mother-infant unit, within which individuation processes start. If
one thinks in terms of an original undifferentiated phase of psychic
life, this then would refer not only to id-ego as intrapsychic potentials, but equally to the psychic undifferentiation of psyche-environ-
ment, of internal and external. Later internalizations, such as those
constituting superego formation, can be conceived as taking place
within a widened and far more complex psychic field, such as the
oedipal situation. The latter also represents a psychic field whose
focal elements, child, mother, father, are relatively autonomous
psychic fields themselves, not just for a nonpsychoanalytic observer,
but also for the child and from the viewpoint of the child. Interactions can now be described as an interplay between external objects and an ego. In the process of superego formation the internality
of the ego and the externality of objects, both previously limited,
become extended and consolidated, and the superordinate psychic
fields widen and gain in complexity.

The subject-object split or differentiation, having emerged in the growth process toward the oedipal situation, is suspended or superseded again in further internalizations which lead to higher orders of differentiation and interaction between subject and object. What becomes internalized—to emphasize this again—are not objects but interactions and relationships. Freud's insistence on seeing the superego not only as a representative of parental authority but also as a representative of the oedipal child's id impulses is in accord with this view. By the internalization of interactions an internal system of interactions, relationships, and connections between different elements and different genetic levels becomes established. This internalized, internally bound force field constitutes, it seems to me, what we call intrapsychic structure.

Despite the revolutionary insights implied in Freud's formulations of narcissism, identification, ego and superego formation; despite the early recognition of the fundamental role of transference and resistance in both analysand and analyst; despite increased understanding of the analytic process and of early developmental stages —despite all these, psychoanalytic theory still clings to the model of a given psychic apparatus and starts out with the assumption of the existence of a primitive individual psyche. The fact that on the physical and biological level we observe a separate organism at birth does not imply that we also deal with a separate psychic organization, however primitive, at birth, and with immanent psychic energies and forces which, as instinctual drives, become secondarily related to objects. I suggest, in accordance with what I said earlier, that we seriously consider the proposition that instinctual drives, as psychic forces, are processes taking place within a field—the mother-infant psychic matrix; and that their character as instincts as well as the character of the emerging individual psyche are determined by the changing characteristics of that field and of its evolution into differentiated but related separate psychic fields. The psyche should neither be conceptualized as an apparatus on which organismic and external stimuli impinge, thus compelling it to perform work, nor should it be conceptualized as originally being a unit of immanent instinctual forces which seek discharge by whatever means they find (discharge by way of "autoerotic" activities or upon or through "objects"). The discharge concept itself is inadequate insofar as it signifies that some amount of energy or excitation is, by whatever means available, emptied out of a closed system.

Instinctual drives, at the stage of the mother-infant matrix, would consist in differentiating and integrating processes within this psychic matrix and not in unilateral processes emanating from the infant. I am not denying the existence of biological needs and urges in the infant; rather, I am saying that instinctual drives as their "psychic representatives," as Freud (1915a) called them, i.e., as motivational psychic forces, are formed by interactions within the original psychic matrix. Instinctual drives, in a further advanced psychic individual organization, have been modified by narcissistic transformations, by the changing of "object libido" into narcissistic libido (and aggression), whereby the relational character of drives becomes to a variously limited degree internalized. This internalization leads to a more complex organization of infantile psychic structure and of the drives themselves. In a schematic way one might say that now a portion of drive elements is deployed internally, while another portion, although modified by narcissistic transformations, continues to be deployed within wider psychic fields. At that stage instinctual drives are "internal motivational forces," but they never relinquish their character as relational phenomena. Their quality and intensity, their mutual balance and imbalance in regard to their fusions and defusions, remain determined by the original and subsequent "environmental contributions." That is, they are determined by the original psychic matrix in which they arose as drives, and are variously modified by present psychic fields of which the individual has become a relatively autonomous constituent.

I believe that such a conception of the origin and nature of instincts is supported by much recent work on early psychic development, drive organization, and individuation (see, e.g., Mahler, 1968; Spitz, 1965; Winnicott, 1965). Far from doing away with intrapsychic structure and conflict (a tendency inherent, for instance, in Sullivan's interpersonal theory), such a theoretical formulation is based on the reconstruction of the individual psyche from its component elements and takes into account the organizing currents which shape the individual psychic structure and its internal conflicts. A theory which starts out with intrapsychic immanent instinctual drives on the one hand, and external objects becoming cathected or introjected on the other hand, presupposes a dichotomy which according to present understanding of early development does not exist *ab initio* and which in many circumstances once it does exist, is loosened or superseded. Such loosening or suspension, under certain conditions, may fall under the category of "regression in the service of the ego." What I emphasize instead is that such regression involves temporary dedifferentiation of subject-object no less than temporary dedifferentiation of intrapsychic organization, that the latter implies the former.

The psychoanalytic process is the arena *par excellence* for studying the underlying psychic activities which enter into the organization, maintenance, and growth of the individual mind. We have become increasingly aware of the fact that this process, although on quite a novel level of operation and organization, repeats and reveals essential features of the formative stages of psychic development. This understanding, implicit in the concept of the classical transference neurosis and the healthier resolution of the oedipus complex in analysis, is being supplemented and deepened by the more recent recognition of the impact of preoedipal disturbances on the analytic process. This had led, when called for, to certain modifications of technique, which are no less psychoanalytic because they take into account insights into and requirements of more primitive stages of development and of mental disturbance. But it is true that reorganization of psychic functioning, where early disturbances play a predominant role, is more questionable. Early, preoedipal, disturbances tend to interfere with the impact of psychoanalytic interventions on our accustomed verbal level of operations, because in such patients the later levels of mental development are not sufficiently stable. Moreover, the earlier a significant disturbance in mental development sets in, the more permanent seems to be its damage. In these circumstances, furthermore, far greater demands are made on the analyst's repertoire of operational psychic levels and on his agility to move back and forth between such levels, so that he finds it harder to be equal to this expanded task.

When Freud (1937) spoke of the professional hazards of analytic work, comparing them to the radiologist's exposure to dangerous X-rays, he alluded to the fact that by analyzing we become part of a psychic force field. A delicate balance has to be kept between becoming damaged by its inherent tensions and strains and resisting its power altogether. If we do the latter, we can neither pursue analytic research nor be of service to the patient, since it is by virtue of the establishment of such a new force field—the psychoanalytic situation —that the patient can resume and reorganize his mental development. The former is the case—and this, too, serves neither research nor the patient—if we overtly or covertly give in to the patient's neurotic demands and entangling propensities, instead of analyzing them. Analyzing them, as we know, means neither gratifying them, by lending ourselves as objects through which instinctual discharge is achieved, nor rejecting them, by lack of response or condemnation.

Analysis of the patient's demands and conflicts in essence involves having him put into words, whenever possible, his feelings, thoughts, fantasies, etc. Recognizing them as manifestations and derivatives of the underlying instinctual conflicts, we then interpret them by fitting them into a wider psychic context. This involves our linking them with the patient's past experience and establishing or re-establishing freer communication between different levels of integration of his past-present experiences. Such linking has been conceptualized by Freud (1915b) as hypercathexis. Hypercathexis, by virtue of the analyst's presence and pressure in that direction, is called forth in the patient as he manages to verbalize his feelings, fantasies, wishes, memories, and conflicts instead of expressing them in nonverbal actions and behavior; and hypercathexis is fostered, significantly augmented, and qualitatively changed by our interpretations if they are accepted, i.e., if the patient, by reproducing the interpretive act, makes it his own.

In his early writings Freud spoke of the patient's verbalization of his feelings in terms of abreaction in words and associative absorption. This implied the recognition that giving words to feelings is not simply a delay of gratification, or not only that, but is a kind of gratification by verbal action, by establishing communicative links between different psychic elements and levels, both within the patient himself (intrapsychic communication) and between the patient and the analyst.[3] I may use the dubious shortcut of saying that the

[3] In this respect we have to distinguish between what we have come to understand, often in a pejorative sense, as abreaction and the concept of abreaction through words as Freud used it in his early papers (see Loewald, 1955).

gratification is a sublimated one—dubious because we do not yet understand much about sublimation, although its connections with identification (as a pathway, as Ernst Kris, in a personal communication, once put it) and with neutralization give us some hints.

If we urge the patient to put his feelings into words and to allow himself to associate freely, and then interpret the material to him, we respond to his longings and conflicts by calling forth his own hypercathectic resources and by providing ours for his use. His hypercathectic resources originated in the infant's and child's fields of psychic interactions with his mother, father, and others. In the psychoanalytic situation these original situations are revived and repeated on new levels and with a new person. The new level, of course, can be operative only to the extent to which it can be based upon and linked with pre-existing, though pathological or underdeveloped, intrapsychic structure and functioning. Words, language, and the linking of what Freud (1915b) called thing representations and word representations, are by no means the only media of hypercathexis, but they do have a special and prominent place in the higher organization of psychic life.

Hypercathexes, according to Freud, "bring about a higher psychical organization and make it possible for the primary process to be succeeded by the secondary process" (p. 202); the operation of hypercathexis has ceased in repression. Hypercathexis, I believe, cannot be adequately understood if we fail to take into account that it originates within a supraindividual psychic field. Expressed in traditional psychoanalytic terms, the essential factor is that cathected objects are themselves cathecting agents. The subject which cathects objects is at the same time being cathected by those objects, although on quite different and not drive-dominated levels of cathexis. The subject (the individual) is not only the subject but is at the same time the object for *his* cathected objects. Object relations are relations between mutually cathecting agents, and the cathecting of each partner is a function of the other's cathecting. Because the individual who cathects, the subject, is an object for *his* cathected objects, the individual can become an object to himself, can gain distance from himself. The higher-order cathecting activity of his libidinal objects (parents) constitutes, as it were, the first hypercathexis. Insofar as the objects' cathecting operations are on secondary process levels (although they are by no means exclusively so), they have the potential of hypercathexes in terms of the subject's psychic processes; and the internalization of relationships makes for what I called the hypercathectic resources of the individual.

III

Psychoanalytic research, in the sense of analyzing another person, and therapeutic analysis are inseparable. As I said earlier, the dichotomy of pure and applied science does not hold in our discipline. But I do not labor under the illusion that a therapeutic analysis consists, or could consist, only of strictly psychoanalytic procedures and interventions. This is decidedly not the case. An actual analysis, as an undertaking extending over a number of years, contains, apart from the attempts to enforce the rules of the procedure, many elements which in themselves are not psychoanalytic, but which are intended to underline, bring back to mind, and promote the specific task of analysis or to prevent the patient from engaging in activities that interfere with the analysis or from self-destructive moves in his life. The less mature the patient is, the more are such interventions at times necessary. While ideally and ultimately such moves are to be understood as resistances and analyzed, these and other types of resistance, especially during earlier phases of analysis, often cannot be dealt with analytically. The foundations for the patient's analytic understanding of his behavior may not yet be firm enough. The patient may for shorter or longer periods of time go along with the analytic procedures not because of his grasp of their rationale but because he wishes to please the analyst, like the child who is afraid of the loss of love or the love object and complies with demands for the sake of keeping the parent's attachment, which is still vital to the integrity of his own psychic organization. We would go along with this as long as it serves the analysis. We utilize this lever with the patient, not by threats, withdrawal or punishment, but by not analyzing such "transference love" prematurely and by relying on it in our educative interventions. These often are similar to educative measures employed by affectionate and sensible parents.

If we look at the totality of an analysis as a stretch of life experience, there are striking similarities with periods of the oedipal phase or adolescence, for instance, with their ups and downs of love and hate, of dependence and rebellion, of clinging and emancipation, submission and self-assertion. Much more has gone into it, from the patient's as well as the analyst's point of view, in terms of personal investment, than strictly psychoanalytic work in the sense of detached, dispassionate research. Parenthetically, I doubt whether any scientific work proceeds in a strictly detached, dispassionate way, motivated solely by the wish to find the truth, except for those most significant moments and episodes which set for us the standard of the scientific spirit.

It also needs to be said that the love of truth is no less a passion because it desires truth rather than some less elevated end. In our field the love of truth cannot be isolated from the passion for truth to ourselves and truth in human relationships. In other fields, too, the scientist is filled with love for his object precisely in his most creative and "dispassionate" moments. Scientific detachment in its genuine form, far from excluding love, is based on it. In our work it can be truly said that in our best moments of dispassionate and objective analyzing we love our object, the patient, more than at any other time and are compassionate with his whole being.

In our field scientific spirit and care for the object certainly are not opposites; they flow from the same source. It is impossible to love the truth of psychic reality, to be moved by this love as Freud was in his lifework, and not to love and care for the object whose truth we want to discover. All great scientists, I believe, are moved by this passion. Our object, being what it is, is the other in ourselves and ourself in the other. To discover truth about the patient is always discovering it with him and for him as well as for ourselves and about ourselves. And it is discovering truth between each other, as the truth of human beings is revealed in their interrelatedness. While this may sound unfamiliar and perhaps too fanciful, it is only an elaboration, in nontechnical terms, of Freud's deepest thoughts about the transference neurosis and its significance in analysis.

In the various perspectives I have tried to sketch, a psychoanalytic investigation is, by its very nature, potentially therapeutic, granted that in order to bring it about, foster it, keep it going, eliminate interferences, many nonpsychoanalytic measures are often called for. In this respect, too, analysis may be compared to surgery.

The work of the surgeon does not consist exclusively in the operation itself. There are preoperative and postoperative procedures, dressings, dietetic measures, and the like. The same *mutatis mutandis* goes for the researcher in any field. In our zeal to be "pure" analysts we tend to forget all this; but we do have to be on the lookout for unnecessary or interfering extra-analytic interventions.

SUMMARY

I have looked at psychoanalysis mainly from the point of view of its being a scientific endeavor. It is far more than that, as is shown in the pervasive influence that psychoanalysis has had on many facets of modern Western civilization. And psychoanalysts should be the last to ignore or disregard this fact. Psychoanalysis, as practiced by some of its best, though often unknown representatives, is an art even more than a science. But here I have looked mainly at its scientific and theoretical face. I have emphasized that as a scientific theory it cannot be content to model itself after the traditional scientific theories constructed by such sciences as physics, chemistry or biology. Their subject matter, as viewed and investigated by these sciences, implies and presupposes a subject-object dichotomy, which is, so to speak, what puts them in business.

Although psychoanalysis took those theories as its model, it soon had to depart from them in essential ways, without being able or willing to make this explicit. The phenomena of transference and resistance as inherent and necessary ingredients of a psychoanalytic investigation do not conform to such a model. Hence, there was a tendency to relegate them to the lower echelon of "clinical theory" and not to admit them to the high plane of "metapsychology," even though Freud spoke of transference, for instance, in Chapter VII of *The Interpretation of Dreams,* in what would now clearly be considered a metapsychological context. The new structural theory, based on the conceptions of narcissism, "primary masochism," identification, introjection, and the formation of the superego, implied and expressed a new awareness of the fundamental importance of object ties for the formation of psychic structure. Although these ideas led further away from the old model, psychoanalysis nevertheless continued to cling to its theoretical premises. In many quarters there still seems to be a tendency to put up a "no admittance" sign when metapsychological considerations point to object relations as being not merely regulative but essential constitutive factors in psychic structure formation.

I have maintained that the psychoanalytic process and deepened understanding of psychotic and early developmental processes reveal the interactional origin and nature of psychic reality, and have expressed my belief that a theory of the mind, of the psyche as it shows itself to psychoanalytic research, should start with the hypothesis of a psychic matrix within and from which individuation proceeds. In this regard I have tried to describe parallels between the psychoanalytic situation as a novel force field and earlier fields of psychic forces within which differentiated and autonomous psychic entities and structures arise and develop.

I have given a brief account of the processes of internalization and externalization which are involved in individuation and continue to be instrumentalities by which individuation in increasingly complex forms takes its course in human life. I have stressed that what is internalized are dynamic relations between psychic elements of a field of which the internalizing agent is one element. In accord with these views I reformulated the concept of instinctual drives and suggested a somewhat novel interpretation of the concept of hypercathexis.

It seems to me that most of the views I have advanced are at least implicit in Freud's work and that of many other psychoanalysts. Perhaps my contribution consists mainly in making some things explicit and drawing some unfamiliar conclusions.

BIBLIOGRAPHY

Freud, S. (1900), The Interpretation of Dreams. *Standard Edition*, 4 & 5. London: Hogarth Press, 1953.
—— (1914), On Narcissism. *Standard Edition*, 14:67-102. London: Hogarth Press, 1957.
—— (1915a), Instincts and Their Vicissitudes. *Standard Edition*, 14:109-140. London: Hogarth Press, 1957.
—— (1915b), The Unconscious. *Standard Edition*, 14:159-215. London: Hogarth Press, 1957.
—— (1921), Group Psychology and the Analysis of the Ego. *Standard Edition*, 18:67-143. London: Hogarth Press, 1955.
—— (1933), New Introductory Lectures on Psycho-Analysis. *Standard Edition*, 22:3-182. London: Hogarth Press, 1964.

—— (1937), Analysis Terminable and Interminable. *Standard Edition,* 23:209-253. London: Hogarth Press, 1964.
Gitelson, M. (1962), The Curative Factors in Psycho-Analysis: The First Phase of Psycho-Analysis. *Int. J. Psa.,* 43:194-205.
Greenacre, P. (1966), Problems of Overidealization of the Analyst and of Analysis. *This Annual,* 21:193-212.
Hartmann, H. (1939), *Ego Psychology and the Problem of Adaptation.* New York: International Universities Press, 1958.
—— & Loewenstein, R. M. (1962), Notes on the Superego. *This Annual,* 17:42-81.
Jacobson, E. (1964), *The Self and the Object World.* New York: International Universities Press.
Kris, E. (1955), Neutralization and Sublimation. *This Annual,* 10:30-46.
Loewald, H. W. (1955), Hypnoid State, Repression, Abreaction, and Recollection. *J. Amer. Psa. Assn.,* 3:201-210.
—— (1960), On the Therapeutic Action of Psycho-Analysis. *Int. J. Psa.,* 41:16-33.
Mahler, M. S. (1968), *On Human Symbiosis and the Vicissitudes of Individuation.* New York: International Universities Press.
Rapaport, D. (1957), A Theoretical Analysis of the Superego Concept. *Collected Papers.* New York: Basic Books, 1967, pp. 685-709.
—— & Gill, M. M. (1959), The Points of View and Assumptions of Metapsychology. *Int. J. Psa.,* 40:153-162.
Sandler, J. (1960), On the Concept of the Superego. *This Annual,* 15:128-162.
—— & Rosenblatt, B. (1962), The Concept of the Representational World. *This Annual,* 17:128-145.
Spitz, R. A. (1965), *The First Year of Life.* New York: International Universities Press.
Stone, L. (1961), *The Psychoanalytic Situation.* New York: International Universities Press.
Webster's New International Dictionary of the English Language, 2nd ed. Springfield, Mass.: G. & C. Merriam, 1956.
Winnicott, D. W. (1965), *The Maturational Processes and the Facilitating Environment.* New York: International Universities Press.

PROJECTION AND EXTERNALIZATION

JACK NOVICK, Ph.D. and KERRY KELLY (London)

Projection was one of the first concepts developed by Freud and a detailed analysis of the topic can be found as early as 1895. It is a measure of the complexity of the subject that despite the long history of its usage there remains considerable confusion and disagreement as to the meaning and applicability of the term. Projection is one of the more frequently used terms in psychoanalytic literature, especially in clinical presentations. It is seen by some authors as basic to all clinical work. Rapaport (1944), for instance, states that the fundamental psychoanalytic postulates of psychic determinism and continuity require a concept like that of projection.

In the current literature it is used as a portmanteau term encompassing such diverse processes as displacement, generalization, transference revival, externalization, and some processes of adaptive mastery. A host of phenomena is described as subject to projection: drives, introjects, aspects of the self, affects, sensations, and structures such as superego and id. Projection is said to be manifest in such varied areas as play, artistic creation, religion, projective tests, and persecutory delusions. Used in this way the term lacks explanatory power, and significant clinical distinctions are blurred. Rycroft's recent definition (1968)—"viewing a mental image as objective reality" —reflects the current broad application of the term. This definition is a resurrection of a pre-analytic usage (Feigenbaum, 1936) and epit-

This paper forms part of a research project entitled "Childhood Pathology: Impact on Later Mental Health," conducted at the Hampstead Child Therapy Clinic, London. The project is financed by the National Institute of Mental Health, Washington, D.C., Grant No. MH-5683-07.

We would like to thank Anna Freud, Dr. J. Sandler, and members of the Index and Clinical Concept Groups for their many helpful suggestions.

An earlier version of this paper was presented at the annual meeting of the Association of Child Psychotherapists in London, March, 1969, and the present version was presented at a meeting of the Hampstead Clinic in July, 1969.

omizes the degree to which Freud's specific psychoanalytic formulations and differentiations in this area have been lost.

In recent years there have been attempts to differentiate some of the processes subsumed under projection. In particular the concept of externalization has been the focus of increased attention (Brodey, 1965; Rapaport, 1944, 1950, 1952; Weiss, 1947). However, this has added a terminological difficulty since those who write about externalization tend to use it synonymously with projection, and it is not clear whether externalization is viewed as a subspecies of projection, as a process distinct from it, or as a more general process with projection as a subspecies. The current state of affairs can best be exemplified by quoting the definitions of projection and externalization given in a recently published glossary of psychoanalytic terms (Moore and Fine, 1967):

> attributed to the external world [p. 24].
> *Projection*—is a process whereby a painful impulse or idea is

> *Externalization:* A term used to refer in general to the tendency to project into the external world one's instinctual wishes, conflicts, moods, and ways of thinking (cognitive styles). It is evident in young children who are afraid of monsters in the dark, in the savage for whom the jungle is populated by evil spirits, and in the paranoiac who sees persecutors all about him. The capacity for externalization may be used constructively in art, poetry, literature, etc. It is also the basis for the Rorschach test . . . [p. 39].

Our interest in this topic stemmed from the fact that clinically we were making distinctions which we were unable to encompass and clearly communicate within the current terminology. The conceptual difficulties can be traced, in part, to the many misunderstandings which exist concerning Freud's use of projection. Freud himself felt that this concept was unclear, and he repeatedly stated his intention to devote a separate study to it (1911a, 1915b).[1] Illuminating as this study would have been, there remains in Freud's extant writings on projection a major source of confusion, which continues to affect current usage. Freud used the term in two dis-

---

[1] Strachey suggests that this may have been one of the "missing" metapsychological papers.

tinct ways which we describe as the psychological and mechanical referents of projection. "Projection" is a pre-analytic term, with major referents in other fields. The literal meaning is "to throw in front of"; hence its usage in relation to the mechanical process by which an image is thrown onto a screen. This usage of projection in relation to psychic processes is a metaphorical application of the mechanical model. It is as if the mind is likened to a cinema projector and said to project internal images onto the blank screen of the external world.

Parallel with the continuing elaboration of a psychological concept of the "process or mechanism" of projection, Freud, from his first to his last usage of the term, employed the descriptive mechanical metaphor. This can be seen, for instance, in his paper on "Screen Memories" (1899). In relation to the "amalgamation" of two sets of fantasies Freud states, "You projected the two phantasies on to one another" (p. 315). Similarly in 1936 he writes, "but these two motives are essentially the same, for one is only a projection of the other" (p. 242f.). A final example will illustrate Freud's explicit use of the term in a descriptive mechanical sense and not as a psychic mechanism or process. In the *Introductory Lectures* (1916-1917) he writes of melancholia as follows: "the object has been set up in the ego itself, has been, as it were, projected on to the ego. (Here I can only give you a *pictorial description* and not an ordered account on topographical and dynamic lines.)" (p. 427, our italics).

The above quotation emphasizes the fact that when Freud used projection in the mechanical sense, he was describing and not explaining the phenomenon in question; in contrast, the psychological concept of projection was meant as an explanation. The mechanical-descriptive and the psychological-explanatory uses of projection are frequently employed in the same paper, and unless one distinguishes between them the theory presented is ambiguous and frequently contradictory. When they are differentiated, it becomes clear that the two referents of the term are used for different purposes. As we shall demonstrate later, the psychological concept undergoes progressive modification so that finally it refers to mechanisms of defense. The mechanical referent of projection remains a "pictorial description" used largely to highlight evidence for the fundamental psychoanalytic assumptions of psychic determinism and continuity. This is especially so in relation to the phenomena Freud subsumed under the projection of "endopsychic" percepts. In 1897 Freud wrote to Fliess:

> Can you imagine what "endopsychic myths" are? They are the latest product of my mental labour. The dim inner perception of one's own psychical apparatus stimulates illusions, which are naturally projected outwards, and characteristically into the future and a world beyond. Immortality, retribution, the world after death, are all reflections of our inner psyche . . . psycho-mythology.

The accent here is on projection not as the explanatory process but as a synonym for "reflection." In subsequent discussions of the projection of endopsychic percepts (1901, 1909, 1911b, 1913) Freud emphasizes the nondefensive "transposition" of the structural conditions of the mind into the external world (1913, p. 91). In each instance he traces the inner source of the external manifestation, using the term projection only to stress that these are reflections of inner phenomena. For instance, the doctrine of reward in the afterlife "is nothing more than a mythical projection" of the endopsychic impression made by the substitution of the reality principle for the pleasure principle (1911b, p. 223).

This use of projection is similar to its current application to the areas of art, religion, projective tests, children's fantasies, indeed all surface manifestations of inner phenomena. It is this reflection of the inner in the external world which Rapaport (1944) refers to as "the projective hypothesis." It is legitimate to use projection in this way, but it should be emphasized that this is a pre-analytic, non-psychological, and mainly descriptive usage. We would therefore suggest that this usage be discontinued since it leads to a situation where all surface manifestations are subsumed under projection, which entails the loss of the specific psychoanalytic referents of the term and strips the concept of any explanatory value. Instead of the "projective hypothesis" one could speak of an "expressive hypothesis" to underline the existence of causal and genetic links between surface expressions of the individual (fantasies, behavior, creative acts, etc.) and "the hidden structures, functions and contents of the

mind" (A. Freud, 1965). It should be stressed that surface manifestations may reflect or express any or all psychic processes, including defenses among which may be the defense mechanism of
projection. The main theme of this paper is the clinical importance
of distinguishing between the various psychic processes since each
requires its own technical approach. To speak of all these surface
expressions as projections, as is currently done, obscures the fact that
defenses require different technical handling than manifestations of
other inner processes.

There are further clinical and theoretical reasons to make the
distinction we have suggested. Although the distinction between
projection as a description and projection as a psychological explanation is relatively clear in Freud's writings, this is not so in the current literature. Thus surface reflections of inner processes not only
are described as projections (which, as noted above, is a legitimate
but confusing usage) but also are explained as being due to projection. This is particularly evident in the area of empathy, where
communication between infant and mother, between patient and
therapist, is attributed to processes of projection (Jacobson, 1964; M.
Klein, 1955). This leads to an equation of expression and communication, which in our view obscures recognition of the patient's resistances to communication. Understanding of the mental states of the
infant or patient on the part of the mother or therapist need involve
neither the child's intention to communicate nor the use of the mechanism of projection. Correct inferences can frequently be drawn from
external expressions before the infant develops the capacity to communicate and despite the patient's intention to avoid communication.

A related issue is the conceptualization of the projective process
in terms of instinctual modes and aims (Abraham, 1924; Malin and
Grotstein, 1966; Jaffe, 1968). Communication is said to occur via
a projective process in which the patient spits out or evacuates something which the therapist then ingests. This is a concretization of a
process which, as Freud repeatedly emphasized (e.g., 1913, p. 64),
takes place in the perceptual system, and thus involves a delusional
or fantasy representation. To say to a patient that he has put something *into* the therapist (e.g., Klein, 1955; Lush, 1968) is to collude
with his omnipotent fantasy, give it the stamp of reality, and provide

the therapist with a rationalization for the acting out of counter-transference feelings.

Returning to Freud's views on projection, once we have excluded the mechanical usage discussed above, we find a psychological theory of projection and related mechanisms which is further advanced than much current thinking on these topics. Under the general heading of projection Freud subsumed five interrelated but distinguishable applications of the concept. We have described the areas of application as follows:

1. Projection as an early mechanism basic to the development of the self
2. Generalization, an aspect of animistic thinking
3. Attribution of cause or responsibility to the external world
4. Externalization of aspects of the self
5. Projection of the drive, or projection proper.

In our view these differentiations should be incorporated into any attempt to conceptualize mechanisms involving the subjective allocation of inner phenomena to the outside world. We would thus achieve a historical consistency the lack of which leads to misunderstandings. More importantly, the differentiations made by Freud are based upon clinical distinctions which are obscured when these phenomena are subsumed under a portmanteau heading.

I

In this section we shall summarize Freud's views on the first three categories noted above, and we will comment on their applicability to current clinical and theoretical issues. The second section will focus on the importance of the distinction between externalization of aspects of the self and projection of the drive.

Projection as an Early Mechanism Basic to
the Development of the self

It is generally accepted that among the major tasks confronting the developing organism are those of integration and differentiation. Specifically, the child must gradually differentiate the self and the outer world. Writers in the field of developmental psychoanalysis and psychology have put forward a number of suggestions concerning ways in which, at various stages, this differentiation might be made. There is, for instance, the action-oriented mode of differentiation (Piaget, 1936), and Freud describes differentiation on the basis of the pleasure principle (1915a). From the adult observer's point of view, such modes will initially lead to faulty, unrealistic differentiation of self and object, but normally this is gradually corrected by experience.

Many authors, especially those of a Kleinian orientation, refer to this initial faulty differentiation as projection. They see projection as a process which occurs from birth on and, with introjection, as a primary mechanism leading to structure formation (Klein, 1932; Heimann, 1952). Whether projection can occur prior to structure formation, especially minimal differentiation of self and external world, is a major controversial issue. Waelder, for instance, states that "conclusive evidence for these early manifestations [of projection] is still wanting" (1951, p. 169). Anna Freud, as early as 1936, pointed out the logical problems created by the Kleinian theory of projection, when she stated,

> we might suppose that projection and introjection were methods which depended on the differentiation of the ego from the outside world. The expulsion of ideas or affects from the ego and their relegation to the outside world would be a relief to the ego only when it had learned to distinguish itself from that world [p. 51].

Proponents of the theory of projection as a neonatal mechanism cite the authority for their view in the writings of Freud, especially "Instincts and Their Vicissitudes" (1915a), and "A Metapsychological Supplement to the Theory of Dreams" (1917). During this period Freud did in fact view projection as an important process in the early development of the self. Under the dominance of the pleasure principle objects which are a source of pleasure are "incorporated" and "a part of its own self" that causes unpleasure projected into the external world, thus creating the "purified pleasure ego" (1915a, p. 136).

However, writers on both sides of this controversy fail to take into account two important points. First, in all genetic statements concerning projection, Freud posits at least minimal structure formation or ego organization prior to the occurrence of projection. The purified pleasure ego which is created by projection and introjection is *not* a primary ego state. Originally, according to Freud, there is a primal pleasure ego, one which is cathected with instincts and capable, to some extent, of satisfying them on itself. It is indifferent to the external world. This primal pleasure ego, "as a consequence of experience" is then forced to take account of reality, thus leading to the "original reality ego." This reality ego *"distinguished internal and external by means of a sound objective criterion"* (1915a, p. 136; our italics). It is only after the development of the capacity to distinguish between internal and external that the processes of projection and introjection come into play in order to create the third phase of the ego, the "purified pleasure ego."[2]

Secondly, most authors fail to note that in his later writings Freud explicity differentiates the early process from projection proper. In *Beyond the Pleasure Principle* he described this same process not as projection, but as "the origin of projection" (1920, p. 29). In his many later investigations in the area of early ego development he does not employ the term projection but uses phrases such as "ascribe to the external world" (1930, p. 66f.).

Since any statement concerning the earliest stages of development must be seen as hypothetical, the question of the occurrence of projection prior to structure formation is essentially a theoretical one. We can add little to Freud's clear formulations, but would stress that to speak of processes involving the subjective allocation of inner phenomena to the outer world before the development of the self and the differentiation of inner and outer is meaningless and confuses cause and motivation (Rapaport, 1960).

Generalization

With the differentiation of the self from the external world, the child's view of the external world, and especially of his objects, will be partly determined by what he knows and feels about himself. Thus as the child becomes aware of himself, he *naturally* ascribes similar characteristics to the object. This is a primitive animistic

---

[2] Even in an earlier paper (1911b), where he described the replacement of the pleasure ego by the reality ego, Freud posited the existence of minimal structuralization ("devices") in order to account for early defensive processes.

mode of thought, appropriate to his relatively ego-centric stage of development. In the current literature, it is frequently described as a result of projection (Eidelberg, 1968; Fenichel, 1945; Jacobson, 1964).

In 1901, Freud explicitly correlates "anthropomorphic" thinking with projection, the dynamic mechanism he discovered at work in paranoia. He continued this line of thought in *Totem and Taboo* (1913), which contains his most detailed examination of animism. The attribution of primitive man's own characteristics to the external world is said to be caused by projection. However, we find in the same work another, more detailed, explanation of animism which does not require the mechanism of projection: animism is a "system of thought" (p. 77), natural to primitive stages in mankind and the individual. It involves the attribution to the external world of those internal characteristics *consciously perceived* by the primitive mind. The animistic system makes use of the technique of magic and is intimately linked with the narcissistic phase of libidinal development and the principle of the omnipotence of thoughts (p. 85).

It seems to us that Freud opts for the latter alternative, because in his later writings on primitive thought he makes no use of projection as a dynamic explanation. In fact, in 1927, he states that projection is not an explanation, but merely a description of what occurs. His clearest description of the process which is involved in animistic thinking is in "The Unconscious" (1915b) where he refers to it as an "identification":

> Consciousness makes each of us aware only of his own states of mind; that other people, too, possess a consciousness is an inference which we draw by analogy from their observable utterances and actions, in order to make this behaviour of theirs intelligible to us. (It would no doubt be psychologically more correct to put it this way: that without any special reflection we attribute to everyone else our own constitution and therefore our consciousness as well, and that this identification is a *sine qua non* of our understanding.) This inference (or this identification) was formerly extended by the ego to other human beings, to animals, plants, inanimate objects and to the world at large, and proved serviceable so long as their similarity to the individual ego was overwhelmingly great; but it became more untrust-

worthy in proportion as the difference between the ego and these 'others' widened. . . . But even where the original inclination to identification has withstood criticism—that is, when the 'others' are our fellow-men—the assumption of a consciousness in them rests upon an inference and cannot share the immediate certainty which we have of our own consciousness [p. 169].

In the interest of terminological clarity, we would call this process "generalization."[3] Following Freud, we see this process as a natural mode of thought, not the defense of projection proper—the child retains conscious awareness of that which he has attributed to the external world. Generalization is the child's major mode of apprehending the unknown and persists to some extent throughout life. Examples are legion: for instance, the infantile sexual theories described by Freud (1908) provide clear illustrations.

The differentiation between generalization and projection is of theoretical importance in many areas,[4] but in our view its major importance lies in the clinical and technical implications. Extensive manifestations of generalization beyond a certain age usually reflect a weakness of the ego due to immaturity, faulty development, or deterioration.

For example, Kevin was an eleven-year-old boy referred to a child guidance clinic for a variety of obsessive-compulsive rituals. He was diagnosed as a neurotic whose major conflict centered around aggression. In psychotherapy he very soon showed conscious fears of

[3] We recognize that the usage of this term in mathematics, philosophy, and academic psychology usually has the connotation of abstract secondary process thinking. However, the dictionary definition of "generalization" conveys precisely the sense of the process we are discussing:
"1. The process of generalizing, i.e. of forming general notions or propositions from particulars.
"2. Quasi-concretely: a general inference.
"3. The process of spreading over every part."
In our view, generalization occurs at every level of mental functioning. What differentiates animistic thinking from sophisticated logical inferences is the operation of other functions such as judgment and reality testing.

[4] For example, it is often assumed that Freud saw projection as playing a central role in superego formation. This is not the case. Freud ascribed the severity of the superego not to the projection of aggressive wishes onto the subsequently introjected object, but to three other factors, one of which was the *natural assumption* on the part of the child that he and the father had similar aggressive wishes toward each other. This is spelled out most clearly in *Civilization and Its Discontents* (1930, p. 128ff.).

being attacked by his therapist. These were seen and interpreted as projections, i.e., as a further attempt to defend against the awareness of his own aggressive impulses toward the object. The child soon became totally unmanageable and was referred to the Hampstead Clinic for intensive treatment. Soon after the start of analysis it became clear that the fear of being killed by the therapist was not based upon a projection but upon a generalization of his own conscious wishes toward all his male objects; i.e., wishing to kill an envied male object, he simply assumed that the object had the same wishes toward him.

Diagnostically, this use of generalization alerted the therapist to other signs of ego deviation, and finally a diagnosis of "borderline" was confirmed. This new perspective on the case led to modifications of technique. Despite positive changes which occurred during the first year of analysis, the use of generalization persisted. At a certain point it became possible to focus on this pathological mode of functioning. The therapist then helped the child to develop those structures necessary to inhibit generalization. By using the therapist as an auxiliary ego Kevin slowly came to accept that he could not know the object's thoughts or feelings (unless these were communicated to him in some way) and that the object was therefore not necessarily like himself and might have thoughts or feelings different from his own. It should be noted that with the inhibition of generalization Kevin remained conscious of his own aggressive wishes, but there was a significant change in the intensity and quality of his anxiety. Only much later in treatment, after considerable ego development, did Kevin make use of projection proper to defend against the conscious awareness of his own aggressive impulses.

While in this example we have emphasized the contrast between a mode of functioning and a defense, i.e., generalization and projection, we are aware that after structural inhibition of early modes has taken place, they may be re-employed for defensive purposes. As a defense, generalization is frequently used to stave off the painful affects attendant upon separation and represents a fantasy fusion of self and object representations. For example, Kevin, at a later stage in his analysis, insisted that the therapist had the same wishes and thoughts as he did himself. It emerged that this insistence represented a fantasy defense against loneliness. Kevin said, "Oh, I wish you did think the same, because then I wouldn't be alone."

Manifestations of the defensive use of generalization are frequently referred to as projections, not only by Kleinian authors, but also by more classically oriented writers, such as Jacobson, who states, "the terms introjection and projection refer to psychic processes, as a result of which self images assume characteristics of object images and vice versa" (1964, p. 46). This view obscures an important clinical phenomenon. In the fusional or merging fantasies, what is said to be projected is not a painful personal characteristic which must be divorced from the self and attributed to the external world, but is rather a conscious inner experience which is extended and *shared* with the object.[5]

Attribution of Cause or Responsibility

During the long period of the child's dependence on his parents, he often attributes to them the responsibility for his thoughts, actions, and feeling states. Gradually the child becomes aware of his growing capacity to execute his wishes in action, to alter both internal and external conditions, and thus assumes or internalizes responsibility for certain of his own actions and thoughts. Anna Freud's description of the developmental line toward bodily independence provides a model of the necessary steps for the internalization of responsibility (1965).

The first type of projection discussed by Freud is the attribution of cause to the external world, and this remains for him a major category (1895, 1909, 1910, 1911a, 1918, 1925). He applies it to the defense against self-reproach, or, in later structural terms, guilt or shame. In his examples we can see that the idea or impulse is retained in consciousness, but the responsibility for it is allocated outside.

There are many examples of this in clinical practice, especially in work with children. It frequently occurs after a period of defense analysis and, as the drive derivative emerges in action or thought, the child may say, "You made me do that," or "You put that thought in my head." For instance, the phallic-oedipal wishes of an adolescent boy emerged in the following form: "You want me to look at my mother's legs." It is striking that there is little discussion of this

---

[5] It would be of interest to examine the possible genetic relationship between generalization and projection. We would suggest that the capacity to generalize is a necessary precursor to the later use of the defense mechanism of projection.

category of projection: it is a common clinical phenomenon, and represents Freud's first conceptualization of projection as a defense.[6]

II

In section I of this paper, we focused on the theoretical and clinical importance of distinguishing between the applications of projection to defensive and nondefensive processes. Concerning Freud's use of projection, we wished to emphasize the line of progressive limitation in the application of the term, the exclusion of phenomena which had initially been subsumed under projection, and the increasing characterization of projection as a defense. We believe it would be helpful if the term "externalization" were to be accepted as the general heading for all those processes which lead to the *subjective allocation of inner phenomena to the outer world*.[7] As a general term "externalization" would refer to processes which might be normal or pathological, adaptive or maladaptive. Such usage would parallel the current general usage of "internalization" under which we subsume a variety of processes: introjection, identification, etc.

Freud differentiated three types of defensive projection. We have already discussed the defensive externalization or attribution of cause. In this section we shall focus in particular on the differentiation we derive from Freud between the externalization of a drive and the externalization of an aspect of the self representation. We would suggest that the term "projection" be reserved for the former process—i.e., *drive projection*.

Although we are aware that the distinction between drive and self representation is an arbitrary one, since these two elements are intimately interrelated—aspects of the self representation are, for

[6] This category is of sufficient importance to warrant a separate study. The internalization and externalization of responsibility can be seen most vividly in child analysis. A starting point might be Anna Freud's discussion of "The Child Analyst as Object for Externalization" (1965, p. 41). A study of this nature would involve discussion of the relations between transference and externalization, the treatment alliance and the internalization of responsibility, and the externalization of structures such as id and superego.

[7] This is a modification of the view advanced in an earlier report on this study (Novick and Hurry, 1969) where "externalization" was restricted to defensive processes.

instance, "colored" by the drive—we still propose that on balance
one can say whether a specific phenomenon is related more to the
drive or to an aspect of the self representation. For example, there is
a difference between the statements, "I am an angry person" and "I
am angry at (I hate) you." The former is an evaluation of the self
representation, the latter a drive expression.

From 1911 onward Freud's most consistent and major use of the
term projection was to denote a reflexive defense against the drive.
Thus, in the Schreber case, he described a paranoid defense against
homosexuality in which *unconscious hate* was projected. The unconscious proposition "I hate him" became transformed into the
conscious thought, "He hates (persecutes) me" (1911a, p. 63). In later
writings (notably 1913, 1922), Freud linked drive projection with
defense against ambivalent conflicts. The last time Freud used the
term projection in this sense was in 1931, when he explained the
girl's fear of being killed by the mother as due to the projection of
her own hostile wishes.[8]

Although the Schreber case is the major reference for most discussions of projection as a defense, it is not generally recognized that,
in the same paper, Freud explicitly differentiated another type of
defensive projection. He wrote that the proposition "I [a man] love
him" could also be contradicted by the formula, "It is not *I* who
love the man—*she* loves him." By means of "the change of the
subject who loves, the whole process is in any case thrown outside
the self. The fact that the woman loves the man is a matter of
external perception" (1911a, p. 64). We would term this type of
projection "externalization of an aspect of the self representation."[9]

We shall discuss the processes of externalization of aspects of the
self and drive projection from two points of view, the development
of the individual, and the effect upon him when he is used as a
target for the externalizations of others.

[8] References to projection also occur in 1936, when it is used in the mechanical
sense described above. See also the posthumously published notes (1941).

[9] This is a cumbersome phrase and in the section that follows we often use "externalization" as a shorthand. The context should make it clear to the reader that we
mean here the specific defensive process of "externalization of an aspect of the self
representation" and not the general heading under which we subsume all the different
types of externalization.

Externalization of Aspects of the Self Representation

With the emergence of the self from the state of "primal confusion" the child faces the extremely difficult task of integrating the various dissonant components of the developing self. When one considers the rapidity of the physical and mental changes which take place in the child between eight and eighteen months, one realizes that the demands made upon his relatively weak integrative function are far greater than at any other period of life. In addition to the integrative demands made by his own physical and mental growth, the object's expectations of the child also undergo rapid changes, and these expectations are transmitted to the child. (Only in adolescence does the individual have to cope with changes which make integrative demands of a magnitude approximating those of infancy.) The earliest conflicts confronting the child in his attempts at integration relate to the existence of dissonant, seemingly incompatible aspects of the self. These conflicts are intensified as some aspects become narcissistically valued through both the child's own pleasures and, more importantly, the parents' response to one or other aspect of himself. Those aspects which are not so valued may become dystonic. Their retention within the self representation will lead to a narcissistic pain such as humiliation. The toddler who falls often cries not only because of the physical pain but also because of the humiliation of seeing himself as unable to walk. One solution is to *externalize* that aspect of himself, for instance, to make the doll or the baby the one who is incapable of walking, thus avoiding the narcissistic humiliation. At this stage of development such externalization is both normal and adaptive.

It is adaptive in that the intensity of the current conflict is decreased sufficiently to allow progressive development to occur. When the child's self image is stabilized at a higher level (through the consolidation of ego skills, the reinforcement of pleasure in functioning, and a general decrease in the intensity of the earlier drive derivatives), he is then able without threat adaptively to integrate many of those aspects previously externalized. Thus the child who is fully capable of walking can again allow himself to crawl without humiliation.

Externalization may also be adaptive in many other ways. It may, for example, be used as a stepping stone on the way to identification.[10] The self is constantly reshaped by changing ego capacities and drive aims. New shapes of the self may be externalized onto contemporaries, in play, onto imaginary figures, fictional characters, etc. In addition to its defensive aspect, this process allows for what may be termed a trial reality test in which, via the object of externalization, the child can assess the effects of and reactions to this new shape of the self. In the light of these effects and reactions he may then be able to accept this new aspect of himself.

Thus, as a transitory phenomenon externalization is a normal defensive process and can be adaptive, particularly at certain phases. However, the extreme or persistent use of this defense at any period of life may have serious pathological effects. It may result in a very restricted personality with important aspects of the self permanently split off and unavailable.

It is a defense not *primarily* directed against the drives or against object-linked anxieties, but is aimed at avoiding the narcissistic pain consequent upon accepting devalued aspects of the self. Object relations are only secondarily involved in this process, and in fact externalization can be used as a defense against object relationships.

Projection Proper

The defense of *projection* proper is fundamentally different. It is motivated by the sequence of fantasied dangers consequent upon drive expression. It is a defense against a specific drive derivative directed toward an object and thus considerable structural development must take place before it can or need be employed. Among other things there must have been a channeling of drive energies into a specific aim and the establishment of the capacity to relate to a whole object. In addition, there must be sufficient ego development to allow for the integration of drive derivatives with ego capacities in the formation of fantasy expressions of object-directed wishes. Thus we would see the use of projection as becoming possible at a later stage than that of externalization—at a stage, in fact, when the capacity to manipulate objects in fantasy has developed to the point where a drive derivative originally directed at an object can be

---

10 We are here following a suggestion made by Anna Freud at a meeting of the Clinical Concept Group.

subjectively allocated to that object, while the self is experienced as the object of that drive derivative.

As a transitory phenomenon the use of projection may be normal at certain phases of development, but in contrast to other processes of externalization it has relatively little adaptive value. It may be seen as adaptive insofar as it represents an attempt to attain, retain, or regain object ties, albeit in distorted form, and thus may presage the emergence of an object relationship. As Freud (1911a) noted, projection could represent an attempt at recathexis of objects following upon a psychotic withdrawal. But from the point of view of the observer projection as a defense is remarkably inefficient for the avoidance of anxiety, except insofar as it makes possible actual or fantasied flight from the apparent source of danger. In contrast to externalization of aspects of the self, which can effectively do away with painful affect, projection may leave the subject a constant prey to anxiety. Whereas externalization of aspects of the self can be seen as a *relatively* simple one-step defense, projection is often the last step in a series of defenses and may in itself occasion the use of further defenses, such as reversal of affect.

CLINICAL AND TECHNICAL IMPLICATIONS

Anna Freud's (1965) recent discussion of externalization and especially of the technical implications of distinguishing between externalization and transference phenomena has contributed greatly to our thinking on these topics.

It was primarily for clinical and technical reasons that we earlier made the distinction between mode of functioning and defense. For similar reasons we believe it essential to distinguish between the two types of externalization outlined above. Extensive use of either defense relates to, and results in, serious ego pathology. However, externalization is more closely bound up with impairment in the integrative function, whereas projection relates to a weakness in the defense system vis-à-vis the drives. Extensive use of externalization of aspects of the self would indicate severe narcissistic disturbance with a very early fixation point; extensive use of projection would indicate severe conflict over drive depression, with a later fixation point, possibly related to the anal phase.

A transitory use of both processes, however, is frequently seen in treatment. While at times it may be difficult to differentiate, from the surface manifestation, which process may be at work, it is usually possible to do so on the lines of the distinctions we have made. Thus a child may say that the therapist is a messy, uncontrolled person. Given that this represents an externalization rather than a generalization, a displacement and so on, it is of value to ascertain whether it is predominantly the messy aspect of the self representation which is being externalized, or whether it is a drive derivative (such as the wish to mess upon the therapist) which is being projected. One can note whether the defense leads to anxiety or relief on the part of the child. The former would indicate the working of projection with the drive allocated to the therapist and the child experiencing himself as the object of the therapist's wish to mess. Here there would be no relief, but the anxiety-driven wish to flee from the situation. In contrast, there is relief when the externalization is the result of the child's need to rid himself of a narcissistically painful self image, for here he will perceive the object as unrelated to himself, as different from himself, and as something which may be ignored, derided, or treated with contempt.

We chose this example to underline the difficulties which may arise in the course of distinguishing between the processes which may be at work, and to point to the child's consequent feeling state and attitude as a valuable indicator. Very often, however, especially in child analysis, the processes can also be separated on the basis of the degree of fit between the externalization and the reality. In the case of projection there is always some degree of fit; i.e., what is projected always has somewhere a basis in reality. There is, for instance, no relationship without ambivalence, so that the child's projection of hostile impulses will always touch upon a core of truth —and in fact the child will frequently hang the projection upon some real event such as a canceled session. In contrast, there may be a very small, or even no degree of fit between an externalized dystonic self representation and the reality. Thus the preschool child who claims that the therapist is stupid and cannot read or function independently is clearly denying the reality of the therapist and simply using him in order to externalize an aspect of himself.

Once the differentiation has been made it follows that interpretation of externalization of aspects of the self must focus upon the need to defend against narcissistic pain, whereas interpretations of projection must focus upon the need to defend against the anxiety related to drive expression.

Michael, a fourteen-year-old boy, spent much of the first phase of his analysis being extremely condescending, sarcastic, and derisive toward his analyst. The material would be purposefully presented in a confusing manner so that the analyst was often left in the dark or made errors in relation to the factual material. This could have been taken as a direct expression of aggression by the patient, or an attempt to ward off anticipated attack from the analyst, an anticipation based on projection. However, Michael's affect and the subsequent material clearly indicated that he was identifying with the powerful, arrogant father and was externalizing the "Little Mike" who had often been laughed at, ignored, and left confused.

The analyst successfully handled this defense by first verbalizing the manner in which he was being viewed by the patient: how he was being seen as a stupid, little boy, and how painful it must be to be treated in this manner. Michael responded by saying, "Like a snot-nose eight-year-old" and could then recount the earlier narcissistically painful experiences at the hands of a condescending father who laughed at him for his ignorance. The therapist could take up the persistence of this image in Michael's current self representation and his attempt to defend against a recurrence of humiliation by externalization. The use of this mechanism then decreased significantly. Michael could accept the fact that he could be ignorant of something without being humiliated and, most important, he could begin to relate to the analyst as a real object.

With the emergence of object-directed wishes toward the analyst, we had the manifestation of projection proper as a defense. Michael's material, and especially his nonverbal behavior, clearly indicated a fear of attack. It should be noted that when Michael was externalizing aspects of the self, he reacted not with anxiety, but with relief. "You've got problems, not me," he would say, but he seemed to look forward to the sessions. However, when projection was used to defend against his hostile wishes, the analytic situation became one fraught with anxiety and Michael would frequently run from or miss his sessions completely. During the hour he would focus on those reality factors which could be experienced as signs of hostility on the part of the therapist, such as the cancellation of a session, the unwillingness to change an hour, or the seeming attack of an interpretation.

The analyst did not disagree with the patient's understanding of these reality events; accepting them as within the realm of possibility, he suggested that what was feared was not just dislike or lack of consideration on the part of the therapist but an actual wish to hurt, possibly kill, the patient. Michael readily agreed that this was his fear, and the analyst could then take up the magical equating of wish and deed as a major factor behind the intensity of the anxiety. This work on the omnipotence of thought led to a significant decrease in the patient's anxiety, the establishment once again of the therapeutic alliance, and the gradual emergence into consciousness of Michael's own aggressive wishes. Subsequent focus on the emphasis on only one side of the therapist, the hostile side, allowed for the uncovering of Michael's intense conflicts over ambivalence and with this the projections themselves disappeared.

Impact of Parental Externalizations and Projections upon the Child

Externalizations and even at times projections are fairly common occurrences within families. It is the extensive and rigid use of these mechanisms by the parents which indicates that pathological processes are at work. In what follows we shall examine the impact upon the child of the pathological parental use of either externalization or projection. This is a subject of great complexity, and here we illustrate only some of our main findings through selected aspects of two cases.

1. Tommy's mother was a woman who could not integrate her view of herself as castrated, damaged, messy. Throughout her life she searched for objects upon whom to externalize this dystonic aspect. Thus all her male objects, including her husband, were extremely messy, damaged, and inferior individuals. From the moment of Tommy's birth until he came into treatment at the age of eleven, the mother perceived him only as a damaged, messy, stupid child. This view of Tommy was not dynamically related to the vicarious gratification of her own primitive impulses. On the contrary, she had little involvement with the child, distancing him from her as far as possible and at times forgetting or even losing him.

At the time of referral Tommy was a prime illustration of what is frequently referred to as "the self-fulfilling prophecy." There was an exact fit with the patterns of the mother's externalization. Despite indications of normal intelligence on psychological testing, he was retarded in all school subjects. He was a regressed, soiling, snot-eating child with little control over drive expression. Most striking was the relative absence of anxiety or guilt in relation to drive expression. What clearly emerged was the presence of a severe narcissistic disturbance with mental pain and conflict rooted in the acceptance of the devalued self and the inability to integrate positive aspects with this conscious self representation.

Outside the immediate family environment he defended against the narcissistic pain almost exclusively by means of externalizations. Despite Tommy's evident relief after having externalized the devalued part of himself, he still could not see himself as clever, competent, etc. A fluctuating and relatively adequate level of functioning could be achieved only by means of a conscious imitation, a type of pseudoidentification with those contemporaries who could manifest the positive qualities he could not accept in himself. Thus, as he later verbalized, "When I pretended I was John I was able to score a goal, but when I was myself I fell in the mud."

Within the family there was little need to externalize the degraded self since the role of the devalued, damaged object was compatible with the needs of all members of the family, especially the mother. The main reason for accepting the mother's externalization lay in the realization, at some level, that despite the mother's distancing maneuvers she needed such a devalued object and that failure to comply with her need would leave him prey to the primitive terror of abandonment.

The father played an important role in Tommy's pathological development by offering him no alternative solution. He constantly reinforced the effects of the mother's pathology by using the same mechanisms along parallel lines. The father viewed Tommy as stupid, girlish, and damaged, and frequently said so to him. Psychiatric interviews with the father revealed the extent to which this view was based upon externalizations of dystonic aspects of himself.

As Tommy began to progress, one could clearly see the extent to which his acceptance of the parental externalizations had been a vital factor in the maintenance of the family equilibrium. Slowly, Tommy became consciously aware of the fact that, in his words, "They put the bad onto me and they feel good." As he gradually overcame the primitive fear of abandonment and could begin to integrate positive aspects within his self representation, his material centered mainly on the sadness of the mother, the chaos in the home, the madness of the family members, and, related to this, his own intense feelings of

guilt. It should be noted that he was guilty not about the newly attained level of functioning per se, but about having deprived the
family of a needed vehicle for externalization. To a certain extent
this material related to Tommy's own feelings, fears, and fantasies,
but to a marked degree it also reflected the reality.

As Tommy's positive development became unavoidably apparent, the family was thrown into a state of disequilibrium and chaos.
The father took to his bed in a state of panic and confusion. The
mother became depressed, disheveled, and totally disorganized. She
consciously viewed herself as useless and unlovable and made a desperate search for a new object upon whom she could re-externalize.

There was another child in the family, George, three years older
than Tommy. Until the time when Tommy began making significant progress, George had seemed like a boy with a well-structured
ego who functioned efficiently in many areas. In the eyes of the
family, including Tommy, George was a near genius. It was George
who was chosen as the mother's new target for externalization of
dystonic aspects, and very soon the family equilibrium was restored
on a reversed basis, with Tommy now seen as the near genius and
George as the stupid, messy, damaged child.[11] Tommy, no longer
fulfilling his mother's most pressing need, now had to cope with the
fact that he was an outsider in his own family. As he said, "I feel
the odd man out. I feel good, but nobody notices me."

2. Mary's mother was a woman who had never been able to
tolerate her own aggression. From childhood on projection had
played a major part in her battery of defenses. Her response to all
objects was one of fear, and she was obsessed by the thought that her
parents would murder her. In relation to her own child she made
use of projection even before the birth, being consciously afraid that
the unborn baby was killing her and eating her up inside. She continued to project throughout the child's development. A most pathogenic feature in her projections was the extent to which they were
hooked onto the reality of Mary's phase-adequate aggressive impulses; Mary's early development intensified the mother's phase-
linked aggressive conflicts. Thus, when Mary was in the oral phase,
the mother feared that Mary wanted to devour her. When Mary
reached the positive oedipal stage, the mother's continuing projection of death wishes now took the form of the fear that Mary wanted
to kill her in order to possess the husband.[12]

---

11 The changing roles of the two brothers represent a highly complex phenomenon
related to many factors in addition to the family use of externalization. A more detailed
report on the two brothers can be found in a paper by Novick and Holder (1969).

12 In this paper we are focusing solely on the role of projection in the pathological
mother-child relationship. It is evident that the relationship is one of great complexity

The extensive use of projection left the mother prey to the constant fear that Mary only hated and wanted to kill her. This image of the child acted as an additional stimulus to aggressive wishes, thus further threatening the mother's defenses. She therefore needed secondary defenses, which could be maintained only provided that the child utilized the same mechanisms, i.e., denied her anger, displaced the hate onto other objects, and reactively stressed the "loving" aspects of the relationship—and this Mary did. She and her mother spent much of their time in mutual assurances of love, the frequent exchange of propitiatory gifts, and the mutual denial of aggression on the part of either partner. Frequently they would discuss their dislike for a shared displacement object.

Unlike Tommy's father, Mary's father did not, on the whole, reinforce the effects of the mother's pathology. Indeed, so close was the bond between mother and Mary that the father remained a relative outsider.

Mary was referred to the Clinic at the age of twelve for school phobia and for sleeping and eating difficulties of marked severity. When Mary was seen diagnostically, all observers were struck by her identification with the mother's defenses. The major conflict related to the aggression toward the mother. Despite the severity of the pathology, there were no indications of a primary ego or narcissistic defect.

Very soon after the start of treatment one could see how ineffective and brittle the defense system was. Primitive aggressive breakthroughs began to occur, each time followed by the intensification of the defenses shared with the mother. It was only with the analysis of the shared defensive system that Mary could become aware of her fear of aggression; at this point the role of projection in her pathology became increasingly apparent. While Mary's own aggressive wishes remained relatively defended, the fear of being destroyed by the mother intensified, and with panic in her voice Mary would say, "She hates me, she'll kill me, she'll eat me alive." Further analysis clearly revealed the largely projective nature of these fears.

This case involves a paradox which can be understood by taking into account the pathological impact of the mother's projections. Mary's ego and superego development had been precocious; for

---

involving other elements, such as the revival of the mother's past object relationships, especially the infantile relationship to her own mother. In general, it is important to distinguish between phenomena related to the revival of past objct relationships and projection proper (A. Freud, 1965; Waelder, 1951). In this case, however, projection was a major defense utilized both within and outside the framework of the revived object relationship.

example, verbalization (including complete phrases) occurred by eleven months of age. Despite such precocious development Mary's defenses remained completely dependent upon the presence of the object and formed no more than a brittle superstructure overlaying primitive and peremptory aggressive wishes. But this could be seen as a direct consequence of the mother's extensive use of projection. By projecting her aggressive wishes onto the child, she constantly revived, intensified, and drew Mary's wishes into the child's consciousness. The normal, developmental evolution of drive expression from direct and primitive to more distanced and less conflictual forms was grossly interfered with. The development of autonomous and adaptive defenses was impeded, and the child was left with no alternative but to use primitive defenses (such as projection itself) and to accept the defenses forced upon her by her mother.

With the working through of pregenital and oedipal hostility toward the mother Mary began to function independently. The mother reacted to the positive changes in her child by making repeated attempts to re-establish the old, shared defense system. When these failed she became extremely disturbed, continued to project her hostile wishes onto the child, but now was increasingly aware of her own aggression. She became terrified that she might act upon her wishes and kill the child. She became consumed with guilt, increasingly disturbed, and made a number of suicidal attempts. A period of treatment reduced the intensity of the disturbance, but she continued her basic pattern of projection onto Mary despite the changes in her child, unlike Tommy's mother, who reacted to his positive changes by shifting the object of her externalizations. Furthermore, whereas Tommy's change affected the entire family equilibrium, Mary's affected the family only secondarily via the effect of the mother's increased disturbance.

Study of the treatment of these and similar cases has led us to the following general conclusions:

1. Children who are the objects of parental externalizations, as in the case of Tommy, manifest relatively little anxiety or guilt over drive expression. Rather, they show a severe narcissistic disturbance with mental pain and conflict rooted in the acceptance of the devalued self and the inability to integrate positive aspects with this conscious self representation. There is a primary impairment of the integrative function of the ego, the maintenance of self-esteem, and the development of an adequate self representation.

On the other hand, in children who are the objects of projection, as in the case of Mary, ego functioning and narcissistic cathexis are only secondarily involved in the pathology. They are subject to intense anxiety and guilt in relation to drive expression. The drives are constantly reinforced by the parental projections, and the development of an autonomous and adaptive defense system is hindered. A brittle superstructure, based on an identification with the primitive superego and defense system of the projecting mother, is created.

2. The extensive use of either projection or externalization by these children can be seen as a "generational" effect which goes beyond identification with the parental defenses.

3. The use of either of these mechanisms by the parents relates not only to severe pathology in the parents but also to a differing pattern of family dynamics. The extensive use of externalization relates to a pathological balance in the family, a closed system (Brodey, 1965) in which all members of the family play interdependent roles. A change in any one member of the family directly affects each of the others and produces a complete disruption of the family equilibrium. Projection, on the other hand, indicates an intense dyadic bond, usually between mother and child. A change in the child directly affects the mother and has only secondary effects upon the other members of the family.

SUMMARY

This study is an initial attempt to sort out some of the problems in an area of great complexity: the subjective allocation of inner phenomena to the outer world. We first separated processes which may have similar surface manifestations, such as displacement, transference, and processes of early differentiation from externalization. Within the category of externalization, we made a further distinction between modes of functioning, e.g., generalization and defenses. Among defensive externalizations we described the attribution of cause, externalization of aspects of the self representation, and externalization of drives, i.e., projection proper. The latter two were discussed in detail, and the differences between them were examined from the point of view of individual development and family dynamics.

BIBLIOGRAPHY

Abraham, K. (1924), A Short Study of the Development of the Libido. *Selected Papers on Psycho-Analysis.* London: Hogarth Press, pp. 418-501.

Brodey, W. M. (1965), On the Dynamics of Narcissism: I. Externalization and Early Ego Development. *This Annual,* 20:165-193.

Eidelberg, L. (1968), *Encyclopedia of Psychoanalysis.* New York: Free Press.

Feigenbaum, D. (1936), On Projection. *Psa. Quart.,* 5:303-319.

Fenichel, O. (1945), *The Psychoanalytic Theory of Neurosis.* New York: Norton.

Freud, A. (1936), *The Ego and the Mechanisms of Defense. The Writings of Anna Freud,* Vol. 2. New York: International Universities Press, rev. ed., 1966.

—— (1965), *Normality and Pathology in Childhood.* New York: International Universities Press.

Freud, S. (1895), Draft H. Paranoia. *Standard Edition,* 1:206-212. London: Hogarth Press, 1966.

—— (1897), Letter to Fliess [December 12]. In: *The Origins of Psychoanalysis.* New York: Basic Books, 1954, p. 237.

—— (1899), Screen Memories. *Standard Edition,* 3:303-322. London: Hogarth Press, 1962.

—— (1901), The Psychopathology of Everyday Life. *Standard Edition,* 6. London: Hogarth Press, 1960.

—— (1908), On the Sexual Theories of Children. *Standard Edition,* 9:207-226. London: Hogarth Press, 1959.

—— (1909), Notes upon a Case of Obsessional Neurosis. *Standard Edition,* 10:155-318. London: Hogarth Press, 1955.

—— (1910), 'Wild' Psycho-Analysis. *Standard Edition,* 11:221-227. London: Hogarth Press, 1957.

—— (1911a), Psycho-Analytic Notes on an Autobiographical Account of a Case of Paranoia (Dementia Paranoides). *Standard Edition,* 12:3-82. London: Hogarth Press, 1958.

—— (1911b), Formulations on the Two Principles of Mental Functioning. *Standard Edition,* 12:215-226. London: Hogarth Press, 1958.

—— (1913 [1912-1913]), Totem and Taboo. *Standard Edition,* 13:1-161. London: Hogarth Press, 1955.

—— (1915a), Instincts and Their Vicissitudes. *Standard Edition,* 14:117-140. London: Hogarth Press, 1957.

—— (1915b), The Unconscious. *Standard Edition,* 14:159-215. London: Hogarth Press, 1957.

—— (1916-1917 [1915-1917]), Introductory Lectures on Psycho-Analysis. *Standard Edition,* 15 & 16. London: Hogarth Press, 1963.

—— (1917 [1915]), A Metapsychological Supplement to the Theory of Dreams. *Standard Edition,* 14:217-235. London: Hogarth Press, 1957.

—— (1918 [1914]), From the History of an Infantile Neurosis. *Standard Edition,* 17:7-123. London: Hogarth Press, 1955.

—— (1920), Beyond the Pleasure Principle. *Standard Edition,* 18:3-64. London: Hogarth Press, 1955.

—— (1922), Some Neurotic Mechanisms in Jealousy, Paranoia and Homosexuality. *Standard Edition,* 18:221-232. London: Hogarth Press, 1955.

—— (1925), Negation. *Standard Edition,* 19:235-239. London: Hogarth Press, 1961.

—— (1927), The Future of an Illusion. *Standard Edition,* 21:5-56. London: Hogarth Press, 1961.

—— (1930 [1927]), Civilization and Its Discontents. *Standard Edition,* 21:64-145. London: Hogarth Press, 1961.

—— (1931), Female Sexuality. *Standard Edition*, 21:223-243. London: Hogarth Press, 1961.

—— (1936), A Disturbance of Memory on the Acropolis. *Standard Edition*, 22:239-248. London: Hogarth Press, 1964.

—— (1941 [1938]), Findings, Ideas, Problems. *Standard Edition*, 23:299-300. London: Hogarth Press, 1964.

Heimann, P. (1952), Certain Functions of Introjection and Projection in Early Infancy. In: *Developments in Psycho-Analysis*, ed. J. Riviere. London: Hogarth Press, pp. 122-168.

Jacobson, E. (1964), *The Self and the Object World*. New York: International Universities Press.

Jaffe, D. S. (1968), The Mechanism of Projection. *Int. J. Psa.*, 49:662-677.

Klein, M. (1932), *The Psycho-Analysis of Children*. London: Hogarth Press, 1950.

—— (1955), On Identification. In: *New Directions in Psycho-Analysis*, ed. M. Klein, P. Heimann, & R. E. Money-Kyrle. New York: Basic Books, pp. 309-345.

Lush, D. (1968), Progress of a Child with Atypical Development. *J. Child Psychother.*, 2:64-73.

Malin, A. & Grotstein, J. S. (1966), Projective Identification in the Therapeutic Process. *Int. J. Psa.*, 47:26-31.

Moore, B. E. & Fine, B. D., eds. (1967), *A Glossary of Psychoanalytic Terms and Concepts*. New York: American Psychoanalytic Association.

Novick, J. & Holder, A. (1969), The Simultaneous Analysis of Two Brothers (unpublished manuscript).

—— & Hurry, A. (1969), Projection and Externalisation. *J. Child Psychother.*, 2:5-20.

Piaget, J. (1936), *The Origins of Intelligence in Children*. New York: International Universities Press, 1952.

Rapaport, D. (1944), The Scientific Methodology of Psychoanalysis. In: *The Collected Papers of David Rapaport*, ed. M. M. Gill. New York: Basic Books, 1967, pp. 165-220.

—— (1950), The Theoretical Implications of Diagnostic Testing Procedures. In: *The Collected Papers of David Rapaport*, ed. M. M. Gill. New York: Basic Books, 1967, pp. 334-356.

—— (1952), Projective Techniques and the Theory of Thinking. In: *The Collected Papers of David Rapaport*, ed. M. M. Gill. New York: Basic Books, 1967, pp. 461-469.

—— (1960), On the Psychoanalytic Theory of Motivation. In: *Nebraska Symposium on Motivation*, ed. M. R. Jones. Lincoln: University of Nebraska Press, pp. 173-247.

Rycroft, C. (1968), *A Critical Dictionary of Psycho-Analysis*. London: Nelson.

Waelder, R. (1951), The Structure of Paranoid Ideas. *Int. J. Psa.*, 32:167-177.

Weiss, E. (1947), Projection, Extrajection and Objectivation. *Psa. Quart.*, 16:357-377.

CLINICAL CONTRIBUTIONS

ON SOME PROBLEMS OF TECHNIQUE IN THE ANALYSIS OF EARLY ADOLESCENTS

MARJORIE HARLEY, Ph.D. (Baltimore)

The aim of this paper is to discuss a few of the technical difficulties which have cumbered my way in the analyses of early adolescents. First, however, I shall briefly review, as I see them, some of the metapsychological aspects of the subphase, *early adolescence*. Since the views of child analysts on the distinction between preadolescence and adolescence are somewhat diversified, such an introduction may be a necessary prelude to the clinical material which I shall include in my discussion of technique.

I have thought it somewhat misleading to characterize preadolescence by the quantitative changes in the drives *in contradistinction to* the qualitative changes which occur in early adolescence. It is, of course, incontestable that in preadolescence there is an indiscriminate instinctual arousal from all developmental levels (A. Freud, 1936); and it is equally incontestable that in early adolescence the biological processes of puberty work toward a qualitative shift in drive organization. But these processes also further augment the quantitative factor, and it is this quantitative factor that largely accounts for the now relative weakness of the ego vis-à-vis the drives. In addition, it is the quantitative as well as the qualitative factor which results in the recathexis of the oedipal strivings with a renewed vigor. As these strivings press toward the surface, the concomitant conflicts may constitute a potentially powerful impediment to the ego's acceptance of genitality and hence a potentially disturbing influence on "the later development of the ego after puberty" (Freud, 1938, p. 191).

Read at the Fifth Annual Meeting of The American Association for Child Psychoanalysis, April, 1970, at Hershey, Pennsylvania. This paper was designed to provide a point of departure for an associated workshop discussion of technical problems in the analysis of early adolescents.

From the foregoing, it follows that I do not question the existence, in early adolescence, of the interplay of forces associated with
the oedipus complex and the attendant structural conflicts. It is
my impression, however, that the recathexis of the oedipal strivings
is as yet a contributing rather than the dominating factor in the
early adolescent's initial attempts to loosen his infantile object ties;
and that these endeavors are motivated at least as much by the ego's
need to repudiate preoedipal protection and comfort, and to move
toward self-reliance and self-direction, as by the need to relinquish
the incestuous (oedipal) bonds. In this sense, they reflect the first
steps on the long road toward the final attainment of adult maturity.
I would further add that they are closely bound up with the maturation of the ego apparatuses and that they draw upon ego as well as
id energies.

In the ego-superego conflicts of early adolescence, the incestuous
strivings obviously play their role, particularly as manifested in the
frequently observed sexualization and resultant externalization of
the superego. Here, nonetheless, in this early subphase of adolescence, I would again see the ego's strenuous endeavors to negate
parental standards as springing in no small measure from the conflictual wishes to establish independence. Further (and in contrast
to the older adolescent), the early adolescent is as yet relatively un-
discriminating in his quest for new values and standards: instead,
self-consciously and protestingly, he is primarily driven to adopt
behavior which is in direct opposition to parental dictates. Underneath, however, his state of mind generally runs counter to his overt
behavior; and his unconscious anxiety and guilt, arising from his
furtively or truculently aggressive methods of self-assertiveness, are
often easily detectable.

The object relations of early adolescence also may be said to have
their own peculiar characteristics. In contrast to the (homosexual)
peer relationships of preadolescence, where it is not so much the
objects that are sexualized as those mutual activities of exploration
of the physical selves and exchanges of sexual knowledge and theories, the bisexual (Blos, 1962) relationships of early adolescence are
often highly libidinized. On the one hand, they provide a displaced
medium through which to enact the various facets of the positive and
negative oedipal triangles; on the other hand, they serve as narcis-

sistic buttresses for acquiring and establishing a new and different status, and as experimental maneuvers for demonstrating one's appropriate sexual role. In any event, these relationships lack those dimensions of emotional richness and depth which mark the ardent friendships and love affairs of later adolescence; and there are as yet, as I have implied, no efforts toward object removal (A. Katan, 1937) contingent on the finding of new (heterosexual) love objects.

I am inclined to conceive of early adolescence, then, within a framework which takes into account a rather wide view of ego development, and which also allows for failures in meeting the new ego and drive demands. It has seemed to me that those pubertal or early postpubertal girls, and those somewhat older boys who are in an analogous maturational stage, whom I would speak of as early adolescents, are in many ways different beings, confronted with a different situation, than the children whom I would regard as still being in the preadolescent phase. To be more explicit, the individual whom I conceive of as an early adolescent has by now, as a rule, attained a more complex level of (autonomous) ego functioning; and he is now faced with a different set of demands, both internal and external. In respect to the internal, there will be new ego tasks among which, of course, the demands to deal with the awakening genital urgencies, to integrate a changing body image into the self representation, and to loosen the infantile object ties are foremost. From the external, there will be demands to meet new standards that come from two directions: from the peer group and from the adult world, so that, in addition, these new standards often will clash. If, however, the individual is burdened with pregenital and preoedipal fixations, or in other ways is ill-equipped to meet the maturational demands for a shift in drive organization and for new modalities of ego adaptation,[1] I would still consider him an early adolescent—albeit one very much in need of treatment. I realize that there may be those who feel that, in speaking of early adolescence, I am not free of discrepancies and contradictions; and that

[1] In my introductory summary of some of the metapsychological aspects of early adolescence, I deliberately excluded the adaptive factor. I am quite in accord with K. Eissler's (1969) statement that neither adaptation nor genetic processes "can be the stuff of special metapsychological categories" (p. 465). I further agree that the topographical factor is indispensable to a complete understanding of mental processes.

there may be others who feel I have placed undue emphasis on the assumption that an individual who is faced with certain phase-specific problems which he is unable to solve, and who retreats to or maintains earlier positions, in many respects is not comparable to the individual for whom the same positions are still phase appropriate.

Against this background I shall discuss a few of the technical problems which I have encountered in the analysis of early adolescents. These problems, which admittedly have occurred to me in a haphazard fashion, have nonetheless tended to organize themselves into three groups:

(1) Problems relating to the initial contact with the early adolescent, that is, to the consultation period;

(2) Problems pertaining to the early adolescent's transference manifestations; and

(3) Problems dealing with the handling of perverse masturbation practices and passive homosexual problems in the early adolescent boy.

I would introduce my comments on technique with the general statement that in working with early adolescents, I apply the analytic method at the point of the first meeting and maintain it throughout the analysis. As with children, I endeavor, however, to adapt my technique to the degree of ego maturation which has been attained and to the particular phase-specific areas of anxiety and narcissistic sensitivity; and I also try to consider the content of my interpretations in the light of the phase-specific tasks to be accomplished. This last applies not only to interpretations which are made but also to interpretations which deliberately are not made lest they hinder rather than augment the developmental processes.

The analytic method obviously presupposes that the analyst present himself, at the outset, in his appropriate role which encompasses interest and empathy, but which does not deviate from neutrality and respects that aspect of the adolescent which is trying to achieve autonomy. By definition, then, it precludes any nonanalytic interventions or manipulations with respect to the patient himself or his environment. I have thought the establishment of this attitude to be essential for the noncontamination of future transference manifestations; and also for the development of the therapeutic alliance, since it sets the stage for the early adolescent's perception of the reality of the analyst as separate from the infantile objects.

It is within the context of the analyst's neutrality that I shall discuss my first thought concerning technical problems in the initial contact.

As we know, the adolescent rarely, if ever, comes for his first appointment with an accurate conception of the analyst's role. In general, we are most aware that we may be viewed as an extension of the parents, as a personification of the old rather than the new, and thus as reflecting old superego standards and a perpetuation of dependence. What we may tend sometimes to overlook is that the early adolescent's picture of the analyst may also be one that carries the attraction of support for instinctual gratification. And this can only mean that this attraction ultimately will be a threat to that part of the adolescent which is seeking instinctual control.

I have thought it is just because we know so well how the resistances to analysis are often especially marked in early adolescence, that we may be overzealous in our efforts to establish rapport. This zeal, then, may trigger countertransference intrusions so that we may unwittingly present ourselves as apart from the primary objects by means other than our adherence to neutrality. For example, we may unconsciously imply, in a manner not always easy to pinpoint, that we are on the side of the adolescent's negativistic and hostile aggressive strivings against the parents, that is, on the side of those strivings which (as I have earlier implied) I believe are rarely if ever totally devoid of some anxiety and guilt. This may result in engendering in the adolescent a spurious sense of power, with the analyst an accomplice, if not the instigator, in his acting out. Or, by trying to convey to the adolescent our understanding and nonjudgmental attitude toward those activities usually condemned, in some measure, by adults, in an equally subtle way we may appear to him as participants in superego corruption.

None of us would dispute the fact that there is no other time in life when the two opposites—regression and progression—draw each other out and set each other into motion to the extent that they do in adolescence. The early adolescent may use his peers as a mainstay for regression in any one or all three of his psychic systems and to bolster him in his battles against his parents. But we know it is a quite different matter if he sees an adult, in this case the analyst, as being in an analogous role. In the latter instance, there is an almost invariable concomitant which either immediately, or as a delayed reaction, will increase rather than lessen his suspiciousness and fears. He may feel he is slipping under the influence of someone who, more powerful than himself, may promote instinctual license and simultaneously seduce him into revealing his sexual fantasies and activities; or, and particularly in those instances where there is a history of an actual childhood seduction, there may even eventuate the unconscious fantasy of this being repeated with the analyst.

I would add it is primarily in those adolescents who are most rebellious and antagonistic, and who may come to the analyst with a manifest and explicit request for support against their parents' restrictions, that the underlying wish to achieve ego control is often especially strong; and that the basic fear of superego and id seduction is often especially marked. Of paramount importance in such cases, then, is that the analyst focus on this wish for control as one of the motivations, or the motivation, for analysis, and that he scrupulously avoid any involvement in the adolescent's externalization maneuvers.

For example, a thirteen-and-one-half-year-old girl obviously had come to my office under coercion. She rested a pad on her knees and wrote for the entire hour. I tried hard, but only once did she speak, when she angrily snapped her answer that she was writing an essay on the evils of the establishment. She made it quite clear that I was in the latter category. At the end of the hour, I verbalized my agreement that she wished no help at this time and left the way open for her to telephone me should she change her mind.

Over a year later, she requested an appointment on the basis that her parents were "driving her nuts." She was obviously upset and I had the sense that her externalization might be a friable one and more in the nature of a face-saving device.

In the course of two interviews, it became apparent, through her derivative communications, that one of her central problems was a fear of loss of control linked to her masturbation conflict. The scenes she provoked with her parents and her older brother were clearly aimed at drawing them into her arena of sexual excitement. Her frequent refusals to go to school were not solely an expression of defiance, as she would have her parents believe, but were associated with the anxiety she experienced at having to sit still in a classroom when her intense sexual excitations threatened to overwhelm her. In a paradoxical way, her emphatic complaints that her parents were exerting too much control and grounding her repeatedly were, unknown to herself, also her way of saying that they were, in fact, depriving her of control; that is, "driving her nuts." For, in her scheme of things, her only means of handling her instinctual pressures was to discharge them through almost unceasing activity with her peers. Yet, by providing her with derivative but anxiety-arousing masturbation outlets, these activities served to perpetuate rather than alleviate her tensions.

This girl opened the first session with a long series of complaints against her parents and an explicit, insistent demand that I advise them to treat her differently: that I recommend she be allowed to go into Central Park and to ride the subways whenever she chose; and that she have no curfew imposed upon her. I listened to her story impassively and when she had finally finished, I said she had told me of her external problems, but I wondered about her internal ones, since it was to these that my kind of work pertained. I maintained this attitude consistently in the face of her alternations between revealing her inner conflicts and then reverting to her demands, which at times were tantamount to threats, for an alleviation of the external. She was enormously relieved when, at the close of our second appointment, we had established between us her need to understand what was going on "inside" so that she could control her feelings instead of allowing her feelings to control her.

Now, in the first hour, when this girl seemed on the verge of speaking of her "hangups," and then hesitated, I suggested it was difficult for her not to regard me as a member of the establishment. She spied a package of cigarettes in an outside flap of my pocketbook and helped herself to one, underscoring that her parents did not know she smoked; and she proceeded to tell me how she had smoked pot, how she *might* decide to "go straight," and indirectly revealed her concern lest she be tempted to try hard drugs. In the course of her second appointment, she told me I should not have made my remark about the establishment. She explained this implied that I was not an adult; it would have been more appropriate had I implied that I was not her mother. The ostentatiously innocent and earnest manner with which she thus chided me was, in one sense, all part of her provocation; but she also had made a valid point. I had felt challenged by this girl, who did not present so easy a picture as I may have depicted. At the moment of my allusion to the establishment, I had been overeager to gain her confidence and there very likely had been a subtle element of seduction in my manner or voice. Later, in speaking of her decision to accept treatment, she again warned me to maintain my appropriate role by paying me a dubious compliment. She compared me favorably with another analyst with whom she had begun analysis two years previously, and from whom she had broken contact after only a few months of treatment. This other analyst was "not a very good one," she said. She had allowed her to break appointments and leave her hours whenever she wished; and, she added, she also had let her "bum her cigarettes!"

My second thought regarding the initial contact pertains to the adolescent's anxiety, as well as his shame and guilt, with respect to revealing his inner life. It has seemed to me that we are so attuned to the threat that this carries for him, so attuned to his narcissistic vulnerability, and so apprehensive lest we frighten him away, that our reluctance to set foot in troubled waters may sometimes deprive him of a valid relief.

The early adolescent, who is willing to consult with an analyst, often has conceded that there is a discernible reason for taking this step. He may well fear, however, that there is another reason. To take an oversimplified example: in the case of an underachiever, the discernible reason may deal with his learning problems. The inner, feared reason may derive from his unconscious castration complex and express itself in a generalized feeling that there may be something "terribly wrong" with him which makes him different; and which the analyst will perceive and thus verify, so that he will be doomed.

If, in the initial contact, we detect this inner reason, and if we are able to bring it out into the open, we may have taken a first step which is no mean one. The underachiever will probably be more relieved than not if we find a suitable opportunity to obtain his acknowledgment that he sometimes feels unsure of himself in ways that transcend the academic area; that these feelings are not easy to define but are confusing and disturbing and amount to his feeling all wrong about himself. His relief will come from our attitude and tone of voice which imply that, in our experience, this sort of feeling is neither unique nor irreversible, but is a problem to be analyzed.

I trust that what I have said will not be construed as my advocating that we abandon caution in our approach to the early adolescent patient; or that I am overlooking the fact that we must be guided by our own experience, sensitivity, and intuition. But I do mean that if we are too ready to augment or even instigate avoidance maneuvers, we may lose rather than gain.

I shall now turn to my two thoughts which relate to problems that I have encountered in the handling of the transference in early adolescents.[2] My first remark regarding transference manifestations concerns the consequences of a technical error which I made when I failed to perceive that the main theme of the analysis, at a given time, was the expression of the patient's transference. In this connection, it is relevant to inject that there have been times when the cathexis of the early adolescent has appeared to be so much vested in his school activities and his peer relationships, or in his initial and experimental attempts at assuming a heterosexual role, that I have not alerted myself sufficiently to the transference manifestations which nonetheless have been active and pertinent.

A boy, not quite fifteen, had been in analysis for a year and a half. An only child, he had entered into a relationship with me in which he strove in manifold ways to elicit those responses which he saw as a means for correction of the emotional deprivations and destructive responses that he felt had been inflicted upon him by his parents; and it should be said that his grievances had some reality basis. His mother had frankly wanted a girl, had lamented repeatedly her inability to conceive again after his birth, and had never welcomed his active, masculine strivings. In his preschool years, he had spent most of his waking hours with a maid who had paid little attention to him. Throughout his childhood, and up to the present, his father had been away much of the time on long trips and, when he was at home, he had been depressed and withdrawn.

---

[2] I should here inject for the sake of clarity that in this paper I am using the term transference in its strict meaning to denote a repetition of past events and experiences, and am not extending it to include all of the patient's attitudes toward the analyst.

I commenced this boy's analysis with the resolution to resist both his overt attempts to force me into gratifying those needs, which he felt had never been fulfilled, and his, at other times, artfully disguised methods to lure me into this role. By the end of the first year of analysis, it seemed that these tendencies had been much lessened. I should add that he was somewhat obsessional, with a proneness toward isolation when his ideational contents became anxiety arousing.

At this time, the boy's main preoccupations had to do with his first serious attempt to have a steady girlfriend whose name was Jane. I cannot elaborate on the content of the analytic hours, with which I am here concerned, save to say that they had to do primarily with his uneasiness in this relationship, an uneasiness which was traceable to his castration complex and his related doubts about the adequacy of his genital. These factors we had already openly touched upon in the context of his masturbation. In any event, for a number of hours, he now offered his own interpretations, mainly through his dreams, of what he saw as the causes for his uneasiness with Jane, linking these to his castration anxiety. He also relied heavily on symbolic meanings (and I feel impelled to say that he did not learn these from me) on which to base his often complex and even fanciful interpretations. His way of thus engaging in what was largely a pseudo self-analysis was highly intellectualized, and I saw this as part of his isolation tendencies when faced with anxiety. For this reason, I interpreted what I thought to be the relevant defense. No sooner had I made this interpretation, when I knew I had inflicted a painful narcissistic hurt; and so I indicated I knew he had taken my interpretation as a criticism. But by this he felt also criticized because I had, as it were, criticized him for feeling criticized.

I next endeavored to speak to his extreme narcissistic vulnerability of the moment in terms of the painful inadequacy we both knew he was experiencing with Jane; and of the inevitable intensification of these feelings at this time, when his anxieties about his genital were in the foreground. However, in my efforts to help maintain this boy's narcissistic equilibrium, I was too unrestrained in the almost soothing understanding I showed as I paved the way for the interpretations I made in subsequent hours. It was not long before he began behaving like a contented child, interspersing his associations with expressions of how "great" analysis was, he was "so much better already"; and of how much he liked my office and also me because I understood him so well. It was then that I realized the extent to which I had been gratifying him.

When I had rearranged my perspective, I could see it had not been his defense of intellectualization that had been the important factor of the moment. He had been, in fact, manifesting a transference resistance in that by enacting his intellectual gymnastics before my eyes, he had been repeating his futile attempts to gain his mother's admiration of his phallic exhibitionism in his oedipal phase. Further, in my ill-chosen ways of trying to undo the narcissistic injury which I had inflicted by repudiating his phallic advances, I had fallen into the trap of encouraging his regression and of providing, on a preoedipal level, that very emotional corrective experience I had cautioned myself to avoid.

We would all agree that certain elements of corrective emotional experiences are probably the *by-products* of all analyses. It also might be interesting to speculate on how much the search for a corrective emotional experience may be phase-specific in adolescence and the various ways in which this may, in general, be implemented. Nonetheless, I believe many of us would agree that the main purpose of analysis is to make the necessary corrections by genetic constructions and the working through of the infantile conflicts. And I have offered this brief sketch to show not only how I allowed an early adolescent's manifest preoccupation with outside activities to obscure my awareness of the transference, and thus to lead me to make a misinterpretation; but also how, in my efforts to undo my apparent yet incompletely understood error, I momentarily ceased to function in my proper role of analyst.

My second thought is concerned with a problem contingent on insufficient understanding of all the ingredients of a given transference resistance. It has relation to an area which has continued to interest me for a long time and on which I elaborated some years ago (Harley, 1961a). Specifically, I have in mind the individual who reaches early adolescence already burdened with an ego which throughout childhood has never overcome a sense of uncontrollability and helplessness in response to instinctual excitations, and whose ego-instinctual balance has always been an uncertain one. These are children who, because of one or several combined genetic factors, usually rooted in the early preoedipal period, but then continuing in new forms or new combinations in the oedipal and even post-oedipal periods, were never able to attain the relative respite from instinctual pressures more commonly associated with the latency years. I am referring to those children who were subjected to excessive and repeated premature genital arousal and who, as will be recalled, were the focus of some of Greenacre's (1952) earlier studies.

The point I should like to make here has to do with the sometimes enormous threat to the early adolescent of this type, which arises from his anxiety lest he be unable to contain his instinctual excitations and associated body sensations and feelings. To say this in other words, it is as though the instinctual changes of puberty, with the attendant assault on the already precarious ego-instinctual balance, threaten to activate the memory traces of the early states of extreme organismic distress arising from the fact that the massive stimulation had exceeded the immature organism's capacity for discharge. It is further relevant that in these cases there tends to be a perpetuation of the excess of aggression linked with the early and premature genital arousal, and which not only results in an increased sadomasochism, but which also contributes to the preservation of the ego's primary, as it were, sense of helplessness in the face of genital arousal.

I learned that in certain situations it was my failure to perceive and comprehend this factor in the early adolescent's fear of his libidinal strivings in the transference that led to an impasse in the analysis. I shall attempt to illustrate this by recalling the patient who first helped me to understand it.

This was a fourteen-and-one-half-year-old girl, who in early prepuberty had erected constricting defenses against her instinctual strivings, and who was approaching the end of her second year of analysis. Up to this point, I had been unable to loosen her defenses against her affects. Suffice it to say that I knew, both from the history and genetic constructions which we had already arrived at, that this girl belonged to that group of overstimulated children of which I have been speaking. She could remember her compulsive masturbation in early latency and recalled how one day the insides of her thighs were so inflamed that she could not wait until her mother had vacated the bathroom; and she had barged in to ease her burning sensations with cold water, even though in so doing she risked revealing the fact of her masturbation to the mother. She had no awareness that she had thus been seeking her mother's aid in controlling her excitement rather than in augmenting it. This I then interpreted. She had hinted at her latency masturbation fantasies when she spoke of the picture games she had played with herself in these childhood years, but insisted that she could remember only the fact that she had imagined a variety of things—that the content of her imaginings she could not possibly recall; and I believed her. Nor did she deny my suggestion that she wanted to keep these fantasies buried away as a means of avoiding the excited feelings they might evoke; but this suggestion yielded nothing further. She was equally insistent that her latency masturbation seemed long ago, like part of the dark ages, and that she now experienced no genital sensations and no desire to masturbate. This, too, I believed.

With this reserve fund of material, I listened to the following dream:

> I was playing football and Harry—a boy in my class—made a pass at me; and I seemed to have forgotten how to play the game and thought it was dodge ball, so instead of catching the pass I dodged it.

She immediately saw the dream pun but seemed not to see the coincidence between the dream boy's name, Harry, and her father's name. Hesitatingly, she said that she thought the dream had to do with the Friday evening, two weeks hence, when Ernie, a sixteen-year-old boy, was to take her to her first dance; and she now volunteered her anxiety lest she not know what to do should he try to kiss her good-night. I approached this anxiety at first in its simplest terms, that is, her uncertainty regarding the expected behavior for her age on her first date with a boy. This yielded no result; nor did my attempts in subsequent hours to approach her underlying sexual fantasies by reference to the forgotten game in the dream, and to her wish to dodge all the picture games of her imagination. She only said I did not understand and that she herself did not understand enough to tell me. But, if Ernie kissed her, she was afraid she *would not know what to do.*

There now ensued a shift in the analysis, the cause of which she easily understood. She turned her attention away from Ernie to me, which obviously meant that she sought safety from the heterosexual (oedipal) dangers in a preoedipal mother relationship. At this juncture, we came up against a period of powerful resistance after she had confessed she was beginning to have "liking feelings" for me, which she feared would increase. In the course of many weeks, I attempted every possible means that I could devise to understand the specific contents of this resistance. For example, I tried to deal with the implied regressive threat in her turning to me for comfort and security; with the fantasy that, as her mother had done, I would increase her excitement rather than help her control it; and I gave interpretations in derivative form of the homosexual implication in her "liking feelings" for me, and of her possible fears of merging into me. Finally, she verbalized her concern that she might even have the urge to hug me. But when I remarked that perhaps she feared she would not be able to control this urge, or even that I would permit her to act upon it, she was convincing in her assurance that she knew full well this urge would not lead to action. She then repeated that I did not understand; she could not explain, but if she "let her feelings come," she would not know what to do. At that moment, I recalled that she had used this same phrase, that is, *that she would not know what to do,* in the context of the good-night kiss from Ernie. It was then that I suddenly understood; and I told her I thought she feared most of all that her feelings would become so strong she would not be able to stand them. Her relief was unmistakable.

After we had repeatedly linked this fear to those early states of intense excitement, which she had sustained when she was so little, and when it was understandable that she must have felt almost as though her little body would burst with such strong excitement, she ultimately dared to experience that immediacy of feeling provided by the positive and negative aspects of the transference; and she could then allow her sadomasochistic primal scene fantasies to emerge in conjunction with her genital sensations. It was also now that she could understand that it was what for her amounted to an almost overwhelming strength of her feelings that lent such reality force to these frightening fantasies. In short, it was her comprehension that her basic fear lest she be unable to contain her feelings was, in one sense, an anachronism that seemed to provide her with the courage to proceed to analyze the pregenital and preoedipal components which had led to her unresolved oedipal problems.

My final remarks have to do with the technical handling of perverse masturbation practices and the problem of passive homosexuality in the early adolescent boy. In this connection, I have in mind those boys whose future psychosexual development appears to be endangered by rather constant perverse inclinations which often have predated the onset of adolescence, and which in themselves are indicators of strong pregenital fixations rather than of temporary drive regressions.

There is fairly general agreement that, in the more usual course of affairs, it is not too difficult to enable the early adolescent boy to speak of the act of masturbation, especially when we approach this in the context of the phase-specific body feelings that a boy of his age is experiencing. More often than not, he will at first deny any concerns, but once the fact of his masturbation is an open one between us, we can slowly proceed to the various anxieties involved. The early adolescent, however, whose masturbation activities are consistently, or for the most part, of a perverse order, will usually strenuously resist any direct mention of masturbation. He may repeatedly make sly references to it, but usually will hastily retreat when we try to pursue these. Yet, in the three such cases I have worked with, I have thought it has been largely this very problem that has kept the adolescent coming.

I would here inject that my findings in respect to the adolescent's attitude toward his perverse masturbation practices are very much in accord with those of Laufer (1968). Laufer states the problem most aptly, I believe, when he suggests that in his cases masturbation could not serve "the function of helping the ego reorganize itself around the supremacy of genitality" (p. 115). He further sees the adolescent's anxiety as arising not only from his belief that this behavior is a confirmation of his abnormality, but also from his awareness of his inability to use masturbation as "trial action" for adult sexual behavior.

In order to provide a setting for my comments on the question of the technique involved in dealing with these and related problems, I shall draw on one more case description as my starting point.

A thirteen-year-old boy eagerly accepted analysis. From the

vantage of both his biological development and his general demean-or, he had the appearance of a fifteen- or sixteen-year-old. He was depressed; although an A student, he was still concerned about his schoolwork; and although president of his class and a surface par-ticipant in most peer activities, he inwardly felt isolated and uncer-tain of his position in the group. He also had been intensely afraid, since early prepuberty, that older boys and men would attack him on the street or in his room at night. In contrast to his urgent request that he commence his analysis as soon as possible, he opened his first hour with what became an oft-repeated refrain for months: "Do I have to come?" No matter how I attempted to deal with this refrain analytically, he retorted that he had to come; he was trapped. He also reiterated that his youth was slipping away too rapidly, that he was not preparing adequately for the future. He emphasized how he wanted to be on his own and counted the years until he could drive a car. Yet he also told, rather wistfully, of his desire to have life remain unchanged; and how, before leaving for weekend or vacation trips, he hid a bottle top in the kitchen so that when he returned it would still be there as a confirmation that "things" were the same. Initially, I saw his mild depression, and his conflicting desires to re-tain his *status quo* and yet to move forward, largely as part of the developmental processes of mourning (Root, 1957; A. Freud, 1958) and of the interplay between regression and progression.

The first material in the analysis dealt with his disparaging, well-nigh annihilating hostility against his father, which soon showed itself as his attempt to obliterate his strong negative oedipal ties. In this context, he portrayed his deep affection for his mother, appear-ing more childlike when he spoke of her, and seeming to regard her more in the light of an all-giving, protecting preoedipal mother than as a positive oedipal love object. Toward me he was formal and po-lite, an attitude which was in marked contrast to his fury that be-trayed itself as he shut the door behind him at the end of each hour. He vehemently heaved it with one hand and then caught it with the other just before it could slam. So violent was his action that one day, unknown to himself, he actually dislocated one of the door hinges. It is noteworthy that behind his defensive exterior, his ex-treme castration anxiety was almost invariably detectable.

It was some time before I realized that his expressed fear and underlying wish to be "trapped," although doubtless related to at least two genetic happenings,[3] at this stage reflected his fear and wish to reveal the perverse nature of his masturbation. His aversion to change reflected his fear of losing his perverse activity, while his concern that he was not preparing for the future was his awareness that this perversion was preventing him from keeping abreast of the forward march of events. His fury against me, which broke through only at the end of almost every hour, was aimed at the negative aspects of the preoedipal mother, now transferred to me: I was the vengeful, castrating, phallic mother who, in this instance, would rob him of his perversion.

For the time being, I shall leave this patient to outline the principles of technique which I found helpful in working with him with respect both to the perverse nature of his masturbation and the passive homosexual fantasies and behavior he also revealed. These principles are essentially the same as those I have used fairly consistently in dealing with passive homosexual problems in early adolescents, albeit in this patient the problem was more a bisexual one in that his masculine strivings and attendant heterosexual stirrings

---

[3] Some of the characteristics and the genetic material of this patient coincide with Greenacre's (1953) findings regarding fetishists. Until he was five years old, he shared a room with his sister, eleven months younger than himself, and this would seem to have been one of the determinants in his proclivity for primitive identification, with a "bisexual splitting of the body image even antecedent to the phallic phase" (p. 92). In the pregenital as well as in the phallic-oedipal phases he sustained traumas of a "castrative type" (p. 89). At two years of age, he was alone with his mother in her bedroom and witnessed her spontaneous abortion. This occurrence, described to the patient by his mother at the outset of the analysis, facilitated his use of it to screen a later traumatic experience in the phallic-oedipal period. When he was four years old, he visited his maternal aunt and six-year-old cousin at a country farm. The cousin fell over a barbed wire fence which pierced his crotch. He was carried bleeding into the house by his mother (that is, the patient's aunt) who placed him on the bed, leaning over him to dress his wound. Not wishing the frightened, younger child to wander around unsupervised, the aunt insisted that he remain in the room while she tended the cousin. In looking back on this experience with his cousin, my patient described how he felt "trapped in a chamber of horror"; and the event became linked with his mother's admonishment of him for masturbating. It was interesting to observe how, in his analysis, he was frequently prone to confuse the image of his aunt bending over his cousin with that of his (castrating) mother; and how, as we worked with this material, a further distortion eventuated in that he began to insist it was his cousin, and not himself, who had been rebuked for masturbating. Throughout the analysis, he manifested a marked body-phallus equation; and his body suffered *"in toto* or in its various parts all of the distresses of castration anxiety" (Greenacre, 1955, p. 192).

could, on occasion, assert themselves more genuinely and forcibly than they could in other such boys.

The first principle I have derived from Anna Freud's (1952) findings through which she demonstrated that the unconscious fantasy of the passive homosexual was an active one since through his active partner he sought to retrieve his lost masculinity.[4] From this she arrived at her formulation that the promise of a cure was a castration threat. In dealing with problems of perverse tendencies, then, I am first of all mindful of the fantasied castration threat implicit in the adolescent's abandonment of his perverse strivings. At this point, I shall return to my patient with the perverse masturbation practices.

When this boy was not far from his fifteenth birthday, and after repeated indirect approaches, I dared to confront him with the possibility that his extreme anxiety in speaking of masturbation stemmed from his feeling that his ways were different from many other boys; and that this might mean to him that he was strange or abnormal. His spontaneous response was: "I knew I was trapped, I can't tell you." To this I countered, not only by underlining both sides of his conflict over whether to tell me or not, but also by saying he might fear that analysis would take away this problem before he was certain he wanted to give it up; and I added it might be hard for him to realize that ultimately it was he and not myself whose power it was to decide whether to change something in himself or not. To this, he blurted out: "I'm a transvestite. Goddamn it, if I give up my paraphernalia, I'll lose my potency." He now told how he put on his mother's underpants and blouse, lay on his back and fondled his penis through the underpants, at that moment consciously identifying himself with a girl; whereupon he removed his paraphernalia, as he called it, lay on his stomach and, now identified with the male role, masturbated to the point of ejaculation which he could not achieve without these preliminaries. He also now told

4 These findings were nicely demonstrated by a thirteen-year-old boy, whom I saw many years ago and who taught me a great deal, especially so since I drove him away from analysis by pursuing too avidly his passive aims. He came back finally when I told him, over the telephone, that I had made a mistake in not conveying to him that I also knew how much he wanted to be big and strong. Soon after his return, he presented me with a series of daydreams, the gist of which were that he was cared for and even "mothered" by famous baseball players. The ending to these daydreams, however, was that through this close contact with these athletes he himself eventually became a great ball player.

how he had initiated this practice in prepuberty soon after discovering his mother's blood-stained underpants in the clothes hamper. Weeks later, he confessed his frequent urge to hug and kiss his parents' men friends and his associated fantasies of anal penetration.

The second principle I have derived from Freud (1931) who, in speaking of activity and passivity, cautioned that we have "no right to assume that only one of them is primary and that the other owes its strength merely to the force of defence." He goes on to ask: "And if the defence against femininity is so energetic, from what other source can it draw its strength than from the masculine trend . . .?" (p. 243).

I endeavor, then, to apply infinite care, in the analysis of passive homosexual problems, to respect openly the boy's attempts at active, masculine behavior, usually refraining from any mention of its defensive purpose save at those times when this is also apparent to him. Even then I remind him that, defensive or not, this is nonetheless also a mark of the way a significant aspect of himself wants to be. I agree very much with Fraiberg's (1961) observation that it is far easier, with early adolescents, to interpret their passive behavior as a defense against their active aggression than it is to uncover and analyze the passive *aims*. But in my experience, I have, nevertheless, found it possible sometimes to bring these passive aims into the analysis and, in some measure at least, to assuage the concomitant narcissistic hurts, by utilizing the opportunities afforded to acknowledge the boy's simultaneous wish to move forward and to claim his active strivings. If he gives danger signals of regressing to the point of a surrender to his passivity, I try to counterbalance this by emphasizing the other side.

In referring to the analysis of passive aims, I do not mean that it is not equally important to analyze the destructive, aggressive fantasies which so often are directed first and foremost against the mother, thus enhancing her phallic, castrating image and furthering the identification with her. For example, my "transvestite" patient, who was now fifteen-and-one-half years old, recounted his "baby fantasies." He would experience rage when thinking of infants because they "just screamed for their bottles and their mothers"; and he would imagine himself sticking pins into them to torture them. What aroused his most violent rage was that they had not learned control, so that he could never make them obey him. The fantasy was, of course, overdetermined: the infants reflected his younger sister with whom he had vied on a preoedipal and negative oedipal level, as well as that passive, infantile aspect of himself which he both cherished and loathed; the pins were the shots he had inordinately feared since early childhood and his turning of passive into active; yet, at the same time, he satisfied his almost boundless masochism by identification with his tortured victims. Yet the uncontrollable infants also stood for his own enormously aggressive impulses which he feared might become uncontrollable. When I interpreted this last element, his association was that he masturbated each day before coming to his hour because somehow he felt that by so doing he would protect me. He took pains also to masturbate before taking a girl out for the same reason, that is, as a protection to her. While masturbating, he felt "aggressive and bad"; when he had ejaculated he felt "passive and good," and quenched his thirst with cold milk. He experienced no aggressive masturbation fantasies, he said, but confirmed my suggestion that he had to keep them away by recalling that while masturbating, he kept popular tunes running through his head over and over again.

In a later hour, he closed his eyes, was silent for only a few moments, startled as he opened his eyes, and explained in surprise that he thought he had fallen asleep and had dreamed his fantasies were not his own but made in a factory. I agreed this might be a comforting dream. At that moment, however, I felt his need for ego support and so I remarked that it was, nonetheless, often easier to understand, and therefore easier to modify or design anew, what one had wrought with one's own hands than to do the same with what others had put together by machine. His ultimate response was to disclose his "little people fantasy," in which he held tiny women in his hands and humiliated them by ripping off their clothes; and thus he felt that he had complete control over them, almost as though he had power over a world of women. The transference allusions in this derivative masturbation fantasy he volunteered without my help; and he also volunteered that it had entered consciousness only twice, but each time as he approached my office.

While we all know by now how rarely, if ever, we can predict whether an adolescent, and especially an early adolescent, will manifest an overt perversion in adulthood, I believe it is of prime importance to begin to analyze these perverse strivings, if possible, in early rather than in later adolescence. Hopefully, this will help to loosen those pregenital fixations which are the cornerstones of the perverse fantasies and their invariable concomitant of unusually strong sadomasochistic tendencies; and it will also hopefully help to reinforce the ego's alienation from the underlying omnipotence fantasies and thereby lessen the danger of their more lasting integration. These narcissistic problems obviously cannot be viewed as those temporary ego regressions of adolescence which ultimately support the forces of progression. It may also be, as I have mentioned elsewhere (Harley, 1961b), that when previous development has predisposed the adolescent toward a weak genital organization, the maturational forces, which now push toward a shift in drive organization, may, in one sense, augment the analytic work.

Further, since it is the constituents of these perverse pregenital fixations which have not only contributed to the unsuccessful oedipal experiences of these patients, but which also tend to bind him to his primary objects, they may prove to be of tremendous hindrance when he is faced with the task in later adolescence of finding new heterosexual love objects. I have more than once been fascinated to note how, as we begin to work through the pregenital conflicts, the analytic hours are sometimes sprinkled with undistorted positive oedipal strivings which seem not to serve defensive aims, but which seem rather to force their way spontaneously and fleetingly into the mainstream of the hour. And I have wondered if somehow, somewhere, the adolescent may not know that the attainment of an undistorted positive oedipal position is essential to his forward movement.[5] This idea may be related, though perhaps very distantly, to Anna Freud's (1958) observations on those war orphans whose adolescence was preceded by a further search for a mother figure; and for whom the "internal possession and cathexis of such an image" seemed "essential for the . . . normal process of detaching libido from it for transfer to new objects, i.e., to sexual partners" (p. 266).

I shall not attempt to summarize my thoughts on a few technical

5 I have been repeatedly reminded over the years of K. Eissler's (1958) comment that adolescence affords a "second chance" for the solution of the oedipal problem.

problems which I have encountered in the treatment of early adolescents. I would rather emphasize that the kinds of patients to whom
I have largely referred, and the samples of analytic material which
I have included, may imply that my analyses of early adolescents
proceed into depth more easily than is the case. My most outstanding
omission has been the often seemingly endless hours in which the
analysis appears to be well-nigh stalemated by the adolescent's preoccupation with his peers and his current crises; and when his apparent uninvolvement with us and the aims of analysis is sometimes
more than discouraging. I have also failed to mention his sometimes
crafty and ingenious methods for concealing his private life, and his
not infrequent adeptness at "playing dumb," so that it may not be
until two or three years later, when he is more settled and a little
more at home with his changing self, that we learn of the things we
failed to perceive at the time; or of the fact that our subtle interpretations, which we thought had gone far afield, had actually hit their
mark. And more than once, I have thought that an early adolescent
had quit his analysis because I had been undercautious in approaching his fantasy life, only to discover, when he returned in later
adolescence, that his leaving was related to his conviction that I
suspected him of a specific bit of acting out in which he was engaged,
when in reality, this possibility had never even crossed my mind.

In closing I would emphasize that I find myself taking increasing
care in determining whether or not the early adolescent's seeming
inability to engage in analysis warrants a decision to interrupt the
treatment until he is older. Such an interruption may at times be
quite necessary. But there are also instances, I think, when he may
be assimilating more than we realize, when our work with those
defenses which might prove to be permanently crippling may be
more effective than we know, and when we may be laying a more
substantial basis for future analytic work than either he or the
analyst is always able to recognize.

BIBLIOGRAPHY

Blos, P. (1962), *On Adolescence*. New York: Free Press of Glencoe.
Eissler, K. R. (1958), Notes on Problems of Technique in the Psychoanalytic Treat-
    ment of Adolescents: With Some Remarks on Perversions. *This Annual*, 13:223-
    254.

—— (1969), Irreverent Remarks about the Present and the Future of Psychoanalysis. *Int. J. Psa.,* 50:461-472.

Fraiberg, S. (1961), Homosexual Conflicts. In: *Adolescents,* ed. S. Lorand & H. I. Schneer. New York: Hoeber, pp. 78-112.

Freud, A. (1936), *The Ego and the Mechanisms of Defense.* New York: International Universities Press, rev. ed., 1966.

—— (1952), Studies in Passivity. *The Writings of Anna Freud,* 4:245-259. New York: International Universities Press, 1968.

—— (1958), Adolescence. *This Annual,* 13:255-278.

—— (1965), *Normality and Pathology in Childhood.* New York: International Universities Press.

Freud, S. (1931), Female Sexuality. *Standard Edition,* 21:223-243. London: Hogarth Press, 1961.

—— (1938), An Outline of Psycho-Analysis. *Standard Edition,* 23:141-207. London: Hogarth Press, 1964.

Geleerd, E. R. (1957), Some Aspects of Psychoanalytic Technique in Adolescence. *This Annual,* 12:263-283.

Greenacre, P. (1952), *Trauma, Growth and Personality.* New York: International Universities Press, 2nd ed., 1969.

—— (1953), Certain Relationships between Fetishism and the Faulty Development of the Body Image. *This Annual,* 8:79-98.

—— (1955), Further Considerations Regarding Fetishism. *This Annual,* 10:187-194.

Harley, M. (1961a), Masturbation Conflicts. In: *Adolescents,* ed. S. Lorand & H. I. Schneer. New York: Hoeber, pp. 51-77.

—— (1961b), Some Observations on the Relationship between Genitality and Structural Development at Adolescence. *J. Amer. Psa. Assn.,* 9:434-460.

Katan, A. (1937), The Role of "Displacement" in Agoraphobia. *Int. J. Psa.,* 32:41-50, 1951.

Laufer, M. (1968), The Body Image, the Function of Masturbation, and Adolescence. *This Annual,* 23:114-137.

Root, N. N. (1957), A Neurosis in Adolescence. *This Annual,* 12:320-334.

A PRECOCIOUS CHILD IN ANALYSIS

KERRY KELLY (London)

This is a report on Emma E., a highly intelligent little girl who was in analysis from the age of four and a half to five and a half. I have called her a precocious child because in many areas of her life she functions at a level appropriate to a child two or three years older. Emma is in the middle rank of her school class, in which most of the children are eight years old; she attends a ballet class with seven-year-olds; her friendships with classmates appear as typical latency peer relationships; her verbal and logical skills are particularly striking.

In this paper I shall describe Emma's development as its history emerged in treatment: the interaction between the environment's demands and Emma's capacities may be seen in the resolutions achieved at each phase of development and the problems remaining for the subsequent phase. Here I hope to show some of the effects of precocity on Emma's pathology. Then I shall examine the ways in which the precocity affected the treatment, in terms of the form in which Emma brought material, and the treatment relationship.

BACKGROUND MATERIAL

The parents' marriage is very unhappy, each partner being disappointed in the other. The father comes from an aristocratic English family and was largely brought up by a governess before attend-

This paper forms part of a research project entitled "Childhood Pathology: Impact on Later Mental Health," conducted at the Hampstead Child-Therapy Course and Clinic, London. The project is financed by the National Institute of Mental Health, Washington, D.C., Grant No. MH-5683-08.

I would like to thank Hanna Kennedy for the help and pleasure of her supervision of this child's treatment.

This paper was presented at a Meeting of the Hampstead Clinic on February 1, 1970.

ing public school and entering a profession. We should note that, despite the father's feeling that his childhood was marked by deprivation and coldness in family relationships, he was able to form a warm affectionate relationship with his little girl. The mother brought herself up, as it were, in a highly disturbed, poor Jewish family, from which her father deserted early in her life. Emma's mother was left by her psychotic mother to the care of various relatives. From this background Emma's mother managed to obtain scholarships for university and postgraduate training. Despite these considerable achievements, Mrs. E. is a disorganized, depressed woman who has severe problems in all her relationships and alternating feelings of arrogant superiority and inadequacy about herself. In the face of her own history of deprivation and her disappointment in the inhospitable reception given her by her husband's family, as well as Mr. E.'s inadequacy as a provider and support, Mrs. E. has focused her aspirations on Emma. Every member of the Clinic staff in contact with Mrs. E. was struck by this mother's excessive identification with her daughter and the degree to which her self-esteem is bound up in Emma's success.

Emma was brought by her mother for treatment mainly because of the deterioration in their relationship: Emma had become passively hostile and resistant. She also was wetting by day and night, had difficulties in falling asleep and then nightmares, and had stopped reading and writing when she was just over three years old. Mrs. E. also reported that Emma was lonely, friendless, and withdrawn from contact with other children in nursery school. The major difficulty in diagnostic assessment lay in determining whether (and to what degree) Emma's regressive behavior was related to difficulties in her own phase development or whether it was reactive to abnormal circumstances, primarily the mother's psychopathology. It was felt, however, that Emma had internalized the external demands and pressures, and her precocious ego and superego development left her prey to intense anxiety and feelings of inadequacy.

TREATMENT MATERIAL

In the first year of treatment, Emma brought material derived from all phases of development. By the end of that year, however, an overall pattern of regression within the treatment situation emerged, parallel with a distinct symptomatic improvement in her behavior at home. Her regressive retreat from being an active, well-functioning schoolgirl to expressing the demanding and passive wishes of an infant was played out in the usual sequence. I would now like to use material from Emma's treatment, not in the order in which it emerged, but to describe her progressive development. In conjunction with this account of Emma's phase-linked wishes, fears, and conflicts, we can examine the external events in her history and try to understand how these contributed to both her precocious development and her pathology.

The Oral Phase

In the Diagnostic Profile we noted the possibility of an oral fixation point in relation to Emma's insatiable wish to be read to and her demandingness for attention, and particularly the recurrence of the themes of loneliness and sadness in Emma's play. In treatment, Emma brought a good deal of material which pointed to oral fixation. Sometimes her wishes emerged directly, as when she sought reassurance that I liked her by asking for extra playthings or gifts to take home; Emma eventually said that she did not really want more toys—she just wanted "more." These demands expressed in oral form both her need for supplies to gratify passive wishes and her feeling that she had been deprived. "More" included the penis and later the breasts and grown-up body Emma wished I could give her. We played endless games in which children were left unhappy or locked alone in their rooms by parents, deprived of their toys and sweets; one such game involved a mother tricking her daughter by taking away the good presents she had promised.

Oral aggression appeared frequently in fantasies of poisoning or being poisoned. These were overdetermined, as the oral mode was often used to express hostility related to later phases, but Emma's ways of dealing with wishes and fears were clearly exemplified here. Early in treatment she initiated a game in which I as the "witch mother" and Emma as the "witch baby" enjoyed enticing people to a tea party where they were given poisoned food, which killed them. We should note here the joint sadism, perhaps a precursor to identification with the aggressor, as well as a self-protection for Emma and an outlet for her own sadistic wishes.

A few weeks later Emma enacted her fantasy of the mother's sadistic handling of the feeding situation. I was instructed to be a baby angry at being sent to bed; as a punishment for my anger I was sent to the hospital where a "nasty nurse gave nasty medicine." Emma gleefully played the role of nurse, and then of the mother, when the baby returned home. As the mother, who wanted to continue the medication, Emma prepared milk for me which would "taste nasty and be too hot," and pretended to force me to drink it, while telling me to cry because I was so thirsty. This material also reflected Emma's current hostility to her baby brother, then a year old, but its relevance here is the content of suppression and punishment for expressing negative feelings and intense needs to be paid attention and fed, and Emma's passive to active role reversal, again with an element of identification with the aggressor.

A great deal of the work in Emma's analysis focused on the meaning which being a baby had for her. In the game I have just described we can see that babies are angry and demanding, and this aspect was played out repeatedly. The other side of Emma's concept of being a baby, the passive libidinal needs, could be seen most clearly in her gradual relaxation in the treatment relationship. Through interpretation of her constant defensive enacting of the role of the active grownup, and her frequently phoney-seeming aggression, we came to understand that it was very difficult for Emma to be, as she put it, "just cosy" with another person. She began by occasionally playing the role of baby in our many games. One of the first times she allowed herself to be the baby was at the end of a session. Emma began to crawl down the stairs very quickly and I said to her, "Be careful, babies need help sometimes." Emma answered, "But it's not always there, so I manage by myself." Eventually she spent whole sessions quietly leaning against me and sucking her thumb as I read to her. It was interesting that her major resistance to interpretation of conflictual material or indeed any approach to the subject of feelings was an implacable demand to be read to; the differentiation between this angry resistance and her acceptance of regressive wishes and the pervasive sadness of the quiet reading sessions was important.

We have some knowledge of the events of Emma's infancy. She was born six weeks prematurely and weighed less than 5 pounds. The mother had decided not to breast-feed, but she reported that Emma took easily to the bottle and was always a happy, contented baby. In addition, Mrs. E. maintained that she started Emma on solids at the age of two weeks. This is implausible and probably not true, but it gives us a picture of what Mrs. E. wanted of her premature and therefore particularly vulnerable infant. Perhaps this cameo of their relationship also helps us understand better how such a highly developed child, with every material advantage, lacked the tolerant gratification usually provided by an "ordinary devoted mother." It appears that Emma's daily care was left largely to *au pairs*. By the time Emma was ten months old, her mother had become severely depressed and found herself unable to go on working. At this point Emma was weaned "overnight" to a cup. According to the mother, Emma made no protest, nor did she ever suck her thumb or fingers in infancy. At eleven months, Emma began to talk well. Within two months, she was also walking. With both speech and motility available at this age, the way was clear for the development of active modes of mastery and an acceleration in ego functions. We might note here Anny Katan's formulations concerning the role of verbalization in the development of reality testing and the ability to delay; she says that children who can verbalize "are able at an early age to differentiate between pretend and real" (1961, p. 188). We shall see later, when I discuss the form in which Emma brought material, how crucial this distinction was for her defenses against the anxiety of being overwhelmed by instinctual wishes. We must set against the advantages of good reality testing the danger described by Anna Freud (1965) of the libidinization and hypertrophy of any one function. Despite the importance for Emma's development of receiving praise and love from her mother for her active and precocious response to the outside world, we can see clearly the residue of her somewhat unsatisfactory oral phase in her sadness and lack of trust. Emma described it well when she explained the "horriblest way to die." This occurred in the context of a game where a witch and fairy were each trying to kill the other. The witch had a plan whereby she would pretend to become friends with the fairy, thus tricking her, and then killing her. Emma said this was the worst way to die "because the fairy would not only be dead, she would be disappointed."[1]

The Anal Phase

At the diagnostic stage, it was felt that Emma's hostile relationship with her mother and the symptom of wetting indicated fixation at the anal-sadistic level. Both anal-retentive and anal-sadistic wishes emerged more or less directly in treatment. Anal-retentive impulses appeared most often in the form of fears of loss of feces or material equated with feces; e.g., Emma deprecated making pretend food from plasticine, because food becomes "pushies," and then expressed anxiety that I would take away all her plasticine. The reaction formation of disgust may be seen here too. She described her excitement at retaining feces until the last minute and said that she did not like actually going to the toilet. To the picture of the meaning of being a baby Emma added anal messing; during a period of treatment which was focused on her jealousy of her baby brother, we often played games in which we, as babies, enjoyed making the room a mess. On one occasion Emma said happily that it was nice to be a baby, because they don't have to pick up the messes they make and no one scolds them for it. At the end of this game she told me to be the mother who uncomplainingly cleared up, while she enjoyed remaining the baby who watched. There were many elements in this, particularly the wishful fantasy of an undemanding mother and Emma's regressive enjoyment of pretend messing. Six months later, however, when Emma had covered the floor with water for herself to swim in, and not for some anonymous baby, she reacted to the mess with anxiety, and solved her difficulty by making me an accomplice: we would clean up together and not tell anyone and everything would be all right because the water had not hurt anything. As

---

[1] The theme of disappointment was a major one in Emma's analysis. It was manifested in many ways, such as in her intense fear that adults would be disappointed in her, with the consequent desperate striving for precocious achievement, and the feeling that she was never good or grown up enough, but the most significant aspect lay in her manifold defenses against her own disappointment in her inadequate mother. Emma's prematurely developed reality testing gave way to blanket denial in the face of her conflicts over the sadness and resentment aroused by her clear perception of her mother's problems and failings. This provided an interesting direct confirmation of the reconstructions made from adult analysis by Sylvan Keiser (1969) in his formulations concerning the role of superior intelligence in neurotic development.

noted in relation to oral sadism, anxiety was allayed by joining with the object.

Later in treatment Emma often retreated to anal modes of expression when she was faced with intense phallic-oedipal conflicts. On these occasions, however, it was noticeable that there was no longer any anxiety linked with the anality itself. For instance, in a period of intense feelings about castration, Emma asked me to accompany her to the toilet because she could not reach the chain. While defecating, Emma began to do sums, but stopped when she reached $11 + 11$, saying, "That's too difficult, because I only have ten" as she stretched out her fingers. Here we could perhaps see a source of her enormous sublimation potential.

The major area in which anal fixation could be discerned was, however, in the relationship between Emma and her mother. Emma's hostile stubborn behavior with her mother was a pale reflection of the response to her internal representation of the mother as a sadistic, demanding, depriving object. This view came through both in the relationship to me (which I shall discuss later) and in disguised form in fantasy games and stories, where, for example, a "mean lady nurse" stole the child's toys because she "didn't like her ever," or the mother "enjoyed being mean." This theme found clearest expression in a fantasy after Emma had undergone a tonsillectomy in the summer holidays. She played a game in which the mother, instead of coming to the aid of the child who was calling for help, joined the gang which in joyful anticipation was plotting to kill the child with the use of their surgical "machines." Again, this was overdetermined, and also expressed castration fears, but the point here is the intensity of Emma's feeling that the mother was untrustworthy and sadistic.

Emma's identification with the victim and the crucial issue of control came through in her remark: "Mummy tells me to do things like Cinderella." Who was in charge and who gave the orders was an area of great conflict and confusion for Emma. This was finally understood after months of interpreting her controlling manner and the reversal of roles whereby she became the adult who told me as the child what I could and could not do. We had some new beads and Emma began to make a bracelet for me. She asked for help in picking up the beads and nodded when I commented on the nice feeling of being a little girl who sometimes needs help. Her tone gradually changed to a more imperative one, "Give me a yellow one, now, immediately!" I remarked on her confusion between a child's asking for help and the grownups' demanding her participation or compliance and Emma stopped and asked, "Should everyone like everyone?" I asked what she thought, and Emma answered that God said they should, then asked what I thought. I replied that God said we should *try* to like everyone because He knew that it made us frightened and unhappy, as she sometimes felt, when she did not like me or other people. Emma then ordered me to make a ring for her, to match the bracelet which she decided to take away from me and keep for herself. I interpreted the orders as a way of saying she did not like me and wondered whether she felt the grownups did not like her when they told her what to do. Emma burst into a jolly song, "I never, never, never, never think that." The importance of this material may perhaps be measured by this sophisticated little girl's reversion to denial, and her subsequent ability to ask me to do things which were difficult for her. We can see here the way in which her ambivalence became linked to control; with the issue of who obeyed whom as the context for the ambivalent relation to her mother, the stage was set for the development of a sadomasochistic interaction between them.

With the material from Emma's history and our knowledge of her mother's pathology to supplement the treatment material, we can trace the development of their battling from the superimposition of Emma's own aggressive and sadistic wishes on the reality of her mother's aggressiveness and demands. When Emma was eighteen months old she requested her mother to leave off nappies and was clean and dry day and night from then until she began to wet some months before referral. This anticipation of the adult's demands could also be seen in treatment when Emma played very busily in the first few sessions; she knew that the person she was going to see at the Clinic would have some things for her to play with. Such a passive to active mechanism was also evident in her leaving sessions before I did, to avoid feeling that I was leaving her. This defense against passivity had been taken up repeatedly, as had her denial and repression of unpleasant things, which Emma called "trying to forget." In the week before a holiday break, which she had refused to talk about, Emma walked out of the waiting room at the beginning of her time, and, holding a comic book up to read, turned straight toward the outside door. I asked her where she was going, and Emma exclaimed, "I forgot," then burst out laughing, finally conscious of her avoidance mechanism.

Around Emma's second birthday, her mother began to have uncontrollable screaming rages when Emma defied her wishes. Mrs. E. herself was frightened by their intensity, and Mr. E. reported that Emma was terrified. Emma's taking charge of herself and anticipating her mother's demands had several effects; first it forestalled the mother's rage; second, it acted as a defense against both Emma's passive wishes and her anger at their nonfulfillment. Third, and most important, this premature internalization of controls laid the foundation for an excessively harsh superego, invested with both the high standards of Emma's demanding mother, whose controlling was experienced as aggression, and Emma's own aggressive impulses, projected onto mother. Some instinctual gratification might also be gained here, since Emma's controlling of herself and domineering of others had for her the meaning of expressing her own hostility.

When Emma was two years old, she was sent to nursery school. She showed no sign of distress at the separation, but gradually became apathetic and bored, refusing to take part in the school activities. It is difficult to know to what degree Emma really withdrew, as her mother had again become quite severely depressed. Mrs. E. may have been reporting her own withdrawal as the child's, but it is clear that school was not a happy experience for Emma, and she was finally allowed to stay home after nearly a year. Emma's brother was born when she was three years old, and once more she was said to show no reaction. A month later she was sent to another school, where the same pattern of unhappiness and resentment appeared, together with the lack of achievement so unbearable for the mother. Emma had, however, learned to read and write at home with the help of the housekeeper. Emma lasted at the second nursery school for only one term. By this time she had regressed considerably: she had begun to wet, she had stopped reading and writing, and her negativism and stubborn hostility to her mother were at a peak. Emma was referred for treatment just before her fourth birthday.

She had then been at home for several months, but her regressive behavior had not diminished and she was having nightmares.

In the autumn of that year a third school was tried, and it was only a few weeks before Emma cried in the mornings and her mother complained about the deterioration in the child's work and play. It was at this point that treatment began, and I could see some signs of increasing disorganization and immaturity in the series of drawings from school which Emma's mother showed me. The mother's exaggeration of this was, however, exemplified by a remark she made when describing a dispute with Emma, then four and a half years old. Mrs. E. said, "Miss Kelly, she was talking like a *little* girl!" Some weeks after the start of treatment, Emma entered school and joined a class for children aged five to six and a half.

The Phallic-Oedipal Phase

It was noted in the Diagnostic Profile that Emma showed signs of having entered the phallic-oedipal phase, and the first year of treatment produced increasing amounts of oedipal material. In the first term of treatment, when Emma was worried that I would forget her during the holiday, she said, "Brothers are bigger than sisters even if they're younger because they have something sisters don't have." This was related to her feeling that she would not be forgotten or left if she were bigger, more grown up, that is, if she had a penis. Emma had a fantasy about the prince killing the "mean sister" whom she equated with "a mother," and then he would live happily ever after with Cinderella. We have already seen how Emma identified herself with Cinderella. The day after Emma had told me with excitement how much she enjoyed the fearful feeling when Daddy tickled her, she asked me about boy ballet dancers. When I remarked that there might be a prince in a story with a princess, Emma said sadly, "But a prince isn't a husband, and I want a husband."

Emma's sadness may have reflected a reality element in her oedipal disappointment. Her father had always been for her a stable loving object; his expectations were not particularly high; indeed there were indications that he expected greater things from his young son, but he was appropriately pleased and proud of Emma's achievements. He reacted negatively, however, to Emma's oedipal advances, and this must have been a shock and disappointment for her, as well as contributing to her retreat from the oedipal phase. In treatment Emma told me a story about a little girl whose mother had gone away as a result of the girl's hostility. To "surprise" her father, the little girl put on her mother's makeup and jewels, but when the father came home, instead of being pleased and surprised, he was "terrified and angry." This accurately described Emma's father's reaction to the fierce competition between mother and child, and the way in which he appeared to join his wife in believing that Emma's fantasy of having him as a husband could come true.

Throughout treatment Emma reassured herself and me that her babyish impulses and intense feelings would disappear soon: "When I'm five" was a frequent phrase. Occasionally direct wishes would erupt in this form, as when she shouted at me that she would be prettier than I was and have more dresses and be bigger than I when she was five. Soon after her fifth birthday, she introduced into the witches and fairies game the variation that the witch always became very enthusiastic about her new plan to kill the fairies and then very disappointed when this failed. Later in the week, when she still could not reach the top shelf in her locker, Emma expressed her disappointment that all the things she had hoped for had not automatically taken place when she turned five. This was understood as related to a fantasy that, as soon as she was grown up, mother would die, and Emma would have father to herself. We should note here that, when this game was being used to understand Emma's anal-sadistic battle with her mother, the fairy represented Emma, and the witch her mother; with the increasing primacy of oedipal rivalry, however, the fairy, very special and grand with pretty clothes, became the mother, and the witch was Emma, with her reprehensible death wishes. The guilt aroused by these wishes was defended against with an elaborate rationalization that distinguished her own feeling from one which she would otherwise condemn. Emma insisted on the distinction between "evil," which was what witches who enjoy the suffering of others are, and "naughty," which people who wish, in anger, to make others sad are.

After the summer holiday following the first year of treatment Emma's relationship with her mother deteriorated again. I felt, however, that this renewed hostility was not due to the pregenital conflicts which had so colored their earlier interaction, but represented

Emma's age-adequate oedipal wishes. There was a shift within treatment to expression of phase-linked conflicts in the transference. At this time Emma alternated in sessions between feelings of miserable inadequacy and fears of what I would do to her. She was meeting the difficulties of the oedipal phase with the same attempts to be a grown-up, successfully in charge of herself, and the same underlying realization of her helplessness and passivity as she had experienced in the face of pregenital conflicts.

Before describing the work of the final term, with the partial resolution of Emma's intense oedipal conflicts, and advancing a hypothesis to explain the changes which took place, I would like to give an account of the progress of the treatment relationship and discuss how Emma's precociously developed defenses affected the ways in which she brought material. Understanding of these aspects of her analysis will add to the picture of the difficulties of her development.

The Effect of Precocity on the Development of Defenses

When Emma entered treatment it appeared that she had partially retreated in the face of oedipal conflicts to the forms of behavior which had served her well in earlier phases. She extended into treatment her controlling relationships and in the first months externalized the helpless compliant child onto me, while she assumed the role of the omnipotent adult. As we have seen, this assumption of control had been used to allay her own humiliation and defend against her passive wishes, had allowed her some sadistic gratification, and, to a certain extent, the active realistic aspect of this behavior had gained her approval and narcissistic supplies from her mother. Emma's precocious reality testing, which in many ways was so important for the development of her ability to satisfy the demands of her environment and master the difficulties confronting her, was pulled into the service of defense against infantile wishes: Emma externalized everything undesirable onto dolls or characters in fantasy games. From these anonymous "pretend" babies, who wanted attention, or enjoyed messing, or sometimes felt angry and resentful, or from the "little girl" who felt she would never be good enough I learned the content of Emma's instinctual wishes and the intensity of her feeling of dissatisfaction with herself.

Sometimes this distinction between pretend and real was carried to extraordinary lengths: once in a game where Emma was the big sister and I was a baby brother, I was allowed to play with some of the toys. When her jealousy became too intense, however, I was allowed only what she called "pretend real" toys. In another such game involving the baby brother, the older person's sadistic use of reality came through when Emma graciously gave me many bits of rubbish from the floor and explained that I as the baby would be pleased with these and think she really liked me because a baby would not know it was really rubbish.

On rare occasions, the pretend-real distinction broke down, and then it was possible to see from the extent of Emma's panic how central this defense was to the maintenance of the grownup superstructure. This happened once in a game in which Emma as the big sister began to hit me as the baby. I held her arm, explaining that I would not allow her to hit me because it frightened her too much, and Emma retreated in panic to the opposite side of the room, saying, "For a minute I thought the baby brother was hitting back." The denial of her feeling experience helped her to measure up to her adult ideal: Emma once told me that we could be ourselves only when we read books—there was no possibility that feelings would emerge in that situation. She could also satisfy the demands of her superego, which were reinforced with intense aggression. Some measure of how much aggression was vested in the superego could be gained whenever I disobeyed the rules, as it were, when I stepped outside the bounds of "pretend" and interpreted Emma's wishes. Then Emma became enraged and told me she hated me for talking about such things.

Emma was well aware of the purpose and methods of treatment; this could be seen both in her resistance and in her pleasure when we had understood something together. Early in treatment Emma reacted to my suggestion that she was worried about why she came to the Clinic with the flat statement, "I don't know and don't tell me." She told me, "I want to play and not to talk"; and when I asked whether she was afraid that I would refuse to let her play, Emma said, "Any day now." She experienced my talking as an assault on her efforts to keep her feelings unreal; as long as we played, she could deny her infantile impulses and keep them at a distance. At a moment when she was struggling against expressing aggression toward her mother, Emma rearranged all the furniture in the room and begged to "leave it this much nicer way."

She derived pleasure from being understood at other times, and displayed her great capacity for self-observation. For instance, she became very angry at the ending of a session and began to throw toys at me. When I verbalized her anger, she was able to change this to a game in which she threw things and we took turns picking them up, Emma laughed and said, "This makes me feel better, but I'm still angry with you." She then accepted my remark that the anger persisted because the wish to stay remained. Frequently Emma understood interpretation as a permission for at least partial discharge and reacted with glee, as well as relief based on the feeling that her wish could not be so bad if I could verbalize it. An example of this was when she was again annoyed by my ending a session and suddenly asked if I wanted her drawing. I suggested that Emma wanted me to want it so that she could punish me for ending the session by refusing to give it to me. Emma was delighted, said, "Say it," and laughed over feeling better.

In line with this good understanding and the distancing defense of "pretend" were the ingenious ways by which Emma could communicate without taking responsibility for the feelings or ideas being expressed. These represented a slight shift in her defenses, based both on analytic work which had given Emma some insight into her use of them, and the pressure of re-emerging impulses.

Emma began a game in which we pretended to be ladies living in separate houses, who could not visit, speak to or even look at one another. She told me to pretend that I was wondering about what she was doing, so I mused out loud about the conflict she was having at that time over talking about feelings of wanting all the toys to herself. She listened intently and finally said, "Pretend I know what you're doing, but I don't want to, and now you don't know what I'm doing." This seemed to be a conscious reference to my use of the pretend game to verbalize her feelings. On another occasion, Emma became very angry when I did not understand her instructions for a game about children being "fixed" in the hospital. She calmed down when I pointed out that the anger came from disappointment, thought for a minute, and said quietly, "I'll do it my way and you do it your way, but you look and then you'll understand, and I won't have to have shown you." At such moments I often had to remind myself that Emma was only four years four months old!

A recurrent feature in her behavior at the end of sessions, when she felt particularly helpless and bossed around by my control of time, was instructing me to take "baby steps" down the stairs. Once when she was especially angry and had projected the anger onto me, that is, she felt my ending of the session as a hostile attack, rather than the usual rejection, Emma told me to "take baby steps so you won't be scary." Soon after this, Emma again ordered me to go downstairs in this way, but then sat down on the stairs looking up at me and said, "If you do baby steps like a grownup, it's not the same as you doing baby steps like a child." She agreed sadly that this meant she really knew I was an adult, but felt better if she could pretend that I was a child as helpless as she.

This realization was a sign that Emma was becoming better able to accept her feelings as her own, but throughout the first year of treatment the timing of interpretations remained a technical problem. In the initial months, when Emma brought abundant material in fantasy games and role play relating to her aggressive wishes and view of adults as sadistic attackers, my attempts to attribute these feelings to Emma provoked panic and violent physical attacks on me, or else Emma would drum her heels on the floor and cover her ears to avoid hearing what I was saying. This was dealt with in three ways: the first was simply physical restraint, accompanied by an explanation that I would not allow her to hurt me because the consequent terror and resistance impeded our work. The reassurance was repeated only about three times before Emma stopped punching me in the head; once, months later, when we were sitting together on the couch reading, Emma leaned back and brushed my hair with her foot. When I verbalized her wish to kick me, she said anxiously, "But you won't let me, will you?" The second response on my part was occasionally to confront her with reality by pointing out that drowning out my words did not make her unhappy feelings go away; Emma reacted to this sort of remark with startled curiosity.

The third and most important way of forestalling these outbursts of anxiety which always led to several days of either busy affectless play or reading comics was to wait and content myself with verbalizing, for example, the "mother's" feeling or the "baby's" feeling in displacement in the game, and commenting where I could on the need for such rigid defense. Gradually Emma began to understand that there was a reason for keeping everything "pretend," but it was a long struggle for her. Just before Christmas in the first year of her treatment, Emma had accepted the possibility of ambivalence and proposed a game: "You be the brother and I'll be the sister and sometimes we like each other and sometimes we don't." She alternated throughout the session between loving and hating the baby. In a hating moment, she stood on the table throwing things around the room, and said, "When the baby's gotten hurt, I don't like him, and when he hasn't, I do like him." I commented only that it was really the other way around. Emma began to cry and said through her sobs, "No, keep it the wrong way round, please Miss Kelly, I need it the wrong way round, it must stay." I agreed and suggested that when we understood why she thought her feelings were so bad, she might not need to keep it the wrong way round, and Emma calmed down.

From material in the weeks just before Emma's fifth birthday and the summer holiday we can see the gradual steps that were being made to link up her feelings about me and the repetitive "pretend" games. Emma kept interrupting a game to ask to take a box of crayons home with her. She seemed to accept my interpretations of her wish to make a link between me and home, and this was also related to my comment several days before when I wondered, after her repeated "I want you to read," what she really wanted from me. When a further link was made to the recent references to birthday presents, Emma said, "I'll have all the birthday presents I could possibly need, so I don't want one from you." She agreed that she was talking about not needing people and said, "Only little girls need other people."

A break of three weeks followed this, because Emma and I were both ill. Emma conveyed that she thought I had really been seeing other children while she was absent. She remarked that she hated it when her mother left the Clinic during her session; I commented that when Mummy stayed in the waiting room she was definitely here for and because of Emma and not paying attention to other people or other children. Emma smiled and began to organize a game in which she was the mother, I was the nanny, and the dolls were the children. By this time the gap between pretend and real had closed to the extent that I was often given adult roles to play, including that of the idealized mother. In this game Emma went out shopping and kept returning with more and more presents for the children. As I dressed the baby doll, I spoke the baby's words, calling for its mother. Emma told the baby to look at all the nice presents, but the baby persisted in wanting its mummy. Emma finally said, "But look what a good mummy I am, bringing you all these things." She would not accept my interpreting this as her response to my birthday present, which had not pleased or consoled her for my long absence. She went on in the game to feed the children, but could not decide if the food was sweets or pills. The children wanted sweets, but the mother kept giving them pills, which they spat out. Emma said they would have to be forced to eat them and remarked, "Mummies get children to do things by frightening them." Thus we had reached a halfway point between her implacable resistance to taking the material of games back to herself and Emma's reinternalization of babyish needs and wishes, with concomitant mellowing of her superego. She had formed an intense attachment to me, while preserving me from the full force of transference feelings by means of her distancing defenses.

The Terminal Phase

At home her parents were very pleased at the reappearance of the competent schoolgirl. All of Emma's symptoms had disappeared and both Mr. and Mrs. E. felt that she was once again a "happy child." Mr. E. had in fact always felt that his wife and I exaggerated the significance of Emma's symptoms and the degree of her suffering. This denial of the distress experienced by the child and his reluctant cooperation in the treatment, based more on his submission to his wife than on belief in Emma's need for help, may have been due in part to his need to defend against awareness of his own reaction to his daughter's sexual advances. Some of the conflict in this area may have been reawakened by Emma's once again approaching the oedipal phase. The parents wanted to withdraw Emma from treatment. I, on the other hand, felt that we were only at this point approaching the crucial area of difficulty, namely, Emma's rigid system of defenses, which, if left untouched, might lead to a pathological character formation and the stunting of her great potential for pleasure and achievement. After much discussion and some working through of the parents' ambivalence to me and to the child's analysis, a compromise was reached: Emma would remain in intensive treatment for one more term.

Emma had been aware of the vacillation about her treatment, and there was a marked change in her use of the treatment situation when she returned from holiday. She began to talk to me about events at home and school and frequently told her mother about things discussed in the session. Both hostility and reproach were expressed directly to me and to her mother.

Emma's characteristic defenses had by no means disappeared, but she now accepted interpretation of the impulse defended against as her own. In a session where she petulantly ordered me around after I had presumed to wonder about her doll's secrets, Emma repeatedly threatened to "spoil all your silly old things." She told me to make a long fence for the queen's palace she was building and as I rolled a piece of plasticine she said, "The receptionist will be very cross with you because you're spoiling the wall." I commented that Emma was the one who was cross with me. She shouted, " I want you to be poor; I want you to be a girl; I want to kill you." This first expression of direct hostility to me as the oedipal mother in the transference contained both Emma's feelings of being castrated—girls are "poor"—and her death wishes, that is, she wanted me to be a girl, rather than a woman, or better still, she wanted me dead. After I had pointed out that it was her own wishes she was so afraid of when she felt the grownups were angry, Emma relaxed. She told me she wished we had not had to change rooms, because everything had been, as she put it, "simple before," that is, she had not experienced such confusing feelings about me. The next day she wanted to read, leaned across my lap and touched my stockings to "see how they feel." She continued to initiate physical contact but responded to my verbalization of her wish to know more about my body with furious orders to read.

We played a hospital game, in which a lady came to the hospital with "a hole in the middle of her back which she wants the doctor to fix." Eventually we worked out that the lady felt something was missing and wanted it put back, and Emma said, "Like a tail." My suggestion that this was a penis like her brother's was met with the indignant denial: "He doesn't have one of those!" Emma switched to a little figure of a buxom nurse and said, "She has those things," then picked up her dress and showed me her own nipples. I remarked that the nurse was like a mother, a grown-up woman. Emma said plaintively, "You don't have those, I can't ever see them." It appeared that this very feminine little girl had made the penis-breast equation, and her reproach to me and to mother was that we had deprived her of these. Her lack of breasts was experienced again as an inability to be grown up, and the narcissistic pain was the same as that felt in earlier phases when she had tried so hard to acquire adult attributes.

Emma made further progress in accepting her own aggressive impulses. We spent a friendly session coloring pictures in a story which Emma said took place in Fairyland. Her definition of Fairyland was that people could be different and look different every day; they could even have green or purple faces if they wanted. When I asked what she would do if she were in Fairyland, Emma said, "You would have a black face and I would have a gold face. You would have the witch face and I would have the fairy face." Here I could take up Emma's fear of the other's aggression and her wish that she did not feel like an angry witch. This was a long way from all the "pretend" witch and fairy games that she had insisted had nothing to do with us. The final bastion of "pretend" fell three weeks later. For several days we had been playing a game with two paper dolls who were little girls who wanted to dress in their mother's clothes, have husbands and babies and everything the mother did. The older sister continually disapproved of the younger's most acquisitive wishes and there was a lot of mutual squabbling. When I suggested that they represented the wish to be grown up and bossy and the babyish impulses respectively, Emma said enthusiastically, "The big part tells the little one she's naughty." This game went on and on, with Emma stressing that the little girls just wanted to play "dress-up" with the mother's clothes. Eventually I commented that they did not want to just *pretend* to be mother, they really wanted to *be* the mother. Emma looked straight ahead and said, in a dazed but passionate voice, "I want everything—get rid of her—I hate her."

While this had been going on, an important related theme appeared in the material. Emma wanted us both to draw pictures, but thought all her drawings were terrible and concentrated on praising mine. When I had finished my drawing she exclaimed, "Oh, it's so nice! May I have it?" She wanted to put a little bit of brown in the blue sky, and when I verbalized her wish to mark it all over with brown because she was so angry that my drawing was better than hers, Emma said miserably, "Yes, but then I wouldn't be able to keep it." It was possible to verbalize her conflict between wanting to have the grownups' nice things and wanting to destroy them vindictively because they were unattainable. This seemed to represent the choice she had always faced between identification and progressive development and a regressive battle. Her choice on this occasion was to add birds to the sky, write her name on the picture and thus make it her own.

At home two days later, however, when she was told that treatment would terminate at Christmas, Emma seemed to experience this as a loss due to her hostility, and regressed momentarily. She wet on the floor, which shocked both mother and Emma, and that night had nightmares and cried out in her sleep. In the days following she began the game with the two little girls which I described above. In the same session in which the direct outburst of oedipal rivalry with mother occurred, Emma went on to a game in which we were both cooks, making "beautiful cakes" for the queen. I was told to make a flower with beads on a plasticine cake, which Emma greatly admired. She used it to decorate the large plain cake she was making, then began to smear the beads off the cake, until it was destroyed. I commented that this reminded me of something. Emma beamed and said, "I know, like when I drew brown all over your picture." She sighed with pleasure when I reminded her that she had wanted to do so, that we had talked about it, and she had not actually ruined the drawing.

A few days later Emma made a boat and asked if I was doing the same with my similarly shaped piece of plasticine. I said it could be a boat or perhaps a bathtub, which Emma found terrifically funny. She immediately joined in, making a soapdish for the bath and floating her boat in it. She asked to take it home, but then decided she wanted me to keep it. The next day we busied ourselves making

cakes again and Emma spontaneously brought up her feeling that
I would see her every day and continue treatment if I liked her well
enough. We had made an elaborate cake with some discussion of
enjoying doing things together which made them turn out better
than if we each worked alone, and this cake Emma took home with
her, saying that it made her feel better about the separation. My feeling about this material was a hopeful one; it presaged Emma's finding a new solution in sharing, rather than a battle over who possessed
more grown-up achievements.

In the few weeks which remained before termination we continued work along these lines. One day Emma brought a book to the
session which her father had been reading to her the night before.
She sat happily with me and talked of how she wanted the cosy reading with me to remind her of being together with Daddy. There
was a story about a little girl pretending her doll was her baby.
Emma's response to my suggestion that she wanted a real baby was a
shy smile and a whispered yes.

The affectionate pleasure conveyed by Emma's account of the
present interaction with her father was very different from the father
she had described as "terrified and angry" at his little girl's oedipal
advances. It appeared that Mr. E. really had reacted negatively and
had rejected Emma's oedipal wishes at first; added to this, however,
was her externalization of superego condemnation of these wishes
—the "angry" father—and of the ego threatened with being overwhelmed by instinctual impulses—the "terrified" father. The happy
togetherness now experienced by Emma and her father was the result of several changes. Most important were the internal changes
which allowed Emma to tolerate her own wishes, to express them
without excessive guilt or shame, and even occasionally to enjoy such
thoughts as having a baby. The real shifts which had taken place
within the family also contributed: the hostile aggressive tension
between mother and child was greatly reduced; Mrs. E. no longer
felt so threatened by Emma and could also allow her more latitude
for age-appropriate behavior; the relief from stress experienced by
everyone in the family helped the parents to move closer to one
another, and both felt that their marriage had a "new lease on life."

In treatment Emma and I talked about her sadness over termination. Emma found these feelings very difficult to verbalize and was

in conflict about her anger. At one point I wrote her a note about how hurt and angry she felt, and afraid that I didn't like her. I wondered whether Emma liked herself. Emma wrote "no," and refused to go any further. When I suggested that we talk about some of the reasons, for instance, that she felt she was too little, Emma wrote, "I know why, but I am not going to tell you." It emerged that she felt it was enough if we both understood the sources of such feelings; it was really too painful for her to go into them again the week before termination. Thus one of the dangers which remained for Emma was her precarious self-esteem. On the very last day, however, perhaps partially as a reassuring reversal of roles, but also sincerely, she told me that she still sometimes felt terrible and wanted to "be Mummy," but at other times "I know I'll be grown up some day."

There are many questions about Emma which remain unanswered, notably the sources of her primary narcissism, which appeared unimpaired. The presence of good *au pairs* and a loved housekeeper as well as her father's affection probably were contributing factors, but we should not underestimate the effect of her mother's love and praise. The mother's aspirations and demands led to an imbalance in Emma's development and perhaps to insufficient gratification at each phase; on the other hand, Emma, with her enormous talents, has been genuinely loved by her mother. The great pleasure derived by both from their now relatively conflict-free sharing of intellectual activities, together with the effects of Emma's treatment in reducing her conflicts over aggression and some reduction of Mrs. E.'s demands, may provide an avenue for a good relationship between them.

With regard to the changes in Emma's treatment, and her use of the situation, many factors appear to be operative. The work of the first year focused on the pregenital conflicts and elucidated the defenses Emma had developed to deal with them. These defenses included denial, passive into active maneuvers, reversal of roles, reaction formation, displacement, externalization, projection, and identification with the aggressor. They partake of a common aim— to get rid of something, in Emma's case, her babyish impulses, which for her included aggression, greed, passive wishes. Emma's defenses were successful against oral and anal impulses, but they were inappropriate for dealing with phallic-oedipal wishes, which involved wanting something from outside—a penis, a grown-up body, a husband, a baby. Here the problem was not how to get rid of something unacceptable, but how to get something unobtainable. When Emma entered the phallic-oedipal phase she had not yet developed a repertoire of defenses which could cope with these wishes, and she retreated to the method which had proved successful earlier, with ample fixations at both oral and anal phases to aid the regression. With the resolution in treatment of some of these pregenital conflicts she was able to move forward once more into the oedipal phase. The appearance of an intense transference relationship to me as an oedipal object at this point was probably a function of the greater amount of libido then available. She seemed to use the old rigid defenses less, and the extreme harshness of her self-judgments diminished. Treatment was terminated with Emma right in the middle of the oedipal phase, but I hoped that with the possibility of a fresh start, she might find her own adaptive solutions to the normal conflict.

SUMMARY

In this account of the analysis of a four-year-old girl I have tried to describe the pathological outcome of the interaction of her high capacities with the extreme demands of her environment. Emma's precocious ego development facilitated the intensification of defense against instinctual wishes; various ego functions were drawn into the service of defense, notably intellectual functioning and reality testing, which were used to preserve a rigid distinction between approved adult behavior, allowed to be "real," and despised infantile wishes and feelings, all relegated to the realm of fantasy and "pretend."

The work of analysis helped to resolve pregenital conflicts and thereby decrease the blanket imposition of rigid defenses. By the end of her treatment Emma was fully established in the age-adequate oedipal phase and was able to acknowledge her own intense feelings.

BIBLIOGRAPHY

Freud, A. (1965), *Normality and Pathology in Childhood.* New York: International Universities Press.

Katan, A. (1961), Some Thoughts about the Role of Verbalization in Early Childhood. *This Annual,* 16:184-188.

Keiser, S. (1969), Superior Intelligence: Its Contribution to Neurosogenesis. *J. Amer. Psa. Assn.,* 17:452-473.

A STUDY OF THE PSYCHOLOGICAL EFFECTS
OF STRABISMUS

EDGAR L. LIPTON, M.D. (New York)

Strabismus, squint, esotropia, exotropia, cast, turn, wall eyes, cock eyes, and cross eyes are terms used to refer to eyes that are deviated from a proper direction so that the visual axes are not both simultaneously directed toward the same point. This situation is considered normal under certain conditions: during the first twelve weeks of life, during sleep, in toxic states, during the later years of life and in death. Subjective symptoms may or may not be present; usually they are not. The defect may or may not be readily apparent to onlookers. For example, "small angle tropias" may have all the annoying symptoms and visual difficulties, but the angle of deviation may be so small that even the trained observer may not be aware of the presence of the squint. The condition is not considered to be a true strabismus, however, if it is chiefly a latent one, appearing only during sleep or in a toxic condition, such as anesthesia (Lyle and Bridgeman, 1959).

Studies of strabismus show an incidence of from 0.6 to 7 percent in normal populations and as high as 51 percent in populations of institutionalized brain-damaged and mentally defective individuals. A fair estimate is that 2 percent of the population either have had or now have the defect in one form or another. There are many forms, the most common being convergence (esotropia or cross eyes) and divergence (exotropia or wall eyes).

Strabismus may occur at any age. While many cases are regarded

A somewhat longer version of this paper was presented at a meeting of the New York Psychoanalytic Society on January 31, 1967.

I would like to acknowledge with gratitude the assistance of the following individuals who gave generously of their time and technical expertise: Dr. Arthur Linksz and Dr. William Ludlam, whose field is ocular physiology; Miss D. Taylor, Miss A. Tibbs, and Miss S. Moore, who are certified Orthoptic Technicians; Mrs. M. Stern, Former Librarian of the New York Psychoanalytic Institute; and Mrs. M. Christ for editorial assistance.

as failures of development from birth, most are noted to begin in the two-and-a-half- to three-and-a-half-year period. The peaks of incidence are during the second to fifth years. It is less common during adolescence or after the climacteric. Convergent strabismus constitutes by far the largest group and almost always has its onset in the first five years of life. With the advent of modern methods, there is earlier recognition and treatment; hence fewer adult cases are now seen.[1]

REVIEW OF THE LITERATURE

There is a paucity of references to strabismus in psychoanalytic literature. The earliest seems to be Breuer's patient Anna O. in the *Studies in Hysteria* (1893-1895). She was said to have developed her convergent squint and macropsia at the bedside of her sick father. She was reported to have "cured" this symptom complex through the talking cure, after one description of the symptom's first occurrence; but we know from Jones (1955) and others that the following year her symptoms recurred.

Freud does not seem to mention strabismus in any of his writings, although visual symptoms, voyeurism, exhibitionism, and visual imagery were of great interest to him (see, e.g., 1910, 1931).

A few papers deal with the Evil Eye concept (Greenacre, 1926; Róheim, 1952) and others with eye symbolism (Abraham, 1913; Ferenczi, 1913; Greenacre, 1926; Hart, 1949; Jones, 1916). Only three papers are primarily concerned with the possible emotional causation of strabismus (Leuba, 1949; Inman, 1921; Rappaport, 1959).

Some psychoanalysts believe that the disorder may well be a psychosomatic or conversion manifestation. Since voluntary musculature and the autonomic nervous system are involved, it cannot be

---

1 Hippocrates recognized a hereditary tendency to strabismus and this is still generally accepted (Adams, 1886; Rappaport, 1959; Schlossman and Priestly, 1952; Stevens, 1899). It is most often considered a developmental anomaly, although encephalitis and physical traumata, with nerve or muscle involvement, are not uncommon causes. Frandsen (1960) in reviewing the literature on the occurrence and theories of causation of squint concludes that often it should be considered a sign rather than an independent disorder (Collins, 1925; Downing, 1945; Guibor, 1959; Hirsch and Wick, 1963; Lyle and Bridgeman, 1959; Schlossman and Priestly, 1952; Waardenburg, 1954).

denied that there may be rare cases of hysterical causation (Biel-schowsky, 1935; Guibor, 1959; Souders, 1942). The evidence available at this time, however, is not at all convincing. In the psycho-analytic literature I have found only one ophthalmologically con-firmed and convincing case; it was reported by Max Schur (1950) as an incidental finding in a paper on another topic.

Ophthalmologists for the most part believe in an organic origin and many seem to be opposed to psychological concepts; yet a fairly large number of writers in that field have noted a high correlation of strabismus with neurotic traits (Fletcher and Silverman, 1966; Gailey, 1949; Guibor, 1959; Harrington, 1947; Lion et al., 1943; Pollie et al., 1964; Schlagel and Hoyt, 1957; Stromberg, 1947). Several writers have noted the onset of strabismus at the time of such stresses as the birth of a new sibling; many have commented on ob-jective improvement in schoolwork and personality following cor-rection of the disorder (Lyle and Bridgeman, 1959; Scobee, 1947).

This paper is based mainly on material from the psychoanalyses of three adult and three child patients of the author. The present study does not differentiate between the different anatomical forms of the condition in the sense of divergence, convergence or vertical forms.

CASE ILLUSTRATION

Mr. T., a twenty-eight-year-old high school teacher, complained of insomnia since leaving home and his mother, and a variety of fears—that her predictions of psychosis and sexual promiscuity would come true; of being alone; of the return of childhood sleep-walking (with the fantasy that he would walk out of a window and kill himself); and certain phobias. He was depressed, anxious about his ability to carry out his new job, and in conflict about his desires to have an affair. He felt quite hopeless about ever being able to get married and lead a normal life.

The patient's father was a retiring and passive man, who had spent many hours playing with his son. In many of their games, visual elements had been prominent: the father would close his eyes and play dead to frighten the child; or they would try to outstare each other until one of them smiled. As a child, Mr. T. frequently pretended to be blind. The mother, a seriously disturbed woman, was given to extreme rages. She severely restricted her son from being active, apparently assuming that movement was sexually motivated. Early in his life she screamed open castration threats at him, and later accused him of sexual delinquency. She resisted his attempts at individuation well into his adulthood. When Mr. T. left home to come to New York in order to separate himself from his mother for the first time and to begin psychoanalysis, her parting curse was that because he left her he would become a male prostitute and go crazy.

Here I do not wish to report on Mr. T.'s analysis, in the course of which he worked with reasonable success on problems connected with his particular oedipal situations—hysterical depressions, phobias, and more especially his difficulties in allowing himself closeness with sexual partners. I wish to focus on an incident which occurred in his fifth year of analysis.

A few months prior to the hour to be reported I had moved to a new office, but had not yet hung my pictures. Mr. T., like another patient with a similar eye disturbance, found facing the blank wall especially uncomfortable, and had voiced frequent complaints about my laziness and about his not having anything to rest his eyes on. During this period he frequently turned on the couch to look at me.

In the course of his analysis, Mr. T. had occasionally had hours in which he suddenly fell silent and I would get the impression that he was withholding a thought. When I said nothing, Mr. T. would try to elicit a response from me by asking a question. Failing in this, he would have the impulse to turn on the couch, get up or make a gross sudden movement. Then in a plaintive voice he would ask me to talk; then couldn't he touch me or couldn't I, just this once, touch him. When this failed, the impulse to move or turn around would overwhelm him and he would find a way to look at me. Occasionally he made a violent statement, or threw the pillow down on the floor, whereupon he would then lie face down or on his side and associate. In the past, I would have helped him to recall and verbalize a memory, usually of a traumatic nature. An enema scene, a primal scene, an illness or a memory of violence would emerge, together with feelings of a nonverbal, helpless, almost dissociated state. On these occasions his excitement and fear would mount, and he would make such statements as: "Things are moving strangely"; "The lamp is moving in front of you"; "You're getting further" or "closer"; "I'm going crazy." Often after such an hour the patient, with a puzzled look, said that there was something he had to tell me, but he did not know what it was. Most of his memories had started as body memories. Some work had also been done on the way in which he manifested his anxiety. His acting out was interpreted as an attempt to undo a previous good hour, and his need to touch the analyst or something in the room as a magical reassurance against the expectation of mother's wrath. The patient often responded by projecting his angry feelings, asking me whether or not I was angry. In the past I had connected these expressions to parental transferences—especially to a mother who frequently had been angry at the patient and who had contributed so much to his masochism.

On the occasion of the hour to be reported, the patient revealed something that had previously not been observed. The silence with the ensuing panic and need for defensive action occurred after he had two simultaneous feelings or thoughts and did not know which to verbalize. He then tried to suppress one so he could say the other, but he did not succeed in this. His panic mounted as, in addition, he felt guilty about doing something wrong. He found the combination of guilt and bodily feelings so confusing and frightening that he feared he was losing control of his mind and was going crazy. He did not feel dissociated but felt enormously threatened by loss of control and loss of feeling of self. Mr. T. then made his usual attempts at regaining control.

This time, however, I responded differently. I suddenly recalled that Mr. T. had once mentioned that as a child he had had a strabismus. I told him that his problems in free associating reminded me of this strabismus. Did he at one time experience a similar conflict over which visual point to focus on? I suggested that his current difficulty in making a choice between two thoughts might be a verbal equivalent of an earlier visual difficulty. Mr. T. immediately developed a diplopia and shortly thereafter a severe headache. Both symptoms lasted for five days.

This hour was followed by a period of great resistance which took the same form as that he had shown earlier in the analysis. However, its intensity and the expressed fears of opening the topic of strabismus were much greater. I learned that the patient usually had analyzed with his eyes closed, ostensibly to make analysis easier. He now objected to associating freely with his eyes open. I interpreted his conscious withholding, about which he felt very guilty, as an unsuccessful attempt at suppression and denial, and related it directly to not looking as well as not understanding. I insisted on two things—that the symptom be analyzed and that the patient was not psychotic. The patient approached this symptom, as he did so many other things, in a phobic manner, and I insisted that the phobia be faced and analyzed. The patient's cooperation brought out that intellectually he recognized the physiological effects of the strabismus (double vision, changes in distance of objects of regard, tilting of the room and the drifting of one image in front of the other, with the resultant feelings of psychological confusion) to be ophthalmological symptoms, but emotionally he experienced these symptoms as signs that he was going insane. Following this bit of analysis and a few weeks of working through, the patient was able to take up tennis, an activity that requires quick visual focusing and which he had previously avoided, enjoy it, and become fairly proficient at it. Mr. T. ceased saying at the end of hours, "There is something I want to tell you, but I don't know what it is." It had been the strabismus.

Mr. T. had what is called an intermittent strabismus. It is a latent form that manifests itself only under conditions of stress such as fatigue or strong emotion. When Mr. T. did not deny or suppress it, he treated it as a shameful and dreaded secret. Indeed, during his childhood it had been erotized so that in a way it was used as a kind of perversion. As a child he liked twirling games, rolling down hills until he was dizzy, and he enjoyed the dangerous feelings and excitement of his eyes going out of control. After some months of analysis Mr. T. overcame his fears of the return of headaches and of insanity; he successfully completed a course of orthoptic training which enabled him to keep his eyes from crossing.

PATHOPHYSIOLOGY OF STRABISMUS

For an understanding of what happened to Mr. T. it is necessary to review the pathophysiology of strabismus (Guibor, 1959; Linksz,

1952, 1961; Lyle and Bridgeman, 1959; Lyle, 1953; Scobee, 1947) because the psychological effects are intimately related to the physical condition of squinting. As Schilder (1935) pointed out, "Every change in the organic function is liable to bring forth with it psychic mechanisms which are akin to this organic function" (p. 33).

Normal eyes function as two parallel *camera obscuras,* darkened chambers having an aperture (usually with a lens) through which light from external objects enters to form an image on the surface opposite. The portion of the retina that has the greatest concentration of visual receptors is called the *fovea;* it is the area of greatest visual acuity; usually each eye focuses on the images toward which that eye is directed so that the images fall on the fovea. The two components of vision are acuity, which tells us what we see, and localization, which tells us where we see. In the squinter the functions of visual acuity and localization have become separated and the visual cortex of the brain, instead of receiving stimuli of images from two approximately similar sights of external objects, receives stimuli from differing objects of gaze.[2] A central sense or perception of two images may occur. Diplopia may be binocular, because each eye transmits different image stimuli, or it may be monocular because stimuli are being transmitted from different portions of a single eye, i.e., from a foveal and from an extrafoveal locus. I shall confine my discussion to conditions of binocular diplopia. The two images may be side by side, displaced vertically or tilted.

Images may also be experienced as superimposed. The experts in vision term this *confusion.* When there is misalignment or deviation of the two axes, both diplopia and confusion may result. Patients characteristically describe optical confusion as one object floating in front of the other. Thus when Mr. T. became cross-eyed, he reported seeing the lamp that was situated to my left as floating in front of him. The floating image is usually reported as unreal, transparent, or ghostlike in appearance.[3]

---

[2] If there are differing degrees of accommodation of the two eyes, as in nearsightedness or farsightedness of one eye, astigmatism, or differing image sizes, so-called aniseikonia, the cortex will also receive discrepant stimuli for those reasons.

[3] If one crosses one's eyes by converging them on a finger in front of oneself while a well-lighted object such as a lamp is in the background, or causes one eye to be deviated by pushing a finger against one eyeball while looking at an object with both eyes open, one is able to observe these phenomena of diplopia and confusion.

Unlike animals without stereoscopic vision of a binocular nature, such as birds which may have two foveas in each eye (Walls, 1942), humans cannot concentrate simultaneously on two markedly different images. Diplopia and optical confusion therefore cause humans to experience a strong subjective sense of discomfort and a psychological sense of confusion. Probably because of the discomfort, attempts at correction are begun fairly quickly. One method is to develop some tolerance for diplopia. This seldom happens naturally, except during the first twelve weeks of life.

A second group of responses to the diplopia could be classified in the category of stimulation to muscle groups. There may be a stimulation to the extraocular musculature so that an external realignment of the muscle groups and visual axis is accomplished. This requires an expenditure of physical energy and a strong attention cathexis. It is noticeable by its absence in those situations in which the attention cathexis is elsewhere and less physical energy is available to hold the squinting eye in place. This happened in the case of Mr. T. during his affect-laden and attention-distracted moments on the couch, or when he was physically ill, greatly fatigued, or "cock-eyed" drunk.

The diplopia may also be responded to by an attempt at intraocular adjustment, e.g., by an accommodation of the lens. This changing of the distance of the focal point will either sharpen an image, making it more dominant, or cause it to blur, rendering it easier to ignore. Accommodation and convergence, however, are reflexively connected so that when accommodation occurs, the visual axis will also be changed in alignment. Judgments of size and distance are in part dependent on our perceptions of divergence and convergence of the optical axis. The eyes converge for closer and smaller objects and diverge for more distant and larger objects. When overconvergence takes place, objects appear to be smaller and closer.

The experiences of Mr. T. when he reported objects appearing smaller and closer might be interpreted as a micropsia, and indeed in this series of strabismic patients he is one of three who reported this.

It is interesting that a review of the very scant English language literature on micropsia and macropsia reveals that several such patients had strabismus (Bartemeier, 1941; Breuer and Freud, 1893-1895).[4]

Some squinters become "alternators" and use each eye alternately for varying periods of time. The most frequent method of adaptation is to ignore one of the two images. This optical "suppression," generally thought to be central and functional in origin, can become, and indeed in most cases does become, long-lasting in one eye. When this functional blindness persists, it is called *amblyopia ex anopsia*. If untreated it usually becomes irreversible in spite of the absence of any demonstrable organic change in either the eye or the brain.

There are several causes of amblyopia ex anopsia, but strabismus is the most common one. Temporary suppression is best demonstrated by thinking of a microscopist before a monocular instrument, looking into the microscope with both eyes open. He pays attention mainly to what he sees in the microscope and ignores images seen by the other eye. It should be noted that in most cases the functional blindness is not complete. Even with very severe amblyopes whose eye tests show a central acuity of less than 20/800 there is a regular use of peripheral vision.

The sense of vision, by way of certain reflexes and of learned responses, plays an important part in our feelings of physical balance and physical orientation. With the onset of a squint both of these may be affected. However, like the judgment of distance, the functions of balance and of spatial orientation are not solely dependent on binocular vision.

For the great majority of persons with strabismus the paradox exists that if there is a marked degree of physical pathology, the method of coping with the syndrome, by its very nature, protects the individual. The eyes usually function as a single organ, somewhat analogously to a centrally placed one. If one eye becomes functionally useless, as happens in the most severe cases, the individuals not only do not suffer very much but are usually quite unaware of the loss. It is the individuals who have the inconsistent strabismus, the

4 An encyclopedia in 1888 included an article on the topic of "Hysteria." Under the subsection, "Disturbances of Sensory Activity" we read: "There are frequent disturbances of accommodation, and false conclusions resulting from them. Objects approaching the eye and moving away from it are seen in different sizes and double or several times (monocular diplopia with macropsia and micropsia)." The author was Sigmund Freud.

intermittent cases like Mr. T., who have the disturbing symptoms, and it is through their greater suffering, even though they have the lesser pathology, that we can learn the most. Much of what follows in this paper has been learned from the analysis of intermittent or latent squinters. It must be borne in mind that, as in the study of psychopathology, the quantitatively greater symptomatology may be extrapolated for use with those who are overtly more normal.

In addition to developmental and congenital or hereditary conditions such as disorders of accommodation and muscle dystonias, strabismus may occur because of physical or toxic injury, tumors, or as a sequela of infections of the brain, ocular muscles or orbit.

Strabismus, like any physical defect, may influence the personality in immediate and long-term ways. The immediate effects are apparent in visual phenomena and in the reactions by the environment to the patient. Long-term effects manifest themselves in various areas of an individual's personality structure: his narcissism, choice of defense mechanisms, attitudes toward affect expression, fantasy life, certain ego and superego functions and their development.

REACTIONS OF THE ENVIRONMENT

The estimated 15 percent of squinters who have had the condition since birth usually have no visual symptoms because one eye has presumably failed to develop functionally (amblyopia of arrest) or because of the ease with which young children are able to suppress one image. They therefore have no inherent visual conflict. For these children the potentially traumatic effect comes mainly from the responses of the environment to this highly visible defect.

The most important adverse reaction of the environment arises if the mother-child relation is distorted because of the child's defect. The mother's anxieties about her child's condition may conjoin with other maternal conflicts. One of these may be due to the parents' responses to reactions in the larger environment. Thus a mother will be concerned not only about her child's vision and physical well-being, but also that other observers will think he is different and possibly stupid and damaged. Whatever the appearance of an odd-looking child may contribute to maternal conflicts, there are frequently the added stresses inherent in a situation where repeated eye examinations increase anxieties and remobilize ambivalent feelings. The parents' burden can be further increased by the necessity of making choices between differing methods and times of treatment, including even being asked to make a decision about elective surgery. An anxious mother may communicate her anxiety to a child and make the child anxious. Perhaps the most important of the several aspects of this problem is the possibility of anxiety in the mother being experienced as aggressive overprotection by the child. This may result in inhibitions of aggression and was seen in several of my patients.

It is unusual for children to complain of the signs and symptoms of strabismus. They are better able to tolerate a diplopia, but may complain of headaches. The symptoms may be of very short duration. The very young person may not realize that the deviant images are something to complain about. There may not be an awareness of the cosmetic flaw until the reactions of peers bring the condition to a forced awareness. No one can see his own eyes without looking into a mirror or at a photograph. (It is because of the lack of awareness in consciousness of his condition that the adult patient may be unable to give a reliable history of the time of onset of the defect.) In addition, because the defect is not directly seen by the child, there is a built-in ease of denial.

If a sibling or other close person has the condition, it may promote earlier awareness. The presence of someone with a similar condition is like having a constant mirror on the scene and this makes denial harder to maintain.

The nature of the repulsion which others experience at the sight of a cross-eyed person seems to be rather different in several ways from the repulsion caused by other physical defects. We usually think of the ridicule of children when they observe a defect in another child as a reaction to castration anxieties with an added sadistic component. In this case the recipient of the ridicule cannot observe the defect in himself, and this may add to perplexity. In addition, in most societies object relations are initially made through individuals looking directly at the eyes. Many people feel uncomfortable when they look at a squinter's eyes. They do not know which eye is being used to look at them and so are confused as to which eye of the squinter they should fixate on in order to maintain contact. One can speculate further that this discomfort may be a result of the narcissistic blow to the onlooker, who is seemingly looked away from; or that it may revive primitive body memories induced by the temptation to cross one's own eyes.[5] This in turn revives the childhood fantasy of crossing one's eyes voluntarily, to then find that one cannot return them to their normal position. Peter Richter[6] has suggested that the repulsion may have something to do with the fact that strabismus is one defect that one cannot observe without the defective person being aware of the observer. Richter suggests that it may revive old guilt feelings about unresolved scoptophilic conflicts.

Another complication brought on by interaction with the environment may later occur if explanations cannot be adequately communicated to the young patients about the use of glasses, drops, an eye patch, or the exercises of the orthoptic technician. The resulting conflicts may become convenient foci for child-parent battles, especially if these take place during or shortly after the anal phase. It is probable that the burden of these battles is heavier than that borne by children who have other types of restrictions and exercises because of the anatomic area involved. Since the eye is a highly drive-cathected area, conflict about the eyes may create extreme anxiety of a castration or annihilation type. When these struggles occur during the anal-urethral and phallic-oedipal phases, they are not only intensified but may very easily become part of sadomasochistic and activity-passivity conflicts.

Squinters commonly desire to hide the defect. For a few individuals shading the eye helps in decreasing discomfort and diplopia. Commonly this has more to do, however, with the reactions of individuals in the strabismic's environment. Onlookers in one way or

---

[5] This may have a bearing on psychoanalytic practice as one of the reasons for the infrequency of the analysis of the symptom. In a discussion of this paper Phyllis Greenacre said: "For a real meeting of the gazes between two people . . . and a comfortable acceptance of this degree of rapport, there must be some mutual focusing. The one person sees himself as acceptable or not to the other in the straightforwardness of the returned visual contact. When the analyst's gaze meets that of the almost unilaterally focused vision of the strabismic patient, he may feel either rejected or rejecting, depending on which side of this identification is the uppermost. The whole situation may make him rather diffusely and preconsciously uneasy. And since analysis goes on on the couch, he may dismiss the preliminary greeting without thinking much about it. One may not wish to be identified automatically in this direct way with someone whose response seems shifty and defective."

[6] Personal communication.

another repeatedly demonstrate anxiety and repulsion in the face of the defect and its possessor. To attempt to hide the defect may become an ego-syntonic mannerism that gradually becomes incorporated into the character structure.

Folklore transmits the culture's common fantasies. Thus it documents popular reactions. One such stereotype is revealed in the folk belief that correlates eyes set close together to evil, aggressive, and predatory motives. One of Shakespeare's plays pictures a cross-eyed man as having a fierce and "fiend-like face" (Dyer, 1884). As a contrast, the heroes of many pulp magazine Western stories are depicted with eyes set wide apart. These folk prejudices have a certain degree of biological validity,[7] which is subjectively also evident in the fact that our eyes tend to deviate externally to their position of divergence when we are relaxed and at rest and tend to converge when we are attentive and pursuing.

In confirmation of the pathophysiological knowledge that strong emotions or debility will bring on a latent strabismus are the phrases relating to feelings and to the condition itself. "Love makes a good eye squint." To be "cross" is a synonym for anger, to be "a cross patch" is to be an angry person. To be cockeyed drunk in Old Irish is to be "cast" (Partridge, 1937).

Further folklore descriptions reflecting reactions of the environment are seen in some humorous tales of men who saw double and were confused. Moreover, in our own culture a few comics use their ability to converge at will for humorous effects.

Conversely, an unfocused look or mild strabismus may be an attractive feature, as many artists have long known (for example, the unfocused look of the Mona Lisa). In at least one culture (the Mayan) squint is esteemed as a trait of beauty and attempts are made to have infants focus their eyes on dangling balls or colored spots painted on the nose in the hope that the children will become cross-eyed. It is when the degree of strabismus or other asymmetry is great that the effect on the onlooker is disconcerting, unaesthetic, repulsive, or productive of great discomfort.

---

[7] In the evolution of the primates from the lower vertebrates (Lyle and Bridgeman, 1959), the position of the eyes has moved forward toward a frontal position from a somewhat lateral direction. The more binocular and more stereoscopic vision is, the more useful it is for predatory purposes.

While a frequently repeated folk saying is that if you meet a cross-eyed person you will have bad luck, one can also find a few instances of the opposite (Gifford, 1958; Hyatt, 1935; Leach, 1949; Opie, 1959; Radford, 1947).

PSYCHOLOGICAL REACTIONS TO STRABISMUS

In the majority of cases strabismus has its onset at two and a half to five years. To appreciate the traumatic possibilities of a squint having its onset in these years of life, let us consider the other phenomena of development and maturation occurring at that time. It is a truism that early development of organ symptoms influences the later structuralization of the personality (Bettelheim and Sylvester, 1949). In the early years the maturing ego apparatuses interact with and are dependent upon physical growth. The child is concerned with such crucial events as the consolidation of motor functions and the fuller control of sphincters and of erect locomotion. At this age he will be moving from the anal and urethral phases to the phallic-oedipal phases. The beginning of abstract thought and object constancy as well as individuation are in the process of establishment. In addition, the superego and ego ideals are about to be formed.

Clearly, for all of these critical processes the function of perception is of crucial importance. Whether or not one can trust one's perceptions will have a bearing not only on one's sense of physical stability but also on self-perception, the body image, reality constancy, and the sense of the self.

According to Schilder (1935), "the whole optic situation determines the feeling concerning our own body . . . the perception of our own body is in no way more reliable than the perception of the outside world" (p. 114). Indeed, our feelings about the outside world are dependent upon our perceptions. The establishment of both animate and inanimate object constancy is, like the body image, dependent on an "average expectable environment" (Hartmann, 1939). We rely on this stability for reality testing, for comparisons and judgment, and for almost all purposive action. This factor is also a prerequisite for superego formation.

In two adult cases the analytic work disclosed that the onset of strabismus at two-and-a-half years had had an effect on their body images. One patient, during the reactivation of the strabismus, described her awareness of the eye as a dead area or as a hole. Mr. T. reported in analysis that he had never been able to draw a face and avoided it even now because of a hesitancy when it came to the eyes. When forced to draw a face he had, as a youngster, always drawn slits for eyes and always represented the eyes as closed. Usually they were automatically drawn with one eye well above the other. A child patient had always had difficulty drawing eyes and had solved the problem by drawing eyeglasses instead. A recent study of the figure drawings of normal three-year-old children (Shapiro and Stine, 1965) confirmed earlier studies which show that once a normal child can draw a head he will be able to draw eyes.[8]

Children react to the onset of strabismus in a way analogous to reactions to other physical or surgical trauma. With regard to the latter, Anna Freud (1952) stated that if the defense mechanisms available to the ego are strong enough to master the trauma, neurotic symptoms or character traits will not develop. If the anxiety is too great, then neurotic symptoms and disturbances of character structure may well occur. Ernst Kris's (1956) concepts of shock or strain trauma (transient or long-lasting) are pertinent here. In a few cases in this series, perhaps owing to a quick pathophysiological adaptation and a good mother-child relationship, there seems to have been no traumatic effect at the period of onset of the strabismus. An important factor in the child's ability to cope with the trauma is his use of the mother as an auxiliary ego, his capacity to borrow her ego strength. Another factor is the state of the child's unconscious fantasy life at the time the strabismus occurred.

Strabismics, like others with physical disabilities, have a greater need for borrowing ego strength because they require additional physical energy and/or attention to compensate for their defective functioning. This may be one of the reasons why strabismus may sensitize the individual to other traumas. We could speculate that these patients are especially vulnerable to poor mothering. This

8 As would be expected in a psychoanalytic practice, I have seen a number of children with squint who, when asked to draw a man, draw figures with obvious strabismus. A series of patients with squint seen in an eye clinic, however, showed a number of strabismic patients who drew figures without any facial or other distortions. Thus, defects in the body image are not an obligatory accompaniment of the physical defect as measured by this test.

seemed true in some of my cases. In those two who had borderline psychotic mothers, there were the added distortions of outer reality. Here the trauma seemed to come from an unstable inner reality conmingled with an unstable outer reality. Mr. T.'s distrust of his visual experience was increased by a mother whose behavior (for example, denying that she had been enraged, or lying to the patient about a happening that he had observed) presented an additional distortion of the outer world. It seems that the perceptual difficulty lends added substance to the parents' attempt to convince the child of a distorted reality.

In two cases the strabismus appeared during the transitional period between anal-urethral and phallic-oedipal phases. One youngster, who was in analysis, perceived the diplopia as meaning that he had X-ray vision, reversing the defect into an asset. His phallic use of visual phenomena, conceived of as a powerful and piercing weapon, was particularly pronounced in his competition with his older and much envied brothers. The other example was provided by Dr. Howard Schlossmann. This patient apparently did not react immediately to the onset of convergent strabismus, but during his adolescence he began to use it for exhibitionistic and aggressively competitive purposes. When he was angry he crossed his eyes in order to frighten his enemies. He changed from a good boy who hid behind glasses to one who began to exhibit his defect like a large phallus. In later years, the eyeglasses that had been discarded with the new-found masculinity were always carried secretly "in case of need," like a spare part. In military service, after the patient had witnessed comrades killed or wounded in battle, he again wore the glasses. Analysis disclosed that the glasses had served as a magic bullet-proof armor.

This patient, like Mr. T., had a period of secretiveness in his analysis. He had successfully suppressed the fact of his childhood strabismus, and became aware of it only when his analysis dealt with material from the transient period between the anal-urethral and the phallic phases.

It is in those cases in which the onset of strabismus occurs during latency, and thereafter, that the subjective complaints of diplopia and discomfort are most common. Presumably this is because as the child grows older, it becomes more difficult to suppress the extra image. This physiological fact has different psychological repercussions dependent upon the person's vulnerabilities. One woman who had a strong ego and efficient defenses was minimally affected by a strabismus occurring during the climacterium. Visual difficulties and severe headaches required minor psychological adjustments, but the optical confusion did not lead to psychological confusion.

The situation was quite different in the case of Mrs. H., who had more unstable and less efficient defenses. She was an actress who came to see me again four years after she had terminated psychotherapy. She thought she was returning to treatment because a voice teacher had instructed her to do some vocal exercises, which included the phrase, "Ma ma ma." It was Mrs. H.'s theory that this had reactivated some early conflicts with her mother that had been incompletely worked through in her earlier treatment. After a few months of analysis another reason appeared in her associations. In addition to the voice lessons, she had been taking acting lessons, and it was two comments of her acting teacher that had served as the more likely precipitating event. On one occasion he had observed that she was using only one side of her body. He also said to her that she was using too much "business" and distracting gestures. These comments revived old anxieties about a childhood strabismus that had not been dealt with at all in her previous treatment. Her strabismus had, of course, connections with old conflicts with her mother and many other areas, but I shall deal here only with the effects as reconstructed in the treatment after a great deal of initial resistance. What apparently happened was that, with the generalized muscle loosening accompanying the climacteric, a previously well-controlled strabismus had recurred. Because of the close reflexive connection of eye function and balance, the patient, in attempts to correct a tilted vision, actually was walking, without being aware of it, in a tilted manner. Preconsciously she had had a revival of old fears that people would see and make fun of her cock eye and so resumed old "mugging," distracting, techniques. Old defenses of denial and suppression were revived. Nevertheless, her anxieties were so great that she returned to treatment. In Mrs. H.'s case the working through of the manifold meanings and consequences of the pathophysiology of the strabismus helped her bear the narcissistic blows of the menopause.

Like any other defect, strabismus is essentially experienced as a

narcissistic blow and there are thus a good many compensatory fantasies, aimed at repairing self-esteem. In my series the persistently
low self-esteem was most impressive. *Each* of the patients I analyzed
thought of himself as "stupid," "ugly," and "different."

If the strabismus interacts with existing areas of psychic conflict,
one expects to find symptom formation or signs of character structuralization, and this was the case in each of the patients I examined.
However, major distortions of character that could be ascribed exclusively to this syndrome were seldom observed. What more often
seemed present was a tendency toward modifications of *styles* of
behavior. In some specific instances they could clearly be seen as part
of multiply determined symptoms; in most they seemed to participate in the formation of character traits.

A noteworthy finding in a few patients, but by no means in all
of them, was a tendency under certain circumstances to lie or to
conceal important events. The connection between this character
trait and strabismus is, of course, emphasized in innumerable folk
sayings and linguistic usage such as "Don't trust someone who doesn't
look directly at you, or a person with shifty eyes." In Old English
the word for a thief was "cross," as was the word for stealing. A
hotel for thieves was a "cross crib." In French the word for cross-eyes
is *louche,* and a *louche* business deal is one that is considered to be
fishy or dishonest. Mr. T. had the impulse and habit for a long time
consciously to withhold information at points in his analysis, although he was quite trustworthy in the outside world and, of course,
for most of his analysis. Another patient found himself telling lies
to girls he was interested in. The parents of the children I was
treating were primarily concerned about their children's tendencies
to lie. Mrs. H., on the other hand, was a compulsive truth teller.
Here the truth telling sometimes seemed to be in the service of a
sadomasochistic tendency, and the strabismus of childhood was a
carefully kept secret.

The germ of truth contained in folklore about not trusting a
person who squints needs a great deal of qualification. It seems to
me that it would be correct to say that this particular defect may
play a part, under certain conditions, in affecting the harmonious
development of the superego. Some strabismics lie; some have overly
strict superegos. Among the many factors involved must be the time

of onset of the defect, the degree of interference with reality testing and of the functioning of vision itself.

In "Vision, Headache, and the Halo" (1947), Greenacre makes the point that stunning visual experiences add greatly to the stress of superego formation. If the strabismus occurs during the third year of life and is accompanied by diplopia, confusion, and tilting of retinal meridians, then these perceptual difficulties may very well serve as a form of visual shock and as such affect the formation of the superego in the same manner as those patients of Greenacre who witnessed violent or bloody scenes. A contradiction to this hypothesis is that most children are better able to tolerate the sudden onset of visual symptoms than adults. Although a child may not react overtly to distortions of perceptions, it is inconceivable that they do not require some forms of adaptation.

In my patients the onset of these visual symptoms was usually recalled in the form of fights about wearing glasses or an eye patch rather than of direct memories of visual symptoms.

We are used to thinking of the importance of the auditory sense in the development of the superego. We think of spoken words in dreams and the element of commands in superego functioning, but visual perception must also have an important place. It must disturb the development of a sense of truth to have a confused and disturbed feeling for the reliability of one's percepts. Most of our perceptions of the world are at least thought of in terms of the sense of vision.

Dorothy Burlingham (1941), writing of the blind, noted that "they are very prone to lie" (p. 43). Speaking of children, she traced this to a wish-fulfilling fantasy: the strong wish to see. Peter Blos (1960) noted a similar phenomenon in reference to the idea that some day in the future the boy with cryptorchidism could hope for the descent of the testicle. Zeckel (1950) has written of the traditional idea of deceitfulness of the deaf. Ruth Mack Brunswick (1943) wrote of the "accepted lies" of women in regard to age and the attainment of orgasm. She suggested that for some women to admit the advance of age or the inability to attain genital orgasms meant giving up the fantasy of eventually having a penis. In all likelihood such wishful thinking can occur in any situation where an individual can compare himself to others to his detriment. Lying in strabismics may be related to a wish that some day the burdensome defect will disappear.

Another form of self-deception can be seen in the previously mentioned attitude toward a squint as though it were a shameful perversion. The individual who expends a great deal of attention on hiding the defect and engages in many subterfuges to hide the defect from himself and others may, like the pervert, be subject to a spread of internal denials and external subterfuges which in turn exert a wider corrupting effect or cause an increased sense of corrupting. This must contribute to low self-esteem.

In the study of specific superego problems one must also consider the development of identifications. We assume intact perceptual functions for the ability to identify. We also assume that a large part of the superego consists of a body of moral values and the person's ability for self-evaluation. These also require intact perceptual processes, as has been suggested by the study of superego development in the blind and deaf. However, the strabismic's problem is less severe because his perception is at most only partially impaired. The crucial problem in the squinter is his distrust of what he perceives.

The impact of strabismus on identifications and superego development is clearly seen in the squinter's low self-esteem. If the person has been subjected to an outside world that reacted to him with repulsion, rejection, and taunting, then the strabismic may in part identify with that hostile outside world and adopt that rejection of himself. Thus a part of Mr. T.'s concept of himself as ugly, stupid, and different was an acceptance of himself as he saw the world seeing him. However, not all squinters have disturbances in superego development.

We would expect early visual problems to sensitize individuals to other traumas. Freud's statement that the ego is first of all a body ego is well established in our thinking not only from the point of view of the mechanisms of defense and the precursors of ego and superego functioning ultimately having their anlagen in body functioning, but also from the viewpoints of maldeveloped ego apparatuses having a distorting effect on new experiences and thus tending to affect character trait formation.

A twelve-year-old boy who strongly distrusted his visual perception—because of a diplopia that he had had since early childhood—was traveling abroad with his family. In a tired state he turned to his father and asked to be led by the hand to the nearby and clearly visible bathroom. This convergence of disorientation and passive wishes is an example of a character structuralization of what had been a necessary defense in the past. Now, under stress, he needed to be shown in the old way, although he had developed adequate vision and coordination. Writing of the blind, Anna Freud (1952) stressed the effects of this passivity and dependence on the masculinity feelings of such patients. A counterpart of this in the female seems to be a tendency toward a heightened masochism and dependence and feelings of genital inadequacy. This is also to be expected if the injury to the developing ego apparatus took place during the anal-sadistic phase or in the period of transition to the phallic phase. If physical activity is interfered with because of perceptual difficulties at that time, it is not surprising to find fixation and regression to earlier levels.

If, as was the case with Mr. T., the strabismus is of the intermittent type, then the function of reality testing may be distrusted although apparently not really interfered with. The individual may then use a more stable sense, such as that of touch, kinesthetic or auditory perception, or a combination of these under circumstances of stress in preference to vision. These provide a much more limited scope in terms of distance, quality, and variety, in contrast to the visual function, and the world narrows to one that more closely approximates that of the blind. The patient then may develop mechanisms of adaptation that we usually find in the blind. Chief among these are passivity and regression to the sense of touch. This was evident in Mr. T.'s acting-out crisis on the couch. He had to touch his pillow to gain a feeling of stability when the room appeared to him to tilt. He would then also look at the pillow. Mrs. H. had to touch the wall at the side of the couch. In both of these patients there were fears of falling, of loss of feelings of self, and, indeed, at these times fears of loss of contact with the current object, the analyst, which seemed to be repetitions of childhood experiences when unstable perceptions of both inanimate and animate objects interfered with feelings of stability in the development of reality constancy. Possibly the well-developed abilities to pay attention to fortuitous sounds made by the analyst and the well-developed verbal abilities of these patients are compensatory adjustments to feelings of deficiency in reality constancy (Frosch, 1966) and of the visual sense.

All the subjects studied, except one, had essentially good object relations, but some of their characteristics seemed directly related to the defect. The schoolteacher, Mr. T., entered all new social situations with a form of social anxiety that was specifically related to his initial anxiety about whether the defect would be noticed by others in the room, and whether he would then have to feel ashamed. Another patient, on entering new situations under the same stress, found herself automatically turning her head away from any new person. She had the reputation of being "snobbish" because of this. She was known as an extremely pleasant and capable person in dealings with all sorts of people via the telephone. In face to face conversations, however, she was extraordinarily anxious and ill at ease. Another person, when he was talking before a professional group, attempted to master his anxiety by using his hands to make all sorts of motions; while they appeared to punctuate his speech, they were actually designed to distract attention from his eyes.

Such mannerisms, defenses, and character traits, while they do not affect the depth of object relations in the usual sense, do exert a detractive force on the personal styles of social relations; in that sense they have subtle effects on the forming of new relationships. Perhaps because the making of new relationships is more difficult, strabismics may have a somewhat greater feeling of dependency on well-established objects. Such dependency may have to do with the feeling of vulnerability that comes with any narcissistic wound, and if, in addition, the function of reality testing is not trusted, there may be a greater tendency to cling to objects as auxiliary egos.

If the person is occupied with compensatory or diverting mannerisms, there may be an interference with a full capacity of empathy because the head-tilting, eyebrow-raising, hand-waving or facial grimacing distracts both the subject and the object from a full communication of nuances of feeling and ideas. If one is attending too much to self and body observation, one has less opportunity to attend to the emotional reality of others.

There may be a tendency to have heightened empathy with ill or defective individuals and a lesser feeling of identification with seemingly normal individuals. This must be very much on a basis of narcissistic identification. Two of the squinters were married to partners who had strabismus.

Dorothy Burlingham (1941, 1961, 1965) and Nagera and Colonna (1965) emphasize that many blind children have a marked inhibition of aggression. They ascribe this to "fear of losing the favor and love of the object, a fear that is . . . transformed into a fear of annihilation caused by extreme dependence on objects for reasons of safety" (p. 274). As in deaf children (Deutsch, 1940), there is a readiness to give up reality and turn to fantasy. The squinters analyzed all had greatly intensified fears of aggression, in spite of their being neither blind nor deaf. Aggressive drives were strong, but direct expression of aggression was inhibited and feared. Defenses tended to be phobic in nature, with a tendency to avoid situations where aggression would be expected. In two of the cases, markedly strong affects—including that of anger—could produce eye symptoms; a third patient experienced dizzy feelings in response to aggressive drive derivatives and because of this sought to inhibit aggression.

When the strabismus has not become stable and the state of being intermittently strabismic or of having diplopia and confusion exists—that is, when optical suppression is not a fixed state—the patient may also be made quite anxious not only by feelings of anger, but by all strong feelings, especially erotic ones. Thus when Mr. T. was with a woman who sexually aroused him, his eye would slip out of line. He would become aware of this either by a perception of his own changed state of vision or else by a perception of the changed look on the woman's face as she noted his eye change. He would then withdraw from further contact with the woman or inhibit his libidinal feeling in the service of pulling his eye back. In addition, he experienced severe guilt feelings. Thus, when his "eye got bad," he was "bad."

Parents of strabismic children can easily tell when the child is fatigued or affected by other stress such as anger, guilt feelings, or anxiety by observing that at such times the strabismic eye is under less control. This has a tendency to prolong for the child ideas of the omnipotence of the mother. Mr. T. and Mrs. H. both had grossly overestimated conceptions of their mothers as all-knowing and all-powerful at much later ages than is usual, although their strabismus was only one of several determinants.

Similarly illustrative was a peculiar inhibition of another analysand who found sexual intercourse impossible when her husband was on her left side. In analysis, the acutely unpleasant feeling was traced to the fact that, in that position, her esophoric and astigmatic eye faced the partner and when she was sexually aroused, her eye became strabismic, whereupon her husband's face turned into a distorted and frightening one. This in turn had made it possible for latent ambivalent feelings to be more easily revived. In addition, the sight of her own nose at these times distracted her and she became preconsciously aware that she was looking cross-eyed. She then feared that her husband would discover her defective and presumably repugnant state. In this case, sexual excitement increased the strabismus, which then interfered with sexual intercourse.

In other instances, the visual experiences accompanying a squint may be sources of excitement and be used as a substitute or equivalent for masturbation.[9] The fears aroused by, and the defenses used against, masturbation conflicts and the attendant guilt feelings extended to strabismus. One such patient feared that the "shameful" strabismic state would become apparent to observers; it would be as if the fact of masturbation were revealed.

If, during earlier years, strabismus occurred during masturbation, this would reinforce guilt about it, because the fantasy about masturbation making one "crazy" would seem to be confirmed by the occurrence of visual symptoms. Conversely, a patient who had displaced his eye defect onto "a defective genital" masturbated to reassure himself about the intactness of his genital. It may be the unconscious link between strabismus and masturbation conflicts that so often creates special resistances to analyzing the meaning of strabismus.

Not only the meaning of the activity but the underlying fantasies may arouse fears. Fantasies and dreams concerning fears of blindness occur much more frequently in strabismic patients than in others.

Two persons reported essentially the same childhood fantasy about the nature of the corrective operation with which they were threatened. Both youngsters thought that the eye in question would be taken out of its socket, turned around, looked at, the muscles cut, and the eye put back in its place. This is of interest not only in its misinterpretation of the actual event. An attempt is made to correct what is essentially the patient's difficulty in being unable to see the

---

9 For example, a patient with micropsia had as a child used his defect for pleasurable purposes, to create what he referred to as his "carnival" feelings.

nature of his defect. The patient compensates via the fantasy for his inability to see not only what the operation may be, but more fundamentally what his eyes look like. It reminds us of the difficulties the little girl has in visualizing the vagina and her compensating both for her lack of a penis and for her difficulty in visualizing the vagina by, in fantasy, placing a penis in the vagina.

On a more conscious level are the fantasies associated with the phenomenon of staring at a person or an inanimate object in an unfocused way. Jacobson (1957) described patients who "turn off" people by closing their eyes and ears. A nine-year-old girl, who did not have strabismus, crossed her eyes and lowered them when she did not want to listen to a scolding parent. Greenacre has referred to the childhood game of unfocusing and pretending that this destroys the person stared at. Mr. T. played this game as a child.

In addition to the fears based on fantasies, there are those that are more directly related to the physical defect. I have previously described the greater dependency on adults which the child who cannot trust his perceptions experiences, a circumstance that also enhances his ambivalence conflicts and fears of aggression and excitement.

Other reality-based fears concern activities involving motion, such as sports where head or eye injury may occur, or driving. Not uncommonly these fears are handled by counterphobic defenses.

Learning Difficulties

For many years optometrists, ophthalmologists, pediatricians, and educators have been seriously concerned about learning problems in strabismics. Indeed, a well-known resistance to sending children into psychoanalytic treatment is to call the difficulty a perceptual rather than a psychological one. The reverse may also be encountered—to call a perceptual difficulty a purely psychological one. We need to take both into consideration, since one usually influences the other.

Along with the high prevalence of body-image problems and distrust of the important sense of sight, difficulties in abstract thinking were anticipated. In my series of patients, this has not been the case, nor have I found gross difficulties in reading.

Some learning difficulties seemed to be related to the child's distrust of his capacity to think. "Is my thinking right?" was a frequently encountered question. A strabismic who had lost his corrective prism eyeglasses reported, "It's bad enough seeing things tilted, but I hate to be thinking crooked too." In this way he expressed the fact that he equated his thinking with his visual perception.

One patient distrusted material learned only by hearing, so that she had to make aural and written material her own by reading it at home, or thinking it through when there was more time for reflection. This was derived from several levels: a feeling of defective reality testing and a time factor especially related to fears of distractibility. Topics that required concentration over long periods seemed to cause more difficulties than those for which quick grasp or memory would serve. In the main, the factors of fatigue and the attitudes of teachers and parents seemed most important.

Reading a book when attention is wandering because of fatigue or ambivalence toward the topic may be paralleled by the strabismic eye wandering so that words from another portion of the page are superimposed on the sentence of immediate attention. If the patient has difficulty in distinguishing whether this is due to physical or mental processes, he may feel that he does not understand what he is reading.

Summary

In this essay an attempt has ben made to trace some of the effects of strabismus on personality development, symptoms, and character formation.

The major thesis has been that strabismus may affect the individual as a unique form of trauma because of certain pathophysiological effects. These may be complicated by the reactions of the individual's environment to the nature of the defect. Of crucial importance is the child's distrust of his own perceptions and the resulting mental confusion. These factors interact with and influence the unfolding of the libidinal drives and aggression, the choice of defense mechanisms, and certain aspects of ego and superego development and functioning. Of great significance is the fact that strabismus usually has its onset at two and a half to five years—a period when the child is confronted by a great variety of developmental tasks.

The focus of this paper has been primarily a clinical one. Using both developmental considerations and illustrative case material, I also attempted to discuss the special relevance of some of the findings for psychoanalytic technique.

I would stress again that these findings are derived from only a small number of analyzed cases. Moreover, only fragments of these analyses were presented here. In only a few of these cases was the strabismus crucial; yet in each individual it constituted a cross of some size to bear, and as such it was well worth examining.

BIBLIOGRAPHY

Abraham, K. (1913), Restrictions and Transformations of Scoptophilia in Psycho-Neurotics. *Selected Papers on Psycho-Analysis.* London: Hogarth Press, 1949, pp. 169-234.

Adams, F. (1886), Airs, Waters and Places. In: *The Genuine Works of Hippocrates.* New York: William Wood, p. 171.

Bartemeier, L. H. (1941), Micropsia. *Psa. Quart.,* 10:573-582.

Bender, M. B. (1952), *Disorders in Perception.* Springfield: Thomas, p. 109.

Bettelheim, B. & Sylvester, E. (1949), Physical Symptoms in Emotionally Disturbed Children. *This Annual,* 3/4:353-368.

Bielschowsky, A. (1935), Lectures on Motor Anomalies of the Eyes: IV. Functional Neuroses. *Arch. Ophthal.,* 13:751-770.

Blos, P. (1960), Comments on the Psychological Consequences of Cryptorchism. *This Annual,* 15:395-429.

Breuer, J. & Freud, S. (1893-1895), Studies on Hysteria. *Standard Edition,* 2. London: Hogarth Press, 1955.

Burlingham, D. (1941), Psychic Problems of the Blind. *Amer. Imago,* 2:43-85.

—— (1961), Some Notes on the Development of the Blind. *This Annual,* 16:121-145.

—— (1965), Some Problems of Ego Development in Blind Children. *This Annual,* 20:194-208.

Collins, S. D. (1925), Strabismus and Defective Color Sense among School Children. *U.S. Publ. Hlth Serv. Rep.,* 1031:1515-1523.

Deutsch, F. (1940), The Sense of Reality in Persons Born Blind. *J. Psychol.,* 10:121-140.

Downing, A. (1945), Ocular Defects in Sixty Thousand Selectees. *Arch. Ophthal.,* 33:139-143.

Dyer, T. F. (1884), *Folk Lore of Shakespeare.* New York: Harper, p. 560.

Ferenczi, S. (1913), On Eye Symbolism. *Sex in Psychoanalysis.* New York: Basic Books, 1950, pp. 270-276.

—— (1916-1917), Disease or Patho-Neuroses. *Further Contributions to the Theory and Technique of Psycho-Analysis.* London: Hogarth Press, 1950, pp. 78-89.

Fletcher, M. C. & Silverman, S. J. (1966), Strabismus: Part I. A Summary of 1,110 Consecutive Cases. *Amer. J. Ophthal.,* 61:86-94.

Frandsen, A. D. (1960), Occurrence of Squint. *Acta Ophthal. Suppl.,* 62. Copenhagen: Munksgaard, p. 149.

Freud, A. (1952), The Role of Bodily Illness in the Mental Life of Children. *This Annual,* 7:69-81.

Freud, S. (1888), Hysteria. *Standard Edition,* 1:41-57. London: Hogarth Press, 1966.

—— (1910), The Psycho-Analytic View of Psychogenic Disturbances of Vision. *Standard Edition,* 11:209-218. London: Hogarth Press, 1957.

—— (1925), Some Psychical Consequences of the Anatomical Distinction between the Sexes. *Standard Edition*, 19:243-258. London: Hogarth Press, 1961.

—— (1931), A Disturbance of Memory on the Acropolis. *Standard Edition*, 22:239-248. London: Hogarth Press, 1964.

Frosch, J. (1966), A Note on Reality Constancy. In: *Psychoanalysis—A General Psychology*, ed. R. M. Loewenstein, L. M. Newman, M. Schur, & A. J. Solnit. New York: International Universities Press, pp. 349-376.

Gailey, W. (1949), The Cross-Eyed Child. *New Orleans State Med. J.*, 101:387-389.

Gifford, E. S. (1958), *The Evil Eye*. New York: Macmillan, p. 216.

Greenacre, P. (1926), The Eye Motif in Delusion and Fantasy. *Amer. J. Psychiat.*, 5:553-580.

—— (1947), Vision, Headache, and Halo. *Trauma, Growth and Personality*. New York: International Universities Press, 1969, pp. 132-148.

—— (1958), Early Physical Determinants in the Development of the Sense of Identity. *J. Amer. Psa.*, 6:612-627.

—— (1960), Further Notes on Fetishism. *This Annual*, 15:191-207.

Guibor, G. P. (1959), *Squint and Allied Conditions*. New York: Grune & Stratton, p. 356.

Harrington, D. G. (1947), Symposium: Psychosomatic Manifestations. *Trans. Amer. Acad. Ophthal. & Otolaryng.*, 52:78-79.

Hart, H. H. (1949), The Eye in Symbol and Symptom. *Psa. Rev.*, 36:1-21.

Hartmann, H. (1939), *Ego Psychology and the Problem of Adaptation*. New York: International Universities Press, 1958.

Hirsch, M. J. & Wick, R. E. (1963), *The Vision of Children*. Philadelphia: Chilton Books, p. 434.

Hyatt, H. M. (1935), *Folk Lore from Adams County, Illinois*. New York: French Printing and Publishing Co., p. 723.

Inman, W. S. (1921). Emotion and Eye Symptoms. *Brit. J. Psychol.*, 2:47-67.

Jacobson, E. (1957), Denial and Repression. *J. Amer. Psa. Assn.*, 5:61-92.

Jones, E. (1916), The Theory of Symbolism. *Papers on Psycho-Analysis*. London: Ballière, Tindall & Cox, 5th ed., 1948, pp. 87-144.

—— (1955), *The Life and Work of Sigmund Freud*, Vol. 2. New York: Basic Books.

Kris, E. (1956), The Recovery of Childhood Memories in Psychoanalysis. *This Annual*, 11:54-88.

Leach, M., ed. (1949), *Standard Dictionary of Folklore, Mythology and Legend*, 2 Vols. New York: Funk & Wagnalls.

Leuba, J. H. (1949), Deux cas de strabisme psychogène. *Évolut. Psychiat.*, 3:353-363.

Linksz, A. (1952), *Physiology of the Eye*, Vol. II: *Vision*. New York: Grune & Stratton, p. 869.

—— (1961), Theory of Pleoptics. *Pleoptics and Light Coagulation*. New York: Little Brown, pp. 747-785.

Lion, E. G., O'Neill, C., & Prager, R. E. (1943), Strabismus and Children's Personality Reactions. *Amer. J. Orthopsychiat.*, 13:121-124.

Lyle, T. K. (1953), Orthoptic and Surgical Treatment of Non-Paralytic Strabismus. *Bull. N.Y. Acad. Med.*, 29:235-248.

—— & Bridgeman, G. J. O. (1959), *Worth and Chavesse's Squint*. London: Baillière, Tindall & Cox, 9th ed., p. 392.

Mack Brunswick, R. (1943), The Accepted Lie. *Psa. Quart.*, 12:458-464.

Nagera, H. & Colonna, A. (1965), Aspects of the Contribution of Sight to Ego and Drive Development. *This Annual*, 20:267-287.

Niederland, W. G. (1965), Narcissistic Ego Impairment in Patients with Early Physical Malformations. *This Annual*, 20:518-534.

Opie, I. & P. (1959), *The Lore and Language of School Children*. Oxford: Oxford University Press, p. 417.

Partridge, E. (1937), *A Dictionary of Slang and Unconventional English*. London: Routledge, p. 999.

Pollie, D. M., Hafner, J. A., & Krasnoff, J. H. (1964), The Strabismic Child and His Psychological Adjustment. *J. Pediat. Ophthal.*, 1:60-63.

Radford, E. & M. A. (1947), *Encyclopedia of Superstitions*. London: Rider, p. 269.

Rappaport, E. A. (1959), Anger, Apathy and Strabismus. *Eye, Ear, Nose & Throat Mon.*, 38:473-482.

Róheim, G. (1952), The Evil Eye. *Amer. Imago*, 9:351-363.

Schilder, P. (1935), *The Image and Appearance of the Human Body*. New York: International Universities Press, 1950.

Schlagel, T. F. & Hoyt, M. (1957), *Psychosomatic Ophthalmology*. Baltimore: Williams & Wilkins, p. 523.

Schlossman, A. & Priestly, B. S. (1952), The Role of Heredity in the Etiology and Treatment of Strabismus. *Arch. Ophthal.*, 47:1-20.

Schur, M. (1950), Chronic, Exudative Discoid and Lichenoid Dermatitis (Sulzberger-Garbe's Syndrome). *Int. J. Psa.*, 31:73-77.

Scobee, R. G. (1947), *The Oculorotary Muscles*. St. Louis: Mosby, 2nd ed., 1952, p. 359.

Shapiro, T. & Stine, J. (1965), The Figure Drawings of Three-Year-Old Children. *This Annual*, 20:298-309.

Souders, B. F. (1942), Hysterical Convergence Spasm. *Arch. Ophthal.*, 271:361-365.

Stevens, G. T. (1899), Historical Notes of Strabismus and Other Anomalies of the Eye Muscles. *Ann. Ophthal.*, 8:143-166.

Stringer, E. (1957), A Case of Eccentric Fixation in an Adult in Which Central Fixation Has Been Restored. *Brit. Orthoptic J.*, 14:61-67.

Stromberg, A. E. (1947), The Psychology of the Squinter. *Amer. J. Ophthal.*, 30:601-606.

Teuber, H. L. (1961), Sensory Deprivation, Sensory Suppression and Agnosia. *J. Nerv. Ment. Dis.*, 132:32-40.

Waardenburg, P. J. (1954), Squint and Heredity. *Documenta Ophthal.*, 7/8:422-494.

Walls, G. L. (1942), *The Vertebrate Eye*. Bloomfield Hills: Cranbrook Institute of Science, p. 789.

Zeckel, A. (1950), Psychopathological Aspects of Deafness. *J. Nerv. Ment. Dis.*, 112:322-346.

ON THE TECHNIQUE OF CHILD ANALYSIS IN RELATION TO STAGES OF DEVELOPMENT

ANNA MAENCHEN, Ph.D. (Berkeley, Calif.)

The technique of child analysis has from its inception always been concerned with development in general. In recent years, however, there has been a tendency to evolve specific techniques geared to specific developmental stages such as prelatency, latency (subdivided into two groups or even into three groups), preadolescence, and adolescence (again subdivided). It seems to me that the growing concern with this issue possibly stems from the application of child analysis to psychotic and borderline children who defy orderly age and developmental categories—and thus also the usual technique of child analysis. We always assumed that once the developmental phases were thoroughly explored, it would be easy to gear the technique to the requirements of each stage. Now the normal developmental stages have been explored, but we still have concerns. When we ask how old the child is, we state his developmental age, but certain syndromes and certain arrests in development are related neither to the chronological age of the child nor to the usual developmental sequences.

Historically, child analysis started as a modified technique of adult analysis, the modifications being necessitated by the immaturity of the child's ego. Child analysis is a well-defined and logical

A version of this paper was presented at the fourth Annual Meeting of the American Association for Child Psychoanalysis, New Haven, March, 1969. A shorter version was presented to the Los Angeles Psychoanalytic Society, February, 1970, and to the Washington Psychoanalytic Society, April, 1970.

Several of the issues of this paper were discussed with the Study Group of the American Association for Child Psychoanalysis.

I want to thank my colleagues whose discussion of my paper helped me greatly: Anna Freud, Drs. Peter Blos, Merton Gill, Stanley Goodman, Calvin Settlage, and the members of the Study Group, which consists of Dr. Joseph Afterman, Mrs. Marion Bradley, Mrs. Eleanor Dansky, and Drs. Philip Spielman, Charles Vieth, Jules Weiss, and Robert Westfall.

technique which fits most cases of neurosis in children. It does not fit the diagnostic categories added to the child analyst's practice and the new and much wider interest in the "dark ages" in the development of the personality—the preverbal stage. Neither does it fit those cases in which fate or environment have interfered with normal development: cases of blind children, cases of seduction, children who lack stimulation for development, etc. (Anna Freud, 1968).

At present the differences between adult and child analysis are shrinking, with the two tending to be equated. This tendency seems to me to stem not only from the "improved" technique, but from a wish of some child analysts to get away from the so-called *un*analytic interactions in child analysis (as if these interactions threatened the very spirit of analysis). Comparing child and adult analysis, one can say, in general, that the analytic attitude is the same, but the technique is different. But when we say that interpretation is the main vehicle in both, then the equation is actually possible.

The salient question is of course in what ways the technique has improved. In what ways did the advancement in ego psychology influence child analytic technique? Together with direct observations (especially in longitudinal studies), ego psychology has greatly increased our knowledge of the early stages of development and their interpretation.

The idea of a "menu" offered a child in his analysis is a very attractive one:[1] we can observe what the patient takes from what the analytic situation offers; we assume that he takes what he needs; and, at times, we base our final diagnosis on this observation. Yet this procedure can lead to errors. Do all of us offer the same menu? Special interests and the personality of the child analyst may create variations in the diet, thus making the evaluation more difficult.

There are other factors that complicate the evaluation of technique in child analysis. Scientific experimentation in technique is hardly possible; we have neither two identical cases nor two identical child analysts, and even the same analyst working with two different cases may not be quite the same analyst. As Anna Freud (1959)

[1] This idea was first presented by Anna Freud in a lecture in New York, 1960. Later (1965, p. 229) she said: "the nature of the child's disturbance reveals itself via the specific elements which he selects for therapeutic use when he is offered the full range of possibilities that are contained in child analysis."

stated, cases can be compared only on the level of method and on the level of material.

In the same vein, I find the concern about the "rate of change" in child analysis meaningless unless we can specify clearly what change we want to produce. Changes of behavior and even the disappearance of symptoms can be achieved much faster than the resumption of normal development, the goal at which child analysis aims. I shall return to this point and give an illustration.

The general approach to the technique of child analysis has not changed fundamentally in recent years. The emphasis is on analysis of defenses and affects—possibly the affects are stressed more prominently at present. As before, our tools are determined by the relative immaturity of the patient's ego.

As to the changes in the technique itself, we have noticeably moved away from "doing" things with the child to talking with the child patient about his feelings and his behavior in and outside the analytic session. We proceed from clarifications to interpretations in the framework of a workable relationship with the child, based on a therapeutic alliance.

The tools of child analysis need no discussion. Whatever "royal roads" to the unconscious are preferred, "All roads lead to Rome." Dreams, play, and transference were all called royal roads at one time or another. The overemphasis of any one of these roads (especially the overemphasis of transference) as the only means of communication leads to a one-sided and possibly lopsided view of analytic material.

Thus, in attempting to get a fresh view on problems of technique, we can use several perspectives: we can look at symptomatology, at transference, at the superego, or at ego functions. The most promising perspective, I believe, is that of the ego functions, which are more readily accessible to observation in analysis (and also outside of it) and thus lend themselves easily to a focus for a comparative study. We are interested in the effects of libidinal regression on ego functions not only because of the impairment it causes through the defensive activity, but also because it involves some regression on the side of the ego. Moreover, we know that developmental failures early in life interfere with the development of precisely those ego functions which are crucial for the use of our classical technique.

Dealing with this topic, I had a choice of proceeding in several directions. Rather than attempt a comprehensive theoretical paper, I shall proceed by outlining (1) child analysis in relation to the specific developmental stages; (2) selected problems of technique; and (3) departures from the standard technique.

CHILD ANALYSIS IN RELATION TO SPECIFIC DEVELOPMENTAL STAGES

From the observational material now available, we have learned that the phases in instinctual development can be recognized not only in autoerotic behavior and in object relationships but also in the development of the ego. These observations have extended our knowledge to earlier ages.

The Young Child

Preschool children are now more frequently analyzed than before. The wishes of the young child can be interpreted, it seems, early in treatment, as Glenn did in the case of Betty, three and a half years old, who suffered from bowel movement retention.[2] Glenn interpreted her wish to be a baby like her younger brother in the first session. We might ask, of course, whether this wish was repressed; and, assuming that it was not, one might raise the question whether this was an interpretation. In this very successful treatment, the child was told that "by playing we will find out"; with this, the play was made a part of communication which Betty used constructively. She even divided herself in two persons (one being the monster girl), a technical device we use with the help of a puppet or an imaginary figure. It is impressive how well Betty demonstrated her defenses and fantasies, and how well she understood what her analyst was saying to her and what analysis was all about.

The forms interpretations take are varied indeed. Glenn, for instance, had to sing his interpretations to Betty. A little boy just entering latency lay down in my study, covered himself up, closed his eyes, and pretended to sleep. I, feeling very much excluded, suggested that he might have a dream. The boy produced many "dreams" and insisted that I close my eyes and tell him my dreams.

2 Unpublished material.

My interpretations took this form. As strange as this picture of a short phase of his analysis might appear, I believe that in this way he came close to free association with the help of a "distancing device," e.g., these are "only my made-up dreams." But we also note that the behavior included regression as well—playing a baby who goes to sleep.

To preserve the analytic situation we are careful to avoid direct instinctual gratification in play and in relation to the analyst. Some analysts are less apprehensive about this issue, but I feel that, e.g., a doctor game with the analyst in the role of the doctor might be much too real. The child's reactions to actual instinctual gratification during analytic sessions can easily be mistaken for a therapeutic alliance (A. Freud, 1969).

Almost all the themes encountered in the analysis of older children are present in the analysis of a very young child, with the exception of the oedipal theme which appears of course only as an overture, as a prelude.

The therapeutic results of the analysis of a young child are striking. The symptoms may be severe, but they can be removed within a year because of the flexibility of the personality at this age. Analysis is usually continued to safeguard the results. The young child's improvement proceeds gradually, which is logical not only because of the "working through" in analysis, but also because the gradual progress in analysis parallels normal development.

Latency

Our views about developmental phases are changing. For example, the latency period was generally considered the golden age in the life of a child, and the golden age for analysis of a child. It is my impression, however, that for some child analysts latency is "shrinking" in duration and importance. As a psychoanalytic research in general, we now place the source of disturbances in earlier phases of development. We think of preadolescence as starting earlier: we wonder how latent latency really is, and we often recommend analysis before latency if we have reason to believe that defenses might cripple some ego functions. We certainly no longer think that it is easier to analyze the child during the latency period (cf. Harley, 1962a, 1967). Anna Freud (1969) feels that although resistance via defense is specially strong during latency,[3] the ego qualities needed for the treatment alliance, insight, and self-observation are important assets favorable for analysis in latency. This point is well illustrated by the cases reported by Erna Furman (1967) and Selma Fraiberg (1965), which I shall discuss below.

The advent of latency can sometimes be observed during the analysis of young children as a developmental step made possible by analytic work (see the case of Billy, reported by Robert Furman, 1967).

The observation that the oedipal theme appears as a "prelude" in the analysis of a prelatency child does not necessarily mean that we always get to analyze this theme in latency children. Geleerd (1967) found that actual oedipal conflicts are rarely prominent in the analysis of latency children; they are things of the past.[4] What we do, she says, is to trace "the vicissitudes of transformations of defenses and sublimations" as a reaction to the "dissolution of the Oedipal complex." On the other hand, the Hampstead Clinic reported striking examples of little girls with male analysts actually reliving their oedipus complex in child analysis. Anna Freud (1969) finds this material impressive, whatever its therapeutic value may be. The different findings are probably due either to the children being in different phases of latency (Williams, 1969) or to structural differences in the personalities of these children, some of whom may not have entered the latency period at all except for their chronological age.

The case of seven-and-a-half-year-old Susan, reported by Erna Furman (1967), provides an illustration of these considerations. Susan, chronologically a latency child, functioned on a more primitive level. She "had been fixated primarily on the level of the need-fulfilling relationship and on that of the ambivalent anal-sadistic relationship." The identifications were unintegrated. My question

[3] Resistance certainly increases at the beginning of latency due to the intensification of defensive activities (Bornstein, 1951). A good example is the case of Becky, who wanted to be "all grown up and do it herself" (McDevitt, 1967).

[4] In contrast, preoedipal material frequently is now prominent in the analysis of latency children. Is it because the patients have changed today (due to changes in the environment), or has the child analyst's interest influenced the picture? Probably it is the latter. In our work, especially with transference phenomena, we pay more attention to the preoedipal mother because the child's relationship to her provides the basis for future development. (See the case of Becky, reported by McDevitt, 1967).

is: how did this influence the technique? Certainly, the technique must have been different since Susan used interpretations as "supplies or gifts within the framework of her infantile relationship." What was clearly shown in Furman's case was "the discrepancy between the intensity of instinctual and affective forces and the relative primitivity of Susan's ego"—a factor which makes it difficult to determine whether Susan was a latency child.

Erna Furman stresses that Susan first had to attain a certain level of ego and superego development before she could actively participate in the analytic work. Only then did analysis help reinstate this child's delayed maturation.

In this respect, Selma Fraiberg's (1965) comparison between five-year-old and six-and-a-half-year-old Roger is impressive. She speaks of the "child's capacity to be an analytic patient at various stages of development," and shows the difficulties in pinpointing variations in technique required at different stages of development. The younger and the older Roger were two different patients indeed. The five-year-old Roger communicated through play, representing his conflict on an imaginary figure. Disowning his conflict, he was free from guilt. His affects were split up and not readily accessible. When Roger got close to the problem, he experienced anxiety which he expressed by an action. The use of play as communication was no secret to Roger, but at the age of five he presented his conflicts as "not real" —a factor that Fraiberg considered "to be the greatest obstacle to analysis at this stage." At six and a half the conflicts were real to Roger. Now he analyzed practically as an adult would. While Roger continued to play, he now mainly talked. Intelligence took over in finding reasons for his actions, thoughts, and feelings. The ability to introspect and to learn appeared. The monolithic "I" was divided into different parts; an awareness of internal conflict was established; and the transference reactions became easier to understand.

Is this latency at its best? Or is it Roger, his symptomatology and his analysis? Maturation certainly played a role in this change, but mostly it was the analysis itself—analysis under a "contract" that made the change so impressive. Anna Freud (1969) comments that "it is analysis which makes the developmental step possible, but it is the developmental step which explains the changed reaction." Or, to put it differently, we can say that child analysis serves as an organizer of the personality and as an accelerator of development.

Preadolescence

Our view of preadolescence has changed as much as that of latency (see Anna Freud, 1949; Harley, 1962b; Kestenberg, 1967; Blos, 1958; and Helene Deutsch, 1944). The attempt to defend oneself against genital excitement by anal or oral regression is a deterrent to development during latency, but it might also be viewed as a "regression in the service of the ego" during preadolescence. I believe that preadolescence is the least understood phase. A few years ago the question was actually raised whether such a developmental phase exists at all (see Panel, 1964b). Is it true that no new instinctual aims exist and that the heightened instinctual cathexis is of a completely undifferentiated character? It is hard to understand why just at the age of ten to twelve the quantity of instinctual energy should increase, unless this increase coincides with the advance toward sexual maturity. Prepuberty is a transition to puberty.

During latency the ego was able to cope more or less successfully with pregenital drives. Can it cope equally successfully with the steadily increasing genital strivings? If the genital drive tends to dominate, a regression to former fixation points would become understandable. When we say that in preadolescence pregenital interests come to the surface, that they are recathected, we do not mean that the child begins to soil again or to suck his thumb. The ego is strong enough to prevent a total regression, but it lacks the support of the parent's auxiliary ego. Applying Jeanne Lampl-de Groot's (1960) evaluation of the ego of adolescents to this age group, which I think one should, one would have to say that the ego is both stronger and weaker. With the genital drives increasing at a time when the auxiliary ego is weakening, the integrity of the self can be maintained by defensive regression of the drives. We certainly observe the imbalance in the ego of the preadolescent. The ego controls suffer, but, more importantly, the increase of the drives demands more defensive activities on the part of the ego. We see the regression of some ego functions, but this ego regression does not correspond to the regression in drives.

This "pregenitality," I would say, is more symbolic than real. It appears in token quantities—anality is expressed not by soiling, but by anal jokes; orality, by voraciousness; exhibitionism, by a noisy "showing off." The increased defensive activity protects the self, but at the same time it also interferes with some areas of ego functioning. So here, too, we observe a complex interaction of progressive and regressive forces. Preadolescence, I would say, is a separate developmental phase, but it is perhaps not a "second edition of infantile sexuality." Preadolescence might be just a digest of it, a short, abbreviated story written under the auspices of a different and a much more mature ego (Maenchen; see Panel, 1964b).

The task of child analysis in this developmental phase is the same as in others: to assess a child's disturbance on the basis of his psychosexual and ego-superego development and to coordinate the goals and the technique to the developmental needs of the child.

Adolescence

If the prelatency child is in the process of organization, the adolescent is in the process of reorganization, to use Kurt Eissler's term (1958). These two phases have in common the state of flux in the personality structure. Some time ago this state of flux was given as a reason against analysis, and the same reason is now given for it. So far we have encountered no stage of development in which we do not face problems of technique. In the analysis of adolescents, it is said,[5] the analyst wants to protect the patient from anxiety, and this interferes with the analytic attitude. I would counter with the question: how much "ego supporting" do we really need in the analysis of adolescents?

Kurt Eissler advises changes in technique and stresses "correct timing." This I see as a variant of our old dictum of a "right interpretation at the right time." I agree with Eissler that we "do not yet have a circumscribed technique for the treatment of adolescents," but we all seem to share his view of the analysis of adolescents, and join him in his "plea in favor of regular psychoanalysis rather than substitute measures."

[5] In this brief section I shall make no attempt to discuss the many contributions to the psychoanalytic understanding and treatment of adolescents made by Anna Freud (1936, 1958), Lampl-de Groot (1960), Blos (1962), H. Deutsch (1944, 1967), and many others.

Eissler makes one point which is particularly important. He states: "When an adolescent enters treatment with a solidified form of psychopathology, . . . psychoanalytic treatment involves no particular technical problem essentially different from its adult counterpart." In these cases the psychopathology dictates the technique. In others, however, the symptoms change from day to day or during a single session, so that "no one technique can fulfill the requirements for the treatment of adolescents" (p. 226).

The concept of flexibility of technique in the analysis of adolescents applies to the analysis of the young child as well. When Eissler says that analysis in adolescents can and should prevent the formation of a fixated reaction to conflict in the ego, I believe this should be a goal in all developmental phases in the life of a child. It is of course more dramatic during adolescence because of the ongoing reorganization.

I would like to present a few of my observations on the analysis of adolescents, using the case of John, which came to my attention. John, an eighteen-year-old, was a good patient. He illustrates the typical vulnerability, mobility of responses, fluctuations, and flexibility so characteristic of this period of reorganization. John's insight was penetrating and quick, but at times it was like quicksand, and he therefore feared it and fought against it. Some libidinization of thinking interfered with insight, and the fear of the intensity of transference acted as a deterrent to using insight. His analyst said, "I have to walk on a tightrope to get at the transference, but I persist."

As a young child, John had shown transvestite behavior. He also had a reading difficulty at the age of six to eight. Now he suffered from an obsessive cognitive confusion and concerns about his masculinity. The therapeutic alliance was based on his suffering and awareness of his illness. His treatment was characterized by a remarkable continuity of analytic material, full affect in relation to childhood material, and persistent translation of the past into the present. His rather ruthless honesty with himself was fed by aggressive drives turned against the self. John's specific resistance was related to his psychopathology: it took the form of "skimming" over analytic work as he had done (and still did) in his reading. John said, "I feel like my neurosis is fighting for its life."

What are the technical issues in this relatively simple case? This patient is on a couch and associates freely; the technique is that of adult analysis. The age-appropriate developmental problems are all present—the "removal" and detachment from the internalized and "real" parents, the hunger for new objects, loneliness, sporadic spurts of activity, and an intense preoccupation with the life and death issues of the everyday world of the adolescent. His analyst feels that any adaptation of technique to this phase might be a problem of the analyst rather than of the patient. Possibly it is the assessment of adolescence by analysts which governs the technique: concern about impulsive actions prompts the analyst to take measures to reduce anxiety, to reassure, and to strengthen the patient's controls.

John is what we would call "a good neurotic," and he is analyzable as an adolescent because he has reached the developmental level of adolescence; he is object-related, which makes transference available. His analysis proceeds methodically.

I agree with Blos (1962) that with the development of a historical sense, adolescents can be analyzed on the model of adults. But a "sense of history" can develop in a careful analysis even earlier. A twelve-year-old boy recently divided his life into "early childhood, a middle period, and then: now." He enumerated all the things which had happened to him and ended the hour by saying to his analyst: "I am okay now."[6] This "sense of history" was due, I think, to the analytic process, which recovered memories, made a reconstruction, and produced structural changes. It also speeded up the developmental process, ushering in a new step.

Technique, then, is dictated not by the symptomatology alone or the developmental stage, but by the actual and particular state of ego functioning in its connection with psychopathology. One could say that it is this causal relation between the state of ego functions and the symptomatology which dictates the technique.

6 Unpublished case reported by Joseph Afterman.

SELECTED PROBLEMS OF TECHNIQUE

Therapeutic Alliance

I now turn to a discussion of specific problems of technique, selecting those which appear in all developmental stages, though in different ways.

I shall begin with the therapeutic alliance. Although it is the starting point of every analysis, we now seem to deplore spending time in developing a positive relationship to the child at the beginning of analysis. As before, we try to establish a therapeutic alliance by promoting the child's interest in and cooperation with the analysis, but in recent years our technique in establishing a therapeutic alliance has become more direct. The interpretations of affects and defenses are used consistently from the very beginning of analytic work. We promote the therapeutic alliance by observing transference reactions, which are then used for interpretations early in the analytic process to convey insight into the conflicts within the child. The "contract" with the patient is a part of this alliance, and there also is an alliance with the parents (Geleerd, 1967).

A very young child not yet three years old was described as having formed a therapeutic alliance during the first half hour (Abbate, 1967). Was the child able to do this because of her age or because of the acute distress which her symptoms, a phobia, caused her? On the other hand, we know of cases that required "special technical measures"—a long period of preparation for analysis (three and a half years or more)—to establish a real therapeutic alliance (see Hamm, 1967). Addressing herself to this problem, Anna Freud (1969) commented that "the treatment alliance is easy to establish at any age and level so long as the child suffers from anxiety against which his defenses are unsuccessful. It is a different matter where defense keeps down anxiety and analysis threatens to set it free."

In order to maintain the therapeutic alliance we still at times "divide" the child patient into two parts, one which is resisting and the other which is seeking help with the symptoms and discomfort, which in the process of establishing the therapeutic alliance has been made ego alien to the child.

Thus I would conclude that the child's ability to form a therapeutic alliance is determined not by his age but by the structure of his symptom and the function it serves in the personality of the individual child.

Communication

Maturational and developmental processes also determine the type of communication. There is a continuum: from body language —to discharge phenomena—to nonverbal imaginative play—to verbal play—and finally to verbal communication with the analyst. The degree of structuralization directly influences the nature of the child's communication in analytic work. Whatever the child "produces," his play included, we learn from it the extent of repression, defensiveness, and transference reactions.

A case I supervised is a good illustration. Daryl, a nine-year-old boy, was developmentally in early latency at the beginning of his analysis. He easily got out of control, teasing his analyst, begging for little things, looking for body closeness. When he was frustrated in the analytic situation, he became destructive. Periodically he left for the bathroom, staying away from the office from five to ten minutes.

During one analytic session, Daryl talked about his dog being in heat, the plans to bring a male dog into the house for mating, and the number of puppies she would have. (From previous material and the parents' reports it was known that Daryl loved the dog and played with her in a sexually excited manner.) He then talked about ghost stories, informing his analyst that he was never scared and that he could not remember any really scary thing happening to him. At this point he complained of a stomachache and had to leave for the bathroom in a most urgent manner.

What was the meaning of this behavior? Was it just action, or reaction to excitement, or memory, or a transference reaction, or a simple discharge? We often try to do a "profile on the spot," usually with little success. Only a careful study of the whole case can explain the meaning of such specific actions.

I do not share the concern of those child analysts who believe that setting realistic limits to the child's destructive motor action deprives them of important analytic material. What we want is a "token" motor expression, which is more open to interpretations than the

unrestricted action which increases anxiety, gives instinctual gratification, and very often is in the service of defense and resistance.

When an aggressive boy (aged eight) approached me with an
open pocket knife, saying that he wanted to cut off my nose, it was
possible to provide a channel for the expression of his wish. I suggested to him that he imagine it instead of doing it. The boy drew a
bird with a very long beak, grabbed an eraser, and proceeded to
erase the beak. In this way no analytic material was lost. Once a student reported that a little girl patient put sand on his hair and
poured water over it. He was proud of his "permissiveness," but I
was doubtful about the unreasonableness of this situation from the
point of view of the child. It is not always easy to provide the children with channels for the expression of their destructive drives
without either distracting their attention or losing important analytic material. However, when the playroom becomes a battlefield,
we lose even more material.

The naming of instinctual urges in analysis is most helpful
when it is combined with interpretations of defenses. It establishes
intercommunication within the child and in this way serves the
progress of integration. Understanding of preverbal communication
helps reality testing and the separation of the self from the nonself.
In this context, too, naming is important (Hartmann, 1951; Anny
Katan, 1961). Geleerd (1967) emphasizes the need to verbalize the
child's feeling "right now." Interpretations of mood, anxiety, and
real happenings in the child's life promote introspection, which we
do not usually find until adolescence. Thus, I would say, we accelerate the development of this ego function.

Free association in child analysis is possible, but it occurs only
sporadically, for instance, as an association to a dream. Fraiberg
(1962) uses the "what pops into your mind" game for this, though
not before latency. I found that a child would close his eyes and tell
me what he saw. A boy of eight wrote to me with his eyes closed (a
double distancing device). These are the sporadic occurrences of
free association.

The point I wish to stress in this section is that we use everything a child says and does as "analytic material"—i.e., everything
conveys some meaning to us—but that by itself does not make it
intentional communication on the side of the child.

Dreams

We know that children in the latency period usually can analyze dreams. But is it correct to assume that a preschool child cannot do that, that he does not feel responsible for his dreams, that he considers them as coming from outside?

Anthony (1964), for instance, states that for the young child, "thoughts and things are not too well differentiated, and matters of mind, like dreams, are given concrete existence so that unpleasant dream characters find their way into the bedroom through an open window" (p. 109).

I have found that the young child's closeness to primary process thinking makes it easier to analyze the "illogical," but it also should make the analyst hesitate and induce him to ask what use the child makes of the analysis of a dream. Does he use it to gain insight into his conflict, or as a regressive game, a "free-for-all" which is silencing the ego?

There are great variations in what different children will do, not only with the analysis of dreams but also with dreams themselves. For example, I worked with a latency boy who was able to "ration" his dreams, which usually swarmed with snakes. He told me that he could control his dreams by "turning them off like a radio" whenever they became too frightening.

Play

During the past decades we have increasingly abandoned "play therapy" because it produced no more than an abreaction; no structural changes followed. In the same way, we are happily moving away from any standardization of play (such as the famous doll house cherished in the past).[7] But we still observe the child at play to obtain some knowledge of his inner world, to understand his conflicts, his behavior at home and at school, to get an impression of where he stands in terms of his development. For example, I learn a good deal from what different children will do with a set of small

---

[7] Any attempt to standardize the toys, to establish fixed patterns according to age groups introduces an element of rigidity that would deprive play of its very nature. I believe that practically anything in one's office or study can be used. A five-year-old boy played with the curtains, making the room dark and light. He was mastering his fear of the dark by doing actively what he was afraid of: being left alone by his mother at night.

animals, both domestic and wild, made of hard rubber which has survived many years of use and abuse. A child of four or five who is not ridden by anxiety will take the animals out of the box one by one, examine them carefully, paying special attention to sexual characteristics; he will name them and play with them indiscriminately. A child of eight will start the same way, but proceed to separate the good animals from the bad ones. After some thought, he will look around for blocks and will build a wall around the bad animals to protect the good ones, or to isolate the wild ones in a zoo. The different way of dealing with these toy animals corresponds, of course, to the normal development of the superego. The bad wishes, the lions and tigers, must be separated, and one has to build up defenses against them. One can add many examples: the indecision of a compulsive child will show itself plainly, or the child will betray his constant hunger for something else by taking up one toy after another and discarding them all. From the child's play we learn something about his wishes as well as his attitude to those wishes. Playing does not involve all the dangers that acting would.

While we continue to observe and learn from the child's play, there have been changes in how we use what we learn from play. In the past we probably regarded play as the child's only means of communication, tended to isolate play too sharply from his other activities, and occasionally even assumed that what we saw in the analyst's playroom was a complete picture of the child's inner life. Although some of us were always cautious in the use of symbolic interpretations, we nevertheless inclined to treat play as an equivalent of free association and analyze it as such. Now we take all these considerations into account to safeguard against arbitrary interpretations.

We still regard play as a communication—as the child's language, which during analysis slowly gives way to talking *to* the analyst and to analyzing *with* the analyst. I agree with those who maintain that direct interpretation of play can be done (and I do it), especially when the young patient understands that his playing is used as a kind of "talking" for a therapeutic purpose. If the analyst does not interfere with the pleasure of playing, the interpretations do not spoil the child's productions in play, including fantasies. Of course, the timing of interpretations is important.

I do not quite agree with Fraiberg (1965) that analysis of fictional characters[8] is useless until the patient recognizes the fears he attributes to them as his own. Fictional characters are, I believe, another "distancing device" similar to those I mentioned previously. As an analysis progresses, we certainly try to dispose of all distancing devices and make the child's conflicts "real," conscious, and accessible to the ego, which then can cope with them.

If play is the royal road to the unconscious, it nevertheless should not be a freeway. (All factors curbing the freedom of play are useful in studying the respective strengths of different forces in the playing patient.)

I have never understood why some child analysts feel that they have to represent reality in playing games according to the rules. This is the responsibility of the child's environment, but it is not the task of the analyst. When a bright boy in early latency wanted me to teach him chess, I told him the rules; but he was scornful of them. What kind of a game was it where a queen could be beaten, but the king could not? We played a new kind of chess: the king was thrown off the board with enthusiasm, but the queen remained. The boy discontinued his strange chess game when he could openly deal with his conflict.

My insistence on his sticking to the "real" rules of the game would simply have cut off this avenue of approaching his underlying conflict and strengthened his resistances.[9]

At one time child analysts themselves engaged in a good deal of role playing, partly enacting the roles assigned to them by the child and partly assuming roles deemed to be indicated by the analytic material. For instance, a child analyst would resort to "playing" the child's defenses. While we certainly could make our point, e.g., by playing out identification with the aggressor,[10] we also realized that

8 There is no sharp dividing line between dreams, daydreams, serialized stories, and play.

9 It is, of course, well known that play, like any other activity, can be used for resistance, either as a regressive form of behavior or as a defense.

10 The most striking illustration of identification with the aggressor I have observed was early in my career as child analyst, when, under the Nazis, a little Jewish boy told me his secret: at night he stood up in his bed, raised his hand, and said, "Heil Hitler!" I did not feel like playing out this defense. I wished I had unanalytic means of help.

at times this involved too much gratification for the child. As a result, we now have less recourse to all forms of role playing.

Transference

In the early years of child analytic work we believed that the child would have only transference reactions but not a transference neurosis because of his great dependence on his original objects, who continued to provide his main emotional gratifications (Anna Freud, 1927; Fraiberg, 1951). However, more recently (1965) Anna Freud pointed out that the relationship of the patient, adult or child, to his analyst, is twofold. With his normal self the patient responds to the analyst as a real person; and with his neurotic part he responds to the analyst as a transference figure. What we find in a child is a combination of transference reactions and normal new object relations.

Most of us agree that transference neurosis, whether "intermittent" or "circumscribed," is a rare occurrence, but it is not determined by the age of the child. Rather, it is connected with the totality of repression of preoedipal material (Fraiberg, 1966) or with the degree of structuralization in the child's personality, as I prefer to put it—the degree to which the child's conflicts are internalized and embedded in his personality structure (see Panel, 1966).

For some child analysts transference is the royal road to the unconscious, and the transference interpretations the main vehicle used while traveling this road. Most child analysts, myself included, disagree with this almost exclusive emphasis on transference. The lasting effect of analysis is produced by the working through of inaccessible material, by the shift from primary to secondary processes of thinking, and by changes in the psychic structure (id, ego, superego). I believe that this cannot be achieved by analysis of transference reactions alone.

Van Dam expressed concern that "the increased activity as a means of communication in the child is not unlike the acting out of adult patients and might result in less energy being available to cathect the analyst. . . . the activity of the child analyst during the session also works toward inhibiting the establishment of the transference neurosis" (see Panel, 1965a). These considerations have worried us for years. If we use, as I do, play as the language of the child, then the activity of the child should not be viewed as "acting out."[11] With respect to the activity of the analyst, this has decreased remarkably, so that the child's difficulty in developing a transference neurosis seems to be much more related to his libidinal attachment to his parents and his dependency on them.

As for myself, in the analytic chair or on the floor with a young child, I am conscious of the fact that I, like any analyst, am not *only* a transference object. To a child the analyst is also an auxiliary ego and superego figure.[12] The same or similar externalizations occur in the analysis of adults. Highly ambivalent patients not only exhibit the ordinary transference phenomena in relation to their analysts; they also externalize one half of their ambivalence onto them.

But there is a difference here between adult and child. As we know, the mature ego of the adult patient is confronted with the dangers which threatened him when he was a child. Figuratively speaking, the animal in the closet was a lion; what makes its appearance is, relatively speaking, a mouse. But with children the repressed does not belong to the distant past: the love object is not a mother image but the real mother. It is certainly much harder to give up a wish and accept the unavoidable frustration while the striving is still in full force and directed toward the original, actual, and present love object. The gratification, at least in fantasy and play in the presence of a transference figure (who is also a new object), is an important part of child analysis.

I have some reservations on the meaningful use of transference interpretation in cases where object relationships have not progressed from the need-satisfying level and where objects are easily interchangeable. But there are published cases which show that analysis was possible even in a case of extreme unevenness of development (Sprince, 1967).

---

[11] One can easily make the child analyst immobile—stay put in his chair—but nobody has yet invented a technique which would immobilize the child patient during analytic sessions.

[12] This use of the analyst has frequently been discussed, for example, by Harley (1967), whose six-year-old patient Anne could distinguish between the analyst in her real role and as a transference figure.

Countertransference

With regard to countertransference, I wish to make only a brief comment. It is, I am sure, an overworked and meaningless term if it is used to cover everything the analyst feels and does in the analytic situation, positive or negative. We should use it in the same restricted and specific sense as we define transference: i.e., we should speak of countertransference only when the analyst uses his child patient as a transference object. This definition automatically excludes the analyst's normal ego reactions, and his positive or negative feelings (for instance, pleasure in a good piece of work, or dislike of ink being spilled on his rug).

Work with Parents

Since the beginning of child analysis, we have included regular contacts with the parents, especially in the case of younger children whose ego functioning is still immature and who lack stable internalizations. However, meaningful contact with and cooperation by the parents are assets in the analysis of older children as well. This work with parents supplements our analytic work with the child, which deals with his intrapsychic conflicts. These will not be altered by attempts to change the environment.

The nature of our work with the parents differs according to the requirements of the individual case. In some instances, the mother's presence during the sessions may be necessary (see, e.g., H. Schwarz, 1950). While her presence can be instructive, it can also become an obstacle. With regard to its being instructive, I believe that the same insight into the interaction between mother and child usually can be obtained by regular interviews with the mother and from the child's analytic material.

While most of our contacts with the mother are geared to increase our knowledge of the child, we must also keep in mind the impact of our communications to the mother. For instance, when I recently read in a report on the analysis of a preschool child that "no advice to mother was given," I wondered whether this was really possible. Perhaps we should say: no advice to the mother was intended. But if we consider the whole situation, and especially also the inevitable transference reactions that appear in the mother's relationship to the analyst, we must realize that "advice" is probably taken by the mother of a young child whether we intended to give it or not.

Opinions differ about the benefit of working with parents of young children. Much has been said about "knowing too much" and "knowing too little" about the child at the start of analysis—both involving risks. I agree with Solnit (Panel, 1965a) and prefer the risk of "knowing too much," especially because I think we never learn too much from the parents, and also because, hopefully, we use what we learn with great care.

Termination

The decision when to terminate depends, of course, on the goals of psychoanalytic treatment, and these have not changed in the course of the years.[13] Child analysis still aims at freeing the energy consumed in neurosis, shifting libidinal positions from fixation points, reversing regressive trends—in short, removing obstacles in the path of normal development.

In this respect, the child analyst can count on a favorable factor that is absent in the analysis of adults, namely, the new energies made available by the child's progressive development. The difficulty in actual practice resides in the evaluation of the degree to which this progressive development can be depended on, an evaluation that directly influences the decision to terminate. Accordingly, we see two trends: (1) to prolong analysis in order to secure the structural changes that have been achieved and to prevent the recurrence of symptoms; and (2) not to prolong analysis: to stop once the obstacles on the path of normal development have been removed. Further analysis, it is believed, might "drain" the ego of the energies needed for mastery (outside of analysis), especially during latency. In this area developmental considerations are of great importance. The analysis of young children is relatively short, and the analyst is rarely in doubt when to terminate it. We seem to be less sure about the structural changes in the analysis of latency and older children.

The topic of termination is a very complex topic, and in this paper I cannot do justice to it. However, I wish to mention one

---

13 The treatment goals of other short-term techniques, even though they may be based on analytic thinking, differ in this respect—a difference that has recently been studied by Heinicke et al. (1965).

point. It seems to me that we have not sufficiently exploited some
sources of information available to us. After we terminate a case,
the door to the analyst's office remains relatively open for "re-entry"
into analysis for children of all ages. If we systematically collected
data on the resumption of analysis of children in different stages of
development, we would be in a much better position to evaluate our
results. The second source would be the pooling of material obtained
in the analysis of an adult who was known to have been treated as
a child (see Ritvo, 1966). While I am aware of the difficulties involved in this procedure, it is an important source of information
that has become available only in recent years as our early child patients have grown to be adults.

DEPARTURES FROM THE STANDARD TECHNIQUE

My discussion so far has dealt with problems encountered in child
analysis when we use the standard technique. But there are cases in
which this technique is not applicable. Before discussing these cases
in detail, I wish to make a few general remarks on modifications of
psychoanalytic technique.

Parameters and Adaptations

We all know that the analysis of a preschool child requires many
"parameters" which often cloud the issue of the proper analytic
technique. During latency we are on much firmer analytic ground. Frequently we lose this safe position again in the analysis of adolescents.

One of the "parameters" is connected with gratifications. The
analytic situation offers gratifications which are not planned, and
their evaluation is not easy; they are inevitably included, I think,
in the "menu" offered. Certainly, gratification of impulses occurs
in the freedom to express them in fantasy and play. This has a
therapeutic value since, as I mentioned previously, it makes it easier
for the child to give up a wish and to accept unavoidable frustrations.
Child analysis provides a controlled situation for play and fantasy,
and makes use of it.

Geleerd (1958, 1967) found that in the treatment of psychotic
and borderline cases some sort of gratification was given "before the
analysis could proceed." I would assume that some sort of gratifica-

tion is given, or taken, by every patient, child or adult, whether we consciously give it or not.

But should we talk of parameters in child analysis at all? In a Panel (1965a) Rangell pointed out that an "adaption of technique" in child analysis is not necessarily the same thing as a parameter in adult analysis. In the same Panel Marianne Kris proposed that we consider "development as a continuum and call the modifications of technique which this requires adaptations, reserving the term 'parameter' for those definite modifications that are brought about by extraneous circumstances rather than by development." Neubauer also cautioned against applying the term parameter to "a modification of technique which applies to the total treatment of the child."

Philip Spielman[14] feels that "parameter" should be used to designate deviations in technique necessitated by the patient's psychopathology (ego strength, nature of anxiety, extent of regression), and "adaptations" should be reserved for modifications in the approach appropriate to different developmental levels (with no pathology implied) and to technical shifts in relation to new developmental phases in the same patient. He also suggests that both terms be distinguished from "errors in technique" which are based on the analyst's incorrect assessment of the child and his needs.

In general I agree with these statements—except that the issues of ego capacity, nature of anxiety, and extent of regression are not always easily assessed, particularly in cases in which there was no orderly progression of developmental phases. And these problems also occur in cases of severe neuroses where child analysis without parameters could presumably be applied.

We strive for a definite model of technique of child analysis, and it seems that we try to get it as close to the model of adult analysis as we possibly can. I wonder why. Are we reflecting the child's wish to be an adult this very minute? The child is not a miniature adult; nor, for that matter, as has often been pointed out, is the model of adult analysis that sharply defined.[15]

14 Personal communication.

15 I have previously mentioned that child analysts feel the need to explain any technical measures which differ from the standard psychoanalytic method (the use of the couch and free association) in spite of the realization that communications coming from the couch are not always free associations and that the reduction of motility induced by the use of the couch does not by itself produce them. Mrs. Isabel

I would summarize this by saying that child analysis has grown up and is developing its own model, that it is moving toward a technique which fits the immature ego and which responds to the developmental needs of the child patient.

Cases Which Do Not Fit

I have mentioned that there are cases in which the standard technique is not applicable. These are the patients with early ego defects which interfere with their adaptation to reality and with the development of the synthetic function. They are usually referred to as borderline or psychotic children.

The literature on the analytic therapy of borderline and psychotic children is far too voluminous to be dealt with in this paper. I mention only the important contributions by Mahler (1968), the work carried out at the Hampstead Clinic (Kut and Sprince, 1963, 1965; Singer, 1960; Thomas et al., 1966), and that of Ekstein (1966) and Frijling-Schreuder (1969). I shall confine my discussion to some specific points suggested by the literature.

Our difficulty in the technique with patients in these groups stems from the difficulty in the precise assessment of their pathology. In this respect the distinction between regression, fixation, and lack of developmental progression is very important, as is the assessment of the degree to which different functions have been firmly established in their personality structure.

We know now that the lack of stimulation early in life interferes with the development of the cognitive function. Can we analyze a child whose mental functioning is severely retarded? To my mind, lack of object constancy also makes analysis hardly possible because it interferes with the use of transference. We miss in the personalities of these patients the fusion of libido and aggression in relation to a love object, and we miss the capacity for real sublimation. We

---

Harris Paret, a child therapist, felt that the wish for the adult model might be powered by the wish of child analysts to gain more acceptance for child analysis in general and for child analysts in particular (especially for those who work with children only). I would think that this very old problem also has some old cultural implications; for instance, "the child is small and the fee should be smaller"; or "the child will grow out of it," meaning that symptoms are not that serious. This general "looking down" on a small child is reflected in the prevalent attitudes to child analysis. But all this is diminishing and may already be a thing of the past.

can undo regression with our analytic technique, but I doubt whether we can undo the early defects in development where some important ingredients were lacking, with the result that such underdeveloped children have an underdeveloped ego that cannot master life (Maenchen, 1968a, 1968b). In these cases, the anxiety we observe is generally not castration anxiety, but is an archaic annihilation anxiety and an ego disintegration anxiety.

In borderline patients the insufficient defense structure frequently breaks down during prepuberty and adolescence. The adolescent tasks are insurmountable for the patient whose equipment is faulty. The major problem of borderline adolescents seems to me to be the problem of loosening the parental object tie, tenuous at best, which is much too threatening because they have achieved only a partial distinction between object and self representations. My question is: how partial is such a partial achievement? So far, our answer is inexact indeed. Unfortunately, our evaluation of personality structure is based on the answer to this question.

If the borderline patient can achieve object constancy through therapy, he will accomplish the task of adolescence better; one has to have or to regain infantile objects to give them up and to find new ones. Some analysts suggest that this task is achieved by incorporating the therapist as an object, and thus modifying the original part objects. The analytic work, they say, is primarily the careful analysis of the transference neurosis. Yet I wonder whether the patient can, at this stage (as an adolescent or even as an adult), pick up trends at the point where failure occurred and, in accelerated development, "catch up" with the evolution of normal personality. The "controlled regression" during therapy seems to be a necessary step in the therapy. The difficulty, in each case, is to ascertain what made the patient regress and from what position. It is also difficult to separate transference manifestations from the other uses of the therapist, as mentioned before. (I have dealt with the subject elsewhere [1968a, 1968b].)

Anna Freud (1965) says "that there are primary deficiencies of an organic nature or early deprivations which distort development and structuralization and produce retarded, defective, and nontypical personalities" (p. 147). I would say that for this category, as well as for the overtly psychotic children, our usual technique does not apply. Whatever the origin of these disturbances, significant modifications of technique are necessary.

A very promising approach is the "tripartite therapeutic design" outlined by Margaret Mahler (1968). Grounded in precise clinical observations and based on psychoanalytic knowledge of child development and its deviations, especially during the separation-individuation phase, this technique aims at giving psychotic children a "corrective symbiotic experience" on the assumption that individuation and independent functioning cannot be achieved without a previous satisfactory "symbiotic" experience.

Borderline children show a wide variety of impulses, which are diffused and not attached to any one stage of psychosexual development. Prolonged analytic therapy sometimes helps the child to catch up on certain developmental sequences. Here the therapy functions as "an organizer" of the personality.

Instead of perfecting our technique in cases in which child analysis is known to be indicated, we seem to be eager to apply it to cases which might not be suited for it. We want to understand these cases, of course, but I, for one, feel uncomfortable when, enthusiastic about a good learning situation in an unusual case, I experiment in technique and am often left in the dark as to exactly what produced the change in the patient, even when the change is for the better.

There is, of course, a very positive side: since child analysis has branched out to include the analysis of borderline and psychotic children, we have become much more aware of oral fixations in the cases of neuroses, and we now study much more carefully the manifestations of the child's early relationships in transference. We have also learned that many neurotic disturbances are superimposed on an ego disturbed early in life (see, e.g., the case of Johnny, reported by Holder, 1968).

In general, I would question the borderline patient's ability to develop a usable transference. I would also wonder about his ability to neutralize energy, though we do not know how much neutralized energy we need for analysis, nor could we measure the quantity needed. This is also true for secondary process thinking. In the continuum between primary and secondary processes the "proper" analysis needs the secondary process thinking (except, of course, in fantasy and play); it needs affect and action in the general functioning of the child analytic patient.

When we analyze a borderline child, his chronological age is relatively unimportant; we are dealing with an arrest of ego development. The bizarre behavior is a product of the uneven development of different ego functions, from highly developed to extremely primitive. Applying our usual technique, we probably get closer to child analysis when the degree of infantilization, or at least some of the ego functions, could be compared with that in childhood neurosis; however, we are confronted not only with a quantitative difference, but also a qualitative one. Our specific technique geared to each developmental stage becomes a shambles when we deal with psychopathology that blocks the development of personality structure. The borderline child is only one example of this.

A different type of example is the case of Christine, an eleven-year-old child who sat motionless in my study. She neither talked nor played. She was cold, negativistic, aloof, and disdainful. She watched me from the corners of her eyes, listened intently to what I said, and she answered direct questions quickly, precisely, laconically. Her beautiful eyes sent flashes of anger and sometimes despair; her pale face was framed by bushy hair, her tall body was a near-skeleton in tasteful clothes. She looked like her own portrait. At the start of analysis, she weighed 76 pounds. She obviously suffered from anorexia nervosa.

Christine had fallen ill a year earlier, apparently after the onset of menstruation (at the age of ten), which subsided soon and did not recur. Changes in her personality followed in quick succession; first to appear was a "Keep Out" sign on her bedroom door; then came withdrawal from all social activities except school, loss of weight, isolation, and lack of communication. At home she moved like a ghost. One year previously she had drawn sensitive pictures and written poems and beautiful stories on being "A Stranger to Himself" and on "The Path of Life." Now she disclaimed interest and even ownership of her profound thoughts. The writing was something she "had to do for school."

After three months of analysis with this silent child, I ran out of interpretations and Christine started to eat again. While still keeping to her rigid diet at mealtimes, this compulsively clean and orderly child began to stuff herself between meals or at night, eating messily with her hands like a toddler. After five months her weight rose to 102 pounds and she grew half an inch.

Christine came from a stable family of professional people. Early in life she had responded to their concept of duty and to the very strict rules by becoming a well-behaved and overly controlled child. The lack of any tolerance for instinctual wishes had fostered strong defenses and severe inhibitions of drives. In her parents' eyes, Christine was an "ideal" child, and they sought help only when her life was endangered.

During the endless hours with this stubbornly silent child, I nevertheless felt that Christine and I were in touch with each other; I learned to understand her subtle body language and translated it to her. From the variety of body language she presented, I select the following example. The left wrist said: "I don't know"; a slight shrug of the right shoulder meant, "I don't care"; an almost imperceptible nod was, of course, a "yes." The laconic verbal responses to my questions came in three different voices: a low short explosion, like a bark, expressed anger; a medium voice was used for everyday things; and then there was also a "little girl's voice" which conveyed affect from the past. If I telescope all her responses, it seemed to me she was saying that her parents were wrong, that they had exaggerated what they told me, that they were away or were not there, and that nobody talked in this family. In general, Christine felt abused and maltreated.

I am presenting the vignette of Christine's case to illustrate my view that psychopathology plays havoc with our wish to formulate neatly a technique of child analysis in precise relation to developmental phases. In addition, this case also illustrates the point mentioned previously on the "rate of change"; the symptom of self-starvation disappeared after three months of analysis, without structural changes in the patient's personality having taken place.

Christine's total resistance in analysis resembled that of uncommunicative preadolescents who are forced into analysis by their parents. But is this the whole story? Here we have an eleven-year-old child, a preadolescent, suffering from an "adult" symptom that is usually found in late adolescents or young adults, who is regressed to pregenitality in most important aspects of her personality. To which developmental phase should the technique be geared in this case? Because of her near-genius intelligence, I found myself talking to her as I would to an adult and I know that I did get across to her; but whenever I felt that I had really reached her, the affect and the voice of a very young child responded to me. Where was the eleven-year-old girl?

Anorexia nervosa is always a puzzle. I am aware that the case of Christine could be described as a "pseudoneurotic schizophrenia." In this presentation I have had to omit much material dealing with Christine's regression to an early libidinal attachment to her mother; her extreme ambivalence; her paralyzing fears of losing control and of intrusion; her denial of feelings, action, and pleasure; her severe inhibition of motility; and her oral sadism. Nor have I described her pathological defenses (overcontrolled behavior and catatoniclike rigidity) against fantasies of oral conception and pregnancy, and her rather old-fashioned and developmentally premature adolescent asceticism. This child was "frozen" with no past and no future, stuck at crossroads (in love and hate, and in rebellion and submission), and exhibited a speech pattern that could be compared to stuttering. Even the normal developmental wish to grow was paralyzed for a year. At the same time there was no real object loss, I think, and there certainly was cognitive appreciation of and adaptation to the environment (angry compliance). In this case we are confronted not with an arrest in personality development early in life but with a severe regression.

As to the technique used in the case of Christine, the typical analytic situation was completely reversed: the patient was silent, whereas the analyst was talkative (offering interpretations by means of "thinking aloud"); and the parents reassured the analyst: "Don't be discouraged, we are not."[16]

CONCLUSIONS

From the very start of child analysis, Anna Freud stressed the developmental point of view as a criterion for the seriousness of a

---

[16] Christine is now twelve and a half years old, weighs 105-110 pounds, and looks a picture of health. Her menses returned; they are regular and she experiences no discomfort. She improved in many ways (she even goes to parties with boys and girls), but she is still silent in analysis and her rigid posture in my study is unchanged.

disturbance and as an indication or contraindication for the use of child analytic technique. The level of development is still our central focus.

While our views of the overriding importance of developmental considerations have been refined but not changed, our views concerning the source of pathology have undergone several changes. In the beginning we attributed it to the environment (first, to seductions; later, to the "rejecting" mother, etc.). We then viewed psychopathology as stemming from the internal psychic constellation. Now we realize that at the time when, from the child's point of view, the "external" is not differentiated from the "internal," the external element can certainly interfere with the internal one; where the mother, for instance, has a problem of "merging" with her child, the separation of the child does not occur. The same is true with regard to "seduction by parents." After Freud had attributed traumatic etiological significance to such events, he found that the most important element was the child's fantasy. Yet now we again ask: what about the impact of the actual seduction?

The current emphasis on ego development seems to relegate instinctual drives to second place (possibly repeating once again the resistance to the theory of instincts), and my emphasis on the ego structure may create the impression of repeating past mistakes. However, we focus on the ego as the area in which we can best observe the interrelations and mutual influences of the instinctual and ego (and superego) development under the impact of the evolving object relations, which in turn have a reciprocal influence on each other. No meaningful study is possible when one variable is singled out and unduly stressed.

It has been said (Loewenstein, 1958) that psychoanalytic technique makes sense only in reference to ego structure and can rarely be derived from symptomatology. I am stressing throughout this paper that symptomatology based on a certain ego structure does influence technique. In child analysis we can usually see the relationship between the syndrome and what the child can use from the help we offer.

However, the symptomatology must be evaluated in the broader context of overall functioning. The central issue in differential diagnosis seems to be, in addition to the structure of the ego, the *type* of anxiety, the *type* of object cathexis, and the *type* of conflict, all of which obviously are interrelated. They all point to specific structural relationships and these, I think, dictate the type of therapy and the technique. When anxiety is not mastered and nicely organized in a neurotic symptom, our technique is not nicely organized either. One could say that actually only symptoms based on intrapsychic conflicts can be analyzed.

Recently I studied three of my cases, following them up after many years. At first glance the symptoms in the three cases were similar—anxiety, restlessness, learning and other disorders—but there were very important differences in the nature of the anxiety and the early ego development. One was an autistic, another a borderline and the third a neurotic patient.

In the autistic child there was no signal anxiety. The undifferentiated anxiety resulted in withdrawal and isolation. This was a case of arrest in ego development during the anal stage with an earlier disturbance in object relations. A constitutional element was found in this case (Maenchen, 1953).

In the borderline case the anxiety was mostly "ego disintegration" anxiety. No specific arrest occurred, the ego remained undeveloped due to twinning in a very specific environment. A constitutional handicap and brain damage could not be excluded (Maenchen, 1968a).

In the neurotic child the anxiety was castration anxiety; the impairment of certain ego functions was due to a severe infantile neurosis manifesting itself in symptoms of inhibition. The enormous amount of defensive work had impoverished the ego energies. No constitutional elements were found in this case (Maenchen, 1936).

The technique of therapy varied enormously in these three cases. It was only in the last-mentioned case, that of a childhood neurosis, that classical analysis was successfully applied. This is the area where we are on sure, familiar ground.

Possibly we ask too much of child analysis, expecting it to overcome environmental disasters and early ego defects. Do we subscribe to an age-old hope, referred to before, that the child will outgrow everything, especially with the help of analysis? I think we all agree that there are unanalyzable children, as there are unanalyzable adults.

We thus continue to search for special techniques best suited to each step of normal development, and we would like to have the same for the abnormal which, as I said before, plays havoc with the age-adequate personality structure, the psychopathology (deviation from the norm) blurring the picture. It seems that we are striving toward a "phase-bound" technique of child analysis which should fit not only the familiar, well-studied patterns, but also the unusual sequences of development.

Until we have succeeded in developing such a "phase-bound" technique, regardless of chronological age and normally expected developmental sequences, it seems advisable to gear the technique of child analysis to the functioning of the ego as we find it. Stated simply, I would say that we analyze the child on whatever level we find him: on whatever level the fixation left him or the regression pulled him back to. The requirements of that, I would think, should determine the technique.

BIBLIOGRAPHY

Abbate, G. McLean (1967), Notes on the First Year of the Analysis of a Young Child with Minimum Participation by the Mother. In: *The Child Analyst at Work,* ed. E. R. Geleerd. New York: International Universities Press, pp. 14-23.

Anthony, E. J. (1964), Communicating Therapeutically with the Child. *J. Amer. Acad. Child Psychiat.,* 3:106-125.

Blos, P. (1958), Preadolescent Organization. *J. Amer. Psa. Assn.,* 6:47-56.

—— (1962), *On Adolescence.* New York: Free Press.

Bornstein, B. (1951), On Latency. *This Annual,* 6:279-285.

Deutsch, H. (1944), *The Psychology of Women.* New York: Grüne & Stratton.

—— (1967), *Selected Problems of Adolescence.* New York: International Universities Press.

Eissler, K. R. (1953), The Effect of the Structure of the Ego on Psychoanalytic Technique. *J. Amer. Psa. Assn.,* 1:104-141.

—— (1958), Notes on Problems of Technique in the Psychoanalytic Treatment of Adolescents. *This Annual,* 13:223-254.

Ekstein, R. (1966), *Children of Time and Space, of Action and Impulse.* New York: Appleton-Century-Crofts.

—— (1968), Impulse—Acting Out—Purpose. *Int. J. Psa.,* 49:347-351.

Fraiberg, S. (1951), Clinical Notes on the Nature of Transference in Child Analysis. *This Annual,* 6:286-306.

—— (1962), Technical Aspects of the Analysis of a Child with a Severe Behavior Disorder. *J. Amer. Psa. Assn.,* 10:338-367.

—— (1965), A Comparison of the Analytic Method in Two Stages of a Child Analysis. *J. Amer. Acad. Child Psychiat.,* 4:387-400.

—— (1966), Further Considerations of the Role of Transference in Latency. *This Annual*, 21:213-236.

Freud, A. (1927), *The Psycho-Analytical Treatment of Children*. New York: International Universities Press, 1959.

—— (1936), The Ego and the Mechanisms of Defense. *The Writings of Anna Freud*, 2. New York: International Universities Press, 1966.

—— (1949), On Certain Difficulties in the Preadolescent's Relation to His Parents. *The Writings of Anna Freud*, 4:95-106. New York: International Universities Press, 1968.

—— (1956), The Assessment of Borderline Cases. *The Writings of Anna Freud*, 5:301-314. New York: International Universities Press, 1969.

—— (1958), Adolescence. *The Writings of Anna Freud*, 5:136-166. New York: International Universities Press, 1969.

—— (1959), Discussion remarks, Berkeley, Calif.

—— (1965), *Normality and Pathology in Childhood*. New York: International Universities Press.

—— (1968), Indications and Contraindications for Child Analysis. *This Annual*, 23: 37-46.

—— (1969), Comments on an earlier version of this paper (personal communication).

Frijling-Schreuder, E. C. M. (1969), Borderline States in Children. *This Annual*, 24:307-327.

Furman, E. (1967), The Latency Child as an Active Participant in the Analytic Work. In: *The Child Analyst at Work*, ed. E. R. Geleerd. New York: International Universities Press, pp. 142-184.

Furman, R. A. (1967), A Technical Problem: The Child Who Has Difficulty in Controlling His Behavior in Analytic Sessions. In: *The Child Analyst at Work*, ed. E. R. Geleerd. New York: International Universities Press, pp. 59-84.

Geleerd, E. R. (1958), Borderline States in Childhood and Adolescence. *This Annual*, 13:279-295.

—— (1967), Introduction. *The Child Analyst at Work*. New York: International Universities Press, pp. 1-13.

Hamm, M. (1967), Some Aspects of a Difficult Therapeutic (Working) Alliance. In: *The Child Analyst at Work*, ed. E. R. Geleerd. New York: International Universities Press, pp. 185-205.

Harley, M. (1962a), The Role of the Dream in the Analysis of a Latency Child. *J. Amer. Psa. Assn.*, 10:271-288.

—— (1962b), Some Reflections on the Identity Problems in Prepuberty. Read at the Cleveland Psychoanalytic Society.

—— (1967), Transference Developments in a Five-Year-Old Child. In: *The Child Analyst at Work*, ed. E. R. Geleerd. New York: International Universities Press, pp. 115-141.

Hartmann, H. (1951), Technical Implications of Ego Psychology. *Essays on Ego Psychology*. New York: International Universities Press, 1964, pp. 142-154.

Heinicke, C. M. et al. (1965), Frequency of Psychotherapeutic Session as a Factor Affecting the Child's Developmental Status. *This Annual*, 20:42-98.

Holder, A. (1968), Theoretical and Clinical Notes on the Interaction of Some Relevant Variables in the Production of Neurotic Disturbances. *This Annual*, 23:63-85.

Katan, A. (1961), Some Thoughts about the Role of Verbalization in Early Childhood. *This Annual*, 16:184-188.

Kestenberg, J. S. (1967), Phases of Adolescence: Parts I & II. *J. Amer. Acad. Child Psychiat.*, 6:426-463, 577-614.

—— (1969), Problems of Technique of Child Analysis in Relation to the Various Developmental Stages: Prelatency. *This Annual*, 24:358-383.

Kut [Rosenfeld], S. & Sprince, M. P. (1963), An Attempt to Formulate the Meaning of the Concept "Borderline." *This Annual*, 18:603-635.

—— —— (1965), Some Thoughts on the Technical Handling of Borderline Children. *This Annual*, 20:495-517.

Lampl-de Groot, J. (1960), On Adolescence. *This Annual*, 15:95-103.

—— (1969), Reflections on the Development of Psycho-Analysis. *Int. J. Psa.*, 50:567-572.

Loewenstein, R. M. (1958), Remarks on Some Variations in Psycho-Analytic Technique. *Int. J. Psa.*, 39:202-210.

McDevitt, J. B. (1967), A Separation Problem in a Three-Year-Old. In: *The Child Analyst at Work*, ed. E. R. Geleerd. New York: International Universities Press, pp. 24-58.

Maenchen, A. (1936), Denkhemmung und Aggression aus Kastrationsangst. *Z. psa. Päd.*, 10:276-299.

—— (1953), Notes on Early Ego Disturbances. *This Annual*, 8:262-270.

—— (1968a), Object Cathexis in a Borderline Twin. *This Annual*, 23:438-456.

—— (1968b), Comments on Dr Ekstein's Paper [1968]. *Int. J. Psa.*, 351-352.

Mahler, M. S. (1963), Thoughts about Development and Individuation. *This Annual*, 18:307-324.

—— (1968), *On Human Symbiosis and the Vicissitudes of Individuation*. New York: International Universities Press.

Panel (1964a), Child Analysis at Different Developmental Stages, rep. G. M. Abbate. *J. Amer. Psa. Assn.*, 12:135-150.

—— (1964b), Prepuberty and Child Analysis, rep. E. Galenson. *J. Amer. Psa. Assn.*, 12:600-609.

—— (1965a), The Relationship between Child Analysis and the Theory and Practice of Adult Psychoanalysis, rep. G. Casuso. *J. Amer. Psa. Assn.*, 13:159-171.

—— (1965b), Latency, rep. T. Becker. *J. Amer. Psa. Assn.*, 13:584-590.

—— (1966), Problems of Transference in Child Analysis, rep. H. Van Dam. *J. Amer. Psa. Assn.*, 14:528-537.

Ritvo, S. (1966), Correlation of a Childhood and Adult Neurosis. *Int. J. Psa.*, 47:130-142.

Schwarz, H. (1950), The Mother in the Consulting Room. *This Annual*, 5:343-357.

Singer, M. B. (1960), Fantasies of a Borderline Patient. *This Annual*, 15:310-356.

Sprince, M. P. (1967), The Psychoanalytic Handling of Pseudo Stupidity and Grossly Abnormal Behavior in a Highly Intelligent Boy. In: *The Child Analyst at Work*, ed. E. R. Geleerd. New York: International Universities Press, pp. 85-114.

Thomas, R. et al. (1966), Comments on Some Aspects of Self and Object Representation in a Group of Psychotic Children. *This Annual*, 21:527-580.

Williams, M. (1969), Latency. Presented at the Fourth Annual Meeting of the American Association for Child Psychoanalysis, New Haven, Conn.

CONTRIBUTIONS OF A GHETTO CULTURE TO SYMPTOM FORMATION

Psychoanalytic Studies of Ego Anomalies in Childhood

DALE R. MEERS (Washington)

Behavior that is "deviant" from conventional expectations is often understood as psychologically "symptomatic." Yet more is asserted than has been scientifically demonstrated with regard to either "normality" or "pathology" (A. Freud, 1965). Cultural norms reflect their ethnocentric origins. In matters psychological, where diagnosis of presenting symptoms depends heavily on behavioral evidence of mental balance or structure, the distinction between cultural and psychological specifications of pathology is blurred. Yet such distinctions are essential to differential assessment of psychopathology in ghetto-reared children (Chess, 1969). Irrespective of the conceptual frame of reference, however, some childhood adaptations can and should be judged as both culturally and psychologically symptomatic, e.g., when psychological adaptation impairs the child's capacity to learn or utilize educational options that are a key to later intellectual, emotional, and social maturity.

Ghetto children suffer socially and psychologically, individually and collectively, from forms of "retardation" which contribute to their 40 percent high school dropout rate (Passow, 1967; Coleman

A condensed version of this paper was presented at the 46th Annual Meeting of the American Orthopsychiatric Association, New York, March 31, 1969.

The author is co-principal investigator, with Reginald S. Lourie, M.D., of the research project discussed here: "Culturally Determined Retardation: Clinical Explorations of Variability and Etiology." Acknowledgments and thanks are due to the Eugene and Agnes E. Meyer Foundation for direct support of this research and to both the Edgar Stern Family Fund and the National Institute of Mental Health, grant #01421, for support of a separate project, "Prevention of Culturally Determined Retardation," from which the present research evolved. The administrative and professional sponsorship of the project is provided by the Children's Hospital of Washington, D.C., and the Baltimore-District of Columbia Institute for Psychoanalysis.

et al., 1966). While educational disadvantages, derivative of ethnic bias (Coleman, 1966), contribute to the problem of intellectual retardation, the very blatancy of the social-political problem obscures an adequate conceptualization of the effect on the child, the nature of the retardation, the reversibility of the dysfunction, etc. It is clear that the majority of professional educators considers the solutions to be basically educational, and this may prove true of the larger percentage of academically retarded children.

We have been stunned by the ghetto child's exposure to physical and emotional trauma, and impressed by his apparent resilience, his adaptation without readily observable, external evidence of neurotic symptomatology. The relationship of trauma to ego stress and compensatory defense organization, commonly observed in analytic practice and explicit in psychoanalytic theory, would appear, on superficial examination, to be disconfirmed by the *non*appearance of symptoms. The ghetto child only rarely evidences the symptomatic behavior conventionally seen in a "middle-class" clinical practice. It is perplexing that clinicians have not conceived of intellectual or academic retardation as a possible "symptom choice" that might be specific to the cultural milieu of the modern ghetto. Such adaptations are hardly unknown in the clinical literature. Fenichel (1945), for example, catalogues an impressive group of analytic authors who have discussed the clinical phenomena of pseudodefect, pseudoimbecility, or pseudodebility (see Bornstein, 1930; Federn, 1930; Jacobson, 1932; Klein, 1931; Mahler, 1942; Schmideberg, 1930, 1938). Indeed, it would be the rare clinician or psychometrician who has not seen children in whom dysfunction of intellect interplays with psychopathology.

As a preliminary effort in assessing the prevalence and characteristics of intellectual dysfunction, we initiated an observational study in 1965. As a consultant from the Department of Psychiatry, I was an observer for about three years in a particular ghetto school, one that seems roughly representative of inner-city schools in general. The teachers, of whom we were particularly appreciative, proved more than perceptive of the symptomatic nature of early childhood problems, particularly those of depressed despondency, of withdrawal and apathy. Both teachers and parents evidenced a surprising readiness to understand dysfunction in terms of illness, rather than obstinance, and to discuss and refer children for treatment *if and where treatment was actually available.* In this context, one may conjecture that Hollingshead and Redlich's (1958) findings (that lower class populations do not perceive deviant behavior as mental illness) may reflect the ghetto parent's defensive rationalization or denial; that is to say, families are unprepared to acknowledge the reality of mental illness in the absence of therapeutic help.

PRELIMINARY OBSERVATIONS: CONTEXT

Our school is located in an area whose residents are preponderantly Negro,[1] with islands of high-rent, high-rise, integrated apartments. White workers and professionals commute daily through and into the area. There is a disproportionately high percentage of rooming houses, liquor stores, bars, and transient males. Income, occupational and educational levels of resident adults are consistent with the vague concept of "ghetto." The ghetto, it should be emphasized, is not simply "physical" and it is demonstrably not homogeneous. The census tracts in which our patients live contain small percentages of adults with declared annual incomes in excess of $15,000 and education into the college years (U.S. Bureau of the Census, 1962). Many live within the ghetto's shadows without sharing its misery or its cultural institutions. The ghetto residents, as discussed here, however, are those physically present; moreover, they are convinced that they are both trapped and sustained by it (Liebow, 1967; Meers, 1969). U.S. Census tract data (1962) document that some 30 percent of the children of the area live in one-parent homes. City-wide data indicate that 30 percent of Negro births are out-of-wedlock (Washington, D.C., 1964), and we suspect that some 60 percent of all families in the area have at least one or more children lacking legitimation. Depending on the index used, this area has either the first or second highest crime rate in the city; the police district's[2] report on this area in 1969 is illustrative: rape: 23; homicide: 29; assault: 465; robbery: 1,354; grand larceny: 1,691; and burglary: 2,269 (Metropolitan Police Department, 1969).

---

[1] Defined here as a social-psychological attribute, presently used interchangeably with the term "black."
[2] One of fourteen police districts of the city.

Other researchers have begun the documentation of the range of physiological and psychological vulnerabilities of ghetto life, e.g., Ainsworth (1962), Blodgett (1963), Lourie (1940), Pasamanick (1946), etc. Prematurity rates and related congenital deficits are perhaps surpassed by the problems of postnatal care where nutritional difficulties are as common as disease or injury. Marital instability is endemic and has bearing on both under- and overstimulation of children of all ages. Multiple pregnancies, maternal ill-health, desertions, placements with relatives, absence of the mother for work purposes, are all common. Overworked, fatigued mothers can be, and often are, grossly out of touch with their children, and "maternal deprivation" occurs in the physical presence of exhausted, depressed mothers (Chess, 1969; Winnicott, 1960). Layman (1970) has reported on the Rorschachs of Negro children with pica and mothers of two other (Washington, D.C.) Negro control groups; she notes a striking similarity of *all* three groups in their impoverished protocols, their vagueness in verbalization, and their considerable expression of inadequacy and inferiority. Some 36 percent of the women gave "sexual responses of a type which in a middle-class white population we would expect to find only in schizophrenics or in patients who are in analysis."

Rather than immoral, however, the older mothers with multiple illegitimate pregnancies appear, in our experience, to be religiously fundamentalist, devout, and driven by their guilt and anxiety. Naomi, our first patient, was the twelfth of her mother's pregnancies; there are seven surviving children born to two, possibly three fathers. This mother's responsibilities define her as unmarriageable and she shuns the idea of being tied to another man. She divorced her first husband while he was serving seven years of a thirty-year sentence for murder. Her second husband was a sadistic alcoholic who episodically shamed and severely beat the mother. Her first psychotic episode was understood as a religious salvation, with total, though temporary, amnesia lasting eleven days when Naomi's mother had determined to kill her spouse. Physically powerful and religiously devout, this mother prays nightly on her knees with her children. Her embarrassment and shame over her own sexual needs are seen only obliquely in embarrassed and occasional confirmation of her daughter's voyeuristic reports (to her therapist).

Virgil, our second patient, has a mother who is considerably younger. Now twenty-six years of age, she has a psychiatric history of three suicidal attempts, from age sixteen onward, and one recent episode in which she was almost killed after taking an overdose of narcotics. She comes from a fundamentalist, religious background and suffers apparent paroxysms of guilt, which are not easily discerned in court where she has appeared for four convictions of prostitution (which supports her drug use). We suspect that the instinctualization of maternal attitudes is not unrelated to the ghetto's incidence of physical assault, shootings, knifings, murders, of breaking and entry, of drunkenness, and rape including that of small children. The potential for instinctual trauma in daily life is tragic and approximates the middle-class neurotic's worst fears (Blau and Hulse, 1956).

Our school lies in the heart of this ghetto. It is *de facto* segregated, 100 percent nonwhite, and varies in enrollment up to 700 children. It is *not* the city's worst school in either physical terms or academic standards. Only 60.7 percent of the fourth graders and 87.5 percent[3] of the sixth graders failed to meet national norms. Our most learned informant estimated that with the presenting problems of both the children and the school some 25 percent of the children remain relatively uneducable; there are a few children graduated who cannot readily read or write. Such impressionistic findings are consonant with the Passow (1967) report's hard data that 40 percent of D.C. Negro children fail to complete high school.

The first grade of school was selected for initial observation since this is an age where the school, presumably, could not yet have impinged on the functional styles or levels of performance, and where we might have a clear view of familial (cultural) determinants of the children's ego functioning. Forty percent of the first grade, of about 125 children, had been designated as unable to use a normal curriculum, and these 60 children had been divided into two remedial classes, one of which became the primary focus of study. Consultation evolved in a pattern affording variability in time of day and day of week, with options for lunch meetings with teachers to discuss both individual and class functioning. Enrollment face sheets, com-

---

3 In 1966. The national norms are established at the 50th percentile, hence an 80.7 percent failure rate is 30.7 percent greater than would be expected.

pleted by parents, gave surprisingly candid family information. In contrast to our expectations, some 90 percent of this special first grade class had *earlier* school experience, either in kindergarten or in first grade the preceding year. School data on these children were unfortunately fragmentary, providing incomplete and (only) atypical absentee information; e.g., nine of these children had an aggregate of 493 days absent in the preceding school year. Other data were obtained from the teacher's considerable knowledge of neighborhood families where several siblings were in school, through parent's visits to the school, etc.

Some 60 percent of this "slow learners" class came from one-parent homes, i.e., as contrasted with 30 percent for the census tract. Yet even the figure of 60 percent does not portray the full extent of marital instability since an unknown percentage of parents designated as married had been *re*married or were living as married in common-law. The mean number of children per family was more than five, but this is also an underestimate since some siblings were not reported, though they were known to be living with other relatives. The diffusion of mothers to individual children, and the frequent total absence of fathers, is evident in families where, for example, three adult sisters and fifteen children lived with the grandmother. Our first child in analytic study has six brothers. When her mother was psychiatrically hospitalized, a twenty-year-old woman recently evicted with her three children became a temporary resident in the patient's home. Without physical, financial, or moral support of a husband, this twenty-year-old was then solely responsible for ten children, all under the age of thirteen. The teachers, incidentally, with Naomi and three siblings in attendance, knew nothing of their mother's prolonged absence when she was psychiatrically hospitalized.

Within the school, the classes observed tended toward a controlled bedlam. It is inaccurate, however, to convey the view that the children were simply action-oriented and impulse-ridden; they also evidenced a profound, if selective, tolerance for noise, confusion, isolation, and passivity. Indeed, one was clinically reminded of passivity as a defense, with an appreciable number of children inevitably preoccupied with private fantasy or even sleep at their desks, oblivious to the omnipresent noise. Depressive affects, the most dramatic and pervasive emotional attitudes in evidence, could have had neurotic or psychotic origins, yet such affects may simply be direct consequences of grief or fatigue that result from reality stresses of an unkind fate. Aggression seemed overcontrolled, and I was particularly impressed that in these years of observation I never observed, within the school, one instance of genuine aggression turned outward in a temper tantrum either in class or on the playground. The only exception reported to me was five-year-old Virgil who attacked and choked a girl in his class, winning our scrutiny and candidacy as our second patient under study.

The prevalence and severity of retardation were perhaps the most striking observations in these classroom sessions. Many of the children seemed hopelessly, passively, indifferent, and, like our first patient, were some two or more years retarded relative to national norms, and this at ages six and seven.

Observational study of classroom functioning proved fascinating, but proved quite inadequate to distinguish between possible cultural or psychopathological contributions to retarded functioning. On the one hand, culturally normative data were simply unavailable; on the other, the children's retreat from adult scrutiny limited any reliable insights to their (possible) psychopathological adaptations. Teachers seem to feel that they can or should be able to distinguish between the educationally deprived, the mentally dull, and the emotionally damaged child. Yet these are rarely mutually exclusive or reliably differentiated by the best of our diagnostic tools. Such problems continue to plague the clinician, even where he is privy to the child's inner life.

ANALYTIC STUDY

Our inability to distinguish between (possible) culturally sustained and psychopathologically required adaptations led to psychiatric screening of referrals (from the school) so as to select a "representative" sample of two "retarded" children who were otherwise, overtly, symptom-free. The magnitude of school problems with such children is more than sufficient to guarantee referral *if* some type of treatment resource is available. Parenthetically, we would note that a recent New York legislative study reported that some 30,000,000 dollars a year is spent on remedial efforts with 10,000 children designated as more "disturbed" than "retarded" (New York Times, 1967).

Hospital programs, independent of this project, provide for relatively complete medical services to the school area's children. Selective screening of cases, therefore, permits collaborative pediatric, psychiatric, and any other recommended studies to provide the fullest developmental and concurrent health data, as well as recommended medical treatment. Collaborative support of the Hospital and the Psychoanalytic Institute provides both senior consultation to our project and the tentative commitment of five child analysts[4] who are prepared to work collectively with respect to data reporting and analysis. Research funding problems have limited our pilot sample to only two children, one in analytic treatment for thirteen months,[5] and the second, seen for an extended diagnostic assessment, who has just begun intensive treatment (five sessions a week).

One of the pilot project's problems is that of uniform conceptualization and reporting of clinical data. Drawing on Sandler's (1962), Bolland and Sandler's (1965), and Bellak and Hurvich's (1967) work in indexing of psychoanalytic concepts, as well as that of the American Psychoanalytic Association (1967), we aspire to elaboration of conceptual handbooks that behaviorally define the terms and concepts of study. Since our preliminary focus is on ego anomalies, the intent is to document such ego functions as integration, synthesis, memory, perception, etc. Such ego functions, ideally, can be examined in their clinical and cultural context to ascertain their attributes. Taking perception as one illustration, we hope to distinguish between (1) idiosyncratic, (2) cultural, and (3) defensive attributes of perceptions that are: internal and external (of self), affective and objective, veridical and distorted, selective and general, etc.

The wealth of data available in any one case is methodologically oppressive in exploratory research. An analytic index provides one option in data control and retrieval. Our intent is the eventual mapping of behavioral norms specific to each child which may also

4 Particular indebtedness and thanks are due Reginald S. Lourie, M.D., co-principal investigator; Gene Gordon, M.D., Robert Gillman, M.D., Mary Flumerfelt, and Lois B. Murphy, Ph.D., for their early and continuing contributions and valued support in the development of this project.

5 Both children have continued in treatment which now extends to two years for the older child and one year for the younger child (March, 1970).

be shared in common with other children so as to reflect (sub)cultural contributions to intellectual style or (ego) inhibition. For instance, we suspect that some behaviors of the ghetto child, e.g., his nominal orality, passive aggressivity, present-time orientation, are syntonic to, if not demanded by, the cultural setting and are *not* inherently pathological. Oral gratifications, a solace for transient hurts or indignities, are also sustained by the social reality that hunger is often a close companion. Where overt, infantile masturbatory exploration is severely punished, as is true in the ghetto, oral displacements are dramatically reinforced.

Like the primary process mentation of the artist, the instinctual openness of the ghetto child can appear (socially) deviant yet be adaptive without necessarily deriving from intrapsychic conflict. It is clear, on the other hand, that some cultural norms mask and rationalize individual psychopathology. Naomi, our first patient, portrays a wide range of verbal anomalies that have been variously (analytically) identified as: (1) specific to her siblings, as in their speaking "nonsense," in word salads which perplex and confuse the mother so that she abandons questioning; (2) a stereotyped "black sambo" (viewed on late night, 1930 style, TV movies), "yah-suh, boss!" with rolling eyes and facial grimaces mimicking stupidity; (3) regressive baby talk, used in spontaneous fantasy to depict the special status of infants of whom little is asked; (4) an argot of the ghetto that can prove baffling to the outsider, a language and syntax that have parallels in the Hawaiian's pidgeon English and the Cockney's slang; and (5) the more typical ego regressions in which normal ego skills are transiently lost, where words are erroneously substituted, misused, etc.

From our two children in analytic treatment, we have miscellaneous information about six siblings, two psychiatrically disturbed mothers, two former husbands, some data on maternal aunts, and a scant history of three generations in these families. As studies in individual sorrow, of apparent social and individual psychopathology, these families' histories stretch credibility.

Case 1

Our first diminutive patient, Naomi, was selected because of her "representativeness," i.e., she had a verbal IQ of 76, a performance

IQ of 87, and a f.s. of 80; she was two years "retarded." Naomi evidenced no presenting, overt psychological symptoms (other than her retardation and tendency to retreat in class into fantasy).

Naomi's mother was initially approached by her child's teacher, who advised that a joint conference (with me) could be set up to assess whether Naomi could have a special opportunity for help. In this first conference, the mother communicated indirectly to me by comments addressed to the teacher, also Negro and well known to the mother. The mother was far more concerned with her elder son, whom she considered explosively murderous; her documentation was impressive. With Naomi, the mother was upset by her outrageous lies (patent fantasies), her stubborn provocativeness, and her tendency to prolonged psychological withdrawals. Yet Naomi wasn't so dumb, as the mother noted and illustrated with an anecdote. Had the teacher seen Naomi's stripes where the mother had "cut her up"? "No?" Then the mother mused: "that's how smart she is! I'd had to give her a whupping, and she was cut up. That evening, Naomi said she had showed you her cuts and then she told me that extension cords [electrical] were for whupping animals, not people. She's right, of course! I shouldn't have done it."

Somewhat later the mother reflected, with slight amusement, on her having cured her eldest son of his lifelong bed wetting. Noting my interest, the mother continued to the effect that she shouldn't have done it, that her sister had later told her it wasn't right; yet it *had* worked! The mother had concluded that the only way her son would believe her would be if she convinced herself first and she worked on her own self-conviction. When suitably persuaded, the mother went to her son's room, and, as usual found him in a wet bed. With a voice of doom, she then made the pronouncement that if the boy wet once more, he could be certain that he would never pee in his bed again. She had promised to cut off his "taddy-wac" and hang it on the end of the bed where it could pee on the floor but never again on the sheets. (The credibility of this threat should be assessed in Naomi's later, analytic material.)

Naomi's treatment has documented that she has episodes of enuresis, like her brothers who are chronic wetters; she has chronic asthmatic attacks, like her mother and her eldest brother (whose asthma is incapacitating during his rages); she is subject to nighttime nosebleeds following tempers with her mother; she is subject to acute flatulence and stomach upsets (that may prove to be a functional colitis). The child (at the start of treatment) retreated to fantasy, at the expense of class participation or attentiveness to her environment. She gave the appearance, to her mother, of mental illness which the mother experienced as similar to her own severe, depressive withdrawal.

The mother relates much of her children's difficulties to separations. The children have been cared for by various relatives, in institutions or foster homes during the mother's twelve pregnancies and her first extended psychiatric hospitalization. During the latter, two of the younger children lost their speech. The eldest, now thirteen, has rages, as earlier noted, which the mother considers homicidal; she is fearful for and of him. The youngest is a failure-to-thrive baby who was just beginning to talk at age three. At age four, one boy became "queer," as the mother put it, wanting to be like her, seemingly in a transient identification that was severely disparaged. All of these children have been separately seen in the hospital's allergy, speech and well-baby clinics, *without* psychiatric referral and without apparent hospital recognition that the separately treated patients (with different surnames) come from the same family.

Our patients' analytic treatment proceeded more like that of middle-class, latency-age children than was anticipated. Naomi's early statement of problems was limited to her convictions of being impossibly stupid. She could not work systematically to master simple educational subjects such as the alphabet or number sequences. Yet she was immediately competent with the complexities of the office's multi-button telephone, a complicated air conditioner, the combination of my briefcase lock, which she had remembered over several weeks of time. Much of the child's nonacademic learning is quite spontaneous and persisting. She can recall contents of my desk which I have quite forgotten. Her recall is selective, episodically excellent, yet alternatively grossly faulty. She is intensely, defensively sensitive about failure. It appears as if she would rather not know and say she doesn't care than to try and then be found wrong. Her memory is particularly susceptible to distortion with respect to relevant adults, e.g., my name, that of her favorite secretary, even her own mother's name, which the child could not remember or use when she tried to telephone her at the hospital. She sustains limited passions for learning, but only briefly, and frequently regresses to a type of talk and play that are emphatically infantile. Naomi gives the clear impression that there is security in ignorance. Fantasy seems a more pleasant refuge, and she notes that Peter Pan didn't have to grow up and didn't have to go to school. Learning often appears to have negative significance, i.e., that a competent child merits even less of a mother's already scant free time.

While this mother aspires to her children's completion of school, and university if this were ever possible, her child evidences no such self-ideals. Naomi suggests that she might eventually become a typist or cashier in a supermarket. Despite her preoccupation with cleaning and correcting things in treatment, however, she has never anticipated working like our cleaning staff whom she constantly sees around the office. Her eagerness with learning, such as it is, seems much like that of a preschool child, to win adult affection and praise. Internalized, autonomous aspirations for academic learning seem absent.

While the child shows no discomfort about her own disheveled appearance or frequent, incidental dirtiness, she is inconsistently compulsive in her fear of germs, e.g., at times she cannot even lick an envelope to seal it. Incongruously, however, she may lick candy off the floor. Her work in treatment has often involved obsessive cleaning up, particularly correcting, erasing, redoing her own mistakes in her attempts at drawing and printing. Her compulsive undoing, erasing, over and over, pre-empted attention in many of her early appointments—giving the impression of obsessional preoccupations of pathological significance (which are not irrelevant to her frequent flatulence and trips to the toilet during the sessions in her first year of analysis).

Open sexuality permeates Naomi's treatment material, and in this respect she clearly varies from middle-class children. From her first psychiatric, diagnostic consultation, the child advised that play with a boy involves sexual passivity, i.e., until "he tries to put his dick in your pussy"—at which time a girl should hit the boy. Current *real* events of ghetto life, drunks who urinate and defecate in the alley behind the house, rapes, two riots with troops and tear gas, knifings, arson, etc., have been noted in treatment, distorted, and then magically diffused by elaboration in fantasy. To illustrate, a (white) policeman had responded to a neighborhood call that a (Negro) woman was on the street, threatening people with a knife. The policeman had approached the woman, was attacked, and then shot the woman in self-defense; the woman died later at a hospital. This event occurred two streets from Naomi's house and one street from her school, during mid-day. Naomi's account started reasonably accurately, then gradually lost its authenticity as she described a boy who was threatened by a woman with a knife, that the gun hadn't been real, that the lady was in the hospital and would be all right. It was impossible to discern whether Naomi "believed" her own rendition. I was impressed that her overlaying fantasy served to obscure the reality, to ignore it by a displacement that was as patently "unbelievable" as the reality Naomi wished to disbelieve.

Sexuality seems to effect selective recall of both objects and letters. The first evidence of sexualization of ego functions came when Naomi, looking for pencils in my desk, found a wood screw and picked it up, asking, "What's this nail doing here?" When I repeated the word *nail*, Naomi replied with a puzzled expression: "Yeah, that's what I said! What's it doing here?" I noted that the nail was usually called a *screw* and Naomi's face flushed as she murmured something indistinct. Clarification, which continued over months of work, documented that Naomi's sexualized associations led to severe inhibitions in her recall or use of words, synonyms and individual letters (of the alphabet), e.g., *screw* equals *chicken-butt* (intercourse), *but* equals *butt* (bottom), *kitty* and *cookie* equals *pussy* (vulva), etc. The child's verbal difficulties do not appear to reflect a conscious or semiconscious suppression of sexualized words. Rather, Naomi finds herself defensively, confusingly using words that she senses are somehow inaccurate, but in that context she is incapable of discerning her own error.

Time and again, week after week, Naomi worked at her alphabet, noting her ability to remember names of people and things and her frustration that she "forgot" the names of some letters of the alphabet, particularly the letter *J*. In her early analytic approaches to penis envy (in a household of six brothers), Naomi became increasingly open in her jokes and drawings. She used "Chinese" as a nonsense language when she feared I might understand too much. Her draw-

ings of Chinese girls led to innuendo, eventuating in the joke that
Chinese girls were different—they wore kimonos so that no one
would know. In one of a series of drawings, Naomi eventually noted
that this Chinese girl had special things underneath, namely, a taddy-
wac (penis[6]). As she said this, Naomi turned to me and explained
most seriously, "That's why I don't like the letter *J*." The name of
the letter had been consistently forgotten when the child had attempted to do her alphabet on frequent previous occasions. Not
understanding Naomi's reference, I conveyed my ignorance in my
facial expression. Naomi rejoined: "Dummy! A *J* is like a taddy-
wac." With this she then spontaneously printed a very legible letter
J, an effort which she had not been able to accomplish on previous
occasions even when she tried to copy my printing of that letter.

Naomi's   psychological   and   Rorschach   responses,   available
through her initial diagnostic workup, had suggested sexual trauma,
probably   relating   to   fellatio.   After   six   months   of   treatment,   it
seemed more probable that sex play was instead cunnilingus (with
the elder brother). With six brothers, this child indicated that all,
including the three-year-old, played with her at "chicken-butt," i.e.,
intercourse.

On her return from her (second) summer break in treatment,
Naomi was strangely intimate and sorrowful. Her continuity of
thought was fragmentary and her exaggerations patently defensive.
With only five minutes remaining in that hour, Naomi spoke of a
fight that she had had with a bigger girl, how she taught that girl a
lesson and had beaten her pretty badly. Yet Naomi volunteered that
she suffered just a little herself. She then raised her skirt to reveal
a row of striped, parallel, scabs, about one quarter of an inch
wide, two to four inches in length, some eight or nine in number,
just below her buttocks. She had suffered a tragic beating. I recalled
with Naomi that her mother had once admitted that she was sometimes crazy-mad, that she had once beaten Naomi this way and had
told me how much she hoped this could be stopped. Naomi, slightly
whimsical and *very* sad, replied, "It *was* my mother, not a big girl.
She missed us when we were away in camp [a fact] and she only did

---

6 One of Naomi's more recent revelations, accompanying her concern about female
body damage, is the fact that she has an umbilical hernia that protrudes about three
fourths of an inch. She is quite certain that she does *not* want this surgically "repaired."

it 'cause she loved me." The mother later elaborated that Naomi and an older brother had been playing at intercourse; the beating was to insure that incest couldn't occur in the family. In this context, one may comment on a pervasive ghetto practice in which parental discipline extends progressively in severity in proportion to the provocative seductions of the milieu.[7] Our patient and her family document the previous findings of Childers (1936) and Pasamanick (1969) that inappropriate and excessive stimulation may be as serious in later years as understimulation is for the infant.

Freud (1919) was *not* optimistic about the efficacy of psycho-analytic treatment for the grossly disadvantaged. What advantages accrue from corrections of pathological distortions in perception when insight may only clarify the cruelty of reality? Naomi's two years of analytic work support a reserved, optimistic hope. Her guilt, deriving from early sexual play and repressed sadistic rage, had fed into her masochistic psychoneurotic interactions with her mother. Naomi effectively provoked her mother's brutal assaults, which served the defensive function of (1) relieving guilt, and (2) of assuring herself that her mother's rages were "reasonable," i.e., *not* insane. The child's therapeutic movement increasingly permits Naomi to cope with her own guilt, thereby limiting her own provocations and consequent beatings; less fearful of her own "madness," Naomi has increasing awareness that her mother's psychotic episodes are a "sickness" (that Naomi is not responsible for).

Cleanliness training may have contributed to Naomi's reaction formations, to her obsessive concern for having things cleaned up and in their proper place. Yet having things in their place is equally fundamental to small children whose mother disappeared, as this one did when Naomi was only five (the children were then placed in institutional care). This child's displacement of affect is striking with respect to separations; e.g., she *casually* commented one day that her mother was in the hospital, that her mother was crazy and had wanted her to help kill the father (long since absent). While this was initially understood as a fantasy, the mother had, in fact, been hospitalized in a suicidal, depressive episode. Yet the child spoke non-

---

[7] Maria Piers was particularly helpful in distinguishing parental sadism from severe punishments engendered by the dramatic threats of the ghetto to a child's safety.

chalantly, then and later, giving the clear appearance that she had been through too many separations and bizzare experiences to permit present grief or fear to overflow her resources. Clinical evidence suggests that her preoccupations in fantasy and her obsessive need to clean up her messes reflect defensive control of emotions that are profound. One may conjecture that since she is unable to face her fears of separation and death in reality, they return to haunt her in displaced form. In illustration, during her first Christmas holiday break in treatment, the mother telephoned me at home asking if I would speak to Naomi who had had a terrible dream and was convinced that it was true, that I was dead, murdered.

Case 2

Our second patient, Virgil, accepted treatment begrudgingly as an opportunity to be out of his kindergarten where he was so consistently lonely, miserable, and angry. He was certain that he was in treatment because he was so naughty. Not unlike Naomi, Virgil never shared his family's secrets with his teachers. I remained "uneducated" for some three months, at which time the maternal grandmother concluded that my indentureship was past, that it was propitious for me to know more. Virgil's grandfather, the only man in the house, was medically retired with a disability pension. He was fearful and rejecting of medical care, though suffering with a severe heart condition (of which he died several months later). He appeared to be a chronic alcoholic who abused and terrorized the household by chronic rages (which alternated with apathetic withdrawal when sober). Virgil's mother, narcissistically attractive and *most* provocative in her attire, was employed in a respectable daytime position. His grandmother appeared as an uneducated but articulate, warm and concerned mainstay of the household. She worked part time as a domestic, and varied arrangements had been used for Virgil's day care during his preschool years.

Virgil is a handsome, nicely proportioned, unusually well-dressed child. His manner is composed, controlled, and a bit autocratic. At the time when his mother (unknown to me) was arrested for prostitution, Virgil was evermore restless at school and resistant to coming for his appointments. His exemplary behavior in therapy then began to change, e.g., Virgil insisted that he wanted to leave the office; he faced the wall in silence, tears gradually emerging, then pouring down his silent face. In a succession of such appointments, muffled sobs would wrack the child's body as tears flowed. Protesting one day that he *would* go, the child crawled under the couch, verbally silent as he kicked the floor in fury. Still purporting that he wanted to go, Virgil then refused to leave, and later was gently, but forcefully picked up and taken downstairs as he struggled in silent fury (to stay). The next week brought his most ferocious outpouring, engendering doubts as to his "treatability."

Early in that hour, Virgil insisted that he *would* leave and return home, on a nonschool day. I had understood and interpreted the child's increasingly open hurt and anger as reflections of (1) his wish and need to control the adults whom he feared; (2) as a "communication" of the intensity of feelings that seemed impossible to put into words; (3) as a measure of his need to keep distant when his anger seemed to threaten his relationship with me (whom he quite liked); and (4) as a passive into active defense where he insisted on going so as to avoid the pain he felt when he was told he had to go. On this occasion, Virgil insisted that he was leaving. Since the secretary was not there to escort the boy home, across two streets, I agreed that he should leave, but he should wait until the secretary could be found to escort him. Virgil's voice then became a sob, a cry, and then a piercing scream that shattered the silence of the entire building. Without a break in volume, the child began to stamp, to swing his arms wildly, then to spit and kick. I made the error, never again to be repeated, of attempting to hold the child's arms. As the boy's kicks landed on the bookcase and his spit expanded, I agreed he should leave without delay, at which point he resisted and was carried downstairs, still screaming without respite (but making no attempt to assault me).

At the bottom of the stairs, Virgil kicked the door furiously, repeating this on a metal water fountain before he blasted out the front door. Fearing the child's judgment was impaired with respect to traffic, I followed Virgil and started to stop him (outside the office). Then sensing the futility of physical controls, I let Virgil go and followed him as he half ran toward the alley at the rear of the office. There, Virgil screamed invictives and threw stones from a distance. The child then disappeared and ran down the alley leaving me perplexed and worried. I returned to the front of the building where I sat and smoked. Virgil reappeared, coming up the street carrying a massive stick that he swung with savage enthusiasm. The child would pause, look up the street at me, pound the sidewalk with his club, and advance another fifteen or twenty feet. Then Virgil crossed the main boulevard, repeated his triumphant march up the other side of the street, keeping me in visual contact. A block distant, he recrossed the boulevard, returned in my direction, but without his club. Approximately 100 feet distant, and across another side street, the boy began walking backward, crossing that street (backward) as he moved to the outer edge of the office building where he ducked around the corner, seemingly disappearing again. From this vantage, the child then made tentative visual overtures, peeking over a wall as he drew ever closer to me.

Virgil's appointment officially ended at that moment and I called out to him that it was time to go home. Virgil, most quietly, benignly, and with an angelic, tired smile ran to me and reached for my hand. His reversal of affect was profound. Thoroughly rung out and quite undecided whether "therapy" could possibly continue thereafter, I advised Virgil that I would personally walk him home (two streets distant). Virgil walked quietly, his hand grasping mine as he murmured, "I've been very bad; I won't be able to see you anymore?" I replied that he had certainly been furious. Perhaps he had needed to test and find out whether I could tolerate and understand his fear and consequent fury when he felt restrained or unwanted.

Thereafter, the education of his analyst having extended somewhat, Virgil had the undisputed prerogative of coming to and leaving his sessions as he needed. His behavior was responsible, but at times his need for emotional distance was impelling and in the middle of a session, e.g., while coloring in a book that touched on white and black, Virgil unexpectedly announced he had to leave, now!

The passions that threaten Virgil's equilibrium appear, in part, as a reflection of daily fears and anxieties, e.g., his loss of his father, assaults by older boys on the street, his mother's absences, her withdrawal while on drugs, etc. But the cruelness of reality is exacerbated by Virgil's defense organization, his systematic isolation and denial of affect which preclude acceptance of other adults' compassion and emotional availableness. Virgil has stoically endured maternal absences, repair of an umbilical hernia (age three), dental surgery under general anesthesia (age four), episodic nasal hemorrhages (perhaps related to his asthma). His mother reports on his toughness, that he did not cry or despair either during his hospital separations or his surgeries. The clinical implications are clear, viz., that early and powerful defensive adaptations were essential for him to cope with his fear of damage and vulnerability to the gross instability of daily family life. His hurts and rages are well encapsulated, and apparently emerge only when Virgil is unable to establish his own control over adults. Even in kindergarten, at age five, the child's message was understood: when he needed to go out, he was (and is) let out. The impact of such chaotic life circumstances and psychological fears on his intellectual functioning can thus far only be guessed at. Unlike Naomi, Virgil does *not* appear "retarded."

Summary Discussion

Our pilot efforts at systematizing psychoanalytic research permit only limited generalization at this time, viz., (1) psychoanalytic study provides data of depth and richness that are simply unobtainable in observational study; (2) such intensive and longitudinal psychoanalytic explorations provide options for definitive documentation of those ego functions which contribute to intellectual function/dysfunction; and (3) as the sample size extends to permit generalization, the analytic indexing of such data offers an empirical, if arduous, potentiality for differentiating between cultural and psychological determinants of varied behaviors.

While the observational study is most limited as a basis for generalization, one may conjecture, however tentatively, on a number of socially significant issues. I concur with Bloom et al. (1964) that if educational remedies are to be effective, even with the "*nondis-*turbed" child, they must necessarily be academically revolutionary, i.e., with extensions of teaching methods that veridically relate to the experiential and motivational needs of this population. Ghetto children and their problems appear anything but homogeneous, and I suspect that one of the fundamental errors of remedial programs is to function as if they were (Borowitz and Hirsch, 1968). Our experience, like Pavenstedt's (1965) in Boston, suggests that social indifference colludes with professional ignorance of "cultural deviance" to obscure a broad range of psychopathology, including severe psychotic, atypical, and psychoneurotic disorders that are not irrelevant to ego impairments and ego dysfunctions.

However bad our ghetto schools are, and some are miserable, a high percentage of children arrive at kindergarten and first grade less than prepared emotionally and intellectually to enjoy the materials and processes of formal education.[8] Few ghetto parents contribute, in the realities of their own experience and interest, models for identification with these educational ideals which the parents nominally share with the general culture. Contemporary ghetto life compounds academic problems since daily experience is fraught with instinctual trauma, not least of these being the realities of terrifying, real danger and interminable discontinuities of residence and caretakers.

Consultative work with teachers suggests that ghetto families are replete with undiagnosed, untreated psychopathology—of which our first samples may prove more representative than we prefer to believe. Yet ghetto children accommodate without the *overt* evidence of phobic, hysteric or obsessive symptom formations more readily observable in the middle class. Deaths, beatings, separations, etc., go unreported to teachers, and such traumas seem effectively encapsulated without symptom formation being discernible to the external observer. Apathetic and depressive behavior in the "retarded" children appears to provide one form of psychological accommodation. Whether such adaptations are necessarily psychopathological, viewed structurally, or whether retardation is a "symptom" that is causally related to such traumas remains the focus of our continuing research efforts.

---

8 There are critics of our school system who fear that such conclusions are a new form of sophisticated prejudice in which racist views of "genetic inferiority" are to be displaced by "cultural inferiority"; that if the culture can be "blamed," the schools are to be exonerated of their failures (Pasamanick, 1969). One should insist, to the contrary, that the special vulnerabilities of the ghetto child demonstrate all the more clearly the futility of preserving educational structures that ignore or discount the ghetto child's developmental and concurrent deprivations and traumatizations.

BIBLIOGRAPHY

Ainsworth, M. (1962), The Effects of Maternal Deprivation. In: *Deprivation of Maternal Care*. Geneva: World Health Organization, Public Health Papers 14, pp. 97-159.
American Psychoanalytic Association (1967), Committee on Indexing, B. D. Fine, Chairman. Ego Index (Ego Achievement to Ego Mechanism) (mimeographed).
Bellak, L. & Hurvich M. (1967), A Systematic Study of Ego Functions. Read at the Spring Meeting of the American Psychoanalytic Association, Detroit.
Blau, A. & Hulse, W. C. (1956), Anxiety ("Actual") Neuroses as a Cause of Behavior Disorders in Children. *Amer. J. Orthopsychiat.*, 26:108-118.
Blodgett, F. M. (1963), Growth Retardation Related to Maternal Deprivation. In: *Modern Perspectives in Child Development*, ed. A. J. Solnit & S. Provence. New York: International Universities Press, pp. 83-93.
Bloom, B. S., Davies, A., & Hess, R. (1964), Compensatory Education for Cultural Deprivation. Read at the Research Conference on Educational and Cultural Deprivation, held by the Department of Education, University of Chicago.
Bolland, J., Sandler, J., et al. (1965), *The Hampstead Psychoanalytic Index*. New York: International Universities Press.
Bornstein, B. (1930), Zur Psychogenese der Pseudodebilität. *Int. Z. Psa.*, 16:378-399.
Borowitz, G. H. & Hirsch, J. G. (1968), *A Developmental Typology of Disadvantaged Four-Year-Olds*. Research Report of the Institute for Juvenile Research, Chicago, Vol. 5, No. 1.
Bowlby, J. (1951), *Maternal Care and Mental Health*. Geneva: World Health Organization.
Chess, S. (1969), Disadvantages of "The Disadvantaged Child." *Amer. J. Orthopsychiat.*, 39:4-6.
Childers, A. T. (1936), Some Notes on Sex Mores among Negro Children. *Amer. J. Orthopsychiat.*, 6:442-448.
Coleman, J. S. (1966), Equal Schools for Equal Students. *Pub. Interest*, 4:70-75.
—— et al. (1966), *Equality of Educational Opportunity*. Washington, D.C.: Department of Health, Education, and Welfare.
Federn, P. (1930), Psychoanalytische Auffassung der "intellektuellen Hemmung." *Z. psa. Päd.*, 11:393-408.
Fenichel, O. (1945), *The Psychoanalytic Theory of Neurosis*. New York: Norton.
Freud, A. (1965), *Normality and Pathology in Childhood*. New York: International Universities Press.
Freud, S. (1919), Lines of Advance in Psycho-Analytic Therapy. *Standard Edition*, 17:159-168. London: Hogarth Press, 1955.
Hollingshead, A. B. & Redlich, F. C. (1958), *Social Class and Mental Illness*. New York: Wiley.
Jacobson, E. (1932), Lernstörungen beim Schulkind durch masochistiche Mechanismen. *Int. Z. Psa.*, 18:242-251.
Klein, M. (1931), A Contribution to the Theory of Intellectual Inhibition. *Int. J. Psa.*, 12:206-218.
Layman, E. (1970), Rorschach Studies of Mothers. In: *Pica and Lead Poisoning*, ed. F. K. Millican & R. S. Lourie (unpublished manuscript).
Liebow, E. (1967), *Tally's Corner: A Study of Negro Streetcorner Men*. Boston: Little, Brown.
Lourie, R. S. (1940), The Recovery of Mental Functioning Lost in Severe Vitamin Deficiency States. New York (mimeographed).
Mahler, M. S. (1942), Pseudoimbecility: A Magic Cap of Invisibility. *Psa. Quart.*, 11:149-164.

Meers, D. R. (1969), *Crucible of Ambivalence: Sexual Identity in the Ghetto.* Family Life Bureau, United States Conference (mimeographed monograph).

Metropolitan Police Department (1969), Crime Index Report for Metropolitan Washington, D.C.

New York Times (1967), Disturbed Pupils Held Neglected, March 26, p. 37.

Pasamanick, B. (1946), A Comparative Study of the Behavioral Development of Negro Infants. *J. Genet. Psychol.,* 69:3-44.

—— (1969), A Tract for the Times: Some Sociobiologic Aspects of Science, Race, and Racism. *Amer. J. Orthopsychiat.,* 39:7-15.

Passow, A. H. (1967), Summary of Findings and Recommendations of a Study of the Washington, D.C. Schools. Teachers College, Columbia University (mimeographed).

Pavenstedt, E. (1965), A Comparison of the Child-Rearing Environment of Upper-Lower and Very Low-Lower Class Families. *Amer. J. Orthopsychiat.,* 35:89-98.

Sandler, J. (1962), Research in Psycho-Analysis: The Hampstead Index as an Instrument of Psycho-Analytic Research. *Int. J. Psa.,* 43:287-291.

Schmideberg, M. (1930), Intellektuelle Hemmung und Aggression. *Z. psa. Päd.,* 4:467-477.

—— (1938), Intellectual Inhibition and Disturbances in Eating. *Int. J. Psa.,* 19:17-22.

U.S. Bureau of the Census (1962), U.S. Census of Population and Housing, 1960. Census Tracts. Final Report p.h.c. (1) 166. Washington, D.C.: U.S.G.P.O.

U.S. Department of Public Health (1964), Vital Statistic Summary. Biostatistics Section. Washington, D.C.

Winnicott, D. W. (1960), The Theory of the Parent-Infant Relationship. *The Maturational Processes and the Facilitating Environment.* New York: International Universities Press, 1965, pp. 37-55

THE VICISSITUDES OF THE "WORKING ALLIANCE" IN THE ANALYSIS OF A LATENCY GIRL

JACK NOVICK, Ph.D. (London)

Although "working alliance" is one of the many terms borrowed from the field of adult analysis, it is one that child analysts not only can borrow, but also can clarify and formulate more precisely. Despite the many important differences between child and adult analysis, the phenomena covered by the term "working alliance" are probably more easily visible in children. Thus far the few attempts at clarifying the term by using childhood material have centered mainly on the child's pathological and normal features that interfere with the initial formation of such an alliance and on the capacities necessary for participation in the analytic task (A. Freud, 1965; Frankl and Hellman, 1962).

It is helpful to differentiate (a) the existence of a capacity, (b) the willingness to use the capacity, and (c) the willingness to use the capacity for analytic work. The first category takes in developmental considerations and pathological interferences with structuralization. If we exclude very young children and those who have experienced gross interference or manifest pronounced ego deviation, then we can assume that most children have many of the capacities necessary for analytic work. However, as Anna Freud (1965) has pointed out, it is natural for children to avoid using capacities such as self-reflection even under ordinary circumstances and to resist its use for analytic purposes. Thus the formation of an alliance is based not only

This paper forms part of a research project entitled "Childhood Pathology: Impact on Later Mental Health," conducted at the Hampstead Child-Therapy Course and Clinic, London. The project is financed by the National Institute of Mental Health, Washington, D.C., Grant No. MH-5683-07.

This paper was presented at a Meeting of the Hampstead Clinic, March, 1970.

I would like to express my gratitude to Mrs. H. Kennedy for her supervision of this case and to Miss Anna Freud and Miss Kerry Kelly for their valuable suggestions.

231

on the availability of certain capacities but also on the willingness to
use them for analytic work.

In this paper I shall focus on the vicissitudes and nature of a
child's willingness to do analytic work, using the treatment material
of a latency child. The case I shall present is an unusual one in that
the child readily entered into a working alliance, thus allowing us
to study in greater detail the motivations for such an alliance. I
shall start with a brief description of the child's development and
the main themes in her analysis.

Case Illustration

Erica will soon be twelve years old. She is now a very pretty,
charming, happy girl who has settled in very well at a grammar
school. Three years ago, at the age of eight years nine months, she
began her analysis at the Clinic. At the start of treatment she was an
extremely lonely, unhappy, and anxious child. She suffered from
many symptoms and frequently experienced what seemed to be attacks of overwhelming panic. She had an intense fear that her
parents would die, was afraid of using strange lavatories, afraid of
monsters and burglars, and worried about the house burning down.
She suffered from severe and persistent stomachaches and headaches
and had lengthy periods of being unable to fall asleep. She had no
friends and lived in a world of fantasy where, as she stated, "If yesterday is more amusing than today, then I will go back to yesterday."
Autoerotic manifestations were frequent, pervasive, and especially
pronounced during periods of withdrawal.

The analysis lasted approximately two and a half years; with the
resolution of neurotic conflicts, the disappearance of symptoms, the
restoration to the path of progressive development, and the firm
establishment of dominance in the latency phase, it was mutually
decided by patient and analyst that treatment could terminate. Follow-up investigation one year after termination indicated that all
positive moves had been retained and the child remained happy,
active, and free of symptoms.

Erica's parents were wealthy, middle-class, university-educated,
cultured South Africans. Although numerous pathological features
were present in the parents and in their relationship with Erica, the

intensity and degree of pathological interference were not marked, and in general they could be viewed as adequate parents. Erica was the eldest of three children, a longed-for child who has remained the favorite of both parents. The parents started a baby album which contained comments on her development from birth onward. The intense joy of the parents is evident in their comments. The baby book reflects their pleasure, but in the interviews with the parents there clearly emerged an equally intense disappointment in this child. It is evident that they had wished for a boy. The persistent disappointment in Erica was a central feature of the parental pathology and became a major theme in the work with both the child and the parents.

The initial disappointment in having a girl soon centered on Erica's congenital eye defect. At about two months of age it was noticed that Erica suffered from strabismus, and she still has no binocular depth vision. A cosmetic eye operation which took place while she was in analysis corrected a pronounced squint. Historical and analytic data indicate that despite the congenital defect and the parental disappointment, there was no gross developmental interference during the oral phase. Erica seemed to have had a good oral period, one which stimulated structural development and provided her with an adequate supply of primary narcissism and positive feeling states. Both speech and motility were somewhat precocious, as she is said to have been walking at about ten months of age and talking by one year.

Erica was sixteen months old when her sister Lou was born and, according to the mother, she showed no signs of distress at this event. Erica could spend hours in what the mother approvingly called "imaginative play," and this self-sufficiency and trouble-free behavior were sources of great comfort and pleasure to the mother. Daytime bowel and bladder control was achieved by the time of Lou's birth, and complete control established soon thereafter. At the age of two Erica had the first of two operations to correct the defect in her eyes. Both operations were unsuccessful. When Erica was three years one month, the third child, Tom, was born. Again Erica showed no sign of upset at this event or any adverse reaction to the second operation, which took place soon thereafter.

When Erica was six years old the parents were forced to give up their affluent existence in South Africa and moved to London. Erica was a bright girl who had always done well at school and had been the favorite of all her teachers. In London she changed schools four times in three years, and her schoolwork and attitude toward school deteriorated. She was still in the top half of her form, but was finding the work increasingly difficult; she hated school and was becoming increasingly frightened of her teacher.

Whereas Erica was considered to be a mature, well-behaved girl, her sister Lou was viewed by the mother as a wild, infantile, and uncontrolled child. Lou was referred to this Clinic for temper tantrums and started analysis six months before Erica did. Little is known of the youngest child, Tom, and the parents claim that he has adjusted well to his new life in England.

Erica was found to suffer from a classical infantile neurosis—a diagnostic assessment to which her treatment was geared. The analytic material disclosed that the major conflicts centered on the oedipal and preoedipal rage toward the mother, the intense rivalry with the siblings, especially Lou, and the pervasive feeling of loss.

Childhood was experienced as a series of losses: loss of the status as the only child, loss of her perfect vision, loss of her penis, loss of the preoedipal mother and oedipal father, and loss of "the happy days in South Africa." She felt that these were lost because she was bad, because she wanted to kill her siblings and her mother, because she masturbated, and because she was damaged, castrated, and helpless to take what she wanted or stop others from stealing what had been hers.

At the behest of a strict superego Erica employed a variety of defenses against the murderous rage, the most prominent among them being reaction formation. This defense was reinforced by the mother's pleasure in having a good, compliant, and "easy to manage" child. As Erica announced with pride early in the analysis, "I won a prize at school for sitting up straight and being good." A more damaging defense was the need to deny and avoid any situation which would stimulate feelings of rejection, hurt, loss, and anger. When these mechanisms became increasingly difficult to maintain, she withdrew from objects into an elaborate fantasy world.

By the start of treatment withdrawal into her "pretend land" had reached symptomatic proportions and had become the characteristic reaction to psychic pain, the defense against object-directed aggressive wishes, a substitute for frustrated libidinal wishes, and a reversal of the painful feelings of helplessness, loss, and castration. In this pretend land she was the queen and the best fighter. With her magic sword and secret tricks she could single-handedly fight off hordes of enemies, kings, monsters, gods, and thousands of soldiers. She could chop off their heads and make them submit. With a signal she could summon thousands of soldiers, millions of rockets, horsemen, and her King George to help her in battle. In pretend land she was never frightened, never hurt, could always overcome any danger, and anyone she killed could be restored to life.

The analytic material indicates that the birth of a rival when Erica was sixteen months and the eye operation at two years were the predisposing factors, whereas the birth of Tom when Erica was three years one month and the second eye operation soon thereafter were the events precipitating the infantile neurosis. With this as a background I would like to focus on one particular aspect of Erica's analysis, her capacity and willingness to do analytic work.

THE WORKING ALLIANCE

The treatment or therapeutic alliance is a relatively new term and was first introduced by Zetzel in 1956. Devoting a major paper to this topic, Greenson (1965) suggested the term "working alliance." Although the term is new, the factors involved in it have always been at the center of analytic interest. From the beginning Freud referred to an alliance between the analyst and the healthy part of the patient's ego. The attitudes of affection, confidence, and hope were, however, subsumed under the positive transference (1913, 1916-1917, 1937, 1940a). Similarly, Fenichel (1941) speaks of the rational transference as the aim-inhibited positive transference necessary for analysis. Other authors (e.g., Sterba, 1934; Zetzel, 1956; Stone, 1961; Greenson, 1965; Loewenstein, 1969) have emphasized that the readiness to form an alliance with the analyst is not transference and should be clearly distinguished from it.

The term seems to have been readily accepted, is now widely used, and is even given official sanction by entry into the glossary of psychoanalytic terms (Moore and Fine, 1967). It is increasingly found in case presentations, and recent articles on child analysis refer to the difficulties and steps in establishing a working alliance with the child (e.g., Harley, 1967; Hamm, 1967).

Rather than discuss in detail the many articles on the therapeutic or working alliance I shall summarize the main points on which there has been general agreement:

1. The working alliance is not transference and should be distinguished from it.

2. The capacity to form a working alliance is dependent mainly on the availability of autonomous and relatively mature ego functions. Past object relationships and a capacity to form reliable, aim-inhibited libidinal ties are also important.

3. The core of the alliance is the patient's conscious, rational willingness to do analytic work.

4. The motivation for such work is the awareness of suffering and the wish for cure.

5. Among the factors which enter into an alliance an important one is the establishment of a therapeutic split between the patient's observing and experiencing ego. This is established through the identification with the analyst's functions.

6. The alliance becomes most apparent at times of heightened resistance and transference.

7. Many patients (e.g., young children, psychotics, delinquents) lack the capacity necessary to form such an alliance; but once the capacities are there and the alliance is established, it is relatively stable and can be called upon at times of intense resistance or transference.

8. The working alliance not only should be distinguished from the transference but is as important as the transference for analytic work.

Recently, however, the validity of these views has been questioned by Loewenstein (1969), and at a series of meetings of the Hampstead Index Group Anna Freud emphasized the need for further research into the phenomena subsumed under this term. In what follows I shall attempt to test the validity of the propositions set forth above by using the material from the analysis of Erica. In order not to preclude the issues involved, I shall head the main section of my paper "Willingness to Do Analytic Work," although I use the term alliance throughout the text.

WILLINGNESS TO DO ANALYTIC WORK

One of the unusual features of Erica's case is her extraordinary capacity for analytic work. Very soon in treatment one could see the high level of verbalization, the capacities to introspect and reflect, to remember, to report and, in general, to do analytic work. For example, in the first week of treatment she spontaneously told me that whenever she had a thought or feeling she did not like, she got an itch in her leg. She then thought so much about the itch that she forgot the painful thought. A little later when I touched on an area of conflict she said, "I just got the itch; maybe what you said made me think of something I don't want to know." Erica not only had the capacities for analytic work but was also willing to use them for this purpose.

As currently defined, Erica could be said to have had a working alliance at the start of analysis. She suffered from her symptoms and neurotic conflicts, and wanted analytic help to be rid of her problems. She knew that the work consisted of reporting thoughts and feelings, and she could accept and build upon the analytic interventions. She was eager to start treatment, never missed a session, insisted on having the full time for each session, and would whine, "unfair" whenever her mother was late in bringing her to the sessions. From the beginning Erica spontaneously viewed treatment as a place where she could safely report her secrets and worries. The willingness to cooperate was clearly present, but what was the motivation?

The Motives for the Alliance

In this section I shall attempt to illustrate that the conscious, rational wish for relief from suffering played a minor role and that irrational motives, especially those relating to the positive transference, were of prime importance.

From the very start it was apparent that Erica's main motivation for treatment was the intense rivalry with her sister Lou and her fantasy that Lou, in analysis, was having a gratifying experience with an adult from which Erica was excluded. Erica's persisting oedipal and preoedipal wish to beat the rival and have exclusive possession of the love object was immediately displaced onto the analyst, and the secrets she so readily divulged represented the secret relationship from which she had been excluded. Analysis became the secret pleasurable activity, the fulfillment of her infantile wishes, and she used all her resources both to maintain this fantasied pleasure and to make others jealous of what she had. She teased Lou at every opportunity and would, for example, dawdle at the end of the hour to make Lou believe that she got more time than Lou did from her analyst. Intent on being the favorite, Erica complied with the rules of analysis and worked hard to be the best patient.

From the very beginning, however, analysis and her analyst had proved to be an enormous disappointment, but she used denial to defend against the pain, avoidance events which could lead to further disappointment, and soon attempted to control the activities in the session to keep it a place of fantasied delight. The more disappointed and angry she became, the more she defended against these feelings by being a compliant, good girl.

There was continued focus on Erica's ambivalence toward analysis and, in one session, when I suggested that she had two feelings about coming and about me, she said "Not about you, but about coming here. I have three feelings; I like coming so I can be alone with you. I like coming so I can tell you my worries, but what I don't like is whenever I want to do something you always ask me why and then I never get to do it." We can see here not only another example of her capacity for analytic work but also the motivation for such work. The first feeling is that she likes being alone with me, and this was the main motivation, i.e., the positive transference. The feeling that she likes having someone to whom she can tell her worries represents the rational motive, but this was now of minimal importance and she said this mainly because she knew this was expected of her. The other feeling, the anger at having her wishes frustrated, underscores the unreliability of an alliance built on the positive transference and warns of the frustrated rage which will soon emerge. However, it is not the analyst but the patient who decides what the alliance is based on. Before the inevitable resistances become too great the positive transference can be used as the basis for important analytic work. There was a further warning in her comment, a warning not to interpret the positive transference while it served as a basis for the alliance, but to use it until it becomes a source of resistance.

Although more intense transference wishes soon began to emerge, in the main they were defended against. By denial and avoidance she could maintain the illusion that analysis was a special treat, that I was a kind and good person, and that she was my favorite. On this basis we could work on her characteristic defenses and major conflicts. She verbalized her intense and pervasive feelings of unhappiness and acknowledged the use of fantasy as an escape from the pains of "earth." Months before Lou's birthday Erica began planning and preparing a gift for her. This provided an opportunity to focus on her reaction formation. She finally said, "The badder I feel the gooder I am." The conflict between the severe superego demands and the id wishes became the center of analytic work as we concentrated on what we termed "the war inside her." The conflict became more intense: eruptions of excitement alternated with periods of good works and good deeds. She did not know what to do. The good deeds pleased mommy and daddy and were safe, but "Oh! so boring!" The fun things were exciting but scary and made her feel naughty and bad.

As Anna Freud (1965) has stated, the tendency to externalize one or both elements of a conflict is natural to children but serves as a major interference with the establishment or maintenance of an alliance. In Erica's case we could see that as the internalized conflict increased in intensity, the externalizations swept aside the positive transference and the rational wish for cure. At times I represented the critical superego, but mostly I became the "silly, stupid, naughty" person who indulged in infantile pleasures or the seducer who stimulated such wishes in her. Analysis became a source of danger and the emerging sexual wishes were experienced as a fear of being attacked by burglars and witches. Her anxiety and the externalization of danger were so intense that this compliant girl who had a strong tie to the analyst announced in the middle of a session that she was going home and walked out. Needless to say, the ambivalence was such that she soon returned and the alliance could be restored. This was not only accomplished by interpreting the externalizations and the fear of me as a seducer, but was also due to her continuing positive transference. She wondered whether doctors had worries; did they worry that they might do harm to children. She acknowledged being concerned about which side I was on in "the war inside her." She beamed with delight when I said I was on neither side since both sides made her unhappy, but I would try and help her find ways of having fun and still feel good and loved. It was this comment which helped re-establish the alliance—not, as it soon proved, on the ideal basis of contacting the rational ego and its wish for cure but by cogwheeling with her persistent infantile hope that oedipal and pre-oedipal wishes could be gratified without guilt, frustration or anger. As she would say later in the analysis when confronted with her unwillingness to relinquish infantile wishes and accept reality, "I always have hope."

To the degree that the positive transference remained within limits it was a useful ally in the analytic process. However, the work done during this period on Erica's defenses and conflicts led to a significant shift in the internal balance. The externalizations referred to above were final attempts to control the emergence of the more intense, primitive transference wishes. With the analysis of this resistance the positive transference no longer served as a basis for analytic work but emerged in full force and set up goals which were antithetical to such work. It started with the request that I take her sledding, and then a furious insistence that I stay with her and not leave at the end of the hour. During the sessions she was no longer interested in understanding her problems but wanted immediate gratification of her wishes. She experienced my leaving at the end of the session as a painful rejection; with uncontrolled rage she would block the exit, hit, kick, bite, and scream.

The total eruption of wishes and rage alternated with a rigid, defensive withdrawal. The information gained during these eruptions was of value and underlined the central nature of her feelings of being rejected, of losing the oedipal and preoedipal object, and how all the feelings of loss had become symbolized by the lost penis. This information was, however, of little use since there was no reasonable ego to which one could impart it. Even during moments of calm the ego was identified with the rigid defense system; interpretations either increased the resistance or cracked the fragile defenses. I was once more faced with the problem of controlling the child.

What had been the main motivation for the working alliance, the positive transference, became the major interference with the continuation of analytic work. The rational wish to be rid of suffering and the willingness to cooperate to this end did not come to our aid, and other means had to be sought to re-establish an alliance. These were found by using what had formerly been an interference with the alliance, namely, Erica's fear of being overwhelmed and her need to be in control of events. Now that the danger was experienced as an internal one, I could use her anxiety and offer my help in providing her with ways of predicting and controlling the id eruptions.

Often, when she withdrew into solitary activity, she made a boat which sailed through dangerous waters, where storms whipped the waves to heights of "10, no 20, no 40 feet high." The waves clearly represented the impulses and I verbalized her fear of being overwhelmed. I told her that experienced sailors could sniff a storm coming before it arrived. They can prepare and then use the waves to go faster instead of tipping over. She was interested in this but could not believe it, and I began predicting when her storms were brewing. I added that verbalizing the feelings would help keep the waves down. By predicting the outburst at its early stages we could catch the process midway between rigid defense and emergence in action. With my help she struggled to control the impulses and spoke of "a funny feeling in my legs." At this midpoint interpretations could be made and accepted. The most important interpretation traced the origin of the transferred impulses to the birth of Lou and related the anger and hurt to the loss of her mother. This link enabled us to effect the first split between the observing and experiencing ego and we began to speak in terms of the little and the big Erica. The relief experienced by the child helped re-establish the alliance. As she controlled the outbursts of rage she began to experience for the first time the stimulus for the rage, the intense pain and sadness over the loss of being the only child. In the sessions, but mainly at home, she now had prolonged crying spells.

Thus far I have tried to illustrate with Erica's material that a clear-cut distinction between the working alliance and the transference cannot be maintained. Despite the analytic ideal that the alliance is based on rational, conscious motives, the patients will provide their own irrational motives for cooperation. The argument may be raised that I have presented material from the early phase of an analysis, at a point when the alliance has not yet been established. I shall therefore examine the child's material at a point nearly a year after the start of treatment. We now had not only the rational wish for cure but also the experience that cooperating with the analytic work brought relief. In addition, Erica had begun to identify with the functions of the analyst and so a part of her ego could at times observe, analyze, and even interpret her experience. We thus seemed to have established the rational and stable working alliance described in the literature. The following material should, I believe, illustrate the continuing importance of the positive transference as the main motive for Erica's willingness to work.

Returning to treatment from her Christmas holidays Erica expressed her enormous pleasure in seeing me again. She had hated the holiday, had been miserable throughout, had been bored playing alone, and had a million things to tell me. Prior to the holiday the work had centered on the anger toward her mother and had led to the first clear signs of a move to the positive oedipal phase. Among the million things she wanted to tell me was a request that I take her sledding. When I refused she did not react with hurt and fury, but this time she split the ambivalence: a male teacher became her oedipal object, while I became a "Mr. Nobody." She read for most of the week, saying, "Reading is my way of not paying attention." Content and defense interpretations met with no success. Although I had become the frustrating, rejecting father who preferred others to her, there was in fact little overt anger and in the main she was completely uninterested in me. After having exhausted all possibilities, I used one of her defensive activities as a way of making contact.

One day Erica complained of being bored and made up a general information quiz to "pass the time." On the following day, when she was engrossed in a book, I put my hand over it and asked whether she could name another book written by that author. She named five. I turned it into a game of "Double Your Money," using the questions she had previously made up. She reacted at first with surprise; then with laughter and excitement she became involved in the game. At a point when I owed her forty million dollars, I said,

"For double or nothing give me three reasons why you haven't been able to talk to me all week." With my support she gave me three reasons. The first reason was, "I feel I can't talk to you. I don't know why, I'm having trouble at home. This is not an answer see, but I get very angry at Lou and Tom. I lie in bed and can't sleep. I say to myself: 'I must tell him, I must,' but I can't." We can see that she suffered and was aware that talking to me would help her, but she could not do so. The reason for this emerged when I suggested that she was feeling sad and lonely. She responded, "I'm not, I feel spring in my bones. I was happy and skipping around the playground for no reason, I don't know why." The reason, of course, as she acknowledged, was her love for the male teacher. In the next session she announced casually and without distress that he had left the school. She really did not miss him and had no need to since the libidinal wishes were now once more in the transference. She wanted me to bump bottoms with her and suggested we go to the next room, which had a couch.

We have seen that the positive transference was a major motive for Erica's cooperation. When it was too intense or too highly resisted it destroyed the alliance. Equally, the alliance was lost when the libidinal wishes were displaced and enacted outside the transference. The ego attitude by itself was not sufficient and she could not speak to me because she no longer loved me. The alliance was re-established when I became, once more, an object of libidinal interest. Having provided fun and excitement, I once more became libidinally cathected. As Erica left the session after our quiz game, she said in a voice filled with delight, "Mommy, mommy, Dr. Novick owes me five million pounds and we did more work today than we've done in all of two weeks."

Identification with the Analyst's Function

All those who have written on the working alliance stress the importance of an element in the alliance that was first discussed at length by Sterba (1934), i.e., the establishment of a therapeutic split between the observing and experiencing ego. They agree further that this is accomplished through identification with the analyzing activities of the analyst. As noted earlier, by the end of the first year of Erica's analysis, such a split had been effected and resulted in an increasing identification with my analyzing activities. One day Erica announced that she had an important question to ask but was too embarrassed to do so. After much avoidance she asked, "How can I learn to read feelings the way you do, the way you can read my feelings?" She wanted to know how long it takes to become a doctor like me. A short while later she told me of an incident with Lou. Lou had complained of a headache and wanted to go to the family doctor. Erica had said that the headaches were due to worries and Lou should tell her Clinic doctor about them.

Increasingly Erica engaged in what one could term "silent analysis"; that is, consciously or preconsciously she worked things out on her own. While much of this working out was of course a defensive intellectualization, a good proportion was true analytic work. The capacity to continue the analytic process independently is, as we know, an important factor in the relative speed and success of the analysis. From the many examples I could quote, the following one illustrates mainly the identification with the analytic mode of thought. I had suggested that there was something she was withholding, to which she replied: "I've been thinking of that and sometimes you're right and sometimes you're wrong. See, I figured there are some things I don't know at all; there are some things I know, but I don't know I know; and there are some things I know, and I know I know, but I just don't want to tell you."

I would therefore agree with those who stress the importance of the identification with the analyst. As this issue is currently presented, however, there is the implication that this is a rational process motivated by the wish for cure. In Erica's case the identification was due, almost entirely, to the nature of her pathology. In the shifting transference reactions I was often the envied rival, the phallic undamaged sister, brother, and father who had stolen the mother from her. The envy focused on the penis; if she could regain this "special tool," all her wishes would be granted. The penis envy was central, and only after repeated interpretations could she begin to envy other attributes of mine, especially my analytic skills. Thus, a wish to read feelings the way I did was powered by the same envy and wish to possess the omnipotent attribute she lacked. Further, I was the longed-for and repeatedly lost object and, as she had done earlier with the mother, she identified with me. Other equally irrational motives played their part such as the passive to active reversal, and just as she had mothered herself she now analyzed herself. The main point, however, is that the rational wish for cure and the conscious awareness that the adoption of an analytic mode of thought would help her played a minimal role in her identification.

I have attempted to demonstrate that Erica's willingness to co-operate was based mainly on irrational motives, especially the positive transference. The reactive compliance, the ambivalence conflicts, and the intense need to be better than her sister also motivated the alliance, but these factors became less pronounced as the analysis progressed. The work accomplished added other forces to the alliance, namely, the identification with the analyst, the experience of relief, hence the conviction that analytic work was effective: and with the significant decrease in symptoms Erica now feared that without continued work these painful symptoms would return. It is at this point in a case that authors often state something to the effect that the treatment alliance has now been firmly established. The case presentation then usually continues with no further mention of the alliance and one is left with the impression that once an alliance is formed, it remains stable and the functions and capacities involved remain autonomous.

The Stability of the Working Alliance

The following material illustrates that all the forces favoring an alliance are in themselves insufficient to overcome the overwhelming effect of the resistances which continue to arise as a natural consequence of the analytic process.

We have already seen that the alliance can be swept aside by resistance to the negative transference, by the emergence of the negative transference, by the enactment of the positive transference in the sessions, by the displacement of positive libidinal wishes and their enactment outside the transference. In addition, we have seen that the intensification of internalized conflicts can lead to the use of externalizations, a defensive process which can overwhelm all the motives for maintaining an alliance (Novick and Kelly, 1970). But there are many other factors that can disrupt an established alliance.

Defenses and the Working Alliance

One day Erica announced that she would be having an operation to correct the squint in her eyes. I verbalized her fear and she agreed. I then said that the operation would remind her of childhood events, i.e., her earlier operations, and this is what would make it frightening. She replied, "I had too many. This will be my third." She then said that she was in shock. She had no real feelings now, but she thought that they would come and she would try to tell me so I could help her. She then added, "Maybe the operation will help us here." This exchange illustrates most of the elements of the working alliance, including the unusual capacity to take a current external event and use it to explore inner processes. However, despite this conscious wish and the continuing force of the positive transference, she was unable to do any work for a prolonged period of time. She seemed unable to turn her attention to her worries or, when one of them emerged, she could not stay with it. She kept saying, "I can't say," or "I can't think about it" or "Let's not talk about it."

The material indicated that, at that moment, this inability was not a resistance due to transference but an interference with the alliance due to the need to defend against painful and frightening material. She was trying to cooperate but was unable to do so.

The breakdown of the alliance at this point could be looked at economically in terms of the distribution of cathexes. Among other things the intensification of defense involves the withdrawal of cathexis from ego functions and its employment as countercathexis. The functions necessary for the alliance are never that highly cathected or autonomous even under the best of circumstances, especially in children. The withdrawal of cathexes for defensive purposes leads to a diminution in the cathexes of those functions necessary for analytic work. The manner in which the alliance was re-established illustrates this point.

The bits which had emerged despite the intensification of defense had been: new operation—old operation—what happens if it's unsuccessful—crying—losing—sadness. While she was involved in a defensive activity, I took six pieces of plasticine and said that these pieces were part of a puzzle that I could not put together. At first she was uninterested in what I was doing, but then became increasingly curious. As I continued to struggle with the parts of the puzzle she took the plasticine and said, "Here! Let me show you. You don't have it quite right." She made a large piece of plasticine and said, "This is the operation. It's the big one. The operation is the main piece, like the middle of a wheel, the other things are like spokes." She verbalized the feelings of loss and anger relating to the forthcoming operation, then picked up the last two pieces, "Old operations" and "Unsuccessful," and said, "I don't know how they fit in. This is the problem, isn't it? And this is where you will help." As we were leaving she said, "It was difficult to talk but once I did, it will be easier now and it won't hurt as much."

The Alliance and Progressive Development

At the beginning of the second year of analysis there was a brief period when a significant positive shift could be seen and, most central, the work on her ambivalence had decreased the level of anxiety and the intense conflict with the superego. Erica could now experience and verbalize her anger at her current objects. The interference with functioning was less pervasive, and age-adequate sources of pleasure and self-esteem were becoming available. In relation to a tea party she said, "It was nice but Mommy spoiled it; she was mean to me when I came back. See how quickly I told you." When I suggested that she might worry about being angry, she said, "Well, everyone feels angry sometimes"; or, when I verbalized her anger at me, she said, "That's not the same as not liking. You see, I like you. I mean Lou doesn't even like her doctor. She told me so." Precarious as it would prove to be, some stability had been reached at a more advanced level of functioning, and defenses were now rigidly employed against the emergence of infantile wishes. I commented on the fact that everyone went through a period when things closed up. She said, "Yes, I know. I've been wondering about that. At night I brought a pad to my bed saying I must write down my thoughts, but they just didn't come." She then told me that she thought of things before coming to the Clinic, but it all closed up when she walked in: "Like putting a letter in the mailbox. When you put it in, it's gone." I wondered where the problems went if she did not bring them here. "So do I," she said, "I can't understand it. I've been feeling fine, happy, and I'm having no troubles, no headaches, and I'm sleeping well."

This material indicates that most of the elements in what is usually defined as the working alliance were present in Erica's case. Although there was no current suffering, she was worried that the happy feelings would not last. She was aware of the fact that verbalizing her thoughts would help and she wanted to work. At such phases of progressive development the motivation for analytic work is lost and the analyst is left without the usual allies. Progressive forces, which we count on for the successful outcome of treatment, can also be a source of resistance. We must then rely on time and, paradoxically, the pressure of the id as an ally for the continuation of analytic work.

Most of Erica's current conflicts had been resolved, but the source of these conflicts, the original infantile experiences, had not yet been touched. Soon thereafter the feelings of rejection together with derivatives of the early death wishes toward her objects emerged. When I interpreted the negative transference as a repetition of the reaction to the birth of her siblings, she brought the baby album and the photographs of herself as an infant. With these external aids to the recovery of infantile memories we began to explore, in depth, her early feelings, wishes, and conflicts.

Libidinal Phases and the Alliance

I have already demonstrated that the transference can both aid and interfere with the working alliance. The illustrations given so far concerned transference in the dynamic sense of the analyst being the object of the drives. However, what is transferred can also be approached from a genetic point of view. We then discover that phase-linked elements also influence the alliance in both positive and negative ways.

Certain attitudes requisite for the formation of an alliance may be rooted in specific phases of development. For example, a good oral period may provide the basic trust (Erikson, 1950), or the basic transference (Greenacre, 1968) which many authors consider necessary for the establishment of an alliance. The anal period may contribute the autonomy necessary for independent analytic work; and the phallic period, the pride and pleasure in achievement. These phase-linked attitudes would constitute aids to the alliance. As an analysis deepens, however, phase-linked wishes, conflicts, and anxieties also emerge in the transference. As a result of this regression ego functions at times become reinstinctualized and then no longer serve the alliance.

In Erica's case this was particularly evident with the revival in the transference of anal-phase material. The conflict now centered mainly on the intense death wishes toward her mother. The important feature at that moment, however, was neither the defended death wishes nor the defenses employed to stave off the anxiety, but rather her absolute refusal to cooperate. As I moved slowly from the surface, she could accept my initial comments, and then said, "That's true, but I don't want to talk about it." One day she came in with two comics, waved them at me, and said, "I'm determined not to talk today." She withdrew completely into reading and masturbating. She masturbated with a defiant look on her face as if daring me to try and stop her and, when I verbalized her anger and unhappiness, she shouted, "Alright, so I'm unhappy. There's nothing you can do about it. You can't help me, fat nose; nobody can help me." The anal fury and death wishes were evident, even to her, but more important was her feeling that I was forcing her and tricking her to get at her thoughts, the way she had been tricked by her mother to give up anal pleasures. Only when I focused on this aspect of the resistance, the withholding and the defiance as linked with anal wishes, could she once more begin to work and face the terrifying death wishes.

Ego-syntonic Pathology and the Alliance

In analysis we deal mainly with the maladaptive, ego-alien solutions to conflicts such as symptoms, crippling inhibitions, the secondary conflicts due to regressions, defenses, etc. Many solutions which measured by an ideal standard we would term pathological are nevertheless ego-syntonic solutions. To take an extreme example, a perversion may serve the adult as a source of comfort and safety and be relatively free of conflict. It is well known that such a solution, unless it can be made a source of conflict, will remain outside the analytic process. These types of solution are frequently found in children, but their conflict-free nature is often short-lived because ongoing internal developments and changing external demands will draw these solutions into a secondary conflict.

In Erica's case an ego-syntonic solution to the feelings of loss, damage, and castration was the fantasy that she had a penis. From the beginning it had been evident that the fantasy of possessing a penis had been the core of her elaborate pretend world in which the magic swords she had waved so omnipotently were but representations of this penis. Extensive work had been done on the penis envy, its relationship to the parental wish for a male child, and the intensification of feelings of castration because of the congenital defect. The rage at those who possessed the penis and the desperate attempt to regain it seemed to have abated, been worked through, and were followed by the wish for a baby. Erica had made substantial progress on all fronts.

On the other hand, Erica referred to her bedtime as her "secret time," but as these secrets frightened her and kept her awake she brought them into the analysis. These secrets involved mainly her masturbation activities and fantasies. There were, however, as she said, "secrets you don't even know." She was in fact correct because at that time there was no evidence that she had retained the fantasy of possessing the penis. It remained outside the analytic process, for it was not a source of conflict but rather served as a comfort and solace. In effect we had what Freud (1940b) referred to as a split in the ego. One part of her ego had accepted reality and on this basis progressive forces had been set in motion. Another part denied it. Descriptively, the fantasy of possessing the omnipotent penis was split off from the reality ego and remained so by virtue of defensive operations such as isolation, denial in fantasy, and, most important, avoidance of object relations. Yet, these defenses contained the germ of future secondary conflicts. The fantasied penis had been her major source of self-esteem, but the analysis of neurotic conflicts had made available alternate and age-appropriate sources. She was doing well at school, had an increasing number of friends, and found immense pleasure in peer activities. For a number of weeks she was in excellent spirits and said, "I feel so happy, so good, I feel I'm way up in the clouds. Do you think the good feelings will last? I hope so."

One day, however, morose and puffy-eyed from sleeplessness, she announced that the good feelings had "crashed" and then withdrew into sullen-faced reading, autoerotic activities, or fantasy games in which she was a champion boxer, skier, football player, etc. When I ventured a comment, she shouted, "Buzz off, leave me alone, I don't like people. I don't like anyone. Just shut up, fat nose." I reminded her that a similar crash had occurred a while back at a time when we had been working on her wish for a penis. I received a swift kick for my efforts; but when I reminded her of how happy she had felt playing with friends, she began to work and we could then take up the causes of the crash.

She was making plasticine structures and suddenly whined that she had lost "the cutter." She became increasingly desperate and as she frantically searched for it she cried, "Where is it, I need it, it's the best tool, it can do everything the other tools can do and even more, I *must* have it." She acknowledged that the tool represented the penis; but when I first linked the crash with a persisting and revived penis envy, she called me a "nit" and said that we had been through all that before. I then confronted her with the fact that she had retained the fantasy of possessing a penis and emphasized that she could do this only at the expense of her object relations. She stood silent and still as if she was deciding something. Again she began the desperate search for the special tool; finally, she sat on the floor, wailing inconsolably and crying, "I need it, I need it." After a while she stopped crying, dried her eyes, found the special tool, looked at it quizzically, and said, "Here, you keep it. I don't think I need it anymore."

The point I wish to emphasize in the above material is that an alliance alone is not sufficient to draw pathology into the analytic process. In Erica's case progressive development had led to an intrasystemic conflict between antithetical sources of self-esteem. Only after the narcissistic fantasy of possessing the penis had become secondarily part of an internalized conflict, could it be drawn into the analytic process.

The relinquishment of the fantasied penis had far-reaching effects. Only now could Erica move away from a phallic competitiveness with equally phallic objects and turn the full force of positive oedipal wishes to her father.

The Alliance in the Terminal Phase of Analysis

By the end of the second year of analysis considerable work had been done on Erica's oedipal conflicts, the guilt toward and the rivalry with the now denigrated mother, and her fear of growing up. Erica had been free of symptoms for a considerable period, progressive development had been restored, and she appeared to be firmly established in latency. It was evident that we could consider the possibility of termination, especially since analysis was now interfering with the normal activities Erica wished to pursue. She introduced the possibility of decreasing the number of sessions, said she felt ready to do so and that if any problems were left, they were probably "titchy" ones which could be handled within the decreased number of sessions. I agreed to this change and made it clear, again with her approval, that we would be working toward eventual termination.

At the beginning of this terminal phase (which altogether extended over a period of twenty weeks) Erica continued to progress, filling the sessions mainly with accounts of her achievements and activities. Soon, however, she entered into a phase of intense resistance during which we were confronted by a revival not only of conflicts and anxiety but also of the presenting symptoms—headaches and stomachaches. This revival was limited entirely to the sessions; both at home and at school she continued to function well. In effect, we had a transference neurosis which allowed us to work through for the final time the infantile conflicts, especially the feeling that she was being forced to give up past pleasures and objects because I was disappointed in her and was turning my attention to the undamaged rival.

In relation to the treatment alliance there is little to add except to reiterate that even in the terminal phase of analysis, a phase in which the strength of progressive forces had become an additional motivation for the alliance, the inevitable resistances and revived conflicts interfered with her willingness to work. The alliance remained neither stable nor autonomous but required technical intervention for its re-establishment. One problem in particular which arose during this phase can be elaborated further.

A few weeks prior to the actual date of termination most conflicts had been worked through, but we seemed to have reached a stalemate in which I could do little to influence the persistent suffering she seemed to be experiencing in the sessions. I finally wondered if she enjoyed being hurt. She said, "Yes, I do, but not too much; just enough so I can feel sorry for myself." After this admission the work progressed quickly through the final conflicts, the idealization of past pleasures, and the guilt for the natural shift of libido from the parents to peers and latency activities. The wish for suffering and the secondary gain from suffering illustrate a point made by Loewenstein (1969) in a recent paper. He states: "the terms 'therapeutic alliance' and 'working alliance' may have the disadvantage of failing to cover the fact that some patients are willing to get well but not to work, while others are ready to work but not to get well" (p. 585).

CONCLUSION

Using the case of a latency-age girl who showed an unusual capacity and degree of willingness to work, I have tried to test the validity of the current views on the working alliance. It is evident that until further research is done into the nature of the working alliance, the term cannot be considered to be on the same conceptual level as that of transference. Rather, it is a description of the willingness to cooperate and the capacities necessary for this task. Were it not for the fact that "working alliance" has now become an accepted analytic term, it might be preferable to use a phrase which is more clearly descriptive such as "the capacities necessary and the motives underlying the willingness to work." Such a phrase would stress the necessity for further research.

In order to obtain a comprehensive list of the requisite capacities and the relative importance of these capacities one could undertake a comparative study of children who can and cannot form an alliance. The metapsychological Profile (A. Freud, 1965) might prove useful for this purpose; for example, it would be of interest to compare the Profiles of Erica and her sister Lou. Lou is at least as intelligent as Erica, has many of the requisite ego functions, and yet, during her years of analysis, seems to have been unable to form or maintain an alliance. On a prelimniary and superficial comparison one can note that, in contrast to Lou, most of Erica's conflicts were internalized, she used mainly autoplastic defenses and had relatively little recourse to externalizations, and superego functioning governed much of her behavior. A more detailed comparison might disclose additional factors necessary for a working alliance. This type of study would be especially useful as a basis for deciding the disposition of cases referred for treatment.

In this paper, however, the main emphasis has been on the manifold motivations for the willingness to work. My disagreement with the current use of the term centers mainly on the view that the working alliance is distinct from the transference, that it is based on the conscious and rational wish to be rid of suffering, and that once it is established it remains stable and is in evidence even at times of intense resistance or transference. The emphasis on conscious, rational motives for the alliance departs radically from the clinical reality. The patient who can consistently maintain the autonomy of ego functions and retain aim-inhibited object ties even under the extreme pressure of analytic regression is either not in need of analysis or is using the split between the observing and experiencing ego as a resistance, as is frequently found in obsessional patients.

The term working alliance was borrowed from adult analysis and applied to the field of child analysis. The child's relative lack of sophistication allows us to study the nature of the alliance in greater detail. I would suggest that what we have seen in the case of Erica applies not only to other children but also to adults. If this is so, then we can say in general that it is not the analyst but the patient who decides what will motivate the alliance. Some of these motives may be rational, but more salient will be the irrational ones arising from the ongoing and revived pathology. As we have seen, even the necessary identification with the functions of the analyst can stem, as in Erica's case, from pathology.

The current view of the working alliance seems to neglect the inevitability and potency of resistance. In general, a resistance can be defined as anything which interferes with the analytic work. There is a constant interplay between the motives for work and the resistances to it, with the analyst's interventions being crucial for the outcome of this struggle.

This leads to the final point, which pertains to the relationship between the role of the analyst and the establishment of an alliance.

The emphasis on the importance of the conscious motives leads inevitably to a modification of classical technique and a stress on the analyst as a real object. According to Greenson (1965) and others, the reality aspect of the analyst and of the analytic situation is of major importance for the establishment of a working alliance. Thus, in a paper entitled "The Non-Transference Relationship in the Psychoanalytic Situation," Greenson and Wexler (1969) state, "Above all, the reliable core of the working alliance is to be found in the 'real' or non-transference relationship between patient and analyst" (p. 29). However, if, as we have seen, the alliance is based to a large extent on irrational motives, then in the analysis of neurotics we can remain within the framework of classical analysis. We then take for granted that the patient's perception of the analyst is based largely on his psychic reality and not on objective facts and that the analyst will use for the alliance whatever motives the patient provides, regardless of whether they are rational or not. The re-establishment of an alliance will depend not only on what the patient brings to the situation or on the "real" relationship between analyst and patient but to a large extent on the techniques employed by the analyst for this purpose.

BIBLIOGRAPHY

Erikson, E. H. (1950), *Childhood and Society*. New York: Norton.
Fenichel, O. (1941), *Problems of Psychoanalytic Technique*. New York: Psychoanalytic Quarterly, Inc.
Frankl, L. & Hellman, I. (1962), The Ego's Participation in the Therapeutic Alliance. *Int. J. Psa.*, 43:333-337.
Freud, A. (1965), *Normality and Pathology in Childhood*. New York: International Universities Press.
Freud, S. (1913), On Beginning the Treatment. *Standard Edition*, 12:123-144. London: Hogarth Press, 1958.
—— (1916-1917), Introductory Lectures on Psycho-Analysis: Lectures XXVII, XXVIII. *Standard Edition*, 16:431-463. London: Hogarth Press, 1963.
—— (1937), Analysis Terminable and Interminable. *Standard Edition*, 23:209-253. London: Hogarth Press, 1964.
—— (1940a [1938]), An Outline of Psycho-Analysis. *Standard Edition*, 23:141-207. London: Hogarth Press, 1964.
—— (1940b [1938]), Splitting of the Ego in the Process of Defence. *Standard Edition*, 23:275-278. London: Hogarth Press, 1964.
Greenacre, P. (1968), The Psychoanalytic Process, Transference, and Acting Out. *Int. J. Psa.*, 49:211-218.
Greenson, R. R. (1965), The Working Alliance and the Transference Neurosis. *Psa. Quart.*, 34:155-181.

—— & Wexler, M. (1969), The Non-Transference Relationship in the Psychoanalytic Situation. *Int. J. Psa.,* 50:27-39.

Hamm, M. (1967), Some Aspects of a Difficult Therapeutic (Working) Alliance. In: *The Child Analyst at Work,* ed. E. R. Geleerd. New York: International Universities Press, pp. 185-205.

Harley, M. (1967), Transference Developments in a Five-Year-Old Child. In: *The Child Analyst at Work,* ed. E. R. Geleerd. New York: International Universities Press, pp. 115-141.

Loewenstein, R. M. (1969), Developments in the Theory of Transference in the Last Fifty Years. *Int. J. Psa.,* 50:583-588.

Moore, B. E. & Fine, B. D., eds. (1967), *A Glossary of Psychoanalytic Terms and Concepts.* New York: American Psychoanalytic Association.

Novick, J. & Kelly, K. (1970), Projection and Externalization. *This Annual,* 25:69-95.

Sterba, R. (1934), The Fate of the Ego in Analytic Therapy. *Int. J. Psa.,* 15:117-126.

Stone, L. (1961), *The Psychoanalytic Situation.* New York: International Universities Press.

Zetzel, E. R. (1956), Current Concepts of Transference. *Int. J. Psa.,* 37:369-376.

A STUDY OF OBJECT LOSS IN INFANCY

ALBERT J. SOLNIT, M.D. (New Haven, Conn.)

We are in a period of history when the concern about man's capacity for destruction has given a sense of urgency to the search for knowledge about the tendency to aggression as an innate, independent, instinctual disposition in man (Freud, 1930). Few will doubt that the adult human being's destructive behavior is unique and a characteristic that distinguishes him from the other animals. "[W]hen terrible things, cruelties hardly conceivable, occur among men, many speak thoughtlessly of 'brutality,' of bestialism, or a return to animal levels . . . as if there were animals which inflict on their own kind what men can do to men. Just at this point the zoologist has to draw a clear line: these evil, horrible things are no animal survival that happened to be carried along in the imperceptible transition from animal to man; thus evil belongs entirely on this side of the dividing line, it is purely human" (Adolf Portmann, quoted by Waelder, 1960). As one index of this power of destructive aggression, which is very likely an underestimate, it has been calculated that 59 million human beings were killed in wars, assaults, and other deadly quarrels between the years 1820 and 1945 (Richardson, 1960). In man the use of aggressive drives against the self can be seen in earliest childhood, especially in connection with the loss of, or deficiency of, care by the love object.

In this paper I shall report observations of a small number of critically ill, hospitalized infants for whom modern medicine had provided lifesaving physiological therapy, but whose recovery was initially blocked by reactions to being separated from their mothers.[1]

Director, Child Study Center and Professor of Pediatrics and Psychiatry, Yale University; Faculty Member, The Western New England Institute for Psychoanalysis and The New York Psychoanalytic Institute.
[1] Certain aspects of these observations have been reported and discussed elsewhere (Solnit, 1966).

257

I shall also present briefly the observations of children attempting to recover from maternal deprivation and discuss their implications based on an elaboration of instinct drive theory.

René Spitz (1965) has pointed out:

> Anaclitic depression and hospitalism demonstrate that a gross deficiency in object relations leads to an arrest in the development of all sectors of the personality. These two disturbances highlight the cardinal role of object relations in the infant's development.
> More specifically, the catamnesis of our subjects affected by these two disturbances suggests a revision of our assumptions about the role of the aggressive drive in infantile development. The manifestations of aggression common in the normal child after the eighth month, such as hitting, biting, chewing, etc., are conspicuously absent in the children suffering from either anaclitic depression or hospitalism. . . . the development of the drives, both libidinal and aggressive, is closely linked to the infant's relation to his libidinal object. The infant's relation with the love object provides an outlet for his aggressive drive in the activities provoked by the object. At the stage of infantile ambivalence (that is, the second half of the first year) the normal infant makes no difference between the discharge of the aggressive or the libidinal drives. . . . In the absence of the libidinal object, both drives are deprived of their target. This is what happened to the infants affected with anaclitic depression.

In a footnote Spitz states:

> My usage of the terms "aggression" and "aggressive drive" has nothing to do with the popular meaning of the word "aggressive." The aggressive drive, "aggression" for short, designates one of the two fundamental instinctual drives operating in the psyche, as postulated by Freud (1920) (and referred to by some authors as "aggressive instinct"). Accordingly, when I speak of "aggression," I do not imply hostility or destructiveness; although at times these also may be among the manifestations of the drive.

Continuing his formulations about maternally deprived infants, Spitz said,

> Now the drives hang in mid-air, so to speak. If we follow the fate of the aggressive drive, we find the infant turning aggression back

onto himself, onto the only object remaining. Clinically, these infants become incapable of assimilating food; they become insomniac; later these infants may actively attack themselves, banging their heads against the side of the cot, hitting their heads with their fists, tearing their hair out by the fistful. If the deprivation becomes total, the condition turns into hospitalism; deterioration progresses inexorably, leading to marasmus and death.

As long as the infants were deprived of their libidinal object, they became increasingly unable to direct outward, not only libido, but *also* aggression. The vicissitudes of the instinctual drives are, of course, not accessible to direct observation. But one may infer from the symtomatology of anaclitic depression that the pressure (impetus, Freud, 1915) of the aggressive drive is the carrier, as it were, not only of itself, but also of the libidinal drive. If we assume that in the normal child of that age (that is, the second half of the first year) the two drives are being fused, we may also postulate that in the deprived infant, a defusion of drives occur [p. 285f.].

The infants suffering from marasmus had been deprived of the opportunity to form object relations. Consequently they had not been able to direct the libidinal drive and the aggressive drive onto one and the same object—the indispensable prerequisite toward achieving the fusion of the two drives. Deprived of an object in the external world, the unfused drives were turned against their own person, which they took as object. The consequence of turning nonfused aggression against the own person becomes manifest in the destructive effects of deterioration of the infant, in the form of marasmus [p. 288].

René Spitz's contributions (1945, 1946; Spitz and Wolf, 1946) along these lines were of critical assistance in successfully treating four infants, reported in this paper, who appeared doomed to the ravages of postinfectious diarrhea. His continuing work (1950a, 1950b, 1951, 1953, 1956) and that of Hartmann (1939, 1950, 1952, 1953), Hartmann, Kris, and Loewenstein (1949), and Schur (1958, 1962, 1963, 1966) enabled us to articulate the theoretical implications of the observations of the illness and the successful treatment of the four infants.

Aggressive behavior is often mistaken as a threat to socialization or to survival. In this paper, I assume, contrariwise, that in the infant and in older children recovering from maternal deprivation it often should be viewed as providing a basis for contacting the object world and holding on to it. From our observations, aggressive be-havior can be understood as the revitalization and redirecting of the drive energies that had been dampened or deprived of attachment to and investment in the world of love objects. The critical question is: to what degree and in what way do the aggressive strivings indi-cate turning toward health and in what way do they indicate a turn-ing toward illness? In the first year of life, what promotes the cling-ing attachment to the crucial human objects and the binding of instinctual striving elicited and directed toward these objects which are essential in creating this environment?

A seven-month-old hospitalized infant died despite the appro-priate physiological and antibiotic treatment of postinfectious diar-rhea. Although the diarrhea had been viral in origin and the infection had yielded to the classical treatment (replacement of fluids and electrolytes while relieving the gastrointestinal system of unnecessary stress), the child's postinfectious diarrhea continued. The baby died despite the biochemical replacements and despite the detailed attention to his physical condition. As we reviewed the death of this unfortunate child, questions about his emotional needs were raised. However, these questions were put aside for a few days when in rapid succession four more infants, five to twelve months of age, were admitted to the hospital with the same condition—an infectious diarrhea in which the infection had yielded to the treat-ment, but the continuing diarrhea and apathy indicated a lifethreat-ening course for each child. Our study did not suggest alterations in the physiological-biochemical treatment, which included electrolyte and fluid replacements as indicated by a careful monitoring of sodium, chloride, and potassium levels.

We made the assumption that emotional replacements would be essential if these children were to recover. It was assumed that the hospitalization was accompanied by a severe deprivation of essen-tial mothering care, crucial libidinal supplies for young children who had a dawning or well-developed specific awareness of their mothers. It was inferred that the physiological depletion caused by the infectious diarrhea had magnified this emotional maternal de-privation not only by sapping the strength and resilience of the babies, but by requiring initial hospitalization on an isolation ward because of the infectious process. Isolation techniques by their pre-cautionary content tend to discourage and decrease physical contact with the young patient. After having spent, on the average, two weeks in the isolation unit, the children were transferred to general pediatrics when they were no longer infectious, and it was at this point that our responsibility began.

Since a rooming-in arrangement for the mothers was not feasible at that time, we decided to arrange for emotional replacements by providing substitute maternal supplies as closely as we could for four infants. We instituted a unit system of nursing in which each of the four children had the same student nurse for each of the eight-hour shifts. Each nurse had sufficient time to provide total care, essential physical and psychological care (libidinal nutrients), for the children to whom she was assigned. The nurses were encouraged to hold, cuddle, talk to, and be very visible to each of the children for whom they were caring. Brightly colored suitable toys were offered in an appropriately playful manner. Monitoring and replacing physio-logical and biochemical ingredients continued in a vigorous and de-tailed manner.

Each of these four children recovered completely. From the ob-servations of their recovery, it appeared that irritable activity initi-ated the recovery process and implied that this was based on a res-toration of instinctual drive energy. Such manifestations not only suggested derivatives of a qualitatively different instinctual drive activity, but also indicated a change in the direction of the drive ac-tivity discharge. Each of the infants was washed out, limp, apathetic, and reduced to a whimper by the time they were transferred from the contagious disease section to the pediatric unit in the same hospital. The infectious process had subsided, but the diarrhea per-sisted. In each case, the return of interest in sucking and in food was preceded by evidence of more body tone, kicking and flailing activi-ties of the extremities, and the expression of a vigorous angry or irritable cry. These activities were assumed to represent manifesta-tions of aggression or aggressive activities.

The nurses initially were alarmed when the children sounded angry and irritable. They fearfully wondered if they were caring for the children incorrectly and tried desperately to soothe them, since they were aware of our consternation and anxiety about the death of the first child. However, reassured by our knowledge that recovery is often accompanied by irritable, disagreeable behavior, the nurses were encouraged to maintain their care. Soon thereafter, the infants again showed interest in sucking and food, the diarrhea began to abate, and the nurses could tell us that the children were now responding in the expected manner and that they were recovering.

The washing-out effects of the diarrhea appeared to have been heightened to an alarming degree by the child's reactions to the loss of mothering attention. These children, five, six, seven, and twelve months of age, were being deprived of maternal care, which in our later thinking we formulated as the loss of the emotional nourishment that can be provided by a need-satisfying figure who had begun to become specific, i.e., constant, in many significant and expectable ways. This vital relationship was seriously compromised by the hospitalization that was otherwise so crucial for the recognition and effective treatment designed to promote the healing and recovery of the insulted body. However, the infants' capacity to use this treatment regime was seriously hampered by the accompanying effects of maternal deprivation. The individualized need-satisfying nursing care enabled each child to have a substitute or replacement maternal presence, and to retain and benefit from the medical treatment replacements he was given. One could say that critical libidinal nutriments were required before essential mineral and caloric replacements could be retained and assimilated. During the acute physical illness, the dawning ego capacities of the infants were overwhelmed by the physiological depletion, as well as by the loss or an unavailability of the maternal love object, the child's auxiliary ego. Thus, even those external and internal capacities for modifying, channeling, and discharging the available drive energies were impaired and unavailable.

Why did irritable behavior appear first rather than behavior that signified the usual evidence of satisfaction and contentment when the nurse played with and cared for her patient as she provided him with loving attention, i.e., libidinal supplies? Probably because the child generally and physically felt irritable and somatically uncomfortable, but also because there was a need-satisfying object, a detectable presence who stimulated and evoked his fussy behavior and its outward-directed discharge. The student nurse actively cared for the child and provided him with meaningful stimulation and with a target for his feelings and behavior. She coaxed the child to pay attention and provided him with a person against whom to discharge those irritable feelings that are the forerunners of later aggressive activity. One could say that otherwise such psychic energies remain attached to and destructive of the self. In the infant, the mental or psychic self and the body are one and the same until shortly before the second half of the first year of life; that is, in the first months of life the child's psychological functioning is represented by the child's physiology.

Hartmann's views provide a further theoretical understanding of these phenomena. He said:

Neutralization of energy is clearly to be postulated from the time at which the ego evolves as a more or less demarcated substructure of personality. And viewed from another angle, we might expect that the formation of constant object relationships presupposes some degree of neutralization. But it is not unlikely that the use of this form of energy starts much earlier and that already the primordial forms of postponement and inhibition of discharge are fed by energy that is partly neutralized. Some countercathectic energy distributions probably arise in infancy. Again, these and related phenomena seem easier to understand if one accepts the hypothesis of gradations of neutralization as just outlined [1952, p. 171f.].

Earlier (1950) Hartmann had declared:

To take again an example from the field of "narcissism": it is of paramount importance for our understanding of the various forms of "withdrawal of libido from reality," in terms of their effects on ego functions, to see clearly whether the part of the resulting self-cathexes localized in the ego is still close to sexuality or has undergone a thorough process of neutralization. An increase in the ego's neutralized cathexes is not likely to cause pathological phenomena; but its being swamped by insufficiently neutralized instinctual energy may have this effect (under certain conditions). In this connection, the ego's capacity for neutralization becomes relevant and, in the case of pathological development, the degree to which this capacity has been interfered with as a consequence of ego regression. What I just said about the bearing of neutralization on the outcome of libido withdrawal is equally true where not libidinal but aggressive cathexes are being turned back from the objects upon the self and in part upon the ego [p. 129f.].

In these children, recovering from a postinfectious diarrhea, the physical illness compounded by the loss of the mother had a retarding and regressive influence on the processes of drive differentiation and the differentiation of the self and the body. This speculation further suggests that the maternal deprivation caused by the hospitalization is experienced as a loss of the need-satisfying object that was also beginning to be perceived as a dependable-expectable-constant love object. The impact of this loss can be formulated energically as the infant's instinctual drive elements remaining relatively undifferentiated and unneutralized. These archaic drive elements are retained by the body and one might say that they have the effect of a catabolic force. Rather than being discharged in a health-promoting interaction toward the mother and other figures in the environment, the deprived convalescing child's interests and energies were withdrawn from the outside world. This withdrawal further deprived the weakened child of libidinal nutrients that were available.

Spitz's observations, though concentrating on the psychological and physical impairments caused by object loss, have implications for the pathological reinforcement that results when physical illness in infancy is compounded by object loss. In his study of the role of aggression, Spitz (1953) stated:

How does this come about? When the separated infant cannot find a target for the discharge of its drive, the infant first becomes weepy, demanding and clinging to everybody who approaches it; it looks as though attempts are made by these infants to regain the lost object with the help of their aggressive drive. Later on, visible manifestations of the aggressive drive decrease; and after two months of uninterrupted separation the first definite somatic symptoms are manifested by the infant. These consist of sleeplessness, loss of appetite, loss of weight [p. 133].

Presumably, physical illness such as an infectious diarrhea could bring about an acceleration of this process, the child's resources be-

ing exhausted by the combined physiological and psychological in-
sults. Spitz continued his formulation:

> Some light is thrown on this question by our observations on in-
> fants suffering from hospitalism: they present a tangible demon-
> stration of the defusion of the two drives. It can be observed
> in the unchecked progression of deterioration in these children
> who were subjected to long-term deprivation of emotional sup-
> plies. The result is a progressive destruction of the infant itself,
> eventually leading to death [p. 134].
> Theoretically we may posit that in these children the aggression
> has been turned against the self, resulting in the shockingly high
> percentage of deaths [p. 135].

In commenting on the contributions of Hartmann, Kris, and
Loewenstein (1949) to the theory of aggression, Spitz further increases our understanding of the process involved in the illness and
recovery of these infants. He stated (1953):

> This approach resulted in several conclusions, one of which is
> that while the internalization, . . . without neutralization, of ag-
> gressive energy in the ego must lead to some kind of self-destruc-
> tion. The authors [Hartmann, Kris, and Loewenstein, 1949] sug-
> gest further that "internalized aggression plays a relevant role in
> the etiology of illness" [p. 126].

Recapitulating, we can say that in this group of hospitalized infants, recovery from a postinfectious diarrhea was hindered dangerously because biochemical replacements could not be retained in the
absence of the love object. The body's capacity to respond to the
biochemical and fluid infusions was restricted until libidinal replacements could be infused at the same time. The nurse, as a substitute
love object, provided libidinal infusions, enabling the child to retain the biochemical and fluid infusions. Lacking the libidinal supplies, the child also lacked sufficient neutralized energies to deal with
aggression directed against the self and to respond to external nutrients.

Further, I would hypothesize that a deficit of neutralized energy
hinders the body's capacity to retain and assimilate physiological replacements. To put it in another way, the retention of physiological
replacements requires a degree of physiological inhibition—a capac-

ity to store and hold against developing pressure—that may be the equivalent of the psychological capacity to postpone or wait. This psychological capacity is dependent on the presence of a counter-cathectic influence or force (Hartmann, 1950), which is directed against the instinctual drives pressing for immediate discharge. To follow this analogy (with all of its risks) of physiological and psychological explanations, just as a child cannot develop if he cannot wait, a child who cannot retain physiological pressure may suffer from a chronic diarrhea that does not respond to biochemical replacement therapy.

The relationship to the active, loving maternal figure is, as studies of the marasmic, institutionalized, affect-deprived child have suggested, a vital and essential protective and nurturing influence on the young child. This formulation is now elaborated to suggest the further consideration that a child's irritable, aggressive reaction may be his first response of recovery and adaptation when psychological and physiological replacements are made available. In such a situation the aggressive energies destructively contained within or directed against the self are now redirected to the external object as the influence of the libidinally invested nurse vigorously stimulated, soothed, and cared for these ailing infants. In this manner, the nurse as an auxiliary ego aided each child's capacity to neutralize instinctual energies, bringing into effect the countercathectic and postponing, inhibiting capabilities. Without these capabilities the children would have been unable to retain stimuli and eventually to utilize the gratifying libidinal relationship as discharging, relieving, soothing, pleasurable experiences. In turn, these processes provided the conditions for continued object relatedness and a neutralization of instinctual drive energies so necessary for ego development and functioning.

In life-threatening situations, the first defense against an external or internal danger is flight or fight. Flight is maturationally not available in infancy, or, for that matter, in any physical illness. The capacity to fight or actively to express aggression in outer-directed behavior requires an object, an auxiliary ego to facilitate the neutralization of instinctual energies and to provide a target against which the infant can discharge his feelings. Thus, the child is encouraged—in fact, coaxed—to respond in an object-related manner. The maternal object provides the helpless infant on the one side with a target against which libidinal and aggressive drive derivatives can be directed and on the other side with the neutralizing, counter-cathectic influences of the auxiliary ego.

The need-satisfying mothering object carries out those ego functions that provide the expectable or required adaptive influences necessary for preservation of life and promotion of growth and development. In the case of the hospitalized infants with postinfectious diarrhea and their recovery described above, it is assumed that with the replacement of the need-satisfying object and the biochemical deficits the child regained the capacity to complain, to engage in defensive behavior, and to develop that physiological and psychological tone compatible with active, adaptive responses.

In our studies of children who failed to thrive due to understimulation and neglect, provocative poorly controlled behavior often appears as restitutive survival and socialization phenomena presenting a paradox of bewildering proportions. These phenomena have been observed in children recovering from relative maternal deprivation in the home, and in those who were placed in a foster home after living in an institution. As the individual child recovered from the disadvantage of understimulation, his pathway to recovery appeared to be characterized by aggressive behavior. This pattern of recovery, namely, aggressive provocative behavior, was often misperceived as undesirable wildness. What could be regarded as the child "coming alive" as his drives were awakened by affection and a responsive environment was often reacted to by parents and foster parents as unacceptable, undesirable, and rejecting of the adults. What the psychologically educated observer might view as tumultuous desirable unfolding behavior is usually experienced by parental persons as intolerable.

I have assumed that this "coming alive" or activation of dormant and often stunted drive capacities produces a disharmony or dysynchronization of impulsive energies and regulative capacities in the individual child. Viewed in this way, the recovering deprived child's drives and his capacities to transform, channel, or ward off the pressures and demands of his revitalized drive energies are out of phase.

Ironically, just as some of these children begin to respond, to "come alive," the (foster) parents feel overwhelmed by their behavior, which is often misperceived as a lack of grace and gratitude as well as a rejection of the parents. In these instances, the foster parents, feeling let down, often bitterly invoke the explanation of "the bad seed" in these children whose background may represent evidences of unacceptable social values for these parents. The natural parents usually also reject such behavior, citing it as the reason they neglected or could not take adequate care of the child in the first place. This latter rationalization is one of many defensive, protective reactions by these parents in their efforts to ward off their own fearful or guilty feeling about their abused or neglected children.

In their follow-up study of institutionalized children placed in foster homes, Provence and Lipton (1962, p. 148) state:

> As time passed the beneficial influence of maternal care, family life, and the enrichment of experience in many areas was increasingly manifest in all aspects of development. The children became more lively, more active, began to learn to play, and to solve everyday problems. They increasingly made relationships with others. In addition, there were other signs of improvement that were not always universally recognized by the parents as signs of growth: they began now to show some provocative, negativistic, and aggressive behavior. This was a time of crisis for some of the parents and children. If the parents saw this behavior as bad or as indicating that they were failing as parents or if they felt rejected by the child, some either gave up in actuality and asked that the child be removed from the home, or withdrew some of the emotional investment and interest that were so important to his improvement. Others realized that such behavior was a necessary step in the child's progress and were able to react to it in a helpful way.

Socializing is a broad concept. It deals with people living together, forming a unit in which the whole is greater than the sum of the parts, embracing considerations as widely separated as social values and biological adaptations. The infant will die or suffer severe developmental impairments if the mother does not feed, stimulate, and protect him in the context of affectionate expectations.

Recent studies of deprived children (Powell et al., 1967) strongly suggest that the biological forces that are associated with skeletal growth are significantly influenced by maternal deprivation. There is a parallel effect on instinctual drive development: the phase-specific unfolding and organizing of psychosexual and psychoaggressive energies are muted and in severe cases seem to be unavailable for involvement with people and human situations outside of the child himself. Failure to thrive is a term that often describes the effect of maternal deprivation on both physical and psychological development. Such paradoxes as temper tantrums representing recovery and easy adaptation to changes in the environment representing illness are clarified by assumptions provided by psychoanalytic drive theory, especially by Schur's recent work, *The Id and the Regulatory Principles of Mental Functioning* (1966). The maturation of instinctual drives, leading not only to the differentiation of libidinal and aggressive drives, but also to other characteristics, is a productive theory-building assumption in that it clarifies the reactions to object loss and the restitutive phenomena of recovery states.

Emotional deficiency, as in institutionalization, can and often does lead to nutritional deficiency and failure to grow, with permanent residual impairments of physical, social, mental, and emotional capacities. The earliest observation of this fact is recorded in the famous experiment in education by Emperor Frederick the Second, in the thirteenth century. Curious about what language a child would first speak if he were untaught—whether it would be the classic languages, Latin, Greek, Hebrew or his own mother tongue—the Emperor instructed the nurses of newborn homeless babies to provide all necessary physical care but never to speak to the children or show any signs of affection. The infants all died at an early age, and the Emperor stated that they could not live without the demonstrated affection and friendliness of their nurses.

Conversely, when a child has suffered such deprivation and replacements of continuing affectionate care are made available, the recovery often manifests itself by behavior that is derivative of the activation and freeing up of instinctual drive energies. Initially the behavior suggests that the drives are poorly fused and not influenced in a sustained manner by ego functions that are also being restored and unfolded in this restitutive or recovery process.

In considering the implications of such observations, it becomes clear that the maturational vitality of the instinctual drives is a critical dimension of the reversibility or permanence of the impairment of development caused by maternal deprivation. Paradoxically, the provocative or demanding qualities of this restitutive behavior are associated with and characterize recovery of drive energy available for survival, biologically and socially.

As has been pointed out by Hartmann (1950) and Schur (1966) as well as others (Provence and Lipton, 1962), the maturational unfolding of psychic capacities and structures, including id and ego functions, tends to follow the patterning characteristic of the species, man. When there are conditions of deprivation, these functions may be lost, stunted or distorted. In providing conditions that promote recovery from these deprivational states, we may expect to see phenomena in which id and ego are dysynchronous and in which id-ego relationships are conflicted and distorted.

Summary and Conclusions

The study of a group of infants recovering from diarrhea and of children recovering from institutional maternal deprivation enables us to elaborate the hypothesis that aggressive behavior may be adaptive, and to suggest that the absence of aggressive behavior may be an alarming evidence of maladaptation. Aggressive behavior in such instances may be viewed as the return of drive energies available for relating to love objects and life in the external world. However, such recovery often proceeds with the return of externally directed drive activity followed by ego development that enables the child to fuse and neutralize drive energies necessary for the recovery and progressive development.

In the first part of this study, maladaptation involved a debilitating physical illness magnified by the persistent loss of the constant love object, the auxiliary ego. With this loss the infant may be said to have a decreased capacity to form countercathexes necessary for curbing and channeling the instinctual drives and their derivatives. The regressed helpless state of these infants suggests that the relatively unmodified drives were discharged within the body with the aggressive components unbound and destructive.

In the study of older children recovering from the affect deprivation that commonly is associated with institutionalization, the rate of recovery and characteristics of the ego and id functions during the recovery period may be uneven and poorly synchronized. This is often misperceived as undesirable provocative behavior which can result in a damaging rejection of the child just when he has expressed his trusting and restitutive responses to the adults who have provided him with the beginning basis for recovery.

BIBLIOGRAPHY

Freud, S. (1915), Instincts and Their Vicissitudes. *Standard Edition*, 14:111-140. London: Hogarth Press, 1957.
—— (1920), Beyond the Pleasure Principle. *Standard Edition*, 18:7-64. London: Hogarth Press, 1955.
—— (1930), Civilization and Its Discontents. *Standard Edition*, 21:59-145. London: Hogarth Press, 1961.
Hartmann, H. (1939), *Ego Psychology and the Problem of Adaptation*. New York: International Universities Press, 1958.
—— (1950), Comments on the Psychoanalytic Theory of the Ego. *Essays on Ego Psychology*. New York: International Universities Press, 1964, pp. 113-141.
—— (1952), The Mutual Influences in the Development of Ego and Id. *Essays on Ego Psychology*. New York: International Universities Press, 1964, pp. 155-181.
—— (1953), Contribution to the Metapsychology of Schizophrenia. *Essays on Ego Psychology*. New York: International Universities Press, 1964, pp. 182-206.
—— Kris, E., & Loewenstein, R. M. (1949), Notes on the Theory of Aggression. *This Annual*, 3/4:9-36.
Powell, G. F., Brasel, J. A., & Blizzard, R. M. (1967), Emotional Deprivation and Growth Retardation Simulating Ideopathic Hypopituitarism: I. Clinical Evaluation of the Syndrome. *New Eng. J. Med.*, 276:1271-1278.
—— —— Raiti, S., & Blizzard, R. M. (1967), Emotional Deprivation and Growth Retardation Simulating Ideopathic Hypopituitarism: II. Endocrinologic Evaluation of the Syndrome. *New Eng. J. Med.*, 276:1279-1283.
Provence, S. & Lipton, R. C. (1962), *Infants in Institutions*. New York: International Universities Press.
Ribble, M. A. (1943), *The Rights of Infants*. New York: Columbia University Press.
Richardson, L. F. (1960), *Statistics of Deadly Quarrels*. London: Stevens & Sons.
Schur, M. (1958), The Ego and the Id in Anxiety. *This Annual*, 13:190-220.
—— (1962), The Theory of the Parent-Infant Relationship. *Int. J. Psa.*, 43:243-245.
—— (1963), Discussion in Panel: The Concept of the Id, rep. E. Marcovitz. *J. Amer. Psa. Assn.*, 11:151-160.
—— (1966), *The Id and the Regulatory Principles of Mental Functioning*. New York: International Universities Press.
Solnit, A. J. (1966), Some Adaptive Functions of Aggressive Behavior. In: *Psychoanalysis—A General Psychology*, ed. R. M. Loewenstein, L. M. Newman, M. Schur, & A. J. Solnit. New York: International Universities Press, pp. 169-189.
Spitz, R. A. (1945), Hospitalism. *This Annual*, 1:53-74.
—— (1946), Hospitalism: A Follow-up Report. *This Annual*, 2:113-117.
—— (1950a), Psychiatric Therapy in Infancy. *Amer. J. Orthopsychiat.*, 20:623-633.
—— (1950b), Anxiety in Infancy. *Int. J. Psa.*, 31:138-143.
—— (1951), The Psychogenic Diseases in Infancy. *This Annual*, 6:255-275.

—— (1953), Aggression. In: *Drives, Affects, Behavior,* ed. R. M. Loewenstein. New York: International Universities Press, 1:126-138.

—— (1956), Some Observations on Psychiatric Stress in Infancy. In: *Fifth Annual Report on Stress, 1955-1956,* ed. H. Selye & G. Heuser. New York: M.D. Publications, pp. 193-204.

—— (1965), *The First Year of Life.* New York: International Universities Press.

—— & Wolf, K. M. (1946), Anaclitic Depression. *This Annual,* 2:313-342.

Waelder, R. (1960), *Basic Theory of Psychoanalysis.* New York: International Universities Press.

THE INFANTILE NEUROSIS

A Metapsychological Concept and a Paradigmatic Case History

MARIAN TOLPIN, M.D. (Glencoe, Ill.)

Freud's concept of infantile neurosis as the endopsychic structure which is the model of the transference neuroses (1909) is the metapsychological construct which underlies his clinical findings regarding the role of the oedipus complex in normal development and in the psychoneuroses (the hysterias and obsessive-compulsive neuroses).[1] It may seem surprising that a concept so deeply rooted in psychoanalytic thinking still requires further clarification and illustration. The concept, however, has been blurred by ambiguous or imprecise use of the term infantile neurosis by Freud himself[2] and by other psychoanalysts. Rather than abandon a term so intimately connected with Freud's most profound insights into the psychoneuroses, it seems preferable to clarify its meaning and to limit its use to its strict metapsychological definition. I shall attempt to do this in the first part of this paper. In the second part, I shall present a paradigmatic case history of a patient whose infantile neurosis was the predecessor and model of his adult hysterical neurosis.

[1] For a review of Freud's writings on the subject of infantile neurosis see A. Freud (1965) and Nagera (1966).

[2] Hartmann (1956) and Kohut and Seitz (1963) have clarified two other notable instances in which Freud at times used his own terms in a metapsychologically imprecise manner which obscured the scientific validity and usefulness of the concepts. I refer to Hartmann's clarification of the ego concept in Freud's works, and to Kohut's and Seitz's clarification of transference as a metapsychological concept distinct from its specific clinical manifestations. The dual use of the term transference neurosis to designate (1) hysteria and obsessive-compulsive neurosis and (2) the new edition of the childhood neurosis which develops in psychoanalytic treatment results from this imprecision. Since it is not my intent to belabor the point of Freud's dual use of his own terms, transference neurosis in this paper designates both of these. The meaning intended should be clear from the context.

The Infantile Neurosis: A Metapsychological Concept

Freud's concept of the infantile neurosis is based on his discovery of repressed infantile sexuality as the chief motive force in symptom formation.[3] He wrote in 1919, "infantile sexuality, which is held under repression, acts as the chief motive force in the formation of symptoms; and the essential part of its content, the Oedipus complex, is the nuclear complex of neuroses" (p. 204). A passage from "Little Hans" (1909) makes the same explicit distinction between symptoms and the underlying motive force:

> . . . let me say in Hans's favour . . . that he is not the only child who has been overtaken by a phobia at some time or other in his childhood. Troubles of that kind . . . are extraordinarily frequent. . . . In later life these children either become neurotic or remain healthy. Their phobias are shouted down in the nursery. . . . In the course of months or years they diminish, and the child seems to recover; but no one can tell what psychological changes are necessitated by such a recovery, or what alterations in character are involved in it. When, however, an adult neurotic patient comes to us for psycho-analytic treatment (and let us assume that his illness has only become manifest after he has reached maturity), we find regularly that his neurosis has as its point of departure an infantile anxiety such as we have been discussing, and is in fact a continuation of it; so that, as it were, a continuous and undisturbed thread of psychical activity, taking its start from the conflicts of his childhood, has been spun through his life—irrespective of whether the first symptom of those conflicts has persisted or has retreated under the pressure of circumstances [p. 142f.].

The infantile neurosis in its strict sense is that *underlying motive force.* Unfortunately, Freud blurred the clarity of this metapsychological concept when he loosely referred to clinically manifest disorders associated with the oedipal stage as infantile neuroses. (In the best known example of this imprecise use he entitled the anxiety hysteria of the four-year-old Wolf Man [1918] an infantile neurosis, while at the same time he made explicit that this particular case was not a favorable one for illustrating the nuclear role of the typical

---

[3] That psychoanalysis as a science, for which Freud laid the foundation, has progressed to further insights about symptom formation based on other models by no means diminishes the momentousness of Freud's original discoveries.

repressed oedipal conflict in later neurosis because the patient experienced neither a normal phallic-oedipal phase nor a typical oedipal conflict owing to the decisive effects of preoedipal pathology on the ego organization. Eissler [1953] has called attention to Freud's unique capacity to investigate mental phenomena in relative isolation from the rest of the personality. The Wolf Man's animal phobia was studied for heuristic purposes to demonstrate the role of a repressed conflict in symptom formation, even though his conflict was a pathological variant of the typical conflict which is central in the pathology of the typical transference neurosis. Freud's emphasis on the patient's preoedipal pathology and severe ego modification has frequently been overlooked.)

Freud's confusing use of the same term to designate two distinct, although related, psychological phenomena, which are on fundamentally different levels of conceptualization (the force and the symptomatic manifestations of that force) has been continued in the literature to the detriment of the clarity of the concept of infantile neurosis.[4] Moreover, this confusion has been compounded by still

---

[4] Anna Freud (1965) and Nagera (1966) continue Freud's twofold use of the term. The confusion associated with this use is apparent in the following statement of Anna Freud's: "in spite of all the links between infantile and adult neuroses, there is no certainty that a particular type of infantile neurosis will prove to be the forerunner of the same type of adult neurosis" (1965, p. 151). The link between the infantile neurosis and the adult neurosis does not lie in an identity of childhood and adult symptomatology as this use of the term suggests. Rather, the link lies in the similarity of the underlying structure of the psyche in which the infantile neurosis constitutes the central pathology and exerts its pathogenic influence on the rest of the personality under those circumstances which enable the walled-off repressed conflict to effect transferences. In fact, Anna Freud emphasized elsewhere (1966) that there are good reasons to expect manifest differences in symptomatology formed by the childhood psyche compared to that formed in adulthood.

It is hardly necessary to mention that it is Anna Freud to whom psychoanalysis is indebted for her continuing clarifications of psychoanalytic concepts. My attempt to clarify the concept of infantile neurosis was stimulated by Anna Freud's discussion of the subject (1965, pp. 148-154), and by her urging psychoanalysts "to formulate clearer pictures of the initial phases of those mental disorders which are known principally from their later stages, and to clear the field by distinguishing between transitory and permanent pathological manifestation [i.e.,] . . . to study the 'natural history' of the adult disorders" (p. 148). The case history discussed in this paper is such a "natural history" of an adult disorder. While it is presented with the intent to delimit the concept of infantile neurosis and to show the specific role of such a structure in specific types of adult pathology, the case also clearly distinguishes between transitory manifestations of pathology and the basic pathology itself; it also demonstrates how, in some cases, symptomatology and even the structure of symptoms may change while the basic pathology remains the same.

another ambiguous use of the term since many psychoanalysts have incorrectly designated pathological manifestations during all phases of childhood as infantile neuroses,[5] overlooking the fact that for Freud the term was virtually synonymous with the ubiquitous nuclear oedipal conflict (A. Freud, 1965; Nagera, 1966). Furthermore, deepening psychoanalytic insights over the past decades into the metapsychology of a wide range of childhood and adult personality disorders indicates that the infantile neurosis is not ubiquitous and universal in personality development, as Freud thought (A. Freud, 1965). The psychopathology and symptomatology of individuals whose development has failed, for any reason, to reach the phallic-oedipal stage of development (or whose development has reached that stage with far-reaching preoedipal pathology) cannot be conceptualized as modeled primarily on the unresolved oedipal conflict or the infantile neurosis. This finding inevitably restricts the applicability of the concept.

Kurt Eissler (1953) pointed out (in an unsurpassed discussion of this issue and its profound implications for psychoanalytic treatment and technique) "that fairly similar symptoms may be combined with two entirely different ego organizations—one barely, the other severely, modified" (p. 118); and that as a rule "symptoms can only remotely be correlated with [the] ego organization" (p. 120) in which they are embedded. (Eissler was comparing the Rat Man and the Wolf Man.) Much discussion regarding the Wolf Man, in particular, and psychopathology in general, has resulted from the failure to distinguish symptomatology and the structure of a particular symptom from the underlying structure of the ego organization in which the symptom occurs (Marmor, 1953; Rangell, 1959; Easser and Lesser, 1965; A. Freud, 1965; Greenson, 1966; Winnicott, 1966). The

---

[5] See, for example, the wide-ranging discussion in "Problems of Infantile Neurosis" (Kris et al., 1954). Both words of the term lend themselves to such general use, whereas Freud used them with a special meaning which psychoanalysts should bear in mind. (The terms infantile complex, childhood neurosis, neurosis of infancy, etc., have the same special meaning in Freud's writings.) Freud used infantile and oedipal interchangeably. Thus, five-year-old Hans illustrated an *infantile* (oedipal) *complex* (1909, p. 147) and the famous wolf dream and phobia "occurred in *infancy*" (1918, p. 120; my italics) at *age four*. To confuse matters further, Freud also used the term "infantile" to refer to any phenomena occurring in childhood, especially in comparisons of children and adults. While "neurosis" usually implied manifest pathology, Freud also used it to designate an unconscious configuration which was often latent.

concept of infantile neurosis implies the particular ego organization which has been considered to be ideally suited for psychoanalytic treatment (Eissler, 1953), and the confusion of the concept with manifest symptomatology hampers the metapsychological diagnosis on which accurate assessments of analyzability are based.

Since infantile neurosis, in its special meaning, is a metapsychological concept fundamental to the understanding of the transference neuroses, its special, restricted meaning merits re-emphasis. The *infantile neurosis is the leading pathology in the transference neuroses*, in contrast to the many disorders in which other factors play the leading role (such as the narcissistic personality disorders described by Kohut [1966, 1968]; the various characterological disorders associated with critical preoedipal regressions and/or fixations associated with significant ego modifications; borderline disorders; psychoses, etc.). An infantile neurosis is the outcome of progressive libidinal and ego development along more or less normal developmental lines, without decisive impairment, so that the child experiences (to a significant degree) the complex conflicts of the phallic-oedipal stage and is faced with the intrapsychic task of mastering the conflicts. A sufficiently unimpaired attainment of the phallic-oedipal level also implies that the ego as a coherent organization has acquired at least the *potential* for relatively optimal adult functioning (e.g., the capacity to maintain an adequate relationship with reality; to realize inherent potentials; to attain the genital stage in adulthood, etc. [Eissler, 1953]). Under optimal conditions the developmental conflict which forms the basis for the infantile neurosis[6] is resolved (and repressed) in such a way that it does not constitute a significant fixation point which will interfere with the subsequent attainment of the genital stage. However, owing to the immaturity of the child's ego which may be unequal to the task of mastery (Hartmann, 1939; Eissler, 1953), the conflicts of the oedipal stage frequently are subject to a variety of insufficient or faulty resolutions. When such a potentially pathogenic oedipal complex undergoes repression, it continues to exist and proliferate in the repressed enclave of the psyche where it is no longer subject to modification by further experience,

6 See Eissler (1953) for a discussion of the implication of this concept: that a normal ego may suffer a neurosis.

the secondary processes, etc., even though growth in other sectors of the personality continues. The repressed, unmastered conflict then constitutes the *central fixation point* to which regression may occur in later life (fixation on the incestuous libidinal and aggressive aims and on the defenses against these aims—including regression—of the phallic-oedipal stage of sexuality). In the event of such regression, the revived and strengthened repressed conflict exerts its influence on the rest of the more or less intact personality by virtue of the fact that transferences across the repression barrier are effected.

In summary, then, the infantile neurosis is not a clinically manifest entity (e.g., phobic or obsessional neurosis) accessible by observation of symptomatology. It is an unconscious configuration in the psychic depths (more often than not a silent one until its existence can be inferred by the outbreak of the neurosis for which it provides the motive force); it involves genetic, dynamic, economic, topographic, and structural assumptions regarding the totality of a repressed, unmastered oedipus complex[7] which may exert a pathogenic influence by virtue of transference.[8] Those later life circumstances which result in regression and reactivation of the conflict may lead to a psychoneurosis if the previously repressed unconscious contents and strivings of the infantile neurosis succeed in penetrating a weakened repression barrier and in attaching themselves to preconscious contents, an eventuality followed by the well-known sequence of defense and symptom formation (Freud, 1916-1917).

I would recommend that clinical disorders, regardless of their stage of origin or their underlying organization, not be referred to as infantile neuroses. These could be described as childhood disorders, neurotic or otherwise, or simply as mental disorders in children. The term infantile neurosis should be reserved for the metapsychological concept that designates the repressed potentially pathogenic oedipal conflict (associated with the phallic-oedipal phase) which is central in the pathology of the transference neuroses. Ad-

---

[7] This totality includes: (1) a specific ego organization (phallic-oedipal); (2) a specific structural conflict (oedipal); and (3) the various mental mechanisms employed to master it, including their consequences for further structuralization of the psyche.

[8] Transference phenomena (some symptoms, dreams, jokes, parapraxes) do not by themselves indicate the presence of such an unconscious structure, nor do they constitute evidence for the assumption that the central pathology resides in the oedipal conflict of the phallic phase.

herence to the specific psychoanalytic meaning of the term enhances the theoretical consistency and clinical usefulness of the concept of infantile neurosis. Diagnosis, by the psychoanalytic method, of such a central unconscious configuration is an indication for classical psychoanalytic treatment. While the more peripheral position of the infantile neurosis in the pathology, or even its absence, may not rule out analysis or analytically oriented treatment, the clinician will not be misled in the expectation of finding a typical, classical analyzable transference neurosis if the concept of the infantile neurosis is correctly understood.

A Paradigmatic Case History of an Infantile Neurosis

THE INFANTILE NEUROSIS AS THE MODEL OF THE ADULT NEUROSIS

The paradigmatic case history of a classical hysterical patient (Eissler, 1953) is presented to show the central pathogenic role of an infantile neurosis in the obsessional neurosis of latency, the adult hysterical neurosis, and the transference neurosis which replaced the latter in the course of psychoanalytic treatment. Each of these, in its turn, was fundamentally simply a new edition of the essentially unaltered infantile neurosis which had remained, for the most part, the silent unconscious core around which occurred significant intrapsychic events, while development also continued in the relatively conflict-free sphere of the personality. When repression partially failed in latency, the symptomatic manifestation of the underlying infantile neurosis was an obsessionallike neurosis. When repression partially failed again in young adulthood, a failure which led the patient to seek psychoanalytic treatment, the symptomatology was even more varied,[9] but the underlying structure of the neurosis was the adult counterpart of the pre-existing infantile neurosis. The specimen case chosen for illustration of this concept has the advantage of having a circumscribed oedipal conflict and a phallic-oedipal fixation uncomplicated by significant preoedipal regressions. It is

---

[9] The changes in symptomatic manifestations—e.g., from obsessional thinking in latency to examination phobia in adulthood—are changes which are more apparent than real since the infantile neurosis was the source of both. What Anna Freud (1966) referred to as the unproductive discussion of Frankie's change from a phobic child to an obsessional adolescent arose, in my opinion, from the confusion of Frankie's phobia with a genuine infantile neurosis.

not intended to suggest that all cases in which an infantile neurosis is at the center of the pathology are as "pure" as this one.

The Presenting Illness and Its Metapsychological Assessment

An intelligent, attractive, shy-appearing twenty-three-year-old man sought psychoanalytic treatment in the midst of a serious emotional crisis. His recent entry into graduate school, in a field in which his father was very successful, had exacerbated a pre-existing anxiety state of approximately one year's duration. Following college graduation he had spent that year abroad on his own, had been unsuccessful in his endeavors, and with these reverses his anxiety state gradually worsened. He was now beset by fears that he could not succeed in competition for a place in the doctorate program. His fears were becoming a reality as he found that in association with severe anxiety his thought processes became disorganized and "childish" during examinations and that the tunes which intruded into his mind distracted him from his task. He had done very poorly on one examination and anticipated failure on his qualifying preliminaries, which were approaching, because he was unable to study effectively in his state of distraction. He felt as though he were six feet off the ground and estranged, from everyone and everything, including himself whom he could not "see" or "know." He felt "wooden," although when he detached himself, as was his wont, he could see this "silly, trembling, scared fellow" in the examination.

When his equilibrium was already improved after a short time in treatment, he added to the picture of the initial symptomatology. He had felt amazed that he was walking around; he had watched himself move, but he had not been conscious of controlling "this person," and had often felt on the verge of blurting out something absurd and inappropriate. Although he had dated since puberty, close relationships with girlfriends had been limited because he "turned off" when sexual intimacy was possible. He feared failure and impotence if he were to attempt sexual relationships, and he was frightened by the fact that on one occasion during his acute misery in Europe when he had been drunk, he had passively endured caresses by a masculine-appearing homosexual. In retrospect he pitied the man to whom he had submitted. He had felt enraged and extremely anxious when the referring analyst, with whom he had discussed the incident, made what the patient took to be a depreciating confrontation of his "homosexual tendencies." He had had to struggle against the urge to depreciate this analyst's recommendation and "chuck the whole thing" in order to maintain his own recognition that he needed psychoanalytic treatment. (This capacity of the adult ego to face anxiety in the service of a realistic goal was one of many indications for a trial analysis.)

The ominous-sounding indicators of a personality in the process of decompensation did not reflect the structure of the underlying ego organization. A trial period of treatment indicated that basically the ego structure was intact and that "the aetiology of his disturbance had been essentially traumatic" (Freud, 1937, p. 220). (Because the etiology was predominantly traumatic, paraphrasing Freud, "analysis succeeded in doing what it is so superlatively able to do; . . . thanks to having strengthened the patient's ego, [it succeeded] in replacing by a correct solution the inadequate decision made in his early life" [p. 220]. Eissler [1953] summed up the findings regarding this case: despite a neurotic solution, which resulted from the immaturity of the childhood ego, "the development and the maturation of the ego organization were not essentially delayed or injured" [p. 123].) Metapsychological assessment of the personality in the initial phase established the diagnosis of hysteria (the manifest symptoms compatible with the diagnosis—anxiety, examination phobia, sexual inhibition, etc.—are not diagnostic in themselves, just as the acute depersonalization and derealization were not diagnostic of impending psychosis). Sample material leading to diagnostic formulation follows. In the 22nd hour the patient remembered a weekend dream which he introduced with: "I want to tell you a terrifying dream." He connected it with having talked about his envy of his father's capacities and his fears that he would not be able to function as an effective adult. (The deeper precipitants, as will be seen from the dream, were the developing—overly intense—transference and an interpretation in the preceding hour concerning his fears whether he could succeed in analytic treatment.)

I was with a woman. I wasn't aware of who she was. Suddenly I was very potent and in control, not overly excited. I had a full erection. I was the active, controlling partner. I pleased this

female [note the distancing defense]. She said, "So you're not
like the others I've known—too quick." She sounded scornful. I
had the feeling I was with J. [current girlfriend], but the face was
not hers, but in the dream it didn't keep me from feeling it was
J. I didn't recognize the face till I woke up slightly. Suddenly I
realized the face was not a part of the body, it was more like a
mask. [Hesitating:] It was a picture of my mother in her early
twenties. I don't like to associate the picture with her. She has
the expression of a flapper who considered herself a naughty
child having a hell of a time—in a way a leer. That's all. I
wasn't emotionally involved. I had no reaction particularly, that's
what's striking. Like I've described. I was the seeing eye detached
from the figure in motion. [Brief pause.] The idea is repulsive
to me consciously. Until I realized what the face was I wasn't
repulsed in the dream itself. There was pleasure with myself.
I was performing well. It haunts me. I know that many troubles
are related to a too strong attachment to your mother—the oedipus complex. An unresolved relationship would lead to difficulty
at my age—homosexuality or impotence.

The assessment of this and similar material was that the beginning of the analysis was having the desired effect. It was promoting
a regression to a repressed oedipal conflict which was capable of
being revived in the transference. The material shows that the
patient's capacity for sexual and intellectual adequacy was burdened
by an unresolved incestuous attachment to the mother of the oedipal
phase. In his wishful unconscious fantasies (elaborated in childlike
form during that phase) his attachment was reciprocated because
his father was impotent and incapable of satisfying his mother. (The
rival in the unconscious transference fantasy that gave rise to the
dream was the male patient—"the others"—whom I saw before him.)
Repressed oedipal strivings to succeed in the areas in which his
father was most successful—with his mother and in his work—were
associated with fantasies of destroying his father's potency and of
replacing the father as mother's lover. To enter his father's profession, to look at, think about, and master the material of that field
had the connotation of sexually entering the oedipal mother and of
emasculating his oedipal rival, as in the dream above.

Symptom formation in this patient had taken place along the
classical path described by Freud (1916-1917, p. 361) in the neurosis
of hysteria: traumatic reactivation of an oedipal defeat initiated

regression to a previous phallic-oedipal fixation (to be described in the next section of this paper); repressed unconscious incestuous and aggressive strivings attached themselves to suitable preconscious contents (girlfriend, academic work, analyst, etc.) when transferences were effected across the repression barrier which had been weakened by the recathexis of the repressed contents of the infantile neurosis; the anxiety and guilt associated with the conflictful wishes then involved these current contents and activities. As the dream and the patient's associations show, emergency defenses—isolation, intellectualization, emotional detachment from himself and his object —were mobilized to bolster failing repression and protected the patient from the full impact of the intrusion into consciousness of the "haunting" and "repulsive" impulses.

However, it is evident from the presenting symptomatology that his anxiety had reached disorganizing proportions and that without intervention the patient either would have phobically withdrawn from the work which occasioned so much anxiety, or failed to succeed in a task so "contaminated" by incestuous connotations, just as he had previously avoided sexual intimacy or had experienced failure if he attempted it. The technical management of an early, overly intense transference reaction is not within the scope of this paper. Suffice it to say that the analytic work permitted fractionalization of this initial, undisguised oedipal transference eruption and the development of an analyzable transference neurosis that was successfully worked through and resolved because of the nature of the therapeutic working alliance. The material that follows is neither complete nor comprehensive, but has been selected with the view of showing the essential continuity of the underlying structure of the infantile and adult neurosis as this continuity was revealed and understood through the analysis of the transference neurosis.

The Revival of the Infantile Neurosis

The adult neurosis was precipitated by events which reduplicated the decisive oedipal trauma that led to the repression of the unmastered oedipus complex. The patient had gone to Europe on a scholarship to work for a "big name" in the field which he hoped to enter. He was perfunctorily examined by the man for whom he was to work for the year, found wanting in some basic information, and assigned to menial tasks. Angry and ashamed at his failure, angry at the "big name" who dealt with him with such indifference, and angry and ashamed that he could not "stick it out," he left the scene of defeat, telling no one. But the attempted flight from failure could not succeed because there was no escape from the return of the previously repressed sense of acute injury associated with his oedipal defeat, and from the return of the unconscious rage toward the oedipal father who had defeated him, which the current failure revived. This return of the infantile neurosis from repression mobilized auxiliary defenses to bolster the failure of repression that involved the whole personality in greater danger of failure: regression to the negative oedipal position, turning the rage against himself, and finally the dangerous split in the ego which made the self and its rage unknowable to him.

In contrast to this failure, he had worked successfully on a high level of research during the previous summer spent in Europe before his college graduation. When the patient had already acquired considerable insight into the unconscious aspect of his ambitions and the unconscious meaning to him of a failure, he reviewed the above events and realized that their sequence should have been reversed: he should have had to start as a beginner before being given the privileges of the advanced researcher (which had been possible because of his father's connections and his own abilities). It was precisely this sequence of events in childhood (first being permitted to occupy what was for him the adult role and then the abrupt "demotion" to the child's role by the "big name") which had led to his inability to master the oedipal conflict.

From the patient's third to seventh year his father's impressive work at first kept the father away from home during the week but permitted weekend returns. This predictable cycle was punctuated by some longer absences on special assignments. In his father's absence the patient, then the only child, experienced what he felt during his first successful work in Europe. In fantasy he occupied the privileged adult position with his mother, and possessed what to him were its most important prerogatives: to be his mother's companion, to sleep with her at times, to sit at the head of the table, etc. His father's regular returns interfered with the fantasy of oedipal victory. His rage at the strange intruder who was on disturbingly familiar terms with his mother and his uneasy fears of what his father would do to him were screened by a memory he placed in his fourth year: a strange man was sleeping on the living room couch; the little boy was bewildered, confused, and angered by the stranger making himself at home, and he imagined that his father would be very angry if he knew of his mother's visitor.

When the patient was seven his father's work no longer required that he travel. The patient experienced then what he was to experience again when he returned to work in Europe with such high expectations. Both times the returning oedipal father had said to the little boy, in effect, "That's my place. Get out." Again, sample material from the transference neurosis shows the basis for this reconstruction of the content of the oedipal trauma. The following dream and associations were reported in the 416th hour of treatment.

I had come here at the regular time and left. I went out to my car and found notes a neighbor or someone had left saying I'd been parked there too long. "What have you been doing? Were you sleeping too late?" There were two people asleep in bed. The insinuation was that I was sleeping here which I wasn't. I am lying down here. It was as though the person who wrote the note wanted *their* car to be in that place. One night last week your husband called to tell me your flu was worse and you'd let me know when and if the next appointment would be [the "if" was the patient's parapraxis; I had been sick for a week and had been unable to call the patient myself]. I was surprised you didn't call. It worried me. I was also interested in what he was like. He was straightforward and amiable. It could be my wish to be here. The idea of someone there in my place has come up before.

It is evident that the patient was re-experiencing in the transference neurosis that the "parking place" beside his mother (in her bed) was his place, not his father's. When he was displaced again from his "place" in Europe, he left in anger. Then the unconscious rage at his returning father precipitated a regression to the safer position of being the injured child who could not threaten his father (the basis for the homosexual encounter), but the price paid for the continued repression of his rage, by then only partially successful, was the threat of disintegration of the cohesiveness of his personality.

By the time the analysis reached a stage when the patient had re-experienced, faced, and finally integrated his aggression, the recovery of his personality cohesiveness was complete; he could again "see" himself and "know" *who* he was because he knew *what* he was. The aggression, which was a repressed part of an alien self since the oedipal "demotion," had to be unknown and trapped within him (repressed), like the crazy, aggressive driver in an early dream was trapped within his car. (The patient's capacity for analytic work had been evident in connection with this early dream when he was able to see that the driver must be himself.)

The oedipal fantasy of victory had for a long time alternated with clear evidence of an intimate tie between his parents and disturbing ideas of his father's anger at him. This fantasy was "smashed" abruptly and traumatically by his father's permanent return (as it was smashed by the analyst's illness when a real husband intruded into the patient's transference fantasies). The adoption of a baby sister around the same time greatly added to the intensity of the traumatic displacement from his special position with his mother, and it traumatically shattered his fantasy that he would give his mother the baby she wanted. The smashing of the oedipal fantasies led, not to the dissolution of the complex (Freud, 1924), but to the repression of the totality of the infantile configuration. Within the walled-off enclave, where it continued to proliferate, uninfluenced now by reality and further opportunities for modification, the wishful fantasy of ultimate victory was never relinquished. His mother was rightfully his "most precious possession" to reclaim from the intruding visitor. In his unconscious fantasies he was the prince deposed by an imposing, but deceitful, priest, foreign diplomat, or other important personage; or he was the wronged victim of an enormous, menacing thief in the night who entered forcibly to steal his valuables. (As the patient's unconscious aggression flourished he became progressively more afraid of the aggrandized father and of his own aggression toward him.) The tenaciously preserved fantasy of the infantile neurosis, which dominated the transference neurosis, was that if he would hang around long enough, he could win back his lost position with his mother.

In the meantime another fantasy consoled him: he could have won if his father had not come home and taken and damaged his other "most precious possession"—his penis. His father's weekend returns and intimate involvement with his mother, which made him feel so injured and excluded, were screened by this memory: one weekend his father borrowed the firebroom, which besides his fire truck was his favorite possession; the father went to a fire, refusing to allow the patient to accompany him, put out the fire with the patient's broom, damaging and ruining it in the process, and then callously ignored the patient's loss and refused to make amends. When the father was no longer simply a weekend "visitor," the seven-year-old was faced with the enraging evidence that, as in the dream, "someone was there in my place," and with the evidence of the parents' tie which contradicted his unconscious fantasy. Late in treatment he said that he either had to accept what was too much for him then, because it made him so angry, or "I had to get around it by changing reality." It was this childhood change of reality in the unconscious fantasies of the infantile neurosis which had such fateful consequences for the adult personality and which shaped the adult neurosis.

When his father returned the child's unbearable rage led to unconscious fantasies of attacking and smashing both parents' sexual organs in order to render them incapable of intimacy, as a revenge against both of them for considering him and his small organ to be inferior in performance compared to his father. The transference dream below followed the patient's affective insight into the fact that he had regarded the "parking place" beside the analyst as his rightful place, and that he regarded the analyst's husband as a threatening intruder whose "amiability" (like his father's) increased the conflict over his feelings of rage and depreciation toward someone (mother and father) who had been so nice to him. During the oedipal phase when the infantile neurosis was elaborated the child's ego interfered with his overwhelming destructive impulses by instituting and maintaining repression. The dream shows the adult's struggle against its transference revival.

A. [his wife[10]] and I were sleeping in bed. The rest of the house belonged to—I guess, her parents. There was another person there. I don't know if this person was sleeping there or was just

[10] The patient married during the analysis.

there. She was a girl around sixteen. A musical occasion was going on and she was there as a visitor. She played the French horn or trombone. A. played violin and guitar. Something made this young girl violently angry. She suddenly became intuitively aware that A.'s parents thought her an inferior musician to A. It made her so angry she started smashing the violin and took her horn to smash the guitar.[11] At this point I sprang up and tried to stop her. The dream dies out. I suppose I was successful. I don't know. I woke up. [Another primal scene dream to be discussed shortly ends with almost the identical associations.]

During his childhood the patient could not leave the scene of defeat that aroused such violent rage, as he left later in Europe. Instead, as in the dream, the child "tried to stop" the destructiveness—the rage and the fantasy of smashing the parents' "instruments" were repressed, the only form of "leaving" then available to his immature ego. The patient first re-experienced his childhood rage and sadism in their transference revival; then gradually he came to understand their consequences—the inhibition of his adult sexual and intellectual capacities.

The Structure and Content of the Infantile Neurosis

The full complexity of the infantile neurosis which necessitated the inhibition described above defies description. However, the unique advantages of the psychoanalytic method for the study of the child through the medium of the adult (Freud, 1918, p. 104) makes possible at least a skeletal account of its development and organization.

The patient's memory of the sight of his mother's caesarean section scar went back as far as he could remember. When he was five his mother underwent a hysterectomy. Under the influence of the oedipal rage at his weekend displacements by his father, his separation from his mother during her hospitalization, and his incapacity fully to comprehend the nature of her operation, he concluded that all of the organs which made her capable of having relations with his father, and of having babies, had been removed. Weaving his early perceptions of the caesarean scar into the later quasi-rational knowl-

---

[11] The unconscious self representation as the enraged girl was not due, as might be thought, to a feminine identification. The self representation was part of a hierarchical defense which will be described in another paper.

edge of a five-year-old about the hysterectomy, he elaborated his fantasies that her organs had been destroyed by himself (at birth) and/or by his father (cf. the primal scene fantasy described below). One of many primitive versions of this childhood fantasy appeared in a dream during the analysis when his longings for sexual intimacy and his fears of his destructiveness were at their height: an attractive used car which he was interested in buying turned out, on closer inspection, to have a totally rusted-out bottom and was therefore worthless. The irony of his unconscious revenge in fantasy, on the mother who, he felt, first aroused and then disregarded his wishes to sleep with her and to give her a baby, was that his original love object was thus forever deprived of "a visitor's lounge" and he, like his father, was forever deprived of "visiting" and leaving a "visitor." (These dream representations of the adult patient's desire for the vagina in intercourse and desire to father a child occurred during the resolution of the transference neurosis when the patient was in the process of integrating the insights into how his sadistic rage toward his mother had led to his fantasies about her missing organs.) The developmental task of achieving genital maturity and fatherhood had been made impossible by the fantasies of the infantile neurosis. His genital impulses were inhibited during adulthood in order to avoid the unconscious re-enactment of his destructive revenge on his new love object; in his unconscious, the latter remained the mother whom he had rendered "worthless" (like the attractive car) as a love object to his father.

Since the patient could not so easily dismiss awareness of his father's clearly visible genital and deny its very existence (as he had denied the existence of the vagina, a denial facilitated, of course, by the anatomical differences), he imagined his father's penis to be so enormous that it could never have entered the tiny mother; or, if it had entered her, *it*, not he, would have been the cause of the destruction of her organ; or, since she had no organ, his father's penis tore and damaged her, created an abnormal or damaged opening, and so forth. The numerous contradictions of this sort which existed in unconscious fantasies (made conscious during the analysis) permitted still another unconscious solution for his rage against his superior father whose genital the mother preferred. (This was the solution which appeared in the early transference dream reported in the 22nd hour [see above].) In this fantasy the father was a flabby, impotent, homosexual who was unable to perform sexually to please his mother, who after all then still preferred her more attractive son. (Obviously this fantasy was given its adult content at a later age than when its prototype was formed; the essential content of the original fantasy— that the parents did not have sexual relationships and that the father would be incapable of such an act with the mother—is a typical latency fantasy.)

All of the patient's fantasies served one purpose: to maintain his denial of the real relationship between his parents. This well-educated and intellectually fairly sophisticated young man had entered treatment with the unshaken conscious belief that his parents had no intercourse since her surgery rendered his mother physically incapable of the act. In spite of the maintenance of his childhood distortion of such a significant piece of reality and its consequences for his own heterosexual development, the favored unconscious defense mechanism—repression—had spared the rest of the patient's ego, which had remained essentially unimpaired and capable of doing analytic work. In fact, however, the defenses had never been entirely successful in eliminating all evidence of the parents' bond, although the profusion of fantasies attests to the continuing efforts to do so. The tie of the patient's ego to reality had been too strong for reality to succumb entirely to repression.

Despite the intensity of the oedipal conflict which eventuated in the infantile neurosis, the phallic level was maintained. His fantasies of competing and winning continued to center around phallic exhibitionism. As some neutralization of the latter occurred, and as his physical development progressed, the shyness and timidity of the five-year-old struggling with his fears of injuring and injury yielded to enjoyment of vigorous athletic pursuits with peers, which provided partial gratification of his unconscious wishes to win because he did excel in several of these. His academic successes provided the same gratification. But the sadistic fantasies of the infantile neurosis also continued on the phallic level and thus centered around his penis. These fantasies made him unconsciously fear the penis as a tearing, penetrating, "shooting" weapon; they also made him fear that his penis, if its activity were not restricted, could suffer the same fate he had imagined for the parents' organs. Substitute satisfactions for these impulses in activities such as hunting were more easily invaded by the destructive impulses toward his father, with whom he often hunted. Echoes of these repressed impulses were conscious at the beginning of the analysis in memories of peculiar feelings of tightness and dread when his father taught him the safe use of a hunting rifle, and in memories of near-accidents to his father when the patient handled the rifle carelessly.

The patient suffered from intense guilt toward the parents whom he also loved, and from intense retaliatory fears aroused by his primitive fantasies of damaging them. But it was neither the guilt nor the fear which led to a partial solution of the oedipal conflict (still another layer of the infantile neurosis)—a solution that was crucial in his adult neurosis. The patient's development in the area of progressive neutralization (Kohut and Seitz, 1963) had been favorable, both because of his good constitutional endowment and because he had essentially conflict-free relationships with both parents outside of the area of the basic conflict. (These relationships with adequately supporting parents with whom he had neutralizing and neutralized experiences also structured his personality. They later permitted the re-establishment of that sufficiently conflict-free working-learning relationship with the analyst, with whom further neutralizing and integrative experiences occurred. These in turn enabled the patient to complete the development of adulthood and adult genitality.) The extensive use of identification led not only to the conflictful identification with the phallic-aggressive father of his fantasies, but also to more neutralized ego identifications with the successful father, thus lending specific features to the oedipal superego. These ego and superego identifications combined in the formation of another solution. This solution, since it was less sadistic, interfered with, but did not entirely halt, his further progression.

At the same time the more conflictful identifications persisted as well. Since his continuing oedipal wishes involved him chronically in the twofold danger of injuring his parents and of retaliative injury to himself, the psyche evolved a compromise fantasy version of the father in which the father retained his genitals and, by virtue of identification, the patient retained his. The cruder version of the emasculated, impotent father was overlayed by the fantasy that the father was a "neuter" man disinterested in sexual relationships. The compromise also involved his mother. From the "worthless" object without a "bottom" she was elevated to the idealized position of a "noble lady" who was above anything as base as sexuality. The patient's identification with the neuter father then made both father and son neuter men who did not have sexual relationships with the "noble lady." Now neither of them possessed her sexually, but she belonged to both of them in a desexualized way, and father and son were allied in masculine pursuits that did not include her. (The patient had, in fact, learned many skills from his father, and they shared a mutual enjoyment of many masculine activities that did not include the mother and sister.)

The transference repetition of this layer of the infantile neurosis made its defensive and protective function clear. When the patient's violent oedipal jealousy and destructive anger had been rearoused and he was terrified by his own sadism which he endeavored to inhibit, he dreamed that a sadistic rapist was trying to enter to attack an unknowing and childlike version of his wife. The acute anxiety aroused by the danger in the dream (the danger of *his* sadistic attack on the analyst who had disappointed him as his mother had) was immediately alleviated when the rapist turned into a pleasant "neuter" man of his acquaintance whose only passion was his work. The innocent child (another version of the "noble lady") had been spared from attack by turning himself and his father into disinterested "neuters." This solution appeased the superego, an introject of the prohibiting oedipal father whose main commands the patient's psyche tried to fulfill by maintaining in repression the childhood incestuous and sadistic impulses, or by inhibiting their enactment when repression failed. The commands perpetuated internally the child's experience with the father of the oedipal conflict (as well as commands of the real father) who demanded, as it were, that "you shall not make demonstrations of any sort that threaten the *status quo* and an even keel," and "you shall not hurt your mother." The patient's occasional angry outbursts, triggered by events that particularly aroused his outraged sense of having been cast off by his mother, produced bewildered tears in the too easily hurt mother, and stern reprimands from the overly controlled and overly strict father who demanded that the patient act his age (control his outbursts) or lose his privileges.

In the main, however, the "neuter" role assigned to his father and himself enabled the child to maintain relatively undisturbed relations with both parents and to enter into what was on the surface an unremarkable latency and adolescence. Because during both phases he was unusually successful in many areas (social, academic, athletic) the patient's personality was enriched and his realistic ambitions and goals for himself expanded accordingly. Thus a relatively stable truce was formed, subject to occasional invasion either by feelings of being crushed and oppressed by his father's excessive power over him, or by what to him were incomprehensible impulses to utter obscenities in his parents' presence or in church (the isolated residues of the unconscious impulses to attack the parents' sexual organs). The feelings of oppression, passivity, and awe toward his father, the result of the negative oedipal conflict, were revived in the analysis as a defense against the transference repetition of the full intensity of his active wishes to win the mother by successful competition with the rival whom he would displace. But the patient had not solved the dilemma of the positive oedipal conflict by a fixation on the negative oedipal posture as a defense because of his innate masculinity, his more neutralized identifications with his successful, masculine father, and because his fantasy of himself and his father as neuter spared him from placing himself in a truly feminine position in relation to his father.

The Infantile Neurosis: Underlying Structure of the Adult Neurosis

The patient's relationships with young women were more strongly influenced by the infantile neurosis and the two solutions of the repressed oedipal conflict which were part of it. The relationships which he had regarded as "normal" and "successful" involved competition for a girl in which he triumphantly won out over another man. But the relationship never progressed to sexual and emotional intimacy, or foundered when either was attempted. He remained the neuter man of his childhood identification with his neuter father because his interest in women could not include either since both were invaded by the infantile neurosis. The relationships in which he felt great distress with himself were characterized by feeling passive toward an idealized girl who, in his fantasies, abhorred sexuality and toward whom he could not make "crude" sexual advances. This was the mother of his childhood fantasy who would be torn or damaged by his sadistic attack with his penis unless it were small and passive, just as he was in relation to her; and she was the mother who had been saved from his attack by his idealization of her as above sexual interests. His involvements with such a girl bordered on bondage, and he became progressively more ashamed and enslaved as he became "unnaturally" demanding of her exclusive attention. As the girl cooled (or, more often, simply did not respond with such total involvement), he felt that he could not exist without her, but it was he who would finally break off the relationship in hurt rage; leaving in this way enabled him to preserve the belief (of the infantile neurosis) that he could have won the girl if he had only persisted.

It was the fixation on this aspect of the childhood solution—faced with the knowledge that he could not succeed, but unable to relinquish the belief that he could—which characterized the prolonged defense transference. The analytic situation with a woman analyst initially aroused the full intensity of the repressed oedipal attachment. The defense which protected the frustrating analyst from his sadistic attack, and which protected his own genital, was a regression to the position of his childhood. He remained the small boy who, although intensely aroused, had to inhibit and disown his active, genital urges to protect himself and the analyst from the destructive rage associated since childhood with his phallic organization. (The patient's unconscious perception of me in the opening phase was that I too was the mother who first seduced and aroused him and then ignored him.)

The patient's "neuter" role made him avoid sexuality during adolescence and young adulthood, but it had permitted him considerable success in other areas until adulthood. Then, when he was driven more and more toward real adult sexual and vocational goals, he was unable to realize them because the repressed phallic sadism of the infantile neurosis dominated the adult genital organization and led to his impotence in the crucial areas in which he had wanted to triumph as a child. His sexual partner remained the oedipal mother, and his academic ambitions were unconsciously equivalent to displacing and destroying the potency of his oedipal father. Premature ejaculation and *ejaculatio ante portas* characterized his first attempts at intercourse—the failure he had anticipated.

As the resolution of the childhood conflicts in the course of the analytic work led to the structural changes in the personality that permitted adult potency, he acquired a new ego function—the capacity for self-analytic work. It was this capacity that led the patient to the deepest insights into the fantasies of the transference neurosis which repeated the essential features of the infantile neurosis. Only the barest condensation of the laborious work of insight is attempted. The patient first called to his own attention a parapraxis repeated during the whole of the analysis, and then, bit by bit during the work of termination, analyzed its unconscious meanings. Following the analytic work on the dream of the sadistic rapist whose entry he tried to bar, he noticed that, although the door to my office was always open when he arrived, he closed it behind him each time he left the office. In fantasy he had barred the entry of the next patient, who appeared in his dreams as the analyst's husband. Each entry into my office had come to have the unconscious meaning of a sexual entry which destroyed the sexuality of the oedipal rival whom he displaced when he entered and took his "parking place" on the analyst's couch. But again as in childhood, reality interfered with his fantasy—he could not rid himself of the knowledge that someone else preceded him, although again he had partially warded off this painful reality by the fantasies of the impotent husband, the "neuter" husband, etc. The analytic hour itself had thus come to signify for him the "short time" that was his alone with the oedipal mother, and it also came to signify the "short time" between entry and ejaculation from which he had suffered. Immediate ejaculation protected the "unfaithful" mother who had another lover from the full fury of his unconscious sadistic attack; and it protected his penis from the unconsciously feared attack by the father whose penis he destroyed in the unconscious act of displacing him as his mother's lover. At the same time his impotence was both the result of, and the means for maintaining, the unconscious identification with the impotent father of his fantasy. Since he suffered intensely from the painful evidence that he did not succeed anymore in reality than his father had in his fantasies, he was protected from his father's revenge. (Another layer of this same complex defensive identification included his identification with the father as sadistic attacker. This was the identification referred to in the discussion of the restoration of his sense of identity as a whole self whom he could know. When the patient protected himself from imagined retaliation by his impotence he was protecting himself from the menacing thief of dreams and childhood fantasies who came to steal his treasures [his penis and his mother]. Among the patient's significant achievements in the analysis was his recognition of himself as the "thief" of whom he had been so terrified—the "little thief" who menaced his father's genital and the genital of his father's love object.)

THE CORE OF THE INFANTILE NEUROSIS: THE PRIMAL SCENE FANTASY

This multi-faceted infantile neurosis which the patient could only repeat but never solve until the analytic process provided the opportunity for its reproduction and "re-solution" (Fleming and Benedek, 1966) had at its core the primal scene fantasy of the oedipal phase. The emergence of the fantasy led to the analysis and the eventual working through of the negative therapeutic reaction,[12] in which the infantile neurosis also played the central role. The patient's resolution of the transference neurosis (the "re-solution" of the infantile neurosis) had been foreshadowed, but the danger still existed that he could leave the analysis as he had "left" the infantile neurosis—with his unconscious fantasy of success preserved and his equilibrium restored, but with his adult capacities still vulnerable to transferences and reinvolvement in the oedipal conflict, the conflict which had led to his fixation at the level of the little boy unable to use adult capacities. The primal scene fantasy was contained in a dream reported in the 463rd hour (during the termination phase) at a time when the patient was overcoming the last barriers between Cs./Pcs. and had revealed (against what was now strong *conscious* resistance) a "playful" enactment of shooting his father "accident-

12 The essence of the negative therapeutic reaction was that: (1) he preferred to leave the analysis (as he "left" the infantile neurosis) with the conscious feeling that he had failed as a man with the analyst with whom he had repeated his childhood longings, because leaving in that way repeated the past leavings which had enabled him to preserve his unconscious fantasy that he could have won if he had chosen to stay; and (2) he was afraid to succeed in the analytic task of successful self-understanding and mastery because that success had not been sufficiently differentiated from the instinctualized meaning of success in the oedipal triangle of his childhood.

THE INFANTILE NEUROSIS 297

ally" (which his reality ego had carefully prevented from becoming an actuality).

> I was standing by a fence in a field where I've hunted doves. I was apparently there hunting doves again. I was taking it very casually [the patient's characterological defense of detachment to protect himself from the unbearable intensity of affect and impulses associated with the scene in the dream]. I was watching a bunch of little birds on the ground like sparrows. Then some other small birds flew in and lit near the others. They were feeding on grass seed. The second group of birds began to attack the first group. They'd hopped onto the backs of the first birds. I didn't know what they were doing. They weren't pecking. They were jumping onto their backs. I didn't like it. I thought it was a bad thing. I thought it was hurting the birds. I had a slingshot with white beans. I tried to shoot at the top birds to shoot them off. I didn't use big stones because I was afraid to hit both. I didn't want to kill the birds. I just wanted to make them go away. I don't remember if I was successful.[13]

The little boy's wish to make his father "go away" (again), the childhood misconception of intercourse as a danger to his mother (the incomprehensible "attack" on her "bottom" by the sadistic attacker), and his own phallic danger to both parents (again by virtue of his identification with his father's role, conceived of as attacking) were the center of the infantile neurosis, of the symptomatic eruption in latency to be described, of the adult neurosis, and of the transference neurosis. The common factor in all of them was that to succeed threatened his love objects and himself with intolerable dangers unless he continued the elaborate compromise formations

---

13 This dream of the transference neurosis bears the unmistakable imprint of the *child's* inability fully to comprehend the nature of the adult sexual act, and its misinterpretation in accordance with the phase-dominant phallic fantasies, which make the small boy's genital equipment—the slingshot and the white beans in the dream above—the attacking weapon, which then came to be feared because of its potential for destruction of both parents in unconscious fantasy. The transferences across the repression barrier of the unconscious murderous intent to the preconscious content, hunting, did not lead (as it might have) to phobic avoidance of hunting, guns, animal phobias, etc. The phase-appropriate hunting activities with the father, during latency and adolescence and on into adulthood, continued because they were sustained by the more conflict-free sectors of the personality, even though they were also subject to transference invasion. The phobic avoidance and inhibition involved the hunting weapon itself—his penis.

which combined minimal satisfaction and success with minimum punishment. The patient's "I don't remember if I was successful" in making the "top bird" go away was a faithful communication reflecting the psychic situation of childhood which he was reliving in the transference neurosis. The negation (Freud, 1925) which appears in that statement did not exist in the walled-off unconscious constellation. The wish to make the father go away "succeeded" all too well in unconscious fantasy, but only at the expense of the crippling alterations of his own self representation and the representation of his oedipal objects. The price of that success was the maintenance of the neurosis. The negation—"I don't remember if I was successful"—arose from that part of the patient's ego which reacted throughout his childhood and adolescence with pain, disbelief, anxiety, and bewilderment to those unmistakable signs of the parents' relationship, from their casual and unselfconscious affection in his presence, to their disappearance behind the closed door of their bedroom from which he was excluded (cf. the screen memory of the fire to which he could not accompany his father). The fact that the patient was not successful in reality, or even completely in fantasy, necessitated the complex fantasy elaborations which convinced only a part of him that his perceptions could be denied. In spite of all the defenses against it, the intact portion of the child's ego did perceive the painful reality—an undistorted perception which eventually enabled the adult ego to resolve the conflicts of the infantile neurosis along typical childhood lines.[14]

---

[14] Again, the resolution achieved during the termination phase can only be indicated schematically. The adult patient re-experienced the childhood longing to be chosen as his mother's lover, and finally the awareness that he would not be chosen because her choice (of his oedipal rival) was a "foregone conclusion." He experienced then, for the first time, the full intensity of the disappointment and sorrow of his childhood, and the disappointment and sorrow associated with the irretrievable loss of a childhood fantasy of success that was unfulfillable then, as it was unfulfillable now with the analyst. It was only then that he turned, with a feeling of deep pride and satisfaction, to the woman he had chosen, and who had openly chosen him as her lover—his wife. This "re-solution" was possible because he had first faced himself as the enraged boy charging to smash his mother's genital because she had found his "inferior"; in this acknowledgment he was able to acknowledge the existence of her vagina that he had denied; and it was possible because he had faced his destructive impulses toward his father, and then restored to *him* the phallic equipment he had rendered "out of order," the restoration which enabled him to see his own adult equipment as that which a real man could use and which "worked" (the material in quotations is from dreams).

Repression of the infantile neurosis failed at two critical points. The failure in young adulthood has been described in connection with the precipitating events and their internal consequences, which led the patient to seek treatment. The earlier failure occurred during latency, when the psyche was still struggling with the prolonged oedipal conflict, when repression was still insecure, and when the original intensities of the conflict were not greatly diminished. Again, it was a combination of specific external factors, as in the later neurosis, which reignited the conflict for which repression could no longer suffice.

The patient lived in an area in which three severe poliomyelitis epidemics occurred when he was eight, nine, and ten years old. Residues of the repressed destructive wishes toward the parents remained in consciousness as terrifying fears, when he was alone in bed at night, that one or both parents would die, fears to which he was especially prone when the day residue had made him particularly angry at his parents. At some time during his ninth year a neighbor playmate died suddenly from a cerebral hemorrhage. He had never really liked this playmate; they frequently quarreled, and he had been angry at him over some scrape just before the child's death. He suffered from the guilty thought that his anger had been instrumental in the child's sudden death. He continued to be very fond of the playmate's mother, a fondness which she reciprocated and which grew after her own child's death. By sheerest coincidence, the neighbor on the other side of his home was a childless woman whose husband had been killed in the war. An unconscious link was formed between the death of the loving neighbor's child with whom he continued his gratifying and affectionate relationship (into adulthood) and the death of the husband who had gone away from home (like his father) and never returned.

His mother's anxious concern about his health during the polio epidemics led her to insist, against his objections, that he nap during the summer afternoons. To induce him to do so, she sometimes let him sleep in her bed and got into bed with him. He remembered one such nap when he awoke to find that his mother had partially disrobed because of the summer heat and was sleeping beside him. (The memory was the childhood component of a traumatic transference dream which initiated the prolonged defense transference in which he assumed the defensive posture of the small boy seduced by an older woman who would be shocked by his active sexual response to her "unknowing" seduction.) The child began to grow more and more fearful that he would get polio as the epidemic continued. He felt intense dread whenever he passed the polio hospital and had terrifying fantasies of what it would be like to be imprisoned there, perhaps never to return. He began to pray that he would not get polio and then to "think superstitiously" in numbers. Any combination of 3's was unlucky and had to be warded off and undone by lucky combinations of 7's. As his superstitions preoccupied him more and more, he began to worry that the worrying itself was unlucky and would cause the very illness he worried about. His "worrying about his worries" increased—and then the crucial blow struck.

When he was ten he became gravely ill with acute bulbar and spinal polio. Although he recovered fully from the paralysis and weakness of both extremities, after a three-month hospitalization and a six-month convalescence, his psyche did not fully recover in the sector of the oedipal fantasies and in that magical realm of childhood thinking connected with these fantasies. To his way of thinking —at that time the secondary process was not yet so securely established that it could counter his magical thinking—his escape from what he regarded as his father's retaliation against him for his destructive attack on both parents was nothing short of a "miracle," and he continued to think in these terms. The real threats to him posed by the polio—another separation from his mother (whom he ambivalently loved, hated, and needed), and permanent injury to his then most highly prized phallic equipment (the musculoskeletal apparatus so valued during his latency)—involved precisely those injuries he had inflicted on his father in fantasy: separation from the mother (as a sexual partner and by death) forever and castration. He remained particularly vulnerable from that point onward to the regressive compromise solutions of the infantile neurosis in order to protect himself and his parents from the ever-present possibility of the magical recurrence of the threat of death or injury. Another of the chance chain of events which had a profound "fit" for his inner life occurred during his year of attempted flight from failure and the return of the repressed rage after his "demotion" in Europe. Again he escaped "miraculously" (from a near-fatal auto accident that almost destroyed his treasured car) and again the escape from death or crippling injury aggravated the developing neurosis, as it had during latency, because of its correspondence to the fantasies of the infantile neurosis.

The repressive mechanism was not sufficient to its task during latency when again, as in the hardly passed oedipal stage, he was exposed to a prolonged castration threat (polio) and to behavior on his mother's part which rearoused his oedipal attachment to her. Before the polio threat his repressed death wishes toward both parents "returned" when conscious anger over some current "injustice" served as a point of attachment for the repressed rage and sadism; isolation then bolstered repression and he had anxious "thoughts" about his parents' dying, but the sadistic fantasies remained repressed; displacement (to the death of the playmate and the dead husband who went away and never returned) likewise bolstered the repression, which the child's psyche needed to protect his parents from his rage. Neither of these phenomena would warrant description as a full-blown obsessional neurosis, however, and neither is an atypical latency residue of the repressed oedipal conflict (A. Freud, 1965).

This still vulnerable equilibrium required yet another trauma for its disruption and for the formation of symptoms. As the inner threats of injury were aggravated by his visions of "withered," unusable legs and arms, or by visions of his death; and, more important perhaps, by his mother's unconsciously infantilizing and seductive behavior, which rearoused his "right" to sleep with her and his rage that his "rights" were violated (except when he had to be "little" and nap, or was sick), the failing repression was buttressed by magical thinking. If he could avoid thinking about 3's (himself, his mother, and his father), he could avoid their injury and therefore his own. The anxiety (the small boy's "worry") aroused by the sadistic fantasies associated with his triangular involvements (3's) was displaced from the revived and reinforced sadistic impulses first to the "worry" about polio and then to the activity of worrying. When he "wor-

ried about his worries," he spared himself and his parents from the
disrupting effects on their relationships that the intrusion into consciousness and overt behavior of his sadistic urges would have had.
(Although the patient suffered acutely from his obsessional anxieties,
he kept his worries to himself. The presence of a childhood neurosis
was not evident to the outside observer.)

It is beyond the scope of this paper to discuss the exact diagnosis
of the latency disorder, nor is it essential to the main thesis whether
this disorder is designated as an obsessional reaction or a genuine
obsessive-compulsive neurosis.[15] However, the fact that symptoms
did break out is relevant to the main theme of this paper. The external stress, with its internal consequences, imposed an additional
burden on the already overburdened psyche which was confronted
with the task of having to integrate the prolonged oedipal stimulation. Had it not been for the polio, the third childhood trauma (following on his father's return and his sister's adoption), the crucial
aspect of the patient's oedipal fixation—the sadistic-phallic urges
curbed by a superego which demanded an eye for an eye—might
have had a less injurious effect on his masculine development. It is
clear that the rearousal of the full intensities of the pre-existing infantile neurosis by the events preceding the polio provided the
motive force for the obsessional disorder of latency. It is also clear
that the traumatic illness, coupled with the obsessional disorder,
further consolidated the position of the infantile neurosis in the
psychic structure where it then continued actively to influence the
further development of all sectors that could be drawn into the
sphere of conflict.[16]

15 Cf. Anna Freud's discussion of the unsatisfactory status of diagnostic categories,
especially for childhood disorders (1965, p. 109f.). The diagnosis in this case is of considerable interest and merits separate discussion since the pathology was primarily
within the thought processes themselves and involved typical "ego devices" to ward
off objectionable contents classically associated with obsessive-compulsive neurosis (A.
Freud, 1966) without significant regression to the anal-sadistic level. The danger
remained phallic.

16 Although this point is debatable, it is highly probable that the accurate diagnosis of infantile neurosis can be made only retrospectively when childhood development
is more or less completed, and when the psychoanalytic method of assessment is
employed, since it is a metapsychological, not a clinical diagnosis. On the other hand,
the psychoanalytic clinician usually makes an "educated guess" about the existence
of this complex structure before undertaking an analysis, at least in the case of an
adult.

Conclusion

A paradigmatic case history has been presented to demonstrate that a symptomatic neurosis of latency and an adult neurosis (replaced by a transference neurosis) had as their point of departure an infantile neurosis, and that they were, in fact, a continuation of the infantile neurosis (Freud, 1909) which was their central underlying structure. Although its symptomatic manifestations changed considerably as the ego faced changing developmental tasks, the underlying infantile neurosis, recapitulated and reconstructed in the transference neurosis, remained the genetic core and the prototype and model for the patient's obsessional neurosis of latency and for the hysterical neurosis of his adulthood. These findings corroborate Freud's description of Little Hans: "a continuous and undisturbed thread of psychical activity, taking its start from the conflicts of his childhood, has been spun through his life—irrespective of whether the first symptom of those conflicts . . . persisted or . . . retreated under the pressure of circumstances" (1909, p. 143).

Summary

In Part I Freud's concept of the infantile neurosis as the model of the adult neurosis was discussed. Distinct from clinically manifest neurotic disorders in children, infantile neurosis has been defined as a metapsychological concept which is fundamental to the understanding and treatment of the transference neuroses (psychoneuroses) in which it constitutes the leading pathology of the personality.

In Part II a paradigmatic case history of an infantile neurosis—the phase-appropriate endopsychic configuration associated with the phallic-oedipal level—was presented to illustrate the concept. In the transference neurosis the patient recapitulated the pathogenic events and solutions of childhood that were preserved in the infantile neurosis. The data abstracted from his analysis demonstrated that the underlying structure of a hysterical neurosis was the adult counterpart of the infantile neurosis. External events which reduplicated the first childhood trauma precipitated the outbreak of symptoms in adulthood. The adult neurosis repeated in its essentials the unmastered conflicts on which the infantile neurosis was based. These conflicts, typically, had their origin in the phallic-oedipal phase of development; at their core was the primal scene fantasy of that phase of personality organization. The ego organization, spared by repression, was left intact despite the intensity of the conflicts, which remained on the phallic level in the absence of significant preoedipal fixations.

The infantile neurosis, the totality of the repressed phase-appropriate conflicts, was pathogenic in this case as a consequence of an unduly prolonged oedipal phase, which was traumatically interrupted. The trauma which shattered the patient's cherished oedipal beliefs led to massive repression of the unaltered beliefs and wishes and the dangers associated with them. The beliefs and wishes continued to proliferate in the repressed enclave of the psyche, influencing the rest of the personality by virtue of transferences which were effected when repression could no longer deal with renewed stresses and fresh traumas. In mid-latency chronic external stress rearoused the full intensities of the oedipal strivings and fears, necessitating additional defenses to augment the repressive mechanism which could no longer contain the recathected infantile neurosis. At that time this internal constellation led to obsessional manifestations. These in association with the continuing chronic stress prepared the matrix on which the new trauma of a severe physical illness could exert a lasting effect on the personality. Although the infantile neurosis was re-repressed after recovery (now without the need for the auxiliary defenses which, had they continued, could have led to permanent ego modifications), a part of the latency child's ego was left with the belief in the reality of the oedipal fantasies; and subsequent development to the adult genital level was halted by the enduring influence of the phallic-oedipal fantasies and conflicts of the infantile neurosis until their opportunity for "resolution" in psychoanalytic treatment.

The case chosen for illustrating the concept of infantile neurosis has the advantage of a paradigm uncomplicated by preoedipal regressions and fixations, but it is not intended to suggest that this is true in all adult neuroses based on infantile neuroses. In most adult neuroses the structure is far more complicated than that outlined above. The paradigm is intended to show the central role of the infantile neurosis in the transference neuroses (psychoneuroses) in which it constitutes the leading pathology and which, for this reason, makes it eminently suited for psychoanalytic treatment by the basic model technique.

BIBLIOGRAPHY

Easser, B. & Lesser, S. R. (1965), Hysterical Personality: A Re-evaluation. *Psa. Quart.*, 34:390-405.
Eissler, K. R. (1953), The Effect of the Structure of the Ego on Psychoanalytic Technique. *J. Amer. Psa. Assn.*, 1:104-143.
Fleming, J. & Benedek, T. (1966), *Psychoanalytic Supervision*. New York: Grune & Stratton.
Freud, A. (1965), *Normality and Pathology in Childhood*. New York: International Universities Press.
—— (1966), Obsessional Neurosis: A Summary of Psycho-Analytic Views as Presented at the Congress. *Int. J. Psa.*, 47:116-122.
Freud, S. (1909), Analysis of a Phobia in a five-year-old Boy. *Standard Edition*, 10:3-149. London: Hogarth Press, 1955.
—— (1916-1917 [1915-1917]), Introductory Lectures on Psycho-Analysis. *Standard Edition*, 15 & 16. London: Hogarth Press, 1963.
—— (1918 [1914]), From the History of an Infantile Neurosis. *Standard Edition*, 17:3-122. London: Hogarth Press, 1955.
—— (1919), 'A Child Is Being Beaten': A Contribution to the Study of the Origin of Sexual Perversions. *Standard Edition*, 17:177-204. London: Hogarth Press, 1955.
—— (1924), The Dissolution of the Oedipus Complex. *Standard Edition*, 14:173-179. London: Hogarth Press, 1961.
—— (1925), Negation. *Standard Edition*, 14:235-239. London: Hogarth Press, 1961.
—— (1937), Analysis Terminable and Interminable. *Standard Edition*, 23:209-253. London: Hogarth Press, 1964.
Greenson, R. R. (1966), Comment on Dr Ritvo's Paper. *Int. J. Psa.*, 47:149-150.
Hartmann, H. (1939), Psychoanalysis and the Concept of Health. *Essays on Ego Psychology*. New York: International Universities Press, 1964, pp. 1-18.
—— (1956), The Development of the Ego Concept in Freud's Work. *Essays on Ego Psychology*. New York: International Universities Press, 1964, pp. 268-296.
Kohut, H. (1966), Forms and Transformations of Narcissism. *J. Amer. Psa. Assn.*, 14:243-272.
—— (1968), The Psychoanalytic Treatment of Narcissistic Personality Disorders. *This Annual*, 23:86-113.
—— & Seitz, P. (1963), Concepts and Theories of Psychoanalysis. In: *Concepts of Personality*, ed. J. M. Wepman & R. W. Heine. Chicago: Aldine, pp. 113-141.
Kris, E. et al. (1954), Problems of Infantile Neurosis. *This Annual*, 9:16-71.
Marmor, J. (1953), Orality in the Hysterical Personality. *J. Amer. Psa. Assn.*, 1:656-671.
Nagera, H. (1966), *Early Childhood Disturbances, the Infantile Neurosis, and the Adult Disturbances*. New York: International Universities Press.
Rangell, L. (1959), The Nature of Conversion. *J. Amer. Psa. Assn.*, 7:632-662.
Winnicott. D. W. (1966), Comment on Obsessional Neurosis and "Frankie." *Int. J. Psa.*, 47:143-144.

ASPECTS OF NORMAL AND
PATHOLOGICAL DEVELOPMENT

NORMALITY AND ABNORMALITY IN ADOLESCENCE

With a Digression on Prince Hal— "The Sowing of Wild Oats"

Z. ALEXANDER AARONS, M.D. (Alamo, Calif.)

This paper is not an effort to deal with the many problems of adolescence, but rather is an attempt to discuss certain genetic factors that are of crucial importance for this developmental period. I shall also examine the main defense displayed, viz., that of "removal" from infantile object ties. The "successful" employment of this defense, peculiar and appropriate to adolescence, leads to what I have termed a "renewal" of object relatedness on a mature adult level in which there is reinvestment of libidinal energy (i.e., depregenitalized and neutralized) in objects and interests. This is a progressive developmental accomplishment that may be expected to occur if object constancy has been secured in early childhood. Preservation of ego ideals, made possible by the establishment of object constancy, will, in spite of the vicissitudes of adolescent discontent and rebelliousness, insure the resolution of conflicts and the constructive employment of psychic energy. In other words, adolescence marks a turning point at which there either may be a reinforcement of pregenitality with its attendant destructive sexualization and aggressivization of relationships, or genitality may be consolidated, sublimations established, and tradition replicated. This "normal" development or resolution of the conflicts of adolescence is predicated upon the preservation of the ego ideal, inculcated but not yet integrated during childhood. The chaos and demoralization of our time are not only provocative of the perpetuation of pregenital fixa-

Presented in part at the Congress of the Philadelphia, Baltimore-D.C., Cleveland Psychoanalytic Societies, June 15, 1969.

tions, but an indicator of failure in the establishment of an imago of the ego ideal in parents and their surrogates.

This paper is desultory in its approach. Observations are made on a prevalent therapeutic attitude, followed by a discussion of certain clinical and theoretical problems. A critical study of the character of Shakespeare's Prince Hal in *Henry IV* illustrates the resolution of adolescent ambivalence and conflict between father and son.

With apology I use the term "normal" to describe mood and behavior that manifestly seem "abnormal." Adolescence is a developmental period that is better described than labeled. It is certainly an emotional testing period in which the drives place ego and superego under the greatest stress. The therapist is warned lest he fall prey to innovations because of the difficulty inherent in the analytic investigation of adolescent psychopathology.

There may be a question concerning the degree to which adolescence is a natural developmental phase, and the extent to which it is conditioned by the society we live in. There are civilized societies, notably in the Orient and aboriginal Latin America, in which adolescence does not exist as we know it (or perhaps its emotional manifestations escape our detection). I refer to those societies in which "the coming of age" coincides with the individual's assumption of work and family responsibilities. Although it may sound facetious, in our society the adolescent period often seems to be designed to delay entry into the labor market and the establishment of family relationships. However, the developmental immaturity fostered too often allows the adolescent impulsively to attempt that for which he is unprepared.

Whether we regard adolescence as preliminary to maturity or a delay in the onset of adulthood responsibility, it must be subjected to analytic research as a developmental phase *sui generis* and explained in terms of its genetic and dynamic determinants and adaptational requirements. Freud (1925) often referred to the "three impossible professions," one of them being the education of children. This "impossible" task applies especially to the emotionally refractory adolescent whose defensive attitude we seek to overcome. Before embarking on the substance of this paper, I would sound a note of realistic pessimism (if not prejudice): if the adolescent is compared with other analytic cases, our understanding of him is least commensurate with our therapeutic success. But this is in the very nature of the case.

Many aspects of adolescent development have been outlined and investigated by analysts. One would think, therefore, that our knowledge of normality and pathology would have brought about a secure therapeutic approach, as in the analytic treatment of adults and children. However, this does not seem to be the case. There is considerable groping for means of effecting a "working alliance" with the adolescent patient in dealing with his resistances. Because of the difficulties, it has been assumed that psychoanalytic techniques must be modified or adapted as, e.g., in the treatment of psychotics. If, however, this means discarding basic rules of procedure—neutrality, abstinence, free association—we may find that analysis has to be relinquished in favor of eclectic psychotherapy. Structural change, the goal of analysis, will not occur, and there is a perpetuation of emotional disturbance into adulthood. On the other hand, we might turn our efforts in the direction of the *application* of our technique to the treatment of adolescent psychopathology. I would, therefore, make a point of distinction between "adaptation" and "application." The former implies a compromise and a modification; whereas the latter refers to the manner in which a technical rule may be used in a given case. There is a precedence for drawing this distinction in common analytic usage. Referring to the application of psychoanalytic principles, e.g., in the behavioral sciences or education, we mean the use of psychoanalytic knowledge to gain a deeper understanding of the subject matter (in terms of unconscious factors and motivations). In regard to the application of technique, we refer, of course, to the means of facilitating the development of the transference and overcoming resistances in the patient. In other words, the emphasis should be upon the artful use of the tool rather than upon how to retool which is often found to indicate that the use of the tool has not been adequately mastered. Again, to illustrate the distinction, the term "adaptation" is used to explain the way in which biological evolution comes about by means of natural selection, implying an alteration in the structure of the organism. When the term is used in psychoanalysis, it refers to one's ability to comply with, and adjust to, the requirements of his reality situation instead of falling into neurotic illness. In education much of the talk about "adapting" educational goals and methods to the supposedly new requirements of society is often an excuse to avoid the problems of educating, and a covert (we might say, adolescent) rebellion against being educated. The point is that "adaptation" implies an alteration, either in a beneficial or harmful way. In regard to psychoanalytic principles and techniques, it usually proves to be a compromise, if not their abandonment. Nor is "adaptation" to be confused or confounded with the extension of knowledge, a legitimate and necessary development for all sciences. In other words, knowledge of adolescence and its psychopathology is predicated upon acquiring a more accurate understanding of its problems through facility in the use of analytic technique in treatment.

COUNTERTRANSFERENCE AND THERAPEUTIC APPROACH

Because, normally, adolescence was a period of turmoil, there is a natural reluctance to relive it in analysis by recall of the actions and feelings that the patient has later come to deprecate. Focusing upon it tends to revive those feelings in both patient and analyst. I refer, in particular, to calling up impulsive reactions that have led to faulty judgments, and the actions that one regrets; also to the painful unhappiness that universally beclouds adolescence. It is a past to dispel rather than to remember. The analyst who has had a bad relationship with his own adolescence will either avoid treating adolescent patients, or, if he does, his identification with them will be employed in the imposition of his unconscious needs, either to rescue his patient, rectify the situation, or repress those strivings found in the patient which the analyst himself failed to cope with in his own adolescence.

Perhaps, it is the adolescent, of all patients, who is most likely to elicit countertransference reactions from the analyst. Countertransference, as we know, is a reversal of the transference situation. Annie Reich (1951) states that it "comprises the effects of the analyst's own unconscious needs and conflicts on his understanding or technique . . . the patient represents for the analyst an object of the past on to whom past feelings and wishes are projected, just as it happens in the patient's transference situation with the analyst. The provoking factor for such an occurrence may be something in the patient's personality or material or something in the analytic situation as such. This is counter-transference in the proper sense" (p. 26).

Margaret Little (1951) suggested that to be able to make use of countertransference is most helpful at crucial times in an analysis; and, I would add, that with adolescents, to be able to do so is often necessary. We utilize countertransference reactions in two ways: by being aware that the feelings provoked by the adolescent patient may be the effects of countertransference; and interpreting this to the patient appropriately and acceptably. To elaborate on the second point, it should be stressed that when a countertransference reaction intervenes and has complicated the analysis, it is necessary that it be recognized by both patient and analyst. The latter should be able to infer that it has been preconsciously detected by his patient and proceed to help him formulate it into conscious expression. When the patient's doubts on this score are removed, Margaret Little points out that this anxiety may be relieved by the discovery that the irrational parental behavior was not necessarily directed against him. Rather, it may well have been a reaction of his parents to their parents under similar circumstances. Needless to say, frankness (not a confessional) on the part of the analyst about his feelings is facilitated to the extent that he is free of primitive impulses, and especially if his sexual feelings are free from the impulse to seduce—in short, if the analyst has no urge to respond in kind to the adolescent's libidinal and aggressive needs.

The need to be a parent, manifesting itself in an authoritarian attitude, is probably the most popular countertransference reaction. However benign it may seem, it will elicit resistance from the adolescent patient. Either quietly or noisily, he will have to reply, in effect, not to tell him what to do; for as we know, in the need to sever parental ties, opposition is inevitable. The need to be a parent may not be readily detected in the permissive and indulgent attitude of the therapist, which may be motivated by a kind of reaction formation (a leaning over backward, if you will) against being authoritarian; or permissiveness may indicate that the therapist is using the defiant adolescent to retaliate against his own parents which the therapist himself was unable to do in adolescence. In either case the therapist counteracts his unconscious tendency to be a parent at the expense of the patient who, in his resistance, is nonetheless unlikely to be receptive. Restriction or permission may be interpreted by the rebellious adolescent as an imposition of authority, the one negatively, the other positively (the parents saying "yes" or "no"). If the patient, seemingly, is in good rapport with the permissive therapist, we might question whether it is because he has been "bribed" by the therapist's appeasement. A familiar defense tactic by the delinquent who wants to have his cake and eat it too is to accept the therapist's indulgence, but in order to keep himself from any genuine attachment remains inwardly contemptuous. In such a situation the adolescent senses the therapist's countertransference. The basic rule of neutrality on the part of the therapist can be seen as not only valid, but essential. It cannot be applied, however, if the therapist's unresolved conflicts over parental identification are imposed upon the patient.

Explanation of the "analytic rule" may be an indicator of how insidiously the need to be a parent may enter the therapeutic relationship. If it is presented as a rule that must be followed or as necessary for the good of the analysis, the therapist may unwittingly appear to the adolescent patient like a dictatorial parent, however benign. In fact, we may doubt whether any imposition or request can be considered benignant by the adolescent so long as compliance connotes submission. If, in contrast, as Margaret Little (1951) says, it can be pointed out that the "analytic rule" is not something that is "required," but rather that in the analytic situation one is free to say everything he pleases, and, furthermore, the therapist is equally free to speak his mind, much may be done to eliminate the onus of parental authority. The patient will soon enough attempt to call forth parental reactions from the therapist who will then find himself in a better position to interpret the transference.

We should consider the implications attached to the need for treatment. Where it is not flagrantly imposed by parents, it is nonetheless to be seen initially as something the adolescent patient would rather not do. If the unconscious need to be a parent motivates a countertransference reaction, the therapist will, upon his evaluation, speak about the "necessity" for therapeutic help instead of indicating to the patient that his unwillingness to undertake treatment is understandable, because it is a burden, and that it would be best if he could work out his problems on his own; however, if he cannot, he may avail himself of therapeutic help. We are reminded here, in this illustration, of the basic rule that the patient must be freely motivated for analytic work to proceed, and how it may be applied to the treatment of adolescents.

The maintenance of "neutrality" in the treatment of adolescents is in need of clarification, for which I refer to Aichhorn's approach to the delinquent. In *Wayward Youth* (1925) he states: "Whoever works with the delinquent should work neither for the persecution nor for the defence. It should be his sole aim to discover the causes which have created the state of delinquency, i.e. to understand the psychic state of which the delinquent action is merely a symptom and, further, to lay bare the interplay of forces which has created the abnormal state."[1]

Every adolescent is a delinquent at least in fantasies attendant upon the rebellion against original love objects. "Understanding" him cannot mean taking his side; it rather means exploring what it is that is threatening in his infantile attachments. He must know that his therapist appreciates his need to establish independence. But it is necessary for him to know also that the rebellion must not become a Pyrrhic victory in which he is destroyed in his efforts to extricate himself from parental and authoritarian relationships. The byword for the therapist is to be "nonparental." The adolescent's transference will soon project the parental imago upon him. The analytic aim, therefore, is to bring the adolescent to the realization that his efforts to force the analyst into a parental role disrupt treatment and represent a way of "acting out" the break with his parents. For an adolescent, a measured degree of acting out on this score may be necessary, and is specific in terms of the requirement of the adolescent developmental phase.

The narcissistic orientation of the adolescent is manifest in his preoccupation with himself, in inflation or devaluation (in either case egocentric), and in being overcome by moods and impulses. Two propulsive emotional forces are ever present and interdependent, viz., the struggle to be free of attachment to parental figures, and the quest for independence and self-identity. If the former

---

[1] Quoted from Anna Freud (1951, p. 53).

is predominant and rebelliousness takes over, the outcome will be delinquency, covert if not overt. Therapeutic efforts, then, are much more difficult if not frustrated. The defiant adolescent is refractory because acceptance of the therapeutic situation and an alliance with the therapist are tantamount to capitulation. At any rate, to both delinquent and nondelinquent adolescent, a narcissistic appeal is necessary. Aichhorn (1925), in discussing the juvenile impostor, an extreme case of object-relationship impairment, speaks of effecting a "narcissistic transference," a projection of the delinquent adolescent's own glorified image onto the therapist, which leads to emulation of the therapist in his fantasies. Eissler (1958), who closely follows Aichhorn, speaks of partially fulfilling the delinquent's wishes, vicariously, as it were, by creating "an illusion of omnipotence" about the person of the therapist whose "knowledge of ways and means to gratify delinquent impulses are vastly superior" (p. 231). The delinquent who has not been able to form stable object relationships makes a libidinal investment in his therapist; or, as Anna Freud (1951) puts it, the delinquent "can become attached to the therapist through an overflow of narcissistic libido" (p. 55).

The narcissism of the nondelinquent adolescent might be viewed positively, i.e., as an effort to gain emotional independence, even though, in order to do so, a narcissistic regressive state is temporarily revived and reinforced. With both delinquent and nondelinquent, it is the adolescent's narcissism with which a therapeutic alliance may be established. With the delinquent, it must be captured and harnessed to the person of the therapist; with the normal adolescent, i.e., one in whom object constancy has been established, narcissism may be treated as a defensive stand taken to ward off what he regards as the parental hold upon him and an encroachment upon areas of newly won independence. In other words, his narcissistic reinforcement of himself is to secure a route to adulthood.

Much of what has been said about treatment so far may be preparatory to analysis, assuming that this may be possible in a minority of adolescent cases. It would be well to determine which cases lend themselves to analysis, but like the question of indications for analysis in adults, it may prove more fruitful, instead of deciding upon criteria, to explore the nature of resistances.

DISPLACEMENT AND OBJECT REMOVAL

This leads us to the crucial issue in the psychopathology of adolescent neuroses: the developmental need to sever libidinal and aggressive attachments to infantile love objects. In analytic treatment an effort is made to effect this cathectic shift nondestructively, i.e., by minimizing the compulsion to act out, universally prevalent among adolescents.

Anny Katan (1937), in her classic paper describing the adolescent ego's conflict with the threatened recurrence of incest wishes, introduced the term "removal" for the defense employed by the ego in diverting libidinal cathexis from the original incest object. She is careful to point out that in the ego's struggle the heterosexual drive must not be impeded in its development toward mature genitality. Displacement alone is insufficient, for it may be undone, or take place in both directions, i.e., not only *from* the incest object, but, as a redisplacement back onto the original object (usually mother) of affects that were intended for other object relationships. Displacement is like a chemical equation in equilibrium with the arrows going in both directions—to the right and left. Displacement, strictly speaking, is a substitution, and does not therefore indicate a decathexis of the original object. The unresolved emotional struggle is simply repeated with someone else. The patient finds another object with whom to replicate the original relationship. Nothing in that relationship has been resolved. As Nunberg (1951) points out, the patient with whom a workable transference is established is able to *experience* the person of the past in the analyst, and transiently to establish an "identity of perceptions," as it were, in which he projects mnemic images of the one onto the other; whereas the patient with whom a transference cannot be brought about seeks to *transform* the analyst (and others with whom he seeks relationships) into the person of the past, usually by trying to make him act in the same way. In other words, he displaces his feelings to indulge in them, not to resolve them. Such a patient is under the sway of a repetition compulsion.

In the adolescent the distinction between "transferring" and "displacing" affects and wishes is difficult to make. There seems to be, at one and the same time, a contest between the need to project mental representations of the parents and the need to free himself from further involvement with them. The struggle occurs with the analyst, as if it were necessary to fight it out with him instead of analyzing it. Thus, the adolescent acts out not only his ongoing parental defiance, but also the break from them that has been planned. This, as we know, threatens to occur in the treatment of most adolescents, especially those in whom ego discerning ability and reality testing are not well developed. The analyst, in attempting to secure a therapeutic relationship with his adolescent patient, may find himself in the dilemma of furthering an incestuous relationship, or of offering himself as the sacrificial proxy for the parents. Neither aspect of the dilemma seems to be subject to analysis because of the patient's compulsive need to act out by the deployment of the wishes he must reject. Displacement therefore is a perpetuation of the conflict, not a resolution of it.

The extent to which there is the need to project and to repeat, to that extent will any relationship tend to become a replication of original relationships rather than an assimilation of identifications leading to an independent self-identity. Adolescence is the final period of development for the resolution of incestuous wishes, and an opportunity for the "neutralization" of drive energy hitherto directed toward the cathexis of original love objects. During this period psychic energy must become mobile and free for reinvestment in new relationships.

Both "displacement" and "removal" are defenses employed by the adolescent in severing infantile object ties, the former against the drives, the latter against the object. Displacement where it occurs alone is insufficient, and it becomes a means of acting out with other objects the fixations and involvements that characterized the relationship with the original love objects. What is required is a cathectic release from these objects in which there is no longer the compulsion to repeat. Anny Katan (1937) shows that "removal" is directional. The equation ceases to be in equilibrium, and has gone to completion in one direction—to the right, and is then irreversible. "The introduction of a new term [removal] for the specific process under discussion seems justified. We are here concerned not with the mobility or displaceability of the libido itself . . . but with a process that occurs once only and that, in case of normality, will never be reversed in the direction of incest" (p. 43). We might add that in this process there has been a neutralization of the drive energy bound to the original love objects.

If the effort to break with incestuous object ties has been unsuccessful, relationships, by and large, remain on a regressive level. There is reinforcement of pregenitality as a defense against genitality, for the latter, it is feared, would facilitate the realization of incest wishes. This is, however, a paradox, because it is only in pregenitality that incest can be maintained, even though it may be manifested genitally. The developmental progress toward genitality is predicated upon a resolution of the oedipal complex at the turn of latency and upon relinquishment of incestual attachments at adolescence. Perhaps the most important aspect of the adolescent's efforts to effect a "removal" is the necessity to counteract the tendency to remain pregenitally fixated upon the incestuous object, for to do so would mean the release of aggression against it. What may be seen in the adolescent revolt of our times is a displacement of destructive aggression against parental surrogates. It is evident that riots, vandalism, and gang warfare are highly libidinized and sadomasochistic. This destructive pregenitality, manifestly impulsive, must be deflected from an attack upon parents and other incest objects. We are not misled, however, for the displacement is a persistence of the pathological pregenitality that the adolescent must divert. The plunge from one impulsive activity into another attests to this. That incest objects must be protected from aggression is evidenced by the guilt and self-destructiveness displayed in the boomerang of adolescent defiance.

Anna Freud (1958) further emphasizes and elaborates upon the "specific nature" of adolescent disorders. What is exclusive and characteristic for adolescence is "that the danger is felt to be located not only in the id impulses and fantasies but in the very existence of the love objects of the individual's oedipal and preoedipal past" (p. 268). The anxiety attendant upon a revival of pregenital and genital fantasies, dormant during latency, compels the adolescent to turn away from his infantile love objects. If the threatening fantasies are primarily oedipal, we find the "normal" adolescent defense of "removal" in operation. Efforts are made to decathect original love objects, not only by a renunciation of libidinal oedipal strivings but by a detachment from the objects themselves—physically by not wishing to be in their presence, emotionally by indifference if not antipathy toward them. The wish to leave home is openly expressed, by the poetic adolescent, often in terms of the stifling of his spirit and curtailment of freedom to express himself. Permissive parents, of course, are far from helpful in their efforts to be "understanding" of the emotive excrescences of their teen-ager, unable to realize that what is required is to hold firm to the conservatism for which they must stand in order to afford him the opportunity to oppose and denigrate. Adolescence is a time when it is necessary to personify the inner struggle in order to free oneself from an emotional invest-ment. The urgency of detachment from the object is indicated by how precipitously it is done, in contrast to the process seen, for example, in mourning. In the latter, "removal" is delayed by a period of reaffirmation of the relationship and of the libidinal ties; relinquishment is then possible.

Pregenitality or Genitality

There is a developmental telos in the direction of establishing new object relations in the normal adolescent's "removal" efforts. In his avoidance of parents and siblings he takes flight to peers with whom relationships are reinforced by conformity. There is a transfer of emotional investment from the family onto the environment, and a diversification of the libidinal investment. "Collective alternates" (to use Greenacre's term [1957]) become available for the adolescent whose object constancy is secure and in whom ego functioning has developed substantially since latency. Peer group affiliations are made, and causes espoused. Although there may be an oppositional orientation to these endeavors, positive motivations are prominent. The activities are both libidinized and idealized; and here I speak not only of the creative, intellectual adolescent of scientific, literary, or artistic talent, but of any other type motivated by success and achievement. One finds in these adolescents much rationalization for their motivation, which is always highly narcissistic. Behind the apparent contempt for parental expectations is the need to become active in the pursuit of a goal rather than remain passively obedient to parental will and judgment. In short, the resources of psychic energy are mobilized for investments in new objects. This is characteristic of normal adolescence, in contrast to delinquency.

Although the lines of demarcation are seldom clearly and easily discernible, there is a basic genetic distinction between "normal" and "abnormal" adolescence. Aside from knowing the nature of the case with which we are dealing, treatment procedure is predicated upon the correct assessment of this distinction. It is as necessary as an evaluation to determine whether a given case is that of a transference or a narcissistic neurosis. I would leave aside, for the present, whether the distinction between "normality" and "abnormality" is due to genetic determinants that are qualitatively or quantitatively different. Certainly the manifestations of disturbance may be assessed in degrees of severity, i.e., quantitatively; however, I believe that genetic explanations are properly concerned with matters of "kind" rather than of "degree."

An examination of the determinants operative in delinquency may serve to delineate normality from abnormality in adolescence. Although its manifestations are protean, delinquency is invariably a negative and destructive reaction to a specific environmental situation, thereby indicating a failure in adaptation which, from the economic point of view, is the result of psychic energy remaining bound to the pregenitality of the drives. From the genetic point of view, the failure to adapt arises from an absence or impairment of object relationships. Rather than define the "norm" for adolescent behavior, we should further our explanation of the developmental determinants and conflicts that result either in delinquency or in the crystallization of an infantile neurosis. We know that certain specific conflicts are inevitable for adolescence, as for infancy and latency, and that the adolescent period is normally a "neurotic" time.

Adolescents are besieged with unresolved conflicts and, for want of a stabilized ego structure, are given to the employment of defensive measures more or less maladapted to the resolution of these conflicts which threaten to interfere with maturity by retarding or preventing it.

The neurotic adolescent is preconsciously aware of conflict and maladaptation, as is evident by affect ranging from embarrassment to guilt, and employment of the gamut of renunciation of object ties, from avoidance to removal. By contrast, the delinquent is relatively undisturbed by conflict, which, in any case, is not the nuclear cause of his disorder. As with children, there may be no feeling of disturbance, only frustration. In the delinquent there is relatively little struggle between regressive and repressive forces; rather, there is an impulsive indulgence of the former. The delinquent's disregard for adaptational requirements and his lack of appreciation for them lead to destructive behavior, outwardly directed. This is the delinquent's primary defect akin to the psychotic's defectiveness in reality testing. The problem of adaptation, if seen at all, is in alloplastic rather than autoplastic terms—"the world must change, not me."

Normality and abnormality may be contrasted in regard to whether adolescence is a period of progression in the direction of genital maturity or a period of regressive reinforcement of pregenitality. To be specific, we may contrast the nature of object relationships, attitude toward sex, aim of aggression, regard for the interrelationship between pleasure and reality principles, and the existence of motivation for work and achievement. I think we may find these to be basic considerations in an assessment of adolescence.

Ernest Jones (1922) attempted to show that adolescence is a recapitulation of infancy. It is not clear, however, whether he meant that during adolescence there is a revival of the experiences of infancy or, simply, that the vicissitudes of infancy determine the course adolescence will take. The latter is a statement of the psychogenetic determination of behavior and the basis of analytic research. Recapitulation, however, can only refer to efforts to retain the emotional investments in pregenitality, aided and abetted by the anxieties attendant upon the challenge of maturity. In normal development the adolescent, bent upon severing infantile object ties and the establishment of emotional independence, makes an effort to rectify his infancy rather than repeat it.

OBJECT CONSTANCY

There is a close correlation between resistance to regression and the degree to which object constancy has been achieved. Adolescence is unlikely to founder upon its vicissitudes if positive object relationships have been secured during infancy and the latency period. Object constancy, if established and maintained throughout early childhood, safeguards object relationships in jeopardy during adolescence. Employment of the defense of removal implies that object constancy has been achieved. This defense is an externalization of the inner struggle to break infantile object ties; it outwardly directs the efforts made by the ego, not yet self-confident, in seeking emotional independence. This defense carries along with it much that is projective. The adolescent constantly protests parental curtailment of his freedom, yet is also seen to welcome it. As much as he longs to get away from home, the adolescent remains, accusing his parents of detaining him. Physical removal from an object that one must avoid is a primitive, albeit at times necessary, means of ending a relationship; whereas indifference, or not feeling affected, is a sophisticated reaction. The point I wish to make is that the defense mechanisms of removal, externalization, and renunciation are all in themselves evidence of cathectic involvement with the objects against which these defenses are directed. They are employed by "normal" adolescents, those who have achieved object constancy in their relationships, in contrast to "abnormal" adolescents who only seemingly remove object ties by withdrawal or defiance.

I think that close observation and analytic investigation reveal that throughout the removal maneuvers that the normal adolescent goes through, an object-constant relationship is nonetheless maintained. Because this is the genetic criterion in distinguishing "normality" from "abnormality" in adolescence, we should briefly clarify the concept of "object constancy." Anna Freud emphasizes that it is more than an inner image or mental representation of the object retained by the child. The capacity of the child to form this inner image, necessary as it may be, is a first step, and still closely connected to the need-satisfying phase. The child may still withdraw cathexis from the object if it fails to gratify his needs. Anna Freud (1968) defines the concept as follows: "What we mean by object constancy is the child's capacity to keep up object cathexis irrespective of frustration or satisfaction. At the time before object constancy the child withdraws cathexis from the unsatisfactory or unsatisfying object. Also in times when no need or libidinal wish is present in the child, the object is considered as non-existent, unnecessary. The turning towards the object takes place again when the need or wish arises. . . . The capacity to retain an inner image comes before object constancy . . . [when] the child takes the step from the object being an object for the id, to being an object for the ego. But that is not the same as object constancy. Object constancy means, on top of that, to retain attachment even when the person is unsatisfactory" (p. 506f.).

The normal upheaval of adolescence depicts the effort to relinquish the object; object constancy, however, once established, is permanent. The situation of the adolescent is compared with a state of mourning (Root, 1957), or termination of a love affair at which time there is a painful decathexis of the lost love object. For a time, there is no libido available for other objects, not until the mourning process has gone to completion. The delay in transferring libido is not only indicative of reluctance to give up the object, but is necessary to effect a transformation of libidinal energy heretofore directed toward the lost object, i.e., a time for this energy to be remobilized and neutralized in respect to the object, then freed for libidinal investment in another love object. This is not simply a displacement which implies that the energy is merely borrowed and may be returned to its original object at any time. Rather, when neutralization occurs, there is an increase in the reservoir of libidinal energy for independent investment in one or many objects and interests. Object constancy establishes the basis for effecting cathectic shifts. It is the genetic code, as it were, for the replication of relationships. The replicated object relationships are not identical with the prototypical one; they have carried out the "instructions" given by the latter.

THE ROLE OF THE EGO IDEAL

Integration of the ego ideal during adolescence may be taken as an indicator of the extent to which object constancy has been secured. The vicissitudes of the adolescent period pose problems for the superego which either will be reinforced, or will prove unable to function in consonance with the ego. I cannot go into the interconnection of ego and superego functioning in this communication, but an outline of the role of the latter is in order for this discussion.

The superego, as the inner agency for parental restriction and prohibition, is well known. We should turn our attention, however, to the norms and ideals that are incorporated and originally derived

from incestuous object ties. A danger during adolescence, as Lampl-
de Groot (1960) points out, is that these internalized moral standards
are threatened in the adolescent's efforts to turn away from his original love objects. To turn away from the one seems to require giving
up the other. Inasmuch as these moral standards have become a part
of the adolescent's personality, a superego disruption may occur. To
disengage oneself from the love object and that for which he stands
is "to disengage oneself from a part of one's own personality." The
struggle that ensues on the part of the adolescent is a fight against the
projection of himself in his parents (or vice versa, of the parents he
sees in himself). But it should be understood that the contents of the
projection are the ideals for which the parents stand rather than
what they are. What has hitherto, during latency, been a source of
ego support is under attack during adolescence. Compliance, which
during childhood has been a pleasure connected with winning parental love and commendation, must be eschewed. Foregoing this
gratification, associated with incestuous wishes, contributes to uncertainty and guilt. Parental omnipotence in which the child participated must be relinquished, and the adolescent must choose to
be left to his own devices. How much is the shyness and awkwardness
of the gawky adolescent a manifestation of uneasiness in attempting
to be on his own?

Giving up the love object with all its omnipotence constitutes a
narcissistic injury and consequent impairment of ego ideals, as
Lampl-de Groot (1960) says. Adolescence is a painful period. The
discovery that parents are not omnipotent—nay, more, the fact that
their imperfections are patently displayed in their actions—is the
reality that supports the adolescent's irrational opposition to the offer of parental guidance and intervention. Mood swings are the
adolescent's manifestation not only of discontent with himself, but
of a despondency born of a new conviction that his parents cannot
solve problems as they could in the days of their omnipotence. The
faith in them that served him well in childhood is shaken. There
are narcissistic injuries concomitant upon this shaken faith. The intellectual adolescent then, becoming acquainted with the problems
of the world, rationalizes his disaffection by pointing to the blunders,
inequities, and barbarousness of our body politic and way of life.

The neurotic adolescent (the norm for our time) has a safeguard against delinquency and personality disintegration in the object constancy long established since early childhood. Relationships based upon it perdure regardless of what occurs to the object, even when it has to be given up. Cathectic energy engendered in the original relationship is available for investment in interests as well as objects; moreover, the latter are cathected by virtue of the interests attached to them. The point I wish to make is that the attributes of the ego ideal, if not sacrificed during the vicissitudes of adolescence, come to stand in lieu of the infantile object attachment to the parents. They are the "collective alternates" for the parental libidinal investment of infancy. The development of ego functions, especially those concerned with thinking and the secondary processes, facilitates the cathectic shift during adolescence. Intellectual pursuits and interests cultivated during latency are at hand to take over the preoccupation with parents and siblings. The adolescent is attracted by the pleasure in actively taking up independent pursuits, a preliminary to sublimations. The two specific means of facilitating the cathectic shift are, of course, work and intellectual activity.

We recognize another forward developmental propulsion during adolescence, viz., to effect cathectic investments which will lead to independence in adulthood. Painful as the relinquishment of object ties is, the narcissistic injury brought about in the liberation struggle may yet be a spur in the search for new objects and interests.

The assessment of normality requires consideration of the adolescent's restitutive efforts in behalf of the survival of his ego ideal. These efforts are countered by the pregenital drives in the service of the destruction of object relationships. In denigrating the object, the rebellious adolescent will inevitably depreciate the ideals for which the object stood.

Only if the ego ideals which the parents espoused for the child can be rescued from destruction and revived, will developmental progress proceed into maturity. Just as the mental representation of the object is retained by the child regardless of satisfaction or frustration (the basis for object constancy), the ego ideal (the collective term for all the inculcated moral standards, ethical values, and aesthetic preferences) during normal adolescent turbulence withstands the attack upon the parents from whom it was originally acquired. To a great extent the sulky attitude of adolescence and labile depressions are manifestations of a narcissism wounded by an ego turning against its own ego ideal. This may offhand sound strange since we are accustomed to think in terms of the reverse. But it is not the ego ideal that castigates the ego, it is the other agency of the super-ego, the punitive and self-critical conscience that assumes this task. Normally the ego questions the ego ideal for a transient period. Surviving the interrogation will depend upon whether the ego ideal has been securely integrated within the superego. The interrogator's narcissism is painfully in jeopardy, and the prosecutor is deeply troubled by the prosecution. Can the ego ideal survive during efforts to relinquish the love objects identified with it? Perhaps only if the latter maintain more than a semblance of superego integrity. The moral chaos of society in which there is conspicuous deterioration of ego ideals readily lends itself to rationalizations for a nihilistic atti-tude. The original representatives demonstrate, all too often, their desertion of the ego ideal in their distorted thinking or demoralized action. The confused college adolescent is thereby provoked into shouting, "Who are you to tell me what to do?" and, "If you perpe-trate immoral and savage destruction in Vietnam, I can riot for a cause in Berkeley."

RENEWAL

Adolescence is a test of object constancy and of the integration of the ego ideal. The two are interrelated, and in order for the ego ideal to survive the vicissitudes of adolescence, object constancy must be secure. The adolescent's wounded narcissism, symptomatically displaying itself in mood swings, self-deprecation alternating with elation, and the feeling of not being understood, are manifestations of the travail his ego ideal is undergoing. Its threatened loss may re-sult in reveling in its overthrow, leading to delinquency; or efforts are made to restore it. The latter path enables the adolescent to progress into adult maturity and the final stage of character forma-tion. The means at his disposal are, first of all, and perhaps most important, the defenses against the upsurge of the drives. However, we should emphasize the importance of the quest for object relation-ships and "collective alternates" for libidinal investment. The "crushes" leading to hero worship, the attachment to "causes" in which drives are sublimated and aspirations realized, the affairs with the arts and sciences sought by the gifted and endowed adolescent are indications that maturity will be achieved. The positive aim is preservation of the ego ideal during the renunciation of infantile object ties. This renunciation at first is confused with the objects, and only later is the distinction made between libidinal object and the libidinal tie, which is internal, held at one end by the child and at the other by the parent (whose own incestuous ambivalence to his child is revived during the latter's adolescence). Preserving original libidinal ties may be considered analogous to need satisfaction, dependent as it is upon the object; the ego ideal, on the other hand, is analogous to object constancy in that it exists independently of an object, is not bound to it, but is free to be invested in diverse objects. This investment facilitates a *renewal* of the ego ideal, illustrated by the gratification obtained in work and peer relationships in which there is mutual participation in a community of *activity* rather than in a pursuit of the object as such. In other words, new objects are cathected by virtue of the mutuality of investment in an ego ideal. I have called this adolescent developmental propulsion (or motivation, if you will) "renewal," referring specifically to the revival and restoration of ego ideals (aspirations and interests) in relationships. These relationships must be other than with the original love objects. A prerequisite is the neutralization of energies bound up with these objects which must take place to effect their desexualization and desaggressivization. Other objects may then be drive-cathected in terms of a mature object relationship. The process of renewal, by perpetuating the ego ideal, serves to carry on and augment tradition.

Siegfried Bernfeld (1938) described a "protracted" type of adolescent which, I think, illustrates a basis for successful renewal efforts. This is the adolescent in whom there are strong creative and productive trends motivated by idealism and moral values—the forerunner of the humanistic spirit. It is referred to as "protracted," if I may interpolate, because, well into adulthood, such a person betrays his youthfulness. The original description was for a type of male adolescent. This might be extended to include the female as well, for, irrespective of sex, this adolescent type is predicated upon an active orientation toward life and the cultivation of ego endowment. Adolescence then becomes a period for the institution and reinforcement of sublimations.

What I have said applies to the normal adolescent in whom object constancy is secure and the process of neutralization is at work in the liberation of energies for the constant renewal of the ego ideal. It is a different story for the delinquent for whom development either ceases or regresses.

The step into maturity is predicated upon the rebellion against parental authority coming to an end, signifying that the issue of the strife has been resolved. A truce, if it is a capitulation of outward compliance, is soon broken by a resumption of hostilities, at least covertly. The scion, in taking over the family enterprise, but in doing so conducts it unsuccessfully, may be perpetuating his adolescent revolt. He may assume the throne, but cannot allow himself to succeed in it. The opposite, carrying on with an exaggerated imitation of personality traits of the parental predecessor, is an identification with a vengeance—Caligula succeeding Tiberius. To wreck one's success or prosecute it is an affirmation of the parental tie, with sadomasochistic pregenitality displayed in either case.

In contrast to the continued indulgence of, or defense against, pregenital and incestual ties is the perpetuation of parental tradition. The superego, established upon resolution of the oedipus complex in prelatency, must be consolidated at the termination of adolescence. The "sowing of wild oats" condoned as a "last fling" may be the means of relinquishing the indulgence of pregenitality. As in mourning, wherein there is reliving in fantasy and recall of the relationship with the lost love object, in the excesses of adolescent riotousness and abandon there is an emotional recapitulation of the past—a reaffirmation of what must be relinquished. The question that can be answered only by the outcome is whether the turbulence of adolescence is a cry of mourning or a consolidation of pregenitality nurtured and encouraged since infancy. I would like to think that an analytic observer, not too distracted by the noise and excessiveness displayed, and knowing about the crucial periods of the patient's childhood development, can make a prediction.

"Sowing Wild Oats "(Prince Hal)

A digression in a classic will illustrate the decathectic efforts that prompt the "sowing of wild oats." We are reminded of Prince Hal,

that adolescent madcap who, with Falstaff as his foil, is the scape-
grace of King Henry. The latter bemoans his paternal fate as compared with Northumberland,

> Whilst I, by looking on the praise of [thy son Percy],
> See riot and dishonor stain the brow
> Of my young Harry. O! That it could be proved
> That some night-tripping fairy had exchanged
> In cradle-clothes our children where they lay,
> And called mine Percy, his Plantagenet [Part I, Act I, scene 1].

The Prince is aware of the grief he causes his father, but he is not
deterred. The need to continue his errant ways leaves him unaf-
fected; it is compelling and takes priority over considerations of state
or person.

> I know you all, and will awhile uphold
> The [unrestrained] humor of your idleness [Part I, Act I, scene 2].

The Prince rationalizes his riotous living which, he declares,
makes righteousness "more goodly and attractive," and relieves life
of its tediousness. To falsify men's expectations of him will make his
reformation commend him all the more, "like bright metal on a
sullen ground." However, behind this adolescent sophistry is a compulsion to continue in his delinquent way a little longer. It has not
yet run its decathectic course. In fact, he will make the most of his
opportunity to be as offensive as possible.

There are two factors that operate in the propulsion to a higher
developmental phase: one is adaptation to biological growth; the
other, and more important, is that the succeeding phase will offer
more gratification than the preceding phase. Under the best of circumstances this is taken on faith, because conviction follows only
upon experience. A motivation, therefore, for "a last fling" is the
reluctance to relinquish a known pleasure for an unknown one.
Furthermore, if little pleasure is derived from adherence to ego
ideals, libidinal and aggressive actions opposed by authority are all
the more indulged if they serve to break parental ties. In a sense,
indulgences are narcissistic love objects, and in giving them up
something of oneself is lost. As in the mourning process, time is required. The adolescent, however, unlike the adult in a state of
mourning, is not sure that he must give up an indulgence; and if

it is in lieu of the love object, yet bereft of the object tie, there is all the more reason for not giving it up. The difficulty is compounded in a society in which material possessions take precedence over relationships.

Complain, protest, and reprimand as he does, King Henry puts up with the Prince. Indeed, he accepts his son's conduct as a punishment for his own offense, and confesses to the Prince:

> For some displeasing service I have done,
> [God] will breed revengement and a scourge for me;
> But thou dost in thy passages of life
> Make me believe that thou art only marked
> For the hot vengeance and the rod of heaven
> To punish my mistreadings. [Part I, Act III, scene 2].

Parental guilt is one motivation for indulging the adolescent. It is passive and filled with a despair. Another motive is unrequited retaliation by the parents against their own parents, using the child for this purpose. This is active in that the parent is an aide and abettor. An example is the mother who becomes the confidante of her daughter's sexual affairs; or the father who boasts of his son's exploits (fair or foul), the emphasis being on the aggression displayed, but without concern for the substance of the action. In such situations, the parents, of course, are seeking a vicarious gratification —most often hostile—through the child. The price to be paid is that the adolescent is given his way, indicated by the parents' *laissez faire* attitude. Seemingly, the adolescent gets along well with his parents, although it is hardly on any other basis than "so long as they don't bother me." He has the upper hand, and when he comes into analysis as an adult, we hear him express regret if not contempt for his parents' weakness and inability to provide external control.

The King's castigation, meliorated by his confession, produces an unexpected contrition on the part of the Prince. Instead of a defiant reply, he begs to be pardoned. He does not seek to be excused (even though he will disprove the false tales), but in sincerity avows to purge and redeem himself:

> I may, for some things true, wherein my youth
> Hath faulty wandered and irregular,
> Find pardon on my true submission [Part I, Act III, scene 2].

The Prince will yet see to it that his father's wish for a Percy in him be even better granted in that he will outshine in "honour and renown this gallant Hotspur." The King is eager to pardon the Prince. It is only through the son's reformation that the father may be absolved of his own sins. I think that the adolescent in such a situation knows this unconsciously and therefore assumes the right to give his parents a hard time. Modern parents, especially the "understanding" ones, are quick in a display of weaknesses and confessionals before their children; and the delinquent can turn this to advantage in pursuing his course. A sincere and courageous admission of mistake or wrongdoing (not a confession) by a father of strong character (such as King Henry) may give the nondelinquent adolescent an opportunity to resolve the issue of the strife. A continuation of the battle of defiance cannot be tolerated indefinitely.

Although he cannot admit it, the Prince is eager to consummate the renewal of the relationship with his father which heretofore was only professed. The opportunity comes when the King, attacked by the Earl of Douglas, is saved by the Prince. The brief scene is great in subtlety. The reality is as firmly entrenched as is the fantasy. First, the King's character and measure of a man are reaffirmed, so there can be no doubt about the worth of the relationship between father and son. The King is no "counterfeit." When Douglas comes upon the King in battle and wonders whether it is really the King, he declares:

I fear thou art another counterfeit;
And yet, in faith, thou bearest thee like a king [Part I, Act V, scene 4].

The Prince then enters, takes on his father's assailant, and fights with him until he flees. In this scene the son saves his father's life, and by this action their roles are temporarily reversed; the son becomes his father's father, protecting him as he in his childhood was protected. This is a reversal that establishes a peer relationship (what one does for the other is equal) which is the necessary step in preparing the son for succession. He not only has to become his father's equal, but the latter must merit the equality.

The tie of dependence is broken by the establishment of a peer relationship—permitting a recathexis of the ego ideal for which the father stood. "Renewal," then, may further be defined as the rescue and reaffirmation of the ego ideal—a sublimation of the love for the father. In the final resolution of the oedipus complex, the son's wish to kill his father is pardoned. This point was well taken by Shakespeare. In the scene, Douglas, who stands for the Prince's attack upon his father, is not killed by the Prince, for how can he, having had the same unconscious design upon the King's life. Even when Douglas is taken prisoner, the Prince arranges for his life and freedom to be spared. He requests of the King, "I beseech your Grace I may dispose of him"; then Douglas is pardoned—the patricidal wish is forgiven. Our question may be, how much is normal adolescent defiance a transient and necessary need to recapitulate the oedipal problem (son vs. father, mother vs. daughter), so that its resolution may be consolidated. The scene concludes with the following dialogue between King and Prince in which the former is overwhelmed by what he interprets in the Prince's action as a return of love and devotion:

King Henry:
Thou has redeem'd thy lost opinion,
And show'd thou mak'st some tender of my life,
In this fair rescue thou hast brought to me.

Prince:
O God! they did me too much injury
That ever said I hearken'd for your death.
If it were so, I might have let alone
The insulting hand of Douglas over you;
Which would have been as speedy in your end
As all the poisonous potions in the world,
And sav'd the treacherous labour of your son [Part I, Act V, scene 4].

What an admission of recent intent!

Here, prematurely, the Prince plays his part, professing his intentions, although he is not ready to carry them through. He "doth protest too much." However, it was the first step in a renewed, but qualitatively different, relationship with his father. He must have yet one more "last fling."

The Prince's words prove truer than his deeds. Unstable and irresponsible adolescent that he is, he is still addicted to merry-making and boon companionship. The King deplores in anguish how badly off things will be after his death upon the Prince's succession.

> . . . when his headstrong riot hath no curb,
> When rage and hot blood are his counsellors . . . [Part II, Act IV, scene 4].

Warwick, it would seem, tries to cover up for the Prince, suggesting that he may be misjudged; he reasons that there may be a rationale for his misbehavior, viz., to learn what it is, so as to reject it.

> The Prince but studies his companions
> Like a strange tongue, wherein, to gain the language,
> 'Tis needful that the most immodest word
> Be looked upon, and learned; which once attained,
> Your highness knows, comes to no further use
> But to be known and hated. So, like gross terms,
> The Prince will in the perfectness of time
> Cast off his followers . . . [Part II, Act IV, scene 4].

Warwick's words are not an apology for the "sowing of wild oats"; rather, a plea for an understanding of its necessity, intolerable as it may be; nor does he indicate that it should be sanctioned.

To understand the reasons, even the necessity for an action should not imply a condonement for it. The so-called "enlightened" parent adheres to a befuddled logic by which to understand the reasons for a misbehavior warrants a permissive attitude toward it. What is required, instead, is that the adolescent know that the parent does not sanction it. Whether some active parental opposition is in order should depend upon the effectiveness of its means. For the superego to wage a successful struggle against regressive drive forces, parents and surrogates must remain constant and firm in maintaining ego ideals, both by espousal and example. A subsidiary but often decisive factor in adolescent defiance is testing to determine if the substance of the matter of conflict with the parents can withstand the assault and, if so, thereby resolve the doubt in the adolescent's mind. This is the principle that the "enlightened" parent fails to understand. Shakespeare does, however.

In the person of the Lord Chief Justice, the King's superego is upheld. In an argument, the test by recrimination is enacted when the Prince (now King Henry V) says he does not think the Chief

Justice believes that the Prince likes him (a projection). The character (integrated superego) of the Chief Justice is revealed in his firm adherence to what is right against the Prince's reproach for being treated severely by him in the past. In the scene it is as if the Prince wants one final proof of what's right, and he seeks it from his father's surrogate. The Chief Justice's words, a paean to the superego, might serve to guide the beleaguered educators of our time (who mistake license for freedom):

> I then did use the person of your father;
> The image of his power lay then in me . . .
> Your highness pleased to forget my place,
> The majesty of power of law and justice,
> The image of the king whom I presented . . .
> As an offender to your father,
> I gave bold way to my authority,
> And did commit you. If the deed were ill,
> Be you contented, wearing now the garland,
> To have a son set your decree at nought,
> To pluck down justice from your awful bench,
> To trip the course of law, and blunt the sword
> That guards the peace and safety of your person:
> Nay, more, to spurn at your most royal image
> And mock your workings in a second body.
> Question your royal thoughts, make the case yours;
> Be now the father and propose a son,
> Hear your own dignity so much profaned,
> See your most dreadful laws so loosely slighted,
> Behold yourself so by a son disdained;
> And then imagine me taking your part,
> And in your power soft silencing your son.

[Then the Prince in reply:]

> You are right, Justice;
> And you weigh this well;
> Therefore still bear the balance and the sword . . .
> So shall I live to speak my father's words . . .
> For in his tomb lie my affections . . .
> The tide of blood in me
> Hath proudly flowed in vanity til now:
> Now doth it turn and ebb back to the sea . . . [Part II, Act V, scene 2].

This dialogue depicts the triumph of the superego effecting a re-unification of father and son in the perpetuation of the ego ideal.

Finally, the approaching death of the King signals the time for discarding rebellious defiance and for the oath of reaffirmation of patrimonial lineage. The Prince is then relieved of his parricidal anxiety and the guilt accompanying it, enabling him to appropriate his father's power with which to carry on the heritage. At the King's deathbed, the Prince puts on the crown, thinking his father already dead:

> Lo! here it sits,
> Which heaven shall guard; and put the world's whole strength
> Into one giant arm, it shall not force
> This lineal honor from me. This from thee
> Will I to mine leave, as 'tis left to me [Part II, Act IV, scene 5].

The premature action of the Prince betrays his unconscious wish to expropriate the crown. In many an adolescent son's rebellious-ness we may assume that delinquency, misbehavior, poor perform-ance, etc., is both an expression of a parricidal wish, via destructive defiance, and at the same time a disavowal of that wish, i.e., by acting unworthily, he disqualifies himself from the succession. Less flag-rantly the latter is revealed in the adolescent's shyness and self-efface-ment. It is the concensus of opinion (with Warwick the exception) that the Prince's succession will be a disaster. Only the Prince knows it will not be so; however, he cannot change his ways until the right time comes. Even so, he misjudges, and there is another open rift with the King. The secret is out, patently displayed in the Prince's impatience, and in the King's suspicion when he exclaims:

> Is he so hasty that he doth suppose
> My sleep my death? [Part II, Act IV, scene 5].

When the Prince becomes aware of mistaking his father for dead, and says to him, "I never thot to hear you speak again," the King replies,

> Thy wish was father, Harry, to that thought;
> I stay too long by thee, I weary thee.
> Dost thou so hunger for my empty chair

That thou wilt needs invest thee with mine honours
Before thy hour be ripe . . .
Thou hast stolen that which after some few hours
Were thine without offence . . . [Part II, Act IV, scene 5].

The King complains that the Prince does not love him, which, of course, is a plea to be assured that he does. There is much protest on the part of both father and son, ending in the final and permanent reinstatement of the relationship. Throughout, each one feels an urgent need to heal the breach between them—the immediate motivation for reconciliation.

CONCLUSION

In every contest between rebellious son and suppliant father we may expect to find an expiation of the guilt that the father bears for his sins. Therefore the relationship between them is jeopardized when the son detects the father's betrayal of the ego ideal he seeks for his son to uphold. The sins of the father weaken the son's resolve. The disappointment with each other is manifest in their mutual antagonism, verbalized by the father, but acted out by the errant son. It may be only through the father's death that a true reconciliation is achieved. It is then that without reserve the father is willing to relinquish his throne to his son, and the latter, in order to achieve his father's potency, espouses the ego ideal.

A differential point of evaluation is whether the adolescent is in revolt against the objects or the demands of the objects. In viewing his manifest behavior it is difficult to make this distinction, although a degree of analytic scrutiny will usually enable us to do so. The cynical adolescent, for example, is seemingly in opposition to what his parents stand for; however, it finally appears that he has suffered profound disappointment over their betrayal of the ego ideals which have been imputed to them. The intellectual adolescent reveals that he is hypercritical of their actions which belie their espoused belief. He then becomes dedicated to value judgments of his own in order to have nothing to do with his parents. In this situation the ego ideal stands in for the parents while they are subjected to the ordeal of severance. The revolt is against them, i.e., what they are, rather than what they stand for. Although originally, in the child's mind, the two were synonymous by virtue of his fantasies of their omnipotence and his need to share in it, the superego, it should be borne in mind, is derived not from the model of the parents but from the parents' superego.

The cynical adolescent illustrates the preservation of the ego ideal. That its manifest content may be different is of secondary importance; what is essential is that there should be an established ego ideal serving to perpetuate tradition and object relationships. By contrast, the "dispositional" (Van der Waal's, 1943, 1946), delinquent bereft of object constancy, has no vested interest in the preservation of ego ideals. Immediate gratification of pregenital drive needs establishes the primacy of the pleasure principle which, as we know, places the delinquent constantly at the mercy of these needs. As Lampl-de Groot (1949) remarks," the delinquent's object attachment is not strong enough to act as a barrier against his instinctual needs, and therefore his ego cannot achieve an adaptation to reality, whereas the neurotic [adolescent] is too dependent upon his object to permit the id more than a limited degree of instinctual satisfaction" (p. 140).

The urgent need for immediate gratification is seldom consonant with an appreciation for the demands of the environment. The adaptational efforts of the neurotic adolescent are to be seen in contrast to the disregard of reality considerations by the delinquent who contrives to manipulate his environment solely for need satisfaction.

There is a positive and decisive contrast between the neurotic and delinquent adolescent in regard to the pleasure principle, viz., a qualitative difference in the experience of pleasure based upon whether it derives primarily from the pregenitality or genitality of the drives. I know this is a statement difficult to prove; and it is not my intention to measure pleasure. Rather, I would suggest that the qualitative difference derives from the source of the gratification. For one thing, we know that in any indulgence fraught with anxiety (and irresistible urgency is a form of anxiety) there is a mitigation of gratification. Pursuing this subject would lead us far afield. My point is that pleasure derived from the pursuit of ideals and the ego functions involved in thinking and the perfection of work skills produce a qualitatively different emotional experience than does the pursuit of immediate drive gratification (surfeited, as it is, with pregenitality). The pleasure principle is drive-oriented, whereas the reality principle is object-oriented. Even if we would question whether greater pleasure comes from adhering to the reality principle, there is no doubt that in that direction lies ego development.

BIBLIOGRAPHY

Aichhorn, A. (1925), *Wayward Youth*. New York: Viking Press, 1935.

Bernfeld, S. (1938), Types of Adolescence. *Psa. Quart.*, 7:243-253.

Eissler, K. R. (1950), Ego-psychological Implications of the Psychoanalytic Treatment of Delinquents. *This Annual*, 5:97-121.

—— (1958), Notes on Problems of Technique in the Psychoanalytic Treatment of Adolescents. *This Annual*, 13:223-254.

Freud, A. (1951), Obituary: August Aichhorn. *Int. J. Psa.*, 32:51-56.

—— (1958), Adolescence. *This Annual*, 13:255-278.

—— (1968), Panel Discussion. *Int. J. Psa.*, 49:506-512.

Freud, S. (1925), Preface to Aichhorn's *Wayward Youth*. *Standard Edition*, 19:273-275. London: Hogarth Press, 1961.

Greenacre, P. (1957), The Childhood of the Artist. *This Annual*, 12:47-72.

Jones, E. (1922), Some Problems of Adolescence. *Papers on Psycho-Analysis*. London: Baillière, Tindall, & Cox, 5th ed., 1948, pp. 389-406.

Katan, A. (1937), The Role of 'Displacement' in Agoraphobia. *Int. J. Psa.*, 32:41-50, 1951.

Kris, E. (1952), *Psychoanalytic Explorations in Art*. New York: International Universities Press; see esp. Ch. 12.

Lampl-de Groot, J. (1949), Neurotics, Delinquents, and Ideal Formation. *The Development of the Mind*. New York: International Universities Press, 1965, pp. 138-148.

—— (1960), On Adolescence. *This Annual*, 15:95-103.

—— (1965), *The Development of the Mind*. New York: International Universities Press; see esp. Chs. 8, 24.

Little, M. (1951), Counter-Transference and the Patient's Response to It. *Int. J. Psa.*, 32:32-40.

Nunberg, H. (1951), Transference of Reality. *Int. J. Psa.*, 32:1-9.

Reich, A. (1951), On Counter-Transference. *Int. J. Psa.*, 32:25-31.

Root, N. N. (1957), A Neurosis in Adolescence. *This Annual*, 12:320-334.

Shakespeare, W. *King Henry IV*, Part I. *The New Clarendon Shakespeare*. Oxford: Oxford University Press, 1964.

—— *King Henry IV*, Part II. *The New Clarendon Shakespeare*. Oxford: Oxford University Press, 1961.

Van der Waals, H. G. (1943), Aanleg en Ontwikkeling. *Mensch en Maatschappij*, 19(4).

—— (1946) [On the Rorschach Test], *Psychiat. Neurol. Bladen*, 49.

YOUTH, GROWTH, AND VIOLENCE

PHYLLIS GREENACRE, M.D. (New York)

The aim of this paper is to investigate from a psychoanalytic angle the nature and course of development in adolescents and young adults of symptoms of unrest leading to violence and in the extreme to bomb throwing, as these have appeared during the present revolutionary period. It is necessary further to consider in what ways the present social situation has cooperated or combined with and exaggerated the ordinary problems of adolescence to such an extent as to involve youth fundamentally in the current revolutionary activities.

Youths and artists have often participated in revolutions, especially in the initiation of their more drastic phases. Students uprisings and protests belong to the revolutionary picture. Nor is this really surprising. Adolescence is a time of marked and rather abrupt growth associated with the maturational changes of puberty. It is a time when with the forward surge of energy accompanying the changes in body size and proportions and especially the maturing of the sexual organs, there is a sudden confluence of stimulations with an awareness of new vistas and expectations in life—with bold ambitions and qualms of apprehensive uneasiness. It is often a time of a maturational crisis in which there is a rearousal and a chance for a new deal of the problems left over from early childhood. At the same time there is a need for a rapid shift in behavior even in day-to-day living. It is often a time of painful emotional revolution with a great variety of external manifestations as well as of inner stress.

REVOLUTION AND THE UTOPIAN IDEAL

Revolutions occur when a group of people becomes so distressed by the conditions of the political government or of the social or religious system under which they live that they make active efforts to overthrow it and form another in its place. Revolutionary movements are commonly focused by specific grievances against a background of generally increasing feeling of unfair treatment. Revolutionary action may be triggered off to become more continuous and more violent in form by some specific event or series of events.

At the same time, there is in mankind a universal fantasy of a place or a condition of peace and harmony where the wants of all will be satisfied. This fantasy, arising in childhood, may remain in consciousness intact or in fragmentary form. But even when forgotten it can exert a powerful influence and contribute to the urgency of dissatisfactions with things as they are. This haven has been represented in myths as an island: Atlantis, Utopia, the Isles of the Blest, and Avalon. In the Middle Ages its existence was regarded as a probable fact and explorers sought to find it. The expectation has been incorporated into many religious as well as political conceptions. It is the Garden of Eden from which we came and the Heaven to which we will go. The fantasy is as ubiquitous as that of the Family Romance to which it is closely related. The ambition to be a glorious deliverer, a world conqueror, or a saintly and persecuted savior may be in part derived from it. To some, the attainment of such a state of grace means a positive and active accomplishment; to others, it is accepted as a passive return to an ideal condition, previously granted but now lost. Underneath this fairy-tale version is a deeply unconscious sense of a time when the parents seemed all powerful and the infant lived through contact with them. This utopian ideal involves the opposing and equally unrealizable wishes to have unconditional love, protection, and freedom granted through parental omnipotence, and also to obtain this omnipotence for oneself. It includes both preoedipal and oedipal wishes in varying degrees. Although dormant for long periods of time, elements in it are activated at times of stress, whether this arises largely from inner conflicts or from external fateful events as well.

Since the utopian ideal occurs so universally characterized by fluctuations between active and passive forms and goes back to the dawn of both individual and collective history, one suspects that it contains deeply rooted biological cravings having to do with the rhythm of alternating rest and activity characteristic of the maintenance of life itself, gradually wearing down to the ultimate and irreversible inertness of death. In man these cravings not only emerge in their primary somatic forms where they are held in homeostatic balance, but are also expressed in the narcissistic functions of the primitive psyche, which, in any case, is the guardian of the soma. They are further directed, protected, and allowed to develop as the innately patterned autonomous functions of the ego become stronger. As the infant grows, these demands for unlimited power and for peaceful rest are experienced first directly in relation to the parents, and subsequently are refined and elaborated into fantasies as the process of individuation advances, and separation is both required and tolerated.

THE BACKGROUND OF NINETEENTH-CENTURY ANARCHISTIC REVOLUTION

In times when inequalities in possessions, power, and privilege between groups or classes of people under the same government have generated frustrations and fulminating resentments, demands for far-reaching change arise and the utopian fantasy may come to life in a full and powerful form. This would seem to be the 19th-century background of the anarchistic philosophy, enunciated by Proudhon and carried on subsequently by Bakunin and Kropotkin. In the endeavor to bring about relief from economic and social oppression, idealistic anarchists developed the vision of a society made up of a federation of small communes whose members would live in a state of harmonious coexistence and equality, each group falling into its own spontaneous organization along the principles of mutual aid and sharing of productivity according to individual needs. The minimal necessary regulation would be by selected administrators rather than by government, which was conceived of as inevitably coercive.[1]

Beautiful as this ideal sounded, it required or assumed an impossible freedom from rivalry, jealousy, and even competitive striving. It took scant account of innate differences in temperament or abilities and attributed resentments to the uneven distribution of

---

[1] For an account of various communistic societies established in the United States during the first half of the 19th century, see Charles Nordhoff (1875). Some of these were anarchistic in origin, but they did not promulgate the use of violence. That attitude was more a development of the last half of the century.

material goods due to the exploitation or enslavement of one group of men by another. There was little realization of the fundamental intrafamily jealousies and rivalries between parents and children and among the children themselves. Consequently it could not be understood that such a state of serene communal existence could not be maintained without a massive repression of hostile aggression which would then be likely to erupt strongly and unexpectedly within the commune, unless it was diverted and absorbed into the fight against the outside: the oppressors. While the actual federation of anarchist communes never became really established, violence toward the government mounted. It was first condoned and then accepted as a necessary tool for the making of an anarchist state, dedicated to the opposite of violence: peace and harmony. Once accepted as righteous, it inevitably soon assumed a fanatical character, which was intensified by the reverberations back and forth of retaliation and counter-retaliation, the need to "get even," which may terminate in an equalization through mutual destruction. It gradually developed in some quarters to a nihilistic aim, which seemed to get a momentum of its own. At any rate anarchism has ever since carried the connotation of violence, since the anarchist's utopian dream of peace became infiltrated with the very characteristic it was dedicated to fighting.

The Anarchists

It is interesting to look at the temperament of the three men, Proudhon, Bakunin, and Kropotkin, who were in the forefront of the anarchist revolutionary movement. Bakunin and Kropotkin belonged to the Russian aristocracy, while Proudhon, the oldest and perhaps the most influential of the three, was a Frenchman, a self-educated man of the people. He was a family man not given to shows of violence himself, but, more than the other two, he was aware of the potential violence in all people. He was an aggressively peaceful man, his hostile aggression being used to form a solid wall against any compromise. He saw the government as a spy system, and the factory largely as a dehumanizing influence in life. He was the coiner of inflammatory sayings: "Property is theft" and "God is dead." His own conscience may have been his God and he relied on it faithfully rather than share a god with a financier. He was probably closer to the feelings of the 20th century than either of the other two. Simple and direct in his writing, he was a pamphleteer rather than a writer of books.

Bakunin, only a few years younger than Proudhon, attributed his liking for anarchism to his unending resentment of his mother's despotism, which had produced in him an "insensate hatred of any restriction of liberty." He was described by a friend as a primitive but complex man, charming, childish, oversize, a braggart, and so unscrupulous that it made a sustained friendship difficult. He loved ideas rather than people and wished to dominate people with them. He was not a family man and in fact was said to be impotent. Like Kropotkin, he seemed to believe that all human beings were basically good, and if only all the evil in them could be destroyed all would be well. His sense of reality was of a tenuous sort: he was unreliable as to money, not a good judge of character, and was repeatedly engaged in fantasies of having established large secret societies which he led in conspiracies. So convincing was he in this role, that he made trouble for a number of people (including the police) who believed him.

Kropotkin was at least a generation younger than Proudhon and Bakunin and lived more than fifty years after their deaths. He came under their influence through reading when he was little more than an adolescent, but did not become active as an anarchist until a little after both had died. After a rigidly conventional education he rebelled against the discipline and formality of the imperial court; and contrary to the wishes of his family he joined an unfashionable regiment in Siberia. While there he read Proudhon's pamphlets and became interested in prison reform, but also spent some time in geographical explorations. This interest remained with him always and rivaled his concern with politics. Not until the age of thirty, did he begin to participate in anarchistic activities while staying in Switzerland. He soon returned to Russia with the idea that he could be more useful to the Revolution there. By the age of forty-four, he had spent five years in prison, two of them in the fortress of St. Peter and St. Paul from which he made a dramatic escape and three in France. From then until four years before his death in 1921, he lived in England, in weakened health. He became more a philosopher and adviser than a participant in anarchistic revolutionary activities. His attitude toward violence was always ambivalent. Early he endorsed it; and at thirty-seven he wrote: "Permanent revolt by word of mouth, in writing, by the dagger, the rifle, dynamite. Everything is good that is outside legality" (Joll, 1964, p. 127). He did not share Proudhon's feeling about the dehumanizing influence of the machine, looking rather to the development of machinery to supply men more plentifully with goods and free them from onerous and degrading tasks. He disliked terrorism intensely; yet he endorsed its use for propaganda purposes and condoned it in "desperate situations." He wrote to a friend: "Personally I hate these explosions, but I cannot stand as a judge to those who are driven to despair" (p. 153). He was concerned lest revenge become an end in itself, but realized that it would characterize revolt for some time to come. Again he saw it as the act of someone driven to despair. But he was firm in his stand that revenge must not be erected into a theory. Like Bakunin, he was troubled by the thought that cruelty might be innate in human nature. He saw hostility as arising only as reaction to mistreatment, and believed that people were by nature only friendly and responsive. He was concerned with the idea of the struggle for survival, especially as Darwin's theories were interpreted by Huxley. He wished to show that survival came about through cooperation and mutual aid by members of the same species and hunted for examples that would support this conclusion. Further, he thought that if all interfering government was abolished, people would live harmoniously in anarchistic communities supporting each other through a spontaneous rise in *mutualism* (Kropotkin, 1902). By the end of his life he seemed to shy away from the term "anarchism." It was by then thoroughly associated with the idea of extreme violence.

THE PRESENT SITUATION

There are some points of resemblance between the rise of violence out of the original ideal of peaceful coexistence of the anarchists of the 19th century and the present apparent increase of violence in the movement which was at first characterized by a dedication to the cause of peace, in the sense at least of the abolition of war and of interracial strife. In this country and in many others, there seems to have developed not only a dependence on violence in the service of dramatic propaganda—propaganda by the deed—which essentially means chronic harassment growing to terroristic proportions, but further in the increasing vision of its use as a direct means of overthrowing the Establishment, which represents not only the government but almost any firmly organized institution in our culture. It is not clear how much this violent destructiveness has been part of a definite plan or even a clear fantasy of clearing the way for a new social order, and how much it has increased through group contagion, rising to epidemic proportions, with demands for instantaneous response and redress, even when such immediacy is not feasible or may not even be possible. Anarchism, in contrast to communism which works through a political organization, has never dealt much with the period of transition, and seemingly depended on the idea of the goodness of human nature asserting itself if the old order was disposed of.

One gets the impression that there is a pattern of protest and demand, which—independent of the ostensible aim—gains secondary values through the gratification of the exhibitionistic needs (a reversal of the feeling of having been ignored) and through the sense of power that a group demonstration affords. This may give a discharge of tension for a depressed, neglected, or mistreated people, but it leads only to chaos if it gains momentum without being channeled into some undertaking for the future, for which a leader, not merely an administrator, is usually necessary. Yet the paradoxical anarchistic ideal of freedom brooks no interference at all, even such as might come from a leader, tolerating only a degree of direction as administration. But leadership and administration are divided by a very thin line. The result then may be that a single leader or a series of leaders take charge; or each individual strives to become a leader responsible only to himself and may see himself in fantasy as *the* leader of the group, as Bakunin's elaborate daydreams of commanding great conspiracies showed. The original naïve and benign theory of anarchy not only took little or no account of innate constitutional inequalities between individuals, whether of intellect or physique, but it was also innocent of awareness of the biological foundation of the various structural elements of family formation. Furthermore, there was scant recognition of the unique interrelation between family patterns and those of society, so intense was the focusing on the class struggle.

Anarchism and Adolescence

But what is of particular interest for this study is the role of the adolescents in the rising revolutionary tide of the past decade. The hippie movement and the civil rights agitation began at about the same time and seem to have gotten impetus from some of the same sources of unrest and mounting dissatisfactions, though they were not definitively united at first. Both contained protests against the long period of wars in which this country had participated, though it had not initiated them. There was undoubtedly a gathering storm of reaction on the part of youth, both black and white, against having the years of their late adolescence and early adulthood and perhaps life itself taken from them by a military service which seemed unending. An atmosphere of war easily spreads even to those who are opposed to war, and in a sense these young people went over to the enemy, became sympathizers with communism of whatever ilk, and in the extreme demanded an anarchistic utopian freedom rather than reforms within a democratic structure.

A large number of the early recruits to the hippie way of life were young people who were primarily rebellious against parents and teachers, and only secondarily became involved clearly in political and social issues. It is hard to say how much the involvement progressed by contagion rather than by clear ideological conviction. They showed their rebellion by "dropping out," turning their backs on family and school, adopting a uniform of poverty, and reducing material requirements to the lowest possible level, as though to demonstrate their freedom from and contempt for the standards which had been expected of them. They were professedly committed to ideals of peace, freedom, and equality, with the latter interpreted in practice as a share-and-share-alike way of life, in possessions as well as in love, which was supposed to rule all. "Make love not war" became a slogan. They might preempt from the outside whatever they felt they needed, with a rationalization not unlike Proudhon's statement, "Private property is theft," to which might now be added, "And theft is justified if there is need." There are striking differences, however, between the communes of the 1960s and the federation of communes as envisioned by anarchist idealists a century ago. The communes of today appeared as though by spontaneous erup-

tion and have been largely the realm of youth; while the earlier ones
hardly existed long in fact, being chiefly the theoretical constructions
of men of mature years and considerable experience. Yet their con-
structs did not prove themselves in practice.

Body Changes and Feelings of Alienation

I have been greatly impressed by the degree of feelings of alienation expressed by some of the commune dwellers of today. It is not
only an alienation in the sense of being at odds with the own family
and with society in general and a conviction of the impossibility of
finding harmony there; but a further estrangement rising from
smoldering anger and going beyond that into a feeling of change in
the individual himself—a "scary" feeling of entering a new state of
being with a separation from the old self and the confrontation with
a new inner configuration which is not yet assimilated. It is a period
of a conglomeration of discrepancies in development with pressures
of activity and interest in many new different and frequently opposing directions. Bewilderingly contradictory impulses exist side by
side and jostle each other for expression. It is obvious that puberty
and the time immediately after it contain many individually as well
as socially determined emotional problems, arising from the physical
sexual maturing and the increasing dominance of the genital urgency.
This occurs before the young person is ready economically, educationally, or in general experience to accept the responsibility of this
new stage in life. It is also obvious that the lags and disturbances in
emotional growth which are left over from childhood may influence
the way in which puberty is experienced.

It is natural that there should be a sense of strangeness and uncertainty with the raising of the curtain on many of the realities of
adult life which have been blurred or denied in childhood, that a
new attitude of criticism develops toward the parents whose short-
comings now loom larger, and that the sense of daring and challenge
which has its own special focus in a new stage of the oedipus complex should pervade the sphere of ego development and heighten
competitiveness in many directions. But the deepest feelings of estrangement, of real alienation, arise with some roots in the stress
associated with the physical changes of puberty. Not only are there
seemingly inexplicable differences in the timing and rate of emer-

gence of pubertal changes between individuals, bringing striking unevenness in comparative body sizes and consequently in interests to
youngsters who have previously held almost all concerns in common.
But even in the single individual the various body parts sometimes
grow at remarkably different rates. The effect on the observer may
be one of absurd incongruity. But in the adolescent there may be a
real ataxia in the sense of self, accompanied by torturing sensitivity.

This dilemma is picturesquely stated in the story of *Alice in
Wonderland,* the little prepuberty girl who, in trying to find her way
into the garden of womanhood, was blocked repeatedly by the unreliability of the functioning of her body. It, as well as its various
parts, was so continually changing size, that it was hard for her to
keep up with them, to know what was hers and what belonged to
someone else; or even worse, whether the change was in her or in
her surroundings. This uncertainty in the functioning of the own
body together with the actual changes in body size and contour
probably subjectively resembles the problems of the infant in the
first two to three years of life when growth is still progressing at
great speed and body functions are being mastered.

Influence of Increased Speed of Communication

But to return to a consideration of other circumstances which
have had a share in bringing about this revolution in which youth
has assumed so important a role. First of all, it is seen against the
background of worldwide revolutionary struggles which are going
on in so many areas as to seem almost confluent. There are differences in immediate aims, methods, and ideologies, but the overall
profession is to establish the freedom and dignity of man and to
abolish poverty and degrading types of servitude. We must question
in what ways technological developments of the century have contributed to this worldwide unrest and revolutionary spirit? Certainly
the increased speed of communication has facilitated the one-world-
ness of all major events. Together with the almost unbelievable
increase in speed of transportation, it has caused a functional shrink-
age in the world's size. People from formerly remote and inaccessible
areas are now readily brought into communication and contact.

This unexpected intimacy requires then a rapid mutual adaptation without enough time for the assimilation and true tolerance of

cultural differences which have their own history built into them. The emphasis is on making changes occur in immediate and tangible ways, rather than by a process of gradual growth. But to move from moment to moment, shutting off each moment as it passes is to undertake to catapult one's self through life in a way which may offer an exciting facsimile of freedom. The lack of continuity and depth of experience may lead to feelings of emptiness which are then countered by further rushing ahead and in the end add to the general tension and unrest. Speed is as contagious as anger, though in a different way. It arouses the competitive spirit even in those who would like to deny it. There is a fear of being left behind which is very close to the fear of loneliness.

The technological gift of acceleration has also made possible the rapid accumulation of people into crowds, and the awareness of power simply through amassment, a fact which has been exploited by and against youth. In a crowd there is a condensation of all the dangers of emotional infection, more rapid but in certain respects not dissimilar to the beginning of viral epidemics. There are other special dangers as well. The crowd not only attracts a great variety of poorly integrated people—and adolescence is in itself a stage at which psychological integration is taking a rather zigzag course—but it tends to bring out regressive behavior and attitudes in many people who would react quite differently in smaller groups. Although verbal communication plays a part, it readily deteriorates to diffusely offensive language and inflammatory rumor.

The excitement is communicated largely by nonverbal contact, actual touching, muscle tension, sense of heat, facial expression, tone of voice, etc. It is like an enormous hall of mirrors with reflections and counterreflections, multiplying and distorting the original image. The primitive introjective-projective mechanism is increasingly at work, as the individual loses his sense of separate boundaries and merges with the crowd. The loss of sense of body self is compensated for by a feeling of expansion and great increase in power. Many students who took part in the early campus demonstrations described an exhilaration amounting sometimes to ecstasy. This in itself promotes a desire for repetition.

In this situation there is an arousal of very infantile sexual and aggressive feelings, mostly pregenital in nature, which become so inflamed as to be susceptible to violent discharge if any incident of violence or even a rumor of violence occurs. Some of the danger also lies in the fact that at this stage of temporary regression in a revolutionary atmosphere, there is often a failure to determine even how or from what source the violence has arisen. The immediate assumption is that it has come from the "other side." The situation reminds one of an infant of eighteen months or so who pounds the floor with his fists and screams "Bad, bad," since it has offended him by his bumping his head on it in falling.

Crowd phenomena are certainly not unique in this time or setting. One has only to think of the Crusades or the enormous gatherings of St. Francis of Assisi to realize how much congregation is a tool in a power struggle, especially if there is a strong sense of righteousness on one or both sides. In the present day, the speed with which a crowd may be gathered, the velocity with which reports of it may be disseminated, and the very size it may attain, make it a formidable weapon, especially as the nature and direction of its discharge may be uncertain.

The Adolescent and Technology

Accompanying the incomparable technological developments in industry in the last hundred years, there has been a corresponding rise in the degree to which science in general and especially the sciences under the general heading of engineering have entered into the actual work of government. In the totalitarian governments of the period of the Second World War there was an effort to control and limit scientific work, and only findings which were supportive to the political ideology of the government in power were acceptable. At present there is a reversal of this trend with a considerable worship of science as offering the hard core of realistic data and the best source of reliable information on which successful government policies may be developed. As a result of this, there is a desire for and sometimes an illusion of the possibility of such a degree of perfection of the systematization of knowledge that human actions and responses might be as predictable and manageable as, for example, girders used in bridge building. This has tended to diminish interest in the humanistic sciences and the subjective aspects of the individual, except as these may be reducible to accurately predictable forces to be taken into account in assessing available manpower in any project (Roszak, 1968). Man thus becomes a secondary part of a machine, and is considered to be a machinelike organization himself.

Technology's contribution to business has been not only the development of machinery for the production of goods but also the influence on the organization of big business enterprises with the aim of making the highest possible profits. This has meant that the men-at-the-top in large industries need not be more than temporarily dedicated to the business in which they may be active at a given time. Nor are they necessarily familiar with the details of the processes of actual production, or in any personal contact with service to the consumer. The highest executives are concerned rather with the production of wealth, and both goods and consumer may become secondary: necessary but otherwise anonymous ingredients. The conglomeration of many different lines of business into one vast empire is an indication of the further deepening of this trend which has gained momentum in the last decade. The day is long past that gave rise to the saying that when a man invents a better mousetrap, the whole world will beat a path to his door.

It is against this background that the young people of today have spent their teenage years. Whether or not they have been clearly aware of the situation, they have breathed it in along with the weekly casualty reports of the Vietnam war. To the children of the poor it comes in some forms and to the children of the rich in others. But the bright, educated, and socially interested young people of whatever class are progressively alerted, and others follow along by contagion. The course they adopt in attempting to direct their own destinies depends on many other elements, perhaps most of all on the nature and depth of the adolescent disillusion they feel in their parents, and how this is interrelated with the new awakening and disenchantment they feel in regard to the current standards of society.

Technology and the Dehumanization of the Individual

As the machine has become larger and more complex, the understanding of its total operation is beyond the comprehension of most men who work with it. Nor is it usually necessary for them to have knowledge of more than a limited portion of the processes involved. The machine seems thus to have outstripped the man, and to be using him rather than being his tool. The product is no longer his product but one in which his share of accomplishment is so small that the product is foreign and alien to him. There is a process of dehumanization in this.

The fact of the displacement of man by machinery was a matter of concern in the organizations of working men that came into being in the 19th century. It was thought then that technology would liberate the man from his more onerous labors and give him leisure for more pleasurable pursuits, provided he got a share in the profits corresponding to the amount of work which had previously been required of him for its production. Proudhon was the conspicuous exception to this point of view for he believed that relieving a man of too much of his work brought a deprivation which weakened him. Proudhon was a man of the people who had been a printer, seemingly with some satisfaction.

As mechanization in industry progressed, and the distance between worker and product increased, it was evident that mechanization also meant standardization not only of the product, but of the work of the individuals connected with it and the basis on which payment was made. Time expended was the readiest common unit. With money the main focus of interest and a diminished competition on the basis of skill between workers, competition naturally turned to a rivalry between the workers (banded together to act in unison) and the employers. Interest in the improvement of the product was sacrificed on both sides in favor of concern for its immediate salability, which correspondingly increased. The struggle between workers and management was thus intensified; and an engineering "science" of negotiating human relationships grew up. In this setting the leadership among the workers was given, not to the master craftsman, but to those who could deal most effectively with the management in terms of the division of profits.

Further, the publicizing of the product assumed greater importance with the multiplication of the media of communication; the business of advertising mushroomed, bringing with it an eccentric relationship to reality. An important aspect of this situation arose from the fact that radio and television permit a vivid, but often specious presentation of the product dealing with its immediate appeal, even before it has been adequately tested for safety, efficiency, and durability. Public consumers act as an uncontrolled practical laboratory in which slowly, imperfectly, and occasionally with disaster to themselves, they carry on the testing. The individual consumer pays for his service rather than being paid for it. Unfortunately many advertising concerns have taken over publicity methods which Hitler announced and used in ways which gave a forecast of what world destruction might be.

Throughout all this there is an "as-if" quality substituted for durability and substance. The individual's relationship to reality is also undermined, and the primary interest in money—which is after all a tangible symbol like a multi-faceted fetish—takes the place of a great variety of experiences and work. Indeed, this seems to involve the illusion that the accumulation of money will bring satisfaction through obviating work almost entirely. With the entrance of cybernetics, the promise is held out that mental work also will be unnecessary for an even larger number of people, and what work is done will mostly involve keeping and feeding the machines. Many people also seem to hold the belief that all problems will be soluble through the acquisition of a complete body of data.

Attitudes toward Work

We come now to consider the possible basic role and significance of work in the individual life under conditions simpler than those which prevail in our culture at present.

I am not able to accept the idea that man is and always has been a slothful creature who will do nothing except under the pressure of dire necessity. It would seem that on this basis the margin of subsistence would be so narrow that it would be a miracle that he survived at all. When this concept of his inertia is coupled with the idea that man is fundamentally violent as well, I begin to feel better about it (Freud 1930, 1933). For I can see that these two opposite aspects of primitive man may be related and have saved him from extinction. I would think that inertia and explosiveness in varying degrees and combinations form the basic rhythms of life: the sustaining and the propulsive rhythms. The sustaining rhythm in which there is a fairly even alternation of tension and relaxation, e.g., in the heartbeat and respiration, is shared one way or another with other animal life, and may in the very beginning have been stamped by the alternation of day and night. But out of this there arose under special conditions a second rhythm which is propulsive and pushes the organism forward gradually making and using an increasing structural complexity.

It is the rhythm which not merely alternates tension and relaxation but one which proceeds by steps of tension and incomplete relaxation until it reaches a peak or climax with relief coming to a modified explosion which stops short of self-destruction and in turn compels and initiates a period of rest. This rhythm is orgastic in form and, in its sharpest contrast of climax and relaxation, it is the source of genital excitement and gratification. It offers an efficient mechanism for the conveying of seminal fluid and, in a less intense rhythmic pattern, is utilized in many body activities especially those of excretory discharge. It is also the basic curve of productive work, i.e., work which is carried on with the aim and attainment of a definite goal which is desired by the worker. However, if the exertion is of the even rhythm of monotony and also is not in the interest of the worker, tedium and aversion result rather than excitement and satisfaction.[2]

So far I have only indicated or implied that work, even in the sense of deliberate conscious effort toward reaching a desired goal, may use certain patterns and directions which are basically part of the constitutional equipment and are set in motion by the forces inherent in growth and maturation. These intraorganism pressures develop as the core of the autonomous ego, but are dependent at first on some cooperation from the maternal environment to give them content and stimulate elaboration. When one sees an infant nursing energetically, one certainly gets the impression of work being done, often with relish, even that certain working hours are preferred and more or less demanded. At each stage of maturational

---

2 The rubbing of sticks together or the twirling of a stick in a small hole in a stone as was done in some Indian tribes in order to make fire furnishes a natural symbolic connection between work and sexual activity, and suggests the fundamental connection between creative work and sexual creativity. It is of some interest, too, that any part of the body may be erotized by repeated rhythmic friction. Tickling by rhythmic stroking of the body may produce either an orgastic discharge with both muscular and genital excitement and release through excretory discharge, or an outburst of rage, depending on the relationship between the tickled one and the tickler.

development there is the same appearance of effort being put forth, at first somewhat at random, followed by a period of faltering and uncertainty, but once the object has been clearly located, the goal-directed activity is nailed down by being repeated with definite intention and appearance of satisfaction in success. There seems usually to be gratification and relief when the definite pursuit is mastered. There is sometimes an after-the-fact practice with trials of variation which have the quality of playfulness.

It is not easy to locate precisely the beginning of the realization of work in terms of its being activity chosen for its future usefulness rather than for immediate gratification. It is possible that there is some dawning awareness of this state of affairs by the age of four when there is some sense of time, as well as of individual identity, but this is not well established. A more definite solidification of the idea of work and of the future occurs with the need to come to terms with oedipal jealousy, and with the extension of sibling rivalry to schoolmates and others outside the family. Certainly the significance of the period of latency must vary greatly in this respect, depending not only on the child's specific environment, but on the influence of the economic condition of the family and the degree to which the child may be drawn into the struggle for existence in an impoverished family setting. In latency, too, there may be a propensity for exploration, and a fairly sophisticated concern with the mechanics of the body together with a related interest in the use and invention of tools, many of which are fundamentally extensions of body parts. During adolescence, however, work begins to assume serious personal significance as a means of livelihood, except in families of inherited wealth.

This also means that with the expectation of accepting responsibility for others rather than a dependence on them, the maturing adolescent feels the need for tools, weapons or some kind of special equipment to meet this change. For the present generation the battle seems to be increasingly one of wits. The relationship between man and his tools begins in infancy and until relatively recently has generally been a close and enduring one and frequently has carried with it an unconscious anthropomorphizing appreciation. Perhaps only the artists will remain regularly in touch with their tools. The most appealing toys of childhood are those fashioned roughly after body parts, or those which simulate the useful implements of adults. But when tools are so built together to make machines, they grossly caricature man. If they discredit and displace him as well, he is liable to outbursts of rage. This is the story of the textile mill workers in the towns of the North of England about 1811-1816. The enraged weavers formed a guerrilla army to attack and destroy the mill machinery. They rode masked and at night, raided the factories, and smashed the machines under the leadership of General Ludd, who may have been a mythical leader since his identity was never known. Their code originally forebade the spilling of blood. But after a strong attack on the raiders by the police, real warfare broke out; and a law was passed making the destruction of a machine a capital offense (Carmichael, 1967). A somewhat related situation was reported in this country in the early part of the present century when a law was passed in New Jersey that any automobile which was responsible for the death of a man should be destroyed at once (without trial?) (Flugel, 1945).

That the machine often represents the threatening father is clear in the dreams of many patients. This connection is strongly suggested in the childhood memories of Herbert Read. At the age of five to six he saw his usually calm father in a terrific rage at a farmhand who had mistreated a mare resulting in a miscarriage. Shortly thereafter he himself went into a state of terror when a "Machine God" (actually a thrashing machine) visited the farm. Later he suffered nightmares which seemed vividly real, of being threatened with extermination by a steamroller which came bellowing and snorting smoke and fire at him. Although Read did not seem to recognize the association of his father with the frightening machine, in another book in which he declared himself an anarchist at heart, he made it quite clear that he was disinclined to accept any political leadership since such leaders turned out invariably to be tyrannical fathers (Read, 1940, 1939). It would seem that in the present more critical period and on a larger stage of life, the Atom Bomb and the computer are magnified versions of Read's thrashing machine and fiery steamroller.

The fanatical young people of today believe they can destroy all evil, some by the passive aggression of total rejection of society—a killing by denial; and the militant others by overt violence fighting the Bomb by bombing. The pent-up energy of youth demands that it should happen at once, without plan or vision of a transition stage to a new culture. Except when the contagious fury of destruction takes over and becomes a blind end in itself, the rationalization seems to be to get rid of everything that is and something good will take its place. This appears essentially as a death and rebirth fantasy which is externalized and put upon society. But back of it is the eternal Utopian dream of a perfect world. This indeed would be a nonexistence, the equivalent of death. For there is nowhere to go from perfection; it is done and over. It is only through variability, fluctuation, differences, and even mistakes that change and possible progress can come about.

This paper has been devoted largely to questions concerning the unusually strong involvement of youth in the current revolutionary activities. Certain important related problems have necessarily been left untouched. Conspicuously, I have not dealt at all with either the *Black problem* or *drugs*. I would regard the drug problem as a secondary social symptom, somewhat similar to a secondary neurotic symptom which arises as a defense but can become malignant nonetheless. The drugs which "expand consciousness" may play a special role, one aspect of which is related to the feelings experienced in crowds, when there is a lessening of the sense of individual boundaries supplemented by an increased expansive identification with the power of the group. This in turn may have qualities of a state of religious fervor.

The Black problem—and the part it plays in the present chaos—deserves two or three volumes, a project in any case beyond the confines of this paper. I would note, however, that since the Blacks have a larger core of reality grievance than the rest of us and a long history of nonviolent rage, they can the more readily join with any other aggrieved group. But their inevitable ambivalence to anything white makes for increased explosiveness. In addition, they are now being called upon to make a more extreme and rapid adaptation to change than is true of any other group in our culture.

It had been my intention to write more specifically about the dominance of anal-sadistic character traits in industrial society (which also strongly influences government attitudes), with an emphasis on mechanical perfection at the same time that it spews forth its refuse in a way that threatens to exterminate us with offal. On the other hand, that same trait, more individually expressed, appears in the young revolutionists' open use of filthy language and of actual feces as weapons of attack during some of the early student revolts.

BIBLIOGRAPHY

Carmichael, J. (1967), *Karl Marx*. New York: Scribner.
Flugel, J. C. (1945), *Man, Morals and Society*. New York: International Universities Press.
Freud, S. (1930), Civilization and Its Discontents. *Standard Edition*, 21:59-145. London: Hogarth Press, 1961.
—— (1933), Why War? *Standard Edition*, 22:197-215. London: Hogarth Press, 1964.
Glover, E. (1933), *War, Sadism and Pacifism*. London: Allen & Unwin.
Joll, J. (1964), *The Anarchists*. London: Eyre & Spottiswoode.
Kropotkin, P. (1902), *Mutual Aid*. New York: McClure Phillips.
Nordhoff, C. (1875), *Communistic Colonies in the U.S.* New York: Harper.
Read, H. (1939), *Poetry and Anarchism*. New York: Macmillan.
—— (1940), *Annals of Innocence and Experience*. London: Faber & Faber.
Roszak, T. (1968), *The Making of a Counter Culture*. New York: Anchor Books, Doubleday.

CHILDREN'S REACTIONS TO THE DEATH OF IMPORTANT OBJECTS

A Developmental Approach

HUMBERTO NAGERA, M.D. (Ann Arbor)

A Brief Review of the Literature

A review of the literature on children's reactions to the death of close relatives must also include papers dealing with their reactions to transitory losses because these have been described as mourning. Furthermore, the very young child always reacts strongly to separation from the important object (mother), regardless of whether he understands the causes of the mother's absence or the meaning of death. Naturally, at certain stages of his development, as Freud (1926) pointed out, the child "cannot as yet distinguish between temporary absence and permanent loss. As soon as it loses sight of its mother it behaves as if it were never going to see her again; and repeated consoling experiences to the contrary are necessary before it learns that her disappearance is usually followed by her re-appearance. . . . In consequence of the infant's misunderstanding of

Although the product of one individual author who remains responsible for its form and content, this paper represents a characteristic example of team research as carried out at the Hampstead Child-Therapy Course and Clinic. The relevant *clinical data* were extracted from the files of several departments of the Clinic or were made available by the therapists of several children treated analytically at this institution. Ample opportunity for informed *discussion* of the subject was offered within the program of the Clinical Concept Research Group, whose members are: H. Nagera (Chairman), Anna Freud (Consultant), S. Baker, A. Colonna, R. Edgecumbe, R. Putzel, W. E. Freud, I. Rosen, A. Hayman.

This paper forms part of a Research Project entitled "Childhood Pathology: Impact on Later Mental Health," which is being conducted at the Hampstead Child-Therapy Course and Clinic, London. The project is financed by the National Institute of Mental Health, Washington, D.C., Grant No. 05683-0607.

At the present time Dr. Nagera is Professor of Psychiatry in the Department of Psychiatry at Michigan University and Director of the Child Analytic Study Program at Children's Psychiatric Hospital.

the facts, the situation of missing its mother is not a danger-situation but a traumatic one. Or, to put it more correctly, it is a traumatic situation if the infant happens at the time to be feeling a need which its mother should be the one to satisfy" (p. 169f.).

The reaction of children of different ages to separation from the parents under a variety of conditions has been studied and described by Anna Freud and Dorothy Burlingham (1942, 1943), Spitz (1945, 1946), Spitz and Wolf (1946), James Robertson (1958, 1962), Bowlby (1960, 1961a, 1961b, 1963), Mahler (1961), and others. Bowlby (1960) considers the reaction of infants, when separated from important objects, as identical with the adult reaction of mourning, a point of view that has been questioned by Anna Freud (1960), Schur (1960), Spitz (1960), and Wolfenstein (1966). Other authors, e.g., Shambaugh (1961), in sharp contrast to Bowlby, agrees with Helene Deutsch, who believes that the "process of mourning as seen in adults apparently differs from that seen in children" (p. 521). Rochlin (1959) states that the adult type of mourning is not common in children.

Fleming and Altschul (1963), studying the effects on adult personality structure of object loss in childhood, found a wide range of repercussions in terms of arrested development, faulty reality testing, impulse control, etc.

McDonald (1964) described the reaction of nursery school children to the death of the mother of one of the children in the group, while Barnes (1964) described the reaction of that child and her younger sibling to the death of their mother. Cain et al. (1964, 1966) studied children's reactions to the death, natural or through suicide, of sibling and parents. They pointed to the multiplicity of dangers encountered by such children during their psychological development.

There is some disagreement in the literature as to the age at which children are able fully to comprehend the concept of death, grasping as well the idea of its finality. Wolf (1958) believes that something similar to the adult comprehension of death is not observed before the ages of ten or eleven, while Furman (1964a) holds the opinion that a two- to three-year-old is capable of "mastering the meaning of death" and a three-and-a-half- or four-year-old has the capacity to mourn. Wolfenstein (1966) has questioned Furman's timetable with regard to mourning. Wolfenstein (1965) described a child's reaction to the death of a parent as an inhibited emotional response and designated as "mourning at a distance" the apparent contradiction existing between the intensity of the grief shown for someone far away (such as President Kennedy) as contrasted with that shown in respect to a close relative (p. 80).[1] Wolfenstein (1966) stated that mourning as "described by Freud did not occur" in the cases she studied (p. 96). In fact, "The painful and gradual decathexis of the beloved parents which the adolescent is forced to perform serves as an initiation into how to mourn. . . . Until he has undergone what we may call the trial mourning of adolescence, he is unable to mourn" (pp. 113, 116).

Laufer (1966) observed in analytic treatment the response of an adolescent whose mother died suddenly of a coronary thrombosis. He stated that the "loss of the oedipal object in adolescence may constitute a developmental interference in the sense described by Nagera (1966)" (p. 291). It is from this angle of *developmental interferences* that I shall approach the question of children's reactions to the death of close relatives.

This brief review of the literature allows us to conclude that different authors disagree on the age at which children are capable of mourning. There are those, e.g., Bowlby (1960), who believe that mourning (in the adult sense) is possible and can be observed from the sixth month of life onward, or, like Furman (1964), who think that mourning can be observed only from the third or fourth year of life onward. There are others, e.g., Shambaugh (1961) and Rochlin (1959), who believe that the mourning process in children and adults differs, and Wolfenstein (1965, 1966), who believes that mourning becomes possible only with the resolution of the adolescent phase, after the appropriate detachment from the parental figures has taken place.

My own view is closer to that of Wolfenstein, that is, mourning as defined by Freud (1917) and as observed in the adult is not possible until the detachment from parental figures has taken place in adoles-

---

[1] Harrison et al. (1967), studying children's reactions to President Kennedy's death, found it necessary to sound a warning note about the reliability of "the descriptions of children's bereavement reactions given by mourning adults." In their data "it was impossible to distinguish between adult misperceptions and confusions, the children's reaction to the tragedy, and the children's reactions to the changes in the adult" (p. 596).

cence. This does not imply that some aspects of the mourning process of the adult mourner cannot also be observed in children as a reaction to the loss of important objects, but I do suggest that there are important differences between the so-called mourning of children and that of adults.

Death of a Relative as a Developmental Interference

For the adult, the death of a close relative is frequently a traumatic event.[2] For the child, death of a close relative such as father or mother can also be a traumatic event, but, even more important, it constitutes what I have described (1966) as a developmental interference and a very serious one indeed.

The mourning that accompanies the loss of an object in adulthood has been rightly described as a process of adaptation (Pollock, 1961). For a time, while the adaptation is worked through, everything else is temporarily suspended until the mourning is completed and the adult mourner resumes a normal life. But the child is not a finished product like the adult. He is in the middle of a multiplicity of processes of development in all sorts of areas and directions— processes that require, for their normal unfolding, the presence of the suddenly absent object. Naturally, in these circumstances it is not sensible to expect that all development will be stopped or a pause produced so that the mourning process, leading to adaptation to the loss, can take place and normal life can be resumed again afterward as in the case of the adult. The pressure of internal developmental forces interferes with the possibility of a pause for mourning. Thus whatever "mourning" is possible under this multiplicity of developmental pressures must take place simultaneously with, and in subordination to, such developmental needs as are

2 As we know, the mere act of talking about a recently lost love object frequently leads to a painful breakdown of the ego. This breakdown is in many ways similar to a traumatically overwhelming experience, with crying, sadness, intense pain, inability to think or to react in an organized and normal way. As time goes by and as the work of mourning proceeds further, the same person will be able to talk coherently about the event without the ego breaking down.

Naturally, the reaction to loss differs according to the intensity of the cathexis, the nature of the relationship, the intensity of the ambivalence, the existence of hostile wishes, and other conflicts. Similarly, as Pollock (1961) points out, the sudden, unexpected death of the love object is usually more traumatic than death following prolonged illness.

appropriate to the age of the child, a situation that is complicated
by the immediate distortions and repercussions of the loss suffered.
It is not sufficiently taken into account that if the relevant objects
are absent, especially during certain stages, it is in the nature of
many of these developmental processes to recreate the objects anew:
to make them come to life in fantasies or to ascribe such roles as
the developmental stage requires to any suitable figures available
in the environment. It is partly this developmental need that opposes the normal process of mourning and the process of gradual
withdrawal of cathexis from the lost object. Thus, relevant objects
are brought to life again and again in order to satisfy the requirements of psychological development. Anna Freud and Dorothy Burlingham (1943) described how "Our parentless nursery-children
. . . do their utmost to invent their own father- and mother- figures
and live in close emotional contact with them in their imagination.
But these products of their phantasy, necessary as they are to the
child's emotional needs, do not exercise the same parental functions.
They are called into life by the infant's longing for the missing love-
object, and, as such, satisfy its wishes. They are the personification of
inner forces, moving in the child, and as such give evidence of successive stages of development" (p. 126).

This does not mean that children who have lost one or the other
parent do not withdraw some cathexis from the memories of such
objects and do not try to find alternative or substitute objects to
which some of these cathexes can be attached. They most certainly
do so, but this process is frequently interfered with by internal forces
that recreate, sometimes in idealized forms, the relationship to the
absent object at the slightest disappointment with the world outside
or the substitute object.

Parents have to educate their children, impose restrictions on the
amount of gratifications allowed (instinctual and otherwise), make
demands, etc. This situation leads, at times, to clashes between the
child and the parents. It is at these points that there is a readiness
(or a facilitation) for certain developments to take place that usually
complicate and introduce more or less serious disruptions in the
emotional growth of these unfortunate children. They may feel, for
example, that all these limitations are imposed on them, or that all
these demands are made, because "she" or "he" is not their real

mother or father, or that all these "unpleasant things" happen because they are not really loved, since they are not their "real" children. Their real mother or father would have been so much nicer, more tolerant and understanding. In short, there is a facilitation in the direction of the idealization of the dead parent and a tendency to split the ambivalence with the positive feelings cathecting the idealized dead parent and the negative ones the substitute parent.

Naturally, this negative cathexis of the substitute parent will have repercussions on the present and future relations between the child and the substitute mother or father. Furthermore, the child's future psychological makeup and future object relations may be similarly harmed by these unwelcomed tendencies.[3]

Another significant factor in children is that the same event, the same developmental interference, will influence development differently. Thus the absence of the father, for example, will acquire new meanings and be reinterpreted in phallic-oedipal terms when that phase is reached, in contrast to the fantasies that accompany the father's absence during the toddler stage.

In this way, developmental interferences, of a detrimental nature, may influence or determine the outcome of subsequent developmental and neurotic conflicts. In the case of the death of a parent, the child is forced to carry on with his psychological development in the absence of one essential figure. This frequently leads to distortions of development and at least tends to complicate the resolution of many of the otherwise normal and typical developmental conflicts of childhood and adolescence. In this way the ground is prepared for a variety of neurotic conflicts that take, as their point of departure, the inappropriate resolution of such developmental conflicts. We have only to consider, for example, that a child who loses his mother or father during or just before the phallic-oedipal phase will find himself handicapped in his attempts to resolve this otherwise typical and normal developmental conflict. Meiss (1952) has described some of these difficulties.

Naturally, the child's need for the parents is quite different from

---

[3] A similar situation exists in the case of adoptive parents. Although early adoption by suitable parents is a most desirable event from the point of view of the infant, the adoptive parent should be aware of the developmentally destructive or at least damaging tendencies that fate has imposed on those unfortunate children who have lost their parents through death or abandonment.

one developmental stage to the next. In the earlier stages the loss of the mother is directly and immediately significant. This is not so in the case of the father except insofar as the mother's mourning and distress will affect her relationship to the baby. Nevertheless, the father's death and consequently the father's absence will become significant in its own right later on, when nature assigns him a variety of roles to play in the development of the child and he is not there to play them.

Finally, in my view, one of the most important differences between the mourning reactions of children and those of adults consists of the fact that the child frequently reacts to the death of a primary object with abnormal manifestations, which in many instances greatly resemble those observed in the case of neurotic conflict or neurosis proper. In other words, they react with anxiety, with multiple forms of regression on the side of the drives, occasionally by giving up certain ego achievements, and by developing abnormal forms of behavior. Though the child is, generally speaking, quite incapable of the prolonged and sustained mourning reaction observed in the adult, he frequently produces instead symptoms of the most diverse nature. They demonstrate the special situation of developmental stress in which he finds himself. Bonnard (1961) has given examples of children who reacted to the parent's death with truancy and stealing. They were seeking punishment out of their sense of guilt for the parent's death. In normal adult mourning such a reaction is not usually observed.

Thus, it seems reasonable to conclude that the death of important objects will, of necessity, produce a serious disruption of the developmental processes per se, quite apart from the special significance that the event may have for the child, according to age, quality of the relationship, intensity of the trauma, special circumstances surrounding the death, the reactions to this event by the remaining important family members, the possible changes for the worse in the child's life circumstances.

The Young Child's Reactions to Loss

Many factors contribute to the specific form of "mourning reactions" observed in children following the loss of important objects. They vary, as I pointed out earlier, according to the different levels of development reached in a number of areas of the personality at different ages. It is for these reasons that I question the validity of some comparisons made between the mourning of adults and children. Naturally, such comparisons show many similarities. Unfortunately, there is an occasional tendency to misconstrue them into identities, or to assume that identical metapsychological processes underlie these superficial similarities.

THE DEVELOPMENT OF OBJECT RELATIONS

In order to understand the reactions of children to loss, it is necessary to examine the role that such objects play at different stages in the child's physical, psychological, and emotional development. By specifying the functions of the object and its contribution to the normal functioning of psychological development, we can highlight what can go wrong or actually goes wrong in the child's development when the object is missing.[4]

Many of the reactions observed in the child have to be understood as the result of the absence of one of the *sine qua non* elements for his normal development and not necessarily as a mourning reaction to the loss of the object (as will be the case in the adult personality). *In short, we must distinguish, in the overt manifestation of the child's reactions to loss, those that are the result of the developmental disturbance introduced by the object loss and the "true mourning reactions to that loss."* At the present time, there seems to be a readiness to lump together these two completely different types of phenomena. Further, as Anna Freud (1960) has clearly pointed out: for a true mourning reaction to the loss of an object to occur, the ego and object relations must have reached a certain degree of development.

Loss during the First Few Weeks of Life

It is easier to ascertain what goes on in the child once he is capable of verbalization. It is more difficult to establish what goes on during the first year of life. Any such attempt has to be tentative

[4] For example, Hoffer (1950) has pointed out that an adequate libidinization of the child's body within the mother-infant relationship is important for the development of his body image.

and highly speculative. Having this in mind, let us ask what "object" means to the young infant.

Many analysts hold the view that the object has no existence of its own to start with in the psychic life of the child. According to Hoffer (1952), it is included as a part of the self, or rather, as an extension of the "internal narcissistic milieu." If we accept this view, a loss of the object at this particular point in the development of the child can presumably be experienced only as a loss of something pleasurable, as a qualitative change in the "internal narcissistic milieu" since no differentiation exists as yet between self and object. Usually, when such a loss occurs at this early stage, a substitute object takes over the mothering function, and if the substitute object is appropriate, the transitory disequilibrium is restored. When suitable substitute mothering is not available, as, for example, in the case of babies living in institutions, we know that although their physical needs may be well attended to, many of the ingredients of "good mothering" are missing. We also know that the development of such babies is affected in a variety of ways because of the lack of appropriate stimulation.

The mother's presence is thus required for the normal development of a number of ego achievements. Her absence through death or abandonment acts as a developmental interference affecting several areas as well as complicating the development of object relationships beyond the need-satisfying stage. For children growing up in institutions, the distance between the quality of the "ideal mothering" (received by babies growing up with their mothers) and the quality of the "substitute mothering" (offered by the institution) is in direct proportion to the developmental retardation and damage observed. In our culture, somebody in the immediate family frequently takes over the mothering function. When this is the case, the baby may show signs of distress with the change of object, but it seems that, at least in the first few weeks of life, a substitute is more or less readily accepted after a short time (Anna Freud, 1952). The distress signs are probably due to his perception of the qualitative differences in handling, general mothering, and the resulting sensory experiences of the "substitute mother figure." The baby's reaction is based not on an awareness of the disappearance of the real mother as an object but on the perception of a change in the quality of his sensory experiences. It is as if the change had taken place in a part of the child's internal narcissistic milieu—that part or extension of what we later on call his self and which, at this undifferentiated stage (in terms of self-object), is still fused with the mother.

Loss After the Second or Third Month of Life

At a later stage, the object *acquires a mental representation of its own in the child's mind as a part object,* according to Melanie Klein, *or as a need-satisfying object,* according to Hartmann (1952) and Anna Freud (1952) . The object is now valued on the basis of its role as a need-fulfilling entity. It is these *need-fulfilling* functions of the object that are important and not the object per se. If during this stage the object is lost or changed, the child will react with more or less marked distress, a response that is probably still due to the marked preference for the familiar and known which are now missing. Although the baby's needs can be satisfied by a substitute object, this is a new, unfamiliar object. The significant difference between the first few weeks of life and this stage is that the object has now acquired a mental representation of its own, even if only as a part object. Nevertheless it has become something independent, identifiable in its own right. It is at this point too that the object starts to be associated with the thing that brings about a particular sensory experience. Thus the baby at the need-satisfying stage notices not only the qualitative changes in the sensory experience of satisfaction (as the younger baby did), but this change is now associated with the change of object. Little by little he becomes more able to discriminate and differentiate such things as differences in the muscular tone, skin warmth, pitch of voice, and breathing rhythms.

Loss in the Second Half of the First Year and Onward

With further development the object is valued independently of its need-fulfilling functions. Toward the end of the first or the beginning of the second year the child reaches the stage of object constancy (Anna Freud, 1952). If at this point the object is suddenly absent, the child's distress is due to the new type of cathexis, which has a special quality, more permanence, and no longer attaches itself automatically to substitute objects even if the child accepts their

ministrations. The example quoted by Bowlby (1960), from Anna
Freud's and Dorothy Burlingham's book *Infants Without Families,*
illustrates this point. It concerns a seventeen-month-old girl who,
on being separated from her mother, said nothing but "Mum, Mum,
Mum," for three days, and who, although she liked to sit on the
nurse's knee and have the nurse put her arm around her, insisted
throughout on having her back to the nurse so as not to see her.

Strictly speaking, it is only at the point when object constancy
has been reached that the nature and quality of the cathexis directed
to the object can at least in rudimentary form be compared to the
level, nature, and quality of the cathexis directed by the normal
adult to his closest objects. It is this special type of attachment
cathexis that determines the intense suffering observed when the object is lost. It is this cathexis that must be withdrawn from the innumerable memories of the lost object and made available for the
recathexis of some new objects. That the quality of the cathexis and
the level of the object relationship are special ones, very different
from that attached to objects during the early stage of need satisfaction, is partly explained by the further development of the ego
which allows for a better discrimination of the object's qualities and
a more clear-cut separation between self and object.

Thus, in my view, it is only from the stage of object constancy
onward that the conditions exist, in terms of object relations, which
make it possible to observe *some aspects* of mourning in children as
the psychological response to the psychologically meaningful loss of
an object. In this respect it shows many resemblances to the mourning responses of adults with clear signs of the three phases described
by Bowlby (1961a), that is, protest, despair, and denial. Superficially
similar responses in the much younger child are based on completely
different reasons and mechanisms, as I have tried to show.

Thus, once object constancy has been established, a common
denominator has been acquired that persists throughout life. Nevertheless, it would be a mistake to conclude that, from this point onward, children's reactions to death could be expected to be uniform
or identical with those of adults. Many other factors, to be examined
next, determine the multiplicity of variations in response observed at
different ages.

The Child's Low Capacity for the Tolerance of Acute Pain

Human beings generally have a limited capacity for the tolerance of acute pain, and in children this capacity is even lower. Wolfenstein (1966) referred to the "short sadness span, which is usual in children." This short sadness span, which can be considered from another angle as a greater flexibility and mobility of the child's attention and interests based on his intense curiosity and the momentum enforced by the developmental processes, can be observed in a variety of ways. Wolfenstein (1965) described how children, in the age range from latency to adolescence, cannot tolerate intense distress for long and quickly bring forward opposite thoughts and feelings (according to our observations the same applies even more so to prelatency children). As she says, "They do not seem able to sustain the process of protracted mourning that we know in adults" (p. 77).[5] She further refers to children aged nine and ten who cried when they heard the news of Kennedy's assassination and yet could not understand why their parents refused to go to the movies that evening as previously planned or were impatient when they could not find their usual program on television.

I have made similar observations in three children (whose ages ranged from four and a half to thirteen) on the occasion of the death of their grandfather, who had lived at their home for three years. Though there was no question that the three children were upset by the grandfather's death, the four-and-a-half-year-old tried to listen to some music on the radio early the next morning, as he was in the habit of doing. He accepted the explanation that the other members of the family were still very sad and did not really feel like having

[5] Helene Deutsch in her paper "Absence of Grief" (1937) was one of the first analysts to call our attention "to the phenomenon of indifference which children so frequently display following the death of a loved person." In trying to account for this she did not consider as completely valid either of the two explanations usually given to account "for this so-called heartless behavior," namely, the child's intellectual inability to grasp the reality of death and the still inadequate formation of object relationships. Her own hypothesis is "that the ego of the child is not sufficiently developed to bear the strain of the work of mourning and that it therefore utilizes some mechanism of narcissistic self-protection to circumvent the process" (p. 13).

the radio on.[6] It was clear that in the following days (until the funeral took place) he was frequently tempted to turn either the radio or the television on. Occasionally he turned it on and off, telling those around that the radio should not be on because his grandfather had died.[7]

The other two children, aged twelve and thirteen, showed clear signs of some sadness at different moments as well as a great deal of empathy at the obvious pain of their grandmother. They would undoubtedly have liked to watch their favorite TV programs, but did not do so out of empathy with the adults. The knowledge that they could watch TV again the day after the funeral also helped them to control the wish.

This type of behavior is, in my experience, quite common up to and including adolescence. It cannot be construed to mean that children do not grieve at all for the lost objects or that some aspect of mourning is not taking place; but it demonstrates Wolfenstein's point that they are hardly able to keep up the process of protracted (and sustained) mourning as we know it in adults. As she points out (1966), "The different ways of reacting to loss according to age often lead to conflict and misunderstandings in the family. The adult . . . cannot understand the seeming lack of feeling on the part of the child. A mother weeping for the father who has died reproaches the child, suffering from an affective inhibition, for remaining dry-eyed" (p. 73).

Object Loss Plus Separation from Other Familiar Objects and Surroundings

We know from the observations of Anna Freud, Dorothy Burlingham, J. Robertson, Spitz, Bowlby, and others of many touching examples of intense and more sustained reactions to the loss of the object because of hospitalization of the child or mother or because

---

[6] This boy's reactions are described in greater detail in the last part of this paper (see the case of P.).

[7] It should not be forgotten that much of the behavior of the adult world under bereavement conditions is a conventional and generally accepted, ritualized type of behavior. This makes little sense to the young child who has not yet come across it and has not introjected it as the appropriate code of behavior under such circumstances. Although many of these rituals are disappearing, in some countries all sorts of rules still exist determining the "official" length of mourning and the severity of the restrictions imposed, according to the closeness of the dead relative, etc.

of absence of the mother for other reasons. But there seems to me to be an essential difference between this group of children and those who have remained in the familiar surroundings of their homes, keeping their rooms and possessions. They have remained as well in the company of other familiar objects even if these objects are, in terms of the mental economics of the child, of less importance than the one lost. The observations of children, by the different authors mentioned, concerned instead children who had suffered not only an important loss in terms of an object but who simultaneously found themselves placed in unfamiliar surroundings with strange people, and who were in some cases faced with the added stress of hospital procedures and medical manipulations.[8] I believe that we tend to underestimate the tremendous importance of perceptual and environmental constancy for the human being and especially for the child. Familiar surroundings and objects, familiar possessions (room, bed, toys, etc.), familiar noises, are important for our well-being.

At Hampstead we have seen many young children who reacted strongly to changes of environment, for example, during holidays. Although they remained with their parents and other relatives, such situations occasionally seemed to trigger a variety of disturbances. Similar distress in the very young child is frequently observed as a response to change of room, cot or bed. Naturally, children's reactions in this respect tend to vary according to age and specific idiosyncrasies.

I believe that some of the differences observed in the reactions of these two groups of children (i.e., those separated from home and familiar surroundings and those staying at home) to the loss of objects can be accounted for partly by the factors mentioned.

8 Anna Freud's and Dorothy Burlingham's observations at the Hampstead War Nurseries concerned children separated from their parents largely as the result of the war conditions. A few children were assigned to a substitute mother and every effort was made for the child to have his "special" person. Robertson's and Bowlby's observations concern mainly children living under hospital conditions, while Spitz's observations concerned, in one case, the reactions to the accidental separation of delinquent mothers and their children who had been living together in a correctional institution. His other observations concerned the development of children in a foundling home in the absence of their mothers and without adequate mother substitutes. Anna Freud (1960) has pointed out that we know in fact little of children's reactions to loss when they remain with the surviving relatives and in their own familiar surroundings.

Denial as a Reaction to Loss

It is natural and normal for the young child to use excessively certain primitive types of defenses such as various forms of denial (in words, actions, and fantasy, or of affect). This factor itself further contributes to making the mourning process of the child somewhat different from that of the adult. As we know, children practically up to the latency period very readily have recourse to denial, especially in traumatic or stressful situations. The low tolerance of the younger child for psychological pain makes this a welcome defense.[9] If denial is the child's primary reaction to loss, its further impact on his development will to a large measure be determined by how the environment deals with this. We know, for example, how frequently adults wish "to spare the child" and withhold important facts from him or, unable to tolerate their own sadness, forbid the child to mention the painful event. (For a further discussion, see, e.g., footnote 10.)

Another important factor is which element of the experience is denied—e.g., whether it is the affect associated with it or the event itself. If it is the latter, it presupposes some understanding of reality, which of course is a function of the child's age.

Reality Testing, Reality Awareness, Reality Adaptation, and Reaction to Loss

Anna Freud (1960) and others have emphasized the importance of relating a child's reaction to loss to his reality awareness. We know, e.g., that at least during the beginning of the second year of life, many children are not yet able to distinguish between dreams and reality. Consequently, events taking place in the dream are treated as pieces of reality, with the result that the child is greatly confused. (Nagera, 1966b). We do not know the implications for the further development of the child at this age if, as it is bound to happen, the lost mother reappears in his dream life; or in which ways this will affect his understanding of the loss and the process of

---

[9] Adults subjected to extreme stress also may resort to denial while the ego gains some time to pull together all its resources in order to cope with more adaptive mechanisms. Frequently the denial lasts only a few instants and takes the form of incredulity, disbelief, the hope that there has been a mistake, that one is really having a nightmare.

detaching cathexis from the object. Naturally, this type of problem does not exist for the older child in whom reality testing is well established and who can clearly distinguish between what goes on inside himself and what belongs in the outside world.

But even in older children one can see difficulties that seem related to the child's limited capacity to grasp intellectually and fully the reality, significance, and finality of death. Freud, in a footnote added in 1909 to *The Interpretation of Dreams* (1900), refers to the remark of a highly intelligent boy of ten after the sudden death of his father: "I know father's dead, but what I can't understand is why he doesn't come home to supper" (p. 254). Recently I had the opportunity to observe the reaction of a four-year-old girl to the sudden death of her father. Her mother was naturally extremely distressed and for several days found herself completely unable to tell the children about the father's death. Once she told them, the little girls seemed to understand and to accept the reason for his absence. Nevertheless, several months later, on her birthday she reacted strongly to the fact that her father had not come to her party or sent her any presents. She was angry and cried bitterly, unable to understand why her father had been so neglectful.

In order to understand her reaction at this point, it is relevant to consider the terms in which the father's death was explained to her. The little girl had been going to Sunday school where she had been told that when good people die they go to God in heaven. Thus, she had been told that her father had been very ill, had died, and had gone to heaven. The mother's adviser who recommended this course of action had a number of considerations in mind. First, the children should certainly be told, and it was necessary to overcome the mother's hesitation in this respect. She seemed agreeable to telling the children in this particular way and reluctant to do it in what she referred to as a "cruder way." Second, they should be given the news in the least traumatic fashion possible. Third, they should be told, so far as possible, in words with which they were already familiar so that they could grasp at least some of the meaning and significance of the event.

Nevertheless, it can rightly be said that the information conveyed to this four-year-old girl was itself an elaborated piece of denial. The story told conveys that the father has changed his physical location to heaven, not that he no longer existed. Yet this is a cultural piece of deception having an almost universal character. Religious and spiritual beliefs are based on the existence of an afterlife. This very fact points to the difficult emotions confronting the human mind when coping with the phenomenon of death and to a certain inability or reluctance to comprehend and accept its finality. Perhaps this can be understood on the basis of the narcissistic and omnipotent elements from the early stages of development persisting in the adult where they then work against the acceptance of a final and total destruction of the self. It is not difficult to see how much more difficult it must be for the child to come to terms with these facts. Further, at a certain stage, all children believe in the omnipotence of the adult world and especially that of their parents, a belief contrary to the idea of the annihilation of the parents. This explains why Peter (four and a half), a child in the Hampstead War Nurseries, having been told that his father had been killed and that he could not come anymore, said: "I want him to come. My Daddy is big, he can do everything."

It is questionable how much the four-year-old girl, referred to above, would have understood if the straightforward facts had been given to her or what she would have made of them. We know that excessive information in certain areas, for example, in the sexual sphere, or information conveyed in terms that are beyond the ego's ability to grasp, occasionally have a traumatic effect on the child. In other cases when the information is beyond the child's comprehension and realm of experience, he just ignores it and continues to build up fantasies whose content is determined in part by the phase of drive development he happens to be in, and in part by his ego ability to organize the data of the observations and experiences into a set of theories meaningful to him (see Freud, 1907).

The Child's Thought Processes and Reactions to Loss

The capacity for abstract thinking is acquired slowly and very gradually. The younger child's thought processes are concrete. Furthermore, even if the child has reached a satisfactory level of abstract thinking, there may still be pockets where, for a number of reasons (not infrequently of a neurotic character) thinking and judgment remain highly concrete. In situations of neurotic conflict, stress, or under the impact of anxiety, there is a tendency in young children to revert to concrete forms of thinking. Barnes (1964) described many instances showing a four-year-old girl's concretization of thought processes and their influence on her reaction. Thus, for example, the child objected to wearing a dress which she had previously liked after her little cousins insisted that her dead mother was now an angel in heaven. The dress had been bought by the mother and was of a type known commercially as an "angel costume." According to Barnes, the anxiety aroused by the synonymity of angels and death made the child refuse to wear the dress. Similarly, the girl became reluctant to take naps at nursery school and preferred sitting on the teacher's lap. She finally explained: "You cannot get up when you want to," a limitation that she associated with being dead and more especially with her mother's death.

Another characteristic of the young child's thought processes is open egocentricity so that he tends to evaluate every event in terms of the repercussions it may have on him. Somewhat later, when the typical egocentricity of the toddler stage has to some extent receded, the child's increased *psychological* awareness of his own helplessness and dependence on the world of objects leads to the same result.

Anna Freud and Dorothy Burlingham (1943) gave many examples of orphaned children in the Hampstead War Nurseries who at the appropriate developmental stage (phallic-oedipal phase) talked "about their dead fathers as if they were alive or, when they have grasped the fact of death, try to deny it in the form of phantasies about re-birth or return from heaven. In some cases this happens under the direct influence of mothers who hide the truth from the child to spare it pain; *in other cases phantasies of an identical nature are the child's spontaneous production*" (p. 107; my italics). The authors further commented: "Visits from the dead fathers are, if anything, mentioned more often than the visits of ordinary living fathers" (p. 108).

The form in which the children expressed the wish for their fathers' return can be understood as a denial of death, but a number of other significant factors must be taken into account. In the examples cited by Anna Freud and Dorothy Burlingham, some children were unable to grasp the full significance and implications of death. In order to give some meaning to it, they used models based on their previous experience and knowledge. For example, for four-and-a-half-year-old Susan, "deaded" is gone away, "far away to Scotland," which does not exclude the possibility of a subsequent return. The different fantasies (perhaps it would be more correct to say theories) that she verbalized can in part be understood as an attempt to grasp the facts.

Thus, Susan must have heard about the army where daddy-soldiers were and that the army was far away. Hence her hope for his return expressed itself in the fantasy that her daddy (who had been in the navy) was in the army which was too far away for him to come. When she thought of him as gone with the navy, she logically concluded that he couldn't come back because "there is too much water."

Thus, while the child's thought processes tend to be concrete and egocentric, they are not illogical in terms of his factual knowledge in other respects, as the following illustrations show.

Freud, in a footnote added in 1919 to *The Interpretation of Dreams* (1900), refers to an observation of a highly intelligent four-year-old girl who was able to distinguish, in contrast to Susan, between being "gone" and being "dead." "The little girl had been troublesome at meal-time and noticed that one of the maids at the pension where they were staying was looking at her askance. 'I wish Josefine was dead.' . . . 'Why dead?' enquired her father soothingly; 'wouldn't it do if she went away?' 'No,' replied the child; 'then she'd come back again' " (p. 255).

For Bertie, another child at the Hampstead War Nurseries, death meant that father had been dismembered into bits and pieces. Knowing that broken objects can be mended and believing what he had been told (that God can do anything He wants), he rightly asked what was delaying God in putting father together. Again, on the basis of his factual information concerning the scarcity or complete lack of many things because of the war, he further concluded: "We have to wait until after the war, then God can put people together again."

All these examples show clearly the degree to which the child's age-adequate thought processes influence his understanding of and reaction to death. He obviously makes efforts to understand the painful events on the basis of his previous knowledge. It is not his fault if the adult world feeds him a great deal of distorted and mis-leading information.[10] His attempts at mastery can only be based on that information. On the other hand, his needs and wishes may at times distort and override factual knowledge (as I have also shown in the section on Denial.)

Ambivalence and Reaction to Loss

Freud (1917) and Helene Deutsch (1937) pointed out that the presence of strong ambivalent feelings leads to a more intense, ex-cessive, or delayed form of mourning in the adult. While we know that in children generally, and especially in the young child, strong ambivalent feelings toward the object world are the rule, we know far too little about how this factor influences the mourning process in the young child.

Having returned to an element of object relations—the theme with which I initially started my discussion—I once more proceed with developmental considerations.

THE OLDER CHILD'S REACTIONS TO LOSS

THE LATENCY PERIOD

Many of the factors described as playing a role in the reaction of the younger child in the death of a close relative are still opera-tive, though in a modified form, during the latency period. These modifications and the relative importance of the different factors in-volved are highly variable from one child to another.

[10] In one of our discussions at Hampstead a colleague described how on a walk he and his two-year-old child had found a mockingbird on the roadside. He tried to shield the child by not referring to the fact that the bird was dead, but the child noticed. The father then decided that they should bury it together. The little boy wanted to know whether the bird was now safe and wished to make sure that no cars could run over it. He also wanted to know whether the bird was a baby, a mummy or a daddy bird, deciding it was a mother bird. More recently he has begun to kill worms and talks freely about this. Anna Freud, commenting on this example, thought that adults frequently try to keep contact with death away from the child at a time when he is interested in and can approach the subject (at his own level). By doing so one surrounds death in mystery, as a dark and secret subject not to be puzzled out and understood. She thought the subject should be treated like the questions about sex. The child should be free to approach it at any age. She further pointed out that the two-year-old frequently approaches injury and death not with horror but with fascination. In the anal-sadistic phase he is most interested in maimed and killed objects. Anna Freud thinks that the adults, by such behavior, are really protecting themselves from the child's sadism.

It is always important, but more especially so in latency, to distinguish clearly between two different aspects of the mourning
process. The first one concerns the question: to what extent can
anybody experience and express the feeling of loss with the consequent signs of sadness and grief? The second concerns the question:
how far is it possible for anybody to proceed with the slow withdrawal of the cathexis previously attached to the lost object so that
the freed energies are available for the cathexis of a new object? The
last process, I believe, is easier for the adult than the child. Complete
withdrawal of cathexis from the lost object will leave the child in a
"developmental vacuum" unless a suitable substitute object is readily found. His emotional development requires the existence of, for
example, a mother figure and her physical death does not alter this
fact in any way and cannot lead to the type of decathexis that will
be observed in the case of the adult. In the latency child developmental imperatives will tend to keep her alive in spite of the ego
knowledge of the reality of the object's death and irretrievable
physical disappearance.

How does the latency child normally handle these two components of mourning? Most observations indicate that latency children deal with serious losses, through death, with massive denial,
including denial of affect and not infrequently even reversal of
affect. This situation seems to be favored or encouraged by our cultural attitudes to death at the present time.

Yet, we will probably agree, on theoretical grounds, that for the
further healthy development of the latency child, it will be better if
he can, within appropriate limits, express and experience the pain,
sadness, anger, and other feelings and conflicts associated with the
loss.

Some authors (e.g., Shambaugh, 1961; Furman, 1964b) believe
that children in this age group can, with profit, experience, and express feelings accompanying the loss of the object if helped to do so
in analysis. At the same time, many of the unresolved conflicts concerning the lost object can be dealt with, and possible obstacles to
further normal development can thus be removed. But the evidence
in this respect is still limited, and only further research and controlled observations can clarify the issue.

As to the second and most important aspect of mourning in

adults, that is, the slow decathexis of the lost object, the evidence seems to point to the fact that the latency child strongly cathects a fantasy life where the lost object may be seen as alive and at times as ideal.[11]

Naturally, a fantasy object is not a suitable substitute for an absent parent, but it may well be an unavoidable alternative, especially if suitable substitutes are not readily available to the child. There is also evidence showing how the child makes simultaneous attempts to cathect certain objects in reality and to give them the mother's role (for example, teachers and, in the case of children in analysis, their therapists), especially if their sex favors such a displacement. Unfortunately, neither teachers nor therapists can perform this role appropriately. Furthermore, in cases where a substitute mother is introduced into the life of the child and the father's remarriage restores the family organization, we can observe very quickly a process of disappointment in the new object which is only partly dependent on the object's ability to play a substitute mothering role. This disarray in the object cathexis may have to be considered as one of the unavoidable consequences of object loss, at least when it takes place at certain times in life. Nevertheless, provision must be made for the fact that some children are more able than others to find the most adaptive solutions amidst these difficulties.

Although the overt, superficial behavior of latency children seems to deny more or less completely the importance of the loss suffered, the child's inner life may undergo significant changes that could seriously affect his later development. There is often, in this age group, no apparent grief or sadness shortly after the event, though an immediate and short-lived sadness reaction is occasionally seen. In the foreground one frequently observes not only denial but a reversal of affects as well. Shambaugh's (1961) description of his patient Henry is typical: "I was struck by his affect. He did not look like a boy who had suffered a loss. Instead, he came to his first interviews as if he were full of energy. He was hyperactive and gay, sometimes even to the point of euphoria" (p. 512). Henry did not talk

---

[11] Not infrequently this fantasy relationship to the lost object is kept secret by the latency child. In one case treated at Hampstead, the therapist, A. Bene, discovered only after many months of treatment that the patient had kept secret an intimate fantasy relationship to a dead sibling for several years of her life.

during the sessions about his home or the mother's death. If this imposed censure was threatened, he reacted with anxiety and anger and on one occasion ran from the office when the analyst alluded to the mother's death.

Nevertheless, as Shambaugh points out, an experienced observer could detect behind this façade many ominous signs. Our experience at Hampstead confirms that latency children frequently respond in this way to the death of an important object. They may not show many overt signs of mourning, but a closer examination shows important evidence of serious disturbances, behavioral disorders, and symptom formation.[12]

ADOLESCENCE

There can be no question that by the time the adolescence phase sets in, all the factors named by different authors as necessary preconditions for mourning in the adult are well established. The adolescent ego development is such that he can understand the full implications and finality of death. His reality testing is firmly established. His awareness of reality and capacity to adapt to it are sufficiently developed. Nevertheless, adolescents shy away from the type of mourning that we know from adults. Their overt behavior and response to loss are significantly different from that of the adult mourner. Yet, they are greatly affected by the loss and react in strong and specific adaptive ways of their own.

How are we then to explain the difference in the mourning response between them and the adult? The significant difference, to my mind, is that the adolescent, as Wolfenstein points out, is still tied to his infantile imagos, generally and more especially so to the parents. He has not yet completed his psychological and emotional development. Their presence is required for his development to unfold normally until it is finally completed. As with the younger child, the sudden loss of such an object through death creates the same situation of developmental stress that I described earlier as a developmental interference.

---

[12] Arthur and Kemme (1964) studied the families of eighty-three disturbed children where death of a parent had occurred. They found "a high incidence of both intellectual and emotional problems either directly or indirectly related to the loss" (p. 48).

The adolescent also tends to recathect the image of the lost object when experiencing certain needs or developmental pressures as was the case with younger children. According to Wolfenstein (1966), "instead of decathecting a lost love object, which is what happens in mourning, children and adolescents tend to develop a hypercathexis of the lost object." According to her, "fantasies of the parent's return are either more clearly conscious or more readily admitted in adolescence than at earlier ages." As she pointed out in 1965: "the death of a parent would find the young adolescent still far from ready to give him up. At the same time conflicting feelings towards the parent would further interfere with pure regret and sadness."

Wolfenstein (1966) and Laufer (1966) have described vividly the reactions of an adolescent girl and an adolescent boy to the death of their mothers. There are many similarities in the reactions of these two adolescents to the loss. I will select from Wolfenstein's case, for the purposes of illustration, some specific aspects of this girl's reaction.

Typically, Wolfenstein describes how Ruth found herself no longer able to cry shortly after the mother's funeral. "She felt an inner emptiness, and as if a glass wall separated her from what was going on around her. She was distressed by this affectlessness, and was subsequently relieved when, comparing notes with a friend whose father had died some time earlier, she learned that the other girl had had a similar reaction" (p. 100).

Again rather typically, after the event Ruth came to her sessions in an elated mood. "She had written a successful humorous composition, in which she congratulated herself. . . . [She] proceeded to detail various embarrassing predicaments she had got into, which she turned to comic effect" (p. 101).

She showed the same tendency as Laufer's patient to isolate her feelings of sadness and despair from thoughts of the mother's death. Any such links established by the therapists, if accepted intellectually, were supplanted by a struggle to capture more pleasurable moods. Similarly, obvious denial of the finality of the loss was overtly or covertly maintained by them.

Clinical Illustrations

a young child's reactions to loss

The first example shows the reaction of a normal boy, four years and eight months, to the death of his maternal grandfather. This example is significantly different from all the others, probably because the lost object was not a primary object. The child had a very close relationship to his grandfather as a favorite playmate, but at no time had the grandfather become entangled in the boy's phallic-oedipal development, which was lived out with his real father and mother as the objects of this struggle. Furthermore, the relationship with the grandfather was free of negative and conflictual elements, as could not easily have been the case with a sibling. The case demonstrates not only the difficulties a child of this age has to comprehend the phenomena of death, but also its repercussions on his phallic-oedipal struggles with the real parents.

P. was a well-developed, likable child whose characteristic approach to life was to master things intellectually. He usually tried very hard to understand what he was confronted with. This attitude also extended to anxiety-provoking situations or events.

Prior to the grandfather's death, P. had had some contacts and experiences with death. The family lived close to a crematorium and P. had often watched the funeral processions and listened to his older siblings' discussion of them. These had stimulated P.'s curiosity at an early age and led him to ask many questions about death.

His more direct experiences with death related to animals, birds or fish. For example, he was greatly impressed by an incident that took place when he was three years of age. His siblings kept cold water fish in an open tank. Once P. heard them saying that the tank was dirty and the water smelly, whereupon he proceeded to put soap powder and perfume in the fish tank, with the result (unexpected, as far as he was concerned) that all the fish died. His siblings, who were greatly upset, accused him of having killed the fish. He was puzzled and guilty. His intention had obviously been to make the water tank clean and he had no idea of the implications of his actions.

Similarly, he had occasionally watched cowboy films on TV with his older brother and sister. When he saw people being shot at and falling down dead, he showed some concern and asked many questions. Until his third birthday, he did not tolerate being shot at by his brother. Although he enjoyed other imaginative role play, he became angry and distressed when his brother pretended to shoot at him, asked not to be shot at, and refused to pretend to be dead. He would, nevertheless, shoot at others and enjoy their pretending to be dead. After P. had moved into the oedipal phase, he no longer objected to being shot at or to pretending to be killed. At the same time he developed the habit of shooting at his father, saying, "You are dead." It was not thought that the child had at this point an intellectual grasp of the meaning of death beyond the fact that it was something bad, that it implied being still, and that one shot only "baddies," enemies or rivals.

The grandparents came to live in P.'s household when he was two years of age. A special relationship developed quickly between the child and his grandfather. They spent many hours playing together every day and a strong tie developed between them. When, at the age of three, P. started nursery school in the mornings, he would immediately upon his return home again be engaged in a game with his grandfather.

Unfortunately, at the time P. was three years of age, the grandfather suffered a stroke which left him handicapped. When they resumed play, P.'s demands were, at times, a strain on the grandfather's strength. Shortly after the stroke, the grandfather developed a serious heart condition that required several prolonged hospitalizations. This further weakened him and greatly reduced his playing with P., but some joint play activities continued to his end.

The grandfather's several prolonged hospitalizations contributed to lessen somewhat the intensity of the tie the child formerly had had with him. P. was always concerned about the grandfather's absences and talked about the grandfather a great deal. Since, on more than one occasion, the family had serious misgivings about the grandfather's life, the children had been made aware of the possibility of his death.

On the day of his death, which happened suddenly, the grandfather, feeling very ill, had returned from a short walk with his wife. He sat in the living room to rest for a moment, but grew worse very quickly. P.'s mother sent P. upstairs with his sister, after explaining to him that the grandfather was ill and the doctor had to be called. P. was soon put to bed and was asleep when the grandfather died.

The next morning P. went to school as usual, still not knowing about the grandfather's death. His mother went to fetch him at the end of the morning, and once they were in the car on the way home, she finally told him.

Mother: P., do you remember that yesterday the doctor came to see grandfather because he was very ill?

P.: Yes.

Mother: Well, he became worse and worse and since he was so old too, the medicine he was given did not help him to get better and he finally died.

P.'s expression became very serious and thoughtful. Then he asked as if to reassure himself he had heard properly: "Did grandfather died? . . . Did he died? . . . Poor grandfather. . . ." Between each phrase there was a pause during which he obviously was thinking hard. Then he asked: "When did he died? Was he at home or had he gone to the hospital?" The mother explained that he had died at home, that it had happened so quickly there was no time to take him to the hospital. After a few moments P. asked: "And where was he when he died?" The mother explained that he was in the living room where P. had last seen him the previous evening. P. was thoughtful again for a few seconds and then asked: "Was he sitting or lying down?" The mother explained that at first he was sitting in the big chair and later was taken to the sofa where he lay down. P. then asked whether the grandfather spoke when he died. He was told he spoke a little just before dying. P. went on: "Did he close his eyes?" "Yes, he did," the mother answered. He remained silent for a while and then asked again: "Did the Rolls Royce from the crematorium come? Did they take him away in a box?" When these different questions were answered factually, he continued his inquest, asking: "How was he, was he dressed up?" He listened with great interest to his mother's reply, then continued: "If I open his eyes and touch them, will he feel it? . . . Does he remember our street?" The mother gave him factual answers. He then said: "Today is a sad day because he died, . . ." After another silent pause, he proceeded to inquire whether each family member knew and what their reaction had been. He excluded only his father.

At this point they arrived home. P. went immediately to the living room and wanted to know exactly in which place the grandfather was sitting before he died. Then he lay down on the sofa where the grandfather died, closed his eyes and said, "Let's pretend that I am grandfather and I am dead." After a moment, he got up and went upstairs to the grandfather's room where he took a close look at everything without saying a word.

During the following days he was slightly excited, after which time he was his usual self again. For two or three days, he talked to the other children in the neighborhood about his grandfather's death. When an uncle arrived from abroad, P. commented that he knew why he had come. When asked why, he replied, "Because grandfather died." As mentioned earlier, he made frequent comments as to why it was that they could not listen to the radio or watch TV until after the funeral.

He said to his father, one or two days after the grandfather's death, on one of the occasions when he was more excited than was usual for him, "It would have been better if you had died too, because then I could do all the naughty things I want."

If we consider his reaction up to this point, it could be said that in his immediately following behavior and verbalizations he showed sadness, "Poor grandfather." There was no feeling of secrecy concerning the death (nor did his family attempt to keep anything from him; all questions he posed were answered). He did not use manic or jocular defenses, as young children often do, nor were there any indications of attempts at denial. Further, as was usual for him, there was a strong attempt to master intellectually all the implications of what had happened and to some extent of the meaning of death by very actively asking a number of questions. Like many children of his age, he associated death with stillness and lack of movement. He also knew, in some way, that in terms of absence, death had a permanent character in contrast with the grandfather's earlier absences through hospitalization. He vaguely inferred that there was more to it that was unclear to him, hence his questions as to what would happen if he opened the grandfather's eyes, or whether the grandfather would feel his touching them, or could the grandfather still think and remember things.

He did not react with the common neurotic responses—usually due to conflict or guilt in respect to the dead person—such as fear of sleep, fear of closing the eyes, or refusing to enter the room where the lost object had died. On the contrary, he was curious and questioning without showing any overt fears, except for the fact that he was slightly uncomfortable when he pretended to be the dead grandfather lying down on the sofa.

In the following days and weeks, while riding in the car, P. would occasionally point out places where he had been with his grandfather or which he knew the grandfather had visited. On the other hand, immediately after the death of the grandfather, P. stopped his early morning visits to his grandparents' room which he had previously made daily as soon as he woke up. They had usually chatted and, while P. had pretended to play his guitar, sung together. At other times of the day which were less reminiscent of this "special" hour, P. continued to go to their room.

Although P.'s reaction to the grandfather's death was surprisingly normal, it nevertheless strained his relationship to his father in the oedipal context. To start with, he moved closer to him and sought his company more frequently as a substitute playmate for the grandfather, but P.'s oedipal rivalry showed clearly and at times interfered with his ability to play with his father.

At about this time the father had to be away from home for three weeks. P. seemed to associate the father's oncoming absence with the grandfather's earlier absences due to hospitalizations and with the fact that these absences were followed by his grandfather's death. His immediate reaction—and he was now obviously under great internal stress—was to try and convince the father to take him along on that trip. He insistently told his mother and siblings that his father would be taking him, though they had explained to him several times why this was not possible. He seemed to accept these explanations. Unfortunately the elder brother teased him occasionally by saying that P. was not going because he was too little but that he, O., and C. were going. P.'s faith was somewhat shattered by his brother's teasing and playful statement. Nevertheless he was able to go to his father whenever this happened, asking, rather pathetically, whether it was true that O. and C. were going. Once reassured, he regained his usual gay composure. However, at the same time he began to reassure the father about how much he liked and loved him, clinging to him more than was usual.

Shortly before the father's trip, P. heard about riots taking place in a city he knew his father would be visiting. He listened very attentively to all comments about these riots and the father's plans for visiting that city. One or two days before the trip, when the father was preparing his luggage, P. said: "Daddy, you better be careful when you are in that place. They can kill people there." In this condensed statement he was able to express simultaneously both his concern and love for the father and his death wishes.

The father's absence passed uneventfully. However, since the father's return—and this may have been a temporal coincidence only—P. showed strong signs of moving away from the "oedipal" mother to other female objects (such as friends of his older sister or other female visitors). He performed for them the phallic-exhibitionistic feats typical for children of his age and usually ended by stating how much he liked them and that he would marry them when he grew up. One cannot but wonder whether this sudden move may have been forced by his need to protect his father from his oedipal hostility and rivalry after his experience of the loss of the grandfather. Be that as it may, one is left with the impression that P.'s oedipal conflicts were greatly reinforced by the grandfather's death. Whereas previously P. had shot at his father, frequently crying out that he was dead, now, after the actual experience of having lost his grandfather, a new real dimension had been added to his hostile wishes and his ideas about death and rivals.

P. is an example of a reasonably normal child who, though showing signs of strain, coped with the event of death in an adaptive way. Many children are less fortunate. The impact on their personality development and the reinforcement of conflicts (developmental or neurotic) will distort their further psychological growth and lead to serious psychopathology, especially so when the object lost is a primary one.

OLDER CHILDREN'S REACTIONS TO LOSS

1. B. was five and a half years of age when analytic treatment started.[13] He was six and a half when his mother was operated on for cancer of the breast, resulting in the removal of one breast and the surrounding tissues. He was seven when the cancer recurred in the form of skin and lung metastases, discoloration of the skin, breathing difficulties, and severe coughing spells. He was seven years eight months when his mother died. I shall focus on his behavior during the period preceding the mother's death and his reaction immediately afterward (for a period of two months).

At the time of referral there was clear evidence of massive oral fixations, disturbances of mood and social-emotional responsiveness with vague fears of being attacked. He was preoccupied with fears and ideas of death, separation, and punishment long before the mother's serious illness became manifest. B.'s mother was aware of the nature of her illness and her impending death (until a few weeks before she died, when she began to deny it). She usually helped B. to deny her impending death when it seemed to her that he needed to do so. Yet, at other times, she was equally sensitive in presenting the truth in a manner designed to alleviate his anxiety and possible guilt. In fact their relationship was, at this point, better than ever before. This seemed due to the fact that she included rather than excluded him from her life—as she had previously tended to do. She was now making a courageous and conscious attempt to help him, wanting to be remembered as a "good mother" after her death.

The analytic material in the months before the mother's death could best be described as seesawing back and forth between denial and awareness of the impending object loss, the latter gaining in momentum the closer the reality of his mother's death drew. For example, B. made elaborate plans for what he would do *with* his mother when he reached the age of ten; or he would figure out what his mother's age would be when he was in college and living away from home, preparing himself, as it were, for the inevitable separation by projecting it into the future.

After the therapist had discussed the possibility that his mother

13 I am indebted to Mrs. C. Kearney, B.'s therapist, for the preparation of the condensed summary of the relevant aspects of the case here presented.

might die even though the doctors were trying everything to make her better, B. said calmly, "Even if everybody dies, Mommy and Daddy, my uncles and aunts, even you, it still wouldn't matter because we are very rich and we would have all the money we need . . . and we would still have each other," referring to his older brother.

B. suddenly became interested in God and professed his religious beliefs. Previously, neither he nor his family had shown any religious interest. He asked, "Would you like better to be liked by God or have many friends? I would like to be loved by God because God can do anything for you . . . He can even make you alive after you die." Motivated by his desire to make restitution to others while his mother was still alive, he began to champion good causes. He identified with deprived children, organizing a "helping club" among his friends to collect money to send to the "starving and homeless children of India." He wanted to invite a boy who had just lost his mother to his house because "nobody wants to talk to him about his mother." In this way he was expressing his understanding of the void created by his (and the other children's) apprehension over the death of this boy's mother. B. asked his own mother to buy a gift for this child which he then took to his house.

B. was particularly impressed with Jesus, who "gave up His life to a bum for stealing a loaf of bread . . . to help him," he added. That he was similarly preoccupied with his mother could be surmised when he told the therapist of the games he was playing with his older brother. They would lie down in the street and, at the last moment, would roll aside to escape approaching cars (counterphobic elements were evident in this behavior). Instead of having to die like the mother he was able to escape death at will. He reassured himself further by stating that boys, having no breast, cannot die of breast cancer. When his identification with Jesus was discussed, he wanted to know if the therapist would give everything she had, "even your life, to make Mommy well." The therapist said that she could not do that, even if she wanted to, because everybody had to live his own life, including him. He would feel sad, but eventually he would be all right again.

Looking back at the material and the child's behavior, one is struck by the fact that B. began looking for another object even before his mother died, and increasingly so as her physical and mental deterioration and withdrawal became worse. This was most notice-able in his relationship to the therapist who became much more of a real person for him. He did not want to leave at the end of his sessions, though he would comment, "Your next customer is here." He implied that the therapist was paid for seeing him and wondered if the therapist would see him "even if my Daddy gets poor all of a sudden." On another occasion he suggested that the therapist could ask a famous baseball player for his autograph, adding, "You could tell him it is for your son . . . he may then give it to you."

B. became more active in seeking physical closeness with the therapist. He came over to her side of the table and ended up sitting on her lap, asking personal questions and looking in her drawers. When he was gently discouraged, he said, "You couldn't marry my Daddy anyway because you are much too old." He wanted the ther-apist to call him by endearing names, provided it was "not 'honey' . . . because this is what my Mommy calls me." He gave the thera-pist permission to call him "Nectar" instead. The loyalty conflict was intensified by the fact that his mother's condition (when he did not deny it) was discussed with him and he then wanted to protect her from his knowledge of it. When the therapist discussed the various aids (e.g., oxygen) his mother needed and mentioned having spoken with her that day, B. cautioned the therapist not to tell his mother about his revulsion when he saw her physical condition. She had developed a deep purplish rash on her neck which he called "a croco-dile skin."

B. had had very little contact with his mother during the week before she died. Although she was at home, she was under heavy sedation and often out of contact with reality; the nurse who looked after her tried to keep the children away from her bedside.

The day before she died, she was taken to the hospital, at a time when B. had his therapy session, and the therapist told him of his mother's hospitalization. B. wanted to talk with his mother on the phone and was able to do so just before she left home by ambulance. He asked her whether it was really true that she was going to the hospital. He turned to the therapist in desperation when he could not hear her low voice and then screamed into the receiver in an effort to reach her, "Speak louder, I want to hear your voice. . . . Mommy, when will you come home?" B.'s face was flushed after this brief last talk with his mother. Holding back the tears, he wanted to play at something: "I don't want to talk about Mommy." With an air of confidence which barely disguised his desperation, he repeated what his mother had just told him, that she would be back within a few days. Following the therapist's comment that this was what his mother would wish most to be able to do—to come back to her family—B. started to cry and, as if he were an outsider observing his own reaction, remarked in wonderment that this was the first time he had cried since coming to his sessions. He accepted the therapist's verbalization of his sadness over the realization that perhaps his mother would not be able to come home by shaking his head affirmatively and asking why she could not die at home. The therapist talked about the special care she needed, the attention of doctors and nurses, the relief of pain. He then confided that he had heard his mother's moaning and coughing at night during the last two weeks, adding, "She caught a cold from me . . . but it wasn't my fault, I caught it from X." When the therapist explained the cough as the symptom of the mother's illness, B. remembered the course of her illness, the "make-believe breast," which had frightened him so originally. He expressed some concern about having been contaminated in his comment, "Can I get her skin?"

B.'s mother died early the next morning. When his father told him, on coming home from school, his first reaction was to call all his friends on the phone to tell them about it. When he came for his session that afternoon, his mood was one of excitement during the beginning of the hour. It seemed that he was turning painful affects into the opposite. He was smiling, giggling, hyperactive with rapid speech. All his mother's things were now his and his brother's; he said, "All her money is ours . . . her clothes . . . we are rich now . . . even her bed and pillow." Laughing hysterically he said, "We'll take her bed and Daddy can roll over and fall off his bed . . . what will we do with all her clothes . . . to whom shall we give them? If Daddy gets married, we won't give her Mommy's clothes . . . would Daddy marry someone we like, would he ask us, how would we know we like her?" B. asked for candy: "I'll need a whole lot today, three, four, six, I'll eat hers, can she still eat candy? . . . She is dead, she can't eat anymore. What would she say if she saw me now? [Therapist: "She could understand that you are really very sad."] I would give everything to make her better again." Correcting himself, he added that he just could not believe that his mother was dead: "I'll never see her again, never talk to her?" He finally broke down crying following the therapist's remark that he would think and talk about his mother because this was the best way not to miss her too much.

In this hour with B. it seemed as if now that the incomprehensible reality had intruded fully, he did not know how to react. A feeling of helplessness rather than sadness seemed to overwhelm him: "Why did R. say 'who cares' when I told him my mother died? What's the date? Write it down." He encircled the date on the therapist's desk calendar and wanted her to put the whole page in his file. When the therapist talked about the bewildering fact that he had talked to his mother only yesterday, he said, "She asked me to speak loudly. I screamed. Daddy said she couldn't hear well anymore—how come?" B. wanted to know whether the therapist would cancel all her appointments to go to the funeral and why she wanted to go when he didn't.

During this session, B. established a pattern of mood swings which he repeated daily for many weeks after his mother's death. He usually began his hour in an excited, maniclike mood, and it often took more than half of his session for him to allow sad feelings to emerge.

It seems to me that B. reacted like a traumatized child, who was overwhelmed by a sudden shock in spite of some preparation for it. He was now under the compulsion to recreate it again and again in order to assimilate it. The traumatic effect seemed related to the overwhelming affects he experienced in spite of the fact that he had "known," discussed, and even reacted, to a certain extent, emotionally to the expected loss.

His behavior continued to show denial and reversal of affect. "I don't mind that Mommy is dead—I can look at TV now; Daddy lets me." He laughed and in a mock effeminate way paraded up and down the room. "I have her quilt and backrest. I want her jewels. I'll be very pretty. I slept in her bed last night." Externalizing the vague inner excitement which had replaced the previous denial of affect, B. giggled and laughed, and often spoke of how glad he was that his mother had died; yet, he would frequently ask what she would say if she could see him now. This was often the cue that he was ready for interpretations of the sad feelings when they were phrased in terms of what his mother "might" think about him, i.e., that she would understand his wanting her things because he missed her terribly much, or her understanding that it hurt him to be sad.

B. described this struggle as follows: "You know, I cried this morning when I woke up . . . because I remembered that Mommy was dead. I read . . . then I remembered again . . . then I went into Daddy's room. [In a sudden panic:] What if my Daddy dies? He could, you know, it's possible. Where will A. [his brother] and I live with aunt? I would love that."

B. constantly worried about what would happen to himself and to objects close to him, as part of the expression of his helplessness and loneliness. "Maybe I am going to be kidnapped. When you went out [of the room] just now, I thought somebody could come in the window and steal me, and you wouldn't even know it because you would believe I was hiding to scare you [a favorite game of the past] and the kidnappers would kill me." He was similarly preoccupied with fears of getting stuck in the elevator of the therapist's office building (like in a casket?), that he might be there for hours and nobody would find him—or miss him. B. tried to keep a picture of his mother in his mind, but her changed appearance during the last few weeks of her life intruded as too painful a memory. In an effort to block out this more recent and realistic image, he brought the therapist pictures showing his mother before her illness. He did this following a visit to the mausoleum, where he seemed to have been overwhelmed by the incomprehensible fact that she was in the casket but unreachable to him. He had wanted to open the coffin: "Would she look funny? She wouldn't have a pink skin. Can she breathe in there? If Mommy wakes up, how will she be able to get out of the casket? Does Mommy have a blanket and sheets in there? Does her sickness go on even when she is dead? I left a peanut butter sandwich there for her."

B. expressed death wishes against the therapist, which the therapist interpreted as a reflection of his sadness and his wish that she had died instead of his mother. He replied, "What if a man came in and tried to murder you? I would run out. If you had magic, you would make Mommy alive again and make her live forever. But everybody would want to do this and there are too many people already."

The therapist had the impression that, although the child was sad and occasionally cried, his mourning process was different from that of the adult. B. more often seemed to feel helpless and lost rather than bereaved. The painful affects of sadness could not be tolerated for extended periods. He would either deny them, reverse them, or try to find substitutes for the mother (without having detached his cathexis from her). After the mother's death, he became a "collector" of friends and had little toleration for being on his own because of the fear of having to face his sadness. When left alone, he was hyperactive, on the run, apparently experiencing an intense feeling of emptiness.

The strong identification with the lost object and the wish to take over all her belongings were partly motivated by strong feelings of guilt due to ambivalence conflicts in his relationship to her. Some time after the mother's death, he verbalized the fantasy that he bit his mother's breast when he was a suckling infant, thus causing her illness and death. With the mother's death, earlier fantasies of terrible things happening to him returned. He had fantasies of retaliation for his own aggression and suicidal thoughts, saying, "What will happen if I jump out of your window? I'll commit suicide by locking myself in the car and suffocating" (his mother had much difficulty in breathing). He finally said, "I'll be buried next to her," thus expressing his wish to be reunited with her.

2. A. A. was sixteen years old when he began his analysis.[14] His mother had died when he was ten years old. His overt mourning response was extremely brief. He immediately developed symptoms and character distortions, which subsequently had an impact on the developmental processes during adolescence.

A. was not told anything about his mother's condition and, just prior to her death, he was sent away to friends on "the pretext" that she was ill. He was informed of his mother's death after the funeral. He was told that she had died of pleurisy. Yet he probably knew that she was seriously ill because he recalled many details connected with

---

14 I am indebted to Dr. J. Novick, the therapist of this case, who wrote the condensed summary here presented.

her illness (e.g., visiting her in the hospital, her needing an oxygen tank, seeing her read the confessional prayer). Nevertheless, he was extremely resentful about not having been told and felt that he had been deceived.

A.'s immediate reaction to the news of the death was to cry, but he soon got over it. At first he missed her and would resent others having a mother. Later he seldom thought about her, and it often seemed to him that he had never had a mother. He probably had no support during the period immediately following the mother's death. It seemed likely that the father's mourning was also aborted. The lack of real mourning in the family and the lack of support during his own mourning combined with other factors to produce in A. a pathogenic reaction to the loss.

Following the loss of his mother A. developed symptoms and serious disturbances. To start with, the loss of the mother revived earlier feelings of oral deprivation. The awareness of oral wishes led to sadness and the consequent frustration of these needs pushed him into a defensive, anal-based, pseudoindependence from the object world. Building on earlier identifications with the mother, A. massively identified with the lost object and lodged his own and the fantasied hostility of his parents within the superego, thus substituting an internalized for a lost relationship and also reinforcing the negative oedipal relationship to the father. A. adopted the mother's rituals, her extreme orthodoxy, her hypochondriasis, her intense fear of death, and her avoidance of social contact. She was said to be unintelligent and mentally ill. A., despite his extremely high intelligence, felt he was stupid and feared that he would become mentally ill. His continuing psychosomatic ailments had numerous determinants, but a basic one was the identification with the hypochondriacal mother. He had a breathing difficulty which, although in part due to a catarrh, probably related to the mother's breathing difficulty during her last few days. He frequently complained of having trouble with his liver—the locus of his mother's cancer.

Finally, the following interferences, in terms of his later development, seem significant. The mother died when A. was in latency. The material suggests that a somewhat brief and fragile phallic-oedipal level of organization had been reached and maintained. The dissolution of the oedipus complex had led to a considerable move into latency with a setting up of the father as the ego ideal, the displacement of cathexis onto oedipal substitutes (aunts, older girls), interest in friends, and the sublimation of drive energy into school, sports, and other activities. However, to a certain extent, phallic-oedipal anxieties resulted in regression to the anal and negative oedipal position. It is probable that A.'s pathology, prior to the mother's death, was within normal limits and did not constitute a threat to further development. The full pathological impact of the mother's death emerged with the onset of puberty and the revival of oedipal feelings. The identification with the mother reinforced an earlier negative oedipal attitude, and the onset of puberty was accompanied by intense homosexual anxiety. The ambivalence previously split between oedipal objects was now directed at the father. Castration anxiety was reinforced by the fantasy that the father had killed the mother. The castration fear was intensified by A.'s identification with the dead mother and by reality events (he had two hydrocele operations). The revival of phallic-oedipal feelings at adolescence led to anxieties of such intensity that A. retreated permanently to the relative safety of the anal position. The death of the mother thus constituted a severe developmental interference.

SUMMARY

In the first parts of this paper I discussed the various factors that determine children's reactions to object loss. The cases cited in the last part demonstrate some of the characteristic responses: the short sadness span; the incapacity to sustain mourning; the massive use of denial and reversal of affect; the inability to grasp the reality of death; the search for substitutes (before the event, if the child was aware of the oncoming death, and after, if he was not); the simultaneous (overt or insidious) symptom formation and the creeping character distortions; the fear of "contamination" causing their own death, often side by side with fantasies of reunion.

Whatever the immediate response, we can conclude that the loss of an important object represents a developmental interference. In the case of P., a normal child, it complicated the ongoing oedipal relationships and perhaps somewhat prematurely pushed the child into relinquishing them. In the case of the two older children who were studied analytically, it was especially apparent that the personality changes introduced by the loss interfered with their subsequent development.

BIBLIOGRAPHY

Arthur, B. & Kemme, M. L. (1964), Bereavement in Childhood. *J. Child Psychol. & Psychiat.*, 5:37-49.

Barnes, M. J. (1964), Reactions to the Death of a Mother. *This Annual*, 19:334-357.

Bonnard, A. (1961), Truancy and Pilfering Associated with Bereavement. In: *Adolescents*, ed. S. Lorand & H. I. Schneer. New York: Hoeber, pp. 152-179.

Bowlby, J. (1960), Grief and Mourning in Infancy and Early Childhood. *This Annual*, 15:9-52.

—— (1961a), Processes of Mourning. *Int. J. Psa.*, 42:317-340.

—— (1961b), Childhood Mourning and Its Implications for Psychiatry. *Amer. J. Psychiat.*, 118:481-498.

—— (1963), Pathological Mourning and Childhood Mourning. *J. Amer. Psa. Assn.*, 11:500-541.

Cain, A. C., & Cain, B. S. (1964), On Replacing a Child. *J. Amer. Acad. Child Psychiat.*, 3:443-456.

—— & Fast, I. (1966), Children's Disturbed Reactions to Parent Suicide. *Amer. J. Orthopsychiat.*, 36:873-880.

—— —— & Erickson, M. E. (1964), Children's Disturbed Reactions to the Death of a Sibling. *Amer. J. Orthopsychiat.*, 34:741-752.

Deutsch, H. (1937), Absence of Grief. *Psa. Quart.*, 6:12-22.

Fleming, J. et al. (1958), The Influence of Parent Loss in Childhood on Personality Development. Read at the Annual Meeting of the American Psychoanalytic Association.

—— & Altschul, S. (1963), Activation of Mourning and Growth by Psycho-Analysis. *Int. J. Psa.*, 44:419-431.

Freud, A. (1952), The Mutual Influences in the Development of Ego and Id: Introduction to the Discussion. *This Annual*, 7:42-50.

—— (1960), Discussion of Dr. John Bowlby's Paper. *This Annual*, 15:53-62.

—— & Burlingham, D. (1942), *War and Children*. New York: International Universities Press, 1943.

—— —— (1943), *Infants Without Families*. New York: International Universities Press, 1944.

Freud, S. (1900), The Interpretation of Dreams. *Standard Edition*, 4 & 5. London: Hogarth Press, 1953.

—— (1907), The Sexual Enlightenment of Children. *Standard Edition*, 9:129-139. London: Hogarth Press, 1959.

—— (1917), Mourning and Melancholia. *Standard Edition*, 14:244-245. London: Hogarth Press, 1957.

—— (1926), Inhibitions, Symptoms and Anxiety. *Standard Edition*, 20:77-175. London: Hogarth Press, 1959.

Furman, R. (1964a), Death and the Young Child. *This Annual*, 19:321-333.

—— (1964b), Death of a Six-Year-Old's Mother during His Analysis. *This Annual*, 19:377-397.

Harrison, S. I., Davenport, C. W., & McDermott, J. F. (1967), Children's Reactions to Bereavement. *Arch. Gen. Psychiat.*, 17:593-598.

Hartmann, H. (1952), The Mutual Influences in the Development of Ego and Id. *This Annual*, 7:9-30.

Hoffer, W. (1950), Development of the Body Ego. *This Annual*, 5:18-24.
—— (1952), The Mutual Influences in the Development of Ego and Id: Earliest Stages. *This Annual*, 7:31-41.
Laufer, M. (1966), Object Loss and Mourning during Adolescence. *This Annual*, 21:269-293.
McDonald, M. (1964), A Study of the Reactions of Nursery School Children to the Death of a Child's Mother. *This Annual*, 19:358-376.
Mahler, M. S. (1961), On Sadness and Grief in Infancy and Childhood. *This Annual*, 16:332-351.
Meiss, M. L. (1952), The Oedipal Problem of a Fatherless Child. *This Annual*, 7:216-229.
Nagera, H. (1966a), *Early Childhood Disturbances, the Infantile Neurosis, and the Adulthood Disturbances*. New York: International Universities Press.
—— (1966b), Sleep and Its Disturbances Approached Developmentally. *This Annual*, 21:393-447.
—— (1967), *Vincent Van Gogh*. New York: International Universities Press.
Pollock, G. H. (1961), Mourning and Adaptation. *Int. J. Psa.*, 42:341-361.
Robertson, J. (1958), *Young Children in Hospital*. London: Tavistock Publications.
—— ed. (1962), *Hospitals and Children*. New York: International Universities Press.
Rochlin, G. (1953), Loss and Restitution. *This Annual*, 8:288-309.
—— (1959), The Loss Complex. *J. Amer. Psa. Assn.*, 7:299-316.
Sandler, J. & Joffe, W. G. (1965), Notes on Childhood Depression. *Int. J. Psa.*, 46:88-96.
Schur, M. (1960), Discussion of Dr. John Bowlby's Paper. *This Annual*, 15:63-84.
Shambaugh, B. (1961), A Study of Loss Reactions in a Seven-Year-Old. *This Annual*, 16:510-522.
Spitz, R. A. (1945), Hospitalism. *This Annual*, 1:53-74.
—— (1946), Hospitalism: A Follow-up Report. *This Annual*, 2:113-117.
—— (1960), Discussion of Dr. Bowlby's Paper. *This Annual*, 15:85-94.
—— & Wolf, K. M. (1946), Anaclitic Depression. *This Annual*, 2:313-342.
Wolf, A. W. M. (1958), *Helping Your Child to Understand Death*. New York: Child Study Association.
Wolfenstein, M. (1965), Death of a Parent and Death of a President. In: *Children and the Death of a President*, ed. M. Wolfenstein & G. Kliman. New York: Doubleday, pp. 62-79.
—— (1966), How Is Mourning Possible? *This Annual*, 21:93-123.

TO CAST AWAY

A Vestibular Forerunner of the Superego

ANDREW PETO, M.D. (New York)

Loss of equilibrium and subsequent falling, usually accompanied by giddiness, are very common transient symptoms and are experienced in a great variety of normal and pathological conditions. Idiomatic expressions point to the fact that the combination of giddiness and falling, or that of solely falling, has, among other factors, a moral connotation. In *The Interpretation of Dreams* (1900) Freud referred to the dream symbolism of falling and stated that in women's dreams it always means a "fallen woman." On the other hand, the expression of "fallen from grace" points to abandonment by a supreme moral or by a merely worldly authority. Expressions like "this is the dizzy limit" symbolize the loss of orientation, the lack of directedness; they contain the element of condemnation and forecast the shadow of appropriate punishment or the expectation of dire consequences. "Giddy with success" also implies an anticipated downfall of the person who has exceeded his appropriate limits. Proper punishment by fate or by authority is assumed to be imminent.

These few examples suffice to point to the thesis of this paper: certain dynamic, adaptive, and structural aspects of primary process thinking indicate that one of the archaic forerunners of the superego has its genetic origins in the sensorimotor apparatus of the vestibular function. This vestibular forerunner includes imagery and fantasies which develop in the course of those traumatic experiences of the child that are part of normal maturational and developmental conflicts.

Presented at the Fall Meeting of the American Psychoanalytic Association, December, 1969, and at the New York Psychoanalytic Society, on May 12, 1970.

Clinical Professor of Psychiatry, Albert Einstein College of Medicine, New York, N.Y.

401

Elements of the evolving ego become part of the maturely and normally functioning superego through the usual projective-introjective processes of preoedipal and oedipal vicissitudes.

When Isakower (1939) wrote on the exceptional role of the auditory sphere as the preliminary stage and nucleus of the superego, he presented the functioning of the vestibular organ of a crustacean as a model for early identifications that lead to the foundation of the superego. He thought that "the super-ego functions like a psychical organ of equilibrium" (p. 344).

I shall consider two models to indicate the presence of the vestibular superego forerunner in a variety of normal and pathological phenomena. The first model is the experience of the child who is passively involved in the game of being thrown up in the air and then suddenly exposed to the pretense of being dropped. This model, which predominantly implicates the father image, will be used in the discussion of dreams, the transference, and depersonalization.

The second model, which predominantly implicates the mother image, is that of the toddler who learns to walk. This active maturational process involves him in ambiguous vestibular experiences and is embedded in the vicissitudes of the separation-individuation phase (Mahler, 1968). This model will receive particular attention in the last section of this paper, while the first model of the universal game will be examined in what follows.

I want to emphasize before further discussion that I do not imply that this vestibular forerunner plays a role in the actual functioning of the mature superego system. Hartmann and Loewenstein (1962) stress the difference between function and genesis, the importance of how much of the antecedents survives, and the related problem of regression. All of the phenomena I am going to investigate present regressive features within the frame of normal or pathological conditions. In the following I attempt to trace the facets and derivatives of a vestibular superego forerunner in a variety of mental phenomena.

THE VESTIBULAR FORERUNNER IN DREAMS

One of the most convincing manifestations of this structure appears in dreams of falling that in many instances include in their

TO CAST AWAY   403

latent content the element of moral decline: "the fall of man." When Freud discusses infantile material present in dreams, several elements of the latent dream material refer in one of the examples to moral "falling," while the corresponding manifest part of the dream reads: "In the Graben she sank down on her knees, as though she was quite broken-down" (p. 202). This was the dream of an "elderly lady" whose previously reported dream (p. 199) also contained the latent element of falling after "rushing about." Freud remarks that these rushings-about "took the place of other, less innocent ones." Freud stresses that whenever a woman dreams of falling, she imagines herself as a "fallen woman." In the latent content of the dream that manifestly contained "falling on the Graben" there are several references to "moral falling"; e.g., the cook who fell on her knees when her thefts were discovered and a maidservant who was "thrown out" because of a love affair. Here Freud also points out that the Graben (an elegant street in Vienna) is a favorite hunting ground for prostitutes. I would like to add here that *graben* means to dig, to bury, and therefore we have here the full circle of sexual and other crimes and sins committed and subsequently punished by a harsh archaic superego that buries the dreamer.

In his discussion of dreams of flying and falling Freud states:

> . . . these dreams, too, reproduce impressions of childhood. . . . There cannot be a single uncle . . . who has not played at letting him [the child] fall by riding him on his knee and then suddenly stretching out his leg, or by holding him up high and then suddenly pretending to drop him. Children are delighted by such experiences, . . . especially if there is something about them that causes a little fright or giddiness. . . . the pleasurable feelings attached to these experiences are transformed into anxiety. . . .
> *I cannot, however, disguise from myself that I am unable to produce any complete explanation* of this class of typical dreams [p. 271ff.; my italics].

I present material from my own practice to illustrate the manifestation of this vestibular aspect of the superego in dreams.

1. A male patient dreamed: A wild woman who at the same time looked rather seductive, was attacking him, and he jumped away in despair from her outstretched arms and into a precipice. He woke

up with a sudden jolt on the floor where he had landed in his actual jump from his bed. The manifest dream indicates, and the associations bear ample evidence of, the involvement of those libidinal impulses which Freud had contended would exist. Moreover, threatening and punishing aspects of the mother image appeared in the latent material and represented a moral conflict on a sexual and professional issue. Real and fantasied dangers could have easily precipitated a "downfall" in the patient's private and professional life.

2. A married woman who was deeply involved in a love affair dreamed: "I was falling off a rock while I was desperately clinging to it." During the same night she had a second dream: "I left my second husband for somebody. I tried to escape and had to jump from the lowest rung of a fire escape. I let it go but grabbed it again and was suspended, clinging to the fire escape."

The patient was fully aware of the moral significance of the dream, understood its symbolic meaning, and knew that it referred to her original guilt feelings caused by incestuous wishes. She had married only once, her present husband, who could be labeled second only if her father was the first. This, however, pointed to the fulfillment of her persistent childhood fantasy that if she eloped with her father and lived with him, he would be happier than ever before since she could give him all the understanding her mother had never been able to do. Thus the dream contained both elements of incest and the punishment for it in the form of being suspended and falling down. Further associations and their transference references produced material that caused giddiness in the session in which the dream was reported and discussed. Giddiness represented the telescoping of libidinal and aggressive reactive feelings that arose as part of the punishing agency's activity. In this way the pleasure of clinging to the archaic incestuous object and of swinging in the air was turned into a punishment of being cast away by it and falling toward the ground where one would be crushed as a penalty for incestuous clinging. On a more mature level, this symbolized the moral meaning of falling below one's standards, social caste, etc.

The Vestibular Forerunner in the Transference

In 1914 Ferenczi described a transference phenomenon:

Many patients have a sensation of giddiness on rising from the recumbent position at the end of the psycho-analytic session. . . . During the session the patient gave himself up wholly to . . . transference to the doctor, and lives in the phantasy that he will always enjoy such well-being. Suddenly this (unconscious) phantasy is destroyed by the doctor's warning that the session is ended. . . . This sudden alteration of the psychic setting, the *disillusionment* (when one feels as '*though fallen from the clouds*') may call up the same subjective feeling as is experienced in sudden and unexpected change of posture— . . . that is to say, to preserve one's 'equilibrium'—which is the essence of giddiness. Naturally at the moment of this disillusionment that part of the *belief in the analysis* that did not yet rest on honest conviction but only on a filial trust disappears very easily [p. 239f.].

Ferenczi's description of a situation that we often observe points to a special case of the regressive revival of being cast away by an archaic superego agency. The transference situation recreates the panic of being abandoned and losing one's balance in childhood. The giddiness is the somatic symbolization of the punishment and its consequences.

Another type is represented by transient depersonalizations during the vicissitudes of the transference neurosis. Such states occur in patients who are in the throes of a suddenly and unexpectedly developed traumatic experience of fantasied rejection that is combined with the equally fantasied threat of abandonment and betrayal. In these instances, dizziness indicates the original libidinal-seductive facet and the threatening moral issue, which signify being cast away in a moral sense as well as in a libidinal sense (loss of love as a form of punishment).

A further syndrome of the vestibular forerunner manifests itself when in the course of regression in the transference the patient's preconscious or unconscious positive feelings are noticed by the superego. Then the punishing aspect of the vestibular superego comes to the fore. The infantile self is pushed away, rejected by the archaic objects introjected in the superego, and the ensuing feelings are regressively experienced as giddiness. The ego experiences the rejection, the feeling of being cast away physically, just as does the child who is rejected and pushed away by the parental figure. Hermann (1926) assumed that the orientation directed by the superego operates silently under normally balanced conditions, whereas in the regressive transference situation both ego and superego function on archaic levels, so that the rejection is experienced in its most concrete primary form, the giddiness of the punitively pushed-away child.

As an illustration I cite the case of a young woman who started complaining about giddiness at certain phases of her treatment. These periods of giddiness disturbed her to such an extent that when they occurred the second time during her treatment she went for a neurological checkup, which was completely negative. These spells lasted from one to two weeks and were followed by periods of positive transference feelings of which the patient was not yet consciously aware during the time the spells occurred. Moreover, I became aware of the premonitive character of the spells only after her acting out with the neurologist. Subsequently I was able to detect fine signs of positive transference in this usually aggressive patient.

In this patient the superego acted at the slightest stirring of a libidinal impulse in a very specific way that may have been determined by the patient's infantile development or by special autonomous factors. The impulse was defended against by regression: the silently operating moral orientation of the superego was pulled into the general regression and pushed away the rejected ego. An intersystemic distancing between superego and ego occurred. The symbolization process, in the course of the transference, led to a moral discarding as a punishment, which in the ensuing regression was experienced as being cast away; the vestibular interplay between the regressed superego and ego was perceived by the patient as actual disorientation, giddiness.

Summing up the role of the vestibular superego forerunner in the regression of the transference we may say that this aspect of the superego exerts a directing, orienting function. If it abandons the ego and the self, the subsequent "loss of balance" indicates moral disapproval and can cause, in the regression, a general transient disorientation of the ego and the self. A situation of "being cast away" comes about and giddiness develops, symbolizing in a somatic regressive form the moral conflict between ego and superego. The ego, in regression, correctly interprets the giddiness as a sign of disapproval by the superego.

THE VESTIBULAR FORERUNNER IN ALTERED EGO STATES

The complex syndromes of depersonalization and related phenomena very often present giddiness combined with a feeling of being lost in reality and within oneself. Giddiness particularly prevails at the beginning of the experience. In the following discussion, I want to stress certain theoretical and clinical aspects of the phenomenon.

The generally accepted theoretical assumption is that in the wake of diffuse anxiety or panic a split in the ego and superego develops (Freud, 1936; Oberndorf, 1939; Jacobson, 1959; Arlow, 1959). This explains the subjective feeling of estrangement and giddiness. What were previously well-integrated functions *and* self images disintegrate in various degrees and for different lengths of time. One part of the self may look at the other part or may feel in some eery way that it is separated from the other part. There is a panicky uncertainty as to which part is the real one. The anxiety and despair are enhanced by a feeling of abandonment. This feeling may be expressed and experienced in a very concrete way. Confusion, despair, losing one's grip on oneself and on the world are intrinsic parts of the experience of depersonalization and related altered ego states.

I suggested in my paper on depersonalization (1955) that these complex phenomena are patterned on the situation that arises when the baby loses the nipple or its substitute from his mouth, either at the end of a satisfactory meal or by an unwelcome interruption. I assumed that even the healthiest and best fed baby who falls asleep toward the end of his feeding must become aware of the physical and psychic loss of the breast and nipple.

The loss of this object, the disappearance of tactile, olfactory, and other stimuli causes disturbances of the body image which have to be coped with. These phenomena are apt to cause transient imbalance of libido and aggression. The greater the trauma (the less satisfied the baby, the less satisfactory the breasts), the greater is the probability of these events. However, in the course of normal development, this physical and psychic loss of the breast and nipple paves the way to introjective-projective processes and toward eventual integration of the lost object representations.

One aspect of this feeling of being hopelessly lost and abandoned is more aptly formulated in clinical terms as a recapitulation of a situation that occurs repeatedly in every child's life. This event is the experience of falling or being dropped under pleasurable or unpleasurable circumstances or in a situation that can be interpreted by the child as "being cast away" by the parental imago, i.e., when he is pushed or dropped either intentionally or unintentionally. Such experiences contain an element of the vestibular-sensory perception of being cast or thrown away and losing support. Projective-introjective efforts to master the feelings integrate the sensory experience into the imagery and into the structural control of this situation. It is quite natural that dizziness accompanies this sudden loss of attachment to the mother's or her substitute's body. This experience is inevitably attributed to the imago that is fantasied as a punishing agency and for this reason is built permanently into the structure of the developing superego. This particular genetic layer of the superego may come to the fore in regressive altered ego states of which depersonalization and its variations are the most common.

My suggestion is that this form of being lost in the frame of the genetic antecedents (Hartmann and Loewenstein, 1962) may in later life become the symbolic re-edition of the above-sketched infantile traumatic situation. Its manifestation accompanied by giddiness is the regressive re-enactment of the intrapsychic abandonment of the ego agencies and of the self by the archaic parental images that are built into the superego.

Schilder (1914) lays particular stress on the disturbances of the vestibular apparatus in relation to depersonalization. He points out that whenever we are giddy, we cannot maintain the unity of our body. He emphasizes the very close relation between the vestibular apparatus and depersonalization, which he suggests is a sadomasochistic negation of the patient's own body, specifically connected with the vestibular mechanisms.

These theoretical reconstructions can be illustrated by case material (Peto, 1955):

Case 1. A thirty-two-year-old woman had suffered from depersonalizations of varying severity since her preadolescence. In the
transference neurosis my "bashing" interpretations precipitated,
among other things, giddiness and feelings of estrangement. The latter represented panic about both unification with *and* separation
from the mother, who was a powerful domineering figure of national
fame in her country. The second half of the patient's second year of
life was a fateful one. Her mother took her on frequent trips of
which she had chaotic memories: of rattling noises connected with
traveling by train, dizziness, desperate loneliness and darkness. Memories of relief while falling asleep in her mother's arms contrasted
with despair because of the mother's disappearance every day when
she went to work.

Thus, the genetic image of the threatening, abandoning superego was closely tied to experiences of giddiness, losing the firm support of mother's arms, and being precipitated into nothingness. The
punishing aspects of this structure were enhanced in her second
year by the birth of a brother.

Case 2. The giddiness, the element of helpless swaying, was
graphically represented in the depersonalizations of a young woman
who felt that "I am a melon *and* a slice of the same melon which is
neatly cut out and gradually removed from the whole. It is a desperate feeling of being in the nothingness and longing hopelessly to become a whole."

Similar phenomena occur as a normal accompaniment of adolescence and preadolescence. The adolescent looks at himself in the
mirror and thinks "Who am I? Is this me?" He feels uncertainty
about his identity and at the same time mild disturbances of equilibrium. I suggest that the ever-present guilt feelings of that age and
the deeply intertwined transient regressions reach archaic ego and
superego layers and revive split-off experiences of being rejected in
a very concrete form—that of being pushed away and feeling giddy
as a consequence of losing ground physically and morally.

This view is supported from quite another field of my experience. While working in a state-controlled outpatient department in
Budapest, I requested some of my patients to sit daily for about
fifteen minutes in front of a mirror and look at themselves without
any purpose, just letting their thoughts and emotions go along. My

aim had been to stir up preconscious or unconscious material and to break through the resistances in order to achieve quick transference phenomena. My reasoning was as follows: people do not usually recognize their resemblance to their parents. Nevertheless, if anyone sees his face unexpectedly in a mirror, he may recognize in himself the features of some relative. The unexpected confronting of the self may cause pleasure *and* sadness and depression because split-off parts may emerge from repression. The reappearance of the parental imagos may revive libidinal as well as aggressive wishes against them and the fear of retaliation on their part.

Those patients who tried had to give up after one or two attempts. They soon slipped into the throes of anxiety which was often accompanied by giddiness, slight confusion, tenseness, breathing and swallowing difficulties. The therapeutic gains were nil, but the theoretical expectations seemed to be confirmed.

The Vestibular Forerunner and the Body Image

The earliest manifestation of vestibular interaction between the ego and the environment is the Moro reflex which disappears after the first trimenon. Moro (1918) elicited this reflex by hitting the infant's pillow with both hands. Thereupon both arms, half extended at the elbows, are spread apart, as are the fingers. The Moro reflex, consisting of an extensor movement of the arms, is the opposite of the startle or fright reaction which is a flexor movement. Moro considered it an atavistic embracing reflex which disappears, in normal infants, after the first trimenon. It is not considered a positional tonic neck reflex; it is exclusively a vestibular reflex (Peiper, 1961).

The Moro reflex is the most archaic phylogenetically imprinted manifestation of disruption of physical support on the mother's part. In the first two years of life the infant is almost daily exposed to situations in which the mother's or father's support in the physical or emotional sphere is lacking or is withdrawn. On such occasions the child inevitably gets into the throes of disorientation on several levels of his mental functioning since at that age physical disorientation may easily precipitate cognitive and affective disequilibrium as well. Schilder (1935) stresses the importance of a unifying agency, the malfunctioning of which causes disturbances of a sensory and cognitive nature. He suggests that in disturbances of the body image as well as in depersonalization and in many neurological syndromes this factor plays an important role. He explicitly states, based on his experiments, that the vestibular apparatus is the most essential element of this unifying agency:

> Under the influence of vertical movements a dissociation occurs in the image of the body, so that a part of the substance of the body goes out of the body in the sense of the positive after-sensation.
> The emanation of the substance of the head out of its frame is of special importance. This emanating substance is the carrier of the localization of the ego [1935, p. 96].
> Dizziness always occurs when the impressions of the senses cannot be united. . . . We deal here with phenomena which have again analogies to what one experiences in vestibular irritation and also during sea-sickness. In sea-sickness the impossibility of adapting movements to the ever-changing surroundings plays an important part, besides the vestibular irritation [1935, p. 113].

Schilder suggests that the child reacts with anxiety and panic to any trauma that threatens the erect posture. The adult responds to similar situations with giddiness. Schilder does not hesitate to consider the vestibular apparatus as one of the ego nuclei in an analytic sense: "We have only to add that where there is a vestibular after-sensation it becomes the carrier of the ego. It is in this respect more important than the body-image based on the other senses" (p. 96). This ego agency, according to Schilder, has originally only indirect correlations to clinging-holding-mastering tendencies and functions. It is a primary "ego component" (an autonomous ego function in Hartmann's sense) that becomes only secondarily cathected with libidinal drive representations. He considers it more important than sucking and clinging.

Schilder (1937) believes that the usual games of lifting and letting the child slide down offer the opportunity, apart from the accompanying libidinal pleasure, to control and keep the proper posture and the equilibrium while playing so that the integrity of the body image can be kept intact. He stressed the significance of the maturational trend to gain better control over one's own equilibrium so as not to be delivered helplessly to the force of gravity.

If we apply Schilder's considerations on the development of the body image to intrapsychic developments and relationships, we arrive at the conclusion that the functional distance between the introjected parental imagos in the superego, and between the ego agencies and the self representations, is a decisive factor in the integrity of the body image, in self-reliance and self-esteem. If through splitting or other processes as in depersonalization, dream formation, etc., the self and/or the ego feel abandoned by the superego, dizziness may develop and the original infantile developmental situation may be repeated intrapsychically as a regressive intersystemic conflict where the original vestibular interdependence is revived and the archaic experience of "not being held" and therefore having "lost one's equilibrium" is re-experienced.

THE VESTIBULAR FORERUNNER AND COGNITION

Combining the topographic model with the structural hypothesis, Hermann (1926) conceived of a subagency having a particular function within the system ego. He drew attention to the fact that thoughts become conscious not solely through visual and acoustic perceptions but also by nonvisual, nonacoustic, but nevertheless conscious, orientation processes. He suggested the existence of a *Bw.* system, an ego agency in the structural sense, which genetically does not correspond to any of the visual-acoustic systems. He singled out a system of orientation and of relatedness, which contains thought symbols that relate to orientation and are conscious in a nonvisual and nonacoustic form. This agency is hypocathected in the manifest dream, where relationships are presented mainly through cathexis of the visual-perceptual system. In contrast, he conceived of talent in logic and mathematics as an ability to operate with the hypercathexis of the relatedness system.

Hermann hypothesized that this thought orientation agency is of vestibular origin since this apparatus is the biological orientation organ. He further assumed that the thought disorder found in sleep and schizophrenia reflects a disturbance of this vestibular ego agency, whereas logical and mathematical thought processes involve relatedness, direction, and orientation, and these correspond to the physiological role of the vestibular apparatus. *Confusion in thinking may be accompanied by the subjective feeling of giddiness, indicating this intricate genetic, dynamic relationship.* The higher the level of consciousness is, the more specialized and structuralized our thought processes are, the more they require this orientation and relatedness agency of vestibular origin.

Hermann's final speculations led him to the assumption that the influence of the superego on the ego is exerted in partly conscious, partly unconscious orientations and directives. He assumed that this ego agency of orientation is one of the superego's agents through which orders and commands and demands are communicated to the ego.

THE VESTIBULAR FORERUNNER AND SEPARATION-INDIVIDUATION

There is a phase in normal development when the ego's balancing operation on all levels and the whole equilibrium of the developing self are closely related to the primary object. I have in mind the period of twelve to eighteen months when the child learns to walk. This may be the most important phase of vestibular operation and direction which encompasses orientation, object relatedness, and directedness in space. The child is caught in a maturational vise: the phylogenetically predetermined maturational process forces him to embark upon walking and expose himself to heretofore unknown vestibular experiences. On the other hand, this same process forces upon him developmental conflicts in the frame of his separation-individuation phase which relentlessly increases the spatial and temporal separation from the primary object that is still an integral part of the child's body image and body self (Mahler, 1968).

Orientation, direction, and relatedness are primarily controlled by the parental imagos, since separation-individuation intrinsically contains the elements of spatial orientation and distance-closeness adaptations. These operations hinge on the orienting and directing attitudes of the archaic imagos. Therefore projection-introjection processes in the second year are closely intertwined with vestibular experiences.

This situation is rendered even more conflict-ridden by the average "good enough" mother's obvious joy in her child's walking, in his attempts at physical separation. The child is thus presented with the image of a mother who fosters and enjoys her child's suffering, which is implicit in separation. On the other hand, the mother's joy encourages the child to go ahead with these strivings. The ensuing identifications are most probably the earliest and possibly most decisive secondary identifications. The intrapsychic structuralizations of these good and bad mother images in the area of supportive equilibrium lay the foundation for some of the earliest conflicts between an archaic superego and ego. The whole process is embedded in the vestibular apparatus's operation. Purely physiological phenomena and accompanying vestibular functions of the ego become coupled with conflictuous mental developments. The mother who, however gently, pushes the child into poorly equilibriumed walking and thereby causes the child to lose control of equilibrium and experience giddiness inevitably becomes incorporated into the early superego. This superego becomes the representative of a powerful image that causes loss of balance and creates giddiness.

On the other hand, the ego develops and learns to operate its equilibrium physiologically. An additional aid to this process is the early secondary identification with the supporting mother. These combinations lead sooner or later to a control of the equilibrium and to silent operation of the vestibular-originated superego forerunner. The early identifications gradually are united with the subsequent parent identifications that raise the level of the original vestibular superego operation into moral and social spheres. However, regressive episodes and sudden or prolonged revival of the original disequilibrium may disrupt the integrated silent operation of the gradually maturing superego. A more turbulent archaic forerunner may come to the fore, and this regression precipitates dizziness which corresponds to its genetic origins.

A simple illustration of what has been sketched above is the following: A fourteen-month-old girl walked happily laughing in front of a newly hired baby-sitter; however, she would walk in front of the well-known and much loved maid only if the latter did not look at her; in the presence of her mother her walking was accompanied by whining and crying. These variations in behavior clearly indicate the degree of the pain and pleasure of separation-individuation with figures who are increasingly invested with love and dependence. These differences in behavior also demonstrate the painfully enforced identification with the "rejecting" aspect of the mother who "forces" the child to walk. Thus, this identification becomes the representative of an archaic mother image that "cast away" the child into the throes of dangers and guilt feelings that are structuralized in the frame of vestibular experiences.

Summary

The experiences of the child in relation to his parents involve him in the vicissitudes of equilibrium, losing control during walking, falling or being pushed away. Further traumatic experiences ensue that are connected with giddiness and concomitant sudden and transient phases of confusion in space and in orientation about the location of the body image as a whole, and in particular the relationship of particular parts of it to one another. These experiences and the corresponding disorientation in thinking are brought into causal relationship to the main oedipal figures and to pleasant *and* unpleasant situations associated with these same figures.

Pleasurable experiences connected with thrills in space like being thrown in the air by an adult or being swung around by the arms of an adult expose the child to a high degree of sexual excitement. Sudden release (being dropped) creates anxiety which in turn may easily be interpreted by the child as a result and concomitant of punishment.

The excitations and the sudden letdown are attached secondarily to preoedipal and oedipal conflicts and thus are drawn subsequently into the structure of the developing superego in the second year. A traumatic vestibular experience turns into a punitive action on the part of the superego. Projective-introjective processes structuralize the threatening aspects of being dropped, losing balance, and the fear of losing hold on people. The concrete, genetic situation of "being cast away" is incorporated in a punishment and guilt complex.

BIBLIOGRAPHY

Arlow, J. A. (1959), The Structure of the *Déjà Vu* Experience. *J. Amer. Psa. Assn.*, 7:611-631.
Ferenczi, S. (1914), Sensations of Giddiness at the End of the Psycho-Analytic Session. *Further Contributions to the Theory and Technique of Psycho-Analysis*. London: Hogarth Press, 1950, pp. 239-241.

Freud, S. (1900), The Interpretation of Dreams. *Standard Edition,* 4 & 5. London: Hogarth Press, 1953.

—— (1936), A Disturbance of Memory on the Acropolis. *Standard Edition,* 22:239-248. London: Hogarth Press, 1964.

Hartmann, H. & Loewenstein, R. M. (1962), Notes on the Superego. *This Annual,* 17:42-81.

Hermann, I. (1926), Das System Bw. *Imago,* 12:203-210.

Isakower, O. (1939), On the Exceptional Position of the Auditory Sphere. *Int. J. Psa.,* 20:340-348.

Jacobson, E. (1959), Depersonalization. *J. Amer. Psa. Assn.,* 7:581-610.

Mahler, M. S. (1968), *On Human Symbiosis and the Vicissitudes of Individuation:* Vol. 1. *Infantile Psychosis.* New York: International Universities Press.

Moro, E. (1918), Das erste Trimenon. *Münch. Med. Wschr.,* 65:1147-1150.

Oberndorf, C. P. (1939), On Retaining the Sense of Reality in a State of Depersonalization. *Int. J. Psa.,* 20:137-147.

Peiper, A. (1961), *Cerebral Function in Infancy and Childhood.* New York: Consultants' Bureau, 1963.

Peto, A. (1955), On So-Called Depersonalization. *Int. J. Psa.,* 36:379-386.

Schilder, P. (1914), *Selbstbewusstsein und Persönlichkeitsbewusstsein.* Berlin: J. Springer.

—— (1935), *The Image and Appearance of the Human Body.* New York: International Universities Press, 1950.

—— (1937), The Relations between Clinging and Equilibrium. *Int. J. Psa.,* 20:58-63, 1939.

FURTHER PROTOTYPES OF EGO FORMATION

A Working Paper from a Research Project on Early Development

RENÉ A. SPITZ, M.D., ROBERT N. EMDE, M.D., and
DAVID R. METCALF, M.D. (Denver, Colorado)

For many years, separately and together, the authors have been conducting research with infants. These investigations have involved detailed observations of infant behavior, electroencephalographic studies, naturalistic studies of mother-infant interaction, and a number of theoretical explorations derived from these and other investigations.

Our recent research efforts have been inspired by Freud's trailbreaking work in *Three Essays on the Theory of Sexuality* (1905). The principal theoretical statements which have guided us were formulated systematically in three publications of Spitz (1958, 1959, 1961).

The following propositions form an overall framework for our research.

1. There is no aspect, activity, function, or structure of the psyche that is not subject to development.

2. Development is the resultant of the interplay of innate and experiential factors which themselves are often inextricably interwoven.

Dr. Spitz is Professor, Department of Psychiatry, University of Colorado School of Medicine, Denver, Colorado.

Dr. Emde, Associate Professor, Department of Psychiatry, University of Colorado School of Medicine, Denver, is supported by U.S. Public Health Service Grant MH-HD 15753 and the National Institute of Mental Health Research Scientist Development Award K3-MH-36808.

Dr. Metcalf, Associate Professor, Department of Psychiatry, University of Colorado School of Medicine, Denver, is currently supported by the National Institute of Mental Health Research Scientist Development Award K5-MH-40275.

3. Innate factors include hereditary aspects and aspects pertaining to intrauterine and intrapartum events.

4. The role of the experiential factors in the inception, unfolding, and structuring of the psychic apparatus has two sources: exchanges with the surround and exchanges within the organism. The latter exchanges consist of interactions between incipient psychic operations and the innate physiological prototypes for some subsequently emerging psychic structures. The maturation of these prototypes takes place as an epigenetic unfolding; as a forward moving, irreversible progressive growth and differentiation, programmed as it were by a maturational clock.

We have set ourselves the following tasks:

1. To collect experimental data which will test the correctness of the theoretical statements in question.

2. To construct appropriate models of the development and structure of the emerging psychic system on the basis of these statements. The value of these models should be tested further by systematic observation and experiment.

3. To demonstrate the explanatory power of these models within the framework of the system of psychoanalytic theory.

We would like to illustrate this approach by some initial findings from this rather ambitious program. These findings are psychobiological in nature and involve behavioral units which are common to every individual of the species. Examples from the current phase of our research include the following areas of development: (1) rapid eye movement states (REM states and REM sleep); (2) quiet, "deep" sleep; (3) effects of stress on neonatal sleep; (4) smiling; (5) normal fussiness.

METHOD AND SUBJECTS

The central strategy of our research project includes the weekly or biweekly study of individual infants from before birth through the end of the first year of life. In addition, cross-sectional studies, involving a larger number of infants, are used to explore hypotheses generated by our longitudinal studies. The design of our project includes alternating home visits and visits to our infant neurophysiological laboratory. During home visits, we make naturalistic observations of the infant, obtain a narrative account from the mother of changes since our last visit, and test the infant's responsivity to a variety of standardized stimuli.

The laboratory visits for electroencephalograms and observations are quite different. After the application of EEG and polygraphic leads, a laboratory recording session begins with a feeding of the infant and continues with a transition into sleep and through about 90 minutes of sleep recording. The recording includes direct observation of behavior, as well as continuous electroencephalogram, electro-oculogram, respiration, electromyogram, and evoked response recording.

To date, twenty-two infants have been studied longitudinally. Of these, thirteen infants have been studied intensively during the first three postnatal months, and nine infants have been studied through the first year. Over five hundred have been studied crosssectionally.

SLEEP INVESTIGATIONS

In common parlance, sleep and sleeping are considered equivalent: one is either asleep or awake. At best, the vernacular distinguishes light sleep from deep sleep with dreams ascribed to one or the other. Psychoanalysis has had, from the beginning, a different approach to the problems of sleep. At the outset, Freud (1900, 1901) was primarily interested in the exploration of dreams, which he recognized as the manifestations of the mental life during sleep. He demonstrated that determinism applies to dreams and all psychic activity in the same way as it applies to the physical world. But his differentiation went further than this. Being primarily interested in the problems of dreams and their elucidation, he noted from the very beginning the possible occurrence of dream states outside of the so-called sleep state, in the form of daydreams. He postulated that (1) sleep would be found to be different from the waking state in its physiological functioning and (2) that specific parts of the brain would be found to be involved in the dream process (1900). Furthermore, he dealt in the same period with a tangential but related phenomenon, that of memory. Freud anticipated modern brain physiology with his proposition of a double registration in the memory systems (1900, 1925). It is interesting to note that, following Freud's investigations, Silberer (1912) discussed the importance of recognizing two qualitatively different kinds of sleep.

Physiological studies of sleep tended to follow two major investigative directions. One direction was that exemplified by the work of von Economo (summarized in 1929) on sleep centers and the neurophysiological work of Hess (1924, 1925), among others. The other direction was that explored for many years by Kleitman (1929). This culminated in the 1953 and 1955 reports, by Aserinsky and Kleitman, which documented *in infants* the cyclic occurrence of episodes of body motility associated with rapid eye movements. This was soon followed by the reports of Dement (1955) and Dement and Kleitman (1957) indicating that a similar rapid eye movement-bodily activity cycle was seen in adults, and that rapid eye movement (REM) periods normally occurred about every 90 minutes throughout a night's sleep; furthermore, these REM sleep periods were found to be associated with a specific EEG and with dreaming. Much of the emergent physiological and psychophysiological research on sleep and dreaming, and its implications for psychoanalytic theory, has been reviewed and discussed by Fisher (1965).

As a result of these pioneering investigations, we now think of sleep as being composed of a number of different stages (I, II, III, IV, I-REM). Each of these stages is described by multiple criteria, which consist of the presence or absence of eye movements, EEG configuration, muscle tone, and sometimes respiratory and heart rate patterns.[1]

From the psychoanalyst's point of view it is of primary interest that two of these criteria appear to correspond closely to propositions advanced fifty years earlier by Freud. The first of these is the finding of greatly reduced muscular activity (via active inhibition) during sleep as measured by the chin electromyogram. We remind our readers that Freud (1900) postulated that the inhibition of motility in sleep not only *facilitates* dreaming, but is also *necessary* for dreaming

---

[1] The concepts, light sleep and deep sleep, are valuable but imprecise and do not refer to sufficiently invariant physiological correlates. Stage IV sleep, the deepest stage of quiet sleep in the human, is associated with very high and steady thresholds to arousal by sensory stimulation. Stage I REM (REM sleep), associated with dreaming, is so unique as to be thought of as a separate state. It has, for this reason, been termed the "D State" by Ernest Hartmann (1967).

to take place. The second of these criteria is the regular occurrence of penile erections during REM sleep—a phenomenon which has been studied by Fisher et al. (1965).

We have been intrigued to find that infant sleep and adult sleep show both significant similarities and important differences. This holds true for behavior as well as physiology. Our investigations of infant sleep were stimulated by these facts in conjunction with the central importance of sleep and dreams to psychoanalysis and the importance of Freud's genetic view.

REM "Sleep" in the Newborn

An initial cross-sectional study resulted in a new conception of neonatal states (Emde and Metcalf, 1970). The combination of detailed behavioral observations and polygraphic recording provided us with information previously not available. In the adult we are accustomed to thinking of rapid eye movements as occurring in sleep. But the matter is not so simple in infancy. In newborns we observe rapid eye movements occurring in a number of different circumstances. Not only do they occur during the sleep cycle when the eyes are closed (*sleep REM*), but they also occur at times when the eyes are open and glassy (*drowsy REM*), during times when the infant is engaged in nutritional sucking (*sucking REM*), and during some times when the infant is fussing or crying (*fussy REM and crying REM*). We established that two trained behavioral observers reached better than 95 percent agreement in judgments of each of these behavioral states.

The states of drowsy REM, sucking REM, fussing REM, and crying REM have consistent electrophysiological correlates—correlates which are also present in the REM sleep of adults and older children. Even though the infant had his eyes open or was engaging in nutritional sucking, or was fussing or crying, he frequently had the same electrophysiology as the type of "sleep" during which the eyes were closed and rapid eye movements were conspicuous. We carried out an independent minute-by-minute study which compared a behavioral observer's interpretation of state with an EEG specialist's simultaneous EEG and polygraphic findings during the same period of observation. In the analysis of nearly twenty hours of data collection from ten normal newborns, the behavioral observer judged a total of 214 minutes to be either drowsy REM, sucking REM, fussing REM, or crying REM states. In the independent judgments of the EEG and polygraph, the electroencephalographer judged over 98 percent of these (or 210 minutes) to be REM states indistinguishable from REM sleep.

We have used the term "undifferentiated" because drowsy REM, sucking REM, fussy REM, and crying REM disappear over the first three months of postuterine life (Metcalf and Emde, 1969). In addition, *neonatal REM* sleep shows a relatively high variability in physiological patterning which tends toward stability over the first three months. These changes are concomitant with another major change in the sleep cycle itself; by three months, sleep characteristically begins with a non-REM (NREM) instead of a REM period. This pattern of sleep onset will from here on remain the same. It is the adult pattern.

EEG Development in Quiet Sleep

It is evident that our EEG studies relate at every step to our behavioral studies. The EEG is used here as one tool in a psychobiological, interdisciplinary research program based on the principles we have already stated. The study of the human electroencephalogram is recent, dating from the work of the psychiatrist Hans Berger in the 1930's. Less well known is the fact that Berger quickly recognized that the human EEG undergoes progressive change throughout life. This is particularly evident from birth to three years. Because of this marked developmental change, the EEG provides excellent opportunity for the study of central nervous system maturation and development. Many workers, notably Ellingson (1967) in recent years, have contributed to knowledge in this domain; it has been our particular area of interest for some time.

In the neonatal period, although awake and sleep EEGs can often be distinguished from each other, this differentiation is sometimes difficult and unreliable, because REM sleep and undifferentiated "nonsleep" REM states share the same electrophysiology. The two main sleep stages, on the other hand, "active" REM sleep and "quiet" NREM sleep, show clearly different EEGs.

The EEG of REM sleep is one of extensive cortical activation and in many ways resembles the EEG associated with the alert, awake state. It shows a low amplitude pattern whose rhythms appear to be fast and irregular. During this state there is activation of many physiological systems as evidenced by extreme variability of pulse, respiration, and blood pressure, by a rise in brain oxygen utilization by REMs, by penile erections, and by increased body motility. Even the lack of muscle tonus during the REM state is not a passive phenomenon, but is a result of CNS activation; muscle tonus is reduced through the mechanism of active inhibition.[2] It is noteworthy that REM-state physiology, for all its inherent variability, changes very little throughout life once its characteristic integrated patterning, loosely present at first, becomes established at about three months.

Quiet sleep also shows many important changes during the first three months, and, in contrast to REM sleep, shows continued development throughout infancy and childhood. The quiet NREM sleep EEG shows waveforms that are more regular, slower, and of higher amplitude than those of REM sleep. During quiet sleep there are no REMS, respirations are very regular, thresholds to arousal are high, and infants are generally motionless, except for occasional spontaneous body jerks or startlelike movements. It can, indeed, be surprisingly difficult to awaken an infant from this state. At about age three weeks, the quiet sleep EEG becomes more differentiated as a result of increased regularity of slow rhythms which replace the previously somewhat chaotic picture of this stage. Four to seven days later (at about five weeks), a momentous EEG change occurs, namely the onset of "sleep spindles." These EEG wave sequences are easily recognizable. We have shown that this seemingly maturational step can be accelerated by the impact of experience (Metcalf, 1969).

At about eight to twelve weeks, quiet sleep shows a further differentiation, the emergence of definable stage II sleep. Stage II sleep is marked by the presence of well-formed sleep spindle bursts and a more characteristic, regular EEG appearance. The onset of sleep spindles probably indicates a complex maturational and developmental step. Existing and partially functioning excitatory and in-

---

2 During REM sleep there is much motor activity, especially of face (smiles, frowns, etc.), hands, and feet as well as body activity (twisting, stretching, etc.). Muscle tonus reduction occurs concurrently and is most evident around the mouth and chin. REM-sleep body motility to this degree is not seen in the adult; the age when change from infant motility toward adult motility takes place is under study.

hibitory brain systems become capable of integrated, self-regulating *interaction*. This step may have primary CNS integrative significance. Part of our research is concerned with searching for behavioral manifestations or correlates of this physiological development.

After the establishment of Stage II sleep at about three months, another kind of quiet sleep begins to emerge. We see here the beginning of adult types of deep, quiet sleep. This form of quiet sleep may be labeled "Stage III/IV." After this integrative patterning is complete, EEG development proceeds in a slower and apparently smooth fashion until about five or six months. When, as part of these developments, sleep Stages, II, III, and IV become clearly distinguishable, three different kinds of deep sleep are formed out of what had been one undifferentiated kind of deep sleep. This is an oft-overlooked and important developmental step, in the course of which a further major EEG pattern emerges, namely *spontaneous* K-complexes.

The K-complex is a specific brief series of waveforms, consisting of conspicuous deviations from the ongoing EEG tracing. K-complexes are similar to sensory evoked responses (Cobb, 1963), and can probably be elicited by sensory stimulation at earlier ages, but they do not occur *spontaneously* during sleep until after five months (Metcalf et al., 1970). When elicited at older ages, there is evidence that the patterned waveform of the K-complex varies according to the psychological meaning of the sensory stimulation (Oswald, 1962).

The K-complex may be considered to be an electrophysiological indicator of CNS information processing. This view is supported by many basic neurophysiological investigations such as those of Dawson (1958) and Barlow (1964). We are intrigued by the fact that spontaneous K-complexes are not seen before five to six months. This may be taken to indicate a new and important step in the capacity of the CNS to respond to itself; i.e., to respond in a patterned and perhaps selective way to processes arising in one part of the CNS and acting on other parts. Therefore, the emergence of spontaneous K-complexes may be connected with the increasing systematic manipulation of memory traces.

Somewhat apart from, but still connected with the preceding, is the question of drowsiness. Up to three months, the observational impression of drowsiness is not paralleled by characteristic changes in the EEG. The latter appear for the first time around three months. It would appear that drowsiness, an important psychological condition, has now acquired a specific EEG pattern. This linkage becomes clearer after six months and continues into the latency period.

Thus it appears that the age of three months is a period of critical developmental importance. EEG and physiological patterns become more clearly organized and systematically integrated with certain behaviors such as drowsiness, sleep behaviors, and sleep cycles. A further, rather abrupt change in the direction of increased differential organization is the development of spontaneous K-complexes during NREM quiet sleep at about five to six months.

Thus our attention is drawn to three nodal points in early EEG development. Our work, in broader perspective, utilizes the totality of EEG development in relation to a variety of behavioral developments, and focuses on these nodal points as "anchor points" of assumed special CNS maturational significance. The three points are aspects of quiet sleep development. They are the development of sleep spindles at four to six weeks, the development of Stage II sleep at about three months, and the development of spontaneous K-complexes at five to six months. A fourth nodal point (resting on the REM-state EEG) is the more complex integration of behavioral, physiological, and EEG manifestations, whereby at about three months undifferentiated REM states disappear and sleep-onset REM is replaced by mature sleep-onset NREM.

Effects of Stress on Neonatal Sleep

Normal hospital routine requires blood drawing from the newborn during the first three days of life. This is performed by pricking the infant's heel with a sharp stylette. We observed that this blood drawing procedure is frequently followed by long, relatively motionless NREM sleep periods. Curiosity about this led us to explore the effects of such a stress-producing (painful) event at this age (Emde et al., 1970). Hospital circumcision, done routinely without anesthesia, was chosen as an independent variable with sleep patterns following circumcision as dependent variables. Circumcision, done by plastibel technique, results in a gradually developing ischemic necrosis of the foreskin which could be expected to produce a continual bombardment of stimulation of pain pathways for many hours.

Results in two observational studies were dramatic. In the twelve hours following circumcision, most infants showed a primary increase in NREM or deep sleep. In a subsequent polygraphic study, normal male infants were observed for a ten-hour period on each of two successive nights. Continuous recordings consisted of electro-encephalogram, eye movement recording, electromyogram, respiration recording, and behavioral observations. Twenty infants were studied on two successive nights beginning at twenty-four hours of age. One half of the infants (control group) did not have circumcisions or heel pricks during the period of study; the other half (experimental group) were circumcised during the beginning of the second night's recording and observation. Eight out of ten circumcised infants showed a major increase in NREM or quiet sleep on the night following circumcision. Percentage increases of this deep NREM sleep varied from 41 to 121 percent. In contrast to this, in the undisturbed control group, the total amount of NREM sleep varied little from the first to the second night—the greatest single increase was less than 3 percent. These results are significant at well beyond the .01 level of confidence.

The cause of this phenomenon is not immediately understandable. A "common sense" guess about the effects of a continual disruptive stimulation at this age is that an infant would sleep less and cry more. Our results showed the opposite. Cirmumcised infants slept *more* and were awake less, and cried for the same amount of time as before circumcision. These results suggest an inborn adaptive mechanism which responds to stress by producing a quiescent state with high sensory thresholds. We are currently in the process of studying individual differences in regard to this phenomenon, as well as the endocrinological basis for it.

SMILING AND FUSSINESS

As derived from the *Genetic Field Theory of Ego Formation* (Spitz, 1959) our research project considers that there are certain periods during the first year when physiological and behavioral development progresses at an increased pace and in a definite normative sequence. It is inferred from that theory that these periods are accompanied by changing thresholds to stimulation and by *affective changes*, which are of crucial significance in the development of social relations. Because of this, we have paid particular attention to the behaviors of smiling and fussiness.

Our investigations have included detailed cross-sectional and longitudinal studies of smiling during the first three months (Emde and Koenig, 1969a, 1969b; Emde, 1970). In the normal newborn, smiling is linked to the states of sleep REM and drowsy REM and occurs as one of many well-circumscribed state-related "spontaneous behaviors." Since it is determined not by external stimulation but by intrinsic physiological rhythms, we refer to it as *endogenous smiling*. It is found with increased frequency in prematures (Emde, McCartney, and Harmon, 1970). We have reason to believe endogenous smiling is mediated through brainstem mechanisms since it was present in a microcephalic infant with virtually no functioning cerebral tissue (Harmon and Emde, 1970). In the normal newborn, endogenous smiling occurs at a mean rate of 11 smiles per 100 minutes of REM period. It is evenly distributed across successive REM periods of an interfeeding interval; thus, it cannot be considered an expression of a "tensionless" or hunger-free condition.

Newborn frowning, on the other hand, appears to be of two types. Like smiling, it occurs as a spontaneous state-related behavior. In addition, during later REM periods of an interfeeding interval and also during wakefulness, it occurs as an expression of distress. Endogenous smiling and endogenous frowning along with other spontaneous REM-associated behaviors wane sharply in the period between eight and twelve weeks.

Exogenous smiling, on the other hand, is not present at birth. It begins as an irregular response which is first elicited during wakefulness at about three weeks of age. It may occur to a wide variety of nonspecific stimuli in auditory, kinesthetic, tactile, and visual modalities, but it is unpredictable, rare, and fleeting. With ensuing weeks it occurs more often, but it does not become predictable until the eight-to-twelve-week period at which time it is best elicited by the visual stimulus configuration which Spitz and Wolf (1946) termed the "essential sign Gestalt" (stimulus consisting of hairline, eyes, nose, and motion). This is commonly considered the time of onset of social smiling or of the "smiling response" (Ambrose, 1961; Polak et al., 1964a; Gewirtz, 1965). Within two weeks after its onset, however, the adequate stimulus for eliciting this response becomes more complex, as three dimensions are required (Polak et. al., 1964b), and very soon after that the face of the mothering person becomes the most potent elicitor. In other words, soon after the eight-to-twelve-week period, exogenous smiling becomes more specifically social and endowed with meaning. As exogenous smiling is becoming more specific and enriched with psychological meaning, endogenous smiling, which is physiologically determined, is decreasing.

In parallel with this countermovement is still another countermovement. In one of our longitudinal research projects (Tennes et al., 1970) we have studied in detail the fussiness which normally occurs in most infants between three and twelve weeks of age. Extreme fussiness at this age has often been characterized clinically as "colic"; although its precise etiology is unknown, several groups have documented the fussiness of this age period (Spitz, 1951; Stewart et al., 1953; Wessel et al., 1954; Brazelton, 1962; Paradise, 1966).

We found fussiness, unrelated to hunger, occurring in all of the infants studied during this age period. By twelve weeks the fussiness wanes and nothing else like it is observed through the first year of life. The time of waning of this fussiness is concomitant with the infant achieving capacities for being a more active regulator of contact with his environment, both in initiating stimulus contact and in terminating it. Again we are struck with the countermovement. As the capacity for mastery and active trial-and-error behavior is increasing, fussiness is decreasing.

Discussion and Psychoanalytic Conclusions

I

In the foregoing we have presented some data from our studies on neonatal development. These form one part of our research program and we selected them because of the developmental parallels and connections they present. These studies are:

1. Neonatal sleep and REM states of infancy.
2. The development of smiling.

3. The development of differentiation of the "mature" form of deep sleep.
4. The effects of stress on neonatal sleep.

Our findings support a number of Freud's theories and the principles he elaborated on the origin, organization, and functioning of the psychic system.

Our data impress us with the operation of two parallel lines acting and interacting in the progressive unfolding of the organism. These are the lines following maturation, the innate; and development, the experiential. They converge toward ever-increasing organization and regulation of the organism's functioning. The rates of change in the development of quiet sleep, the REM state, and smiling parallel each other in their progression. This progression is gradual from birth until the postnatal age of about six weeks, where we have found an important turning point in the nature of the interaction between maturation and development.

In the six weeks following this first turning point, the changes accelerate, with mounting evidence of incipient awareness and psychic functioning, to a second turning point in the third month. We have designated this turning point the emergence of the first organizer of the psyche. It is marked by clearly defined modifications in the behavioral pattern of the same three areas (quiet sleep, REM states, smiling). These modifications run parallel with a change in the EEG pattern, which has become organized and in which sleep spindles have appeared (see Table 1).

Until age six weeks the EEG pattern present when the above-mentioned behaviors were observed, was categorically different from the EEG patterns associated with a comparable behavior in the adult. After age six weeks, an increasing organization of the rather undifferentiated neonatal pattern begins to become rapidly evident. Sleep behavior becomes more specific; it approaches more and more the adult form. A good example of this is REM sleep, which represents 60 percent of total sleep in the neonate and only 20 percent in that of the adult. After the first turning point, the REM percentage decreases progressively. After the second turning point (age two and a half months) REM stages, which until then appeared indiscriminately during both sleep and apparently awake periods, disappear completely from the nonsleep periods.

TABLE 1

	0-6 weeks	6-12 weeks	10-12 weeks
REM STATE	Occurs during behavioral sleep (eyes closed), drowsiness, nutritional sucking, fussing, and crying.	Occurs decreasingly during drowsiness, sucking, fussiness, and crying.	Occurs *only* during behavioral sleep and is more patterned from the physiological point of view.
	Neonatal Pattern: sleep begins with a REM state.	Continued neonatal pattern.	Neonatal pattern disappears; "adult" pattern of sleep onset is now present.
QUIET SLEEP	EEG rhythmic activity becomes organized at 4-6 weeks. No EEG spindles before 4 weeks. Spindle bursts first seen at 5-7 weeks.	EEG rhythmic activity is poorly differentiated between "light" and "deep" sleep. Spindles become more defined.	Stage III/IV EEG sleep ("deep" quiet sleep) begins to differentiate from stage II. Spindle maturation complete. Hypersynchronous drowsy pattern begins to emerge after 12 weeks.
SMILING	*Endogenous:* Occurs during sleep REM and drowsy REM at a rate of approximately 11 per 100 minutes.	Occurs at the same rate or at a slightly decreased rate.	Endogenous smiling wanes.
	Exogenous: Irregular response during wakefulness: elicited by a wide variety of stimulation in visual, auditory, tactile, and kinesthetic modalities.	Occurs with increased frequency, but is still irregular and in response to nonspecific sensory stimulation.	A regular response to the "essential sign Gestalt."
FUSSINESS	Endogenous nonhunger fussiness appears during the latter part of this period (3-6 weeks).	Intermittent bursts of prolonged nonhunger fussiness.	Prolonged nonhunger fussiness disappears.

The development of smiling is another example of this unfolding. We found that smiling shows that the endogenous physiological origin of this behavior decreases progressively during the first six weeks; in the second six weeks it is progressively displaced by a psychologically determined behavior. As endogenous smiling decreases, there is a proportionate increase in exogenous smiling. The stimulus for exogenous smiling originates in the surround, whereas the endogenous smile occurs as a function of innate internal rhythmic processes. The exogenous smile begins as a response to a wide variety of stimuli and progressively is transformed into a specific response to the human face. After three months, the endogenous smile occurs mainly in REM sleep and is not a prominent behavior. In other terms, while the endogenous smiling had the characteristic of physiological rhythmicity, the exogenously determined behavior has the characteristic of awareness continuing into anticipation. Exogenous smiling represents a turning from inside perception (response to inner stimuli) to the perception of the surround. In terms of motivation, the progression goes from tension discharge to awareness with active exploration and anticipation. The latter is a specifically psychological process.

From the viewpoint of the psychic apparatus, we see at this age the emergence of a number of psychic structures (e.g., memory, anticipation, meaningful directed response). These psychic structures are modeled on neonatal physiological processes, which we have called "prototypes" (Spitz, 1958). Each of these physiological processes has its innate phylogenetically predetermined maturational trajectory, and develops independently from every other one. Under the influence of the first organizer of the psyche, situated at age three months, they tend at certain maturational levels to form a range of predictable relationships with each other. They become coherent. But this maturation does not proceed alone, uninfluenced by other factors. At all developmental levels maturationally guided processes are turned into developmental processes as a result of the adaptations enforced by exchanges with the surround and the organism's response to them.

In this sense, postnatally, the concept "maturation" is a useful construct, even though *unrealizable: all is development.* For development is the resultant of the constant interactions between environment (or experience) and the innate: these interactions operate at all levels, whether molecular, cellular, or organismic.

Maturation, as a functional reality, is that aspect of development which provides potentialities on the one hand, and limitations on the other. Organizers, particularly in the context of this discussion, were first described (Spitz, 1958) as "emergent, dominant centers of integration . . . [forming a] field of forces from which a dominant center of integration, the first organizer of the psyche, will emerge." Development is not blind. It is responsive to the surround in terms of the *law of effect*. In the ontogenesis of individual behavior the law of effect plays the same role as that played by natural selection (through survival) in phylogenesis.

Conversely, maturation is blind, for it is the product of phylogenesis over geological time spans. Development, through the impact of experience, is the means through which maturationally given potentialities are realized. It is one of the *inducers of organizers*. Organizers are formed out of species-specific, innate potentialities and directions, interacting with the species-unique demands of the surround.

Organizers introduce a new *modus operandi* into the psychic system. Indeed, we believe that *the psychic organizer is equivalent to the development of a new modus operandi through adaptive exchanges*. The organizer of the psyche is not a physical structure; it is not even a psychic structure. It is the emergence and establishment of a different way of processing the psychic givens. It introduces a better adapted way, which takes advantage of the opportunities offered by the surround. With this different way, the integration of these givens on a higher level of complexity becomes possible. From here on the new, more adapted *modus operandi* becomes predominant in the psychic processes. This will obtain until, at the next level, the growing complexity and number of elements achieved through the instrumentality of the organizer make a new step necessary. That step is the development of the next and more advanced *modus operandi* which will constitute the next organizer. As the term states, a more complex, more highly integrated reorganization of the psychic givens will now begin.

Postnatally the distinction between maturation and development becomes therefore increasingly constrained: by the same token a boundary line between psyche and soma becomes ultimately meaningless. During the earliest postnatal days, approximately the first two to three weeks, physiological or somatic aspects of development are predominant as determinants of observable behavior. During this period, interactions between innate and surround become involved with an increasing variety of experience. The interactions increase in complexity and simultaneously become progressively more organized. These early patterned constellations of innate behavior and adaptive functioning, which culminate in volitional behavior and physiological adaptation, tempt one to speculate about their relationship to early ego or "pre-ego" development.

An outstanding example of the role of physiological prototypes for later psychic development and structure is breast-feeding behavior, and its "intaking" aspects in the neonate (Erikson, 1950; Spitz, 1957).

Examining this earliest physiological process and its interplay with differential experience sheds light on its emergence as the physiological prototype of an ego nucleus. Psychic structures will encroach on the discharge processes which this nucleus provides. These psychic structures will in turn modify the functions of the ego nucleus to the point where their origin becomes unrecognizable, though they will continue to contain evidences of their somatic beginning.

In studying the prototype potentialities of neonatal sleep for subsequent development of the psychic system, of its structure, of its organization, of its activity, we have followed certain principles which have been outlined elsewhere. (Spitz, 1957, 1958, 1961; Spitz and Cobliner, 1965). These principles are:

1. Psychic activity, function, structure, etc., are not innate.
2. What *is* innate is:

    (a) the variable capacity for learning and adaptation;
    (b) the capacity for making use of neurophysiological and morphological givens for coping with the environment.

However, the physiological way the innate copes with its environment is not the way the psyche does it. The prototype is not a blueprint for a future psychic entity. It provides the available means for the later developing psychic structure and the limits within which they can operate. We realize that when we say "structure," we are taking liberties with this term. Though the subsequent development certainly is structured, it mostly is rather a *modus operandi* (e.g., defense mechanisms) and more rarely a coherent psychic structure (e.g., the superego). The *modus operandi* itself is not homologous with its physiological prototype. In view of the adaptive requirements of development, a direct continuation of the prototype is most unlikely. What will develop is an analogy that we must explore in the spirit of Robert Oppenheimer (1956): "One has to widen the framework a little and find the *disanalogy* which enables us to preserve what was right about the analogy." In this spirit, when examining neonatal sleep as a possible physiological prototype for later psychic functions, we shall stress more how it differs from sleep in the adult than dwell on the obvious similarities.

Furthermore, the neonate, during "nonsleep" periods, which could pass for "wakefulness" in the adult, shows undifferentiated REM states. The neonate begins behavioral sleep in a REM state; whereas the adult falls asleep in a NREM state. And while the adult shows a generalized diminution of motor activity during REM sleep, the neonate is behaviorally active despite paradoxical suppression of muscle tonus.

These differences suggest that REM sleep probably serves a different function in the neonate. In the adult, REM states are connected with dreaming. What, we may ask, would correspond to dreaming in the neonate? The very fact that the organism is compelled to adjust neonatal sleep to the adult pattern within the first three postnatal months suggests that the neonatal sleep pattern is probably not suitable for the function sleep will have to perform after the emergence of the first organizer. It is highly probable that an interference with this adjustment would encroach upon the development of a sharp demarcation of diurnal wakefulness and, concurrently, with the perception of reality.

The function of sleep and REM in the neonate is categorically different from their function in the adult. It is a good example of the uses of *disanalogy,* for it permits us to sense where analogies lie— not where we expect them. For instance, the neonate's REM activity is triple that of the adult. Yet what can correspond in the neonate to dream activity, that rich mental life of the adult during REM sleep? And, even more significantly, in studies of premature infants, the percentage of REM activity increases in inverse proportion to the gestational age of the subject.

We need hardly argue that the psychic content, the material of dreams, is as yet nonexistent in the neonate, and *a fortiori* in the premature. We cannot therefore consider neonatal sleep and its REM activity in the same line as sleep REM in the adult. In the neonate's first three weeks of life, REM states are present, both during apparent wakefulness and sleep. We therefore come to the conclusion that they probably represent the operation of maturational processes in the CNS of the neonate, which are primarily related to physiological processes and hardly influenced as yet by experience. In our opinion, these maturational processes are part of an unfolding genetic progression, phylogenetically preformed for an average expectable environment. The processes involve the establishment, by practice and channelization, of the necessary connections within the CNS as well as in CNS behavioral integration.

What then does neonatal sleep represent? In our opinion, a physiological prototype for later function. It is sleep behavior in transition from an exclusively physiological phenomenon to adult sleep, a psychophysiological phenomenon. Neonatal sleep occurs during an existence practically devoid of interference from the surround, let alone exchanges with it. Conversely, adult sleep includes, among its functions, the enormously important psychic function of discharging the tension originating during the previous day's exchanges with a rich, varied, and ever-changing surround, probably with the help of the dream.

It is then not surprising that, by comparison with adult sleep, prototype REM sleep is poorly organized. But in the neonate it only takes three months of development to organize it. Three months is that developmental level at which a number of other psychic phenomena also converge, forming on the one hand a rudimentary ego organization, initiating on the other the preobjectal stage in the formation of object relations. And it is precisely at this level that the physiological patterning of the REM state becomes consistent. Now the REM state becomes firmly linked with behavioral sleep and can no longer be confused with wakefulness. Sleep spindles become definitely established in the sleep EEG.

If REM physiology in the adult belongs exclusively to behavioral sleep, then it has no place in the psychic life of directed, volitional action. After the three-month level, action, whether in the motor or mental sphere, will become increasingly incompatible with the REM state. Can this provide an explanation of the spectacular decrease of REM activity after the ego becomes established?

At the present state of our knowledge the linking of adult REM sleep with dreaming permits us only the assumption that during dreaming a CNS activity is going on. Some aspects of these linkages will become clearer when problems related to memory, object formation, and perhaps mental representation will have been adequately investigated.

One thing is certain: REM sleep is neither the cause nor a direct result of dreaming. That is evident from the difference of its role in the neonate and in the adult. REM sleep is the indication of specific ongoing processes in the CNS: in the neonate these processes are exclusively physiological. In the adult the vast realm of the psychological is added.

The ages at which REM and EEG pattern changes appear in the infant are quite suggestive through their convergence. The organization and structuration of sleep spindles in the EEG pattern and their maturation are coterminous with the appearance of the smiling response, the behavioral indicator of the first organizer. At the same period the REM states become limited to behavioral sleep. The adult "pattern" of NREM sleep onset also becomes established. Independently, as a result of certain theoretical considerations, we also situated the emergence of the preobject as well as of a rudimentary ego structure (Spitz, 1957) at this stage. Lastly, we may ask whether it is the progressive patterning of EEG and REM states which is one more indicator of the emergence and structuration of the first organizer of the psyche.

II

As happens so frequently, answering one question makes us aware of more unanswered ones. We concluded that prototype sleep in the neonate represents a transition from physiological sleep to sleeping as a psychophysiological function in the adult. But if REM sleep is an indication of a specific CNS activity in the neonate, then it may well correspond more to the adult's waking mental activity than to adult REM sleep.

What then would be the function of the neonate's NREM sleep in terms of prototypes? Should we assume that it corresponds to Engel's (1962) "conservation-withdrawal" to stress? Our finding that the neonate's response to circumcision consists in a spectacular increase in NREM sleep certainly supports this hypothesis. If so, of what is this the prototype?

Evidently there are quite a number of defense mechanisms of which one might think: denial, repression, withdrawal, regression, etc. One might even consider the neonatal NREM response as a possible prototype for defense *as such.*

However, in our opinion these initial observations are not sufficient for drawing such fundamental theoretical conclusions. Much more research will be needed to establish the further developmental steps which will follow this first one. We will have to observe the subsequent modifications of behavior in the course of the first year before drawing any conclusions.

The same can be said of the problem of the age of the onset of dreaming. Our work does not yet bear on this, inasmuch as we have not yet adequately investigated problems related to memory, object constancy, and mental representation. Furthermore, any useful speculations will require solution of the problems of dream reporting (or of reasonable inferences about dream experiences) during the first two years of life. We may remind the reader here that Freud's daughter dreamed the "strawberry dream" when she was nineteen months old (Freud, 1900).

Recent dream and sleep research (some of which has been noted here) again raises the question from a different direction. Is there any evidence from the physiological study of sleep in general and REM sleep (associated with adult dreaming) in particular that sheds light on the age of onset of dreaming?

We do not know of any studies of infant REM sleep which explore this question. We have already mentioned our EEG work on the ontogenesis of quiet NREM sleep (stages II, III, IV) culminating in the development of spontaneous *K-complexes* at about six months. We would suggest that the development of this CNS information-processing signal is a prerequisite for CNS readiness to support dreaming during sleep. It is known that there is occasional mental content also during NREM sleep. It may be that both kinds of sleep are necessary for dreaming. One possibility is that NREM sleep favors the more formal, secondary process aspects of day-residue processing, while REM sleep subserves the rich, associational, affect-guided psychic activity of dreams as generally understood.

These findings lead us to search carefully for the relation between developing integration of the physiological system and the development of psychic structures of ever-increasing complexity, i.e., ego development. We ask ourselves whether the appearance of *spontaneous* K-complexes can be brought into meaningful statistical relationship with behavior at somewhat more advanced stages of development, when object constancy is achieved (Hartmann, 1952; Spitz and Cobliner, 1965), or insight behavior becomes manifest in problem solving.

Many more problems confront us and the opportunities for research in the field of prototypes are numerous. We will not touch on them in our present report, reserving these problems for our future publications on the subject. But we will end with a brief discussion of the methodology of our research on prototypes. By this time, prototypes have a long history. After Freud, Hartmann (1939) was the first to take up the concept of prototypes as the explanatory principle for some ego defenses. As discussed elsewhere (Spitz, 1961), a number of authors approached the tempting problems of prototypes with very little actual definition of the term prototype. We therefore thought of establishing criteria for identifying a physiological entity as a prototype. Although it is easy to detect similarities in one respect or another between a psychic phenomenon and some physiological process, that does not make it a prototype.

We believe that in our present report we have demonstrated the usefulness of two such criteria, both genetic in character. One is the criterion of convergence of different developmental lines (Anna Freud, 1965). The process of psychological development of any physiological prototype or rather of its component elements, be they behavior, function, EEG, physiology, etc., will inevitably mesh with various other developmental processes, progressively converging to a point where they become coterminous and interact to form what we have called an organizer of the psyche. They are the constituents of the organizer and, at the same time, components of the subsequent changes in the development which arise from it. We believe that in a prototype such a convergence should be demonstrable as a developmental line—a line that leads from the prototype itself to the end result.

Our second criterion is equally genetic. For, to become a credible physiological prototype for a psychic entity emerging much later, the prototype must be the starting point of a developmental line. Accordingly, it can be observationally, mensurationally, and experimentally followed in its development. Decrease of physiological component elements can be quantitatively demonstrated. Their replacement through psychic devices, mechanisms, structures can be observed and the modification of the EEG verifiably be demonstrated.

This is what we have attempted to show in our present report. These are the principles we are applying to the other projects of our research program.

And this is indeed an application of Oppenheimer's recommendation to explore the disanalogies. For analogies can be found everywhere. But the genetically progressing series of disanalogies forms the meaningful coherent link for us, leading from physiological inception to psychological completion.

Accordingly, we would like to conclude by offering a whimsical recommendation for psychoanalytic developmental research: "Take care of the disanalogies; the analogies will take care of themselves!"

BIBLIOGRAPHY

Ambrose, J. A. (1961), The Development of the Smiling Response in Early Infancy. In: *Determinants of Infant Behavior,* ed. B. M. Foss. New York: Wiley, Vol I, pp. 179-201.
Aserinsky, E. & Kleitman, N. (1953), Regularly Occurring Periods of Eye Motility and Concomitant Phenomena During Sleep. *Science,* 118:273-274.
—— —— (1955), A Motility Cycle in Sleeping Infants as Manifested by Ocular and Gross Bodily Activity. *J. Appl. Physiol.,* 8:11-18.
Barlow, J. S. (1964), Evoked Responses in Relation to Visual Perception and Oculomotor Reaction Times in Man. *Ann. N.Y. Acad. Sci.,* 112:432-467.
Berger, H. (1929), Über das Elektroenkephalogramm des Menschen. *Arch. Psychiat. Nervenkr.,* 87:527-570.

Brazelton, T. B. (1962), Crying in Infancy. *Pediatrics*, 29:579-588.
Cobb, W. A. (1963), The Normal Adult EEG. In: *Electroencephalography*, ed. D. Hill & G. Pharr. New York: Macmillan, p. 246.
Dawson, G. D. (1958), The Central Control of Sensory Inflow. *Proc. Roy. Soc. Med.*, 51:531-535.
Dement, W. C. (1955), Dream Recall and Eye Movements During Sleep in Schizophrenics and Normals. *J. Nerv. Ment. Dis.*, 122:263-269.
—— & Kleitman, N. (1957), Cyclic Variations in EEG During Sleep and Their Relation to Eye Movements, Body Motility, and Dreaming. *EEG Clin. Neurophysiol.*, 9:673-690.
Ellingson, R. J. (1967), The Study of Brain Electrical Activity in Infants. In: *Advances in Child Development and Behavior*, ed. L. P. Lipsitt & C. C. Spiker. New York: Academic Press, Vol. 3, pp. 53-97.
Emde, R. N. (1970), Endogenous and Exogenous Smiling in Early Infancy. Read at the American Psychiatric Association, San Francisco, Calif., May 13, 1970.
—— Harmon, R. J., Metcalf, D. R., Koenig, K. L., & Wagonfeld, S. (1970), Stress and Neonatal Sleep. Submitted to *Science*.
—— & Koenig, K. L. (1969a), Neonatal Smiling and Rapid Eye Movement States. *J. Amer. Acad. Child Psychiat.*, 8:57-67.
—— —— (1969b), Neonatal Smiling, Frowning, and Rapid Eye Movement States. *J. Amer. Acad. Child Psychiat.*, 8:637-656.
—— McCartney, R. D., & Harmon, R. J. (1970), Neonatal Smiling in REM States: IV. Premature Study. *Child Develpm.* (in press).
—— & Metcalf, D. R. (1970), An Electroencephalographic Study of Behavioral Rapid Eye Movement States in the Human Newborn. *J. Nerv. Ment. Dis.*, 150:376-386.
Engel, G. L. (1962), Anxiety and Depression-Withdrawal. *Int. J. Psa.*, 43:89-97.
Erikson, E. H. (1950), *Childhood and Society*. New York: Norton.
Fisher, C. (1965), Psychoanalytic Implications of Recent Research on Sleep and Dreaming. *J. Amer. Psa. Assn.*, 13:197-303.
—— Gross, J., & Zuch, F. (1965), A Cycle of Penile Erection Synchronous with Dreaming (REM) Sleep: Preliminary Report. *A.M.A. Arch. Gen. Psychiat.*, 12:29-45.
Freud, A. (1965), *Normality and Pathology in Childhood*. New York: International Universities Press.
Freud, S. (1900), The Interpretation of Dreams. *Standard Edition*, 4 & 5. London: Hogarth Press, 1953.
—— (1901), The Psychopathology of Everyday Life. *Standard Edition*, 6. London: Hogarth Press, 1957.
—— (1905), Three Essays on the Theory of Sexuality. *Standard Edition*, 7:125-243. London: Hogarth Press, 1953.
—— (1925), A Note upon the 'Mystic Writing-Pad.' *Standard Edition*, 19:227-232. London: Hogarth Press, 1961.
Gewirtz, J. L. (1965), The Course of Infant Smiling in Four Child-Rearing Environments in Israel. In: *Determinants of Infant Behavior*, ed. B. M. Foss. New York: Wiley, Vol. III, pp. 205-248.
Harmon, R. J. & Emde, R. N. (1970), Spontaneous REM Behaviors in a Microcephalic Infant (in preparation).
Hartmann, E. (1967), *The Biology of Dreaming*. Springfield: Thomas.
Hartmann, H. (1939), *Ego Psychology and the Problem of Adaptation*. New York: International Universities Press, 1958.
—— (1952), The Mutual Influences in the Development of Ego and Id. *This Annual*, 7:9-30.
Hess, W. R. (1924, 1925), Über die Wechselbeziehungen zwischen psychischen und vegetativen Funktionen. *Schweiz. Arch. Neurol. Psychiat.*, 15:260-277; 16:36-55, 285-306.
Kleitman, N. (1929), Sleep. *Physiol. Rev.*, 9:624-665.

Metcalf, D. R. (1969), Effect of Extrauterine Experience on Ontogenesis of EEG Sleep Spindles. *Psychosom. Med.*, 31:393-399.

—— & Emde, R. N. (1969), Ontogenesis of Sleep in Early Human Infancy. *Psychophysiology*, 6:264.

—— Mondale, J., & Butler, F. K. (1970), Ontogenesis of Spontaneous K. Complexes. *Psychophysiology* (in press).

Oppenheimer, R. (1956), Analogy in Science. *Amer. Psychol.*, 11:127-135.

Oswald, I. (1962), *Sleep and Waking*. New York: Elsevier.

Paradise, J. (1966), Maternal and Other Factors in the Etiology of Infantile Colic. *J.A.M.A.*, 197:191-199.

Polak, P. R., Emde, R. N., & Spitz, R. A. (1964a), The Smiling Response to the Human Face: I. Methodology, Quantification, and Natural History. *J. Nerv. Ment. Dis.*, 139:103-109.

—— —— —— (1964b), The Smiling Response to the Human Face: II. Visual Discrimination and the Onset of Depth Perception. *J. Nerv. Ment. Dis.*, 139:407-415.

Silberer, H. (1912), Symbolik des Erwachens und Schwellensymbolik Überhaupt. *Jb. Psychoanal. & Psychopath. Forsch.*, 3:621-660.

Spitz, R. A. (1951), The Psychogenic Diseases in Infancy. *This Annual*, 6:255-275.

—— (1954), Genèse des premières relations objectales. *Rev. Franç. Psychanal.*, 28:479-575.

—— (1957), *No and Yes*. New York: International Universities Press.

—— (1958), On the Genesis of Superego Components. *This Annual*, 13:375-404.

—— (1959), *A Genetic Field Theory of Ego Formation*. New York: International Universities Press.

—— (1961) Early Prototypes of Ego Defenses. *J. Amer. Psa. Assn.*, 9:626-651.

—— & Cobliner, W. G. (1965), *The First Year of Life*. New York: International Universities Press.

—— & Wolf, K. M. (1946), The Smiling Response. *Genet. Psychol. Monogr.*, 34:57-125.

Stewart, A., Weiland, J., Leider, A., Mangham, C., & Ripley, H. (1953), Excessive Infant Crying in Relation to Parent Behavior. *Amer. J. Psychiat.*, 110:687-694.

Tennes, K., Emde, R. N., Kisley, A. J., & Metcalf, D. R. (1970), The "Stimulus Barrier" in the First Three Months of Life (in preparation).

von Economo, C. (1929), *Die Encephalitis Lethargica*. Berlin & Vienna: Urban & Schwarzenberg.

Wessel, M., Cobb, J., Jackson, E., Harris, S., & Detwiler, A. (1954), Paroxysmal Fussing in Infancy, Sometimes Called Colic. *Pediatrics*, 15:421-434.

THE BASIC CORE

ANNEMARIE P. WEIL, M.D. (New York)

In earlier papers I expressed the opinion that neurotic development and symptomatology are ubiquitous, that they are bound to occur with ego and superego development. I further proposed that the substructure on which neurotic symptomatology is built be evaluated as "normal" and "healthy" or as disordered. While previously I applied this idea primarily to disturbed development, I shall now consider the full range of possible variations in the fundamental substructure, which I now call the *fundamental layer*. This range extends from harmony to imbalance. This paper will attempt to relate these variations to the striking differences found in neonates and young infants.

It is my opinion that the interaction between the infant's equipment and early experiential factors—an interaction that aggravates or attenuates initial tendencies[1]—will lead, after a few weeks, to the emergence of a *basic core of fundamental trends* with which the infant enters the symbiotic phase.[2] It is this basic core which places each infant within the range of variations mentioned above. The characteristic tendencies of this basic core give rise to and intertwine with later psychic development, yet remain more or less evident as a fundamental layer.

The neonate's congenital equipment (genetic heritage plus irreversible paranatal influences) represents a combination of con-

---

From the Child Development Center, New York.

Presented at the First Annual Symposium on Child Development, sponsored by the Women's Medical College; Section of Child Psychiatry (Chairman, S. Kramer); and the Philadelphia Psychoanalytic Society; Philadelphia, June 13, 1970.

[1] This is a thought often stressed by Ernst Kris (see, e.g., Ritvo et al., 1963).

[2] I deliberately do not mention the age at which an infant enters the symbiotic phase because this differs so much in different infants. I believe that with our present knowledge about the varied faculties of the newborn, our ideas concerning the length of the "normal autistic phase" will have to be revised.

genitally given potentials in different spheres of functioning, the functions being related to the autonomous anlage as well as to the ego-id nucleus.[3] The limits in each sphere as well as the fact and ease of modifiability are genetically given. In other words, each child has in each sphere—e.g., intelligence (apparatus) or emotional development (object relatedness)—a certain span of potential developments, with the upper and the lower limits constitutionally given. (Constitutional variations of this span explain why not every child responds in the same way to the same kind of care.)

Sander (1962) has drawn attention to the fact that the earliest interactions between the mother and the neonate lead to an important initial adjustment: the formation of a first "regulatory stability" with regard to such fundamental rhythms as feeding, elimination, sleeping, waking. I believe that this early regulatory stability—or relative lack of stability—is part of the basic core, which already contains directional trends for *all* later functioning.

An infant of a few weeks, in the beginning of the symbiotic phase, already has distinctive characteristics.[4] There are differences with regard to his mood, his need for activity, and his dawning relatedness to the environment, especially the human one. There are the smiling, beaming, "picture book" baby; the serious and thoughtful one; the somber and distressful baby; the apathetic infant; and many others.

At the beginning, and even more so at the height of symbiosis, the specific initial cores—which range from considerable harmony to considerable disharmony—become discernible. The cores consist of recognizable trends and potentials in different spheres. These trends allow us to draw inferences with regard to the dawning ego, such as object relatedness, resilience, anxiety potential, and types of the libido-aggression balance. These trends foreshadow the ego's strengths or weaknesses.

3 I follow Hartmann's proposition (1952) regarding the two parts of the ego. One, the autonomous, nonconflictual part, is represented by the apparatus whose "maturation follows certain laws which are also part of our inheritance. They will gradually come under the control of the ego; on the other hand, they act on the ego and its subsequent phases of development" (p. 18). The other, conflictual, part is conceived as a structure that evolves from the ego-id nucleus. This structure is characterized by the integrative capacity and other budding ego functions, such as the capacity for object relationship, reality testing, and acceptance of the reality principle.

4 "Type of baby" is for me a category of necessary information about a child.

Several factors contribute fundamentally to the later personality. The first is the congenital equipment. After a few weeks of the infant-mother interaction, the basic core will emerge. At that time it is already characterized by a definite degree of stability and harmony, features that will remain as a fundamental layer. Subsequently, the impact of the separation-individuation process will leave an important mark on the developing personality of the child, not only on its structure but also on the content of his mind. With the achievement of object permanence and eventually of object constancy, which implies that the child has a mental representation of the parents and their demands, we find the beginnings of more or less internal conflicts that manifest themselves in simple developmental disturbances (Anna Freud, 1965) or more marked preneurotic disorders. The next decisive factor, intertwined with the others, is the psychosexual development, which gives rise to predominantly internalized conflicts and neurotic disturbances.

It should be emphasized that experiences can alter potentials (within limits), but they cannot create them. There is, however, another aspect that has to be kept in mind: what Bela Mittelmann used to refer to as "Heredity goes on."[5] Genetic factors are decisive not only at conception, but they continue as a kind of developmental blueprint (as twin studies have shown).[6] This genetic blueprint also determines the extent and degree to which each child can withstand later stresses. A child who seems to have overcome early imbalances quite well may nevertheless develop an acute psychosis in adolescence —just as a diabetic condition suddenly becoming manifest at forty is genetically determined at conception.

THE MANIFESTATIONS OF INDIVIDUAL
VARIATIONS IN THE BASIC CORE

The basic core will determine where in the range of potential trends a baby is situated. At one end we have infants who are potentially sturdy and adapt easily; at the other end are infants who

---

[5] Personal communication. See also Hartmann and Kris (1945).

[6] I have seen children in excellent adoptive placement who had severely burdened heredity and initial imbalance, which was attenuated by excellent early care to a subclinical or subliminal schizoid adjustment. Nevertheless, occasionally such a child then broke down in adolescence with more severe and overt pathology.

have a brittle makeup, hypersensitivities, greater anxiety potential, limited resilience, and a lesser degree of object relatedness.

The literature abounds in investigations on individual differences among neonates and young infants, from the neurophysiological to the behavioral-observational points of view (with or without using psychoanalytic conceptualization). Fries was probably the first who applied psychoanalytic knowledge to infant observations and elaborated on their implications. She related the "congenital activity type" to early mother-infant interactions, psychosexual development, potential ego development, the choice of defenses, and potential psychopathology (Fries and Woolf, 1953). Greenacre (1941, 1945) believes that the birth experience of each child acts as an organizer and may determine the degree of narcissism—perhaps adding to a later anxiety potential in some children.

More recent studies have described individual differences in neonates and very young infants: "qualitative and quantitative individual differences in autonomic function apparent within the first days of life" (Richmond and Lustman, 1955, p. 274); "individual differences in central and peripheral nervous system organization and reaction" (Lustman, 1956, p. 93); "congenital differences in reactions to sensory stimuli" (Bergman and Escalona, 1949, p. 340). Korner (1964) stated: "individual differences in the neonate's way of dealing with internal and external stimuli may reflect derivatives of . . . primary endowment factors" (p. 70). Sander (1962) emphasized the importance of the early interactions with the mother and spoke of the resulting "synchronization" and regulatory stability of fundamental functions (sleeping, waking, feeding, elimination) which the mother-child dual unit—to use Mahler's phrase (1968)— is able to achieve. Chess et al. (1959) described "early reaction patterns that are unique and persistent."

Many investigators seem to agree that the interaction between the infant's congenital equipment and his specific early environment leads to behavioral manifestations the intensity and timing of which make for the many variations among infants. I would emphasize, as I have in the past, that it is the *extremeness of manifestations in many spheres* that makes certain infants conspicuous as vulnerable, possibly deviational, especially if their heredity is burdened (Weil,

1953a, 1953b, 1956). There are other infants with less severe deviations who show some weaknesses and unusual sensitivities, which may diminish either spontaneously or as a consequence of an especially helpful environment. How well such an infant enters into and passes through the symbiotic phase will depend largely on how successfully his mother is attuned to his specific needs.

In considering the full range of basic cores in infants—not merely the vulnerable ones at one end—I find myself thinking of aspects of behavior which enable us to draw inferences with regard to the infant's autonomous endowment as well as to his ego-id core. They fall into categories which resemble those I have used to describe deviational children:

General patterning and maturation of physiological functioning as well as tension and anxiety potential;

precursors of ego development—i.e., capacities indicating incipient ego strength or weakness; precursors of object relations; some initial functioning according to the reality principle; beginning trends toward neutralization; resilience to regression—all of which influence the ego-id balance;

and the early libido-aggression balance.

General Patterning and Maturation of Physiological Functioning

All neonate behavior is neurophysiologically determined and at this primitive level of functioning all behaviors are still interrelated to a considerable degree. However, some behavioral manifestations remain in the neurophysiological realm for a longer time and influence psychic structure formation indirectly, while others become more directly part of that structure.

I would now like to describe two types of infants (referred to as A and B). Each illustrates one end of the spectrum of potential basic cores: harmony and imbalance. It is of course understood that many variations exist between these two extremes and that behavioral manifestations are not always so densely clustered. (It is assumed that both infants are full-term, had a good pregnancy and delivery history, and good Apgar scores.)

Infant A is moderately active, with a moderate startle. He sucks well, his states are distinct, and he cries little. He has a good capacity for discrete communication (Wolff, 1959) so that his "ordinary devoted" mother can easily respond to his needs—she can soothe him with feeding, holding, or stimulation. Hence, a "regulatory synchrony" (Sander, 1962) is soon established. There are increasing periods of alert inactivity (Wolff, 1959) with visual pursuit movements directed toward external stimuli. Good interaction ensues: he roots well, sucks well, scans, and focuses on his mother's face. Soon there will be eye-to-eye contact between them, adding to the mother's delight. In other words, good functioning and interaction are associated with the development of the autonomous ego apparatus (increasing perception and memory) as well as the ego-id core. All this will soon lead to some initial introjection and then to dawning awareness.

Although such a baby seems almost a little too "average expectable," he still has innumerable, individually quite specific possibilities for later structuring and dynamic development. This development will be determined by many other genetic factors—such as instinctual endowments and growth rates, which intermesh with the infant's experiences and his parents' expectations—to make him the unique, colorful individual he will become, with his own particular inner conflict solutions or neurotic disturbances.

At the other end of the continuum of different basic cores—from harmonious and well-balanced to less harmonious and imbalanced—is type B. (Two examples of this type will be given, both of which show extremes and unevennesses in their functioning and their maturational processes.) B[1] might be a child with a very low threshold, who is extremely hyperactive—a tense hyperreactor with a self-perpetuating startle. He becomes upset in reaction to minor stimuli and awakens easily. His states are indistinct or few; for example, he might just sleep or else go into excited crying spells (like the case published by Brazelton, 1962). Hence, there is not much alert inactivity—that most important state which enables the infant to become acquainted with the outside world. There is poor capacity for discrete communication; he is hard to console; and it is difficult to help him regain homeostatic equilibrium. He shows irregular patterns of sucking, feeding, and sleeping, in addition to a great deal of distress. He is confusing to his mother, even if she is experienced in child care. As a result, there is an unusually prolonged period of asynchrony.

B^2 on the other hand is an underreactor, with a very high threshold: he is hypoactive, sleeps most of the time, and communicates poorly—not even communicating his needs. He might prefer not to be handled at all and be happiest when he is left alone.

Such behavioral manifestations are related to neurophysiological immaturity. However, they often persist for an unusually long period as part of the uneven maturational patterning. *The differences in the timing of maturation and in the intensity of manifestations make for the differences in the functioning of these infants; and extreme manifestations in too many spheres make for pathology.* Bender (1942, 1947) was the first to describe the unevenness of patterning in the very disturbed, schizophrenic children. Such infants with burdened heredity, who later developed into psychotic children, were observed from birth by Fish (1957). Bergman and Escalona (1949), Brazelton (1962), and others have also described such pathological development from infancy on; and I have described the milder forms in this range of deviation (1956).

How such infants, whether of the A type (the moderate, apparently healthier one) or of the B type (the extremes, of which two examples are described), continue to develop depends on genetic as well as experiential factors.

Let us consider a baby of type B in early interaction with his mother. Such poor starters, interacting with an unempathic mother in a continuous negative feedback, may have a poor chance for good adaptation and therefore develop a more or less severe ego deficiency. In fact, for many such infants even an "ordinary devoted" mother is not enough.

Some of these children, however, may be more fortunate. Certain poor starters—perhaps not the most extreme cases—reach a certain degree of harmony and balance, although they may do so at a somewhat later than usual time. This can happen if their genetic endowment includes modifiability (and/or later modification of the basic core), and if they have extremely devoted mothers who are especially gifted for appropriate cueing. It seems to me that some of these infants, upon being rescued from, or growing out of, perpetual stress and threat of disorganization, constitute a group of especially alert, sensitive, discriminatory, perceptive, and gifted children. It was

Bergman and Escalona (1949) who drew attention to the fact that unusual sensitivities may be the forerunner of psychosis and severe failure of ego development in some children, while in others the same handicaps, under adequate maternal protection—substitution for the deficient protective barrier—may become unusual advantages. More recently (1966) Easton expressed similar thoughts, describing a case that seemed to take this fortunate line of development. Much also depends on other factors that foreshadow ego strength, especially those related to the primary object.

I shall now take up some of the specific behavioral manifestations of the neurophysiological variations I have described and indicate *what inferences can be drawn* from them *with regard to future ego development.*

Excitability implies an imbalance between the protective barrier and the infant's capacity to deal with and integrate stimuli. The resulting stress reactions carry with them a greater tendency to disorganization and regression, as Leitch and Escalona (1949) have described in detail. Perceptual hypersensitivity, with accompanying stress and tension, may also foreshadow a later anxiety readiness (anxious expectation of the new, for example, or a noise hypersensitivity that may become fear of noise). Richmond et al. (1962), in their differentiations of newborns on the basis of physiological behavior, suggest the possibility that "heightened and abrupt reactivity endows the individual with an alarm system, which rapidly and easily signals danger, whether symbolic or real" (p. 90).

Hyperactivity and hypoactivity are related to both drive endowment and possible ways of future pathways of discharge. If we follow Escalona's expansion of Fries's concept of "activity type" into the concept of "zest, availability of energy, and resilience to stress," we can draw inferences with regard to future ego strength, especially since Escalona and Heider (1959) found this to be a continuing characteristic that can be successfully predicted.

Indistinctness of state not only will impede the interaction with the mother and the achievement of synchrony, but it may also act as an impediment to the infant himself, as Korner (1964) has pointed out, by limiting his capacity to anticipate and possibly also his capacity to discriminate between inner and outer stimuli. Similarly, state-boundness (Korner, 1964)—the overly strong influence of inner stimuli—will diminish the frequency and the degree of alert inactivity, i.e., the periods during which the infant is accessible to the object world, both animate and inanimate. State-boundness will delay reality testing and the infant's relating to objects; it may thus influence the intensity of his emotional attachments. Moreover, overwhelming strength of need tension such as hunger may impede the capacity to delay and, hence, the development of the reality principle.

To summarize: perceptual sensitivity and responsivity; activity or energy type; different constellations of state with their differing effect on organization; degree of alert inactivity—all these are important facets of the neurophysiologically and experientially determined basic core. When these characteristics mature at appropriate times and manifest themselves in proper intensity, development will be facilitated. In contrast, when they are out of kilter, they will lead to various degrees of further imbalance.

It follows that the fortunate infant—the one with a moderate threshold and a better initial capacity to integrate stimuli; who is resilient to regressive disorganization; less under the pressure of instinctual needs; in whom there is better balance between ego and id —such an infant would be better able to assimilate outside stimuli at an earlier time. He would be better able to exercise his ego apparatus, to perceive, remember, discriminate, test reality, as well as to anticipate and delay, and hence move toward the reality principle.

More Direct Precursors of Ego Development

Above all, as a result of his greater ease in absorbing outside stimuli, the infant's object directedness is freer to unfold and to become associated with the developing awareness of the human object. It should be stressed, however, that such freedom from inner stimuli fosters, but does not necessarily lead to, object directedness. In the sphere of object directedness, facets of behavior pass from reflexive, neurophysiological reactions to psychological ones in an almost sequential continuum.

Object-directed behaviors have from the very beginning a considerable psychological impact on the mother. Rooting, molding, scanning are followed by gaze fixation, eye-to-eye contact, and then by smiling,[7] although there is not always a predictable continuum between them. Not every well-rooting baby, for example, will be a good smiler. However, one often feels that both rooting and smiling are part of a good neurophysiological endowment, which permits sufficient energies to be directed outside (unlike the situation in the hypoactive child who neither roots much, nor communicates much, nor smiles much).

The directing of energies to the outside and the welcoming of new stimuli, animate and inanimate, precede the specific reaction to the human partner. Many investigators (e.g., Meili, 1957; Chess et al., 1959; Bayley, 1937) believe that neonates and young infants already show a definite ease, or lack of ease, in assimilating new stimuli, and that this greater or lesser capacity to assimilate stimuli continues in later, more or less positive reactions to the unfamiliar human being. This original response is very different in different infants. Again, the degree of outward-directedness has a direct bearing on the basic core.

In addition to the earliest interaction with the mother, there are also important intersystemic interactions that foster or delay the development of object directedness. A good capacity for discrete communication; a greater amount of alert inactivity, attention cathexis, and more intense focusing; stimulus need as well as early developing memory for experienced need satisfaction—all these may foster the development of a dawning awareness of (and reaction to) the mother. (The early development of these faculties and the degree to which they are developed make for qualitative differences.) Hence, the ego apparatus will influence the precursory ego function—the relation to the object; just as an early reflexive smile may facilitate, if only in physical patterning, a later smile (Korner and Grobstein, 1967).

Most important for the infant's development is the interaction with the mother who, if she is an "ordinary devoted" mother, responds to, or even helps, the neurophysiological forerunners of object directedness—such as the ease in being held, contact comfort by her finding the best form of soothability, e.g., talking, looking, or holding. The infant's capacity for communication facilitates the

[7] That genetic neurophysiological factors are important for these reactions is borne out by the concordance of eye fixation and smiling in identical twins, even if they are of different birth weight (Freedman, 1963).

mother's cueing and *her* reaching a state of confidence. She responds
to the scanning of her face. She will enjoy even more the delightful
eye-to-eye contact with her child (all the more so when it becomes
discriminate) and the even more delightful smile, followed by cooing, anticipatory excitement, especially as that too becomes increasingly discriminate and focused on her. A mood of mutual delight
becomes established, and the infant starts to express the desire to
make this "especially interesting and gratifying spectacle last," to
paraphrase Escalona (1968). If he is left alone and awake for any
length of time, he complains. On the other hand, his capacity to
wait for need satisfaction increases as soon as the mother is in view—
that is, a confident expectation develops on *his* part and with it the
capacity for anticipation and delay.

The above describes an infant at one end of the spectrum of
object-directed behaviors. At the other end of the spectrum is the
infant who shows various deviations or distortions in the timing and
intensity of behavioral traits, in a degree sufficient to impede object
directedness. These might be manifested by reactions such as hypersensitivity; a poor capacity for communication; lasting unpredicta-
bility of states; negative reaction to new stimuli; and even the complete gaze aversion and nonsmiling of the future autistic child. As
always, between the two extremes there are many variations and
shadings.

The earliest interaction between mother and infant determines
whether initial tendencies will spiral more toward the extreme or
will instead become modified and modulated. A mother's handling
may draw out her withdrawn infant a bit more, or she may capitalize
on his lesser need and thus allow him to become even more withdrawn, within the limits of his given genetic endowment.[8]

Wolff (1961) expressed his conviction that eye-to-eye contact is as
important in the development of social interchange as it seems to be
for all adult communication. In an interesting study, Robson (1967)
investigated the establishment of eye-to-eye contact between mother

---

[8] However, a mother who is not empathic may also overrespond to the early smiler
and keep him overstimulated, to the point of transitory disorganization. Escalona
(1963) has drawn our attention to the fact that identical maternal behavior may be
experienced completely differently by different infants and have completely different
effects on them, depending on their temperamental makeup. A great deal also depends
on the mother's ability to distinguish between needs and desires.

and infant. He conjectures that if this face-tie is not established, or if its quality is such as to foster disruption and distress, the infant will experience varying degrees of interference in forming his earliest, and probably also his future, human relationships. Enduring deviations in eye-to-eye contact, he believes, will go along with disturbances in emotional attachment.

Eye-to-eye contact is followed within days by the smile—so well known, investigated, and discussed as the first "organizer" (Spitz, 1965) and the forerunner of ego development. With this first organizer, the "dialogue" (Spitz, 1953) between infant and mother takes on more definite shape, and gradually the infant also introjects the mother's moods. If further development proceeds smoothly, the symbiotic phase will be characterized by an increasing richness of communication.

There are many quantitative and qualitative variations in the infant's type of emotional response. I was quite struck by the fact that an infant I observed, who could already smile, did not smile back at the mother's smiling face, but consistently stared at the mother's print dress with which he was quite familiar. In other words, he preferred to exercise an ego apparatus (perception) rather than a dawning ego function (object relatedness). I am of course not surprised when another infant immediately responds with eye contact and a smile to a really warm and devoted mother. But I was somewhat surprised to see a smile appear equally fast in an infant who had a well-cueing but only intermittently devoted mother. Smiling seems to be an especially good indicator of how *some infants can make the most out of the least, while others need the most to arrive at very little.* The ability to break down maternal neglect (Dennis, 1938) or to accept it and the degree of resilience to neglect seem to be other genetically determined characteristics.

Usually, smiling and cooing soon become associated with the gleeful joy that is so typical of an emotionally well-endowed and well-cared-for infant in the early part of the symbiotic phase. Although this core of social responsiveness, as well as of mood, seems to indicate a potential for a good future object relatedness, and although some investigators do find continuity between these factors, not all investigators are in agreement about this (e.g., Escalona and

Heider, 1959). I believe that the discrepancies in the degree of continuity which appear in follow-up studies are due to the subsequent important influence of the separation-individuation process. True, the reactions of the first few weeks do show trends with regard to object directedness; these trends, however, may be modified by ensuing interactions, especially during the separation-individuation phase, as Mahler (1968) pointed out. Unsuccessful individuation; mood disturbances; developmental disturbances, later on compounded by distortions in the psychosexual development may thwart such basic trends considerably, just as the genetically predetermined maturational shifts may alter apparent potentials.

In which way do behavioral manifestations allow us to draw *inferences with regard to the precursors of ego development and the ego's relative strength or weakness?*

We all wonder at what point physiological reactions become psychological. Wolff (1965b) connects the shift from the physiological to the psychological with the infant's increasing capacity for alertness to and expanding interest in environmental events. Spitz (1965) is convinced that "the transition from the somatic into the psychological is uninterrupted and that therefore the protoypes of psychic ego nuclei are to be found in physiological functions and somatic behavior" (p. 104f.).

Among the trends that allow us to draw inferences, those having to do with the ego-id balances are especially important, as Alpert, Neubauer, and myself (1956) have pointed out.[9] This balance depends on the threshold for inner drive tension and the maturational rate of its shift. In an infant who is too much and too long at the mercy of his instinctual needs, the development of dawning ego functions and the evolving ego structure are likely to proceed more slowly. If instinctual needs are overwhelming, then the use of the ego apparatus may be slowed down, and with it the capacity to delay, the development of confident expectation, the first "stage of object relationship" (Benedek, 1938), and the acceptance of the reality principle.

There are also individual variations in the balance between instinctual need and the need to function. An adequately heighten-

---

[9] Korner and Grobstein (1967) call it "the different distribution in ego and id endowment" (p. 685).

ing threshold for inner and outer stimuli fosters a dawning capacity for concentration. As always, of course, this is in relation to adequate environmental stimulation. Provence and Lipton (1962), among others, not only documented the effect of understimulation but also that of excessive stimulation. They describe infants in whom overstimulation led to severe sleeping disturbances early in life.[10]

Wolff (1965a) states that the neonate's capacity for attention cathexis is derived from neutral energy "bound within the apparatus" (p. 824). This is in accordance with Freud's assumption (1923) of an original "neutral" energy and Hartmann's (1955) "noninstinctual" energy reservoir. Wolff implies that this original energy becomes neutralized energy only at a later stage of development—a proposition with which I agree. Can we assume, then, that the young infant's capacity for concentration, the intensity of his attention cathexis, permits us to draw inferences with regard to his future potential capacity for neutralization? The assumption that this capacity for concentration may be a forerunner of the capacity for neutralization is supported by the findings of Escalona and Heider (1959). They concluded that an infant's attention span—his capacity for concentration (i.e., the intensity of his response and the absence of distractibility)—is an enduring characteristic that can reliably be predicted. We see in infants different tendencies to persist—for example, in their efforts to repeat and practice their chance vocalizations or to practice and observe their experimental finger movements.

Activity needs, if adequate, will further catalyze attention cathexis: if they are overly strong, they will interfere with attention cathexis; yet they must be strong enough to allow for the necessary tension discharge.

On the basis of my foregoing considerations I would postulate the existence of a rudimentary, precursory, organizing function that regulates the balance between threshold and tension discharge, thereby permitting a harmonious absorption and integration of stimuli. Spitz (1965) states that "an integrative tendency . . . leads from the organic, that is, from embryology, into psychology and into

---

[10] See also Coleman and Provence (1957) and Ritvo et al. (1963).

the developmental sphere" (p. 104). Sander (1962) also feels that "integration is the essence of organization from the beginning" (p. 24), and he suggests that the early potential for synchronization can be correlated with, or may be the forerunner of, the integrative function.

It is my opinion that an incipient integrative, regulatory function is already involved in synchronization as well as in the successful assimilation of stimuli (the balancing of input of stimuli and tension discharge). I would, furthermore, assume that this integrative function greatly influences the degree to which the basic core is harmonious. The harmoniousness of the basic core also depends on the degree to which the mother has been attuned to the special needs of her infant.

Another dawning ego characteristic is emotional expressiveness, which may already be considerable in an infant at the beginning of the symbiotic phase. With this, the prevalence of pleasure may become obvious—pleasure in instinctual need satisfaction, pleasure in human contact, and pleasure in functioning (Bühler, 1930).

The Balance between Libido and Aggression

In our earlier paper on "Variation in Drive Endowment" (1956), we indicated that the original strength of the aggressive drive does not itself determine the nature of later traits. The balance also depends on channelization, the degree and kind of externalization, and the further contribution of individuation and psychosexual conflicts. Mahler (1970) expressed related thoughts concerning the importance of the libidinal valence.

It is my opinion that an infant, at the beginning of the symbiotic phase, already shows signs of his particular style of channelization of the aggressive drive (fused with the libidinal drive). He shows this in his "energy reservoir," in his vigor and forcefulness in general (for example, in his sucking), in the investment of his attentive behavior, in the use of his ego apparatus, in the level of his need to function, and in the intensity of his pleasure. This capacity to invest and persist—which is of course linked once again with neutralization —helps in the consolidation of ego nuclei. Greenacre (1960) has drawn attention to the fact that through moving his hands and looking at them, the infant establishes a first rudimentary awareness of the sense of self. Hoffer (1949, 1950) has expressed similar thoughts about the distinction between self and not-self in the somewhat older baby.

The degree of admixture of the aggressive drive also becomes apparent in the vigor and forcefulness with which the infant expresses his delight in human contact, or his preferences and dislikes, or his moods. As the inner systems mature, the threshold for proprioceptive stimuli is heightened and the infant becomes increasingly aware of the mother, the pleasure-unpleasure balance[11] usually shifts in favor of pleasure, unless the infant experienced early and persistent distress.[12] In addition to the libido-aggression balance, there is a balance within the aggressive drive, namely, between vigor and assertiveness on the one hand and negative moods on the other. As was the case in other areas, in this sphere of drive balances we will again encounter variations of potential trends that are typical for each child.

SUMMARY

Neonates differ from one another from the very beginning. This is due to variations in their equipment.

Each child is born with a unique physiological equipment, which, in each sphere, allows for a certain span of further development—within constitutionally given limits. The ease of modifiability is also constitutionally given.

The early interaction between the infant's equipment and the mother's attunement results in a basic core, which may range from greater harmony and potential for ego structuring and ego strength to considerable imbalance and vulnerability. The infant begins the symbiotic phase with this basic core, in which the mother's caretaking has already attenuated or aggravated the original trends.

An aggregate of behavioral trends constitutes this varying basic core in different children. These trends can be inferred from the infant's observable behavioral manifestations. They relate to

[11] Spitz (1953) said: "At this point (i.e., after about two months of life) we can begin to distinguish manifestations of pleasure in the child from manifestations of unpleasure, and frequently of rage. Phenomenologically we can speak of observable manifestations of the libidinal drive on the one hand, and of the aggressive drive on the other" (p. 128).

[12] My belief is (and Greenacre concurs with this) that early persistent distress may, in addition to the anxiety potentials described by her, foster an aggression potential. With the longer persistence of primary narcissism, both fusion and neutralization of the aggressive drive become impeded.

early physiological and maturational patterning, sensitivity, and responsivity, including a potential for anxiety; precursors of ego development, earliest directedness to the human object, a potential for neutralization, a beginning integrative function, an incipient ego-id balance; and the libido-aggression balance.

Characteristics of the basic core will persist, clinically recognizable as a fundamental layer, although the separation-individuation process and the psychosexual development will intertwine with this basic core in manifold ways and add significant structural and contextural imprints.

The basic core will partially determine individual nuances of the character of healthier persons or the symptomatology of our patients. It is such different nuances in pathology that have sometimes veiled the clinical picture in the greater variety of patients we now see. Considering this basic core, or fundamental layer, in the evaluation of our patients may help to unravel the intertwined development and to clarify some of the often rather diffuse diagnostic aspects—just as understanding and helping parents to understand this basic core may safeguard them from potentially damaging interactions between themselves and their child.

BIBLIOGRAPHY

Alpert, A., Neubauer, P. B., & Weil, A. P. (1956), Unusual Variations in Drive Endowment. *This Annual*, 11:125-163.
Bayley, N. (1937), Environmental Correlation of Mental and Motor Development. *Child Develpm.*, 8:329-341.
Bender, L. (1942), Childhood Schizophrenia. *Nerv. Child*, 1:138-140.
—— (1947), Childhood Schizophrenia: Clinical Study of One Hundred Schizophrenic Children. *Amer. J. Orthopsychiat.*, 17:40-56.
Benedek, T. (1938), Adaptation to Reality in Early Infancy. *Psychiat. Quart.*, 7:200-215.
Bergman, P. & Escalona, S. K. (1949), Unusual Sensitivities in Very Young Children. *This Annual*, 3/4:333-352.
Brazelton, T. B. (1962), Observations of the Neonate. *J. Amer. Acad. Child Psychiat.*, 1:38-58.
Bridger, W. H. (1962), Sensory Discrimination and Autonomic Function. *J. Amer. Acad. Child Psychiat.*, 1:67-82.
Bühler, C. (1930), *The First Year of Life*. New York: John Day.
Chess, S., Thomas, A., & Birch, H. G. (1959), Characteristics of the Individual Child's Behavioral Responses to the Environment. *Amer. J. Orthopsychiat.*, 29:791-802.
—— —— —— & Hertzig, M. (1960), Implications of a Longitudinal Study of Child Development of Child Psychiatry. *Amer. J. Psychiat.*, 117:434-441.
Coleman, R. W. & Provence, S. (1957), Environmental Retardation (Hospitalism) in Infants Living in Families. *Pediatrics*, 19:285-292.

Dennis, W. (1938), Infant Development Under Conditions of Restricted Practice and of Minimum Social Stimulation: A Preliminary Report. *J. Genet. Psychol.*, 53:149-158.

—— & Dennis, M. G. (1940), The Effect of Cradling Practices Upon the Onset of Walking in Hopi Children. *J. Genet. Psychol.*, 56:77-80.

Easton, K. (1966) Neonatal Behavior, Mother-Baby Interactions, and Personality Development. *N.Y. State J. Med.*, 66:1874-1882.

Escalona, S. K., (1963), Patterns of Infantile Experience and the Developmental Process. *This Annual*, 18:197-244.

—— (1968), *The Roots of Individuality*. Chicago: Aldine Publishing Co.

—— & Heider, G. (1959), *Prediction and Outcome*. New York: Basic Books.

Fish, B. (1957), The Detection of Schizophrenia in Infancy: A Preliminary Report. *J. Nerv. & Ment. Dis.*, 125:1-24.

Freedman, D. (1963), Hereditary Control of Early Social Behavior. In: *Determinants of Infant Behavior III*, ed. B. M. Foss. London: Methuen; New York: John Wiley, pp. 149-159.

Freud, A. (1965), *Normality and Pathology in Childhood*. New York: International Universities Press.

Freud, S. (1923), The Ego and the Id. *Standard Edition*, 19:3-66. London: Hogarth Press, 1961.

Fries, M. E. & Woolf, P. J. (1953), Some Hypotheses on the Role of the Congenital Activity Type in Personality Development. *This Annual*, 8:48-62.

Geleerd, E. R. (1960), Borderline States in Childhood and Adolescence. In: *Recent Developments in Psychoanalytic Child Therapy*, ed. J. Weinreb. New York: International Universities Press, pp. 154-171.

Greenacre, P. (1941), The Predisposition to Anxiety, Parts 1 & 2. *Trauma, Growth, and Personality*. New York: International Universities Press, 1969, pp. 27-82.

—— (1945), The Biological Economy of Birth. *This Annual*, 1:31-51.

—— (1960), Considerations Regarding the Parent-Infant Relationship. *Int. J. Psa.*, 41:571-595.

Hartmann, H. (1938), *Ego Psychology and the Problem of Adaptation*. New York: International Universities Press, 1958.

—— (1952), The Mutual Influences in the Development of Ego and Id. *This Annual*, 7:9-30.

—— (1955), Notes on the Theory of Sublimation. *This Annual*, 10:9-29.

—— & Kris, E. (1945), The Genetic Approach in Psychoanalysis. *This Annual*, 1:11-30.

Hoffer, W. (1949), Mouth, Hand and Ego-Integration. *This Annual*, 3/4:49-56.

—— (1950), Development of the Body Ego. *This Annual*, 5:18-24.

Korner, A. F. (1964), Some Hypotheses Regarding the Significance of Individual Differences at Birth for Later Development. *This Annual*, 19:58-72.

—— & Grobstein, R. (1967), Individual Differences at Birth. *J. Amer. Acad. Child Psychiat.*, 6:676-690.

Kris, M. (1957), The Use of Prediction in a Longitudinal Study. *This Annual*, 12:175-189.

Leitch, M. & Escalona, S. K. (1949), The Reaction of Infants to Stress. *This Annual*, 3/4:121-140.

Lustman, S. L. (1956), Rudiments of the Ego. *This Annual*, 11:89-98.

Mahler, M. S. (1963), Thoughts about Development and Individuation. *This Annual*, 18:307-324.

—— (1968) (in collaboration with M. Furer), *On Human Symbiosis and the Vicissitudes of Individuation*. New York: International Universities Press.

—— (1970), Study of the Separation-Individuation Process and Its Possible Application to Borderline Phenomena in the Psychoanalytic Situation. Freud Anniversary Lecture, New York Academy of Medicine.

Meili, R. (1957), *Anfänge der Charakter Entwicklung: Beiträge zur genetischen Charakterologie, I.* Bern: Hans Huber.

Provence, S. & Lipton, R. [Coleman] (1962), *Infants in Institutions.* New York: International Universities Press.

Richmond, J. B. & Lustman, S. L. (1955), Automatic Function in the Neonate. *Psychosom. Med.*, 17:269-275.

—— Lipton, E. L., & Steinschneider, A. (1962), Observations on Differences in Autonomic Nervous System Function between and within Individuals during Early Infancy. *J. Amer. Acad. Child Psychiat.*, 1:83-91.

Ritvo, S., McCollum, A. T., Omwake, E., Provence, S. A., & Solnit, A. J. (1963), Some Relations of Constitution, Environment, and Personality as Observed in a Longitudinal Study of Child Development: Case Report. In: *Modern Perspectives in Child Development*, ed. A. J. Solnit & S. A. Provence. New York: International Universities Press, pp. 107-143.

Robson, K. S. (1967), The Role of Eye-to-Eye Contact in Maternal-Infant Attachment. *J. Child Psychol. & Psychiat.*, 8:13-25.

Sander, L. W. (1962), Issues in Early Mother-Child Interaction. *J. Amer. Acad. Child Psychiat.*, 1:141-166.

—— Burns, P., Julia, H., & Stechler, G. (1968), Some Changing Research Questions in a Study of Early Mother-Infant Interaction: Part I (unpublished paper).

—— Stechler, G., Burns, P., & Julia, H. (1970), Early Mother-Infant Interaction and 24-Hour Patterns of Activity and Sleep. *J. Amer. Acad. Child Psychiat.*, 9:103-123.

Schaffer, H. R. & Emerson, P. E. (1964a), Patterns of Response to Physical Contact in Early Human Development. *J. Child Psychol. & Psychiat.*, 5:1-13.

—— (1964b), The Development of Social Attachments in Infancy. *Monographs of the Society for Research in Child Development.* Vol. 29, Serial No. 94, 3, pp. 5-77.

Spitz, R. A. (1953), Aggression: Its Role in the Establishment of Object Relations. In: *Drives, Affects, Behavior*, ed. R. M. Loewenstein. New York: International Universities Press, pp. 126-138.

—— (1963), Life and the Dialogue. In: *Counterpoint: Libidinal Object and Subject*, ed. H. S. Gaskill. New York: International Universities Press, pp. 154-176.

—— (1965) (in collaboration with W. G. Cobliner), *The First Year of Life.* New York: International Universities Press.

Weil, A. P. (1953a) Certain Severe Disturbances of Ego Development in Childhood. *This Annual*, 8:271-287.

—— (1953b), Clinical Data and Dynamic Considerations in Certain Cases of Childhood Schizophrenia. *Amer. J. Orthopsychiat.*, 23:518-529.

—— (1956), Some Evidences of Deviational Development in Infancy and Early Childhood. *This Annual*, 8:271-287.

—— (1960), Discussion of Geleerd, E. R.: Borderline States in Childhood and Adolescence. In: *Recent Developments in Psychoanalytic Child Therapy*, ed. J. Weinreb. New York: International Universities Press, pp. 171-174.

Wolff, P. H. (1959), Observations of Newborn Infants. *Psychosom. Med.*, 21:110-118.

—— (1961), Observations on the Early Development of Smiling. In: *Determinants of Infant Behavior II*, ed. B. M. Foss. London: Methuen; New York: John Wiley, 1963, pp. 113-138.

—— (1965a), The Development of Attention in Young Infants. *Ann. N.Y. Acad. Sci.*, 118:815-830.

—— (1965b), The Natural History of Crying and Other Vocalizations in Early Infancy. In: *Determinants of Infant Behavior IV*, ed. B. M. Foss. London: Methuen; New York: John Wiley, pp. 81-109.

—— & White, B. L. (1965), Visual Pursuit and Attention in Young Infants. *J. Amer. Acad. Child Psychiat.*, 4:473-484.

VULNERABLE PERIODS IN THE EARLY
DEVELOPMENT OF BLIND CHILDREN

DORIS M. WILLS (London)

This paper, which describes three periods of particular vulnerability in blind children, owes much to Fraiberg's recent report on
blind infants (1968). The first period in particular, before the blind
child can grasp on a sound cue, is one that she described very
graphically; here it is discussed further and some additional observations are cited.[1] In the course of learning to understand the
dangers inherent in the development of children who have a specific
sensory handicap which slows down and changes certain processes,
we may even hope to gain insights which could at some later date
be applied to children with unknown, unspecified sensory handicaps
such as those which may be linked with autism and brain damage.

Perhaps we should first remind ourselves of the part that sight
plays during the very early years of the ordinary child's life. From
the very beginning it has of course a vital role in the mother-child
relationship, both in maintaining contact between them and in
facilitating interaction. Even at four weeks the child is beginning to
watch the mother's nearby face when she feeds or talks to him
(Sheridan, 1960). Gough (1962) has further illustrated this by recording on film the immediate lifting of the child's eyes to the mother's
face as she regards him during the early weeks of breast and bottle

The work with blind children is part of the Educational Unit of the Hampstead
Child Therapy Course and Clinic and as such is maintained by the Grant Foundation,
Inc., New York. The research work with the blind is assisted further by the National
Institute of Mental Health, Bethesda, Maryland.

I am very grateful to Dorothy Burlingham, H. Kennedy, and A.-M. Sandler for
helpful suggestions and would like to thank C. Legg and other members of the
Research Group on Blind Children at the Hampstead Clinic for making their records
available.

[1] This paper was originally drafted for a weekend Conference on Handicapped
Children of the Royal Medico-Psychological Association in September, 1968. Hence
the selection of special periods and hence the framework of the argument.

461

feeding. By six weeks or so the child smiles in response to the sight of the mother's face (the blind child smiles about the same time, but more fleetingly, in response to her voice or touch [D. G. Freedman, 1964; Fraiberg and D. A. Freedman, 1964]), and by six months he is described as "visually insatiable" and able to follow the adult's movements across the room.

Sight also plays a major role in attracting the child away from preoccupation with his own body to interest in the world around; even at one month he will notice a dangling toy at four to six inches range and follow its movement briefly. By three months he is watching his own hands in front of his face and begins mutual fingering, which will run alongside, and lead on to, the use of the hands for other purposes, e.g., touching the mother, playing with toys, and so on.

Throughout the early years, sight continues to further the mother-child relationship. The child can keep visual contact with his mother even when she is not attending to him; he watches her face for changes in mood toward him; in addition, he can interact with her in a way meaningful to both, and thus one which directly fosters the development of this relationship.

As to the inanimate world, exploration involving gross movement is from the beginning well motivated by the visual attractiveness of the people and things he sees around him; and the acquisition of skills in building, ball play, and so on is easy for him and also visually satisfying.

The impact of blindness on a child's development is probably most serious at this early stage of his life, when, on the libidinal side, he has to establish the cathexis of his objects, and, on the ego side, he has to organize his experience. In spite of their serious handicap a number of blind children do develop satisfactorily. However, there is an unduly large proportion of deviant blind children with no other demonstrable damage who cannot be educated, and there are histories of curious breakdowns in the course of some children's development which also make them ineducable. Moreover, there are a number of blind children who arrive at school with personality distortions, ranging from a plethora of autoerotic habits, parroting, and poor orientation, to excessive anxiety and withdrawal, problems which generally disappear more or less as they grow older.

Two reasons are usually adduced for these: the possibility of additional brain damage of a kind which cannot be pinpointed, and the assumption that the parents have failed to stimulate the child in the early years of his development.

The possibility of additional brain damage is a matter for the medical profession, but the second reason appears to merit further attention here. Is it in fact the case that these considerable problems arise merely because the parents overprotect and understimulate the blind child? No doubt in some cases this plays a part, but observation suggests that the blind child has to surmount many difficulties in the course of his early development that do not confront the sighted child; that he is, during this period, extremely vulnerable; and that most mothers need ongoing help and support if they are to cope successfully with the task of bringing him up.

It is to three of these vulnerable phases in early childhood that attention will be drawn in this paper.

1. The first is the long period before the blind child reaches for and locates a toy on a sound cue alone, and its implications.[2] This is chosen for two reasons—because such reaching is the outward and visible sign of the blind child's having become aware that objects in the noncontiguous world have substantiality; and because it shows a move away from interest in the child's own body and the things in immediate contact with it, and in his mother's body, to interest in the world around, a move we take largely for granted in the sighted child. Observation of the blind child makes us more aware of the degree to which these developments are mediated by vision and motility. As Gesell (1941, p. 259) puts it, the blind child's "major developmental problem is to achieve some degree of extroversion."

2. The second phase is the long period when the blind infant remains tied to the familiar and to routine even when mothering is optimal; this goes with a tendency to revert to earlier modes of functioning and persistently to cling to these in response to upsetting experiences, especially to disturbances in the parent-child relationship.

[2] This topic is ably described by Fraiberg not only in her 1968 paper but also in an earlier paper (Fraiberg, Siegel, and Gibson, 1966). It is perhaps of interest that research topics crystallize in different places at the same time, as we at Hampstead have also been studying the blind child's ability to reach and locate on a sound cue since the early 1960's.

3. The third phase is the period when the young child is acquiring an inner representation of the object and object constancy, leading on to some fusion, some compromise, between aggressive and libidinal feelings, and their expression to the object. In more general terms, this is the period when the fate of the blind child's aggressive impulses in relation to the object is being decided.

THE PERIOD BEFORE THE BLIND INFANT REACHES FOR A TOY ON SOUND CUE ALONE

There has been a tendency to assume that the early development of the blind child proceeds much like that of the sighted, and, while this has had a positive effect in that the people around the blind child have provided him with normal opportunities, it begs some important questions: How does this modify his development in general? How does he circumvent this major sensory handicap; and, in this instance, how does it modify his ability to widen his interest from his mother to the world around?

In fact, from the moment the blind infant begins to grasp, his developing interest in the world around must start on its somewhat different course, since hearing cannot further his grasping in the way that sight can (A.-M. Sandler, 1963). By the age of five months the sighted child can locate and grasp on a *visual* cue; the blind child needs much longer before he can locate and grasp on a *sound* cue, a much more difficult task. Selma Fraiberg (1968) describes how, at five months, if a sound-making object is placed within easy reach of the blind baby's hands, he remains motionless, although he is alerted. The same response occurs if the bell on the cradle gym is rung a few seconds after the baby rang it himself. Her eight babies would reach on a sound cue alone between the seventh and twelfth month, with six out of eight of the babies succeeding between nine and a half and twelve months.[3] Fraiberg states that she credited one success on the infant's part and that twenty or thirty trials might be

---

[3] Norris et al. (1957) say, of the sixty-six blind children in their intensive study, that nearly all of the children observed at six months were able to grasp on contact, but typically grasped objects within reach only at nine months. It is not made clear whether "within reach" in this context means locating and grasping at hand level in front of the child, or anywhere around the blind child's head in the way that a sighted child can.

given if he would tolerate this. She points out that this lateness in reaching means that the blind infant's hands, on which he must so greatly rely, give him little information and power of action for a dangerously long time; that, compared with the sighted infant, he lives in a sensory void from which objects emerge from time to time and make contact with his hands; as a result his personality may remain centered on his own body and appetites.

While I have from the beginning tried to evoke this reaching behavior in blind babies and did so during my fortnightly visits to Simon and Cynthia, to whom reference will mainly be made, I have never persisted to the extent described by Fraiberg. This may in part be the reason why in these children the reaching behavior occurred only at a later time. What was striking in Simon and Cynthia was the interaction between the developing ability to locate and grasp toys in this way and the ability to move nearer to or further from the source of sound:

Simon,[4] a three-months premature infant, was at fourteen months just beginning to reach for a toy on a sound cue. At the same time he started in a baby walker and was soon able to go out of the sitting room in it and find the kitchen doorway near where his mother was. (Like many blind children, he never crawled.) This ability to move a great deal nearer to, or further from, the source of sound, so making it louder or softer, seemed to speed up his understanding that sounds *had* a source and could be located, since by sixteen months he was able not only to reach for, but to locate, toys that were rattled anywhere around him when he was sitting still.

The same interaction was observed in Cynthia (between twelve and eighteen months). Her mother would clap her hands in front of, and around, the child as she sat facing the mother on her knees, and Cynthia soon learned to reach for them. However, the mother reported that Cynthia would not reliably reach for a toy on a sound cue alone (nor could I elicit this) until she started to crawl and walk.

These examples underline the importance of the child's being able to move himself bodily nearer to, or further from, the source of sound, either by crawling or walking, at the appropriate age. Not

4 For causes of blindness, see Appendix.

only does this appear to facilitate the ability to locate on sound and show the infant that many sounds he hears have a cause; it also enables him to explore many objects in his world of which until then he had been totally unaware (unlike his sighted counterpart, who has observed them for a long period). The literature includes studies of deviant blind children who were immobile during the first three or four years of life, and, as Fraiberg and Freedman (1964) indicated, there may be a link between early immobility and later deviation[5] (see also Keeler, 1958).

The danger is, of course, not only that the blind child will fail to find out about, and so cathect, the world around him but that his cathexis will remain centered on his own body for far too long and show itself in rocking, wishing to be handled, and so on at an age when these are inappropriate.

The Prolonged Period When the Blind Child Remains Tied Closely to the Familiar and to Routine

The blind child's tie to the familiar has been described in the literature; and we have observed it in some of the children referred to our nursery school. It is usually ascribed to the mother's failure to stimulate the child during infancy. While this may well be a contributory factor, observation suggests that blind children cling to the familiar, especially in those areas where blindness interferes with mastery, and refuse to move on even when the mothering is good. This takes us back to the thesis put forward by A.-M. Sandler (1963) : "that the development of blind and sighted children follows roughly parallel courses for about twelve to sixteen weeks after birth, but that at the time of transition from the first (predominantly passive) oral phase to the second (predominantly active) phase, the ego development of the blind child pursues a course which results in his passive self-centeredness and *lack of striving toward mastery at later ages*" (p. 346; my italics). A.-M. Sandler takes the view that this is a specific ego deformation in blind children dating from the end of the first quarter of the first year, which occurs as a consequence of their handicap.

---

[5] Janet's case history (see p. 476) exemplifies this.

While this statement in general appears to be true,[6] we must remember that one of the blind child's main activities in infancy—listening—is often not visible to the observer. The relative lack of active striving will affect some areas of development more than others. For example, feeding appears to be a specially vulnerable area where the child frequently shows arrests:

Cynthia was breast-fed for six weeks. During the first year the mother did not succeed in getting Cynthia to accept spoon feeding, although the mother had had no such difficulties with her two older children. At about fourteen months Cynthia's bottle teat began to wear out, but she refused to try a new one. When it finally wore out completely, she ate nothing from breakfast until lunch the next day. After much patient effort the mother induced Cynthia to accept some food from a spoon, but she took it only while she was on her mother's lap. Since her second birthday (she is now two and a half years old), Cynthia has been persuaded to sit in a little chair to eat, but has insisted on a bottle or at least a cuddle on one of the parents' laps afterward.

Looked at from the side of the ego, these arrests certainly show a lack of striving for mastery in the feeding area (and also some opposition to the mother). However, on closer examination it will be seen that the arrests are due not merely to passivity at each stage. Cynthia behaves as if the new steps—eating off a spoon to supplement the bottle; sitting in a chair instead of on mother's lap—had little to recommend them compared to the known pleasure of always feeding from the bottle, always on mother's lap. She puts considerable energy into preserving the *status quo* at each stage; in fact, her behavior suggests a tie to the familiar, an arrest in development, rather than a fixation, because, as Nagera and Colonna (1965) remark in another context, if sight were restored, we would expect this difficulty largely to be dissipated. Sight would initiate the wish to move on, and provide the impetus to what we call mastery.

Cynthia (two years old) not only refused to feed herself, but, as was the case with other of our blind children, it was hard to get her to hold the bottle or play with food. For her, feeding was the

---

[6] For instance, it is the adventitiously blind adults who appear to strive to better their lot, while the congenitally blind, on the whole, appear to accept it.

mother's function. Perhaps any encouragement to self-feeding implied for her some withdrawal on the part of the mother.

In the case of Sarah, another well-mothered child (whose peripheral vision developed toward the end of the first year), feeding has always been a major problem and has to this date (she is now five and a half years) remained too closely tied to the mother-child relationship.

While the sighted child shows the same difficulties—an unwillingness to move from bottle, to spoon, to self-feeding—these are rarely so acute because the child has been *active* in bringing many things to his mouth since his early months. He can turn passive into active by feeding his mother (blind infants do not appear to do this) and, stimulated by vision, he imitates, even if he does not compete with, the eating of siblings and adults around him.

Willingness to bite mother and siblings, but *not* new food substances, was also observed in some of our blind children:

When Cynthia (two years) was beginning to feed from a spoon, she occasionally still bit her mother and siblings, but she would not bite a piece off a sponge finger and she screamed when a piece was put in her mouth.

Saul, twenty months, a backward blind child, bit his mother, according to her report; but he refused to bite off a piece of banana when it was placed between his lips.

This suggests that some caution must be exercised in the assumption that refusal to bite food always stems from a taboo on biting the mother; it seems rather, in the blind child, to be a difficulty in mastery, a dislike of the new substance which remains strange without the introduction that sight can give. (From a limited number of cases, one gains the impression that blind toddlers do not eat things they come across, like the sighted toddler, though they may mouth them. It seems as if there is a step between mouthing and eating, biting and eating, which some have difficulty in taking. This step goes largely unnoticed in sighted children.)

These various difficulties in the feeding area need understanding, and great patience, on the part of the mother if she is to establish normal feeding patterns without upsetting her relationship to the child in the process.

In other areas the blind child's difficulty in mastering new experiences also results in his clinging to the familiar:

Sarah would not walk on grass the first time that she was introduced to this.

Cynthia has only recently, in her third year, been coaxed to get into the big bathtub with her siblings; even then she tolerates only brief dips.
She usually wears a hairband. When her mother did her hair in two bunches, she insisted on having the hairband as well.
She usually wears pajamas with feet at night, but has now grown out of the largest size available. Wearing the new footless pajamas and feeling nothing against her feet, she cried until her mother added socks.

These children not only cling to the familiar experience but also to the familiar routine:

When Sarah was nineteen months old, her mother had planned to let her play with a bowl of water in the garden for the first time during my visit. She set out the bowl, and removed Sarah's frock to keep it dry. Sarah backed away and appeared uninterested, though she liked it when I splashed the doll in the water. She seemed unable to cope with this bowl of water in the wrong place and with undressing at the wrong time. She herself would not touch the water.

Older children, who can talk, sometimes throw light on these early happenings:

During Sam's fifth year I always met him in the waiting room at 10 A.M. in order to maintain routine. After many months, I decided to greet him on the steps or even in the road if we arrived at the same time. When I did this, he began the session by re-enacting what was omitted—my coming into the waiting room, greeting him, and bringing him out.

Such ties to routine suggest that the blind child is struggling to organize his experience, and that a known routine is one of his safeguards against confusion.

It is true that the very young sighted child also likes the familiar experience and the familiar routine. However, during his long periods of gazing around in the first year he has been able to familiarize himself with a wide range of experience, and vision gives him an ongoing means of mastering small changes in routine.

As mentioned earlier, this tie to the familiar is accompanied by a tendency to revert to earlier modes of behavior in response to up-setting experiences, especially those connected with breaks in the parent-child relationship.[7] Not surprisingly, Cynthia showed this in the feeding area when her mother was suddenly hospitalized for five nights because of a miscarriage; during this time Cynthia visited her twice:

Cynthia, at sixteen months, was left in the care of her grand-parents in her own home. On her mother's return she showed the initial avoidance and subsequent clinging that is usually observed in sighted children. For the following two and a half months she refused the spoon, which she had recently started on, and took noth-ing but bottles or something off her mother's finger.

This reversion to an earlier feeding relationship with the mother is potentially less dangerous than the turning back to his own body by Simon, a child who spent his first five months in the hospital:

Simon had learned to jump in a bouncer before my visits started Subsequently, he had many enjoyable times jumping while his father held his hands. At eighteen months, when he was put to bed at night, he started jumping compulsively in his cot until his hands were blistered. The jumping had several determinants, but one of them was obviously a reversion to interest in his own body because of the break in contact on being sent to bed. The father responded to this by renewing the contact and "reading him to sleep" (Simon understood a little but did not talk properly). As a result the jump-ing soon stopped.

Some time later Simon was circumcised in the hospital. He re-acted to this, not by a withdrawal but more normally, by a sleep disturbance, which meant he got up and went to find his parents.

Compulsive behavior also occurs in the young sighted child, but is usually of temporary duration. However, in some blind children the tendency of such behavior as jumping and rocking to persist makes it particularly desirable to deal with it quickly.

---

[7] This links with the more dramatic and massive regressions seen in the sample described by Fraiberg (1968).

The fact that the blind child remains tied to the familiar and to routine, reverts to earlier modes of behavior, and withdraws easily suggests that we should be chary of assuming that the parents have overprotected or understimulated the child until we know more about the developmental difficulties with which they have had to contend.

The Period when the Fate of the Blind Child's Aggressive Impulses to the Object is Being Decided

Nagera and Colonna (1965) comment that the tendency of blind children to cling to anyone present does not mean that they have not reached object constancy,[8] that such behavior is for the purposes of survival. (However, some blind children may take longer than sighted children to reach this stage.) Nagera and Colonna also noted that the children (ranging in age from four to eight and a half years) complied with the wishes of their important objects, especially with those of the mother, to a degree hardly seen in sighted children of the same age. These blind children showed a tendency to inhibit any form of overt expression of aggression against those objects on whom they were dependent.[9]

Dorothy Burlingham had previously (1961) suggested that the blind toddler seemed to be prevented from treating the mother aggressively by the general limiting of his muscular activity, and that the death wishes of the blind child in the phallic phase were inhibited by his very great fear of losing the object, that is, by his dependency.

Looking at blind children of school age, either those who have been in treatment or those whom we have known since early childhood, one is struck by their difficulty in dealing with aggression, whether its expression is inhibited or not, by the many devices they use to cope with it, and by the bizarre results.

With these disturbances in mind, it is obviously important to pay

[8] By object constancy is meant that stage when the child can maintain a positive inner image of the object, irrespective of either satisfaction or dissatisfaction (Anna Freud, 1965).
[9] Since Nagera and Colonna were also using Hampstead Clinic case material, some of the children they studied are also cited in this paper.

particular attention to the period of growing individuation during the second and third years, when the child finds himself in collision with his mother and must learn that the loving mother can also be the angry mother, that he can love and hate the same person. In the sighted child this realization leads not only to object constancy but also to some compromises in feeling and behavior toward her and not to the constant ambivalence or almost total suppression of aggression that is seen in some blind children.

However, unlike in the two vulnerable periods described above, where the setbacks can be observed during the child's first three years and are mitigated but not averted by work with the mother, these acute problems around aggression are on a different level and can, to some extent, be averted by drawing the mother's attention to them. For this reason they are not easily studied *in statu nascendi* because the observer's very presence tends to prevent their development in such an acute form. One is alerted to the dangers of this period of development mainly by observation of the later disturbances in the blind child. Thus, before describing observations of blind children during their second and third years, I shall first consider the possible reasons for the blind child's difficulty in dealing with his aggression toward objects in an age-adequate fashion.

Blindness probably delays the perception of the object as a whole.[10] At what stage does the blind child regard his mother's many and varied ministrations as emanating from a single being like himself?

When Cynthia, at seventeen months, reached for her mother's clapped hands in front of her when they were by then on her knees, she may in fact not have known that the mother had only one pair of hands (and one thinks of many-armed Indian statues in this connection).

Sarah's mother thought that Sarah understood "Noggy" (the name for the cat) as an entity before she understood "Mummy" or "Daddy" in this way because she could more easily feel the whole

---

[10] Omwake and Solnit (1961) put forward the hypothesis that "without vision from birth, the child has a considerable difficulty in transforming perceptual experiences into mental representations" (p. 401). Fraiberg's observations support this; indeed, she believes that the blind child evolves some kind of stable object concept only between the ages of three and five years. However, Fraiberg's definition of object constancy (1969) differs from that adopted by us.

cat. Being able to do this exposed her to a less bewildering variety of sensations.

Before the blind child has acquired a concept of bodies by playing such games as finding mother's nose, then his own, etc., he probably has only a very vague, piecemeal image of his mother. The number of different sensations (touch, smell,.sound, etc.) with which she presents him are not easily unified without the vision of her as a whole person. It is also possible that the visual aspect of the mother changes less than her voice does when she is angry; she still has the same face and outline, whereas her voice may become harsh and much less recognizable. For example, Omwake's patient, Ann, asked, "Where does the loving go when the scolding comes in the voice?" (Omwake and Solnit, 1961, p. 352).

These considerations raise the question whether a blind child who is left with the sound of his mother's scolding voice and who cannot see her face relax may not sometimes fail to realize that the voice still belongs to the loving mother, may indeed believe that the loving mother has gone away, and that there now is a different, angry, mother. *In fact, the blind child may be in serious trouble if he does not have a sufficiently stable inner representation of his mother as a basically loving person by the time he clashes with her.* This lack may account for the strange withdrawals from all objects seen in some young blind children. It would also throw a different light on the mechanism of splitting for defensive reasons so often seen in older blind children: this splitting may rest on a *primary* failure to perceive the loving and angry mother as one person.[11]

That blind children may have a vague and not very stable image of their objects is further suggested by the way in which they use denial and fantasy.[12]

Miss Omwake reports that she had to interrupt Ann's treatment for two months due to illness. On her return Ann (in her fifth year)

[11] A rough analogy to this would be those cultures where the people deduce from natural phenomena separate good and angry deities (a god and a devil) as against those where the people deduce a single good and loving deity who *becomes* angry.

[12] Heron (1961) has reported that adult subjects in a state of temporary perceptual deprivation tended to hallucinate in the sense of "perception without object," though the majority did not imagine what they "perceived" to be "real."

wanted her to talk like the maid at home. She kept up this demand until her anxiety was sufficiently reduced for her to inquire about the nature of Miss Omwake's illness some twenty sessions later (Omwake and Solnit, 1961).

Sam, during his sixth year, was seen by Mrs. Sandler while I was away. When he recalled her one day, he said, "Pretend you're Mrs. Sandler."

A sighted child could not do this because he would perceive the facts. He would initiate pretense of this kind only for a short game, whereas these blind children wished to deny or change their companion. Such vague piecemeal imagery must lead to vague and piecemeal inner object representation, which in turn facilitates denial and other distortions of reality by defense and fantasy, thus laying the ground for later character disturbances.

If we accept that some young blind children have difficulty in reconciling the loving with the angry mother because of their piecemeal image of her, and that their vague perception of the object facilitates denial and fantasy, then we must apply these ideas to our examination of the blind children's troubles with expressing aggression. As mentioned earlier, when blind children are angry they cannot easily discharge their anger because they feel themselves too dependent on the holding object to risk estrangement. They cannot easily use ways open to the sighted child, such as turning passive into active in play and other activities. Being incapable of easily imitating *actions,* they have difficulties which are reflected in the behavior of the nursery school children.

It may be said that problems around handling aggression are found in most, if not all, neurotic children. But there is a difference between them and blind children which is a matter of degree. In neurotic children these problems rarely result in such gross personality distortions perhaps mainly because neurotic children are much less dependent on their objects for survival in the very early years and so can discharge some aggression both physically and verbally with less risk during that period.

In the nursery school we have frequently been struck by the compliance, passivity, and inhibition of aggression in the blind children. In some of them no doubt the aggression is fully unconscious, and the impulses have been repressed or projected. In others we get hints that the impulses, although still conscious, are perhaps too primitive and archaic to be fully accepted by the child's relatively mature ego; that they can find no ego-syntonic expression, or none that will not endanger the blind child's object relationships. Sam gave hints of this:

In spite of my constant attempts during Sam's fifth and sixth years to show him his cross feelings with me when they arose, Sam scarcely expressed any such feelings himself. He very rarely allowed himself a normally aggressive fantasy in play, since he insisted on using me, and not a teddy, to act it out. When he could be induced to substitute a teddy (as the victim), the oral-sadistic fantasies he occasionally produced were startling. In his eighth year, when he was still very docile in behavior, his mother said that, on television, he would listen only to gun fights and battles, but not to peaceful programs, presumably using these for externalization. It seemed that the aggressive impulses toward the object were largely inhibited and repressed, but that some were still available. Now at last, in his ninth year, he is beginning to show more aggression, of a kind, toward both his schoolmates and me.

What is it that may be going on in these children, not only in those who control object-directed aggression while remaining aware of it, but also in those who repress it fully? Here we are fortunate in having analytic material to turn to.

Of the four analyzed children, Winnie, who was treated by Miss C. Legg for two years from the age of four and a half, presented the picture of a depressed child in the nursery school, giving the impression by her posture that "she had all the cares of the world on her shoulders." At home she rarely expressed aggression toward her deaf mother. However, in the more permissive atmosphere of the treatment hour, the underlying extreme ambivalence of the sadistic phase emerged. She made assaults on both oral and anal levels, attacking the therapist and the things in the room physically and verbally by using anal and sexual swearwords. Expressions of hate and love followed one another quickly; physical attacks on the therapist alternated with caresses. Miss Legg referred to one such piece of behavior as "a dramatic exposition of the nonfusion of libidinal (erotic) and aggressive drives." She then referred to Anna Freud (1949), who stated that where there is such a lack of fusion, the "pathological factor is found in the realm of erotic, emotional development which has been held up through adverse external or internal conditions, such as absence of love objects, lack of emotional response from the adult environment, the breaking of emotional ties as soon as they are formed, deficiency of emotional development for innate reasons" (p. 41). Miss Legg points out that Winnie had experienced all four of these prerequisites for nonfusion: her father had died, her mother was deaf, she had undergone hospitalizations, and she lacked inner visual representation of love objects.

Of these four possible prerequisites for nonfusion, two were present in other blind children. They lacked inner visual object representations and most had undergone hospitalizations. The question arises how Winnie would have developed without her therapist's help in dealing with such ambivalence.

Janet began to walk only at the age of three. She went to a Sunshine Home at four and a half years. She was treated by Mrs. H. Kennedy from the age of eight and a half years over a period of four years. At the beginning of treatment Janet was thought to be ineducable. Inhibition of aggression toward objects was a major problem; and Janet's compliance hid a passive resistance, one of the results of which had been this pseudodefectiveness. She maintained a quasi-symbiotic tie with her mother, toward whom she was unable to express aggressive impulses. Her dependence on her mother led to splitting and idealization; she thought *other* people, not her mother, had sent her away to school. However, this idealization was contradicted by Janet's persistent play activities which depicted the mother as angry, shouting, and complaining. The perseveration demonstrated Janet's failure at integration. It appeared as if these aggressive fantasies about her mother could be neither mastered nor repressed.

At the same time Janet had very many fears. While it is appropriate for blind children to have more fears than sighted children because they often lack full understanding of situations, the fact that some of Janet's fears lessened with interpretation of her aggressive feelings demonstrated that they were another device for dealing with her unmanageable aggression by projection.

Celia was referred to the clinic because of difficult behavior in school and depression. She was treated by Miss Legg from the age of seven for about three years. While Celia had had violent outbursts at the blind school to which she had been sent at the age of four, she saw her mother as powerless to prevent this and herself as having to do what the headmistress decreed. During treatment, her hostile feelings emerged in the transference but were quickly defended against; when, for instance, after a stream of aggressive questions she was asked what *she* thought, her reply was that she was only thinking about "God bless Miss Legg." In a later report Miss Legg remarked on the quantity and quality of this aggression. Celia also suffered from acute, but not widespread, fears.

These three children all showed unusual problems in handling their aggression toward their principal objects (and these observations can be supported from other cases). Winnie swung from libidinal to aggressive behavior, while the other two employed various devices to deal with it: withdrawal, denial, splitting and idealization, and projection which leads to hampering fears.

The fourth child who was analyzed, Helen, did not demonstrate the same problems as the other three, and reference to her early history showed that in fact she had had some sight until three years of age. She had therefore not been so dependent on her mother during her second and third years, and may also have been able to build a more stable image of the mother.

The deductions made from the problems in object relationships of these older disturbed blind children can be applied to our work with mothers of blind children during the first three years of life, when these relationships are being laid down. As mentioned earlier, children of mothers with whom we have worked consistently have not shown these problems in their development, although the following examples demonstrate that dependence on their parents presents fertile grounds.

When Simon was eighteen months, his parents noticed that he withdrew or "sulked" on the rare occasions when they needed to scold him. They therefore attempted to retain contact with him subsequently, either by voice or by sitting near him, in this way supporting his idea of them as basically safe loving parents. Several months later, when he was moving more freely, the mother reported that when she refused Simon's request to get him a toy because she was upstairs working, he would go out and run up and down the back garden, which she understood as a discharge of his annoyance.

When Cynthia[13] was two years, her mother occasionally had to smack her, after several warnings, because Cynthia would bite her

[13] Cynthia was fortunate in having had a peaceful early life, with only two brief visits to the hospital, which were well handled.

siblings when they got in her way. (She had largely given up biting her mother.) The mother said she always took particular care to comfort Cynthia after such a scolding.

When Cynthia was two and a quarter years, I was able to observe such a biting episode. The father was playing Scrabble with the two older children. Cynthia went across and felt the board, probably to find out what was going on. Her brother resisted this, and she became very tense, as she always did before biting. The father scolded her gently; she burst into tears and had to be picked up and cuddled by her mother.

A sighted child could have watched the game and in this way participated, but a blind child cannot do this. Thus she may not only have to give up expressing aggression toward the siblings and withdraw to solitary play, but she may also refuse to have anything to do with the punishing parent.

The existence of this tendency was clearly observed a few weeks later. After a recent smack from her father, Cynthia refused to take food from him for a whole week. (The mother, with whom Cynthia was in constant contact, could smack her occasionally without any such repercussion.) In blind children whose mothers handle aggression with less insight such withdrawals sometimes spread to such a degree that the children refuse all contact with adults, on whom they must so greatly rely.

While any blind child's ability to handle aggression toward his objects depends on many factors, special attention should be paid to this particular area. When mothers are alerted to the potential dangers, they usually handle such situations quite well. Tendencies to cramp the child's expression of aggression in order to have a "good" child are generally overcome by the interest in furthering his development and in having a more normal child who can use his aggression in socially acceptable ways.

However, though the mothering may be adequate, the early life experience of many blind children is disagreeable and even traumatic due to the need for hospitalizations and various medical interventions. We should therefore encourage mothers to give such children as much positive experience in the early years as they can. For instance, they should keep the child in close contact and try to avoid further separations; they should look for enjoyable experiences for him, and so on. This would elicit his emotional libidinal ties with his objects, provide a better balance between his libidinal and aggressive impulses toward them, and enable him to make some compromise, some fusion, in his feelings and their expression.

While the blind child's development needs optimal handling throughout, it seems that the vulnerable periods in his early life are, at least to the unsophisticated observer, somewhat different from those of the sighted child. For this reason, it may be both important and rewarding to call the mother's particular attention to them.

APPENDIX

Causes of Blindness

With the exception of Sarah no child had more than light perception.

Celia:	retrolental fibroplasia
Cynthia:	blindness probably due to a deteriorated retina
Helen:	retrolental fibroplasia
Janet:	pseudoglioma; eyes removed at four months
Sam:	retinoblastoma; eyes removed at six months
Sarah:	retinitis pigmentosa; has peripheral vision but must learn Braille
Saul:	retrolental fibroplasia
Simon:	retrolental fibroplasia; born twenty-eighth week of pregnancy, weight 1 lb. 15 oz. (survivor of twins)
Winnie:	congenital cataract; one month premature, weight 6 lbs. 1 oz.

BIBLIOGRAPHY

Burlingham, D. (1961), Some Notes on the Development of the Blind. *This Annual*, 16:121-145.
—— (1964), Hearing and Its Role in the Development of the Blind. *This Annual*, 19:95-112.
Fraiberg, S. (1968), Parallel and Divergent Patterns in Blind and Sighted Infants. *This Annual*, 23:264-300.
—— (1969), Libidinal Object Constancy and Mental Representation. *This Annual*, 24:9-47.
—— & Freedman, D. A. (1964), Studies in the Ego Development of the Congenitally Blind Child. *This Annual*, 19:113-169.
—— Siegel, B. L., & Gibson, R. (1966), The Role of Sound in the Search Behavior of a Blind Infant. *This Annual*, 21:327-357.
Freedman, D. G. (1964), Smiling in Blind Infants and the Issue of Innate vs. Acquired. *J. Child Psychol. & Psychiat.*, 5:171-184.

Freud, A. (1949), Aggression in Relation to Emotional Development. *This Annual*, 3/4:37-48.
—— (1965), *Normality and Pathology in Childhood: Assessments of Development*. New York: International Universities Press.
Gesell, A. & Amatruda, C. (1941), *Developmental Diagnosis*. New York: Hoeber, rev. ed., 1960.
Gough, D. (1962), The Visual Behaviour of Infants in the First Few Weeks of Life. *Proc. Roy. Soc. Med.*, 55:308-310.
Heron, W. (1961), Cognitive and Physiological Effects of Perceptual Isolation. In: *Sensory Deprivation*, ed. P. Solomon et al. Cambridge: Harvard University Press, pp. 6-33.
Keeler, W. R. (1958), Autistic Patterns and Defective Communication in Blind Children with Retrolental Fibroplasia. In: *Psychopathology of Communication*, ed. P. H. Hoch & J. Zubin. New York: Grune & Stratton, pp. 64-83.
Maxfield, K. E. & Buchholz, S. (1957), *A Social Maturity Scale for Blind Pre-School Children*. New York: American Foundation for the Blind.
Nagera, H. & Colonna, A. B. (1965), Aspects of the Contribution of Sight to Ego and Drive Development. *This Annual*, 20:267-287.
Norris, M., Spaulding, P., & Brodie, F. (1957), *Blindness in Children*. Chicago: University of Chicago Press.
Omwake, E. B. & Solnit, A. J. (1961), "It Isn't Fair": The Treatment of a Blind Child. *This Annual*, 16:352-404.
Sandler, A.-M. (1963), Aspects of Passivity and Ego Development in the Blind Infant. *This Annual*, 18:343-360.
Sheridan, M. D. (1960), *The Developmental Progress of Infants and Young Children*. London: H.M.S.O.
Wills, D. M. (1968), Problems of Play and Mastery in the Blind Child. *Brit. J. Med. Psychol.*, 41:213-222.

APPLICATIONS OF PSYCHOANALYSIS

CULTURAL DEPRIVATION

A Clinical Dimension of Education

SEYMOUR L. LUSTMAN, M.D., Ph.D. (New Haven, Conn.)

If our primary, and presumably most treasured, asset is our children, no one seriously concerned with the future can deny the pivotal role of education. Any multidisciplinary group charged with planning for generations to come, however divergent their initial focus, must inevitably converge on our schools. This is not only "where the children are," but is an enterprise which commands the nation's largest professionally trained group of workers. If we would but permit our economic and technological power to be brought to bear, the ethical imperative for appropriate facilities and settings could be fulfilled easily. As a system, education remains the ideal hub for a network of consultative talent extending to all areas of life. In point of fact, a sound basis for such a substantive network already has been laid. Accordingly, the educational mission—viewed either as a limited or as an extended area—is crucial and urgent by any set of priorities.

Nevertheless, schools are embattled and in disarray; educators are an unappreciated, beleaguered, and underpaid profession; work fatigue, insecurity, frustration, and consequent job change remain inordinately high; and the magnitude and complexity of the tasks at hand are increasing at a disconcerting pace. Criticism of schools, teachers, and teaching has not always been constructive in tone or intent, nor helpful by design. This is increasingly true of the present. It characterized the decade past as the school preempted the center of our political turbulence. Advice and demands, though plentiful, have not always been far-seeing and altruistic—with either children,

From Yale University, Child Study Center and Department of Psychiatry. Chairman, Task Force IV, Joint Commission on Mental Health of Children.

teachers or their collaborative work in mind. The lack of humility and the frank opportunism on the part of many politicians, parents, students, teachers, and members of the behavioral sciences have been startling as well as offensive.

And yet, even without such issues of self-seeking territoriality, we are faced with an astonishing, almost inconceivable proliferation of perplexing and divergent needs. From day to day we are presented with numerous redefinitions of the goals of education, which have one fact in common—more and more is asked of it. Physical health, mental health, and a multitude of developmental responsibilities formerly believed to be firmly lodged in the home, parents, families, and a host of other societal institutions such as the church, industry, medicine, psychoanalysis, social work, welfare, the law and the police are now considered integral to the province of education. In the stress of events, we have not had time to weigh these institutional alterations in function, let alone time to plan.

Since no solutions are at hand, and there is every reason to anticipate continued pressure and flux, it is unfortunate that the resultant confusion is held forth by many as presumptive evidence of the school's failure. This is grossly in error. It is more likely evidence of a painful and difficult period of transition—one that will continue for some time to come.

I think this state of affairs has been intensified and deepened by a subtle misapplication of political, social, and economic values to some aspects of education. I speak specifically of egalitarianism, which correctly applies to many social, economic, and civil-libertarian issues, but which nonetheless obfuscates individual differences in educational capability and educational need.

The blurring fails to recognize one of the major conflicts within education which echoes our society. I refer to the balance of individuality and sociality. We will one day have to ponder the degree to which our respect and striving for individuality are compatible with, or locked in contentious struggle vis-à-vis, the demands of our particular kind of society with its gamut of contending and militant views.

At the moment, the problem-solving processes (not necessarily planning processes) at the national and institutional level are locked into heroic issues of social need. At the same time, the individual teacher is locked into the individual needs of individual children. The head and the tail are not yet synchronous.

The teacher knows well individual differences of educational capability and need. Yet, it has become difficult to speak of differences without raising the pejorative accusation of "elitism." Nowhere is this clearer than in our university graduate departments of the performing arts, where many students stubbornly confuse "power" with talent, gift, and creativity.

Planning, on an individual or institutional level, demands discourse of the whole range of needs. In the world of the basketball player, a boy who is seven feet tall, gifted, and trained is the "elite." In the world of the race-horse jockey, the same boy is handicapped. I hope that it is possible to discuss such differences, stripped of their contentious social values as judged by different interest groups. I am speaking of innate and experiential resultants as reflected in the sense of individual differences in all of man's biological and psychological characteristics.

I would like to return for a moment to the issue of the tasks of education. If, in addition to the responsibility for cognitive development, we enlarge the school's mandate to include character development, delinquency, drug abuse, sexual enlightenment, and a host of mental health problems—society must assume that task but must maintain a crucial attitude and construct a more felicitious atmosphere in which to work.

The redefinition of education must retain the historic and traditional scope of its mission; it must not distort, destroy, or deflect the teaching profession; it must broaden that profession's knowledge and capability without overwhelming it or rendering it helpless by conflict; and last, although a consortium of local and federal politicians, parents, students, community organizations, behavioral scientists, and well-intentioned laymen may participate, the ultimate control of *educational activity* must reside within the appropriate group —education itself. The teaching profession must be supported and actively helped to make itself attractive as a satisfying career—one that can compete successfully in the recruitment market for talent; one that can hold its practitioners after their training when they are so desperately needed. Professional status must be enhanced, pay increased, and new career patterns as well as new career ladders be created. If this is not done, we will have the poorest qualifications in those situations where the best are minimal standards.

This requires the educator to become a senior partner in a field that requires the broadest definition, even if inclusiveness increases the risk of a platitudinous tone. One such definition of education in schools would include those gifted aspects of art, those scientifically based techniques and sequential procedures—flexibly used—to maximize the probability for human development. This retains cognitive development and specific content, but permits the inclusion of pediatric care, inoculations, repair of teeth, ways of involving parents and the broader community, nutrition, etc., in addition to the usual and new curricular experiences addressed primarily to content. This was part of the planning and part of the impact of "Operation Head Start." This was never intended to be a program *exclusively* concerned with the "cognitimorphism" of children in terms of IQ points. The increase of IQ points with nursery school experience—whatever that means—was documented in the 1930s. It is possible to retain and enhance that goal (cherished by so many), and still address oneself again to the developmental concerns that psychoanalysis has by tradition shared with teachers.

Psychoanalysts have never made "demands" on educators. Their collaboration is an old and fruitful one characterized by mutual benefit. The atmosphere and spirit of that collaboration goes beyond the shared interest in children. It is true that in a substantive sense, from the viewpoint of the educator, psychoanalysis has been helpful. It has presented a theory of normal and deviant psychological development of inestimable value. From the viewpoint of psychoanalysis, it has been encouraged by the old and immediately perceived view of education as an important period and place to minimize or hopefully prevent disordered development. In addition, psychoanalysis has drawn many of its most distinguished members from the ranks of educators.

The attitude of which I speak was described best by Ernst Kris (1948):

> . . . the relationship of psychoanalysis to education is complex. In a first approach the inclination may be to characterize it as one between a basic science and a field of application. Psychoanalytic

propositions aim at indicating why human beings behave as they do under given conditions. The educator may turn to these propositions in his attempts to influence human behavior. The propositions then become part of his scientific equipment which naturally include propositions from other basic sciences. In any relationship between a more general set of propositions and a field of application outside the area of experience from which these propositions were derived, a number of factors must be taken into account. The more general propositions, in this instance those of psychoanalysis, must be formulated in a way that permits their operation in a field, here that of education. The process of application is likely to act as a test of the validity of the propositions or of the usefulness of their formulation. Hence we are dealing not merely with a process of diffusion of knowledge from a "higher" to a "lower" level, from the "general" to the "applied" field but with a process of communication between experts trained in different skills in which cross-fertilization is likely to occur [p. 622].

I shall not review the history of this common effort—it has been made available many times, in admirable form, by Anna Freud (1931, 1946, 1954), Aichhorn (1925), Bernfeld (1925), and others. An excellent psychoanalytic review has just been published by Ekstein and Motto (1969). The impact on nursery schools as experienced by a leading educator has been detailed by Omwake (1966).

IMPULSE CONTROL

Although there is great merit in conceptualizing the educational process as an integrated unit extending from prekindergarten through the university, I shall restrict my comments to the primary grades. My focus will be on the issue of impulse control since my interests are with those formative and developmental tasks of early childhood most related to the ability to use a school experience, however it is constructed. My conclusions are drawn from many years of intensive observations and consultation to the Yale University Child Study Center Nursery School, four inner-city prekindergarten programs, access to several inner-city primary schools, the analysis of a number of impulse-ridden children, and several research projects on impulsivity in culturally deprived children. Two of these studies have been reported (Lustman, 1966).

SEYMOUR L. LUSTMAN

It is my impression that the development of impulse control is one of those key developmental syntheses which signifies the presence of the host of other psychic functions necessary to permit school learning. A child must be able to sit still, to attend, ultimately to concentrate for increasing periods of time in order to perceive, receive, organize, retain, recall, and creatively use knowledge. An internal structure must be developed, sustained, and maintained by internal and external forces. It must ultimately be powered by an inner motivation in order to permit the child to replace internal organization for disorganization in class and outside of it. I am not suggesting that the need for external support, appreciation, and narcissistic supplies ever ceases—but inner structure must be there and cannot be substituted by an exclusively external agent. In other words, the presence of the extraordinary developmental feat of inner control of impulse means that the child can probably use a school experience—although adults can then debate the appropriate or relevant content and forms of presentation. Those are problems of a different nature than the inability to use a school experience because of a developmental deficit which must first be remedied.

In those children where this does not come about, or where it only partially occurs, one is left with an impulse-ridden, uncontrolled individual unable to relate to school, and where the probability of severe trouble in adolescence and later life is enhanced. This is clearly related to the vicious cycle of learning problems, rejection by adults, frustration evolving from no significant experience of success, and in some to the sequelae of severe pathology, dropouts, and delinquency. I add delinquency because of the relationship of superego to control of impulse.

Of course, the scale of inner control ranges from its complete absence to its massive presence. The latter is accompanied by loss of spontaneity, restricted creativity, and characterized by the severe constriction and inhibition noted in some middle-class children in school. Both are developmental problems—one too little, the other too much—which do not augur well for a reasonably harmonious life in school and thereafter.

Either extreme can probably occur in any socially defined group because the number of factors feeding into the development of internal control are numerous and interacting. They are both qualitative and quantitative matters. A variety of causally related sequences can precede similar phenomenological behavior.

However, the prevalence of impulse-ridden children in the so-called "culturally disadvantaged" population is impressive enough to warrant the attempt to relate it to factors within this group. This is not to say that it is universal—but it does seem to be the major impediment to teaching and learning in the poverty-ridden segment of our population.

For the psychoanalyst, this is rooted in the idiosyncratic patterns of object relations which occur in the atmosphere of the family, or whatever substitutes for the usual family's child-rearing functions. However, when speaking of families and familial relationships within the so-called culturally disadvantaged population, one must remain quite clear that this is not a homogeneous population. The common element for this categorization is poverty, not family structure. The population shares most aspects of political, social, and economic disadvantage—but family structure, function, and values vary. The primary family unit ranges from intact families (mother, father, and children together) to incredibly disorganized, ever-changing, and tenuous relationships, the variations of which defy easy categorization. Value systems range from middle-class ideals and hopes to no discernible values other than survival. The range of obstacles and handicaps has been eloquently and accurately described elsewhere in our general as well as sociological literature. Poverty needs no review here. However, the quality of object relationships experienced and established in poorly structured or unstructured "families" and "living arrangements" is incontrovertibly causally related to impulse control.

The problem of child rearing in this sizable group of people is not yet the responsibility of either educators or psychoanalysts—although both have helped and continue to try to help. It is assumed that our culture, if it is to survive, will make every conceivable effort to cope with, if not solve, the problems of housing, employment, meaningful participation in community life, involving the caretaking person with the child and both with the educative process. The war on poverty has a massive literature that is not the topic of this paper.

For my purposes, I would like first to generalize, for a moment, on the impact that teaching culturally disadvantaged children has on

the teachers I have known. Except for the few gifted and extraordinarily committed teachers, the prevalence and unremitting quality
of impulsivity, over a period of time, can have a devastating effect
professionally and personally. Teachers, as all professionals, tend to
judge themselves by the standards of their training as superimposed
on their own unconscious motivations for career choice. Some may
be unconscious missionaries, but most, at least in part, share a professional identification as an imparter of, or guide to, knowledge.
As she is forced into the unhappy role of a disciplinarian, there is a
frequent concomitant feeling of an inability to "reach" her pupils.
She may begin to question seriously her talents, her training, her
vocational choice, and her future. In addition to such professional
conflicts, there are deeper inner conflicts which will be stirred or
augmented. Similarly, there is constant exposure to the volatile
conflicts of parents as well as militant community forces. Little work
satisfaction, professional fatigue, and chronicity may conspire to
cause withdrawal from the children. Contagion and disorganization
of children who are coping—but with emerging and still fluid ego
skills—is regressive for them, and the teacher may find herself feeling forced to a partisan protective position. This may result in
greater irritability and "scapegoating" of the disruptive children.
The class day may degenerate into a fierce, exhausting, inner and
outer struggle centered around control—control of herself and of
her pupils.

In talking to teachers, particularly the young, idealistic, and inspired teachers, one is impressed with the additional burden they
must bear as elements of social, religious, and racial prejudice
emerge within themselves, their colleagues, students, parents, the
administration, and community organizations.

In such a crucible, projection as a defense is common. The original challenge and desire to help is in danger of being replaced by
a view of her students as having lamentable aberrations to ultimately
attributing malevolence to the impulse-ridden child.

Within the first three grades many teachers experience profound
relief when these matters are discussed. Insight into the superficial
aspects of their own conflicts as well as some understanding of the
developmental aspects of impulse control can be helpful. Nevertheless, I have not been impressed by the overall effect of the teacher's

greater tolerance, understanding, and comfort on the child's impulse disorder. This is not the case with middle-class children, who are markedly affected by such changes in the teacher.

There seems to me to be a marked difference between the impulsivity of the culturally deprived nursery school child and that of the middle-class child, a difference that goes beyond the higher incidence. In the middle-class child who has a true impulse disorder, there always seem to be elements of object relatedness in the behavior. This usually takes the form of some manipulativeness and elements of a power struggle reminiscent of the earlier anal development. The impulsive behavior is, even though uncontrolled, channeled to some degree into meaningful and communicative behavior, in part directed to the teacher, in part displaced onto the teacher, and always onto the parents. This is quite understandable to most teachers and can be handled effectively and helpfully by many.

The deprived group is more immature. Their behavior is less manipulative, less directed, less communicative, and more unfocused. It seems to be more random, frequently purposeless, and characterized by greater distractibility. Inanimate and human objects are rarely used appropriately for any period of time. Behavior occurs more like constant motion with diffuse generalized bursts of activity best described as a "collective monologue" of behavior similar to Piaget's (1923) collective monologue of speech. It glances off of toys, other children, and rarely the teacher—but has almost nothing to do with the teacher (whose name the child may not know). The presence or absence of the teacher has no demonstrable effect on the behavior. However, the strains are so great that the teacher may superimpose an attribute of "badness" on the child which is at least comprehensible, even if incorrect.

In this setting, the teacher becomes deprived, the children's actual and potential deprivation is increased, and an inexorable process of disenchantment and debilitation may ensue for all.

However, the damage to the child is unique for it may be the last opportunity to set in motion the developmental forces he so desperately needs. This can be placed within the context of the psychoanalytic theory of development, but more than that, within a "psychoanalytic learning theory." Such a learning theory would be fundamentally very different from that variety of learning theory which has preoccupied American academic psychology. Except for the largely forgotten Gestalt psychologists, and individuals like Lewin and Piaget, the theories are behaviorist and lean heavily on conditioning paradigms. They are being promoted very earnestly for school use in the form of operant models, machine teaching, and "programmed learning."

To my mind, such theories are not "incorrect" in the sense that man cannot be conditioned—obviously some things can be "learned" via this mode. The error lies in assuming that conditioning is the *only* or even a basic mechanism by which man learns. It reduces man's great gift—his ability to learn—to a mindless response. It leads to such remarkably simplistic and inconsequential theory building as Skinner's (1957) account of the human acquisition of language. The pitfalls of behaviorism have been discussed by Chomsky (1959), von Bertalanffy (1967), Simpson (1967), and Koestler (1967), to name but a few. The reasons for its persistent interest among parents and some educators lie beyond the scope of this paper.

The danger is not theoretical, but lies in the educational practices to which it leads. Koestler makes the point that the original anthropomorphism of the rat now leads to a "ratomorphism" of man. Koestler concludes his scathing review by saying, "It is impossible to arrive at a diagnosis of man's predicament—and by implication at a therapy—by starting from a psychology which denies the existence of mind, and lives on specious analogies derived from the bar-pressing activities of rats" (p. 18). Ludwig von Bertalanffy sees the danger as moving toward a sociology of "robot man," constricted by a "behavioral engineering" tantamount to "functional decerebration"—a new fate for man, i.e., "menticide." The pressure for a "national curriculum" rigidly programmed by behavioral engineers would be particularly devastating to the culturally deprived child for whom it seems particularly aimed. The ethics of such applications of social science may be similar to those of the physical sciences, and reminds me of Max Born's (1968) "nightmare" statement. "The political and military horrors and the complete breakdown of ethics which I have witnessed during my lifetime may not be a symptom of an ephemeral social weakness but a necessary consequence of the rise of science. . . . This is no prophecy, only a nightmare" (p. 58). It is not only science that is involved here, but the uniquely American technological imperative.

For me, the replacing by teaching machine, or rigid programmed reinforcement, of the extraordinary need for intense *human* relatedness is the ultimate deprivation of the culturally deprived. One must not confuse automatized, mindless behavior for man's ability to make rational and responsible decisions. One must not tamper too much, if at all, with the dignity, grace, and creativity of which man is capable. Certainly not for a seemingly expedient counterfeit "intelligence." It represents a particular danger when it is seductively tied into a machine technology and held forth as a simple technique to increase cognitive content *and* control of behavior—both major concerns of our troubled society.

There have been relatively few attempts to explicate a psychoanalytic learning theory, although its importance and existence have always been taken for granted—insight is a learning term (Piers and Piers, 1965; Ekstein, 1969; an explicit psychoanalytic learning theory was a matter of primary interest to David Rapaport). It does not concern itself directly with the development of intelligence or those aspects of human thought subsumed under cognitive development. However, its concepts of primary and secondary process are important developmental modes of thinking as well as feeling and behaving. In the main, as related to schools, it is concerned with those aspects of internalization and psychic structure building related to characterological development. Such a learning theory would follow an epigenetic schema from direct and immediate instinctual gratification to controlled, delayed, directed, and even symbolic gratifications. Sublimation as a process would be of extreme importance. It would developmentally relate frustration, or the absence of gratification, to the learning of differentiation. Memory of gratification-frustration and ability to use secondary process would be central to the development of reality testing. Insight as a psychoanalytic learning process is related to, but quite different from, its use in Gestalt psychology. The affective components, progressive internalization and maturity, and the achievement of motivation at a greater distance from direct gratification are implied in Ekstein and

Motto's felicitious "From learning for love to love of learning" (1969).

Mastery in repetitive play and subsequent fantasy is of crucial learning importance to the age group I am concerned with. To the extent that psychoanalysis would ever concern itself directly with cognition, there is every reason to believe that it would evolve a theory consonant with the genetic epistemology of Piaget.

For our purposes the prime applicability of this kind of "learning process" is that it occurs only within the framework of incredibly intense human relationships. These are the vicissitudes inherent in the development of object relatedness. Object relations not only are brought about by human need and human development, but also act as the organizers of psychic function and by their phase-specific crises impel further development. Through processes ranging from conscious imitation to unconscious processes of the varieties of identification, they leave their lifelong imprint. If this does not occur at the appropriate time, or in the intense experiential drama of the home (or other caretaking methods), there is scientific warrant to wonder if it can ever be completed. However, if an effort is to be made short of the impossible and impractical foster home concept, one comes to the school and the teacher.

PSYCHOANALYTIC IMPLICATIONS FOR CULTURAL DEPRIVATION

A complex mental function such as internal control of impulse is an astonishing achievement of advanced development signifying delay, thought, binding of energy, reality testing, awareness of self and others, and degrees of empathy and sympathy. It demonstrates the internal presence of moral values, whatever their cultural content, and the ability to experience and use anticipatory as well as retrospective guilt and anxiety in signal form. Although there are many prestages, and all aspects of this do not occur at once, in its synthetic and multiple function aspects it is well established with the appearance of a definitive superego.

Viewed from a structural theory framework, I would think of it as a complex psychic function resulting from a *superordinate* structuralization. It involves a hierarchical stratification of drive derivatives and defenses with both ego and superego elements having, by temporal interaction, intertwined on ever higher levels of function. Cognitive development depends to a significant degree on this prior step. While it is clear that cognitive development and personality development are related, and seem to continue apace, there is no compelling evidence that cognitive development has a major formative and abiding impact on personality. Training in one cannot be expected to have a generalizing effect on the other—although many psychologists make this assumption. For example, studies in the cognitive development of moral values and judgments (Piaget, 1932), while of interest and value in their own right, have no direct correlation with moral behavior or the experience of guilt. As a matter of fact, there is an imposing body of clinical evidence which demonstrates that knowledge of rules and cognitive moral judgments in no way preclude social psychopathy. On the other hand, characterological psychopathy such as impulse disorder always interferes with learning and cognitive development to a greater or lesser degree.

How can psychoanalytic theory and experience continue to be put at the service of educators? I do not believe in "Freudian schools" and I know that there are many individual ways in which to help and areas in which to start or continue such efforts. Obviously, I think the richest and most commanding problem is the area of impulse control and behavioral morality. Not that I want quiet rooms filled with "good" children. Rather it is that I consider inner control, as described, a problem in schools to which psychoanalysis has the most to contribute. It is also a "target" psychic achievement by which to assess many other aspects of the readiness for, or ability to use, a school. To use psychoanalytic propositions calls for the latitude to develop different kinds of schools, teachers, and programs to meet the different *developmental* needs of this large group of children.

For them, the educational experience must attempt to mobilize and capitalize on the internal impetus to development. If one retains as his anchor the central relevant issues of dropouts, delinquency, learning disorders, and psychopathology, he is led to those aspects of development that are mediated via the kinds of learning described above and mediated only through object-related experience.

Predicated on object constancy and intensity of relationship, this process produces and depends on periodic increases in intrapsychic tension which must reach an unbearable intensity—thereby imposing on the child the need for resolution. Without this, there is arrest, fixation, and distorted development.

Via internalization processes, internal structures are built (which are characteristic for the specific object relationship) and enable the child to delay and control his impulsivity. This process includes aspects of the moral development we attribute to the superego. Object constancy and developmental crises are, I suggest, core prerequisites.

As stated above, it is my impression that the degree of disorganization and impulsivity in the culturally deprived population correlates with the degree of tenuous relationship within the family. There are of course more complicated situations in those instances where clear identification processes with impulsive adults are the major causative factor. At any rate, the disorganized poverty family offers no basis upon which to form the kind of object ties needed for the developmental process.

It may prove fruitful to reconstruct the primary school in an ungraded fashion, devoted to overcoming this primary object deprivation and capitalizing on the child's hunger for human objects. This shifts the emphasis to object ties with the teacher rather than cognitive development in terms of content and IQ scores. In this context external regulation may still become internal control.

Under the imperative of a cognitively based curriculum for all, grades are organized by an orderly progression of content, teachers have become specialized by grade and further specialized by content within grade. The idea of compensatory education has resulted, by and large, in the introduction of even more specialization and loss in individually sustained contact. This is clearly valuable for those children who are secure enough in their development to use it, i.e., those with reasonably secure family ties. It is bewildering to the others and may be harmful.

If one decides that the primary need is object relationships, some obvious experiments come to mind. The first problem is to make the teacher *the* crucial, or *a* crucial, person. This calls for small groups of children, and specially selected and trained teachers, amply supported by expert help designed for their needs as well as the children's.

In essence it is an attempt to give the child, via the teacher, what he has never had: a prolonged, consistent, almost exclusive relationship with an adult who cares for him. To bring this about may require the assignment of *one* teacher to teach *all* content herself and to remain with the same small group of children for perhaps eight years. This is in sharp contrast to our current cognitively based educational patterns with their aforementioned specialization. At present, with yearly teacher change, the child is expected to relate to a large number of primary teachers and an infinite number of subject specialists. This is not helpful to the child who has not had the opportunity to invest deeply in one adult, let alone the few inconstant adults available.

Within this framework, a systematic research effort must be made to delineate circumstances and techniques by which the object tie to the teacher can be most rapidly and firmly enhanced. The work of Anna Freud is succinctly applicable, and if I may paraphrase her (1965b), the best interests of the child and the probability of his continued development will be enhanced if *three needs* are fulfilled and safeguarded. First, the need for *affection*. By teacher selection and support, by small numbers, by genuine responsibility, and by long-term proximity, the chance for this may be enhanced. Second, the need for *stimulation*. The committed teacher's ability to elicit inherent functions and potentialities becomes most meaningful under the conditions described. Third, the need for *unbroken continuity*. In part, this is to prevent further damage to and dulling of feelings attendant on separation. However, within this context, it is designed more to encourage the intensity of relationship crucial to *induce* development. It may call for experimentation with periodic introduction of a male teacher or one male-one female team teaching. It would seem probable that within such an extended period of responsibility, "crisis and rescue" situations will occur which will further enhance the object tie. Consistent and prolonged firmness by one teacher may make possible the internalization of benevolent control via identification. In such a program, content would not be ignored, but would aid and be aided by the focus on object constancy, object ties, and intensity of relationship.

Conclusions

It seems to me that no culture has ever survived with but one kind of institution—any more than it can survive with a "Tower of Babel." An institution has the same basic architectonic principle at work that biology has; i.e., function determines structure. We have been singularly ineffective in the attempt to use the middle-class school structure in culturally deprived areas. We must evolve new kinds of schools and new experiential educational programs for a significant portion of the deprived population. Although deprived in every sense—including cognition—a significant group of this population is deprived in almost all areas of personality development. These children cannot use the middle-class school structure, and they seriously compromise the other children who can. Their presence in the usual teaching situation makes it difficult for the teacher to function in a way that is helpful to any or gratifying to herself. The hallmark of those who need this special planning is the degree to which "impulse control" has not developed.

I would suggest some experiments in educational function and structure based on the following five psychoanalytic theoretical propositions:

1. Psychic development, like biological maturation, appears to have an intrinsic motor force of its own. Anna Freud (1965a) has called this the child's need to complete development. This can be noted in analytic counseling of parents, where by holding a few things constant, the developmental momentum can be counted on to carry an oedipal child into latency rather than into the distorting prolongation of the oedipal phase. Just as development can be impeded (Provence and Lipton, 1962; Spitz, 1945, 1946, 1959), there are biological and psychological elements which maintain or give fresh impetus to the momentum of development. Biological factors can be seen to contribute to this process in adolescence. All psychological impetus comes from the vicissitudes of the individual's genetic history of object relations. Significant people are necessary to bring about the appearance and development of psychic functions and can be called "organizers" in an analogue to biogenetic development.

2. The astonishing interaction of innumerable and complicated relationships, events, states, and affects causes development to occur

in a hierarchical and spiral fashion. An achieved developmental phase not only sets the stage for further development but also may act as the organizer or stimulus for further development. For example, in such a hierarchy, an ego function such as "self-awareness" (Freud, 1914; Hartmann and Loewenstein, 1962; Jacobson, 1964; Lustman, 1966) not only is a precursor but stimulates self-regulation and organization. This may be a crucial inducer to superego development in the child capable of entering and resolving the oedipal phase.

3. Following a thought of Ernst Kris, crises—after the fashion of phase-specific crises—may also serve as points of organization and stimulus for development. Whether they become the nidus for arrests and fixations or progression may depend on the quantitative factor and accordingly is related to the theory of trauma. Internal discomfort must reach an *intense, but optimal* height to force the child to progressive resolution without the sequelae of either no resolution or the regression and fixation of extreme trauma.

4. For the purpose of certain kinds of research, many aspects of psychoanalytic human development may be conceptualized in learning theory terms. As a limited learning theory this differs dramatically from existing learning theories of academic psychology. Although many differences exist, the primary one is that it occurs within the context of intense object relationships and is not particularly related to such concepts as "reinforcement" or "gratification." It is a learning theory addressed to character development, not to academic content. The key modes of "learning" are the internalization processes.

5. Viewed from the point of view of the structural theory, a complex psychic function, such as internalized impulse control, is itself a *superordinate structure* involving a hierarchial stratification of drive derivatives, defenses, with both ego and superego elements intertwined on ever higher levels of organization. What we call the synthetic function of the ego is usually credited with this task. It may well be that the hierarchy itself is the cohesive and organizing element. Impulse control does not become structuralized definitively until the superego does—from which time internalized moral codes (whatever their cultural content) participate in control. Cognition alone (primarily an ego function) must rely on superego elements to

effect this inner state. Otherwise control remains external in the form of the teacher, the cops, etc.

All of these propositions point to the hypothesis that prolonged and intense object ties with one teacher may act as inducer and organizer of psychic function. Once started, the developmental process may get some continuity by virtue of its own force and momentum. The continued and intense relationship may maintain further development by its relationship to crises and their organizational and inducer potentiality. The development of impulse control is the target set of functions by which to select children who need this kind of special educational experience—and is the set of functions by which it can be assessed.

Based on these propositions, I suggest the experiment of assigning *one* (specially selected, specially trained and supported) teacher to a small, nongraded group of impulse-ridden, culturally deprived children. This primary relationship should be of a long enough duration—perhaps eight years—to insure object constancy and unbroken continuity for the child.

The teacher should have genuine, prolonged responsibility for her children. She should teach all content to them, although enrichment can be introduced as usable by the children. The "curriculum" should shift from its focus on content to a primary focus on human object ties. Affection, stimulation, and *absolute, unbroken continuity* are deemed crucial for such an experiment in safeguarding the best interests of the child. It is hoped that within such a setting, developmental impetus can be induced in these deprived children.

It is of interest that such a modification would fit into what two leading educators (Fantini and Weinstein, 1967, 1968) call a "contact curriculum." In their terms the modifications call for the curriculum to be flexibly geared to unique needs of individual schools; that it move from a symbolic (academic) base to an experiential base; that experientially it be immediate in its orientation (rather than past or future); that it shift to social participation (doing) rather than academic participation (knowing); that it explore reality; and that the emphasis move from a sole concern with cognitive content to an "equal emphasis on affective, inner content" (1968, p. 50).

In this troubled era, I must close by repeating that while focusing on education, I am in no sense suggesting exclusion of the existing families, however disorganized. Quite the contrary is indicated—with vigorous social, political, and economic efforts to aid adults. More than that—vigorous research efforts are needed to develop psychological aids to this population.

I have been almost exclusively concerned with ways of making maximal use of the teacher as a *crucial object* in the lives of children. This is with the hope of offsetting the unfortunate circumstances which deprived them of human object ties necessary for development. It is with the hope of setting into motion developmental forces and maintaining developmental momentum. Frequent change of teacher, introduction to a bewildering number of specialty teachers will not enhance the possibility of intense relatedness, which psychoanalytic experience insists is the single most important variable in this problem.

BIBLIOGRAPHY

Aichhorn, A. (1925), *Wayward Youth*. New York: Viking Press, 1935.

Bernfeld, S. (1925), *The Psychology of the Infant*. New York: Brentano, 1929.

Born, M. (1968), *My Life and My Views*. New York: Scribner.

Chomsky, N. (1959), A Review of B. F. Skinner's "Verbal Behavior." *Language*, 35:26-56.

Ekstein, R. (1969), Psychoanalytic Notes on the Function of the Curriculum. In: Ekstein & Motto, pp. 47-57.

—— & Motto, R. (1969), *From Learning for Love to Love of Learning*. New York: Brunner Mazel.

Fantini, M. & Weinstein, G. (1967), Taking Advantage of the Disadvantaged. *The Record: Columbia University*, 69:1-12.

—— —— (1968), *The Disadvantaged: Challenge to Education*. New York: Harper & Row.

—— —— (1969), *Toward a Contact Curriculum*. New York: Anti-Defamation League of B'nai Brith.

Freud, A. (1931), Introduction to: *Psycho-Analysis for Teachers*. London: Allen & Unwin.

—— (1946), Freedom from Want in Early Education. *The Writings of Anna Freud*, 4:425-441. New York: International Universities Press, 1968.

—— (1954), Psychoanalysis and Education. *This Annual*, 9:9-15.

—— (1965a), *Normality and Pathology in Childhood*. New York: International Universities Press.

—— (1965b), Three Contributions to a Seminar on Family Law. *The Writings of Anna Freud*, 5:436-459. New York: International Universities Press, 1969.

—— & Burlingham, D. (1943), *Infants Without Families*. New York: International Universities Press, 1944.

Freud, S. (1900), The Interpretation of Dreams. *Standard Edition*, 4 & 5. London: Hogarth Press, 1953.

—— (1914), On Narcissism. *Standard Edition*, 14:67-102. London: Hogarth Press, 1957.

Gill, M. M. (1964), *Topography and Systems in Psychoanalytic Theory [Psychological Issues*, Monogr. 10]. New York: International Universities Press.

Greenacre, P. (1945), Conscience in the Psychopath. *Amer. J. Orthopsychiat.*, 15:495-509.

Hartmann, H. (1947), On Rational and Irrational Action. *Essays on Ego Psychology.* New York: International Universities Press, 1964, pp. 37-68.

—— (1955), Notes on the Theory of Sublimation. *Essays on Ego Psychology.* New York: International Universities Press, 1964, pp. 215-240.

—— (1960), *Psychoanalysis and Moral Values.* New York: International Universities Press.

—— & Loewenstein, R. M. (1962), Notes on the Superego. *This Annual,* 17:42-81.

Jacobson, E. (1964), *The Self and the Object World.* New York: International Universities Press.

Koestler, A. (1967), *The Ghost in the Machine.* New York: Macmillan.

Kris, E. (1948), On Psychoanalysis and Education. *Amer. J. Orthopsychiat.*, 18:622-635.

Lustman, S. L. (1966), Impulse Control, Structure, and the Synthetic Function. In: *Psychoanalysis—A General Psychology,* ed. R. M. Loewenstein, L. M. Newman, M. Schur, & A. J. Solnit. New York: International Universities Press, pp. 190-221.

Mahler, M. S. (1963), Thoughts about Development and Individuation. *This Annual,* 18:307-324.

Omwake, E. (1966), The Child's Estate. In: *Modern Perspectives in Child Development,* ed. A. J. Solnit & S. Provence. New York: International Universities Press, pp. 577-594.

Peller, L. (1946), Incentives to Development and Means of Early Education. *This Annual,* 2:397-415.

—— (1956), The School's Role in Promoting Sublimation. *This Annual,* 11:437-449.

Piaget, J. (1923), *The Language and Thought of the Child.* London: Routledge, 1932.

—— (1932), *The Moral Judgment of the Child.* Glencoe, Ill.: Free Press, 1948.

Piers, G. & Piers, M. (1965), Modes of Learning and the Analytic Process. *Selected Lectures: Sixth International Congress of Psychotherapy.* London, New York: S. Karger.

Provence, S. & Lipton, R. C. (1962), *Infants in Institutions.* New York: International Universities Press.

Simpson, G. G. (1967), The Crisis in Biology. *Amer. Scholar,* 36:363-377.

Skinner, B. F. (1957), *Verbal Behavior.* New York: Macmillan.

Spitz, R. A. (1945), Hospitalism. *This Annual,* 1:53-74.

—— (1946), Hospitalism: A Follow-up Report. *This Annual,* 2:113-117.

—— (1959), *A Genetic Field Theory of Ego Formation.* New York: International Universities Press.

von Bertalanffy, L. (1967), *Robots, Men and Minds.* New York: Braziller.

Waelder, R. (1930), The Principle of Multiple Function. *Psa. Quart.,* 5:45-62, 1936.

TRANSITIONAL TUNES AND MUSICAL DEVELOPMENT

MARJORIE McDONALD, M.D. (Cleveland)

The Suzuki Method of Violin Teaching

Following World War II Shinichi Suzuki, a Japanese violinist who managed to survive many tragedies inflicted on him by the war, determined that he would dedicate his life to teaching music to young children. Forsaking the possibility of a career as a college teacher or a performer, Suzuki instead took over an abandoned kindergarten in Matsumoto and turned it into a music studio. There he taught the violin to small children, some as young as three years of age. He gave a simple explanation for his unorthodox choice of pupils. "Children learn their native language in a natural fashion—properly taught, they can learn music the same way!" (Nickels, 1968, p. 5).

Suzuki proceeded to develop a system of teaching stringed instruments to young children which has become widely known under the name, "talent education." This system has had both strong supporters and strong critics, as evidenced by the mixed reactions to the first Annual Conference, in Japan in 1954, when several hundred young violinists played works ranging from "Twinkle, Twinkle Little Star" to the Bach Double Concerto. Some hailed it as a musical achievement and others regarded it as sheer exhibitionism. The Suzuki method first gained attention in the United States in 1958 when a film about it was shown to a meeting of string teachers at Oberlin, Ohio. Since then the system has become increasingly popular in this country. There have been innumerable Suzuki workshops for string teachers, and Suzuki has appeared in person, sometimes with his own pupils, at many of them. He has been accorded many honors, and respected musicians such as Joseph Szigeti and Pablo

503

Casals have lauded his revolutionary contribution to the art of string teaching. Eminent musicians, trained by Suzuki methods, are beginning to appear on the international music scene (Nickels, 1968; Suzuki, 1969).

An English translation of Suzuki's book, *Nurtured by Love*, has only recently been published (1969). In his Introduction Suzuki describes the great revelation that he experienced, in his early thirties, at his "discovery" about the learning of language.

> Oh—why, Japanese children can all speak Japanese! The thought suddenly struck me with amazement. In fact, all children throughout the world speak their native tongues with the utmost fluency. Any and every Japanese child—all speak Japanese without difficulty. Does that not show a startling talent? How, by what means, does this come about? I had to control an impulse to shout my joy over this discovery.
>
> But no one else seemed the slightest bit impressed. It was just taken for granted; people in general think that the ability children display is natural. At my excitement, half of my listeners were startled, and others just thought me absurd. Nevertheless, my discovery actually had a great meaning; it made me realize that any child is able to display highly superior abilities if only the correct methods are used in training [p. 9].
>
> Why do all children possess the marvelous ability to speak their mother tongue quite effortlessly? Therein lies the secret of how to educate all human ability [p. 97].

It is Suzuki's goal to teach children as young as three years of age to play the violin and to do so in a manner which resembles as closely as possible the way children have learned language. Recognizing the importance of the parent in this process, Suzuki begins by teaching the parent, who plays a small-size violin such as the child will later use. As the parent plays and enjoys the instrument, the child spontaneously wants to join the activity. He then attends both private and group lessons with his parent and soon is participating himself, enjoying the violin as a new toy. As he has learned language from his parents, so he learns the violin, at first from them, and later from his teacher and from group play sessions where he is exposed to older and more advanced pupils. The emphasis is always upon having fun through playing music.

There is much that is sound, on both a psychological and a musical basis, in Suzuki's methods. To a psychoanalyst his method has more merit than his psychological explanation of it. He idealizes childhood as a time of supreme happiness, denies drives and conflicts, and minimizes the significance of hereditary and constitutional factors. It is his belief that, with loving teaching, talent can be "inculcated" (p. 110). The term for this method, "talent education," must be understood to mean "talent inculcation."

Suzuki's own musical development is of special interest. He came from a family of samisen makers (a Japanese three-stringed instrument, resembling a banjo). His father's researches into the history of this instrument led to an interest in the Western violin, and eventually his father converted the family business into a violin factory. Not only did his father thus bring the violin to the people of Japan, but his factory became the largest producer of violins in the world (at one time reaching 400 violins and 4,000 bows a day). Suzuki himself always thought of his father's violin factory as a toy factory until, at the age of seventeen, he heard a recording of Mischa Elman playing Schubert's "Ave Maria." He writes of this experience:

> To think that the violin, which I had considered a toy, could produce such beauty of tone! . . . Elman's "Ave Maria" opened my eyes to music. I had no idea why my soul was so moved [p. 79].

This profoundly moving experience led Suzuki to take up the serious study of the violin at the late age of seventeen years. (He constantly denies, however, even when in his early twenties he went to Germany to study, that he was a serious and ambitious musician.)

In Germany he had another profoundly moving experience in which he received an exalted appointment from Mozart. After listening to a performance of the Mozart Clarinet Quintet he experienced a temporary paralysis of both arms and was unable to applaud the performance. He had a typical "belle indifférence" reaction to his short-lived conversion reaction. He writes of the experience:

> It was Mozart who taught me to know perfect love, truth, goodness and beauty. And I now deeply feel as if I were under direct

orders from Mozart, and he left me a legacy, and in his place
I am to further the happiness of all children [p. 91].

It is my impression that this special summons by Mozart came at
the height of a loneliness he could hardly permit himself to acknowledge. (Indeed he refers especially to the "piercing sadness" of the
Quintet's second movement, and sees Mozart as answering life's sadness with a "loving affirmative" [p. 92].) He was an Oriental in Germany, having difficulty in finding a suitable teacher, and perhaps
increasingly faced with his own limitations as a latecomer both to
the violin and to Western music. So the man who started too late
was ordained by the most noted musical child prodigy of all time to
become the teacher of little children. And the man whose father
once produced the world's largest supply of violins may well have
become the man who has produced the world's largest supply of
violinists.

That a preschool child can learn to play anything on the violin,
let alone a Baroque concerto, holds as much fascination for a psychoanalyst as it does for a musician. Both must ask the question:
how is such an achievement possible? The psychoanalyst must also
ask: how can it possibly harmonize with ordinary prelatency tasks of
personality development? Do the music lessons act as a developmental interference, or is it possible that, as with learning language,
the learning of music might even *promote* personality development?

In an article for string teachers I attempted to answer these questions through a consideration of both the failures and the successes
with the Suzuki system (McDonald, 1970). I discussed the inevitable
failures that result when preschool music lessons are experienced by
the child as a developmental interference—e.g., when they repeat a
toilet-training struggle between child and parent; when they foster
a neurotic exhibitionism.

Much more intriguing are the reasons for the success of the
Suzuki method. Musicians tend to point first to the remarkable personality of the method's founder. Childless himself, Suzuki has demonstrated a lifelong selfless devotion to children and he works tire-
lessly in behalf of their development. "Today Dr. Suzuki seems to
thrive on a schedule that might well kill a younger man. One of his
biggest sorrows is that he no longer has much time to spend with

the small children he loves. He coaches the teacher-trainees, travels around the country as needed to hold conferences, to help a discouraged teacher, to inaugurate a new class, to discuss revision of his method books" (Nickels, 1968, p. 5).

Yet the Suzuki charisma does not cover the story. The Suzuki system appears to incorporate certain essential ingredients that we would expect to find in any well-run psychoanalytically oriented nursery school. One or both parents must participate actively with the child in a pleasurable musical experience. The parent plays the violin with the child and attends and participates in the music lessons as well. Thus the child's first experience with a teacher is not complicated by a needless separation anxiety brought on by the parent's sudden desertion. Further, the strong parental cathexis of child, teacher, and music acts as an essential catalyst. It makes possible a gradual transfer of parental authority to the person of the teacher, and it promotes a pleasure not just in music but in the activity of learning, producing, and sharing it. These methods all promote learning as a progressive development of an ego skill, and minimize the possibilities that it will be detoured into developmental drive conflicts.

The question of inherent musical talent in the child as a determining factor in the method's success must also be considered. However, Suzuki has demonstrated time and again either that no unusual musical talent is needed for very young children to learn and enjoy music, or else that the population at large has a higher level of musical talent and a greater capacity to enjoy music than is generally recognized.

There is nothing I have presented so far about either the failures or the successes of the Suzuki system that will come as news to a psychoanalyst. But neither have I offered any explanation about why learning the violin might have a special place in the life of a musical preschooler. Suzuki points the way to an explanation with the simple statement of his philosophy, "Children learn their native language in a natural fashion—properly taught, they can learn music the same way." This statement, placing music on a par with language, has a natural appeal, but nevertheless it bears some scrutiny.

Ordinarily children learn to verbalize long before they can possibly learn to play the violin. They do so in part as a way of preserving and enjoying the vital emotional tie to the parents. In the first two years of life the child maintains this tie largely through primitive imitations and identifications with the parents. To be with the parents means to be at one with them, a part of them, and like them. The learning of language becomes for the child a part of this pleasurable imitation and identification. But as a child learns language he acquires a new way of communicating with his parents. The *verbal* communication promotes his reasoning powers. He develops a sense of separateness and independence in his mental functioning, and he gradually relies less and less upon primitive imitations and identifications to preserve the all-important tie to his parents.

When he arrives for his violin lessons, at three or four years, his ways of learning still draw quite heavily upon these early processes, but in addition they have advanced to include more independent intellectual reasoning powers. The mind of a three- or four-year-old is less amorphous, less a porous sponge, than that of a one- or two-year-old. Hence Suzuki's statement that children can learn the violin as they learn language seems to me to tell only part of the story. It does not allow for a developmental increment between a one- or two-year-old and a three- or four-year-old. (I am unprepared to take up the cultural differences in Oriental and Western societies as they affect timing and balance between early identification processes and later mechanisms involving more secondary process thought.)

Yet, in likening the learning of language and music, Suzuki seems to be saying more than is immediately apparent. He rightly suggests, in this comparison, that musical development can begin at the same age and in the same way as language development—long before violin lessons are possible. If given the opportunity, the infant and toddler will "absorb" music at the same age and in the same way that he absorbs, shares, and responds to language, as an auditory expression of the emotional tie with his parents. This very early musical development then provides a favorable foundation for introducing the violin as the *next* forward step at three or four years. Learning to play the violin becomes comparable to learning more words and sentences as the *next* forward step in lingual development.

In his book Suzuki gives a captivating account of an experience with a five-month-old baby's response to music. The baby, Hiromi, was attending her six-year-old sister's group violin lessons, cradled in her mother's arms.

> Hiromi's sister, Atsumi, six years old, was daily practicing at that time the Vivaldi A-minor concerto, as well as listening to the record every day. So Hiromi grew up hearing this music daily from the very beginning. I wanted to know what effect this had on a five-month-old baby. I announced that I would like to play something, and stood up with my violin. When everybody was quiet, I started playing a minuet by Bach. While I played, my eyes did not leave Hiromi's face. The five-month-old already knew the sound of the violin well, and her eyes shone while she listened to this piece that she was hearing for the first time. A little while later I switched from the minuet to the Vivaldi A-minor concerto—music that was played and heard continuously in her home. I had no sooner started the piece when an amazing thing happened.
> Hiromi's expression suddenly changed. She smiled and laughed, and turned her happy face to her mother, who held her in her arms. "See—that's *my* music," she unmistakeably wanted to tell her mother. Soon again, her face turned in my direction, and she moved her body up and down in rhythm. This baby, just five months old, had shown that she knew the melody of the Vivaldi A-minor concerto [p. 17].

(At four years Hiromi was herself playing the same concerto, and at ten years she was writing to the Professor to send him her poetry and musical composition which had won first place in a national contest.)

My curiosity about the *earliest* stages of a child's musical development, aroused by my interest in the Suzuki system, led me to formulate a hypothesis. It seemed to me that some children, who have experienced music from birth onward as an integral part of the loving motherly and fatherly caretaking environment, might make use of music in a very particular way. My hypothesis is that these children find in music their own special "transitional phenomenon." Some may even select from a musical repertory a special "transitional tune," just as another child selects from among his toys a special transitional toy. (It seems very likely to me that Hiromi, for example, could have selected a transitional tune as a very young infant, and perhaps it was even the tune supplied by her sister, Atsumi, in her daily playing of the Vivaldi Concerto.)

WINNICOTT'S TRANSITIONAL PHENOMENA AND THE AUDITORY SENSE

Psychoanalytic interest in "transitional phenomena" has focused almost exclusively upon tangible objects which infants use as their first "not me" possession—objects which make their appeal through sight, smell, feel, and taste. A musician would have to ask why the sense of hearing is not included in this list of significant sensations. In his original article on the subject (1953), Winnicott has not ignored the auditory sense. The following quotations from this article will serve the dual purpose of reviewing his concept of transitional phenomena and crediting his recognition of auditory sensations as included in these phenomena.

> I have introduced the terms 'transitional object' and 'transitional phenomena' for designation of the intermediate area of experience, between the thumb and the teddy bear, between the oral erotism and true object-relationship, between primary creative activity and projection of what has already been introjected, between primary unawareness of indebtedness and the acknowledgement of indebtedness (Say: 'ta!').
> *By this definition an infant's babbling or the way an older child goes over a repertory of songs and tunes while preparing for sleep* come within the intermediate area as transitional phenomena, along with the use made of objects that are not part of the infant's body yet are not fully recognized as belonging to external reality [p. 89, my italics].
> . . . there may emerge some thing or some phenomenon—perhaps a bundle of wool or the corner of a blanket or eiderdown, *or a word or tune* [my italics] or a mannerism, which becomes vitally important to the infant for use at the time of going to sleep, and is a defence against anxiety, especially anxiety of depressive type. Perhaps some soft object or type of object has been found and used by the infant, and this then becomes what I am calling a *transitional object*. This object goes on being important. The parents get to know its value and carry it round when travelling. The mother lets it get dirty and even smelly,

knowing that by washing it she introduces a break in continuity in the infant's experience, a break that may destroy the meaning and value of the object to the infant.

I suggest that the pattern of transitional phenomena begins to show at about 4-6-8-12 months. Purposely I leave room for wide variations. . . .

As the infant starts to use organized sounds (mum, ta, da) there may appear a 'word' for the transitional object. The name given by the infant to these earliest objects is often significant, and it usually has a word used by the adults partly incorporated in it. For instance, 'baa' may be the name, and the 'b' may have come from the adult's use of the word, 'baby' or 'bear' [p. 91].

Winnicott stresses the normality and ubiquity of transitional phenomena and postulates that they may exist more often than is generally recognized by the caretaking adults. He considers their obvious use as a defense against infantile anxieties and as a focal point for expression of later (anal and phallic) drive conflicts arising in the course of ordinary development. In addition, he views the transitional experience as important in the development and maintenance of reality testing and as an early determinant in the evolution of creativity. In his preface to an article by Stevenson (1954) he writes:

The transitional object is also not the same as the next soft toy. It can be said that the next one must be acknowledged as coming from the world. The infant is expected to say "ta" and in this way to make an acknowledgment of the gift. The transitional object comes from the environment, as we know, but it is essential to understand that from the infant's point of view it was created by the infant. There is no question of saying "ta," because the object was in use before the word "ta" could be formulated and before the acknowledgment to the world had become meaningful. In respect of these transitional objects the parents, as it were, conspire not to challenge the origin. They easily see that the thumb is part of the child and that the next toy or teddy bear or doll is a gift, but with regard to the object in question they undertake to refrain from challenging the infant as to its origin. There is a madness here which is permissible because it belongs to this stage of the infant's emotional development. The madness is that this object is created by the infant and *also* it was there in the environment for the infant's use [p. 200f.].

As I have recounted, it was a curiosity about the success of the Suzuki system which led me to hypothesize that some children select a special "transitional tune" as an early step in their musical development. Winnicott's inclusion of musical sounds and tunes in his original description of transitional phenomena offers a verification of the concept of a transitional tune.

Another verification can be found in the psychoanalytic literature in a brief clinical paper, "About the Sound 'Mm . . . ,'" by Greenson (1954).[1] He describes an unusual sensation which appeared during the analysis of an adult patient and lasted for several days, during which time it proved to be analyzable.

> [The patient] felt a constant pleasant humming sensation in his lips. Although no audible sound came from him, he felt as though he were making the sound 'Mm . . .'. . . .
>   The humming sensation was a manifestation of a sense of contentment and well-being. . . . The sense of well-being was recognized to be a repetition of those few occasions in his life when he believed himself to be his mother's favorite. . . . [It] also represented a successful denial of quite the opposite feeling, of being abandoned and deserted [p. 234].

Further analysis of the "Mm . . ." sound, through a dream fragment concerning a piece of velvet cloth, led to the soft woolen blanket which the patient had fondled as a part of his pleasurable experience of sucking on his mother's breast. Throughout his life he had required this blanket or substitutes for it in order to be able to go to sleep. Thus the "Mm . . ." sound and the soft woolen blanket both appeared to be components of the patient's transitional phenomena. Greenson's postulations about the sound "Mm . . ." as both a shared experience with the mother and a means of pleasurably remembering her in her absence recall Winnicott's criteria for transitional phenomena.

> The musical quality of this 'Mm . . .' sound is probably related to the fact that the contented mother hums cheerfully herself as she feeds her baby or rocks it to sleep. She hums by way of her

[1] In this work Greenson does not use the word "transitional" and it appears likely that he was unfamiliar with Winnicott's work, published in 1953. Greenson's paper was presented in 1953 and published in 1954.

identification with the baby's pleasurable satiation and thus echoes a sound she felt as a child. The 'Mm . . .' indicates a sense of contentment and satisfaction [p. 235]. Apparently it is the sound produced with the nipple in the mouth or with the pleasant memory or expectation of its being in the mouth [p. 238].

Greenson does not mention whether music came to have any special significance in the course of this patient's development.

TRANSITIONAL TUNES: LULLABIES AND CRADLE SONGS

A transitional tune has to be a familiar tune, frequently filling the atmosphere between parent and child. It has to provide a shared and comforting experience. In that the infant hears it himself, he probably initially experiences the sensation as though it were a part of himself, just as mother herself does not at first exist as a person distinct and separate from himself. At first he does not, and indeed is not capable of, asking about the tune's origins or who "possesses" it. When he finds a way to reproduce the tune—by command performance, or later on by singing it himself or playing a recording of it—he can feel himself to be in charge and the originator of the experience. Where once he was dependent upon his parents to produce the musical comfort, he gradually becomes able to control its production himself. The particular tune is *his own choice,* just as the transitional toy is the child's own special choice made from a whole collection of toys. The value of this transitional phenomenon is that it is a creative way for a small child to master separation and aloneness and at the same time begin to acquaint himself in a pleasurable way with the external world. When the transitional phenomenon is an auditory, musical, one, it would seem that music has claimed an early and very likely a lasting importance in the child's life. It may even be that a transitional tune is an essential early step in musical development. Early music instruction, for a child who has taken this first step, would seem natural, even necessary, and almost irresistible.[2]

2 The musician, Wilhelm Friedemann Bach, grew up in the musical atmosphere of the large Bach family and received his musical instruction from his father, Johann Sebastian Bach. In her recorded comments on the "Two Part Inventions," composed

I hope to collect further evidence in support of my hypothesis about transitional tunes and their place in musical development by exploring three sources of information. First, I am interested in collecting examples of transitional tunes observed by music teachers and parents of young children. Here is an illustrative example:

A precocious little girl (she had a large vocabulary before the age of one year) was accustomed to hearing music all the time. Her father, a professional musician, taught and practiced in his home, and the child could not help but sense that both parents loved music, as they loved her. She was little more than a year old when she developed the habit, upon awakening and discovering herself alone in her crib, of calling out, "Play Bach, Daddy!" Her loving father would respond by playing the child's favorite tune—the second Bouree from Bach's Suite IV in E Flat Major, for unaccompanied cello. Bach's Bouree was this baby's special lullaby. I believe it was a "not me" sound, shared between her and her parents, yet often available on command when she felt separated from them. That is, she could "create" its performance. This child has since grown into a successful and likable college student, and her ambition is to become a member of the Bach Aria Group.

Second, I hope that biographies and autobiographies of musicians may yield examples of transitional musical phenomena in the early development of these talented and creative people. A beautiful example is quoted in an interview with the violist, Ernst Wallfisch, in which he describes the role of music in the first six years of his life (Arazi, 1969, p. 7):

Music played such a big part in my life from the beginning it seems, and I can recall much . . . my father was a business man and an amateur violinist . . . music was his big hobby . . . chamber music especially . . . his circle of friends included many like him and chamber music seemed to be part of living. . . . I can remember as a very small boy all of these people in our home talking, laughing, smoking cigars, and making music . . . at first

---

by Bach for his nine-year-old son, Wilhelm Friedemann, Wanda Landowska remarked, "What today is for us erudition was for Wilhelm Friedemann daily bread and life experience" (RCA Victor LM-2389). Daily bread is not only a commonplace, but a necessity of life.

A musician friend who grew up in a large family of musicians once told me of the surprise she felt, as a very small child, when she discovered that every family in the neighborhood did not routinely spend their evenings together playing chamber music.

all I recognized were the different sounds and the many moods of what they played . . . as I grew older, I began to separate the composers, the rhythms, the harmonies . . . *I can remember being lulled to sleep by all these sounds,* and being put to bed with all of these sounds swirling through my thoughts . . . *sometimes I would awaken a few hours later, and I could still hear the music sounding through the house* . . . to this day, whenever I hear certain works played by a quartet, it brings back a flood of memories of many things and people . . . *yes, I was thoroughly imbued with the spirit of music from the cradle* so it seems [my italics].

Third, I hope to make a collection of lullabies and cradle songs. The very word, "lullaby," confirms that it is a song intended to serve as a transitional tune. It is of echoic, onomatopoeic origin, being composed of "lull" and "bye." (A similar imitative word, based on "lull," exists in several other languages.) It is a song which soothes the baby while expressing a separation, a good-bye (or a goodnight, as the child narcissistically withdraws into sleep).

The words of many lullabies tell of the absence of an important person (parent, older sibling) and assure the infant of that person's return. But for the preverbal child, it is the comforting *tune,* originally supplied by the parents, which must convey the feeling message. The *words* are as much to express and soothe the empathic distress of the adult for the lonely baby as to convey a verbal message to the infant. The words of the lullaby, "Bye, Baby Bunting," are illustrative:

> Bye, baby bunting,
> Father's gone a-hunting,
> To fetch a little rabbit-skin
> To wrap the baby bunting in.

> Bye, baby bunting,
> Father's gone a-hunting,
> Mother's gone a-milking,
> Sister's gone a silking,
> Brother's gone to buy a skin
> To wrap the baby bunting in.

In this traditional tune the rabbit skin seems to be offered as a potential transitional object.

In some lullabies it appears that the melodic line of the music may be intended to convey to the infant a sense of separation and safe reunion. Just as his rocking cradle will return to a low point of rest, so will the missing person return and his tension be relieved. Contained in the soothing melody may be a wide interval, expressive of a momentary high point of tension in the music, which is then followed by a rhythmic rocking return to a lower resting pitch. Two of the best-known lullabies, "Rockabye Baby" and Brahms's "Lullaby," both contain such suspenseful intervals.

MUSICAL DEVELOPMENT

Finally, I would like to return to the question of whether the Suzuki system of teaching the violin to preschoolers could be consistent with and even promote personality development. I believe that this question can be answered affirmatively, with certain qualifications. The child must, of course, have the motor coordination necessary for playing whatever instrument is introduced and the instrument must be of a suitable size. (Suzuki violins come as small as "one sixteenth" size.) The music lessons must not conflict with other developmental lines or with the resolution of drive conflicts, which is so important a task in prelatency development.

Most important, the music lessons must harmonize with a natural developmental line for music within the child's total personality development. Ideally, and perhaps even necessarily, a line of musical development is opened up by favorable musical experiences in the first few years of life, before music lessons are a possibility. (I include among such favorable experiences a "transitional tune" stage.) Then preschool music lessons do not pose a new assignment, nor do they induce a new developmental line. Instead they contribute to a line of musical development which is already in progress, and through their contribution they foster a healthy expansion of the child's developing personality.

A developmental line for music can be constructed as follows. (The successive steps along this line bear many similarities to the steps in the developmental line, "From the Body to the Toy and From Play to Work," as described by Anna Freud (1965, pp. 79-84).

1. At first the infant's babbling is an autoerotic activity which

is only rhythmic or musical by accident. The mother's talking and singing and her performance of instrumental music in the child's presence is not discriminated from the autoerotic "music" activity of the child.

2. The child "creates" his own special music, a transitional tune, by transferring onto this "creation" the musical properties both of himself and of his mother (or parents). The tune, as a musical transitional phenomenon, becomes cathected both with narcissistic and with object libido. It is the child's special lullaby. (The child may also choose a musical toy for a transitional object—a cuddly toy containing a music box which plays his lullaby for him.)

3. Interest in a limited range of musical transitional phenomena broadens into a wider interest in the world of music. The transitional functions of the first musical interests fade out gradually, although the child's own "lullaby" may retain its special function at bedtime and at times of special stress.

4. Somewhere after the third birthday the first musical instrument can be given to the child. For him this instrument has the appearance of a new toy. He may regard it as a successor to an actual toy instrument, or perhaps to a cuddly toy containing a music box inside it. His first pleasure, if the instrument is a violin, may be in scraping and scratching sounds and in the motor activity of producing them. The sophisticated musical ears of the parents must relax sufficiently to permit sharing the child's pleasure in this unmusical production. At the same time it may be necessary for the parents to protect the child from destroying the instrument altogether, as a result of lingering ambivalent, clinging, destructive impulses from the anal stage of development.[3]

5. Pleasure in disorganized play with the musical instrument evolves into a pleasure in more organized ego activity. Child and parents enjoy together the child's production of harmonious, rhythmic tunes upon the musical instrument. (If all goes well the child may progress from "Twinkle, Twinkle Little Star" to the Bach

---

[3] Suzuki regarded the violin as a toy until the late age of seventeen. Some artists have a conscious recall of the early experiencing of their instrument as a toy. In an interview with a local music critic, a young violin soloist with the Cleveland Orchestra, a member of a noted family of musicians, described such a recall. At the age of four years he broke his violin across his knee, and his parents then replaced it with a metal violin.

Double Concerto!) In time the child's main pleasure derives from his musical achievement, rather than from the indiscriminate playful production of sounds. Along with this pleasure in achievement he becomes less dependent upon the tie to his parents for experiencing his own musical pleasure.

6. The achievement of pleasure in "play" at music evolves into an ability to achieve pleasure through "work" at music. Greater impulse control, neutralization, sublimation, and the transition from the pleasure principle to the reality principle effect this change from play to work. In the adult personality music finds its place as an important sublimation. It may become a vital hobby or a full-time professional activity.

The sequence of steps in Suzuki's "talent education" methods conforms closely to the natural developmental line for music which I have just outlined. First the parents are encouraged to provide and share with the child a pleasurable exposure to music in some form, from birth onward. According to Suzuki, the parents introduce music as they introduce language to their child. Later the child's interest in the violin is naturally aroused through witnessing his parent's pleasure in playing the instrument. To this end the parent, whether a beginner or not, must take violin lessons himself, as a preliminary to the child's lessons. Suzuki calls this step "training the parent rather than the child." He says: "Until the parent can play one piece, the child does not play at all" (p. 106). As the child's interest is awakened he begins to attend the parent's lessons as an auditor. (These may be both individual lessons and group lessons, where other parents and children listen and play together.) When the child wants to try the violin he is given his first tiny, but real, instrument, just as he would be given a new toy. Suzuki says, "We encourage them to 'play' with the violin. . . . We encourage them to think of it as fun" (p. 106f.). The parent's lessons are expanded to include the child, who shares with his parent both the relationship with and the instruction offered by the teacher. As the child progresses on the violin he joins group lessons with other young musicians, much as a nursery school child gradually acquires the ability to play with and enjoy other children. Suzuki emphasizes this timely group play as an important part of the fun for children. His observation is that parents who bring a child only for private instruction and regard the group sessions as unnecessary are parents who do not understand his methods and cannot succeed in applying them with their children. As the child grows the spirit of fun leads him on, almost imperceptibly, into the spirit of work and in turn to the development of his full musical ability.

Suzuki's own informal headings, in the brief account of his violin training methods which he includes in his book, could well serve to express his own conception of a developmental line for music: "We encourage them to think of it as fun." "We encourage them to 'play' with the violin." "A game to begin with, the spirit of fun leads them on." "Five minutes every day [leads to] three hours every day." "The development of ability is absolutely reliable." "We amaze the world."

SUMMARY

The Suzuki method of teaching young children to play the violin roused my interest in musical development and led me to the concept of a "transitional tune" as an important early experience in the development of some musicians. In his original article on transitional phenomena Winnicott included sounds and tunes among the wide range of normal transitional experiences.

Confirmation for the concept of a transitional tune comes from direct observation of young children, from biographical and autobiographical accounts of the early lives of musicians, and from music itself, in the form of lullabies and cradle songs. The word "lullaby" is an onomatopoeic word, composed of 'lull" and "bye," and thus a lullaby is a song offered to an infant as a lulling comfort at the time of a separation. By definition, the lullaby is a song intended for use as a transitional tune, and the words of many lullabies express this function of the music.

Finally, I have proposed a developmental line for music, in which the "transitional tune" stage occupies an early and probably an important position. The success of Suzuki's method of teaching the violin to young children seems to be based on its close adherence to and support of this natural developmental line for music.

BIBLIOGRAPHY

Arazi, I. (1969), One Plus One Equals One. *Amer. String Teacher,* 19(1):6-10, 26.
Freud, A. (1965), *Normality and Pathology in Childhood.* New York: International Universities Press.
Greenson, R. R. (1954), About the Sound 'Mm. . . .' *Psa. Quart.,* 23:234-239.
McDonald, M. (1970), The Suzuki Method, Child Development, and Transitional Tunes. *Amer. String Teacher,* 20(1):24-29.
Nickels, C. (1968), Who Is Suzuki? *Amer. String Teacher,* 18(4):4-5.
Stevenson, O. (1954), The First Treasured Possession. *This Annual,* 9:199-217.
Suzuki, S. (1969), *Nurtured by Love: A New Approach to Education.* New York: Exposition Press.
Winnicott, D. W. (1953), Transitional Objects and Transitional Phenomena. *Int. J. Psa.,* 34:89-97.

A PSYCHOANALYTIC CONTRIBUTION
TO PEDIATRICS

BIANCA GORDON (London)

With a Foreword by

ANNA FREUD, LL.D., D.Sc. (London)

Foreword

Work with pediatricians and hospital personnel does not belong to the early extensions of psychoanalytic activity. The application of psychoanalytic child psychology moved very gradually from the understanding of the child's emotional relationships within the family to the understanding of his behavior in nursery school and school, his learning potentialities and inhibitions, his first ties with playmates, his first encounter with community standards, his compliance with or revolt against the teachers' authority. In accordance with the specialization of work in the children's field which obtained at the time, this knowledge was shared only with the professional workers who were engaged with the psychological side of the child's life such as nursery school teachers, teachers, child guidance and juvenile court personnel, while concern with the child's or adolescent's physical health or ill-health remained strictly a medical concern, untouched by insight into the complicating emotional factors.

The gap between mental and physical aspects of child development was closed then, increasingly, due to two separate advances in the psychoanalytic study of the child. One was the move of investigation from the later to the earlier years of childhood, especially to

This work is a contribution by the Hampstead Child Therapy Clinic to preventive work in the community, and is supported by the Grant Foundation of New York.

the first and second year. At this period of life any mental experience such as anxiety, distress, impatience, rage, frustration, etc., may be discharged in the form of physical upsets such as the disturbance of sleep, food intake, elimination, etc., while any bodily discomfort, pains, intestinal upsets may cause emotional upheavals in the form of unhappiness, distress, anxiety. In short, psychosomatic reactions are the order of the day, and the links between physical and mental processes are inescapable for the analytic observer.

The second line of inquiry was concerned with older children and the fluctuations in growth and structuralization of the personality which are due to the general influence of bodily illness on mental development. What was explored in detail was the meaning to the child of a massive influx of unpleasure, of motor and dietary restrictions, of surgical interventions, of nursing care, etc., with special regard for the regressions in libidinal phase development and ego functioning which are the frequent consequences of experiences of this nature.

Nevertheless, it remained difficult to engage the medical world's interest in these studies, and the first effective breakthrough in this respect was made not on the basis of such interactions between body and mind but via the plight of ill children who have to be taken to a hospital. It was the emphatic description of the *separation anxiety* of hospitalized infants which succeeded finally to convince a number of doctors and nurses that, to be therapeutically effective, the care for a child's ill body needs to be complemented by concern for and attention to his psychological needs. In fact, the general public's readiness to acknowledge the importance of separation anxiety threatened for a while to overshadow the equally important impact of the illnesses themselves.

To set the record straight again, it needed systematic work as described by Bianca Gordon in the following pages and carried out by her in connection with the outpatient and inpatient departments of major children's hospitals. Perhaps, in the distant future new training programs in pediatrics and nursing will equip all hospital staff with sufficient knowledge of emotional factors to insure enlightened management of their child patients. But, until the time when this happens, pediatricians will have to rely on consultation with a psychoanalytically trained advisor; ward sisters and nurses will need instruction and guidance of the same kind; medical social workers and hospital teachers will learn from such help to use their professional skills to the best advantage. Above all, as illustrated by Mrs. Gordon's paper, the psychoanalytic consultant will be an indispensable figure in the maternity wards and infant clinics where the opportunities for preventive work are almost limitless.

Such work is already being carried out in some selected centers in England as well as in the United States. But it is still waiting for its introduction into children's hospitals, pediatric wards, and infant welfare clinics on the widest scale.

A Psychoanalytic Contribution to Pediatrics

After undergoing a period of consolidation and perhaps inevitable isolation, psychoanalysis is extending its scope and is making a contribution to community services, particularly in the area of mental health. This is a task it must undertake and, indeed, one by which its social value will be judged.

Each area of knowledge needs contact with other disciplines, not only in order to contribute to them, but also to receive stimulation from them. This being so, analysts have a duty to discover how best to put their knowledge to work wherever it can contribute to a better understanding of both individual and social problems.

The analyst is equipped for work outside intensive analysis because of what he learns from patients whom he has treated intensively. Individual long-term treatment offers opportunities to the analyst to experience and to study under a microscope, as it were, his patients' emotional and behavioral manifestations and their thought processes. It is possible for him to draw on his experience of intensive analytic treatment and to apply this to therapeutic consultations in which a patient is not seen frequently and over a long period of time.

A psychoanalytic contribution to pediatrics not only is desirable from the point of view of preventive and therapeutic work, but is also necessary for a further and socially significant development of psychoanalytic thinking and practice. Moreover, the need for psychoanalytic contributions is increasingly felt by those concerned with mental health and there has already been some significant involvement in allied fields. In recent years, the insights of psychoanalysis have proved a useful tool in less intensive forms of treatment. They have played an important part in maternity and infant welfare work and in pediatrics; that is to say, in situations not involving gross psychopathology.

The object of this paper is to describe and discuss briefly two projects which have used psychoanalytic methods in conjunction with normal pediatric practice. The first concerns work within the pediatric and obstetric departments of a group of hospitals; and the second, a more recent venture, an experiment with interdisciplinary and interhospital study groups on the effect of illness and hospitalization on children. Both are an attempt to integrate the various skills of our respective disciplines in order to help the sick child and his family.

I would like to talk first about my work at the hospitals. It is now thirteen years since Anna Freud asked me to work with Dr. David Morris, Consultant Pediatrician of the Woolwich group of hospitals, and with his staff. I was at that time a child psychotherapist, had worked with the mothers of babies and young children at infant and maternity welfare centers, and had also been concerned with the training of doctors and health visitors. The aim of this assignment was to introduce the practice of mental health into hospital pediatric departments, and to help the staff of these departments, doctors, medical social workers, and nurses, toward a better psychological understanding and to develop the skills needed for an analytically oriented approach to their work, to case problems, and to interviewing. For this purpose a suitable framework had to be created within which this teaching could take place. Training was the fundamental object and was therefore given special emphasis throughout.

I saw my function not as providing textbook information but rather as helping the staff by practical means to approach and appraise the emotional problems of the children and parents whom they met. To provide opportunity for teamwork in which training can be accomplished through direct participation, we introduced three devices. First, the Special Clinic was established to cater to the psychological needs of children referred to the pediatric outpatient department because of psychosomatic illnesses and behavior problems.

Secondly, two years later, the Pediatric Conference was set up.

An extension of our work in the Special Clinic, this was a forum for consultants, junior medical staff, nurses, social workers, and medical students, to discuss the psychological problems of inpatients. Thirdly, a Maternity Ward Round has extended team activity to the problems of babies and their mothers. We referred to these ventures as the "Woolwich Experiment." In what follows I shall describe some of the basic methods and techniques employed in these three aspects of our work.

The Woolwich Experiment

The Special Clinic

The Special Clinic, which used to meet weekly and now meets fortnightly, was originally staffed by the pediatrician, the medical social worker, and myself. For the last few years, however, it has been run by the pediatrician and myself alone.

Children whose problems do not appear sufficiently severe to warrant referral to an overworked and distant child guidance clinic are selected by the pediatrician after they have undergone a careful physical examination in order to exclude the possibility of organic disease. When a child is referred to the Special Clinic, the pediatrician explains to the parents the purpose of the setup. At the beginning of our joint meeting he also gives a brief explanation of the function of each member of the team, he introduces me as a specialist in children's problems. He will point out that the child's problems appear to be wholly or partly emotional and that, in the Special Clinic, we can devote more time and attention to the emotional aspects of problems than is possible in the extremely busy outpatient clinic. The presence of the pediatrician is important. He is the first and main contact with the patient and his parents and is thus able to offer continuity of treatment. In addition, his participation serves to reassure the parents that the medical aspect of the child's condition is not neglected.

The parents and their child are interviewed by the team for about forty-five minutes, which enables us to see from four to six cases during a session. The interview takes place in an ordinary outpatient consulting room, around the doctor's desk. We have found it useful to keep toys in the room in order to help anxious

children feel less frightened in strange surroundings, and to gain
insight into the child's state and problems by observing his reaction
to the play material and his parents' reaction to his play. Parents
are encouraged to talk freely about their child's condition and problems and about their own feelings. After each interview, the material
is subjected to a careful scrutiny of the case, the technique used, and
the areas which had been chosen for interpretive interventions.

One might ask: how is it possible to carry out psychotherapeutic
work in a group setting, since this type of treatment is ordinarily
associated with a confidential face-to-face interview between two
people? However, our initial fear that the patient might suffer in
some way by being exposed to an interview in the setting of a small
conference proved unfounded. Why is it that people are prepared to
discuss their most intimate, and often painful, problems in the presence of two or three strangers? I would like to suggest that a patient's
willingness to do so depends to a considerable extent on his expectations. Thus, a person seeking the help of a psychiatrist is not likely
to accept the presence of more than one consultant, whereas the
anxious parent coming to a hospital does not normally expect privacy
and often has little hope of much personal attention and interest.
To these parents, therefore, the relatively private and intimate setting of the Special Clinic presents a serious attempt to meet their
problems. Moreover, at their first appointment, few parents anticipate that they will eventually talk about very personal feelings and
thoughts. Later on, having established a relationship with the team,
they tend to be highly motivated to do so.

Far from having produced any evidence of adverse reactions from
the parents, the Special Clinic has made a positive contribution to
the therapeutic work itself. By avoiding strong transference and
dependency feelings toward *one* consultant, regressive tendencies
could often be restrained. It may well be that the relatively weaker
individual attachment resulting from the team setting is more con-
ducive to the parents' needs for independence and self-reliance. But
the actual therapeutic work of the Special Clinic, although very important, remained secondary to the central purpose of providing
training. For this reason we were forced to select our patients very
carefully. It will be appreciated that, in a district which lacks, as

is often the case, adequate child guidance facilities, one has constantly to guard against the temptation to act as a service clinic. Although, inevitably, the clinic did provide a service, by virtue of its very existence, this never obscured the primary intention of the project. Had we allowed this to happen, the clinic's training role would have been jeopardized.

In choosing cases we tried to pursue a number of specific interests which have developed since the start of our work. Thus, priority is now given to work with mothers with the following problems:

Screaming babies;
Sleeping and feeding difficulties;
Maternal reaction to the premature birth of a baby;
Children born with a congenital deformity;
Children born with a mental handicap;
Blindness
    Blind children of sighted parents;
    Sighted children of blind parents;
Bereavement in the family
    Helping parents to deal with the death of a child;
    Helping a child to deal with the death of a parent;
Battered babies;
Follow-up cases of young children originally seen by the team as babies;
A longitudinal study of a boy with a congenital absence of sensations of pain.

The majority of patients are seen from three to six times. These we refer to as our short-term patients. Our long-term patients are seen fortnightly or monthly over a period varying from six months to two years.

Over the years, the Special Clinic has built up considerable experience with such cases, particularly with the screaming babies and the sleeping and feeding disturbances in the first weeks and months of a child's life. Much material has been collected, and we hope to report in the future in detail on each of these specific areas of work.

It is interesting to note that the Special Clinic has very few cancellations or absentees. This would seem to be due largely to a thorough and careful selection of referrals by the pediatrician as well as to effective preparation of the parents concerned. However, it would also suggest that people respond to the opportunity to express their problems and feelings freely. As our work was done in a district providing a good cross-section of the community, it further indicates that this applies to members of all socioeconomic groups.

Another point worth commenting on is the very active participation of many fathers in the treatment. This is all the more interesting since no special attempts have been made to encourage husbands to attend with their wives. This high degree of participation, less usual in child guidance clinics generally, was maintained not only at initial diagnostic sessions but also for more prolonged casework. Moreover, it was not confined to fathers from any particular social class. While it is difficult to be certain why a father is prepared to be actively involved, it would seem that the traditional exclusion in our culture of the father from the feminine function of infant care is gradually being abandoned, and it is now often possible to interest fathers in the care of their children from the very beginning.

Our experience further suggests that the general public shows an increasing willingness and ability to relate not only behavioral problems but also physical symptoms to the psychological difficulties of the individual child, and to his relationship to other members of the family, including his father. It is also possible that a hospital, with its aura of prestige, scientific knowledge, and equipment, still commands greater respect and confidence among parents than does the child guidance clinic.

The Special Clinic was not designed to turn pediatricians into child psychiatrists; rather it attempts to expand their medical roles by adding new areas and new skills. In trying to provide medical personnel with a psychologically oriented technique, we were faced with the difficulty that medical training has accustomed doctors to take a much more active role with patients than is here desirable. Their training with its emphasis on decisiveness and control, on early diagnosis, management and treatment tends to hamper them in a situation requiring greater passivity.

Knowing what to observe and how to observe is fundamental in this type of work. So is the knowledge that the presenting conditions of a problem are, and have to be, treated as part of the total person. It is essential that we are perceptive not only to verbal but also to nonverbal communications, that we recognize significant patterns in the patient's behavior, and that we learn to select the salient points from the session.

However, perception of any kind involves our own emotions, and observations are easily colored or distorted by the interference of our own subjective attitudes and needs. If this is true of observation in general, how much greater is the danger to objective observation in our particular work, involving as it does problems of parent-infant relationship. Almost inevitably, such problems evoke in the worker powerful emotions relating to his or her own life experiences. For this reason, colleagues should, whenever possible, be given an opportunity to share the interviewing experience, so that they can learn to scrutinize and sharpen their perception.

We are concerned with developing this basic skill of observation through the clinical experience of the Special Clinic because our work consists of and depends on scrutinizing and using small segments of what is often a very complex situation. As the worker, in this setting, cannot investigate long and detailed histories, he must be particularly alert to all the detailed elements of the session itself. From these he learns to build up a picture of the significance of the presenting symptom, and with it of the total problem and its deeper implications. As a teaching method, the joint interviewing was found effective by my colleagues, confirming the value of participation. It proved particularly suited to the communication of techniques of careful observation in the interview situation.

I should like to comment on the approach of the Special Clinic to short-term therapeutic work with parents. Parents' attitudes toward their children are determined by their own early childhood experience and by unresolved conflicts. Conflicts which may have remained latent until the birth of the baby tend to be revived by the birth and lived out in the parent-infant relationship, especially in the feeding situation.

Pediatric practice provides many examples of psychosomatic conditions in children resulting from the unconscious needs of one or both of their parents. A mother's inability to gratify her child's needs more often than not stems from the fact that *she* did not enjoy a satisfying relationship with *her* mother. Her attitudes have been shaped by her whole life; in fact, the problem is one which extends over past generations. However, unresolved maternal conflicts do not always originate in an unsatisfactory feeding experience. Other childhood events, such as the arrival of a sibling, can give rise to them. In that case, a mother unconsciously identifies her baby with that *hated* brother or sister, and feelings, fears, and hostile desires belonging *not* to her baby but to that intruder in the past are generated. She then does not perceive the baby as her child, but regards him as the parent or sibling responsible for her early suffering, feeling again the pain, rejection, and despair belonging to this early period.

Although it cannot be the aim in this type of short-term therapy to treat the parent's personality problems, it is essential to explore those aspects which now contribute to her difficulties with her child. In doing so, we are helping the mother to disentangle herself and her problems from her child, so that she can begin to relate to him as a separate person. Thus, the isolation and recognition of the parent's problems are the central tasks in this type of work. An awareness of this will minimize the frustration both of parents and doctors, the extended period of anxiety, and the wasting of precious medical time on the repeated requests for physical examinations which so often otherwise occur.

Two real dangers must be avoided when parents turn to us at such a time. First, as we do not perform the function of a family doctor or health visitor, we should not allow ourselves to be drawn into giving advice. Not only should we explain that there are no easy, practical solutions, but we should also avoid prescribing remedies and thereby perhaps reinforcing a dependence on authoritative figures. Secondly, acceptance and experience of personal success are essential for satisfactory parenthood, and demonstrations of what parents often regard as superior and esoteric knowledge may well increase their sense of inadequacy and failure. All our efforts should therefore be directed toward mobilizing the parents' inner resources and supporting their self-esteem. We can do this most effectively by helping them see that they themselves are capable of finding a solution which answers their own and their child's needs. Our knowledge and skill should be used to help them think and discover how and why present difficulties have been caused.

Where this is achieved, an important step will have been taken toward creating the necessary conditions for the child's healthy development, during which he will be able to unfold freely and express his needs and potential. Those who seem to benefit most are mothers seeking help during the first weeks or months of their children's lives. The most common problems are feeding, sleeping or screaming difficulties, or an ill-defined fear that something may be organically wrong with the baby. We have seen many desperately unhappy, screaming, inconsolable babies transformed into satisfied, responsive, and thriving ones, often after only a few sessions. Naturally, the effects of such changes are not confined to the infant, but profoundly affect the whole family.

The Pediatric Conference

The Special Clinic remains the focal point of our work, but our interest has gradually widened to include other aspects of hospital care of children and their families. In due course the second venture of the Woolwich Experiment, the Pediatric Conference, was instituted. This forum, which is composed of consultants, junior medical staff, nurses, social workers, medical students, a play leader, and the psychoanalyst, meets at the Postgraduate Medical Centre.

The Conference concerns itself with the social and psychological problems of sick children and their families, paying special attention to emotional problems associated with specific childhood diseases, and to the problems of terminal care, death in the ward, and problems arising from mothers and young children staying in the hospital together. Discussions are recorded by the junior medical staff, which enables continuity of care to be maintained in a situation where the staff is constantly changing.

The aim of the Pediatric Conference is to create among the staff the realization that the concept of a sick person must include consideration of his mind as well as his body. The focus is on the whole child and his family. History, social data, assessment of the child's development, as well as the observed behavior of the child and his family are reported and evaluated. In our discussions of children in this forum, we try to concentrate on such questions as:

Who is this child?
What are his relationships with the important people in his life?
What is the sum total of his experiences so far?
What stage of development had he reached before his illness, his operation, or his accident?
How, and to what extent, can his treatment be helped by the answers to these questions?

The meetings have provided opportunities to discuss aspects of child development via observed case material. The value of this information in relation to the treatment of a child's illness has been clearly demonstrated, and appreciation of its importance by the consultants has led to more attention being given to such aspects by the junior medical staff. But the training of these same people remains a problem, and a more effective teaching method must be evolved. Difficulties arise because junior medical staff are harassed by very heavy clinical commitments during the six months they stay in the department. And this happens at a stage in their careers which is focused on obtaining higher medical qualifications. I have the impression that some of them see our discussions and concerns as only of secondary importance to the "real thing"—medicine. With this group, I think, we have not succeeded in overcoming the artificial division between physical and psychological care in pediatrics, and this has led at times to a lack of spontaneity on their part in bringing forward problems for discussion in this forum. However, the situation is different with those who are aiming to specialize in child psychiatry or pediatrics. The problem of reaching through to all junior medical staff in training is presently occupying senior members of our team.

The multidisciplinary character of the forum, within a large and very busy group of hospitals, has considerably improved the atmosphere necessary for total care of the patient. By fostering communication between members of the different professions, the meetings have enabled members to define their own professional roles more clearly and then to integrate these separate roles to provide a more effective service. Benefit has also been derived from the opportunity to verbalize tensions which can otherwise easily interfere with teamwork.

These Pediatric Conferences have become an integral part of our work and increasingly, in recent years, have aimed at improving all aspects of hospital care for the child. They have helped to establish a closer link between the nursing and the medical staff and between the work of the Special Clinic and that of the ward. It was, therefore, encouraging that consultants such as the cardiologist, neurosurgeon, and surgeons joined the Conference when a case of special interest to them was to be discussed. When it was felt that the time was ripe to widen the circle, we invited general practitioners and representatives of the local Health and Education Authorities and Children's Department. Initially, most of the visitors came by invitation to take part in a discussion concerning one of their patients. Eventually, however, some joined in regularly, whether or not they had a patient in the ward, in order to learn about particular psychological aspects of illnesses and their treatment.

The Conferences have achieved several important modifications in hospital practice. In 1958 we helped to gain permission for unlimited visiting, with the results that more mothers of under-fives stayed with their children in the specially designed cubicles, while opposition to the scheme gradually weakened.

It had been felt for some time that the local authorities had not been sufficiently aware of the work carried out in the pediatric departments, and that there was a growing need to follow up patients, after their discharge from a hospital, in the community. At the request of a group of school medical officers, I have, for the past two years, held monthly seminars with them. These seminars are designed to deal with problems encountered in their work at infant welfare centers and in the schools. The group is currently engaged in working out a study project concerning the personalities and pathology of "battering parents." It is our plan to involve the health visitors in this research. These contacts with representatives of the Local Health Authorities are a further link with the community.

The Maternity Ward Round

The latest development of our work, the Maternity Ward Round, reflects a shift toward greater emphasis on prevention. As a result of this, we now see a far higher proportion of very young children; we deal with babies from birth and can help them by means of early work with their mothers. The Ward Round is conducted by the pediatrician, the ward sister, myself, and, occasionally, the obstetrician. Its main purpose is to give all mothers of newborn babies an opportunity to discuss anything they wish in relation to their babies, to themselves, or to their older children whom they have had to leave at home. Before the ward round, the team is briefed by the sister about the mothers to be seen, in order to avoid the disturbing effects of discussing personal details in the mothers' presence and within hearing of the other patients. Since this round is conducted as a matter of routine, most mothers find it natural to express what is worrying them at the time. The kind of questions most frequently raised refer to:

Breast or bottle feeding;
Demand or schedule feeding;
The problem of wind in the newborn baby;
Physical abnormality ("Is my baby normal?");
Familial diseases;
The effect on older children of the mother's absence from home;
Circumcision ("Should my boy be circumcized, and if so, when?");
Methods of birth control;
Sterilization;
Stillbirth.

The team pays special attention to feeding disturbances, to signs of undue restlessness in either mother or baby, and to babies with some mental or physical abnormality, regardless of whether or not the mothers recognize or complain about them. The team is also on the alert for indications of maternal problems arising from premature births. Interest in this much neglected area was stimulated by an infant who was presented as a case of autism at the age of two and a half years: his difficulties in relating were subsequently found to be causally connected with his mother's intense estrangement and feeling of loss following the premature delivery.

Several important advantages have emerged from the introduction of the routine ward round. First, it has made early intervention in troubled situations possible. This is obviously important if the infant is to be allowed optimum conditions for his development. At the very least, prompt attention can give valuable temporary relief from tension by reducing the impact of pathological maternal reactions, and even this temporary respite would justify the creation of such a service. Secondly, the ward round serves to inform mothers about the Special Clinic at which they can be seen by appointment and it encourages them to make use of this in the event of later difficulties. We are particularly anxious to convey to the mothers that they should feel free to return to us and to reassure them about the continuity of our interest and care after they have returned home. Thirdly, as a result of these ward rounds, there now exists a good liaison between the team and the consultant obstetrician. In addition to numerous consultations and informal discussions of psychological problems encountered in obstetrics, we have occasional joint ward rounds in the maternity unit. This liaison benefits both the mothers and babies, and the nurses and junior medical staff. It is also a most effective means of overcoming the artificial dichotomy between physical and psychological care in obstetrics.

I would like to see more time being given to this aspect of the work. Reliance on referral of patients by the staff, as opposed to direct appeal from the mothers themselves, can result in only obvious conditions coming to our notice. There is a danger of neglect of conditions which require more time for recognition and exploration. A further relevant point is that, unless there is more time available, the shy mother, who is often more inwardly anxious, will have greater difficulty in making use of this service. There is great potential in this sphere of work. Once it is accepted that a good and mutually satisfying mother-infant relationship is the very basis of mental health, any work done with the nursing couple is the most important aspect of preventive psychiatry. With the necessary skill and experience, it is possible to effect a relatively quick response from parents during the neonatal phase. During this early period of her baby's life, a mother is very close to her own infantile experience and to the unconscious problems associated with it. Hence it is easier than at any other time in her life—outside a psychoanalysis which aims at reaching these early stages—to penetrate to this unconscious level of her experience. At this time the mother is most highly motivated to obtain help because of great pressure from two sides. On the one hand, there is the baby who in his own right demands satisfaction; and, on the other, there is internal pressure arising from the intensity and brevity of this period. There is an unconscious awareness that the very short period of early motherhood is providing a second chance of reliving and thereby coming to terms with unresolved aspects of her own childhood experience.

Benefits of the Woolwich Experiment

Doctors, psychologists, social workers, and students from various disciplines, not only from this country but also from overseas, have taken part as observers in these three facets of the Woolwich Experiment. Such visits not only give people of diverse professions the chance to study the sick child in the hospital, but also help them to realize the importance of good communication between the various specialists concerned with an individual case. We are anxious to show that specialization can and should be accompanied by a fuller knowledge of all relevant aspects of the child's life; aspects which, although not in the specialist's own sphere, are nevertheless an integral part of the child's background. For example, it must benefit the medical and nursing staff concerned with the sick child to have a picture of the child's home and school background, just as it must help the child's teacher to know about the nature and problems of the child's illness.

The type of work done at the Woolwich group of hospitals can also prove a valuable adjunct to the training of child psychotherapists and analysts, especially if the periods of observation come at a time when the student is not yet called upon to be actively involved in the details of everyday clinical work. In the hospital situation he can witness a much broader spectrum of psychopathology in childhood, and the symptoms *in statu nascendi*, than he is likely to encounter once his attention is focused on the intensive study of a very small number of individual patients.

These visits have another incidental, but nevertheless important, function, particularly for students of psychoanalysis. They demonstrate the extremely difficult conditions which face medical and nursing personnel in the actual hospital setting, and they draw particular attention to the very serious limitations imposed on the staff by sheer lack of time. All this tends to instil in the prospective therapist or analyst a salutary measure of respect for, and a more tolerant attitude toward, cursory investigation of problems, snap decisions, or a superficial type of casework, the value of which he might otherwise deprecate.

STUDY GROUPS ON THE EFFECT OF ILLNESS AND HOSPITALIZATION ON CHILDREN

The promotion of interdisciplinary cooperation, although important and fostered by the Pediatric Conference and the encouragement of visiting observers, was not central to the work in the Woolwich group of hospitals. However, another project—the inter-hospital study groups on the effects of illness and hospitalization on children—places very special emphasis on interdisciplinary cooperation. Indeed, the multidisciplinary character of the study groups was intended as an experiment in communication between the professions represented. It was hoped that the development of a common language and approach would help the various specialists in their own work situation.

Since the sick child and his family are in contact with, and helped by, a number of workers who, by their presence, if not always by design, exert an influence on the child, it seemed obviously important that as many of them as possible were represented in the study groups. With this in view, the study groups (the first started in February, 1968 and the second early this year) included a wide variety of people, mainly in senior positions: social workers, pediatric ward sisters, doctors, a hospital play leader, a matron, psychologists, teachers, and psychoanalysts.

Our interest in the effects of illness on children (the motive force behind the formation of the study groups) was aroused by the considerable amount of recent comment on the adverse effect of separating children from their homes by hospitalization. Work at the hospitals had shown us that relatively little is known or documented about the meaning which illness, accidents, burns, surgical intervention, and bodily restraint have for the child patient. There is no doubt that separating a child from his normal environment produces its own very important, sometimes traumatic effects which must be known and taken into account. Yet, however valuable and relevant the appreciation of this aspect of hospitalization is, those of us who work with sick children and their families are becoming aware that many of the emotional difficulties of the child patient cannot be sufficiently understood and explained only in terms of separation experiences. They relate more fundamentally to the actual illness and to its effect on the particular child, whether he is nursed at home or in a hospital.

During home visits we notice the same emotional and physical reactions in the sick child as we find in the hospital. That is to say, a child may regress, be hostile, listless, depressed and withdrawn wherever he happens to be during the acute phase of his illness, although separation from home does at times, but by no means always, aggravate his emotional and physical condition. I have felt for some time that there is a danger in using separation as a blanket explanation for the ill child's emotional condition, and I fear that such a single factor explanation may obscure other, possibly more complex and fundamental problems. We need to look at the illness as such, in the hope that we may more fully understand its meaning and impact, and thus be in a position to act appropriately in our total management of the child patient, whether in the hospital or at home.

Our project is based on the hypothesis that physical illness affects the emotional state of the child, and that specific diseases may produce their own specific effects. If this is so, better knowledge of the general emotional effect of illness and of the effect of specific diseases is a necessary condition for the successful management of the sick child wherever he is cared for. Only thorough observation will yield more definite data about the total effects of sickness. Such observation must be free both from experimentation and from the dangers of too narrowly defined hypotheses, whether about the reactions of different types of children or the effects of specific diseases. Data obtained through unbiased observation might ultimately lead to detailed hypotheses, but in the meantime our task is to observe as much as possible. We must not restrict our vision or allow it to be influenced by preconceived ideas which conflict with our stated aim of study and discovery.

Training in direct observation of children is fundamental to the work of the study groups. The aim is to obtain as full and real a picture of the child as possible, without reference to case files and without discussion with the hospital staff. These observations, written up in detailed reports, are discussed within the framework of a seminar, and describe not only observed material but also the subjective reactions of the observer. Observations carried out specifically for the study group, rather than reports of past or even current cases, are essential to our work because even experienced workers have rarely observed a child in the strict sense of the word. Even when some observation was carried out in the course of professional activity, it usually focused mainly on one or another specific physical or emotional aspect rather than on the total state of the child. By virtue of going into the ward, not as members of the team concerned with the child's treatment but purely as observers, members of the study group, free from any departmental responsibility, can give their undivided attention to the child. Further, in making direct observation the basis of a study group, each member is encouraged to report all that he has observed and not to select aspects which he regards as especially interesting or problematical.

The task undertaken by the observer is, therefore, not to look for a particular piece of behavior or emotional manifestation, but to note carefully as much as is realistically possible of what does and does not happen during the visit. With this task in mind the observer will be basically passive, though not distant from the child. He will respond to the child but not initiate activities and discussions. As an observer he will certainly not interpret to the child any of his behavioral manifestations, verbal or nonverbal. In the seminar, the group will then attempt to understand the reported observations where possible, or will decide to wait for further experiences which might help to clarify the problem.

All this is, of course, much easier said than done. Observers are human beings and not measuring instruments; they cannot but be affected by the pains and worries of a sick child and cannot but react to these in accordance with their own personal makeup. The natural tendency is that they will wish to help alleviate suffering, i.e., to do something. Therefore, an important task of the group is to try to minimize the danger to observation arising from such personal involvement. This can be done only by openly recognizing one's own feelings and reactions and by discussing them. The continuing attention to this aspect, the assessment of the role of the observer and his involvement, must be one of the basic and most important functions of any group task of this kind.

The children selected for observation are those able to express themselves and to communicate. They have also been admitted recently and are expected to stay for at least two weeks so that the observer can visit them on at least two occasions, when he spends from three quarters of an hour to an hour at the bedside of the child in the ward. To prevent our study of the effects of illness from becoming too diffuse and in order not to dissipate our energies too much in the early stages, we decided to restrict the number of problems chosen for observation and to limit our observation to children in the hospital. We have concentrated on orthopedic conditions, diabetes, obesity, asthma, and congenital heart disease. Once the work has progressed beyond the present stage, we hope to be able to widen its scope, to study a greater variety of illnesses, and to make observational studies of sick children in their own homes.

Conclusions and Summary

Our experiences with the Woolwich Experiment—the Special Clinic, the Pediatric Conference, and the Maternity Ward Round—suggest that the technique of teaching within the framework of joint clinical commitments is a dynamic method of training experienced personnel. The knowledge gained by the team will be of permanent benefit, and I feel confident that the personnel involved, both medical and nonmedical, are determined to continue this type of work and are capable of doing so.

Thirteen years may be considered a long time for the introduction and assimilation of a basically different approach to pediatric casework. However, we must bear in mind that our endeavor to train specialist staff depended not only on the modification of professional and personal attitudes but also on a basic change of climate, in a setting colored by the very firmly established and often rigid traditions inherent in both the medical and nursing professions.

In the development of this particular service, three phases are distinguishable in the process of assimilation. First, there was an eager, unquestioning, wholesale acceptance of the psychoanalytic approach. This was then followed by a fairly strong reaction culminating in skepticism, resistance to and rejection of what did not turn out to be the desired magic formula. Finally, there was a more sober, experienced, reality-based use of relevant insights and methods. That is to say, once curiosity and interest had been aroused there was a dangerous tendency toward oversimplification and an overenthusiastic and sometimes superficial use of these principles. This was accompanied, to varying degrees, by the belief that there is no clear boundary between the function of the hospital staff and that of the psychoanalyst, and that the former could assume the latter's function. This inevitably led to disillusionment. However, repeated confrontation with complex psychological problems tended to have a sobering effect, leading to an awareness that psychoanalytic work, far from being magical, is more complex than was thought.

This sometimes painful awareness marked an important stage. Further painstaking clinical work, patient cooperation between members of the team, and repeated experience of sometimes very striking clinical results led to a deeper, reality-based respect for psychoanalytic methods. This was accompanied by better discrimination of which psychoanalytic skills could be used by the nonanalyst as a useful adjunct to his own profession.

It is now clear that the change in outlook, both in the outpatient department and in the ward, has been a fundamental one, which is bound to develop further along progressive lines. Moreover, the work done in one particular hospital can be expected to affect that of other hospitals and similar institutions. This interaction has, in fact, already taken place in a most encouraging way. One-time members of the hospital team, including doctors, medical social workers, and sisters, have moved on to positions in other hospitals, where they have taken the opportunity of introducing a similar type of service or part of this service.

The formation of the interhospital study groups was a logical extension of the work done in the Woolwich hospitals and offers a valuable opportunity to learn more about the contributions of different disciplines to a common task. The work of these study groups helped members become aware of the significance of their individual experiences when they are contributed to the fund of combined knowledge. The function of the seminars is, therefore, not only to teach and collectively explore new areas of understanding but to coordinate, consolidate, and evaluate the corporate body of facts, experiences, and viewpoints which group members have individually accumulated. This provided us with valuable data which are bound to enrich our understanding of the meaning of illness to children.

Apart from its main objectives, this work has had other benefits. In discussing their observations, members have concerned themselves increasingly with problems of ward management, nursing, medical procedures, and hospital structure, and have felt the need to question and reappraise them. In this way, we have made a modest beginning in influencing current practice in this sphere of work in a number of hospitals, including some of our teaching centers.

The ventures I have described show that there is a need and readiness on the part of hospital personnel to make use of psychoanalytic skills which are relevant to their problems and applicable to preventive and nonintensive therapeutic work in the field of pediatrics. Throughout, I have tried to focus attention on the importance of a dynamic approach to the problems of infants and parents in the wards and in the outpatient departments. Above all, however, I hope that my remarks have indicated ways in which a climate of opinion favorable to such developments may be created. The principles and techniques outlined in this paper are, in my view, capable of being used in antenatal and maternity clinics, infant welfare centers, and pediatric departments by appropriately trained workers able to recognize and treat early manifestations of psychological problems. Prevention of psychological disorders cannot be the task of child psychiatry alone; but it *must* be the task of child psychiatry and child analysis to establish good contacts with those in other fields responsible for child care so that they may benefit from the knowledge and experience of these specialized disciplines. Many child care workers, educators, and physicians know a great deal about the environmental factors in the child's life. It is by virtue of this knowledge that they can make their own very important contribution to preventive work.

Finally, in my experience, the analyst also benefits considerably. I have been enriched by what I encountered and learned in the hospitals. Being accustomed to dealing with a few patients in the tranquil atmosphere of the consulting room, I feel great respect for the way in which the hospital staff deal with many complex cases and make crucial decisions, while working under constant pressure of time and in extremely difficult conditions.

The benefit derived has, therefore, I trust, been mutual. I hope that the two projects which I have described will go some way toward justifying the assertions made at the beginning of this paper: that psychoanalytic insight and methods have much to contribute to preventive and nonintensive therapeutic work in the field of pediatrics.

CONTENTS OF VOLUMES I-XXIV

CONTENTS OF VOLUMES I–XXIV

Maternal Stimulation, Psychic Structure, and Early Object
Relations: With Special Reference to Aggression and Denial
(1962)   17:265–282
RUDNIK, R., see WEILAND & RUDNIK (1961)

SACHS, L. J.
On Changes in Identification from Machine to Cripple (1957)   12:356–375
SALDINGER, J. S., see COREN & SALDINGER (1967)
SANDLER, A.-M.
Aspects of Passivity and Ego Development in the Blind Infant
(1963)   18:343–360
—— DAUNTON, E., & SCHNURMANN, A.
Inconsistency in the Mother as a Factor in Character Develop-
ment: A Comparative Study of Three Cases. With an Intro-
duction by *Anna Freud* (1957)   12:209–225
SANDLER, J.
On the Concept of Superego (1960)   15:128–162
—— HOLDER, A., & MEERS, D.
The Ego Ideal and the Ideal Self (1963)   18:139–158
—— & JOFFE, W. G.
Notes on Obsessional Manifestations in Children (1965)   20:425–438
—— KAWENOKA, M., NEURATH, L., ROSENBLATT, B.,
SCHNURMANN, A., & SIGAL, J.
The Classification of Superego Material in the Hampstead
Index (1962)   17:107–127
—— & NAGERA, H.
Aspects of the Metapsychology of Fantasy (1963)   18:159–194
—— & ROSENBLATT, B.
The Concept of the Representational World (1962)   17:128–145
See also JOFFE & SANDLER (1965)
SARVIS, M. A.
Psychiatric Implications of Temporal Lobe Damage (1960)   15:454–481
SCHAFER, R.
The Loving and Beloved Superego in Freud's Structural
Theory (1960)   15:163–188
SCHARL, A. E.
Regression and Restitution in Object Loss: Clinical Observa-
tions (1961)   16:471–480
SCHMALE, A. H., Jr.
A Genetic View of Affects: With Special Reference to the
Genesis of Helplessness and Hopelessness (1964)   19:287–310
SCHNURMANN, A.
Observation of a Phobia (1949)   3/4:253–270
See also SANDLER, DAUNTON, & SCHNURMANN (1957),
SANDLER, KAWENOKA, NEURATH, ROSENBLATT,
SCHNURMANN, & SIGAL (1962)
SCHUR, H.
An Observation and Comments on the Development of
Memory (1966)   21:468–479
See also GREEN, SCHUR, & LIPKOWITZ (1959)

WALLERSTEIN, J., see EKSTEIN & WALLERSTEIN (1954, 1956), EKSTEIN, WALLERSTEIN, & MANDELBAUM (1959)

WALLERSTEIN, R., see RAMZY & WALLERSTEIN (1958)

WANGH, M.
  The "Evocation of a Proxy": A Psychological Maneuver, Its Use as a Defense, Its Purposes and Genesis (1962)   *17*:451–469

WEIL, A. P.
  Certain Severe Disturbances of Ego Development in Childhood (1953)   *8*:271–287
  Some Evidences of Deviational Development in Infancy and Early Childhood (1956)   *11*:292–299
  See also ALPERT, NEUBAUER, & WEIL (1956)

WEILAND, I. H. & RUDNIK, R.
  Considerations of the Development and Treatment of Autistic Childhood Psychosis (1961)   *16*:549–563

WEISSMAN, P.
  The Childhood and Legacy of Stanislavski (1957)   *12*:399–417
  Shaw's Childhood and *Pygmalion* (1958)   *13*:541–561

WERMER, H. & LEVIN, S.
  Masturbation Fantasies: Their Changes with Growth and Development (1967)   *22*:315–328

WHIPPLE, B., see JESSNER, LAMONT, LONG, ROLLINS, WHIPPLE, & PRENTICE (1955)

WIEDER, H.
  Intellectuality: Aspects of Its Development from the Analysis of a Precocious Four-and-a-half-year-old Boy (1966)   *21*:294–323
  ——— & KAPLAN, E. H.
  Drug Use in Adolescents: Psychodynamic Meaning and Pharmacogenic Effect (1969)   *24*:399–431

WILKIN, L. C., see JACKSON, KLATSKIN, & WILKIN (1952)

WILLER, M. L., see COOLIDGE, TESSMAN, WALDFOGEL, & WILLER (1962)

WILLS, D. M.
  Some Observations on Blind Nursery School Children's Understanding of Their World (1965)   *20*:344–364

WINESTINE, M. C., see DEMAREST & WINESTINE (1955)

WINNICOTT, D. W., see STEVENSON (1954)

WOLF, K. M.
  Evacuation of Children in Wartime: A Survey of the Literature with Bibliography (1945)   *1*:389–404
  Edouard Pichon: *Le Développement de l'Enfant et de l'Adolescent* (1945)   *1*:417–423
  See also SPITZ & WOLF (1946, 1949)

WOLFENSTEIN, M.
  Some Variants in Moral Training of Children (1950)   *5*:310–328
  A Phase in the Development of Children's Sense of Humor (1951)   *6*:336–350
  Children's Understanding of Jokes (1953)   *8*:162–173
  Mad Laughter in a Six-year-old Boy (1955)   *10*:381–394